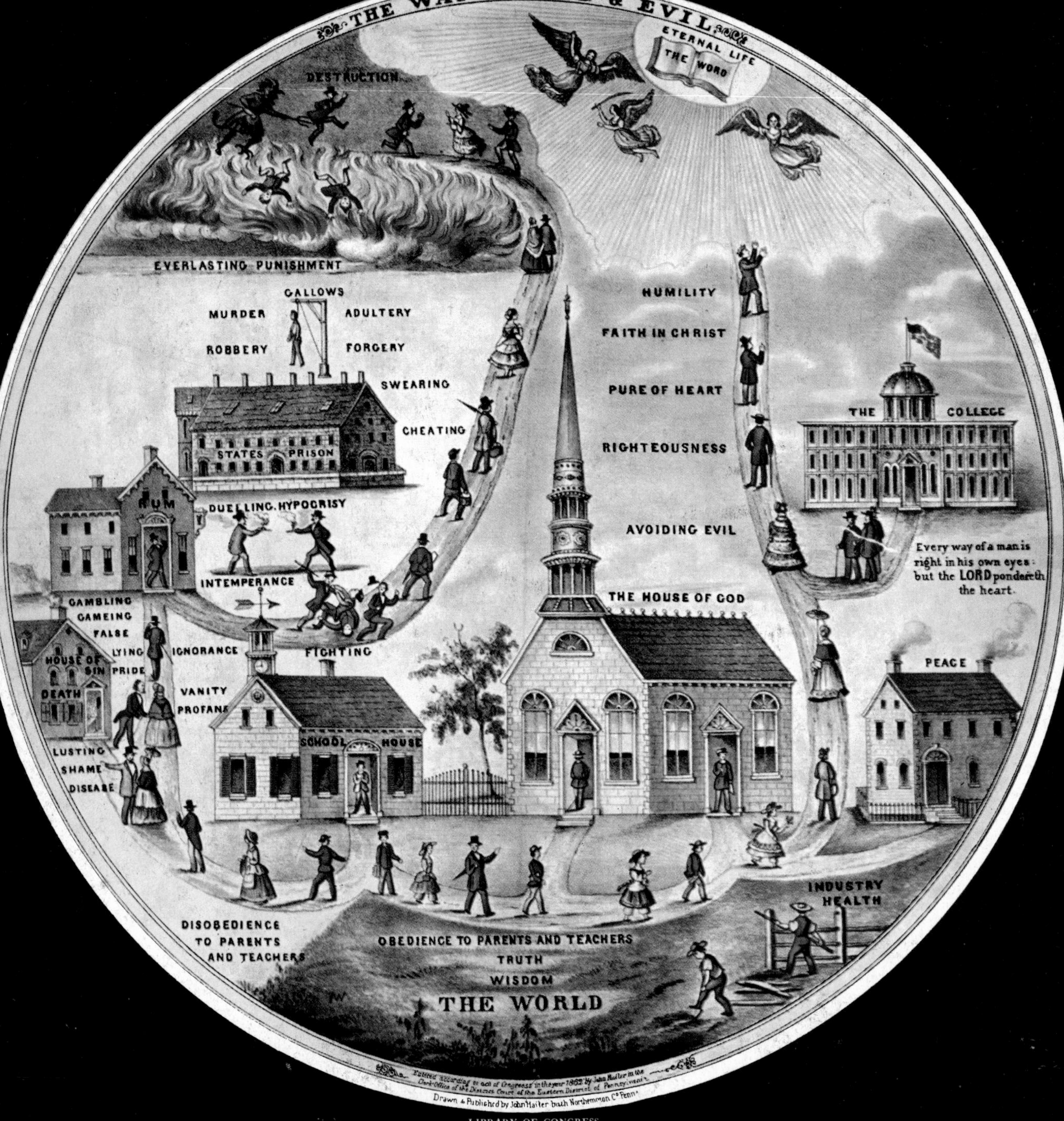

THE WAY OF GOOD & EVIL

ETERNAL LIFE
THE WORD

DESTRUCTION

EVERLASTING PUNISHMENT

GALLOWS

MURDER   ADULTERY

ROBBERY   FORGERY

SWEARING

CHEATING

STATES PRISON

HUMILITY

FAITH IN CHRIST

PURE OF HEART

RIGHTEOUSNESS

AVOIDING EVIL

THE HOUSE OF GOD

THE COLLEGE

Every way of a man is
right in his own eyes
but the LORD pondereth
the heart.

DUELLING. HYPOCRISY

RUM

INTEMPERANCE

GAMBLING
GAMEING
FALSE

LYING
PRIDE

HOUSE OF
SIN

DEATH

IGNORANCE   FIGHTING

VANITY

PROFANE

PEACE

SCHOOL HOUSE

LUSTING
SHAME
DISEASE

INDUSTRY
HEALTH

DISOBEDIENCE
TO PARENTS
AND TEACHERS

OBEDIENCE TO PARENTS AND TEACHERS

TRUTH

WISDOM

THE WORLD

Entered according to act of Congress in the year 1862 by John Hailer in the
Clerk Office of the District Court of the Eastern District of Pennsylvania

Drawn & Published by John Hailer Bush Northampton Co Penn

Stories of
GREAT CRIMES
& TRIALS

from
AMERICAN HERITAGE
MAGAZINE

Introduction by
OLIVER JENSEN

Published by
AMERICAN HERITAGE PUBLISHING COMPANY, INC., NEW YORK
Book Trade distribution by
McGRAW-HILL BOOK COMPANY, INC., NEW YORK

AMERICAN HERITAGE
PUBLISHING CO., INC.

PRESIDENT AND PUBLISHER
Paul Gottlieb

EDITOR, AMERICAN HERITAGE MAGAZINE
Oliver Jensen

GENERAL MANAGER, BOOK DIVISION
Kenneth W. Leish

EDITORIAL ART DIRECTOR
Murray Belsky

Library of Congress Cataloging in Publication Data
Main entry under title:
Stories of great crimes and trials.

1. Crime and criminals — United States — Addresses, essays, lectures. 2. Trials — United States — Addresses, essays, lectures. I. American heritage.
HV6779.S76   364'.973   74-4031
ISBN 07-032465-4
ISBN 07-079385-9 de luxe boxed set with *The American Heritage History of the Law in America*

CONTENTS

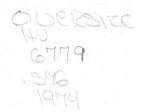

INTRODUCTION

In December of 1954, when we started issuing AMERICAN HERITAGE, the editors aimed at painting history with the widest possible brush, covering almost every aspect of human behavior in this country, and not excluding, of course, a few strokes at our misbehavior. But that after twenty years we should have published so much about crime and gone into so many legal cases as appear here we find at first astonishing. And in putting together this book we have omitted a good number of other cases, notably a series on Supreme Court decisions, because they are contained in other ways in the companion volume to this one, *The American Heritage History of the Law in America*. When one reflects on the record, however, one can see how, even without conscious design, we came to report so much about these matters. America is a law-conscious as well as a litigious society. It is not by accident that the courthouse in any town or city is such a busy place, because a great deal of our political and social history winds up there.

That we go to court so often, and linger there so long in a mass of appeals and pleadings, is a phenomenon traceable no doubt to the formidable number of lawyers among the Founding Fathers, and the esteem in which we seem to hold the profession. If we did not, would we elect so many of them to high office? If we did not, how could we have today the largest number of lawyers in the world, both absolutely and relatively? According to a study made in 1968, the latest with comparative statistics, the United States has 300,000 practicing attorneys—one for every 659 persons; in the British Isles there are 21,000—one lawyer for every 2,579 Britons. In France there is one for

every 4,385 people, in Germany one for every 3,636, and in the Soviet Union one for every 2,625. (It is not so astonishing that 23,000 of the 93,000 Soviet lawyers are judges and *prosecutors*.)

If we have four times as many lawyers per capita as Britain, ours have an awesome amount of crime to deal with—ten million *serious* crimes per year in the United States. We have thirty times as many violent crimes per capita as Great Britain, ninety times as many as Holland, even five times as many as neighboring Canada, slightly infected no doubt by its proximity to the rattle of gunfire in the United States. The National Crime Commission, which reported these depressing figures in 1969, went on to point out that the United States, with a two hundred million population, suffered fifty times as many murders by gun as the nearly similar total population of England, West Germany, and Japan combined. America, alone of modern big countries, has no national gun controls, thanks in large part to the National Rifle Association lobby. And our crime rates have only been increasing since 1969, especially as to violent crime and rape. Six out of every ten women interviewed in 1972 told the Gallup Poll that they were afraid to go out alone at night, which takes the United States back to the kind of conditions which prevailed in early eighteenth-century London, before the creation of modern police forces.

Ironically, it can be argued that the settled parts of that earlier America, in which so many of the acts of murder and mayhem in the first two sections of this book took place, were safer by day or night than most major American cities today. Such stories as the murder of old Captain White of Salem, of the Borden fam-

6

ily of Fall River, and of the little mill girl found hanging in Tiverton, Rhode Island, won their notoriety as much from their rarity as from their horror. Our murderous ways today, and our gun-toting habits, have an honest history; they go back to frontier traditions, when a man had to be ready for whatever came, whether Indian, highwayman, or wild animal. That tradition of violence remained with us in the racial struggles of the South and the anarchy of the lawless West of the post-Civil War era; in Section VII we examine some of its tragedies, not to mention the false glamour with which Hollywood and television have invested some of its most pathological murderers and infamous drabs, as heroic figures for the children to emulate. That violence can infect our political life as well was our tragedy both during the last century and this one. It seems to have no end.

Our busy courthouses, of course, have had to deal with more than murder and violence. They have also been concerned with political struggles, matters of high principle, aborted revolutions — like John Brown's, or Nat Turner's — and an assortment of swindlers. In a landscape so full of evil, a genial con man stands out like a wildflower, thorny for the unwary but a spot of cheerful color nonetheless. We have included several of this engaging fraternity. Our court calendar also offers, marked "unsettled," cases which may never be concluded as long as there are lawyers, historians, or partisans to argue them. Was Sacco guilty and Vanzetti innocent, as Francis Russell claims? Did Aaron Burr, whom the late John Dos Passos pursues through a nearly incredible career, really mean to add treason to his other crimes?

Great lawyers stalk our courthouses, silver-tongued performers like Patrick Henry and Daniel Webster, and skillful defenders, too, like Samuel Leibowitz destroying the case against the Scottsboro Boys, and old John Adams, taking the unpopular course and winning the legal battle for Captain Preston, whose redcoats had fired at the Boston rioters of 1770. It is the skill and the tricks of learned counsel, the patient brilliance of detectives, and the unanswered questions about the prisoners at the bar that lend to this whole topic its continuing fascination. We invite our readers into this collection, with its whiffs of other times and customs, its very human passions, its humors, and its horrors.

Crime is, despite our attempts to regard it all with equal disapproval, a strange combination of tragedy and farce. If a man murders his wife, it is a tragedy, but if a man like Johann Hoch, described in *The Lady-Killer,* methodically marries and murders some thirty wives in a row, playing Schubert to them on the zither before the wedding and dosing them with arsenic afterward, as neat and precise as an assembly line, one struggles to maintain the sense of outrage; the numbers, and the gullibility of Hoch's eager widows, verge on comedy. With the particular we sympathize, with the mass we find comprehension hard. But crime, and the game of wits that plays about it, is the very stuff of history, even though one might wish, looking about the crowded courtrooms of America, with their assortment of footpads, muggers, and high political defendants, that we may someday have a little less of it.

— Oliver Jensen,
Editor of AMERICAN HERITAGE Magazine

The Mark of Cain

By CHARLES P. CURTIS

The YOUNG DEVILS and DAN'L WEBSTER

Salem, Massachusetts, in the 1830's, was a city of some 14,000. Merchants and sailors, shopkeepers and ship chandlers, owners and bankers and insurers, doctors and lawyers lived in its red brick and white wood houses. Neighbor and trader with more of the rest of the world than any other port of the United States, Salem in the spring of 1830 was pressing its prime. In Samuel Eliot Morison's neat phrase, "the movement from wharf to waterfall" was beginning. But wealth had not quite yet made prudence a virtue, and the great shipowners were still adventurers as well as the leaders of Salem society.

One of these shipowners was Captain Joseph White, eighty-two years of age and as wealthy as he was elderly. To get to his house one walked down Essex Street, past the rooms of the East India Marine Society, where the captains met for news and reminiscence; past the side streets that led toward the harbor, where spars slanted against the sky and the smell of tar and new canvas filled the air. Only a little farther along stood the Captain's big white house, set back behind its elms. It backed along Brown Street, and just beyond, off Essex Street on Newbury, was the Salem Common, with a wooden rail fence around it and a gate surmounted by a gilt eagle.

At six in the morning of April 7, 1830, a man rushed out of Captain White's house and dashed across the street. A little later, a doctor came and disappeared into the house.

Captain Joseph White had been murdered. The man who had dashed out was Benjamin, his man of all work. When he had come down to open the shutters and light the fire, he had found a back window open, the strip of metal that usually barred it standing against the wall, and a plank set against the outside sill. Upstairs, the door of the Captain's bedroom was open, and when Benjamin went in the Captain lay in bed. He was quite dead, and not yet cold. Calling Lydia, maid and cook for the last sixteen years, Benjamin told her that the Captain "had gone to the eternal world" and that he would go and call the neighbors. Lydia had heard nothing. There had been no one else in the house that night.

The doctor who answered Benjamin's summons was named Samuel Johnson. He found the Captain lying

When four aristocratic

triumphant. But these

on his right side, his left temple fractured by a blow heavy enough to kill him; in addition there were thirteen deep stab wounds, six over the heart and seven under the left arm, which the assailant evidently had lifted up for his purpose.

As word of the murder got around, consternation gripped Salem. Instantly, everybody became a suspect, even Captain White's highly respectable nephew, Stephen White. He had the run of the house, and he was understood to be the heir to most of the Captain's fortune. Stephen was staying then in Boston at the Tremont House, but from April 7 on he took care to be seen frequently in Salem. A Committee of Vigilance was formed the day following the funeral, after a public meeting in the Town Hall and a great harangue by the Reverend Henry Colman, whose church Captain White had attended. The committee met in Stephen's office, and he gave a thousand dollars to it.

Another member of the family was suspected, young Captain Joe Knapp. Also a respectable young man, and a member of the East India Marine Society, he had commanded one of Captain White's ships, the *Caroline,* and he had married pretty Mary Beckford, the Captain's favorite great-niece and daughter of his housekeeper. How angry the old man had been! But young Mary had gone ahead, and now the Knapps were living on Mrs. Beckford's farm in Wenham, a good six or seven miles away. There they had been on the night of the murder, along with Mrs. Beckford herself, who was visiting them.

As the weeks passed, rumors persisted. That death —even death by violence—should come to a Salem man off the coast of Sumatra, or in the Spanish Main, or almost anywhere else, was a thing to be expected. But here in Salem, and on Essex Street! Doors were bolted for the first time in living memory. Pistols and dirks were promptly sold off storekeepers' shelves, and more had to be ordered from Boston. Sword canes became more popular than Malaccas.

Rumor multiplied the number of suspicious-looking characters who had been seen lurking along Brown Street behind Captain White's house that night. Suspicion continued to mount, until people began wondering even about their own kin. The Benjamin Crowninshield girls, writing their weekly newsletter

to their father in Congress, expressed apprehension that their "Cousin Richard"—he was the black sheep of that great Salem family—"would be found to have had a hand in it." We must suppose that the Committee of Vigilance had more than this to go on when "Cousin Richard" Crowninshield and his young brother George were arrested on May 2. Black sheep though they were, as Crowninshields they belonged to one of the wealthiest, most elegant, and most distinguished families of Salem.

There had originally been five Crowninshield brothers, and all had served on the family's ships. One had died at sea. Of the other four, Benjamin and Jacob had gone into politics. Ben had been Secretary of the Navy and later had succeeded Jacob in Congress. George was the dandy of the family. After retiring, he built the first American yacht, then eclipsed it with a second, the famous *Cleopatra's Barge.*

Even Richard, the ne'er-do-well of the family and father of the two Crowninshields now in the Salem gaol, had distinguished himself—in a left-handed way. When he went into bankruptcy it was his case, *Sturgis v. Crowninshield,* in which Chief Justice Marshall upheld the constitutionality of bankruptcy statutes.

All in all, the Crowninshields were a prominent clan; but quite naturally, now that he was a prime suspect in the murder of Captain White, it was young Richard, aged twenty-six, who took the attention of the town. We know very little about him—less, certainly, than did his cousins when they wrote to their father in Washington. Richard was dark, bold, and intelligent. Like the rest of the family, he had no respect for conventionality; unlike them, he had no respect for law, either. He was the admired leader of all the rascals in Essex County.

For two weeks, the Committee of Vigilance got no further. A couple of bad Crowninshields in gaol was the best they had to offer an outraged and anxious community. Then on May 14 Captain Joseph J. Knapp, Sr., young Joe's father, received a threatening letter. It came from Belfast, Maine, and it demanded $350, "the refusal of which will ruin you." The letter was signed "Charles Grant, Junior."

The senior Captain Knapp was even more respected

blackguards were jailed for a brutal murder, justice seemed

were no ordinary criminals, and justice needed eloquent help

than his son. He had owned ships that sailed out of Salem and others that he had shared with Captain White. Recent adversity had led him to make an assignment to his creditors, but he remained a respected and beloved member of the Marine Society. This letter made no sense to him. He showed it to his son Phippen, who had gone to Harvard, and together they consulted young Joe. He simply laughed at it, and told his father he should take the letter to the Committee of Vigilance. And so he did the next day. Here was a clue, and the committee thought it warranted retaining Rufus Choate, a brilliant young lawyer who had come to Salem only two years before.

It was easy enough to pick up "Charles Grant" in a small community like Belfast, Maine. He turned out to be a thoroughly disreputable character, whose real name was Palmer. Not long out of Thomastown Prison, where he had served two years for burglary, he was a shoddy witness, and he told a sorry tale.

The two Crowninshields had told him that young Joe Knapp had offered them and Knapp's brother Frank a thousand dollars to kill old Captain White. The three Salem men had asked Palmer to join them in the murder for a share of the fee. When he refused, they told him it was a joke. But later Palmer heard that the fee had indeed been offered, and he had written to Joe Knapp to see if there was anything in it. He had, he claimed, addressed the letter to Joe's father by mistake.

Palmer was brought to Salem, and the two Knapps, Joe and Frank, were arrested and joined the Crowninshields in gaol. Salem breathed a sigh of relief.

The Knapp brothers were scarcely settled in their cells when Joe was visited by his pastor, the Reverend Mr. Colman, now a prominent member of the Committee of Vigilance. Convinced that Joe was guilty, Mr. Colman had come to get him to confess.

He visited the gaol three times that day, and Joe finally agreed to tell all—but only if Frank consented. Here Mr. Colman needed some help, and he took Phippen, Frank's brother, with him to Frank's cell.

Who can hope to know what was said? Phippen later recalled that Frank had said, "I have nothing to confess—it is a hard case, but if it is as you say, Joseph may confess if he pleases." The Reverend Mr. Colman's memory of the conversation was somewhat different. According to him, Frank "thought it hard, or not fair, that Joseph should have the advantage of making a confession, since the thing was done for his benefit, or advantage." And the pastor recalled that Frank had added, "I told Joe when he proposed it, that it was a silly business, and would only get us into difficulty."

Joe finally admitted his guilt privately to Mr. Col-man, but the minister knew that in order to obtain a written confession—with or without Frank's assent —he would have to offer Joe a pledge of immunity, and for that he needed authority from the attorney general. He rode at once to Boston, stopped at the Tremont House to tell Stephen White the good news, saw the attorney general, and got his written pledge not to prosecute Joe if he would confess and testify for the state against the others. With this in his pocket, Colman rode rapidly back through the night to Salem.

At one o'clock the next afternoon he and two other members of the committee, Dr. Barstow and Mr. Pettiplace, met at the north steps of the Howard Street Church. There, following directions Joe Knapp had given him, Mr. Colman put his hand into a rat hole under the steps and drew out the club that had killed Captain White. Now back to the gaol, to give Joe the attorney general's pledge, and to get his confession down in writing.

Joe now had more need of a lawyer than a clergyman, and Phippen Knapp had gone to Boston to get one. He was lucky: he was able to retain Franklin Dexter and William H. Gardiner, leaders of the Boston bar; they would take on Phippen's close friend and classmate, Robert Rantoul, for their junior. Phippen could not have done better.

Mr. Colman had promised Phippen to wait for his return before going to see Joe again and take his confession, but Phippen wasn't back until three o'clock, and Colman couldn't wait. When Phippen came to Joe's cell, Mr. Colman refused to let him in until he had "finished his business."

This was not until seven that evening, when Joe finally signed the confession, which Colman had written out in his own hand. Joe's part in the murder turned out to be sordid and mercenary. He had said to his brother Frank, as far back as February, "I wouldn't begrudge a thousand dollars that the old gentleman was dead." If the Captain's will were destroyed, his money wouldn't all go to Stephen; half would come to Mrs. Beckford, Joe's mother-in-law, and thence through her to him.*

* Apparently Joe Knapp shared Salem's assumption that Stephen White was the principal heir, but in this he was tragically mistaken. Like many another close-fisted Yankee, the Captain kept his financial affairs to himself. His will, dated January 8, 1830, and filed for probate on May 4, less than a month after he was murdered, divided his fortune among his nephews and nieces and their descendants; Mary Beckford, Knapp's mother-in-law, received $15,000—less than some of the legatees, more than others. Stephen White was named executor, but a thorough examination of the will—still on file in the County Court House in Salem— makes no specific cash bequest to Stephen and contains no residuary clause. [Ed.]

Webster Enters the Case

Webster, by G. P. A. Healy

The killing of the venerable Captain White was so mysterious and frightful that it attracted widespread attention before Senator Daniel Webster stepped on the scene. But his consent to appear for the prosecution gave it unprecedented notoriety.

In the summer of 1830, Webster, in his forty-ninth year, was at the absolute height of his fame—the Cicero of America, the matchless orator of the Dartmouth College Case, the Plymouth Oration, and the more recent Reply to Hayne, and not yet the perennially disappointed candidate for the Presidency. He had been elected in June, 1827, to the U.S. Senate.

Webster had had his own personal sorrows as well as his public triumphs. In January, 1828, his wife of twenty years, Grace Fletcher Webster, died after a painful illness, and his second wife, Caroline Le Roy, did not have an equally restraining influence upon him. Webster, always a free spender, lapsed deeper and deeper into debt.

In January, 1830, a bridegroom of only a few weeks, Webster reached his eloquent zenith in his Reply to Hayne, and from that moment he was regarded as the outstanding spokesman for the Union. When the twenty-third Congress closed its first session on May 31, Webster made his way, in the slow fashion of those days, back to New England. While in the capital, he had read of the White murder; and his friend, Justice Joseph Story, had written him from Cambridge giving some of the gory details. Stephen White, the man who invited Webster to enter the case, was Captain White's nephew and had married Judge Story's sister; White's daughter later married Webster's son, Fletcher. Many ramifications of this crime gave it the aspect of a family affair.

Harriet Martineau, in her *Retrospect of Western Travel* (1838), told how the rusticating statesman was persuaded to assist in the prosecution of the Knapps:

"A citizen of Salem, a friend of mine, was deputed to carry the request. . . . Mr. Webster was at his farm by the seashore. Thither, in tremendous weather, my friend followed him. Mr. Webster was playing checkers . . . My friend was first dried and refreshed, and then lost no time in mentioning business. Mr. Webster writhed at the word, saying that he came hither to get out of the hearing of it. He next declared that his undertaking anything more was entirely out of the question, and pointed, in evidence, to his swollen bag of briefs lying in a corner. However, upon a little further explanation and meditation, he agreed to the request with the same good grace with which he afterward went to the task. He made himself master of all that my friend could communicate, and before daybreak was off through the woods, in the unabated storm, no doubt meditating his speech by the way. He needed all the assistance that could be given him, of course; and my friend constituted himself as Mr. Webster's fetcher and carrier of facts. . . . At the appointed hour, Mr. Webster was completely ready."

Webster was badly needed at Salem, for the attorney general, Perez Morton, fifty-nine years out of Harvard College, was aged and infirm, and the principal counsels for the defense, Dexter and Gardiner, were by no means novices. But a still stronger motive was his desire for money. The prospect of a thousand-dollar fee could not be ignored by a man periodically harassed by his creditors. His eight-dollar-a-day salary as senator would hardly have paid his wine bill.

Unquestionably Webster earned his fee—and more. He spent seventeen humid summer days, from August 3 to August 20, in Salem, when he might have been resting or fishing at his farm in Marshfield. Furthermore, after the conviction of Frank Knapp, he returned to Salem in November to devote six more days to the trial of Joseph Knapp—for which extra labor he received no fee whatever.

The public excitement during this trial was described as "prodigious." On August 15 the Salem *Gazette* reported, "Hundreds of individuals were gathered around the Court House, being enabled by the powerful voice and distinct enunciation of Mr. W. to hear the greater part of his address to the jury from the street."

Daniel Webster returned to Marshfield in late August, apparently quite satisfied with the convictions, his own speeches, and his remuneration. He did not attend the hanging of Frank Knapp, and when George Crowninshield was tried in November, Webster had to keep an engagement in the Rhode Island courts and could not go to Salem. At this trial the government was represented only by the attorney general and the solicitor general. George, although far from being a paragon of virtue, was quite rightly acquitted.

—*Claude M. Fuess*

Frank said he didn't have the pluck, but he knew who would—the Crowninshields, Dick and George. Joe answered: "I told him, well, I didn't think they would, but he could go and see." Frank did go and see, and some time later Joe met Richard Crowninshield, who showed Joe the tools he would do it with, a club and a dirk. On the morning after the murder, Joe's confession continued, Frank came to the farm at Wenham and told Joe how the deed had been done. About ten o'clock on that fateful April night, Richard Crowninshield had met Frank Knapp in Brown Street, had told him to go home, and then had himself gone into the house by the back window, which Joe had previously unbarred. Richard had met Frank again about eleven. Then they had separated and gone home. A fortnight later, Joe Knapp said, Richard came to the farm and "I gave him one hundred five-franc pieces," and "Richard Crowninshield informed me that same evening, that he had put the club with which he killed Capt. White, under the Branch Meeting House steps."

Here by rights this sordid tale should end, with assurance that Justice would easily triumph and the four blackguards would hang. And so it would have ended, had not Justice run into difficulties.

Dick Crowninshield, in his cell in the Salem gaol, undoubtedly knew that Joe Knapp had confessed. The Committee of Vigilance, in a burst of pride, had revealed it to the newspapers. Dick read all about it, and gossip had the run of the gaol. So, Dick mused, Joe had taken the easy way out!

Hence it happened that one day, as lawyer Dexter was visiting his client, Frank Knapp, he heard his name called. He stepped over to the window of the cell. Dick Crowninshield wanted to ask him a question. If Dick were to die suddenly, could anything be done to George and Frank? No, Mr. Dexter said. Crowninshield pressed his question. Mr. Dexter said he was sure of it. The Supreme Judicial Court had held, some ten years before, that where no principal has been convicted no accessory can be convicted; and that since the law presumes every man innocent until he has been proven guilty, no one can be tried as an accessory until someone has been proven to be the principal in the crime.

Having delivered this legal opinion, Mr. Dexter went home to Boston. Late that night his wife heard him pacing the floor, and asked him what was the matter. "I had a talk with Richard Crowninshield today," he said, "and now I am led to believe they are all guilty."

Who knew better than Richard Crowninshield that he and he alone was the principal in this crime? He had met Frank Knapp on Brown Street and had left him, urging Frank to go home. He believed Frank had done so. Perhaps he had, and had then come back, for he was there after the murder, curious about how it had come off. At most, Frank had done nothing more than hang around. As for his brother George, Richard Crowninshield knew very well that *he* had spent the night "at Mary's." If that Boston lawyer knew what he was talking about—and he seemed to—Richard Crowninshield thought he saw a way to keep Frank and George from hanging. Joe was looking out for himself, damn him. He had taken the easy way. Dick would now take the hard way.

The next day, Nehemiah Brown, the keeper of the gaol, stopped and called at Dick's cell, but got no answer. Brown looked through the wicket. There was Dick, hanging at the grating by two silk handkerchiefs knotted together, his knees bent and not more than a foot from the floor. It was an exceedingly deliberate suicide, and a gauntlet thrown in the face of Justice!

As soon as Rufus Choate explained the legal consequences of Dick's removal as principal, the Committee of Vigilance was quick to see how serious the challenge was. It appeared to be more than an aging attorney general could cope with, even with the confession Mr. Colman had obtained from Joe Knapp.

Stephen White, as a member of the committee, met the challenge by retaining the great Daniel Webster for a fee of one thousand dollars.

On the third of August, 1830, as much of Salem as the courtroom would hold jostled and scrambled in. The lawyers were already at their tables, taking papers out of their green bags—the attorney general and Webster at the table nearest the bench; Dexter, Gardiner, and Rantoul at the defense table behind them.

Then "three young men, well and rather genteelly dressed, and of fair presence," as one newspaper put it, were brought into the dock. But only Frank Knapp was to be tried. For he was charged as the principal now, with Joe Knapp and George Crowninshield as his accessories. They could not be tried until Frank had been convicted. Now they were remanded.

Nineteen prospective jurors were rejected by peremptory challenges, and eleven more for cause shown, before a jury was impaneled. Justice was choosing her representatives on earth with care, here in this case between the Great Man Eloquent and a young blackguard of Salem.

The fact of the murder was quickly established by Benjamin, Captain White's manservant; by Lydia, the cook; and by Doctor Johnson.

Now the attorney general called Joseph J. Knapp, Jr., to the witness stand, and inquired of him if he was willing to be sworn. But Joe shook his head, and said nothing. "On advice of counsel," the attorney

The scene of the crime: Captain White's stately house on Salem's Essex Street.

general remarked. Dexter denied it. So did Gardiner and Rantoul. Joe had, indeed, asked Dexter if he had better testify, and had been told: "You must decide for yourself." Joe had muttered, "It won't do."

"Perfidy to the State and to the Government which would have saved him!" Mr. Webster was to call it. But that was not quite true.

It was now incumbent on the Reverend Mr. Colman to summon up his best memory of what Frank had said to him and Phippen; and he did so very well indeed. Then Palmer, the shoddy witness. There was also testimony from a boy who worked for Mrs. Beckford in Wenham—a tale of what he said he had heard Joe and Frank say on the other side of a stone wall against which he had been "nooning." It was damning enough, but scarcely survived cross-examination.

Still, it was becoming very plain that Frank had been an accessory. Yet Dick Crowninshield's ghost was haunting this court room. Could Webster make the jury believe that Frank as well as Dick had been a principal, and not merely an accessory? Could he prove, to put it in legal language, that Frank had been "present, aiding, and abetting the murder"?

There were many witnesses who *thought* they had seen Frank Knapp on Brown Street that evening, but none was certain; and there was no unanimity on how the man had been dressed. Some said he had worn a dark frock coat, others that he had worn what Frank usually wore, a camlet cloak. Even if Frank had been there, what could he have done to aid and abet Dick from so far away? Brown Street ran behind the White mansion, toward the Common; it was three hundred feet away through the Captain's garden.

What if Frank had been on Brown Street only to be informed of the result? Mr. Dexter asked the court to instruct the jury that in such an event Frank could not be convicted. The court agreed: "If the defendant did nothing more than this, he must be acquitted." But there was nobody to tell the jury that Dick had sent Frank home, and that he had come back only to find out what had happened. Not even Frank himself, for those were the days before a defendant could take the stand on his own behalf.

Webster's closing speech was not so well reported at the time that he did not feel it necessary to embellish it for publication later. But we can easily imagine the impact of his eloquence, particularly the great passage on suicide:

Meantime, the guilty soul cannot keep its secret. It is false to itself; or rather it feels an irresistible impulse of conscience to be true to itself . . . It *must* be confessed. It WILL be confessed. There is no refuge from confession, but suicide.

At this point Mr. Webster paused, as a dash in his revised version indicates; and someone sitting close by said, loud enough to be heard "—and suicide *is* confession." Mr. Webster picked it up, and concluded, "And Suicide *is* confession."

Yes. There was no gainsaying that. But may it not also be something more? May not a man take his own life with as much love as he can lay it down for his friends?

It was going to take more than eloquence to convince the jury that Frank was "present, aiding, and abetting" this murder. And Webster was not quite persuasive enough. The jury was out all one afternoon, all the next day, and still could not agree the following morning. At three o'clock that afternoon, the foreman reported that "there was not the least probability of their ever coming to an agreement."

Dick Crowninshield's suicide and Joe Knapp's refusal to testify against his brother had saved Frank, but Justice has greater staying power than the gallantry of the wicked. Another jury was promptly impaneled, and the case was tried all over again.

This time the testimony that Frank was on Brown Street that evening was more satisfactory. Justice had been outraged, and testimonial truth sought firmer ground. One of the four witnesses to Frank's presence, Peter E. Webster,

John Pimlott

had not been able to swear positively that he had seen the prisoner; nor was he any more positive now. But the memories of the other three had improved: from "can't swear positively" to "have no doubt"; from "I judge it was Frank" to "I can swear positively"; from "My belief is" to "I've no doubt."

So this time the jury found Frank Knapp guilty, and on September 28, 1830, "very neatly dressed in a dark cloth frock coat, blue pantaloons and light vest . . ." he was hanged.

Joe Knapp's trial followed. By refusing to testify against Frank he had forfeited his immunity, which the attorney general had pledged him only on condition that he make a complete disclosure and testify fully and truly. Now the written confession he had made after receiving the pledge (his oral confession, given to Mr. Colman the day before, was not competent evidence) made short work of him. He had made it in the hope of immunity. His "It won't do" had been a gallant act, but for it he paid the same price Dick Crowninshield had paid. On December 31, 1830, Joe Knapp, too, was hanged.

George Crowninshield, the last of these four young blackguards, took his trial lightly, even gaily. To be sure, he had been in town that night, he admitted, but he had an alibi. He had spent the night safely in bed with one Mary Bassett, and it was his good fortune that another lady could testify to it, one Mary Jane Weller. Mr. Dexter called her "a most precious witness, a most infamous woman, of lewd character." Lewd and infamous she may have been, but Mary Jane Weller *was* a precious witness—how good may be judged from her cross-examination:

Q. What sort of weather was it the next day?
A. You know as well as I do. I am not going to answer any such silly questions. I've told my story and I don't want to be made fun of.

Thereupon, it is recorded, "on a suggestion from the Court, counsel desisted from a cross-examination."

Salem by now had had its fill of the hanging of young men, however vicious. The jury acquitted George Crowninshield, and he lived to a good old age, whatever his youth had been. He died in 1888, stoutly maintaining to the end that it was not his brother Dick, but Stephen White, who had murdered the old Captain.

Between its grim beginning on a Virginia plantation and its surprising end at a great New York estate, the career of Nancy Randolph involved many of the famous figures of the post-Revolutionary era. The lovers, the scorned ex-suitor, the cheated wife, all four were cousins in a great southern dynasty. This tale of hate and "honor" is recounted by a descendant of Edmund Randolph, the first Attorney General of the United States

By FRANCIS BIDDLE

SCANDAL AT BIZARRE

The story of Anne Cary Randolph, called Nancy, is strangely interwoven with that of her spectacular cousin, John Randolph of Roanoke, and touches other famous names in unfamiliar moments; it gives us a glimpse into the intimate history of the times. Her career opened with tragedy before she had come of age, pursued a course of wretchedness and poverty while she was still a young woman, and ended, as she was touching middle age, in serene happiness and contentment.

At seventeen she was tried, with her sister Judith's husband, for the murder of their child—and acquitted. For the next fifteen years, with the mark of adultery and—by the laws of the time—incest on her sleeve, she lived with Judith at Bizarre plantation, and with her sister's two children, St. George, a deaf-mute, and Tudor, who became a consumptive. These years of poverty and repugnance, the shadow of her sister's hatred poisoning the air, suggest the pattern of *The Sound and the Fury*, for Faulkner might as easily have written about these Randolphs of Virginia as he did of their brothers under the skin in Mississippi.

Nancy's story was dramatic enough to have been long remembered, yet history seems almost to have forgotten it. Her lawyers in the trial that shook the state of Virginia from end to end were Patrick Henry and John Marshall; but Beveridge in his life of the Chief Justice makes no mention of the case. He may have thought it too nasty for comment. Jefferson's daughter Patsy was a witness, yet Jefferson never referred to it in his vast correspondence except indirectly, when he wrote Patsy that he "saw guilt in but one person," but not in Nancy. He urged his daughter never to fear to extend her hand to save another "lest you should sink yourself." He hoped Patsy would preserve her cousin "in the peace and love of her friends."

There was a saying in Virginia that only a Randolph was good enough for a Randolph. Certainly the Randolphs were constantly marrying their cousins, and almost every actor in Nancy's drama was related to her and to the other characters. The relationships tend to confusion. Two families are particularly involved— John Randolph of Roanoke, and his two elder brothers, Richard and Theodorick; and Nancy Randolph

---

For fifteen years after her acquittal, Anne Cary (Nancy) Randolph lived at Bizarre amidst poverty and degradation. The only known portrait of her—seen on the preceding page—shows Nancy after that experience, in her mid-thirties. It is a pastel by James Sharples, completed soon after her marriage in 1809 to Gouverneur Morris.

---

and her sister Judith. Nancy and Judith and their brothers, "Possum" John and Thomas Mann Randolph, Jr. (who had married Martha—called Patsy—Jefferson), were second cousins of the three Randolph boys. Nancy was full of the delight of living, hot-blooded, careless, haphazard. She carried her gaiety and affection through the most trying and tragic passages of her strange career. Judith was plain, pious, serious, and terribly frustrated by life. She married her cousin Richard, the eldest brother, when she was sixteen. After her mother died, and her father had re-married, having lost a substantial fortune by acting as surety for a friend, Nancy went to live with Richard and her sister Judith at Richard's plantation, Bizarre.

The three Randolph boys at one time or another were all in love with Nancy, who seems to have had an irresistible charm for men. John she turned down, taxing him with his impotence—this at least he came to believe. To Theodorick she became engaged—and he died in eight months. Richard—handsome, intelligent, and his brother John's idol—not long afterward became Nancy's lover.

The first act of this incredible melodrama began at a house party at Glenlyvar, the country place of the Randolph Harrisons. Richard and his wife; Nancy; John; and a young cousin, Archibald Randolph (Mrs. Harrison's brother), who was also attracted by Nancy, drove over to Glenlyvar from Bizarre on October 1, 1792. Nancy, wrapped in a thick cape, was so weak she could hardly get to the second floor, where her room was next to that of Richard and Judith. The Harrisons slept on the floor below. In the middle of the night Nancy woke screaming, and was given laudanum —so Harrison was told—to quiet one of the recurring hysterical fits from which she suffered. Later that night the Harrisons heard someone descend the stairs and return. The next morning Nancy was still in bed, wrapped in blankets. There was blood on the pillow-case and along the stairs.

The house party broke up. Old Esau, a slave, whispered to Harrison that a foetus of a white child had been carried out into the yard and placed on a wood-pile. He had seen bloodstains on the shingles where a hound sniffed.

The story spread and before long was all over the South: the dead child was Nancy's and Richard's, and they had murdered it. Were the Randolphs stronger than the Commonwealth of Virginia? Would the state dare indict them? The taverns buzzed with allusions to Richard and his trull. Finally the gossip reached home to Richard. After consulting John Marshall—through his grandmother he was one of the Randolph tribe, with eight years still to go before he would be appointed to the Supreme Court—Richard sent an open letter to his stepfather, Judge Tucker, for publication. That, it was thought, would force the authorities to take action, and seemed to him the only way he could obtain public vindication. "My character has lately been blackened," he wrote, "with the imputation of crimes at which humanity revolts, and which the laws of society have pronounced worthy of condign punishment." The charge against him had spread far and wide, and had daily acquired strength in the minds of his fellow citizens. It would take too long to refute these calumnies by private suits against their authors; and he had therefore resolved on this method to present himself before the bar of public opinion. "Calumny to be *obviated* must be confronted." If the crimes imputed to him were true, his life was the just forfeit to the laws of his country. He was giving notice that on the first of April, 1793, he would appear before the Cumberland County Court, and render himself prisoner to the court or any magistrate of the county there present to answer any charge whatsoever that any person might think proper to allege against him. The only favor he could ask of his accusers was "to step forth and exert themselves for conviction." His supposed accomplice would "meet the accusation with the fortitude of innocence." The letter was printed in the *Virginia Gazette and Chronicle*.

Gouverneur Morris, shown in a companion pastel to Nancy's, served in the Continental Congress, was minister to France and a Federalist U.S. senator.

It was a courageous challenge. Richard must have known what it would mean if the Commonwealth prosecuted, and the case were tried. They would all be dragged into the witness box—Judith and Nancy, John and Archibald, the Harrisons; and Nancy's aunt, that peering, vindictive old busybody, Mrs. Carter Page, who had been sniffing around her niece ever since she had begun to show her changed condition. Under the Virginia law a slave could not testify against a white person, so that old Esau would not be allowed to swear to what he had found. Richard's lawyers must have told their client that there was no evidence of murder —of adultery, yes—but not of murder.

On April 29, 1793, Richard and Nancy were held without bail by sixteen gentlemen justices for feloni-

ously murdering a child, said to be Nancy Randolph's.

Richard also retained Patrick Henry for five hundred guineas to try the case with Marshall, a very large fee for those days. Henry was past his prime at fifty-six. He was infirm and less active in his practice, and would be dead in half a dozen years; but he was still the darling of the plain people, one of them; and, unlike his younger associate Marshall, was a tough old lion, brutal in cross-examination, and a spellbinder who could convince you against your will. Everyone flocked into Cumberland to hear old Patrick Henry defend young Richard Randolph. They were all so young— Richard, twenty-five; John, nineteen; Judith, twenty; and Nancy, seventeen.

The family divided sharply, some testifying to Richard's intimacy with his sister-in-law, others not willing to admit any impropriety. Richard's uncle, Major Carter Page, who had been an aide ,to Lafayette, opened the case for the Commonwealth by swearing that Richard and Nancy were very fond of each other, they "were very good company for themselves," and the witness had seen them kissing and embracing. He had noticed Nancy's increase in size. His wife, who could never forget that she was a daughter of Archibald Cary, the speaker of the Virginia Senate, testified to Nancy's pregnancy. She had heard Judith complain of the intimacy between her husband and sister and begun to watch them. She had noticed a change in the girl's figure, and a moodiness which Mrs. Page did not ascribe to colic. She had asked her niece if she could examine her to determine whether she was a virgin, but was flatly and impolitely refused. Mrs. Page's worst fears were soon confirmed. One evening on her way to her chamber, she passed Nancy's door, which was closed, and heard her niece talking to her colored maid. The door was locked, but Mrs. Page could see inside through the keyhole. Nancy stood absolutely naked before her mirror, combing her hair, and her aunt saw that she was pregnant. She also heard Nancy ask her maid if she did not think that her mistress was smaller, and heard the girl say: "Ain't so. Truth is, you belly gettin' bigger."

Patrick Henry rose to cross-examine. Was she on terms of intimacy with the Bizarre family, and was it her custom to inspect her niece on every visit? "I am not accustomed to pry," answered Mrs. Page, trying to look haughty—it was her duty as an aunt to determine Nancy's condition. "Duty alone compelled you to look through a crack in the door as she prepared to retire?" he asked her gravely. She acquiesced. Whereupon Patrick Henry, with his "inimitable power of exciting ridicule," asked the witness which eye she peeped with; and when laughter drowned her answer, "Great God," he cried, "deliver us from eavesdroppers!"

Patsy Jefferson Randolph, twenty-two, was called by the prosecution, but turned out to be a cool and unflustered witness for her sister-in-law. Yes, Mrs. Judith Randolph had asked her if she knew a remedy for Nancy's "colic," and she told Mrs. Randolph that she could get some gum guaiacum, an excellent remedy for that ailment. It was dangerous if taken in too great quantities by a pregnant woman, she had added, for then it might produce abortion. She sent Miss Nancy a portion a few days later. On cross-examination Patrick Henry asked if she wished to give the impression that she had sent the medicine to Miss Nancy with any belief that she desired to produce such a result. On the contrary, Patsy answered, it was the best remedy for the colic from which Nancy was suffering miserably. She had known of cases where more gum guaiacum was given to a pregnant woman without producing any ill effect.

But Judith's testimony was the most impressive of all. She knew that her younger sister and her husband had been lovers, and that their child was born on that first terrible night of the house party. For the rest of her life she would show in every act and word how much she detested Nancy. But at the trial Judith perjured herself on the stand for the family name, to keep the family "honor" out of the gutter. Patrick Henry thrust at once to the heart of the charge. "Mrs. Randolph," he said, "common gossip has brought charges to this Court that your husband committed murder that night. A new-born child, his child, delivered of your sister in that inner room, was carried by Mr. Randolph, scandalmongers say, out into the hoary night and cast cruelly on a pile of shingles. I ask you, Mrs. Randolph, if you saw anything to indicate so heinous a crime was perpetrated."

"I saw nothing," she answered firmly.

Judith swore that her husband did not go downstairs for any purpose all that night; he was sleeping by her side, although she could not sleep at all. Could Richard, Henry pressed her, have carried the body of a child from her sister's room, and downstairs, as the prosecution claimed, without Judith's knowledge? "It could not have happened," she said—he would have had to pass through her room, where she lay awake all night, and she must have known. And, under cross-examination by the Commonwealth's attorney, repeating every detail of that horrible night, hour after hour, unflustered and cool, she stuck to her story.

After hearing the evidence the sixteen justices dismissed the case, and John Marshall noted, in the careful account he made of the trial: "The friends of Miss Randolph cannot deny that there is some foundation on which suspicion may build; nor can it be denied by her enemies that every circumstance may be accounted for without imputing guilt to her. In this situation, candor will not condemn, or exclude from society a person who may be only unfortunate." It now seems to be accepted that Nancy had a miscarriage, but that she and her lover were not guilty of murder.

But if candor did not condemn, the world did.

The four cousins went back to Bizarre—Judith, Nancy, Richard, and John. Judith was desperate —family honor was cold comfort when she knew that her husband and sister had been lovers. Shortly after the trial, she wrote to Mary Harrison: "My health is very bad, indeed so much have I suffered lately, both in body and mind that I much fear that a few *months* will put an end to my troubles in this world, neglected and thrown off by all whom I once fondly relied on." She watched the lovers constantly with a bleak and morbid jealousy gnawing at her heart. Were they still paramours?

For the next fifteen years Nancy lived in a degradation that constantly grew more humiliating in the squalid intimacy of Bizarre. Her life, she wrote twenty years later, differed "from any servant's only in this. I received no wages but was permitted to sit at table where I did not presume to enter into any conversation or taste of wine and very seldom tea or coffee." She was deprived of the use of her harpsichord. She loved riding, but was not allowed a horse, or any leisure for reading. "Months in succession," she recalled, "have been devoted to the needle (for Judy cherishes not a latent spark of affection for me) when my intellect absolutely languished for a little indulgence." She must be taught to expiate her sin. She must earn her living and keep her place. Each day, after Richard's death, she must clean out the chamber pots—that would relieve a slave for other duty.

Richard died in 1796, three years after the trial, and Judith was later to accuse her sister to John Ran-

One of Richard Randolph's lawyers was Patrick Henry, at 56 an old and broken man, but as a lawyer still "as complete an artist as the times afforded."

dolph of poisoning her husband. The accusation was without foundation. There has been a suggestion that Judith herself caused his death, changing a recipe which called for a *half-grain* of tartar emetic, to be mixed with calomel, jalap, opium, and oil of aniseed, to read *ten grains,* and telling Nancy to mix it and give it to Richard to relieve his pain. Ten grains were enough to kill. Judith—this story runs —put the original recipe in the pocket of Nancy's apron. Richard vomited, writhing in agony. He lived for a few days longer, without Judith's sending for a doctor—it was not necessary, she told an English traveler who had stopped with a letter of introduction from Colonel Beverley Randolph. There was a terrible thunderstorm, and she said that Dr. Smith might not come; she herself would nurse her husband through the night. The next day the doctor came, and all the next night until he died Judith nursed Richard, and dosed him constantly—but not as Dr. Smith had directed. Nancy was too terrified to interfere. She was afraid of Judith, who had got hold of the prescription. Early in the morning Richard died. Of the three brothers only John was left.

John inherited Bizarre from his brother, but was seldom there, and the sisters lived alone with the two children. It was a strange atmosphere for the two boys to grow up in. Nancy loved them both and helped to bring them up. St. John, who was nicknamed "the Saint," was sweet and affectionate, and devoted to his aunt. He had a fine, sensitive, friendly face and gentle manners. He could not understand very much. Tudor liked his aunt, too—it was hard not to love her—until he was told as he grew older by his mother and his Uncle John that she was a murderess. Tudor was always in wretched health, slowly decaying. Like his Uncle John, it was not hard for him to hate.

Now that Richard was dead, Judith lost all self-restraint. She ordered Nancy's meals served to her in her room or in the kitchen. Nancy must work out of sight, and not go to her room until Mrs. Randolph had retired for the night. Judith was seeing strange visions, losing her self-control in fits of anger, on the edge of convulsions . . . Finally, a note written to one of the slaves by Nancy, beginning "Dear Billy Ellis," telling him to polish the andirons, fell into Judith's hands. She accused Nancy of sexual intercourse with a black, screaming at her, ordered Billy whipped, and locked Nancy in her room. When John Randolph arrived he directed Nancy to leave the house at once . . .

In a few years Bizarre burned down. Tudor, who was at Harvard, developed consumption. John wrote a friend:

Affliction has assailed me in a new shape. My younger nephew, whom you saw in Georgetown a few years ago, has fallen, I fear, into a confirmed pulmonary consumption. He was the sole hope of our family. He is now traveling by slow stages home. What a scene awaits him! His birthplace is in ashes; his mother worn to a skeleton with grief; his brother cut off from all that distinguishes man from the brute beast. My own reason has staggered under this last cruel blow. All is chaos and misery.

But not for Nancy. Toward her the gods at last turned a smiling face. It was in 1808 that she met Gouverneur Morris at "old Mrs. Pollacks'" boarding-house in Greenwich Village. He expressed a wish, as Nancy years later wrote a friend, "that some reduced gentlewoman would undertake to keep his house, as the lower class of housekeepers often provoked the servants to riot in his dwelling." He was a friend of her father's and remembered her as a child at Tuckahoe, bursting with vitality, galloping her pony over the plantation, following her father about, curtsying in her funny, long dress to Mr. Jefferson when he came to stay with them. He had brought back a French chef and French coachman from Paris, and they were always quarreling with his black house-servants. He wanted only peace.

He began to correspond with Nancy. He offered to help her, and when she thanked him, said he did not want her gratitude. He vaguely remembered the events that brought distress into her family, but she should not dwell on them. If they were ever alone she could tell him "her tale of sorrow." He asked her to come to Morrisania to manage his house. She did not accept at once, but teased him about other "housekeepers." There had been only two, he said, one of them "a tall, well-made good-looking woman of low birth and education: assuming to have so much of vulgar dignity as to offend my servants . . . Certainly I have never approached either of them with anything like desire."

His diary notes that on April 23, 1809, he drove "to Armstrong's tavern and after breakfast brought home Miss Randolph of Virginia who had arrived from Con-

21

necticut." On Christmas Day he added, "I marry this day Anne Cary Randolph. No small surprise to my guests." Two years later Nancy was pregnant, and Morris, returning from Albany, wrote in his diary, "dear, quiet, happy home." It was not like any other entry in that witty and robust record of his love affairs, as when, for instance, he recorded in Paris that after dining with Adelaide de Flahaut and joining "in fervent adoration to the Cyprian Queen," he left her "reclined in the sweet tranquility of nature well satisfied."

Gouverneur Morris had a shrewd understanding of people, and of their foibles and vices and jealousies, but his resulting skepticism had not dried up a natural friendliness and generosity. And he idolized his wife. He had heard of Tudor's illness in Cambridge, and suggested to Nancy that they get the boy to Morrisania —it would do him good. Reluctantly she acquiesced— she was still fond of her nephew, but she did not trust him. Accordingly, in July, 1814, Morris wrote John Randolph a friendly letter expressing his hope that Tudor and his mother would come to stay with them. They would find "a comfortable home, an affectionate sister, and a good friend." John responded to this "friendly and interesting letter" in the same tone. Meanwhile Tudor wrote his aunt asking for money, and the desired sum was sent him. Almost immediately he arrived, was put to bed at once, and treated for a hemorrhage by the famous Dr. David Hosack, summoned from New York. In October Judith came, followed in two days by John Randolph.

Tudor whispered to his uncle that his Aunt Nancy was indulging in "lewd amours," and that his earliest memories of her had been that she was an "unchaste woman." Probably John Randolph did not at first take his nephew seriously, for (according to Nancy's credible account) when he left in two days he thanked Morris, and kissed Nancy affectionately. He bade her remember the past, and those who once loved her. She must not think too harshly of her own kin. To Morris he expressed gratitude for what he had done for Tudor.

On his way up to Morrisania, John Randolph had fallen down a steep staircase in Philadelphia and injured his shoulder. On his way back the coach in which he was riding overturned, and his leg was painfully wrenched. By the time he reached New York, descending at Mrs. Brandish's boardinghouse, he was in agony, and insisted on a dose of opium.

Then David Ogden, a great-nephew of Gouverneur Morris, stepped in. From the beginning Morris's nephews and nieces were bitter about his marriage. His niece Gertrude Meredith went so far as to write him a protest, telling her uncle that he had committed a folly and had acted undutifully in not consulting

her. His answer was politely, almost amusedly restrained:

I can only say to the first that I have not yet found cause to repent, and to the second that I hope you will pardon me for violating an obligation of which I was not apprized . . . If I had married a rich woman of seventy the world might think it wiser than to take one half that age without a farthing, and, if the world were to live with my wife, I should have certainly consulted its taste; but as that happens not to be the case, I thought I might, without offending others, endeavor to suit myself, and look rather into the head and the heart than into the pocket.

David Ogden wanted his uncle's money; the Randolphs, Nancy's disgrace. If Morris could be made to believe that his wife was unfaithful and even dangerous, their separation might follow, and Ogden would eventually inherit the share of his uncle's fortune which he felt was his by right.

Ogden sought out Judith—they had both come to New York—and they compared notes. She probably told him that Nancy had killed not only her baby but the child's father. With this accusation Ogden went to see Randolph, lying in bed with his crippled leg, and assured him that Mrs. Morris was unchaste, she was engaged at that moment in a love affair, and Mr. Morris was in danger. John was inclined to agree, to believe anything evil about Nancy. He sent for Judith. She agreed with Mr. Ogden, and talked of the fatal dose that had killed Richard. John must save Mr. Morris. Tudor, following his mother, reminded his uncle of Nancy's "love letter" to Billy Ellis. John's old hatred of Nancy flared up—she had rejected him as a suitor, knowing him to be impotent, in favor of a black! Inflamed, half-mad, tortured with doubt and jealousy and pain, he wrote a brief note to Morris, saying that he wished he could withhold the blow—but he must do what he would have Morris do to him, "under a change of circumstances." With the note he enclosed a long letter to Nancy, charging her in violently intemperate language with murder and the intention to murder.

"Madam," he wrote, "when at my departure from Morrisania I bade you 'remember the past,' I was not appraised of the whole extent of your guilty machi-

Also at Randolph's side was the great John Marshall—capable, said a contemporary, "of developing a subject by a single glance of his mind."

nations . . . My object was to let you know that the eye of man as well as of that God of whom you seek not was upon you, . . . to rouse some dormant spark of virtue if haply any such should slumber in your bosom." He was now convinced that she had destroyed the child of which she was delivered in October, 1792.

Tudor had told him, John continued, that his Aunt Nancy had been responsible for Richard's death in 1796. When he found her mind running upon poisonings and murders, his suspicions were strengthened. After her intimacy with one of the slaves—*"your dear Billy Ellis, thus you commenced your epistles to this Othello!"*—she could no longer stay at Bizarre. Subsequently, he was informed by a friend in Richmond, she had declined "into a very drab." Tudor had said to him that as far back as he could remember she had been an unchaste woman. And now at Morrisania he saw "a vampire that, after sucking the best blood of my race, has flitted off to the North, and struck her harpy fangs into an infirm old man"—Morris was then sixty-two—whom she had made a prisoner in his own house "that there may be no witness of your lewd amours"—had she driven away his friends so that there would be no witness to his death? Before this letter reached her ear, he concluded, it would have been perused by Mr. Morris, who sooner or later must unmask her "unless *he too die of cramps in his stomach.*" He hoped never to see her again.

Apparently Morris was not greatly disturbed by the letter. To Randolph Harrison he wrote: "Mr. Randolph's communication gave me no concern, for Mrs. Morris had apprised me of the only fact in his possession, before she came to my house, so that her candor has blunted the point of his arrow." Yet, although he had received the letter on November 1, he did not show it to his wife until January. We do not know what passed between her and her husband. He confided nothing of their talk to his diary. He may have been frightened, his confidence at times shaken, wondering if cramps in the stomach would follow when she mixed his medicine, or cooked something delicate for him with her own hands. But he did not give her up. We can imagine him sending for her and saying, very simply: "My dear, this is a letter which your cousin of Roanoke sent me to give to you"—and then watching her as she read it, turning crimson, turning pale, trembling, looking up at him when she had finished. "Let me tear it up," he may have suggested, "the poor fellow is obviously mad." But instead of destroying it the extraordinary woman, proud and disdainful and very frank about almost everything, wrote John a long answer, and sent half a dozen copies not so much to her friends as to his political enemies in Virginia, so that both letters remain for posterity to brood over.

Richard's life, Nancy told Richard's brother, knowing what would most deeply wound him,

is now beyond the reach of your malice, but his fame, which should be dear to a brother's heart, is stabbed by the hand of his brother. . . . Our unwarranted trial took place, Sir, in a remote County of Virginia more than twenty years ago. You have revived the slanderous tale in the most populous city in the United States. For what? To repay my kindness to your nephew by tearing me from the arms of my husband and blasting the prospects of my child!

He had alluded to one of Shakespeare's best tragedies. He must be convinced by now that he had but clumsily performed the part of "honest Iago." Happily he had not found in her husband a headlong, rash Othello. For a true description of what on this occasion he had written and spoken she referred him to the same admirable author: "It is a tale told by an idiot, full of sound and fury, signifying nothing." She must have felt proud of her rejoinder as she signed her name—"Anne C. Morris." She would admit to her bastard; but never defame Richard's memory by acknowledging that the child was his.

Two years later Morris was dead. His will gave his wife Morrisania, and a comfortable income; and, "in case my wife should marry, I give her six hundred dollars per annum, to defray the increased expenditure, which may attend that connexion." He left all the residue of his estate to his son, providing in case of his son's death that his estate should go to his nieces and nephews and their descendants "in such proportions as my wife shall designate." He was a just and generous man, not without a sense of irony.

Fall River Legend

Seventy-one years after the murders, doubt persists, and if you were to ask, "Was she guilty?" the chances are a good twenty-to-one that the answer would be affirmative. The law may protect a defendant from double jeopardy, but it cannot prevent the public from passing judgment. What might be called the public's "case" against the rather plain young woman began long before the Commonwealth of Massachusetts brought her to trial. It commenced, in fact, the day after the bodies of her father and stepmother were found. Rumor and half-truth spread like wildfire, feeding on the smouldering flames of fear, creating almost overnight a legend that has never disappeared. The story, as it began to build during those first hours, went something like this: On the hot, humid morning of August 4, 1892, in an angular frame house on Second Street, in Fall River, Massachusetts, Mrs. Andrew Borden was brutally hacked to death by someone wielding a hatchet or an axe. Somewhat later, in another room of the house, her husband was similarly dispatched. The news that a respectable couple had been murdered in their own home in broad daylight brought the town's normal activities to a standstill; two hours after the crime was discovered, thousands of hot, angry people were milling about in Second Street, muttering, questioning, venturing opinions, wondering where the mad killer would strike next, who the next victim would be. Before nightfall the town's newspapers had taken over the case, describing the murder scenes in all their gory detail and hinting broadly at suspects.

Now, almost any news about Andrew Borden would have been enough to make the mill town sit up and take notice; he was a silent, sour man who had made money as an undertaker and as exclusive agent for Crane's Patent Casket Burial Cases, who was now an extremely well-to-do banker and real estate owner. It was common gossip that neither of his daughters, Emma or Lizzie, got on well with their stepmother, whom Borden had married twenty-seven years earlier. But Emma, it seemed, was out of town when the murders were committed. Lizzie had found her father's body on the sitting-room couch and sent the hired girl, Bridget, for help; a little later Bridget and a neighbor discovered Mrs. Borden in the upstairs guest room, lying face down in a pool of blood. So suspicion soon fastened upon the thirty-two-year-old Lizzie, a slight, ordinary-looking girl with brown hair and a habit of saying just what was in her mind.

First Lizzie had killed her stepmother, townsfolk said; then, after cleaning her hands and clothes, she had busied herself about the house for an hour and a half, sewing, ironing, reading a magazine, waiting for her father to return from downtown. After he came in, stretched out on the couch, and dozed off, she attacked him with the same weapon she had used on Mrs. Borden. Again she removed the blood from her clothes and from the axe (all within the space of ten minutes, and so effectively that later chemical tests revealed no trace of it), then called for help. Someone said she never shed a tear when the bodies were discovered; the maid Bridget was said to have heard her laugh coldly when her father entered the house; there was talk that she had tried to buy poison the day before the murders; someone said she was seen burning a dress afterward.

Five days after the crime an inquest was held; two days later Lizzie Borden was arrested and held without bail pending trial. Meanwhile the wildest theories and rumors gained currency. But most damning of all was the verse—those unforgettable four lines of doggerel, sung to the tune of "Ta-ra-ra-boom-de-ay," which condemned her forever in the public mind, no matter what any court might decide:

> Lizzie Borden took an axe
> And gave her mother forty whacks;
> When she saw what she had done
> She gave her father forty-one.

In June, 1893, the trial opened in New Bedford, and for thirteen days the jury heard a great deal of conflicting testimony (much of it highly embarrassing to the prosecution), and witnessed a brilliant performance by the defense attorney. One of the most telling accusations made by the prosecution was that Lizzie had not been in the barn behind the house between 11:00 and 11:15 on the fatal morning, as she claimed—that she had, in fact, been bludgeoning her father to death at that very moment. A sensation of the trial was a surprise witness for the defense, an ice-cream peddler who maintained stoutly and credibly that he had seen a woman, dressed as Lizzie purportedly was, emerging from the barn just when she said she had.

When the trial ended, the jurors were out for a little more than an hour before bringing in a verdict of "Not Guilty." Spectators in the courtroom applauded, and an editorial writer for the New York Sun summed up the trial: "A chain of circumstantial evidence is strong only if it is strong in every necessary link . . . The chain tested at New Bedford the past twelve days was proved fragile indeed, not merely at one place, but in almost every link."

Legally, the defendant was acquitted. Theoretically, her ordeal was over. But the public considered her guilty—guilty by innuendo, if nothing else. Not even her death in 1927 ended the trial of Lizzie Borden. Books and plays were written about her, eventually there were movies, a television show, a ballet. Finally, Edward D. Radin came to her defense with a fine book, *Lizzie Borden: The Untold Story,* that argues her innocence convincingly while revealing the falsehoods behind the legend. There the matter might rest at last, were it not for the cruel verse: "Lizzie Borden took an axe, and gave her mother forty whacks . . ."

—*Richard M. Ketchum*

Crazy Bill had a down look

Quaint pictures and a grim story tell of prejudice and mob passion in upstate New York of the 1840's

By JAMES TAYLOR DUNN *and* LOUIS C. JONES

The scene of the murders. In this primitive painting, old Mrs. Wyckoff fights Freeman in front of the farmhouse.

It was a great event in the upstate New York villages of the Finger Lakes country, during the late 1840's, when George J. Mastin came to town with his "Unparalleled Exhibition of Oil Paintings." First there appeared broadsides on barn doors and in tavern barrooms describing the fourteen huge paintings (8 x 10 feet, most of them) and promising a religious and historical lecture by Mr. Mastin explaining the paintings; there would also be clog dancing by the Erin Twin Brothers, comic songs and a demonstration of phrenological reading.

A day or so after the broadsides were posted came the show and its impresario. The paintings, done on bedticking and rolled up in a long, stout wooden box, were transported from town to town in a farm wagon and carefully hung in the sheds of the local tavern, or in the ballroom, if it were big enough. The show was always at night when twenty flickering candles added movement and excitement to the crude but vivid and forceful work of the unknown artists. Sometimes Mastin would take out his violin and fiddle for dancing. Fiddling and phrenology, lecturing on history and religion, were his pastimes; by trade a tailor, he was later to be a country storekeeper and farmer. He lived a long life over in Genoa and Sempronius, from 1814 to 1910, and seems to have enjoyed himself all the way.

A man could understand without any difficulty the pictures that George Mastin had hired some good sign or carriage painters to do for him. When he lectured before each picture, it all seemed very moving and very real. Five of the canvases were scenes right out of the Bible. Then there were five exciting pictures from American history. But the great drawing card was the series of four which depicted in horrifying, bloody detail the murder of the spectators' own good neighbor, John G. Van Nest, his wife, his baby son, and mother-in-law—all four of them brutally stabbed to death in a few minutes by that crazy colored fellow, Bill Freeman, in their home just south of Auburn.

From mid-March, 1846, to the summer of 1847 the Van Nest murders were a favorite topic of conversation in those parts. They raised a lot of questions. For example, how could you tell if a man was crazy? And if he was crazy and committed a murder, was that any reason not to hang him? And why would a man like ex-Governor William H. Seward, one of the leading lawyers in the state, of his own accord and for no fee, defend this villain?

Bill Freeman was born in the small upstate New York village of Auburn in September, 1823, and all the cards were stacked against him from the beginning. His father, who died insane, was a freed slave; his mother, part Negro, part Indian, a heavy drinker. One uncle became a wandering lunatic and an aunt died early and mad. Despite the fact that Auburn was to become a station of the Underground Railroad and the home of its most famous conductor, Harriet Tubman, it was also a community which long retained strong Copperhead sympathies. The colored population was completely isolated, without any benefits from cultural influences and deprived of the privileges of church and school.

When he reached the age of seven young Bill was put out to work as a servant boy. He was remembered from this time as being not much different from any other boy—lively, smart and active. At times he was lazy, trying to avoid work, and occasionally he ran away. He laughed, played, was good-natured and "talked like other folks."

During those difficult, formative years Freeman came under no good influences. Three times he was arrested for minor offenses, first when he broke open a peddler's cart in front of the Bank Coffee House. A short while later he fled via canalboat after stealing some of Jonas Underwood's chickens, was quickly apprehended and brought back.

In the spring of 1840, the Widow Godfrey of Sennett Township, five miles north of Auburn, lost a horse. Young Bill Freeman, then in his middle teens, was suspected and arrested, but freed after examination by a local magistrate. Some weeks later the Godfrey horse turned up in Chemung County where it had been sold by another Auburn Negro, Jack Furman. Furman, who knew of Freeman's previous arrest, immediately accused the youth. On Furman's testimony, Bill Freeman was convicted and sentenced to five years in prison.

From September, 1840, to the same month five years later Freeman was locked up at the State Prison in Auburn. During the first year of his imprisonment, Keeper James E. Tyler ordered Freeman flogged for not doing his full quota of work. Instead of complying with Tyler's order to strip, Freeman attacked the keeper who took a piece of basswood board a half-inch thick and struck the prisoner over the head, splitting the plank. This was followed by a heavy flogging.

From this point on, Freeman's mood darkened and a serious deafness developed (a post-mortem was to disclose a diseased temporal bone and a broken eardrum). "It was as though the stones of my ears dropp'd down," he stated, "as if the sound went down my throat." Orders had to be given several times before he would understand and seldom did he hold up his head and look a man in the face. "Crazy Bill," the keepers commented, "always had a down look."

His sense of betrayal, bitterness and loneliness added to the misunderstanding of others. The foreman of the dye house considered Freeman "a being of very low, degraded intellect, hardly above a brute, and I treated him so." Whenever Freeman would cry that the floggings hurt him so he couldn't sleep, they would lay the cat on his back with added force.

When Freeman was released from the Auburn State Prison on September 20, 1845, few people recognized him. For the next five and a half months Freeman earned what living he could by sawing wood, although few wanted to employ him. For his room, he helped his landlady, Mary Ann Newark, carry laundry up from the New Guinea section of Auburn to the village. At home he always sat and but seldom spoke. If he said anything, it was mostly about their not paying him at prison. He felt that since he had been put away without cause, he should have his full recompense for those five years of hard work. "There wouldn't anybody pay me," he kept brooding.

It wasn't until March of the following year that Freeman decided to do something about this injustice. First, he visited the farm of Martha Godfrey whose stolen horse had sent him to prison. He ate a cake she put out for him, could bring himself to say nothing of his grievances. Later he stopped for five minutes at a home three miles south of Auburn, a well-kept frame farmhouse on the road which skirts the west shore of Owasco Lake. Here at John Van Nest's he asked unsuccessfully for a job. Freeman next sought a warrant for the arrest of the man (or men—he couldn't make himself clear) who had put him in jail. At the Auburn office of Magistrate Lyman Paine he flew into a passion when this demand was refused.

The dark storm brewing in his twisted mind became more oppressive. On Monday, March 9, Freeman purchased a knife. On March 12, Freeman said to himself, "I must begin my work," the work of vengeance and requital. Reaching Owasco Lake, he took the shore road down to the west side. He paused at two or three places, but it wasn't far enough out to begin.

The moon came up, shimmering on the recently fallen snow. It was cold. When Freeman reached the farmhouse of John G. Van Nest he decided that the time had come. Here was where he should begin his work.

Within the house, the Van Nest family was preparing for bed. It was almost 9:30 and a visiting neighbor had just left. The master of the house, 41-year-old John G. Van Nest, justice of the peace, supervisor and highly respected farmer, was warming himself in front of the stove in the back kitchen. His wife Sarah was about to step out the back door. His mother-in-law, Mrs. Phebe Wyckoff, had taken their oldest child Peter and retired to the north front bedroom. Helen Holmes, Mrs. Wyckoff's great-niece and adopted daughter, had gone with young Julia Van Nest to their bedroom. Cornelius

Van Arsdale, the new hired man, was already upstairs, and the youngest in the family, two-year-old George Washington Van Nest, was asleep in the sitting room.

Freeman walked around to the rear of the house. As he approached the door of the back kitchen, Mrs. Van Nest stepped out. He met her with a strong upward sweep of his knife, inflicting a single deep wound in her abdomen. Screaming, she ran to the front of the house, was let in, collapsed on a bed and died a few minutes later. Freeman immediately entered the back door, where he met Mr. Van Nest who died almost instantly, stabbed in the chest and the heart. The murderer then struck the sleeping two-year-old baby George with such ferocity that the knife passed completely through the body. He next attacked the hired man.

Though severely wounded in the breast, Van Arsdale managed to drive Freeman from the house. Out in the yard the murderer slashed at 70-year-old Mrs. Wyckoff, who had armed herself with a butcher knife and run outdoors. Badly wounded, she nevertheless managed to cut Freeman's wrist so severely that, as he later said, "My hand was so hurt, I couldn't kill any more." Clad only in a flannel nightgown, the undaunted old lady fled across-field a quarter mile to the next neighbor south to spread the alarm. In the meantime, within the house, Van Arsdale stumbled to the parlor floor where he slumped against the wall while Julia Van Nest and Helen Holmes tried to comfort the dying Georgie. All reason gone, Freeman came back to the house, kicked at the door, peered in the window, and then was gone into the night. Two days later Mrs. Wyckoff died at Brooks' farmhouse, bringing Freeman's toll to four.

Within a matter of minutes after the massacre began, Freeman was on his way, riding Mrs. Wyckoff's aged and uncertain horse down the road toward Auburn. The animal did not last long. Just the other side of the village it fell and Freeman stabbed the beast for hurting him. He stole another horse and continued the flight to Schroeppel, in the southern part of Oswego County, which he reached at two in the afternoon.

At Schroeppel he was arrested. On Saturday morning the prisoner was driven to the Van Nest home, where he was greeted by an excited, revengeful mob demanding that he be lynched.

By moving fast, however, the authorities were able to spirit Freeman away in a covered wagon. A terrible commotion followed him into the village of Auburn and as the wife of ex-Governor William H. Seward wrote in a letter to her sister, "I trust in the mercy of God that I shall never again be a witness to such an outburst of the spirit of vengeance as I saw while they were carrying the murderer past our door."

Something of the horror that beset the dark farmhouse comes through in this depiction of the fatal attack on sleeping little George Van Nest, who was slain with one blow.

In vivid and slightly unrealistic strokes, the painter attempts to show the scene in the stricken home after the murders, with the crazed slayer of four people peering in at the window.

Final scene in the traveling picture story, of course, had to be the hanging. As it happens this picture had no relation to the actual facts, as ailing, demented Bill Freeman died in his cell.

The first voice of reason to be raised was that of a clergyman, Reverend John M. Austin of Auburn's Universalist Church; while deploring the murders, his pity went out to the demented Negro and placed the blame on the indifference of the community to their colored population: "Is not society in some degree accountable for this sad catastrophe?"

He characterized the Auburn Negroes as "victims of unworthy prejudices which compel them to exist under circumstances where they are exposed to imbibe all the vices, without being able to become imbued with the virtues of those around them; who can wonder that they fall into crime?" John DePuy, Freeman's brother-in-law, testified that white men had made this murderer what he was, "a brute beast; they don't make anything else of any of our People but brute beasts; but when we violate their laws, then they want to punish us as if we were men."

Another voice in the wilderness was that of ex-Governor Seward, then a private lawyer and Auburn's most influential citizen. When no one would undertake the defense of Freeman he offered his services, thereby bringing the wrath of the entire village down upon him. Seward held the viewpoint, not yet generally accepted, that the insane were not responsible for their acts.

Judge Bowen Whiting announced on June 24 that there would be a preliminary jury trial to determine Freeman's sanity. Seward and his law partners volunteered their gratuitous services and appeared for the prisoner. State Attorney General John Van Buren, son of Martin Van Buren, and the district attorney of Cayuga County represented the people. The trial lasted ten days and in spite of the tremendous evidence of Freeman's insanity, the jurors brought in the verdict that the prisoner was "sufficiently sane in mind and memory, to distinguish between right and wrong."

On July 10 Freeman went before a second jury, this time on trial for his life. Once again the best of authorities were presented by Seward in an attempt to persuade the jury that the murderer was completely insane.

The trial itself was a travesty, where every possible insult and calumny was heaped on Freeman and on his defense. Even Seward's masterful summation, which was called the most impassioned that ever passed his lips, went almost unheard. On the twenty-third Freeman was quickly found guilty, and the following morn-ing Judge Whiting sentenced him to be hanged on September 18.

Seward, continuing his valiant fight on behalf of Freeman, obtained a stay of execution. In October Mrs. Seward paid a visit to the jail with her husband. There she found Freeman with only a few feeble glimmerings of memory. "I was affected to tears by his helpless condition," she wrote to her sister. "I pray God that he may be insensible to the inhumanity of his relentless keepers. He stood upon the cold stone floor with bare feet, a cot bedstead with nothing but the sacking underneath and a small filthy blanket to cover him."

It was on February 11, 1847, that the State Supreme Court handed down a ruling reversing the judgment of the local court and ordering a new trial. In a letter written four days later, Seward called on Dr. Amariah Brigham, head of the State Lunatic Asylum in Utica to submit the names of "one hundred of the most intelligent physicians throughout the State of New York and abroad" who might give evidence. But no trial was ordered. Area newspapers continued to enmesh the case in local politics. They even accused all concerned of taking part in a Whig conspiracy to build up Seward.

To ailing, demented Freeman, languishing in his cell at the Cayuga County jail, his feet heavily ironed, all this meant nothing. For many weeks he had been failing and those who saw him were convinced that he had become a perfect idiot. He died on Saturday morning, August 21, 1847. A post-mortem examination was held and Dr. Brigham summed up the sad case of Bill Freeman in these few words: "I have very rarely found so extensive disease of the brain in those who have died after long continued insanity, as we found in this instance; and I believe there are few cases of chronic insanity recorded in books, in which were noticed more evident marks of disease."

The great furor created by crazy Bill Freeman was in its time spread far and wide by the press, but certainly no reporting could have compared with the sense of immediacy and intimacy that came to those who saw the events dramatized in George Mastin's paintings. The last of the series shows, with Hogarthian effectiveness, the hanging of Freeman which the court ordered and for which the community profoundly hoped. The death of Freeman not only forestalled his hanging, but it also vindicated William Seward. As time passed the people realized that the tragedy involved more than four needless murders.

By BROOKS W. MACCRACKEN

THE CASE OF THE *Anonymous Corpse*

Among *causes célèbres* the Hillmon case is unique; it was not a criminal case and no famous or notorious persons were involved. Murder may —or may not—have been done, but there was no murder trial. It was only a young woman's suit against three life insurance companies, the question being whether she was or was not a widow. Yet it was a political and legal storm center for nearly a quarter of a century, from before the assassination of Garfield until after the assassination of McKinley. It coincided with the rise of the Grangers and the Populists and the coming of the trust busters; and for all of them it was a ready-made and graphic story of the constant struggle of the little people against the forces of big business.

The case began in 1878, at Lawrence, Kansas. John W. Hillmon, aged thirty-three, was a roving cattle herder without visible property or means, currently resident in Lawrence. His most valuable asset was the friendship of Levi Baldwin, who was known in Lawrence as a cattleman with money. In the fall of 1878, Hillmon cemented this friendship by marrying Baldwin's cousin Sallie Quinn, a pleasant and popular waitress. Bride and groom set up light housekeeping in a room in a lodging house, while Hillmon planned how he might improve his fortune and give Sallie the good things she no doubt deserved. Baldwin let it be known that he would help his old friend and new cousin acquire a stock ranch in the Southwest, if Hillmon could find one. Unfortunately, the Southwest was still prey to Indians, wild animals, and other dangers that a loving bridegroom might want to avoid.

Baldwin advised that before Hillmon set out to seek a suitable ranch he insure his life against these dangers. If this would not save Hillmon's scalp it would at least protect his wife. Baldwin introduced Hillmon to the proper insurance agents, and Hillmon applied for and received policies for $10,000 each from the New York Life Insurance Company and from the Mutual Life Insurance Company of New York. Then, in December, 1878, he left for the Southwest in the sole company of a coadventurer, John H. Brown of Wyandotte, Kansas. They took the Atchison, Topeka & Santa Fe to Wichita,

where they hired a wagon and horses. Hillmon returned to Lawrence for a few days in January and in February. While there, he again saw the insurance agents and obtained a third policy—this one for $5,000—from the Connecticut Mutual Life Insurance Company. On the urging of one of the agents, and after some protest, Hillmon allowed himself to be vaccinated against smallpox on February 20. This kept him in Lawrence for a few more days; but about the first of March he went back to Wichita, where he again met Brown, and the two of them headed into the south-Kansas country.

On March 17—St. Patrick's Day—1879, at a campfire on Crooked Creek near Medicine Lodge, Hillmon was accidentally shot and killed. Or so it was claimed. The three insurance companies, which owed his widow $25,000 if it were so, were doubtful that the dead man at the campfire was Hillmon. They knew of two or three Kansans who had recently tried to fake death for the insurance money that was in it.

In 1879 Medicine Lodge had not yet become famous as the home of Carry Nation, "The Smasher," or of "Sockless" Jerry Simpson, the Populist leader; but the editor of its new weekly paper, being of a literary and sardonic turn of mind, had made a somewhat lasting commentary on the time and the place by naming his paper the Medicine Lodge *Cresset*, after the cressets of oil which, according to Milton, were used to light the palaces of hell. The cynicism of that christening was shared by the insurance companies whenever they received an unusual claim from Kansas country.

Sallie Hillmon and Cousin Levi Baldwin insisted that the body *was* Hillmon's. There was only one actual witness to the truth—Brown—and he told two contradictory stories. After about a year of fruitless negotiation, Sallie Hillmon filed suit for her money. In the next twenty-three years the case was tried six times, before six different juries, and went twice to the United States Supreme Court. For three quarters of a century it has been a "leading case" in the law of evidence.

What aroused the suspicions of the insurance companies from the first was the fact that Baldwin and

Was the dead man by the campfire the heavily insured John Hillmon, the unemployed Frederick Walters, or an unknown drifter? The United States Supreme Court pondered

Description of JOHN H. HILLMON at or about the time of disappearance, 1879

AGE—About 37 years of age, 5 feet 9 inches, well built, broad shoulders, erect and weighed 140 to 150 pounds.

HAIR—Dark or brown, when worn long curls upward or outward.

FOREHEAD — Broad, broader through temples than at cheek bones.

EYES—Either dark gray or hazel; very bright, intelligent and well separated.

NOSE—Prominent and slightly Roman, faint scar on bridge which shows white when he laughs, end of nose tipped very slightly to the right.

BEARD—Has worn full beard, but prefers moustache and imperial, is of light brown, several shades lighter than hair. Moustache of medium thickness and length and worn hanging over mouth.

MOUTH—Medium size, with under lip drooping slightly.

TEETH — Prominent when he laughs, with left upper incisor missing or black, probably missing. Teeth may now (1889) be generally defective.

HANDS—Medium size and shapely with long fingers.

FEET—Very proud of his feet, which are small, wears a No. 7 fine boot easily, heavy boots No. 8 probably.

LIMBS—Long, body short in proportion.

SCARS—Ugly scar on right hand (or left), at base of thumb, extending along thick of thumb through crotch and over on upper side, wide as though made by burn or brand. It is the result of a tearing injury and not clean cut.
Small scar on back of head on a line with top of left ear, about an inch long. Cut shoe, hair must be it.

Frederick A. Walters

John W. Hillmon

The body in the coffin, said the insurance companies, was probably that of Frederick A. Walters—certainly not that of John W. Hillmon, whose description they ardently circulated in the hope that someone would find him alive. As a matter of policy, Mrs. Hillmon had reasons to hope otherwise.

Hillmon had themselves sought out agents and asked for the policies, whereas all good prospects were expected to wait for agents to seek them out. Later investigations revealed that Levi Baldwin, the reputed cattleman with money, was in fact bankrupt, or at least very hard-pressed by his creditors. One of them he had told—in March, 1879, before Hillmon's death was reported—that he and Hillmon "had a scheme under 'brogue' and that if it worked out all right he was all right." After Hillmon's death was reported, Baldwin put off another creditor by saying that he had arranged to get $10,000 of Hillmon's life insurance. Worst of all (or, from their point of view, best), the insurance investigators learned that in the summer or fall of 1878, before Hillmon applied for his insurance, Baldwin had allegedly had an odd conversation with a doctor. He wanted to know how long it would take a dead body to decompose after it was buried; and then he had archly asked if it would not be "a good scheme to get insured for all you can, and get someone to represent you as dead, and then skip out for Africa or some other damn place?" All that might have been in jest, but subsequent events aroused a natural suspicion that it was in earnest.

We can be certain of very few of the facts in the case, but it is at least safe to say that Hillmon and Brown had no adequate conception of the litigation they were starting when they left Lawrence in December, 1878. Hillmon might have had some foreknowledge of his coming fame, because for the first time in his life he began a diary. (Cynical people believed he wrote the diary just for the purpose of having it planted on "his" dead body, where of course it was found.) It wasn't a very great diary. Despite the fact that he and Brown were going, so they said, to look for a stock ranch, there was not much in the diary about that. The entries chiefly described the weather and the country.

January 6 . . . This kind of weather will make one almost curse camp life, and himself for being so silly as to start on a trip of this kind during the winter months. . . . The sun goes down tonight dark with snow and wind. I think it has been as blustery an afternoon as I have ever witnessed. This kind of weather is what will condemn this part of the country for stock. It will be almost impossible to save near all of the stock . . . .
February 8 . . . I think I have never did as hard work in my life as I have done in the past six weeks. It is killing me almost by inches to loaf around and do nothing as I have been doing of late. . . .
February 23 [back home in Lawrence] . . . Don't see as there is any good to grow out of me trying to keep track of my misdeeds, while I am apt to err as any one. And that I would be sure ashamed not to make a memorandum of, and only show up the best parts as others have done before me. . . .

That was the last entry in the diary when it was found in the dead man's clothing at Crooked Creek. Hillmon and Brown had made camp there on the evening of March 16. The nearest farmer, about three quarters of a mile away, called on them the next morning. In the afternoon, according to Brown, the two spent some time shooting. About sundown, Brown said later, he went to put the gun in the wagon and somehow caught the hammer of the gun and discharged it. Hillmon, standing by the campfire some twelve feet away, was hit in the back of the head and killed. Brown seized him by the arms and swung him away from the fire, but could not save his life or prevent his face from being singed by the flames. Brown's actions then were all very prompt and correct. He immediately went for the farmer who had called on them, and next morning Brown and the farmer went for a justice of the peace, George Washington Paddock. An inquest was held on the spot. Then they took the body to Medicine Lodge, the nearest burying ground, where another inquest was held. Brown wrote the widow a proper letter and gave it to Paddock to send to her:

Medicine Lodge, March 19, 1879

Mrs. S. E. Hillmon:
I am sorry to state the news that I have to state to you. John was shot and killed accidentally by a gun as I went to take it out [sic] of the wagon, about 15 miles north of this place. I had him dressed in his best clothes, and buried in Medicine Lodge graveyard. I shall wait here until Mr. Paddock hears from you. If you will leave me to take charge of the team, I will dispose of them to the best advantage, and take the proceeds, and when I come back to Lawrence I will relate the sad news to you. Probably you have heard of it before you get this letter.

Yours truly,
JOHN H. BROWN

Levi Baldwin came to Medicine Lodge at once, without Sallie, and he and Brown neatly fenced the grave. Then three men came from Lawrence to view the corpse for the insurance companies. They insisted that the body be disinterred, and that being done, they promptly declared that it was not Hillmon. Because of this dispute the body was sent to an undertaker in Lawrence, where it was finally seen by the "widow," minutely examined by physicians, and elaborately photographed.

A third and much more formal inquest was held. Brown, Baldwin, Sallie, and about a dozen others identified the body as Hillmon's. Honest persons at Medicine Lodge and elsewhere who had seen Brown and Hillmon on their trip said the body was Hillmon's, or at least that of the man they had seen with Brown. But the insurance companies produced two or three dozen persons who had known Hillmon at Lawrence

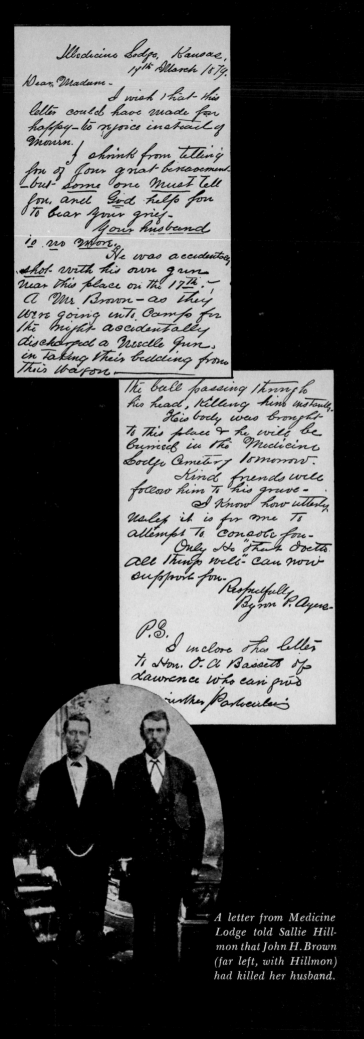

A letter from Medicine Lodge told Sallie Hillmon that John H. Brown (far left, with Hillmon) had killed her husband.

or other places, who said the body was not his. The undisputed facts were that the corpse was wearing Hillmon's clothes except for his hat, which had been burned, and his shoes, which were somehow lost. The corpse measured five feet eleven inches; the face was marred by burns, but a perfect set of teeth was preserved, and there was a vaccination scab on the arm. The measurement corresponded with Hillmon's height as stated on the insurance policies, but an insurance doctor and some other witnesses swore that Hillmon was actually only five feet nine. (The insurance doctor said he had forgotten to report the shorter measurement to the company until the dispute arose.) There was medical testimony to the effect that Hillmon's vaccination in Lawrence in February would not have left a scab like the one on the body; but the effect of this was undoubtedly lost on the jury because one of the insurance doctors had carefully removed the scab from the body and never returned it. There was a nose scar that some said they remembered on Hillmon; but there was no sign of other scars and marks that Hillmon was said to have had. In particular there was much testimony that Hillmon had been missing a tooth. Sallie denied that; she said her husband's teeth were perfect, like those in the dead body. Sallie was not very good at descriptions. Before the body had arrived at Lawrence the insurance men had tried to get her to describe her husband, but she would say only that he had more hair than her questioner, who was bald. The insurance witnesses, on the other hand, were precise in their recollections of Hillmon's physical peculiarities—considerably more precise, indeed, than they were when cross-examined about the equally obvious peculiarities of other locally well-known persons.

With some of this evidence before them and the insurance lawyers in back of them, the inquest jury brought in a finding that the body was that of an unknown man *feloniously* shot by John H. Brown. The effect of this verdict on Brown was impressive. He went for help to his father, who lived in Wyandotte, and wrote another letter to the "widow":

Mirs Hillmon i would like to now where Johny is and How that business is and what i shall doe if any thing. Let me now threw my Father.

JOHN H. BROWN

His father sent him to a locally influential lawyer-politician named Buchan—the Honorable State Senator W. J. Buchan. In the many trials of the case the insurance lawyers liked to refer to Buchan as Brown's "own attorney"; but what pay Buchan received—some $600 or $700—came from the insurance companies.

The court of appeals called his conduct "unprofessional," but he seems to have thought of himself as an arbitrator. In any event, after discussing Brown's difficulty with him and his father, Buchan went to see the agents of the insurance companies; returned; discussed the situation again with Brown; and then someone—allegedly Brown—concluded that Brown should turn state's evidence, and that Buchan should arrange a deal with the insurance companies. Brown would make a complete confession and get Mrs. Hillmon to surrender the policies, while the insurance companies would take no steps to prosecute the Hillmons, Baldwin, or Brown. Buchan prepared the "confession" in the form of an affidavit:

... Along about the 10th day of December, 1878, John W. Hillmon, Levi Baldwin, and myself talked about and entered into a conspiracy to defraud the New York Life Insurance Company and the Mutual Life, of New York, out of some money to be obtained by means of effecting a policy or policies on the life of said John W. Hillmon. Baldwin was to furnish the money to pay the premiums . . . . Hillmon and myself were to go off southwest from Wichita, Kansas, ostensibly to locate a stock ranch, but in fact to in some way find a subject to pass off as the body of John W. Hillmon, for the purpose of obtaining the insurance money aforesaid. We had no definite plan of getting the subject. . . .

[On the 5th of March] we left [Wichita] on our second trip. . . . We overtook a stranger on this trip, the first day out from Wichita, about two or two and one half miles from town, who Hillmon invited to get in and ride, and who he (Hillmon) proposed to hire to herd and work for him on the ranch as proposed to be located. This man was with us during all this trip. Hillmon proposed to me that the man would do to pass off for him. I contended with him that the man would not do to pass off for him . . . and I protested, and said that was going beyond what we had agreed, and something I had never before thought of, and was beyond my grit entirely. But Hillmon seemed to get more deeply determined. . . . Pains were taken not to have more than two of us seen together in the wagon. . . . Hillmon kept at the man until he let him vaccinate him, which he did, taking his pocket knife and using virus from his own arm for the purpose. He also traded clothes with him. . . . This man appeared to be a stranger in the country, a sort of an easy-go-long fellow, not suspicious or very attentive to anything. His arm became very sore, and he got quite stupid and dull. He said his name was either Berkley or Burgess, or something sounding like that. We always called him Joe. He said he had been around Fort Scott awhile, and also had worked about Wellington or Arkansas City. I do not know where he was from, nor where his home or friends were. I did not see him at Wichita that I know of. I had but very little to say to the man, and less to do with him. . . . I frequently remonstrated with Hillmon, and tried to deter him from carrying out his intentions of killing the man.

The next evening after we got to the camp last named [on Crooked Creek], the man Joe was sitting by the fire. I was at the hind end of the wagon, either putting feed in the box for the horses or taking a sack of corn out, when I heard a gun go off. I looked around, and saw the man was shot, and Hillmon was pulling him away around to keep him out of the fire. Hillmon changed a daybook from his own coat to Joe's, and said to me everything was all right, and that I need not be afraid. . . . He told me to get a pony . . . and get some one to come up. He took Joe's valise, and started north. . . . I have never heard a word from him since. . . .

I make the above statements in the Hillmon case as the full and true facts in the case, regretting the part I have taken in the affair.

Brown executed and swore to this affidavit on the fourth of September, 1879. At the same time he gave Buchan written authority "to make arrangements, if he can, with the insurance companies for a settlement of the Hillmon case, by them stopping all pursuit and prosecution of myself and John W. Hillmon, if suit for money is stopped and policies surrendered to companies."

Then began a period of correspondence and visits between Brown and Sallie Hillmon. He first had a midnight rendezvous with her at Baldwin's house, told her what he had done, and got her to meet Buchan. She did so on several occasions—and once stayed at Buchan's home at Wyandotte for three weeks. She was always in need of funds, and did not hesitate to ask him for train tickets or money that she could not get from Baldwin. In September she wrote Buchan from Ottawa, Kansas, that:

. . . it will never do for you to come to my sisters. I will tell you the reason when I see you. . . . I will be obleged to ask you to send me enough to bye my Ticket to your city. . . . I did write that letter to Riggs & Borgholthaus [her attorneys] have got no answer and don't want any.

I will be on the Wendsday's Train without something offle happens.

In September, 1880, Sallie gave Buchan a full "release" of all her interest in the insurance policies; but she did not have the policies themselves. They were in the hands of Baldwin's lawyer, who refused to give them up, saying he had a lien on them for $10,000. Buchan showed her Brown's statement and the agreement of the companies not to prosecute him; but then, somehow—perhaps at her insistence—Brown's statement got torn up and dropped into a stove. (Later, when negotiations with her finally broke off, it was remembered that the stove was unlighted, and the pieces of the statement were fished out and preserved.)

The situation grew more and more puzzling. Despite all her friendly visits with Buchan, Sallie evidently never made any statements of fact that were inconsistent with her previous claims, or contrary to any of her testimony in the case. If she had, Buchan was not the man to have kept it secret. Indeed, it may be just as likely that Sallie was playing a game with Buchan as that he was spinning a web for her. The fact is that Buchan got no further results. The policies were not surrendered. Sallie's "release" had no legal effect. Only Brown's statement, rescued from the fireless stove, took its place among the mass of evidence served up to six juries. But soon after Sallie filed her suit and it became clear that he was in no real danger of criminal prosecution, Brown—can it surprise you?—repudiated his "confession" and reverted to his original story. With not unreasonable caution, Sallie's lawyers took Brown's deposition before the case came on for trial, and had him repeat his original story of how he had accidentally shot Hillmon. The insurance lawyers cross-examined him for nineteen days, but they were unable to get him back to the tale he had told in his written "confession."

Up to this point the insurance companies' conclusion that there had been a conspiracy was based on their own natural suspicions, the odd remarks of Levi Baldwin, and the written "confession" of Brown. As late as the summer of 1879 they thought the body was that of one Frank Nichols, who had disappeared from Wichita; but he turned up. Then perseverance and luck brought them evidence concerning another person whose description might fit the dead body.

In Fort Madison, Iowa, there lived the parents, the sisters, and the sweetheart of a young German named Frederick Adolph Walters. Fred had left that town to seek his fortune about a year before the occurrence on Crooked Creek. During this year he had wandered around Missouri, Iowa, Nebraska, and Kansas, spending time in various towns, including Wichita. On the first of

March, 1879, a few days before Hillmon and Brown left on their final trip, Walters wrote his sister a letter from Wichita:

I in my usual style, will drop you a few lines to let you know that I intend leaving Wichita on or about March 5th, with a certain Mr. Hillmon, a sheep trader, for Colorado, and parts unknown to me....

At about the same time he wrote his sweetheart, Alvina Kasten, a longer letter dated March 1, 1879:

Dearest Alvina:

...I will stay here until the fore part of next week, and then will leave here to see part of the country which I never expected to see when I left home, as I am going with a man by the name of Hillmon, who intends to start a sheep ranch, and as he promised me more wages than I could make at anything else, I concluded to take it for a while, at least until I struck something better. There is so many folks in this country that have got the Leadville [mining] fever, and if I would not have got the situation that I have now, I would of went there myself; but as it is at present, I will get to see the best part of Kansas, Indian Territory, Colorado and New Mexico. The route that we intend to take would cost a man to travel from $150 to $200, but it will not cost me a cent; besides I get good wages. I will drop you a letter occasionally until I get settled down, then I want you to answer it (you bet, honey).

Thereafter time passed without further letters to sweetheart, sister, or family, though previously Fred Walters' letters in "usual style" had been steady and regular. When his new silence extended into weeks and months, the family became alarmed and began to make inquiries. The inquiries eventually came to Lawrence, and from there someone sent the family photographs of the controversial dead body. These they immediately declared to be pictures of the missing Walters. There was even a mole on the back of the dead body in just the place where the new witnesses swore Walters had had a mole. To be sure, his sister said that he had had a scar on his ankle, received from a dog bite when he was twelve years old; the doctors' minute examination of the dead body in Lawrence had revealed no ankle scars, but the scar might have disappeared over the years.

The Hillmon case was now popularly reduced to a single question: Was the dead body Hillmon or Walters? There were several difficulties with the Walters theory. All the testimony identifying the body as Walters was based on photographs of a weeks-old corpse with a burned face. Apart from such identification there was nothing to connect Walters with Hillmon and Brown except the letters to his girl friend and his sister. No one was ever produced who had seen Walters with Hillmon or Brown, or who had seen Walters near Crooked Creek or Medicine Lodge. And if Brown's

WANTED: THE TRUTH

Was It Hillmon or Was It Walters?

THIS IS THE QUESTION.

Plenty of Testimony on Both Sides of It.

TO THE JURY BEFORE LONG.

Who Ft. Madison People Believe It Was.

All Agree That the Photographs Bear a Strong Resemblance to Frederick Adolph Walters, Formerly of That Place.

It begins to look as if the Hillmon case would go to the jury either the last of this week or the first of next. This will be rather remarkable, considering that the last trial consumed seven weeks. Judge Williams has ___ ys dow___

"confession" is referred to, there is nothing in it that is completely consistent with the Walters letters. If Hillmon hired Walters in Wichita, either he did not tell Brown about it or Brown's "confession" was not forthright. The name "Berkley or Burgess" which Brown cited in his statement is certainly not "Walters"; "Joe" is not a likely nickname for "Frederick Adolph"; and the travels that Brown ascribed to Joe do not correspond with the known travels of Walters.

So the letters from Wichita were the only real support of the Walters theory. Their genuineness was not questioned, and the inferences drawn from them seemed inescapable in the light of Walters' complete disappearance. Sallie's attorneys tried to destroy the effect of the letters in two ways—factually (by pointing out to the jurors that Hillmon was a very common name in Kansas and that the letters did not say "John Hillmon") and legally (by objecting that the letters were "hearsay" and as such inadmissible in evidence).

For at least two centuries the rule against hearsay has been one of the foundation stones of the law of evidence. Indeed, about the time of the Hillmon case, an Alabama court declared that this rule had been one of the rights guaranteed to Englishmen by the Magna Charta. This was more than a slight historical error, but it showed the reverence that courts and lawyers have had for the rule. Chancellor James Kent, the author of America's first great law book, gave this reason for the rule against hearsay:

A person who relates a hearsay is not obliged to enter into any particulars, to answer any questions, to solve any difficulties, to reconcile any contradictions, to explain any obscurities, to remove any ambiguities; he entrenches himself in the simple assertion that he was told so, and leaves the burden entirely on his dead or absent author.

Popular faith in the cross-questioning of witnesses was expressed by the commercial Mr. Moulder, in Anthony Trollope's *Orley Farm:* "It is the fairest thing that is. It's the bulwark of the British Constitution. Trial by jury is, and how can you have trial by jury if the witnesses are not to be cross-questioned?"

There are and always have been exceptions to the hearsay rule, to allow for statements made by one who cannot be in court for questioning but who is nonetheless presumed to have told the truth—deathbed statements, or routine business entries, or confessions of something which it would be to his interest not to confess. But Walters' letters were not his dying declarations, though his doom may already have been sealed when he wrote them; they were not confessions or admissions of anything that Walters could have been expected to want to conceal. The insurance lawyers argued that the letters were a kind of business entry;

but a man's business ought not to include his love letters.

The legal question was not resolved for twelve years. At the first trial, in 1882, the letters were admitted in evidence, despite objection; but the jury disagreed seven to five, and no verdict resulted. So the case was retried in 1885, with the same result, except that the division in the jury was six to six. On the third trial, in 1888, Judge O. P. Shiras refused to admit the letters in evidence, and then the jury brought in a full verdict for Sallie Hillmon for the amount of the policies plus accumulated interest. The defendants appealed to the United States Supreme Court; and the Kansas state superintendent of insurance (who had been of counsel for the insurance companies in the second trial) included in his annual report a full account of the evidence in the case, reporting that which had been admitted by the court and some which had not, and adding comments of his own, mostly favorable to the companies. (This report, as republished in *The Principles of Judicial Proof* by the late, great writer on the law of evidence John Henry Wigmore, is the principal authority for many of the statements in the present account.)

In the first hearing before the Supreme Court, in 1892, the insurance-company attorneys apparently presented no sound theory by which the Walters letters could have been held admissible, and we are told that the point was "miserably argued." Nevertheless, the Supreme Court justices voted unanimously to decide in favor of the insurance companies on general principles, thus reversing the lower-court findings and clearing the way for a new trial.

The preparation of the Supreme Court's opinion was assigned to Justice Horace Gray, who could be relied upon to find a precedent for the decision if anyone could do so. He was the most learned and resourceful member of the court—a Harvard graduate, a former chief justice of Massachusetts, an heir to wealth, and a thorough Bostonian. Typically, his opinions were larded with judicial citations and legal principles. Yet we are reliably told that even he was in "dense darkness" about how to justify the admission of Walters' letters, until a suggestion came from his young legal secretary's father, James Bradley Thayer, professor of evidence at the Harvard Law School. Together Justice Gray and Thayer brought forth a new legal theory and adorned it with their authority. A man's intention, they said—whenever that intention is a distinct and material fact in a chain of circumstances—may be proved by his own contemporaneous oral or written declarations. For truly, how better can we find out what a man thinks than by what he does or says at the time? And was not Walters' intention to leave Wichita with Hillmon the sheep trader a distinct and material fact in the chain of circumstances that may have led him to Crooked Creek? To be sure, as the professor knew, no court would have allowed Walters' letter to be admitted in evidence if he had written his sweetheart, saying, "I have left Wichita with Hillmon the sheep trader." Such a letter would indisputably have been hearsay. But the learned professor suggested that there was a logical difference between a hearsay account of a past fact and Walters' personal expression of his then present intent; the Supreme Court agreed.

Justice Gray's opinion (Insurance Company v. Hillmon, 145 U.S. 285) is famous among lawyers. Generations of them have debated whether such a distinction between a past fact and a present intention is sound or unsound. Forty years later, Justice Benjamin Cardozo, speaking for the Supreme Court in Franklin Roosevelt's day, said the decision in the Hillmon case "marks the high water line beyond which courts have been unwilling to go."

But the legal points of the decision were lost on the Kansas public of the nineties. To them the real question was one of motive: Who was being made the victim of conspiracy—the insurance companies or the Kansas widow? These were the years of full flood for the People's party in Kansas and the Midwest. One Mary "Yellin" Lease rode all over the middle border, telling the farmers that "Wall Street owns the country" and urging them to "raise less corn and more hell." At their first national convention—in Omaha on the Fourth of July, 1892—the Populists declared:

We meet in the midst of a nation brought to the verge of moral, political and material ruin. Corruption dominates the ballot-box, the Legislatures, the Congress and touches even the ermine of the bench. . . . From the same prolific womb of governmental injustice we breed the two great classes—tramps and millionaires.

To those Kansans who followed the Populists, the Hillmon case was a heroic contest between the wealth of Wall Street and a poor, defenseless widow of Kansas whose cause involved the very good name of the state itself. They had no more faith in the motives and ways of the insurance companies than the companies had in Hillmon. Wealth had paid the doctors to lose Hillmon's vaccination scab; wealth had paid Buchan to extort a false confession from Brown and to deceive Sallie; and in everything the hand of wealth and influence was fashioning a crown of thorns and a cross of gold for one poor, weak, bereaved woman. When the insurance companies persuaded one of Hillmon's old girl friends and his sister and brother-in-law to take the witness stand to testify that Hillmon had a blackened or missing front tooth and not, like the corpse, a perfect set of teeth, those with Populist leanings called the brother-in-law a wretch and the girl friend a spiteful old maid, and accused the insurance companies of buying their false testimony.

Sallie's lawyers scorned the defense's accusations. "Such a conspiracy as the defense alleges must [if true] result in lasting separation from his young wife—the blighting of both their lives forever—her lifelong misery and his eternal damnation." If, they said, the arguments of the insurance lawyers were to be believed, "Hillmon must have been a marvelous man. One of a party of three, traveling through a settled country, camping out, and stopping at houses, he succeeded in concealing one of the party through the entire journey from Wichita to Medicine Lodge. Not only that, but he vaccinated him, made it work, kept the protesting Brown at bay, and succeeds in his conspiracy." Finally—and mark you—"These insurance companies with boundless wealth and inexhaustible resources at their command, with agents scattered the world over, with . . . years to operate in, have failed to find Hillmon. . . . With all their money and all their power they have never been able to find a vestige of Hillmon."

Defending themselves against this sort of attack, the insurance companies at first hinted that Hillmon's whereabouts were known to the authorities, and that it would be only a matter of time before he would be produced. When time passed and he was not brought forth, they pictured him as a "typical Western bravo," and it was "surmised that the detectives are more afraid of him than desirous of getting the reward for his capture." But no one ever found Hillmon.

Walters never showed up either; but Sallie's lawyers had no difficulty in explaining that they never had the money and the resources to search for *him*.

Between 1892 and 1897 two more trials were held (the fourth and fifth of the series) and two more juries disagreed. In 1897, when the Populists were in control of the Kansas state administration, Sallie's lawyers took a new tack; and Webb McNall, as superintendent of insurance, denied Mutual Life a license to continue to do business in Kansas, because "I am satisfied that your company has not dealt fairly with the plaintiff, Mrs. Sallie E. Hillmon, in refusing to pay the death loss and in the litigation of the same pertaining to her deceased husband." When this came to the attention of federal judge John A. Williams, who had presided at the fifth trial, he promptly had a federal grand jury bring in an indictment against the superintendent of insurance for interference with the rights of litigants in his court, and on the petition of the insurance company he issued a mandatory injunction against both the superintendent and the attorney general of Kansas, enjoining them from interfering in the insurance company's transaction of business in Kansas. Apparently no one actually went to prison, but the insurance companies continued in business. By this time New York Life had thought it wise to settle with Sallie Hillmon, but the other two, Mutual Life and Connecticut Mutual, continued to contest the case.

The sixth trial began in October, 1899. In the course of it the trial judge surprised the defense by ruling that Brown's "confession" of conspiracy against the insurance companies, and Baldwin's conspiratorial remarks about Hillmon, dead bodies, and insurance, were not proper evidence against Sallie since she was not charged with being a party to the conspiracy. This ruling so weakened the case for the insurance companies that the jury brought in a verdict for the plaintiff. Mutual Life then gave up the battle and paid; but Connecticut Mutual made 108 assignments of error and appealed. The circuit court of appeals affirmed the trial court, but on further appeal the Supreme Court, in 1903, again reversed the judgment and ordered a new trial.

The opinion was written by Justice Henry Billings Brown of Michigan. He had had the misfortune of losing the sight of one eye shortly after he was appointed to the court in 1890, but with his good eye he had no trouble seeing that the "widow" stood to benefit from the conspiracy whether she was a party to it or not, and in his view the whole case was simply one of "graveyard insurance." (Even the annual premiums of $600 for the life insurance were more than Hillmon had ever earned in a year.) This time, however, the court was not unanimous. Two of the justices dissented—Justice (later Chief Justice) Edward White of Louisiana and Justice David Brewer of Kansas, who had himself presided at the second trial and was presumably more intimately familiar with the case than any of the justices. They wrote no dissenting opinion,

but perhaps they agreed with the words of the circuit judge, Amos M. Thayer:

This case has been pending...for more than 21 years, and it would be a matter of great regret, and a reproach to our method of administering justice if, after six laborious and lengthy trials, an error had crept into the record of such consequence as to require reversal.

In any event, a seventh trial was then too much to contemplate even for the parties themselves; and a settlement with the last of the insurance companies was finally reached. (Counting accumulated interest, the "widow" eventually received a total of $35,700 from the three companies.) She had been for some years happily remarried, with no apparent apprehensions of bigamy; and whether or not her *sang-froid* was justified, it would not be too long before a future Chief Justice of the United States, Charles Evans Hughes, would gain first fame by his investigation of New York life insurance scandals.

The truth in the Hillmon case is as debatable today as it was when it began. Some twenty years after the last court decision the dean of Kansas journalists, T. A. McNeal, in a book of reminiscences, *When Kansas Was Young*, would express the novel opinion that Hillmon did conspire to defraud the insurance companies, but that something went wrong and he was really killed at Crooked Creek. McNeal is entitled to respect because he began his newspaper career on the Medicine Lodge *Cresset* in the spring of 1879, just after the first inquest; and if in the next fifty years or so either Hillmon or Walters had ever been heard from, McNeal would have reported it. However, his little book does not reveal how or why he came to his odd conclusion.

You now have all the facts and theories that are known; perhaps the best way to conclude is with the words with which Justice Brewer, a son, grandson, and nephew of clergymen, concluded his charge to the jury in the second trial:

Consider all the facts in the case. Fear not. Be just; and may that infinite Being, who from His unseen throne in the center of this mystic universe, who sees and knows the very fact, help you to be strong and guide you to truth.

About nine on the morning of Friday, December 21, 1832, John Durfee, a farmer of Tiverton, Rhode Island, was driving his team through his stackyard when he noticed something inside swaying against one of the five-foot stakes. Leaping forward, he saw the body of a woman. Her knees hung six inches above the ground; her legs were bent backward, the toes balancing on the grass; her head lolled forward from a cord attached six inches below the top of the stake. Durfee tried to lift her with one hand, while loosing the cord with the other, but small as she was, her weight was too great for him. He shouted for help. In a moment his father, with Bill Allen and Ben Negus, the farm hands, ran up from the darkness. Allen cut the cord with his knife, and they laid the body on the ground.

The dead woman's black hair cascaded from the pleats of her calash—the "bashful bonnet," it was often called. Her cheeks were frostbitten, and her tongue was caught between her teeth. Her brown cloak was hooked up the front, except at the very top. Beneath it, one arm hung straight, and one was bent up to her breast, as if to ease the cord at her throat. There were gloves on her hands, and half of a comb in her hair; the other half they found outside the stackyard. Her shoes lay together a few inches to her right, with a red bandanna beside them. On the "fog"—last year's dead grass—there were no footprints, for the ground was frozen. The noose by which she hung was not the slipknot, but what farmers call a double hitch and sailors, a clove hitch. The cord was three-strand hemp, no thicker than a goose quill. It cut into her neck just below the right ear, and her right cheek rested against the stake.

Tiverton is one of the townships in Newport County. Durfee's farm lay half a mile below the Massachusetts line at Fall River. Someone ran into the village for Elihu Hicks, the coroner, and someone else to Fall River for a doctor. Hicks arrived within an hour. Picking a jury from the gathering crowd, he swore them in inside the stackyard. Then the body was carried to Durfee's house under a horse blanket, with straw beneath the broken neck.

By this time there were two Fall River men who could identify the body: Dr. Thomas Wilbur and the Reverend Mr. Bidwell of the Methodist Church. Dr. Wilbur examined it with the help of the female bystanders. Beneath the petticoat was the imprint of two hands. When Aunt Hannah Wrightington asked Dorcas Ford what she thought they proved, Dorcas whispered, "Rash violence!"

The girl was Maria Cornell—her full name was Sarah Maria Cornell—of Mr. Bidwell's own congregation. The minister sent Durfee to Mrs. Hathaway's in

The
MINISTER

By GEORGE

The Meeting of Rev. E. K. Avery and his Victim.

In attempting to reconstruct the strange circumstances of Maria's death in farmer Durfee's stackyard, the con-

40

pregnant Maria Cornell's murder,

was a guilty hypocrite concealed by

legal process in 1833 New England

and the
MILL GIRL

HOWE

The unsuspecting girl was strangled by the scoundrel ere she became aware
of his cruel intention.

temporary artist who made these woodcuts had, like
press and public, prejudged the Reverend Mr. Avery.

Fall River, where Maria had boarded, to fetch her effects. Durfee soon returned with a trunk and a bandbox, and with Mrs. Hathaway herself. In the bandbox Hicks found a letter, undated and unmailed, addressed to Bidwell. He made the minister read it aloud:

Sir: I take this opportunity to inform you that for reasons known to God and my own soul I wish no longer to be connected with the Methodist Society. When I came to this place I thought I should enjoy myself among them but as I do not enjoy any Religion attall, I have not seen a well nor a happy day since I left Thompson campground. You will therefore please to drop my name from [the Bible Class], and I will try to gain all the instruction I can from your public labours. I hope I shall feel different some time or other. The Methodists are my people when I enjoy any Religion. To them I was Indebted under God for my spiritual birth. I once knew what it was to love God with all my heart once felt God was my father, Jesus my friend and Heaven my home but have awfully departed and sometimes feel I shall lose my soul forever. I desire your prayer that God would help me from this.

Yours respectfully,
Sarah M. Cornell.

Beside it, under her trinkets and ribbons, lay three letters addressed to her—one yellow, one pink, and one white—and a soiled scrap of paper, dated the very day before. Hicks read it aloud:

If I should be missing, enquire of the Rev. Mr. Avery in Bristol. He will know where I am gone. Dec. 20. S.M. Cornell.

Bristol, Rhode Island, lies across Mount Hope Bay in full sight of Fall River and Tiverton. The Reverend Ephraim K. Avery, a friend and fellow laborer of Bidwell's, was the minister of the Methodist Church there. On hearing Avery's name, Bidwell took horse through Fall River, round the head of the bay, and down through Warren to Bristol. It was seven o'clock when he reached that town. He whispered the news of the suicide to his friend, outdoors in the dark, on the narrow dog-leg of Wardwell Street, where Avery lived. Avery did not ask him to spend the night, and we can guess he would have declined. Bidwell rode home.

The deputy sheriff for Fall River was a young sleuth named Harvey Harnden. Hicks and Harnden spent Saturday morning over the three remaining letters found in the bandbox, which led them to suspect Avery of murder. However, the coroner's jury, when it returned its verdict, was more cautious:

On viewing the body of said Sarah Maria Cornell, here lying dead, upon their oaths [they] do say that they believe the said Cornell committed suicide by hanging herself upon a stake in said yard, and was influenced to commit said crime by the wicked conduct of a married man, which we gather from Dr. Wilbur, together with the contents of three letters found in the trunk of said Cornell. And we the jurors aforesaid, upon their oaths aforesaid do say the aforesaid Sarah Maria Cornell in manner aforesaid came to her death by the causes aforesaid.

Not content with this, Harnden, with Hicks, Durfee, and another man, crossed on Sunday by bridge to Aquidneck Island and by horse ferry to Bristol. The four called on Squire John Howe, justice of the peace for Bristol, and asked him to hold Elder Avery on suspicion of murder. Durfee swore out the complaint. Reluctantly, the Squire promised to send the constable that evening to arrest the suspect, and set a hearing for the next Wednesday, the day after Christmas, with his colleague Levi Haile from the neighboring town of Warren.

On Monday, back in Durfee's barn, Dr. Wilbur performed a post-mortem on Maria's body, exhumed for the purpose. If she had lived, he told Harnden, she would have borne a daughter in five months. A second jury then returned a new verdict, accusing Avery of being the "principal or accessory" in her death.

Maria was then buried against a stone wall in the very field where she had been found, with prayer read by Elder Bidwell to a tearful, angry crowd. That evening—December 24, 1832—Harnden, amid cheers and groans, presented the new verdict to a meeting in the Lyceum Hall at Fall River, promising that it should reach the two justices when their hearing opened two days later in Bristol. The citizens appointed him to head a "committee to aid the inhabitants of Tiverton."

Pending the hearing, Squire Howe had released Avery in his own recognizance. The Parson, a self-confident man of thirty-seven, engaged three lawyers, to whom he admitted easily that he had known Maria Cornell in meeting at Lowell, Massachusetts, before being stationed in Bristol; that he had seen her once since then, at Elder Bidwell's revival meeting in Fall River on October 19; that on December 20, the day before her body was found, he had crossed the ferry from Bristol to Aquidneck Island for a stroll, as the ferry master could testify; that he had returned to the ferry at nine o'clock, too late to cross, and had slept at the ferryhouse; that the Fall River men might claim to have seen him in their village, but that Mrs. Jones, who lived on the west side of the Island, could testify to seeing him cross her field in the afternoon, much too late for him to reach Fall River and return to the ferry by nine.

"Sister Jones," he told her solemnly, "my life is worth thousands of worlds. Can you not recall that you saw me in the afternoon?"

But Mrs. Jones shook her head. She had seen a stranger in the *morning*, and could not even be sure whether what he carried on his shoulder was a walking stick or a clam hoe.

On Christmas Day, in those still-Puritan times a holiday of no importance, a hundred men of Fall River chartered the steamer *King Philip* for an invasion of Bristol. They swarmed up from the dock and surrounded the parsonage, even forcing their way into the sinkroom. Avery, who had performed a marriage that very morning, listened upstairs with his family. While William Paull, the Bristol sheriff, stood helpless on the outskirts, one stouthearted Bristolian faced the mob.

"What do you want?" he asked them.

"We've come for Elder Avery and will have him dead or alive," said Harnden.

"That you shall not," answered the Bristol man, and shoved him outdoors. There might have been a lynching if the bell of the *King Philip* had not rung just then. The crowd trooped down, empty-handed, for the return trip to Fall River.

Next morning the hearing opened in the courthouse on the Bristol Common, just beside Avery's white-pillared chapel. Luke Drury, Collector of the Port, acted as clerk. The room was filled from morning to night. The squires were strict. They refused to examine Harnden's three letters, and when he asked Dr. Wilbur to describe Maria's condition, they refused to accept an answer. On January 7, they discharged Avery on the grounds that the complaint was signed by a private citizen (Durfee) instead of by the coroner, and that there was not much evidence against Avery anyway. That very evening Harnden read their verdict to an ugly crowd which overflowed the Congregational

WALLIS E. HOWE, FAIA

Two sketches by the late Wallis E. Howe show the Bristol, Rhode Island, courthouse (left) where Avery's case was originally dismissed, and the Colony House in Newport (right) where the minister later stood trial

Church in Fall River. If the Bristol court would not bring Avery to justice, he promised them, he would do so by himself.

Avery, whose life was in danger from the Fall River mob, sought advice from the Reverend John Bristed, the Episcopalian rector of Bristol. He might not expect comradeship from his colleague, but he could expect wisdom, for Bristed had been a lawyer in New York before taking orders. He advised Avery to leave town till the excitement died down.

Avery got out of Bristol just in time. Harnden had persuaded Judge Randall of the Rhode Island superior court to issue a warrant against Avery for suspicion of murder, with a request for extradition in case he had fled to another state. Now Harnden, arriving an hour after Avery left, was told by a neighbor that a carriage drawn by two white horses had picked Avery up outside the feed mill and headed northward. Above tiny Rhode Island lay the breadth of Massachusetts, and beyond it, like fingers spreading from a palm, the upper states of New England, and beyond them, Canada, where the fugitive would be safe.

The sleuth did not give up the chase. He hired a horse and sulky, disguised himself in a fur cap and pea jacket, and set out in pursuit. In turn he visited Providence, Pawtucket, Attleboro, Wrentham, Dedham, Boston, and finally Lowell, suspecting that his quarry had hidden there among his—and Maria's—former congregation. But nobody in Lowell had seen Avery. It was January 18 by now, and at night in the American

for his life. A member of one of New England's most famous families, Mr. Howe was the father of George Howe, the author of this article, and the grandson of the Bristol magistrate who first judged Avery innocent.

House, the sheriff oiled a sheet of paper, laid it over the innkeeper's gazetteer, and traced on it the roads of southern New England. They all led to Boston; he should have searched there more thoroughly.

I then left Lowell [he writes] stopping but seldom for the reason that at most of the public houses through that part of the country, including the whole distance to Boston . . . a man must be proof against most gasses and obnoxious exhalations in order to withstand the effluvia of new rum. Yet there are several houses in the [district] that are cleanly and well-kept, and in which a man can sit down and feel himself at home, and be well entertained. But in some others, on going into the barroom, the first question put to you will be, "Mister, how fur are you going this way? What may I call your name, Sir, if I may be so bold? 'Taint any of my business, sir, but what's your business up this way. What's the news down to Gineral Court?"

Arriving in Boston, he picked up the trail of the two white horses. The landlord of the Bromfield House had seen a certain Elder Gifford drive in behind them on January 10. Harnden remembered Elder Gifford as an observer sent down to the hearing by the New England Methodist Conference.

Gifford was cornered by Harnden's knowledge of his journey from Bristol. After they had exchanged promises—that Gifford would not warn Avery if Harnden did not betray Gifford—he weakly suggested that the sheriff try Rindge, New Hampshire.

Next day [i.e., on Sunday, January 20], having crossed the state line, Harnden picked up a New Hampshire deputy sheriff named Edwards. There were not many Methodists in Rindge, said he, and those few all lived close together on a country lane just off the northbound pike.

Harnden appealed for reinforcement to Edwards; he called in a young man who drove a bread cart, and so knew the Methodist road. He eagerly promised to "keep dark."

The three men bedded down at Colonel French's tavern in Fitzwilliam, north of the Methodist road. After a few hours' sleep, Harnden dispatched the other two southward, with orders to reconnoiter the road en route. He promised to meet them at noon in the public house at Rindge.

But when the posse gathered, he found that Edwards had learned nothing; it was clear that he had spent the morning in the bar. The baker, however, traveling the road in his sleigh, had heard there would be a Methodist prayer meeting that evening at a certain Captain Mayo's, three miles north of the village. Harnden ordered him to attend it in the guise of a repentant sinner and to stay through it to the end.

The baker started off without supper, only to return before Harnden and Edwards had finished their pie and ask for some himself. He had been unable to survive the prayer meeting. Accompanied by his aides, Harnden then drove the baker's sleigh to Captain Mayo's. He opened the door without knocking. Two men and a woman sat in the keeping room with a single candle before them. He asked for Captain Mayo. A stocky man with a pipe in his hand allowed he was the Captain.

"I am here after *Ephraim K. Avery,*" Harnden announced.

"Ephraim K. Avery?" the Captain repeated slowly, moving his pipe to his lips and back again.

"Yes sir," said Harnden.

"*Ephraim K.* Avery!" Mayo repeated, as if there were more than one. "I never knew such a man as Ephraim K. Avery."

"*I* know such a man," said Harnden grimly. "I have come a great way after him; I came on *purpose* after him, and I *must* have him; and Capt. Mayo, the better way is for you to go to the room where Mr. Avery is, tell him a Mr. Harnden is here and wishes to see him, and let him come forward; for he is in your house, and if he comes not forward I shall search your house, for I *must* have him."

At this point Mrs. Mayo slipped into another room, closing the door behind her. Getting no help from the Captain, Harnden started the search alone, taking a single candle. While his posse guarded the doors, he explored both floors and even lifted the trap door to the attic. On the way down he met Mrs. Mayo, who whispered to him from the dark, "You seek innocent blood."

He threw open the door of a second-floor room, where a low fire burned in the fireplace. A candle before it was extinguished, but the wick still smouldered. Finding the room empty, he went downstairs again, where his eye fell upon a closed door that had been open when he passed it before.

I thought to look behind the door [he writes] and should have done so earlier, if the object of my search had been so large about the breast as most men. I must give the gentleman credit for requiring less room than I thought possible for any man to do.

Avery had been hiding behind the door, and now he was taken at last. He had grown a beard and wore green spectacles. Harnden took him by the hand.

"Do endeavor to overcome this agitation," Harnden said; "you need fear no personal violence, you shall be kindly treated."

Then for the first time he heard Avery speak.

"I suppose you cannot legally take me from this state, without a warrant from the Governor," he said weakly. "Have you such a warrant?"

Harnden showed him Judge Randall's warrant, and after Avery had packed, Harnden drove him back to Rindge in the baker's sleigh.

Next morning the posse disbanded. Harnden carried his prisoner by stage to Boston. Back at the Bromfield House, he found Colonel Bradford Durfee of the Vigilance Committee waiting with money and congratulations. The next day he pushed on toward Rhode Island. The citizenry waited at the crossroads. During the chase excitement had been intense through the countryside, for it was not only Avery, but Harnden, also, who had disappeared. Rumor had spread that the minister had escaped to Canada or to Cuba—even that he had been a pirate in the West Indies for ten years, before taking the cloth. It was reported that Harnden had chained him in irons and was exhibiting him for a fee on the return from Rindge—a charge Harnden denied.

Late in the afternoon of January 23, the coach reached Fall River, and on the twenty-fifth Harnden handed his prisoner over to the sheriff of Newport County, Rhode Island, at the state line, not far above Maria's hastily dug grave. The grand jury for the 1833 term of the Supreme Court of the state of Rhode Island and Providence Plantations then indicted the Reverend Ephraim K. Avery for murder in the first degree.

His trial opened on May 6, in the lower hall of the eighteenth-century Colony House (then known as the State House) on the Newport Parade. It took 101 talesmen to produce a jury of twelve.

Five hundred spectators crowded into the pillared courtroom. Reporters came from as far away as Philadelphia, but the law forbade them to publish their stories while the trial was still in progress.

Avery pleaded not guilty. He spoke in a firm voice, holding his right hand in his breast pocket. Thereafter he sat silent, for the law did not allow the defendant in a capital case to testify. He was clad in a brown surtout; in place of a collar he wore a white handkerchief knotted at his neck, and he hid his eyes behind the green spectacles.

The prosecution was led by Albert C. Greene, the state's attorney general, whose high stock, in his portrait, seems to lengthen the disdainful egg-shaped face above it. To defend Avery, the Methodist Conference hired a team of lawyers headed by Jeremiah Mason of Boston, after Daniel Webster the smartest and dearest advocate in New England. Like Webster, he had been a senator of the United States. He stood six foot three, with one shoulder higher than the other, but the voice that issued from his enormous frame was a falsetto

This primitive contemporary woodcut shows Farmer Durfee, arms thrown up in shock, finding Maria's body in his stackyard.

squeak. The whole courtroom leaned forward as the two lawyers unfolded the story of Ephraim Avery and Maria Cornell.

Lowell, Massachusetts, at the falls of the Merrimack River, was the industrial show place of America. In 1820 it had been a barren waste. Ten years later it had fifteen thousand inhabitants and seven newspapers. Brick cotton mills, up to seven stories high, lined the watercourses, each capped with a belfry and surrounded by snug green-shuttered boardinghouses. Most of the workers were farm girls, who looked to a short experience in the mills as an introduction to life, much as their brothers looked to a few years at sea.

Among the factory hands was a little black-eyed sparrow of a girl named Maria Cornell, who stood only five feet tall. Born at Rupert, Vermont, in 1802, she had been apprenticed at twelve as a seamstress in Norwich, Connecticut, by her widowed mother. Mason showed that she had been discharged from Norwich for breaking the heddles on her loom; that she had lost other jobs—at Jewett City, Connecticut, for promiscuous behavior, and at Dorchester, Massachusetts, for calling the Methodist elders "a pack of damned fools." She had also been dismissed from the Methodist congregation at Slatersville, Rhode Island, for lewdness. Who, asked Greene, could blame them for reading her out of meeting? She did not blame them herself, Mason answered.

In 1828, repentant, she had moved to Lowell to work as a weaver in Appleton Mill Number 1. Her wages were $4 for a six-day week, of which $1.25 was withheld by the company for lodging and meals at her boardinghouse. In 1830 the Conference stationed the Reverend Mr. Avery in the growing mill town. He was thirty-three then, and must have looked as he did now in the box: a good six feet tall, with dark hair brushed up in front and curling long behind. He had a round chin, lank cheeks, and full lips. He had come first from "York State," where he had tended store for his father, a wounded veteran of the Revolution. He had studied medicine before divinity and was something of a naturalist as well.

With his invalid wife, Sophia, his five-year-old boy Edwin and his infant daughter Catherine, he took lodgings at the house of a Mr. Abbott. There was a study for him on the ground floor—the devout called it the Prophet's Chamber—with shelves for his collection of minerals, a couch of his own, and a separate door to the street. While Sophia spent her days upstairs with the children, he would take his tall cane after breakfast and tramp the countryside—no one knew where—till it was time for tea and evening prayer at home.

Maria was one of his flock. His rectitude, perhaps, served to reawaken the Devil within her. He had not been in Lowell a month before she stole a piece of muslin from a store; it was retrieved from within her shawl. She even rode out with a young man to the nearby village of Belvidere, where, says the State's testimony, "They called for a chamber and he treated her with wine."

When Avery heard this story, he threatened to expel her from meeting. She promised to reform again; she

45

offered to work without pay as his servant if he would relent. But young Edwin, Mason proved, had once told his mother, as if it were a trifle, "Pa kissed Maria in the road." Then the neglected lady forgot her meekness and, when Avery wanted to hire Maria to do housework, refused to have her in the house. Pious and penitent though she might be, the minister could not keep such a magdalen in the church. In October of 1830, five months after reaching Lowell, he read her out for theft and lewdness. She took the road again, this time to Somersworth, across the New Hampshire line.

Though she could not live with the Methodist Church, she could not live without it either. Avery had warned the Reverend Mr. Storrs of Somersworth. Storrs testified that when, as gently as he could, he had excluded her from a "Love-Feast" (a religious service for those who profess to have experienced a "second blessing"), she had cried to him, standing tiptoe with her arm across her breast, "You think to triumph over me now. But what care I for Mr. Avery and the Methodist Church? I will have my revenge, though it cost me my life."

She struggled through a year at Somersworth. Then on June 1, 1832, she fled with her loneliness to Woodstock, in the northeast corner of Connecticut, to join her sister Lucretia, who was married to the tailor Grindell Rawson. He made her his bookkeeper, and she wrote out his bills in a bold, clear hand.

Although the doors of Woodstock meeting closed against her, she managed to join a Bible class at a hamlet called Muddy Brook. And no one could bar her from the camp meetings which abounded in the countryside. Their whole purpose was to save lost sheep. Card sharps, horsejockeys, liquor peddlers, and fallen women, among the hundreds who truly sought redemption, flocked to the great circles cleared among the pines. The crowd would sway on the narrow benches set up before the preachers' stand. Delegations from neighboring villages pitched white tents at the edge of the woods and laid their provisions on the center table, where they were shared by all.

The camp meeting at Thompson, Connecticut, only a few miles from Woodstock, opened on Monday, August 27, 1832. On Tuesday John Paine, the Woodstock expressman, dressed in a dark coat, light pantaloons, and a green-lined palm-leaf hat, drove Maria to Thompson and dropped her, with bandbox and hamper, at the Muddy Brook tent. By this time Avery had been rotated from Lowell to Bristol, Rhode Island, which lies sixty miles southeast of Thompson—a long trip by chaise, even for a man in good health—and Avery, four days before, had broken his ankle on a

stone wall and fainted from the pain. Though he limped as he walked, and was not even on the list of preachers, he drove to the meeting. At Thompson he boarded in the Plainfield tent. Between meals he sat with the preachers in the stand or rested in the official tent behind it.

The prosecution did not claim that he knew Maria would be there and admitted that he did not meet her till Thursday, the last day of camp. That morning at six o'clock the horn blew for sunrise prayer. As the echo of Amen died away, the Reverend Elias Scott warned his colleague that there were bad characters on the ground. Avery nodded; he had seen Maria gazing up at the stand, and when he caught her eye, she turned her back on him. He agreed with Scott that it was their duty to warn the Muddy Brook tent master of her character and took the stern assignment on himself. He listened to the preaching from ten o'clock till noon. He took dinner with Plainfield, and tea with Weston. At 7:25 P.M. the horn sounded for the last service. Half an hour later, after the prayer of dismissal, the Thompson meeting was over for another year.

Of the next hour the only word is Maria's own, written to her sister in a letter submitted by the State:

I went up and asked to talk with him. "There is no room for us at the tents," he said. "Go along further and I will overtake you." He did overtake me, outside the fence, and we passed on, arm in arm, into the woods. When in the woods some distance, he asked me to sit down, and I did. I asked him if he had burned my letters, the ones I wrote him from Somersworth, asking to be retained in meeting. "No, but there is one condition on which I will settle the difficulty." About this time he took one of my hands and put one of his own into my bosom. I tried to get away from him, but could not. Afterwards he promised to burn the letters when he returned to Bristol.

A month later she discovered her plight. Her only salvation, she wrote to her sister on November 18, was to hide again. This time she chose Fall River, a bustling village of five thousand. Next to Lowell, it was New England's fastest-growing mill village, and as the fish hawk flies it is only four miles from Bristol. Three times a week the *King Philip* plied between the two, on her way to and from Providence; and the stage, through Warren, ran twice a day. On October 3, Maria set down her trunk at a boardinghouse and started work the next Monday in the weave-shed of the Anawan Mill. She tended four looms. In the twelve-hour workday she could run off 130 yards of cloth, for which she was paid a half cent a yard. In good health, she could make sixty-five cents, or four shillings—for some people, fifty years after the Revolution, still reckoned in shillings and pence.

On Friday, October 19, Avery, as Parson Bidwell's

guest, preached at the evening service in Fall River, as he had told Squire Howe. The night was not so dark but that a passer-by saw a short woman, at the edge of the emerging crowd, pluck at the sleeve of Avery's cloak. The evidence of what they said is again from Bidwell's testimony.

"Mr. Avery," Maria whispered, "I want to speak with you."

He turned to look down at her. "Maria, I do not wish to have anything to say with you."

"You must. I want you to say you will not hurt me here. You have ruined me at Somersworth and Lowell."

"Say rather that you have ruined yourself. I have never wanted nor tried to hurt you, Maria, but I can give no such promise. It is only just that Elder Bidwell should be warned."

"Nobody knows me here," she insisted, "and will not unless you tell them. Don't tell them, will you? I mean to behave myself well."

"That will be seen," he answered, pushing on after the Bidwells, "I shall talk with you tomorrow."

He came to see her the next evening, Maria wrote her sister, and she spent an hour with him.

He said . . . that if that was my case [the unborn child] was not his, and said I must go to a doctor immediately; said he had burned my letters—if he had have known what would have happened he would have kept them—said I must never swear it, for if that was my case he would take care of me—spoke very feeling of his wife and children—said I must say it belonged to a man that was dead, for, said he, I am dead to you—that is, I cannot marry you. He owned and denied [his guilt] two or three times. . . . I pledged him my word and honor I would not expose him if he would settle it. Therefore you must not mention his name to anyone . . .

What the result will be I know not. . . . I do not, however, wish you to do anything for me till I send you word. . . . The girls make from 3 to 4 dollars per week in the summer, but the days are short now and the water is low now. We can't do very much . . . I do not want for anything at present. I have kept at home except on the Sabbath, but the methodists begin to know me and say good morning Sister, as I go to the factory. I am glad that you have plenty of work. I hope you will get along with help. . . . You must not forget you have a sister in Fall River. My love to Mother. You must burn this letter. Farewell. Your sister,

Sarah M. Cornell.

The folded yellow letter in her bandbox, unsigned, bore the Bristol postmark and the date November 13, 1832:

Miss Cornell— . . . I will do all you ask, only keep it secret. I wish you to write me as soon as you get this, naming a time and place where I can see you, and wait for my answer before I come . . . I will keep your letter till I see you, and wish you to keep mine, and have them when I see you. Write soon—Say nothing to no one. Yours in haste.

On Monday, the twenty-fifth, Avery set off from Bristol by Chadwick's stage for a four-day prayer meeting in Providence. On Tuesday morning, dressed in the black goat-hair cloak called a camlet, he stepped aboard the *King Philip* at her dock. He handed a pink letter to Orswell, her engineer, with a tip of ninepence, and asked him to leave it for Miss Cornell at Mrs. Hathaway's in Fall River. (At the trial, Orswell identified the letter, which was the second found in the bandbox, but could not positively identify Avery because of his green spectacles.) That evening Maria received it:

Providence, Nov. 26, 1832

Dear Sister:

As I told you I am willing to help you and do for you. As circumstances are, I should ratther you would come to Bristol in the stage the 18th of December and stop at the Hotell and stay till six in the evening and then go up directly across the main street to a brick building neare to the stone meeting house where I will meet you and talk with you. When you stop at the tavern either inquire for work or go out on to the street in pretense of looking for some or something else and I may see you. Say nothing about me or my family. Should it storm on the 18th come the 20th. If you cannot come and it will be more convenient to meet me at the methodist meeting house in summerset just over the ferry on either of the above *eve'g* I will meet you there at the same hour or if you cannot do either, I will come to fall river on one of the above evenings when there will be the least passing, I should think before the mills stop work. . . . When you write, direct your letter to *Betsy Hills* and not as you have to me. *Remember this.* Your last letter I am afraid was broken open. Wear your calash not your plain bonnet. You can send your letter by mail.

Yours &c,
B.H.

Betsy Hills was the crippled niece of Mrs. Avery who helped with the housework. Inside the flap was a postscript: "—Let me still enjoin the secret. Keep the letters in your bosoom or burn them up."

But he did not wait for her to come to Bristol. On the eighth, ten days before the assignation, he walked the fourteen roundabout miles to Fall River. He bought a half-sheet of white paper—the third found in the bandbox—scribbled a note on it, sealed it with a purple wafer, and dropped it at the post office in the penny box for local delivery:

—I will be here on the 20th if pleasant at the place named, at six o'clock. If not pleasant, the next Monday evening. Say nothing, etc.

The twentieth was the day before John Durfee had found Maria's body in the stackyard.

After noonday dinner, Avery started out from his house in Bristol. He wore his peaked walking hat and the same brown surtout he wore later in the courtroom. He carried a red bandanna under his arm with a package in it. He eased his limp on a walking stick. There were no spectacles on his nose. At the foot of Ferry Hill in Bristol, two miles from home, he shouted across to George Pearse, the ferryman, who was tied up on the Island side. Pearse brought the horse scow over, apologizing that he must charge sixteen cents instead of eight, since he had to cross twice. He ported the sweep and clucked to the pair in the deck stalls; they plodded the disk of the treadmill; the paddles began to turn, and the scow edged into the channel.

Waving his cane toward the west side of the Island, Avery told Pearse he was out for a ramble, in spite of his still-lame ankle. He aimed to call on Brother Cook, four miles down-island. On the way, he thought to look at the Butt's Hill Fort, where his father had fought in the Revolution, and perhaps at the coal deposits on the western shore. Pearse saw him limp up the hill to the windmill on the crest, and then out of sight, with his cane to help him.

Eastward in Fall River, at four that afternoon, Maria asked her overseer to excuse her for the rest of the day. Lucy Hathaway promised to watch her looms—one was broken anyway—for the half hour that remained till dark. Maria walked home to her lodging, changed to her brown cloak and calash, and went out, telling Mrs. Hathaway she would be home early. At the same time, a little beyond the Tiverton bridge connecting the Island to the mainland, Annis Norton saw a dark-spectacled six-footer, in a snug snuff-colored surtout and tapered beaver, striding uphill toward Fall River.

"At that rate," laughed Annis, "he'll reach Ohio by sunrise."

The sun set at half past four; the moon would not rise till ten. In the dusk, on the hill just short of Fall River, Benjamin Manchester and Abner Davis were blasting rock. Having kindled their shavings, they ran to the shelter of a stone wall. At that moment a stranger, taller than common height, climbed the same wall farther down. "Look out," they shouted to him. He halted till the rock had stopped falling, then started across the field. He climbed the opposite wall into John Durfee's pasture. Durfee saw him too, dark as it was. The stranger gazed at Durfee's stackyard, then squared his shoulders, and passed into the dusk, toward Fall River.

There, in Lawton's Hotel, a clock peddler was eating supper. At quarter of six a long-legged stranger with dark glasses on his nose walked into the sitting room and ordered supper too. He wore a fur cap and had no cane. While waiting for his food he walked into the bar and returned with half a tumbler of brandy, which he drank neat at the trestle table, without speaking to the peddler. Having eaten, he paid Margaret Hambly, the waitress, and walked out into the dark.

At seven o'clock, Zeruiah Hambly, Margaret's mother, happening to open the door with a lantern in her hand, saw a tall man and a short woman, arm in arm, walk down the lane in the direction of Durfee's farm. At half past seven, Eleanor Owen heard shrieks from the same direction. She was washing the tea dishes in the sinkroom, but kept on washing them.

Everyone went to bed early, to save candles. But at 9:10 P.M. John Borden, on the Tiverton side of the bridge, passed a stranger striding from the direction of Fall River; and a few minutes later William Anthony, on the Island side, foddering his cattle late, saw a figure come from the same direction and disappear toward the ferry. The moon was not yet up.

Whoever the stranger was—if indeed there was not more than one of him—the Reverend Ephraim K. Avery soon afterward awakened Jeremiah Gifford, who tended the wharf on the Island side of the ferry. Gifford resented being roused from his four-poster. He peered at the wooden clock on his mantel; the hands just lacked quarter of ten. The minister asked to be ferried to Bristol.

Gifford grumbled that it would be inconvenient. The wind was high, and it was very cold.

Avery persisted, saying that his family was unwell and needed him at home.

The ferryman still refused. He did, however, give Avery a room for the night. The minister was up at five for an impatient breakfast. He crossed as the sunrise bell sounded from the Congregational Church in Bristol and trudged up Ferry Hill, reaching home in time for a second meal. In the afternoon he, Mrs. Avery, and their son walked downtown for tea with Mrs. Nancy Gladding, who testified that he was cheerful and affable; his demeanor was that of a Christian and a gentleman. Soon afterward, as we have seen, Elder Bidwell brought him the news of Maria Cornell's death.

The State had a hard time drawing a description of the corpus delicti from the ladies who had laid it out, and one of them snapped, "I never heard such questions asked of *nobody*."

Attorney General Greene described it anyway, to the courtroom's horror, while Avery sat impassive behind his spectacles. The crowd's hatred for him spread to encompass the black-robed elders who attended him. When the gentle Bidwell entered the courtroom, someone called out, "Here comes another of the damned murderers."

Mason, on the other hand, was waked up one night by a man who said an angel had appeared at his bed-

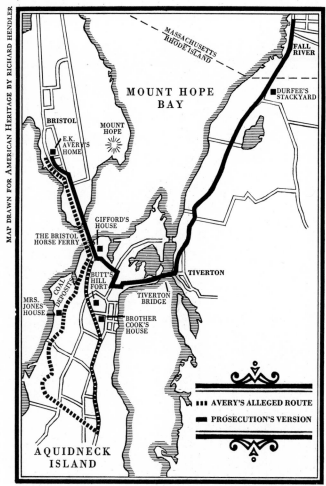

MASSACHUSETTS
RHODE ISLAND

FALL RIVER

MOUNT HOPE BAY

DURFEE'S STACKYARD

BRISTOL

MOUNT HOPE

E.K. AVERY'S HOME

GIFFORD'S HOUSE

THE BRISTOL HORSE FERRY

TIVERTON

BUTT'S HILL FORT

COAL DEPOSITS

TIVERTON BRIDGE

MRS. JONES HOUSE

BROTHER COOK'S HOUSE

■■■ AVERY'S ALLEGED ROUTE
■■ PROSECUTION'S VERSION

AQUIDNECK ISLAND

On December 20, 1832, the day of Maria's death, Mr. Avery set out from his Bristol home for a long walk. He claimed he visited Aquidneck Island, but neither Mrs. Jones nor Brother Cook—nor anyone else—could substantiate his story. The prosecution charged that he met Maria by prearrangement in Fall River, killed her at Durfee's farm, then came home.

post to tell him, "Mr. Avery is innocent of this crime," and immediately vanished. He begged to take the stand with this evidence, and Mason said he might do so, provided he brought the angel with him.

No one had seen Avery at the places where the defense claimed he had spent the afternoon—not at the Fort, nor at the mine, nor at Brother Cook's. The only people he had met on the Island—a boy driving sheep and a man with a torn hat—could not be found, nor had anyone else seen them. Mrs. Jones, being a Quaker, would not take the oath but despite the minister's solemn admonition that she had seen him *after* noon, affirmed that her stranger had passed in the morning. Jane Gifford, the ferry master's daughter, swore that Avery had told her he "had business with Brother Cook"; Cook swore he was away from home all day. Mason countered that Avery had not told Jane he had

actually *seen* Cook; and besides, Jane had been read out of meeting just as Maria had.

On the other hand, none of the witnesses who claimed that Avery had gone to Fall River could surely identify him. The red bandanna at Maria's feet looked like the one that Pearse had seen him carry, but could not be proved to be the same. Harnden hired two boys to walk from Lawton's Tavern to the ferryhouse, to show there was time for a murder on the way. It took them an hour and a quarter, but they admitted on cross-examination that they might have trotted a little going downhill. He bought a forty-dollar patent lever watch to prove that the Bristol bell was half an hour slow; but this evidence must have been prompted by civic jealousy, for it did not affect the final outcome of the case.

Greene called 78 prosecution witnesses. Mason, for the defense, called 160, mostly clergymen to prove that Avery's character was good and women to prove that Maria's was bad. He produced an expert on penmanship who deposed that the three letters were forged and a cordwainer who swore that a stranger—not Avery—had given him a letter to deliver to Orswell at the *King Philip* on the very morning the state claimed Avery had delivered his. By a miracle of coincidence both letters were pink and both were addressed to Miss Cornell in Fall River. Brother Jillson of Providence testified that Brother Avery could not possibly have reached the *King Philip* between the services at sunrise and at nine, as he had shaved and eaten breakfast in between.

Mason implied that Maria had forged the three letters and then hanged herself to incriminate Avery. To support this likelihood, Miss Louisa Whitney, for the defense, stated that the clove hitch was used by weavers like Maria and herself to repair the harness of their looms. On the stand she tied one and drew it taut at her own neck, amid the gasps of the courtroom. Another weaver, for the State, denied that she had ever used a clove hitch.

Mason saved his heaviest artillery for the end. He called Dr. Walter Channing, professor of midwifery and medical jurisprudence at Harvard, who declared it was impossible to tighten a clove hitch on anyone who resisted. Using the report of Dr. Wilbur's post-mortem, he proved by a dozen authorities that Maria's unborn child could have been conceived *before* the Thompson camp meeting.

Greene summed up for seven hours, and Mason for eight. Justice Eddy then charged the exhausted jurymen, who retired with a hand bell at seven o'clock on Saturday evening, June 1. The case had lasted four weeks—longer, Mason told the jury in his closing arguments, than any previous trial in the history of the republic's jurisprudence.

On Sunday morning the jury was still locked up. Most of the spectators went to church. At noon, after a hearty dinner, courtesy of the State, Foreman Trevett rang the hand bell. The sheriff called the jurymen to their box and tolled the bell in the tower of Colony House. At this signal the men instantly left church, leaving their wives behind. In five minutes the courtroom was full again.

For a breathless quarter hour the sheriff had to hunt for Jeremiah Mason, while jury and prisoner stared at each other in profound silence. At last he lumbered in. The trial ended thus:

CLERK: Gentlemen of the Jury, have you agreed upon your verdict?
JURY: We have.
CLERK: Who shall speak for you?
JURY: Our foreman.
CLERK: Mr. Foreman, what say you? Is the prisoner at the bar guilty or not guilty?
FOREMAN TREVETT: Not guilty.

For the first time Avery showed emotion. He passed his hand under his glasses and held it to his eyelids for a moment. Then he took off the glasses for good. The clergy crowded up to shake his hand; the rest of the audience filed out to the Parade, muttering its disgust. Avery was discharged. In half an hour his friends had him aboard a sloop which wafted him in three hours, with the wind behind her, to Bristol. The village had not expected a verdict on the Sabbath, but the word soon spread. A crowd followed him from the wharf to Wardwell Street but let him enter the house alone.

"Sophia," they heard him say, "I am freed from the thrall."

She toppled forward in her chair.

The news of his acquittal appeared in newspapers all over the country. He preached in his own meetinghouse on Sunday and in Boston the next Sunday. In the week between, the Methodist Conference, which had charged him with adultery, absolved him and voted that "in view of brother Avery's confinement and afflictions, and the influence they have had upon his health and constitution, the Bishop is hereby respectfully requested to give him such an appointment and relation to the church, as will afford him the most favorable opportunity of recovering his health."

Bishop Henning reappointed him to Bristol, with an assistant. But the notorious preacher could not face the crowds who flocked to hear him. He had been acquitted, but the trials had ruined him. Mason's fee of $6,000 had almost ruined the Methodist Conference.

Leaving his family at home, Avery began a speaking tour of vindication. But he was hissed at Hartford when he rose to preach on Ephesians 2:8 ("For by grace are ye saved, through faith, and not of yourselves"). At his benefit sermon in Richmond, Massachusetts, the collection was hardly enough for his horse's oats. In Boston, when he was recognized in the street, a mob of five hundred threatened to hang him. A straw effigy of him, kneeling in prayer with a rope at his neck, was set up outside Durfee's stackyard, and so frightened a young sinner of Tiverton that he put one around his own neck and hanged himself.

Avery's letters to Maria were hawked in colored facsimile at the news parlors. Drury wrote an account of the hearing, and Hallett, clerk of the court, one of the trial. Harnden's story of the capture at Rindge sold thirteen thousand copies. In New York the Richmond-Hill Theatre presented a melodrama called *The Factory Girl, or the Fall River Tragedy*. Lurid accounts of the case, with woodcuts, appeared throughout the country. And though Avery published his version of the facts in a so-called *Statement*, it convinced nobody.*

Before the end of the year he fled to his wife's family in Connecticut, but suspicion and mockery pursued him. Finally he resigned from the ministry to move out west. He bought a fifty-acre farm in Lorain County, Ohio. In the quiet reaches of the Western Reserve he lived out the blameless life of a farmer with Sophia and the children until he died, with suspicion outrun, in 1869.

His estate amounted to $111. Sophia sold his buffalo robe and sleigh to pay for his gravestone. The Lorain *Constitutionalist* gave him this farewell:

> *Servant of God, well done;*
> *Thy glorious warfare is past;*
> *The battle is fought, the victory won,*
> *And thou art crowned at last.*

Whether Maria or he had tightened the clove hitch, she had had her revenge.

---

* Among the published curiosities of the Avery case is a sixteen-page purported confession—to adultery but not "wilful murder"—entitled "Explanation of the Circumstances Connected with the Death of Sarah Maria Cornell, by Ephraim K. Avery." It bears the legend: Providence:/William S. Clark, Printer/1834/Price 12½ cents. It turns out, however, that there was no printer named Clark in Providence around that time, and that this document was a deception, published in New York and sold for a quick profit before the fraud could be detected.

Male & Female

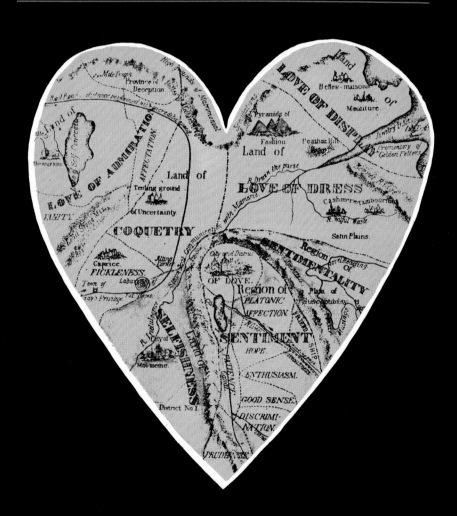

Sarah Althea Hill was a rosy-cheeked, blue-eyed beauty of the Golden West, with spirit and a temper. By her own testimony—if no other —she could shoot a pistol straight and "hit a four-bit piece nine times out of ten." During most of the eighteen eighties she was the sensation of San Francisco, and before she was through—in 1889—she had involved three of California's most prominent men in a scandalous case that eventually required three Supreme Court decisions. The men were Senator William Sharon, king of the Comstock Lode; David S. Terry, sometime chief justice of California; and Justice Stephen J. Field of the United States Supreme Court. Before it was all over, Justice Field had been given a bodyguard; as things turned out, he needed one.

Senator Sharon was a widower of great wealth in a time when wealth had license. He had come to California with the forty-niners, and through speculation in real estate, banks, and silver (culminating in Nevada's fabulous Comstock Lode), he had amassed more than fifteen million dollars. In 1875 the Nevada legislature elected him to the United States Senate, although his opponents pointed out that he was really a resident of San Francisco, where he had his office and owned the most extravagant estate on the coast as well as the largest, finest hotel in the West—the Palace. He was a little man, neither stately in appearance nor statesmanlike in conduct—but he was shrewd. His enemies berated him as a man of suspicious deals and licentious living. Apart from business and poker, his pleasures were Byronic poetry and pretty girls—and being a widower with grown children, he saw no reason to curb his instincts for voluptuous living.

Sarah Althea Hill entered Sharon's life in 1880, when he was sixty and she was in her late twenties. The orphaned daughter of a respected Missouri lawyer, she had been brought up in a convent, and in 1871, while still in her teens, had come to California with her brother.

When Althea reached San Francisco she had a small inheritance, which she gradually dissipated in stock speculations. In the summer of 1880, when her speculations and her personal affairs were at a particularly low ebb—she had tried to commit suicide because of unrequited love for a San Francisco lawyer—she met Senator Sharon, who generously offered to give her some points on stocks. At his invitation she called on him at his office several times to "talk stocks"; but they always ended by talking about themselves. On one of her calls Sharon asked her to let him "love her" and said he could give her $500 a month. (Sharon later testified that that was the regular proposal he made to his mistresses.) Althea declined, whereupon he raised his ante to $1,000.

ALTHEA

Senator Sharon's Discarded Rose

Blood Flowed at

as They Ambushed

By BROOKS W.

This is demure Althea, dead shot but, she said, easy mark for old men.

BEDLAM AT THE BAR

THE JUDGES

Packed a Pistol, Her Lawyer a Knife.

Their Last "Appeal,"

a Federal Judge

MACCRACKEN

This is the rich senator, elusive but always ready for a frolic. Was he, in fact, Althea's victim?

At this point their later recollections of events diverge. As Althea remembered it, she immediately rose to depart, saying, "You are mistaken in your woman. You can get plenty of women that will let you love them for less than that." Sharon then put his back against the door and protested that he was really in love with her and wanted to marry her. That was different. She said (or said she said), "If that is what you want we will talk about that." "Then," according to the subsequent court summary, "the question arose as to how they should be married. He wanted the marriage secret: he had a liaison with a woman in Philadelphia who would make trouble if she heard of it, and that might injure his chances for re-election to the Senate." Sharon told Althea that under the civil code of California they could marry one another simply by agreeing in writing to do so; and indeed, Section 75 of that code did recognize a written declaration of marriage in proper form if followed by cohabitation as husband and wife. Then, she said, he had her sit down at his office table and, consulting some law books, he dictated to her this declaration of marriage, which she wrote on note paper and they both signed:

In the city and county of San Francisco, state of California, on the twenty-fifth day of August, A.D. 1880, I, Sarah Althea Hill, of the city and county of San Francisco, state of California, aged 27 years, do here, in the presence of Almighty God, take Senator William Sharon, of the state of Nevada, to be my lawful and wedded husband, and do here acknowledge and declare myself to be the wife of Senator William Sharon, of the state of Nevada. SARAH ALTHEA HILL.

August 25, 1880, San Francisco, Cal. I agree not to make known the contents of this paper or its existence for two years, unless Mr. Sharon himself sees fit to make it known. S. A. HILL.

In the city and county of San Francisco, state of California, on the twenty-fifth day of August, A.D. 1880, I, Senator William Sharon, of the state of Nevada, aged 60 years, do here, in the presence of Almighty God, take Sarah Althea Hill, of the city of San Francisco, Cal., to be my lawful and wedded wife, do here acknowledge myself to be the husband of Sarah Althea Hill. WILLIAM SHARON, Nevada, August 25, 1880.

That fateful instrument having been signed, and her honor thus protected, the secret bride and groom separated without benefit either of clergy or of honeymoon—he to Virginia City, Nevada, and she to her home in the Galindo Hotel in Oakland. Within a month the Galindo burned down, and she moved to the Baldwin in San Francisco. There Sharon came to her, and for a while he was with her almost constantly. But soon he became afraid that their being together so much was creating a good deal of comment. He asked

53

her to move to the Grand, which was connected to his own hotel, the Palace, by a bridge that made confidential access to one another easier. He wrote a note to Mr. Thorn, the manager of the Grand, introducing "Miss Hill, a particular friend of mine, and a lady of unblemished character and of good family. Give her the best, and as cheap as you can."

For a few months, apparently, the bridge between the Palace and the Grand was a bridge of love. He furnished her room as she wanted it and he gave her (by coincidence?) $500 a month expense money. She had many of her meals and spent many a night with him at the Palace. She gave a musicale for him at the Grand and he had her and some friends for week ends at his country mansion, Belmont. She even attended, she said (though Sharon denied it), the great reception he gave for the wedding of his daughter to a titled Englishman, Sir Thomas Hesketh. "I used to go everywhere with Mr. Sharon," she testified later. "He scarcely went anywhere that I did not go with him—either riding or driving, or attending to business, that he did not take me with him."

Thus for a year or a little more. Then he began to accuse her of revealing his business secrets and private affairs, even of stealing his papers. Once, according to Althea, he demanded that she sign a paper that she was not Mrs. Sharon; he offered her the usual $500 a month if she would. She denied his accusations, declined his offer, and refused to sign his paper. But finally she took $7,500 in cash and personal notes payable to "Miss Hill," and gave him a receipt and some sort of release of claims. Then he had the manager of the Grand give her a notice to vacate her room. When she delayed the hour of her going, Sharon had the room door taken off its hinges and the carpets taken up. She then decided to avoid the further indignity of being thrown out.

For a time she stayed at the home of Martha Wilson, "a poor, nervous little Negro woman" whom she had employed as a seamstress and from whose restaurant she had been used to having her breakfasts. Later she moved to a house in a more fashionable neighborhood and asked a Negro woman who was known as Mammie Pleasant to furnish it for her. As described later by a federal judge, Mammie Pleasant was "a shrewd old Negress of considerable means, who has lived in

San Francisco many years, and is engaged in furnishing and fitting up houses and rooms, and caring for women and girls who need a mammie or a manager, as the case may be." For some reason—it may be that Mammie had once been a slave girl of Althea's family in Missouri—it was to this protectress that Althea confided the story of her "marriage" to Senator Sharon.

It was said (but Althea denied it) that Mammie persuaded her to try voodoo charms on Sharon to win back his affection. Allegedly Mammie showed her how to put black powder around his chair and white powder between the sheets of his bed and advised her to take one of Sharon's socks and one of his shirts and bury them under a corpse in a newly made grave. Whether

Althea's champion, David Terry, once the chief justice of California, was a dangerous duellist.

with or without voodoo, Althea was back in favor with the Senator for a time in 1882, but not for long. In the summer of 1883 Mammie took her, with her precious declaration of marriage, to Mammie's lawyer, George Tyler. Tyler needed and called in more eminent cocounsel. Among them was David Terry, a former chief justice of California. With him Althea seems to have made a genuine hit.

Terry was a tall, strong, fighting man from Texas. Although he was over sixty when he met Althea, he had all the quickness and penchant for wild passions of a much younger man. He claimed to adhere to the chivalry and the code of honor of the old South; and no man had ever safely challenged his readiness or his ability to defend his code— at law or with his bowie knife. He had fought in the Mexican War and, like Sharon, had come to California with the forty-niners. He settled in Stockton, became a leader of the Know-Nothing party, and in the early fifties was elected a state supreme court judge. In San Francisco, he was drawn into a fracas with the Vigilance Committee and wounded one of the vigilantes. The committee demanded that he resign from the bench, but he refused. Within a year the court's chief justice died, and Terry succeeded to the post.

In 1859 he challenged Senator David Broderick— then the political leader of the state—to a duel on a point of personal honor. Terry won the duel and killed Broderick, but witnesses claimed he had fired before the count. Terry's friends and defenders insisted that Broderick had fired first, accidentally or otherwise. Whatever the truth, the incident made

Terry a sort of California Aaron Burr; he left the state, joined the Confederate Army when the Civil War began, and rose to the command of a brigade. After the war and a brief sojourn in Mexico, he returned to Stockton and resumed his practice of law and politics; but he never regained a position of real leadership, except as a sort of elder statesman for the malcontents.

Now, in the summer of 1883, he joined George Tyler in the case of Sarah Althea Hill.

In September, Althea made a public disclosure of her claim that she was Sharon's wife, and on her behalf William Nielson, a journalist, had him arrested for adultery with another woman. Her claim of marriage was a sensation. Sharon vehemently denied it, said it was blackmail, and vowed he would spend all his millions in defense before she would get a penny. His lawyers filed suit in the federal court, alleging that Althea's precious marriage document was a fraud and a forgery and asking that the court compel her to give it up and cancel it. She replied with a suit in the state court at San Francisco, asking for a divorce and a property settlement. For over six years the two suits went from court to court and from hearing to hearing, and brought forth some twenty published judicial opinions, three of them by the United States Supreme Court.

The trial of Althea's divorce suit began in March of 1884, without a jury, before Judge Jeremiah Sullivan of the superior court of San Francisco. It continued, off and on, until September. In court, Althea told her story with a goodly number of embellishments, many of them rather transparently false. She produced a sheaf of notes from Sharon written in the fall and winter of 1880, all to "Dear Allie" and all to the general purport of "come up and see me." One, toward Christmas, said, "Come over and join me in a nice bottle of champagne, and let us be gay before Christmas. If you don't come over and take part in the bottle, I may hurt myself." Also she had a number of letters written in 1881 to "My dear Wife." Sharon replied that the "My dear Wife" had been forged. In any event, the letters were quite innocent of love, or of any domestic intimacies other than this sort of thing: "My Dear Wife: Inclosed send you . . . the balance, two hundred and fifty [dollars] which I hope will make you very happy. . . . Yours, S. April 1st."

BOTH: BANCROFT LIBRARY

Althea's nemesis in the courts, and the man she stalked outside, was Supreme Court Justice Field.

Sharon, however, produced a number of letters from Althea that *were* intimate and that delighted the readers of the San Francisco newspapers. Althea wrote this one, for instance, when Sharon was insisting that she get out of the Grand and leave him alone:

My Dear Mr. Sharon: I cannot see how you can have any one treat me so—I, who have always been so good and kind to you—the carpet is all taken up in my hall—the door is taken off and away—and it does seem to me terrible that it is you who would have done it. . . . Oh, senator, dear senator, don't treat me so—whilst everyone else is so happy for Christmas, don't try to make mine miserable—remember this time last year—you have always been so good, you don't act so—now let me see you and talk to you—let me come . . . & be to me the same Senator again—don't be cross to me—please don't—you know you are all I have in the world . . . I know it is not in your nature to be so hard to one that has been so much to you—don't be unjust —Say I may see you.

Another, which came to be known as the "Us Girls" or "Egg and Champagne" letter, had been written when they had made up and were temporarily pals again in the summer of 1882:

My Dear Senator: Won't you try and find out what springs those were you were trying to think of today, that you said Mr. Main went to, and let me know tomorrow when I see you? And don't I wish you would make up your mind and go down to them with Nellie and I, wherever they be, on Friday or Saturday. We all could have nice times out hunting and walking or driving those lovely days, in the country. The jaunt or little recreation would do you worlds of good, and us girls would take the best of care of you, and mind you in everything. . . . I am crazy to see Nell try and swallow an *egg in champagne*. I have not told her of the feat I accomplished in that line, but I am just waiting in hopes of seeing her some day go through the performance. As I told you today, I am out to Nellie's mother's for a few days, 824 Ellis Street. What a lovely evening this is, and how I wish you would surprise us two *little lone birds* by coming out and taking us for a moonlight drive. . . . 'Twould do you good to get out of that stupid old hotel for a little while, and we'd do our best to make you forget all your business cares and go home feeling happy. A.

Sharon's lawyers did not find it difficult to underline the unwifelike quality of those letters. And even her own testimony made it easy to say that Althea had done other unwifely things. At one time she had hidden in Sharon's room to see him and another woman undress and go to bed together—it was a good joke. At another time she had hidden her friend Nellie behind Sharon's bureau while Althea and the Senator went to bed together. Althea had hoped that Nellie would overhear Sharon call her "wife"; but apparently her hope was not fulfilled.

Althea's supporting witnesses were not particularly impressive. Her two Negro friends testified that as early as 1881 she had showed them the declaration of marriage, but "poor, nervous little" Martha was most befuddled on cross-examination, and besides, she couldn't read. Mammie, on the other hand, was almost too positive about the whole thing. She proudly admitted to having made Althea's "fight" her own, and to having advanced her $5,000. Althea claimed also to have told an uncle about her marriage to Sharon, but the uncle was not called as a witness, nor did she call her other available relatives to her aid. It is altogether probable that they were glad to be left out of the mess. A girl named Vesta Snow testified for her, but Vesta's reputation was of the doubtful kind. And so it went with all of Althea's witnesses.

Judge Sullivan, a distinguished Catholic, concluded that Althea had lied in some particulars; but on the essential points he believed her—Sharon had signed a legally binding declaration of marriage with her and had called her "wife." If Sharon had not meant the declaration to be real, he had seduced her by trickery. Althea was of good family, and had been educated in a convent; Sharon himself had said that her character was "unblemished." So the Judge was sympathetic when her counsel spoke of her as "an ungathered rose" who had become "the rose of Sharon." He granted Althea a divorce and $2,500 a month alimony. Said Althea: "I am so happy, I feel just like a young kitten that has been brought into the house and set before the fire." Sharon promptly appealed from the decree, and at the same time pressed his petition in the federal court to have the declaration of marriage adjudged a forgery and cancelled.

Althea's lawyers made every possible objection to the jurisdiction of the federal court to hear Sharon's case, but they were overruled by the federal judge; an official examiner was appointed to take the testimony of the witnesses and to report to the court. The examination took six months. Sharon and his lawyers spared no effort or expense. They hired the most celebrated experts to examine the declaration of marriage and to testify against its authenticity. They persuaded some of Althea's erstwhile companions to come into court and bear witness against her. They even persuaded one lawyer to testify (over the vehement objections of her trial attorneys that the testimony was a violation of the lawyer-client privilege) that she had once asked his legal advice about what proof she needed to sue Sharon for breach of promise of marriage.

Althea responded to all this by letting loose her spirit and her temper in an onslaught of contempt and derision the like of which has seldom been witnessed in our courts. She sneered at the lawyers, the witnesses, and the examiner, and took to carrying a pistol in the courtroom.

One day, while Sharon's lawyers, William M. Stewart and Oliver P. Evans, were questioning a witness, Althea, ignoring them, sat reading a deposition made about her by a woman acquaintance. The deposition was unfriendly, and Althea did not like it. First she muttered, then she shouted for the proceedings to halt. The examiner remonstrated, but that only fanned her indignation. "When I see this testimony, I feel like taking that man Stewart out and cowhiding him," she shouted.

I will shoot him yet; that very man sitting there. To think he would put up a woman to come here and deliberately lie about me like that. I will shoot him as sure as you live; the man that is sitting right there; and I shall have that woman, Mrs. Smith, arrested for this, and make her prove it. I say no jury will convict me for shooting a man that will bring a woman here to tell such things on me. They have never dared, when they put me on the stand, to ask me a question against my character yet—never dared. If they have got so much against it, why didn't they dare ask me some questions when I was on the stand?

Several times the presiding officer sought to end her tirade, but she refused to be silenced. "They shall not slander me," she said. "I can hit a four-bit piece nine times out of ten." She drew a pistol from her satchel and dangled it in her right hand, pointing it idly in the direction of Evans, assuring him all the while that she was not going to "shoot you just now, unless you would like to be shot and think you deserve it." When her fury was fully slaked she allowed the examiner to take the pistol from her. He made a special report of her conduct to the federal judges.

Enter now upon this fevered scene the third and most prominent of the California gentlemen whose lives were entangled with that of Althea Hill. Stephen J. Field, associate justice of the United States Supreme Court, was then on circuit in California, and the report of Althea's pistol-waving came to him and Circuit Judge Lorenzo Sawyer. In those days Supreme Court justices were required to hear cases on circuit when the full court was not in session in Washington. Field's circuit included California, and there he went each summer to assist Judge Sawyer and the district court judges, Mathew Deady and George Sabin. Field was one of the nation's most remarkable and self-confident jurists. In his legal and moral principles he was an assertive doctrinaire, his mind seldom in doubt, his actions never hesitant, and his manner so often offensive that he had acquired a number of enemies. Nevertheless, as a judge he was widely admired, and his appointment to the Supreme Court had been applauded all over the country. Like Terry and Sharon, Field had come to California with the forty-niners and had learned the value of courage and firearms. He had written California's first civil code, and in 1859 he had succeeded Terry as chief justice of California. Abraham Lincoln had appointed him to the Supreme Court in 1863, and there he was to sit for thirty-four years and seven months, longer than any other justice in the history of the Court.

In August, 1885, when Althea first came before him, Field was just under seventy years of age, and with his full beard, bald and lofty dome, broad forehead, long nose, dark eyes, and stern visage, he looked like a judge out of the Old Testament. In fact, he was the son of a Connecticut minister. Two of his brothers had followed their father into the church; a third, Cyrus Field, had laid the Atlantic cable; a fourth, David Dudley Field, was a great New York lawyer who did much to improve American civil procedure but who was also involved with Jay Gould and Jim Fiske in the Erie Railroad scandals. At one time Justice Field aspired to the Democratic nomination for the Presidency, but he had too many political enemies.

Justice Field was not one to tolerate Althea's theatrics. He and Judge Sawyer promptly ordered the marshal to see to it that in the future she would come into the examiner's presence unarmed. When one of her lawyers, George Tyler, suggested that a gun was sometimes necessary for protection in court, Justice Field gave him a lecture: "Any man, counsel or witness, who comes into a court of justice armed, ought to be punished, and if he is a member of the bar, he ought to be suspended or removed permanently. That is the doctrine that ought to be inculcated from the bench everywhere. So far as I have the power, I will enforce it."

Tyler protested, "Where witnesses do come armed—"

"Then report the fact to the court; that is the proper way."

"That will not stop a bullet."

Judge Sawyer spoke up: "Then arrest the parties in advance, and put them under bonds, or apply to the court to have them examined and disarmed before permitting them to enter the court. The laws are very severe."

Tyler again demurred. "The laws are very severe, but it is harder on the man that gets the bullet."

Justice Field answered him, "I don't mean to say that there may not be times in the history of a country, in certain communities, when everybody is armed. That was the case in the early days of California, when people travelled armed; but at this time, when the law is supposed to be supreme, when all good men are supposed to obey it, and where counselors are sworn to obey the law and to see it properly administered, the carrying of arms into a court cannot for a moment be tolerated."

That was Field's first encounter with Althea. David Terry was not involved. Some weeks later the taking of the testimony was at last completed, and 1,723 pages of it were sent to Circuit Judge Sawyer and District Judge Deady, Justice Field having by then returned to Washington. Terry then made the argument for Althea, but to no avail. The two judges concluded that the declaration of marriage was a forgery; they ordered Althea to surrender the declaration for cancellation, and perpetually enjoined her from alleging its validity or from making any use of it to support any "right claimed under it." In addition, Judge Deady gave her a gratuitous moral lecture:

... [As] the world goes and is, the sin of incontinence in a man is compatible with the virtue of veracity, while in the case of a woman, common opinion is otherwise. ...

And it must also be remembered that the plaintiff is a person of long standing and commanding position in this community, of large fortune and manifold business and social relations, and is therefore so far, and by all that these imply, specially bound to speak the truth, and responsible for the correctness of his statements; and all this, over and beyond the moral obligation arising from the divine injunction not to bear false witness, or the fear of the penalty attached by human law to the crime of perjury. On the other hand, the defendant is a comparatively obscure and unimportant person, without property or position in the world. Although apparently of respectable birth and lineage, she has deliberately separated herself from her people, and selected as her intimates and confidants doubtful persons from the lower walks of life. ... And by this nothing more is meant than that, while a poor and obscure person may be naturally and at heart as truthful as a rich and prominent one, and even more so, nevertheless, other things being equal, property and position are in themselves some certain guaranty of truth in their possessor, for the reason, if none other, that he is thereby rendered more liable and vulnerable to attack on account of any public moral delinquency, and has more to lose if found or thought guilty thereof than one wholly wanting in these particulars.

In this undertaking, doubtless, the proverbial sympathy

of the multitude for an attractive young woman, engaged in an affair of this kind with an immoral old millionaire, was largely relied on to make the conspiracy successful. But in a court of justice such considerations have no place. . . .

A woman who voluntarily submits to live with a millionaire for hire ought not, after she finds herself supplanted or discharged, to be allowed to punish her paramour for the immorality of which she was a part, and may be the cause, by compelling him to recognize her as his wife and endow her of his fortune. If society thinks it expedient to punish men and women for the sin of fornication, let it do so directly. But until so authorized, the courts have no right to assume such functions, and, least of all, by aiding one of the parties to an irregular sexual intercourse, to despoil the other, on the improbable pretense that the same was matrimonial and not meretricious. . . .

But I cannot refrain from saying, in conclusion, that a community which allows the origin and integrity of the family, the corner-stone of society, to rest on no surer or better foundation than a union of the sexes, evidenced only by a secret writing, and unaccompanied by any public recognition of each other as husband and wife, or the assumption of marital rights, duties, and obligations except furtive intercourse, more befitting a brothel than otherwise, ought to remove the cross from its banner and symbols, and replace it with the crescent.

To Althea, the sting of this decision was eased by two new developments. Sharon had died before the decision was given—albeit he had left a will in which he made his final, solemn testimonial that she had never been his wife. More important, on January 7, 1886, two weeks after the decision, Althea and David Terry were married by a priest. For over a year she and her case had been a solace and a diversion to Terry. His wife and five of his six sons had died, one by suicide, and he had need of a gay and high-spirited woman. His marriage to Althea ended him socially, but when that became obvious he remained all the more true to her. "They shall not brand my wife a strumpet," he said, over and over again.

Terry believed that the federal court's order had died with Sharon. He did not trouble to appeal it. Althea did not obey it. It was, he said, "an ineffective, inoperative, unenforceable pronunciamento." Meanwhile, Sharon's lawyers, now representing his children, pressed the appeal from Judge Sullivan's earlier divorce decree. In two years they got the California supreme court to reduce the alimony from $2,500 a month to the $500 that had been Althea's allowance from Sharon, but that court still recognized Althea's marriage to him as lawful. Consequently his children asked for a new trial and spent large sums of money to elect some new California judges.

They then filed a petition in the federal court to revive its order on Althea to surrender her marriage

FROM *David S. Terry*, BY A. E. WAGSTAFF, 1892

The long-simmering feud which had pitted Althea and her husband, David Terry, against Justice Field came to a violent climax on August 14, 1889, in the depot dining room at Lathrop, California. Terry suddenly attacked the Justice, who remained seated at the table. Thereupon Field's bodyguard, David Neagle, drew a pistol and shot him dead.

contract; they had deliberately waited until her time to appeal from the order had expired. Legally, Terry was outmaneuvered; but Althea was cocksure of the popularity of her case. One day in the summer of 1888 she and her husband were riding on a train when she saw Judge Sawyer sitting in the same car. She pranced up to his seat and taunted him. "I will give him a taste of what he will get bye and bye," she said, and leaned over and yanked his hair. Terry laughed and said, "The best thing to do with him would be to take him into the bay and drown him." The Judge asked the marshal to have deputies present the next time the Terrys came into court.

Justice Field was again on the California circuit that summer, and along with Judges Sawyer and Sabin he heard the petition to revive the federal order. The judges brushed Terry's arguments aside, and in a unanimous opinion read by Field they revived the order against Althea.

While Justice Field was reading his opinion, Althea and Terry sat at the attorneys' table directly in front of the bench. Althea fidgeted nervously with her satchel. Suddenly she stood up and addressed the bench: "Judge, are you going to take the responsibility of ordering me to deliver up that marriage contract?"

Coldly, Justice Field looked down upon her and said, "Be seated, madam."

Defiantly, she kept on. "How much did Newlands [Sharon's son-in-law] pay you for this decision?"

Field spoke to the marshal. "Remove that woman

from the courtroom. The court will deal with her hereafter."

She sat down. "I won't go out and you can't put me out." Then, as the marshal strode up to her, she sprang up and struck him in the face with both hands. "You dirty scrub! You dare not remove me from this courtroom."

Terry rose to his full height beside her. "No man shall touch my wife. Get a written order." When the marshal replied, "Judge, stand back; no written order is required," Terry struck him in the mouth with all his might. A general melee followed, in which a swearing Terry and a scratching Althea were subdued and taken from the courtroom. In one of the scuffles a bowie knife was wrested from Terry's hand. A loaded pistol was removed from Althea's satchel.

The court promptly adjudged them both guilty of contempt and ordered them to prison, Terry for six months and Althea for one. On September 17 the Terrys filed a petition to revoke the order, but Justice Field denied it. He wrote:

... Why did the petitioner come into court with a deadly weapon concealed on his person? He knew that as a citizen he was violating the law which forbids the carrying of concealed weapons, and as an officer of the court—and all attorneys are such officers—was committing an outrage upon professional propriety, and rendering himself liable to be disbarred.... Therefore, considering the enormity of the offenses committed, and the position the petitioner once held in this state which aggravates [the offences] ... the court ... cannot grant the prayer of the petitioner; and it is accordingly denied.

The Terrys appealed twice to the U.S. Supreme Court—from the revival of the order on Althea to surrender her marriage contract, and from the order imprisoning them for contempt. They lost each appeal. Then the California supreme court—with a majority of newly elected judges—finally decided that Judge Sullivan's original decree in Althea's favor was not supported by the evidence. The state and the federal courts were at last agreed that she was a perjurer, a forger, and a fallen woman. The only court now left to her was public opinion.

To this she and Terry made prompt appeal. Terry wrote a series of long letters to the San Francisco *Call*, attacking the honesty of the judges and especially of Field. He reviewed Field's career, emphasizing some old scandals and concluding, "He has always been a corporation lawyer, and a corporation judge, and as such no man can be honest." In conversations, Terry called the judges "all a lot of cowardly curs" and he would "see some of them in their graves yet." Once he said he would horsewhip Field, and "if [he] resents it, I will kill him." Several times Althea said she would kill both Justice Field and Judge Sawyer, and she did not attach any conditions to her threat.

These and other wild statements were duly reported in the papers, and reached the eyes and ears of Washington officials. Field's friends advised him to keep out of the California circuit the next summer, but he was too proud a man to take such advice. He was still the same Stephen Field who had come to California in the gold-camp days and had published *Reminiscences of Early Days in California,* filled with tales of his own bravery. "Shoot and be damned!" he had once told someone who had threatened him. Now that he was a Supreme Court justice he was no less defiant. The Attorney General, however, advised the local United States marshal in California to furnish him a bodyguard; and the marshal appointed David Neagle.

Denouement came on the fourteenth of August, 1889. The afternoon before, Field, accompanied by Neagle, took the train for San Francisco from Los Angeles, where Field had been hearing a case on circuit. Their route went through Fresno, where the Terrys were living. There, in the middle of the night, Neagle saw David Terry and his wife board the train. He told Field. "Very well," the Justice said, "I hope they will have a good sleep." But Neagle slept no more that night. He told the conductor that he was apprehensive of trouble, and asked that a warning be sent to the officer at the station in Lathrop, where the train would stop for breakfast in the morning. Just before they reached Lathrop, Neagle suggested to Field that he could get a good breakfast at the buffet on board the train. But the judge did not realize what he was driving at, and said he preferred to have his breakfast at the table in the station. Neagle replied, "I will go with you." They were among the first to be seated.

Shortly afterward Terry came in, and Althea followed a few feet behind. When she saw Field, she turned on her heel and rushed back to the train for her satchel. While she was gone her husband chose a table and sat down, whereupon the manager went up to him and said, "Mrs. Terry has gone out to the car for some purpose. I fear she will create a disturbance." Terry replied, "I think it very likely. You had better watch her and prevent her coming in." When the manager left to do so, Terry himself rose from the table, went around back of Field, stopped quickly, and slapped the Justice viciously on both sides of his face. Neagle sprang to his feet, calling out, "Stop! Stop! I am an officer." But Terry gave him what Neagle later recalled as "the most malignant expression of hate and passion I have ever seen in my life" and made as if to reach for his bowie knife. Instantly Neagle raised his pistol and fired twice. Terry fell to the floor—dead. Field had not risen from his chair.

Just then Althea rushed back to the room, an open satchel in her hand. The manager stopped her, grabbed the satchel, and took from it a loaded revolver. Then she became hysterical, calling out for vengeance and denouncing everybody as murderers.

Field and Neagle identified themselves; but Lathrop was near Terry's old home, Stockton, and Althea was surrounded by his friends. On examination it appeared that Terry had been unarmed. Despite Justice Field's protests, a sheriff took Neagle to the county jail at Stockton, and Field had to proceed to San Francisco alone. The affair was an immediate sensation and the idea gained currency that Field and his man had deliberately provoked Terry's assault so as to have an excuse to kill him. At Stockton Althea swore out a warrant for the arrest of both Field and Neagle for the murder of David Terry.

The arrest of a Supreme Court justice on such a charge was not a matter to be treated lightly. The sheriff apologized, but Field was unperturbed. His words were copybook material: "Proceed with your duty; I am ready. An officer should always do his duty. I recognize your authority, sir, and submit to the arrest. I am, sir, in your custody." He was not long in jeopardy. Habeas corpus proceedings were begun, but before they could be acted upon, the governor of California ordered Field to be freed from the arrest, lest his prosecution on Althea's charge become a "burning disgrace" to the state.

Neagle, however, was in real trouble. He had undeniably killed Terry, and whether a jury in Terry's home county would ever believe Neagle's claim of justifiable homicide was at least doubtful. He was forced to apply to the federal court for a writ of habeas corpus, and there was serious question whether the federal court had any right to free him. The legal answer depended upon whether Neagle had been acting "in pursuance of a law of the United States," and admittedly there was no specific statute that provided for him to act as Field's bodyguard. Moreover, there were those who felt that because of the personal hostility of the federal judges to the Terrys it would be a grave mistake for the federal court to assert control of the case. They argued that the determination of Neagle's guilt or innocence should be left to the local authorities of the state of California. But the federal court, Judge Sawyer presiding, overruled all objections and ordered Neagle's release. The state's attorneys appealed to the United States Supreme Court.

Field did not sit on the case, but he got Joseph Choate, then the country's most famous advocate, to represent Neagle. In 1890, in the last, the longest, and the most unprecedented of the Supreme Court's opinions concerning Althea, a majority of the justices held that, in protecting their brother Field against threats of violence, Neagle had been acting "in pursuance of a law of the United States," and it was not necessary to find a specific statute. The majority opinion was written by Justice Samuel Freeman Miller:

In the view we take . . . any duty of the marshal to be derived from the general scope of his duties under the laws of the United States is 'a law' within the meaning of this phrase. It would be a great reproach to the system of government of the United States . . . if there is to be found within the domain of its powers no means of protecting the judges . . . from the malice and hatred of those upon whom their judgments may operate unfavorably . . . If a person in the situation of Judge Field could have no other guarantee of his personal safety, while engaged in the conscientious discharge of a disagreeable duty, than the fact that if he was murdered his murderer would be subject to the laws of a State and by those laws could be punished, the security would be very insufficient.

Justice L. Q. C. Lamar and Chief Justice Melville Fuller joined in a long dissenting opinion, the crux of which was:

. . . [We] think that there was nothing whatever in fact of an official character in the transaction . . . and the courts of the United States have . . . no jurisdiction whatever in the premises . . . [we] cannot permit ourselves to doubt that the authorities of the State of California are competent and willing to do justice; and even if the appellee [Neagle] had been indicted and had gone to trial upon this record, God and his country would have given him a good deliverance.

So Neagle was released. Field presented him with a gold watch inscribed "as a token of appreciation of his courage and fidelity to duty under circumstances of great peril."

David Terry's friends and partisans continued to see the whole matter in a different light. They wrote articles and pamphlets further presenting Althea's version of the story and attacking Justice Field and the courts. But for Althea, that was all; her cases were over and done with. After a time she had nothing left, not even her mind. In 1892 Mammie Pleasant, still her friend and protectress, had her committed to an asylum for the insane, and there she lived until her death, some forty-five years later.

A HUSBAND'S REVENGE

By THOMAS J. FLEMING

Is it all right to shoot your wife's lover?
Do you have to catch him *flagrante delicto?*
What if your victim is district attorney?
And if you are a member of Congress?
Now come with us to Washington, D.C., in 1859

"District of Columbia, County of Washington, to wit: The jurors of the United States for the county aforesaid upon their oaths present, that Daniel E. Sickles late of the county of Washington aforesaid, gentleman, not having the fear of God before his eyes but being moved and seduced by the instigation of the devil, on the 27th day of February in the year of our Lord 1859, with force and arms at the county aforesaid, in and upon the body of one Philip Barton Key, in the peace of God and of the said United States then and there being, feloniously and wilfully and of his malicious aforethought, did make an assault; and that the said Daniel E. Sickles, a certain pistol of the value of two dollars, then and there charged with gunpowder and one leaden bullet, which said pistol he, the said Daniel E. Sickles, in his right hand, then and there had and held, then and there feloniously, wilfully, and of his malice aforethought, did discharge and shoot off, to, against and upon the said Philip

Barton Key . . . and wound him, the said Philip Barton Key, in and upon the left side of him . . . a little below the tenth rib of him, the said Philip Barton Key, giving to him, the said Philip Barton Key, then and there, with the leaden bullet aforesaid . . . a little below the tenth rib of him, one mortal wound of the depth of ten inches and of the breadth of half an inch; of which said mortal wound, he, the said Philip Barton Key, then and there instantly died."

On Monday morning, April 4, 1859, this sonorous legal jargon was read before the packed benches of a dingy courtroom in Washington's City Hall. Outside, police battled a mob of frustrated citizens who were burning to join the lucky few as spectators at the legal circus of the decade. The victim, forty-two-year-old Philip Barton Key, was none other than the district attorney of Washington, D. C., and the son of the man who had writ-

After the slaying, Key's body was carried to the Washington Club, where the inquest was held.

61

ten "The Star-Spangled Banner." Philip Key was a handsome, mustachioed widower who stood at the very top of the capital city's social register. The assailant was the Honorable Daniel E. Sickles, second-term congressman from New York City, Tammany Hall figure, confidant of President James Buchanan. But the motive—Sickles' reason for shooting Key down in Lafayette Square, just a block away from the White House—was at least as sensational as the crime. "You villain, you have defiled my bed and you must die!" That, according to an eyewitness, was what the stocky congressman had roared as he blasted the tall, unarmed aristocrat with bullets from a derringer. Adultery! In an era when sex was rarely mentioned in public, official Washington—and the nation—reeled.

A few minutes after Key had breathed his last on the floor of the nearby Washington Club, Sickles had surrendered to his friend, silver-haired United States Attorney General Jeremiah Sullivan Black. After a brief stop at his own home, where he picked up some personal belongings, Sickles and a crew of prominent friends, including the mayor of Washington, James Berret, rode to the city jail. There he stoutly declined bail, declaring that his only wish was a swift trial. If the Congressman suspected his incarceration would not hurt his cause, he was right. His transfer to the warden's quarters after four days of fighting bedbugs in the jail was ignored by the public, who seized upon Sickles as a heroic defender of family honor. (The prisoner did himself no harm by asking for, and getting, a visit with his five-year-old daughter, Laura, and later calling for the company of his pet greyhound, Dandy.) Few if any stopped to consider the weight of official power and wealth on Sickles' side. His strong friendship with the President dated from his service as secretary of legation during Buchanan's ambassadorship to the Court of St. James's. In addition, Sickles had in his three years in Washington won a significant niche in the upper reaches of capital society. His ample house, known as the Stockton mansion, shared Lafayette Park with the handsome residences of the Adamses, the Taylors, the Blairs, the Slidells. This elite, plus scores of other Cabinet and congressional notables, had flocked to Sickles' Thursday night "at-homes," where the food and drink, served by the incomparable Gautier, king of the capital's caterers, were invariably first class. Presiding over these occasions, bedecked in magnificent jewelry and wearing the latest gowns, was Sickles' young, darkly beautiful wife, Teresa. It was frequently claimed that the thirty-nine-year-old Sickles, an aristocrat in his own right with the blood of Knickerbockers and Van Sicklens in his veins and a millionaire father in New York, had his eyes on the Presidency. This dream had vanished, of course, in the

roar of his pistol on that fatal Sunday afternoon. But not a little of the influence he had banked in three industrious years was still highly negotiable.

Nothing underscored this more than the powerful battery of legal counsel Sickles now arrayed around him. Heading his staff were two crack New York attorneys, portly James Topham Brady, famed for his rapier wit and deft examination of witnesses, and tall, majestic John Graham, considered to have no peer when it came to swaying a jury with persuasive eloquence. Both were close personal friends of the Congressman. Also a devoted friend was the third man on the team, Edwin McMasters Stanton. Lincoln's future Secretary of War was famed for his ferocious courtroom demeanor. Witnesses quailed before his violent eyes, which peered from a massive head crowned by black curly hair and adorned with a thick crop of whiskers; Stanton resembled an Old Testament prophet in full cry. Finally, to give his team a local veneer, Sickles added four Washington attorneys: suave Philip Phillips, former congressman from Alabama, and Messrs. Chilton, Magruder, and Ratcliffe. Against this talented team the District sent only one man, plodding, bull-necked Robert Ould, who had been Key's assistant district attorney. Friends of Key were so mortified by the obvious imbalance that they begged the President* to appoint a special counsel to bolster the methodical Ould. Buchanan declined to lower the odds in favor of his good friend Dan, and only at the last moment did Key adherents provide a fund to retain J. M. Carlisle, considered the flower of the District bar.

Still Sickles, sternly sequestered from his attorneys in the large, cratelike prisoner's dock, remained the underdog in the public eye. Prospective jurymen were excused by the dozen because they admitted their sympathies lay with the indicted congressman. The jurors finally selected were all sturdy middle-class types—grocers, farmers, a tinner, a shoemaker, a cabinetmaker. But Sickles and his attorneys undoubtedly cast a nervous eye on the foreman, Reason Arnold. He was a staunch member of the Know-Nothing party, which was noted for its antagonism to Tammany's habit of sheltering foreigners and Catholics in its political wigwam. True, honest tradesmen could usually be depended upon to sympathize with any man who defended the chastity of his marriage bed—but Dan Sickles was not just any man. He was decidedly unique, and this was one among several reasons why his attorneys decided that under no circumstances would they permit him to take the witness stand.

Outside the courtroom, meanwhile, some of the very large problems involved in Sickles' defense began to show in the newspapers. The New York *Evening Post* declared the Con-

---

* The district attorneys for the District of Columbia were, like the judges, presidential appointees.

gressman "a person of notorious profligacy of life ... a certain disgrace has for years past attended the reputation of being one of his companions ... the man who in his own practice regards adultery as a joke and the matrimonial bond as no barrier against the utmost caprice of licentiousness—has little right to complain when the mischief which he carries without scruple into other families enters his own."

Also in New York, George Templeton Strong confided to his not-yet-famous diary, "Were he [Sickles] not an unmitigated blackguard and profligate, one could pardon any act of violence committed on such provocation. But Sickles is not the man to take the law into his own hands and constitute himself the avenger of sin."

Others recalled how Sickles in his bachelor days had squired a luscious courtesan named Fanny White around town; she even accompanied him to Albany when he was elected to the state assembly. Less certain was the rumor that after his marriage, when he left his pregnant wife in New York to go to London with Buchanan, Sickles took Fanny White along and insolently introduced her to Queen Victoria. From his earliest days in Tammany, Sickles had had

While his friend Butterworth watches appreciatively, Sickles gives the protesting Philip Barton Key the coup de grâce.

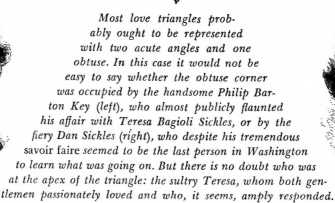

*Most love triangles prob-
ably ought to be represented
with two acute angles and one
obtuse. In this case it would not be
easy to say whether the obtuse corner
was occupied by the handsome Philip Barton Key (left), who almost publicly flaunted
his affair with Teresa Bagioli Sickles, or by the
fiery Dan Sickles (right), who despite his tremendous
savoir faire seemed to be the last person in Washington
to learn what was going on. But there is no doubt who was
at the apex of the triangle: the sultry Teresa, whom both gentlemen passionately loved and who, it seems, amply responded.*

a reputation as a brawler, ready to attack or defend with fists, pistols, or bowie knife. This, and a consistent disdain for paying his debts, had him frequently in court. The more people remembered, the more unlikely became Dan Sickles' posture as a defender of marital fidelity.

The first and most crucial move was in the hands of the prosecution. Would solemn District Attorney Ould attack in his opening statement only Sickles' crime—the fact of homicide which the defense could hardly deny—or would he include the character of the defendant? Undoubtedly Messrs. Brady, Graham, and Stanton breathed a subtle sigh of collective relief when Ould proceeded to concentrate his fire on the deed. In vivid terms Ould underscored the armed power of the assailant and the helplessness of the unarmed victim, also noting that Sickles chose Sunday to accomplish his "deed of blood." The prosecuting attorney called the Congressman "a walking magazine, a temporary armory, a moving battery . . . like a piece of flying artillery on a field of battle." He pictured Key as in poor health, and armed with nothing but an opera glass which he vainly flung at Sickles when the assault began. This, Ould solemnly declared, was "murder, no matter what may be the antecedent provocation in the case." The prosecution now proceeded to summon a parade of witnesses who titillated the courtroom with hair-raising recollections of the murder scene. James H. Reed, a wood and coal dealer, told how Key took cover behind a tree after the first shot (which apparently missed), then crumpled to the ground after the next shot and was hit a second time while lying

on the pavement begging, "Don't shoot." Except for the flung opera glass, there was no evidence of any resistance by the terrified victim.

But Washington and the press were more astonished by the District Attorney's failure to call another witness— Samuel F. Butterworth. A Tammany sachem, Butterworth had happened to be in Washington on political business when Sickles discovered the truth about his wife and Key. Butterworth had called on Sickles in response to a note asking his advice on what course the injured husband should take. As they talked, Key appeared in Lafayette Square and began making signals toward the Sickles house with his handkerchief. It was Butterworth who rushed out of the house alone and detained Key long enough for Sickles to go upstairs, find and load both his derringer and a revolver, and rush out to kill him. Butterworth would have been a hostile witness, and Ould knew that if he called him to the stand he would be legally barred from cross-examining him; but a first-class attorney would have taken the risk because the mere fact of Butterworth's actions cast an aura of calculation over the crime—the very point for which Ould was contending. Instead, Ould let the defense seize the initiative and ask the court to *require* the prosecution to put Butterworth on the stand, as well as an even closer friend of Sickles', George Wooldridge, who was in the Congressman's house when the murder was committed.

A lively argument ensued. Carlisle, Ould's associate, maintained that the defense was making this demand to win "the pleasant cross-examination of the counsel for the prisoner, and protect [Butterworth and Wooldridge] from what might be the unpleasant cross-examination of the counsel for the prosecution." Seventy-three-year-old Judge Thomas H. Crawford, described by one lawyer as "a sharp-featured old gentleman with a bald head somewhat shaped like that of a chicken," ruled it was not necessary for "the United States" to bring Butterworth and Wooldridge to the stand, since more than enough witnesses had already been produced to describe the bloody deed. But Sickles' lawyers had made their point. By getting the prosecution to back away from Butterworth they had in effect cancelled him out as a threat to their client. They then comfortably ignored him for the rest of the trial, and only later did the prosecutors and the public learn that Mr. Butterworth had left town before the proceedings began.

The defense also showed their coolness under fire when the prosecution placed in evidence the derringer pistol and ball that had killed Key. James T. Brady blithely noted that while the bullet had been positively identified as the one that killed Key, no one on the prosecution side had identified the gun. In a burst of verbal gymnastics Brady implied that the murder weapon might belong to Key, an assertion that brought outraged gasps from the prosecution.

Ould's performance had been feeble, but he nevertheless rested his case, and the defense opened with a thunderous oration by John Graham. In rolling, ponderous periods, Graham seized on Ould's sarcasm about Sickles' profanation of the Sabbath and converted it into a bludgeon of defense. Who had profaned the Sabbath, the injured husband or "a confirmed, habitual adulterer . . . besieging with most evil intentions that castle where for their security and repose the law had placed the wife and child of his neighbor"? Sickles, Graham contended, was acting in self-defense when he killed Key. No matter that under the law of the District of Columbia a wronged husband could sue an adulterer for damages. The law, he said, was almost ludicrously inconsistent on this point. "If an individual comes into your house and lies upon your bed against your will, he commits a trespass and you can repel him by force. If an individual comes into your house and lies with your wife and robs her and you of that which cannot be restored and for which no recompense can be made, can you not repel this invasion by force? Can your wives be used with impunity when your furniture can not?" There was only one possible answer to this contradiction, thundered Graham. "If society has not protected you in the possession of your wives, it is proof conclusive that society meant that your right to their possession should remain as at nature and that the right to protect the purity of your wives is a natural right which you can assert, even to the extent of killing whoever seeks to deprive you of it, as much as you can kill for the purpose of protecting your

own lives." It is, he declared, a right "given by the law of God."

Quoting Shakespeare, the Bible, and judicial examples ranging all the way back to the Roman Empire, Graham elaborated this defense of the "higher," or "unwritten," law. He combined a shrewd use of the Bible and his own wits to plug up the most obvious hole in Sickles' case—his failure to kill Key for two full days after an anonymous letter had informed him that the District Attorney had made him a cuckold. Pointing out that Absalom waited two full years to kill the violator of his sister, Graham proceeded to argue that if the law permits a husband to kill an adulterer caught in the act, it is equally permissive if the seducer is caught "so near the act as to leave no doubt as to his guilt." Was this not precisely what had happened between Sickles and Key? The Congressman did not invite the debonair district attorney to stroll past his house on that fatal Sunday afternoon and wave his adulterous handkerchief at Mrs. Sickles' window. "Is it possible that under these circumstances," Graham asked the jury, "Mr. Sickles could have acted in cold blood?" Indeed, he went on, Sickles' provocation was so enormous that he was, from a legal point of view, insane. Graham proceeded to dwell on Key's professed or avowed friendship with Sickles; he pointed out that Key had retained his job as district attorney largely because Sickles had interceded with President Buchanan for him. With heavy sarcasm he emphasized the hypocrisy of Key's private conduct when contrasted to his public station. Finally, Graham stressed two cases: in 1843 a New Jersey jury acquitted one Singleton Mercer, charged with killing the man who had raped his sister; more recently in a Washington criminal court trial presided over by the same Judge Crawford and prosecuted, ironically, by the late Philip Barton Key, the jury had acquitted one Jarboe for exacting the same revenge for a similar reason.

Graham talked for almost two full days, a feat even in an era of massive eloquence. His performance drastically altered the trial's center of gravity. Thereafter the defense was in possession of the initiative, while Ould and Carlisle found themselves playing the unpleasant role of obstructionists.

This became sensationally apparent when Brady attempted to place in evidence the trial's *pièce de résistance* —the confession that Congressman Sickles had extracted from his tearful, hysterical wife the night before he killed Key, after detective work by his friend George Wooldridge had convinced him that she was guilty. Bridget Duffy, Mrs. Sickles' maid, identified the paper, written in her mistress' hand, and told how the confession was produced after an angry scene punctuated by shouts and cries in Mrs. Sickles' bedroom. At the Congressman's request, Bridget had signed it as a witness, and a young woman friend of Mrs. Sickles', Octavia Ridgeley, had done likewise.

"This paper," Brady declared, "we propose to read in evidence. It is Mrs. Sickles' statement to her husband:

" 'I have been in a house in 15th Street with Mr. Key. How many times I don't know. I believe the house belongs to a colored man. The house is unoccupied. Commenced going there the latter part of January. Have been in alone with Mr. Key. Usually stayed an hour or more. There was a bed in the second story. I did what is usual for a wicked woman to do. The intimacy commenced this winter when I came from New York, in that house—an intimacy of an improper kind. Have met half a dozen times or more at different hours of the day. On Monday of this week. And Wednesday also. Would arrange meetings when we met in the street and at parties. Never would speak to him when Mr. Sickles was at home, because I knew he did not like me to speak to him; did not see Mr. Key for some days after I got here. He then told me he had hired the house as a place where he and I could meet. I agreed to it. Had nothing to eat or drink there. The room is warmed by a wood fire. Mr. Key generally goes first. Have walked there together say four times—I do not think more; was there on Wednesday last, between two and three. I went there alone. Laura was at Mrs. Hoover's. Mr. Key took and left her there at my request. From there I went to 15th Street to meet Mr. Key; from there to the milk woman's. Immediately after Mr. Key left Laura at Mrs. Hoover's I met him in 15th Street. Went in by the back gate. Went in the same bedroom, and there an improper interview was had. I undressed myself. Mr. Key undressed also. This occurred on Wednesday, 23rd of February, 1859.

" 'Mr. Key has kissed me in this house [i.e., the Sickles house on Lafayette Square] a number of times. I do not deny that we have had a connection in this house last spring, a year ago, in the parlor on the sofa. Mr. Sickles was sometimes out of town and sometimes in the Capitol. I think the intimacy commenced in April or May, 1858. I did not think it safe to meet him in this house, because there are servants who might suspect something. As a general thing, have worn a black and white woollen plaid dress and beaver hat trimmed with black velvet. Have worn a black silk dress there also, also a plaid silk dress, black velvet cloak trimmed with lace, and black velvet shawl trimmed with fringe. On Wednesday I either had on my brown dress or black and white woollen dress, beaver hat and velvet shawl. I arranged with Mr. Key to go in the back way after leaving Laura at Mrs. Hoover's. He met me at Mr. Douglas's. The arrangement to go in the back way was either made in the street or at Mr. Douglas's as we would be less likely to be seen. The house is in 15th Street between K and L Streets on the left-hand side of the way; arranged the interview for Wednesday in the street, I think, on Monday. I went in the front door, it was open, occupied the same room, undressed myself and he also;

went to bed together. Mr. Key has ridden in Mr. Sickles' carriage and has called at his house without Mr. Sickles' knowledge and after my being told not to invite him to do so, and against Mr. Sickles' repeated request.

" 'Teresa Bagioli

" 'This is a true statement written by myself without any inducement held out by Mr. Sickles of forgiveness or reward, and without any menace from him. This I have written with my bedroom door open and my maid and child in adjoining room, at half past eight o'clock in the evening. Miss Ridgeley is in the house, within call.

" 'Teresa Bagioli' "

District Attorney Ould excitedly declared that this document could not possibly be included as evidence. It was a communication between husband and wife—parties who were excluded by law from testifying for or against each other. Brady replied with equal vigor that the statement was indeed admissible because it accounted for Sickles' state of mind at the time of the homicide. Back and forth wrangled Brady and Ould, each citing cases to support his contention, until the court adjourned for the day.

If Judge Crawford had his doubts about the relevance of Teresa Bagioli Sickles' confession, the Congressman and his attorneys did not. They proceeded to release it to the press, where it promptly made front pages around the world. Family, friends, and acquaintances of the lovely Teresa must have shuddered with disbelief, not only at the content of the confession but at the husband who could use it so ruthlessly. Sickles had been an intimate friend of Teresa's father, a noted New York opera impresario, and of her grandfather as well. He had known her from infancy, and had persuaded her, over considerable protests from her family, to abandon her convent education and marry him when she was only sixteen.

J. M. Carlisle opened the proceedings on the next day of the trial with a long, passionate speech against admitting the confession. Did the paper tend to show that the act committed the day after it was written was either justifiable homicide or manslaughter? he cried. It did not, unless His Honor held to the doctrine laid down by the other side—that no amount of time was sufficient to cool down the mind of a man under such provocation, and render him observant of the law of God and man. Was it evidence to show the prisoner's insanity? He would like to see what expert would declare "that such a declaration as this would tend to produce insanity in all or in a majority of cases. It would depend upon the moral and intellectual condition of the person."

Now Carlisle revealed for the first time his real role in the trial. If Ould, who held his job at the pleasure of the President, was afraid to strike at Buchanan's friend, Carlisle had no such inhibitions. There were, he said, two classes of men who could resist the insanity such a confession might cause. One was the convinced Christian, who would on his knees "pour out his supplication to Him who alone can bind up the broken heart." Then there was the second, "safe, quite safe from insanity, from such a blow as that—the confirmed adulterer, the open, shameless profligate—the man nurtured in brothels, the man breathing all his life the atmosphere of adultery and seduction . . . Now, to offer evidence of the fact of the adultery with the prisoner's wife as the ground to impute to him insanity, necessarily opens inquiry of the sort I have indicated. . . ."

This threat to explore the less than sanctified bypaths of Sickles' love life might have made some attorneys blanch. But it only seemed to make Sickles' triumvirate, especially Edwin Stanton, press on with even fiercer determination to get every last ugly fact of Key's adultery into the record. Perhaps they were influenced by Carlisle's inability to reach the jury's emotions, for all his rhetoric. "Nervous of manner yet cold of heart," as one eyewitness described him, Carlisle was a little too smooth for the role he had assigned himself.

Judge Crawford, after a recess, ruled Teresa's confession inadmissible because it would destroy before the law the "confidential identity" of the husband and wife. Unruffled by this ruling—a technicality that did nothing to erase the impact of the confession on the emotions of the jury—the defense summoned various witnesses. Bridget Duffy proceeded to describe Sickles' agitation on Sunday morning: how she saw him "come into the room crying aloud, his hands tearing his hair and in a state of distraction." More important was her description of Key's appearance in Lafayette Park, waving his handkerchief in a slow rotary motion. She told how the Sickles greyhound, Dandy, rushed out and fawned on Key, who ignored him. Sickles' good friend, George B. Wooldridge, confirmed these details. But when Brady attempted to lead Wooldridge into a discussion of what he had discovered about Key and Mrs. Sickles in his detective work the day before the killing, the prosecution once more objected.

This was too much for Stanton, who seized the center of the stage with a scathing attack on the prosecution's tactics thus far. He condemned Ould and Carlisle for their "thirst for blood" and begged the judge not to exclude evidence "in order that vengeance might obtain the blood of this prisoner." At this Ould leaped to his feet crying that it was sheer malice on Stanton's part to accuse a public prosecutor of being actuated by a thirst for blood. He vowed he would let his conduct in the case stand before the court and the world "in contrast with the disreputable rant" that Stanton had exhibited. Obviously, he declared, Stanton had been assigned the role of "the bully and the bruiser." Ignoring a mutter of protest that rose from the audience, Ould insisted he would stand by his oath and continue to call Sickles' deed murder, no matter what the defense called it.

Stanton met the District Attorney head on. He insisted that under the law Ould was defending, his client would be led to the gallows "by those who are malignantly seeking for his blood." He added that he did not have the honor of Ould's acquaintance "and after his language just uttered, [did] not desire it." This produced an uproar of approval in the courtroom, with much shouting and stamping of feet. It required considerable effort by the district marshal and his assisting officers to restore order.

In jail, the warden let Sickles stay in his own quarters instead of a cell; there he kept his dog and received guests.

Robert Ould, chief prosecutor

"Of course it is true that there are exasperations, and extenuations, and anger that conquers the will and the conscience, and strikes in an almost unconscious fury. But *ought* it to do so? Ought a man to be negatively praised for losing his moral control? Do we justify an engineer for not bridging precisely the worst abyss of all? The moral sense of every man is given him ... for the trials that tear at his heart-roots. That sense may be overborne, and the man commit a crime as black as the one that exasperates him; but he is then not a man to be pitied as if he were a victim—he is to be pitied as a criminal. He may have more excuse than the seducer. But because the seduction of a woman is a crime, the willful murder of the seducer does not cease to be a crime also.

"And ... remember ... the real victim of the tragedy ... a wayward girl fascinated to her ruin. If you hasten to pardon crime to him who sins through hate —will you deny forgiveness to her who falls through love: Tenderly, tenderly, pious souls!

"Owning her weakness,
Her evil behavior;
But leaving with meekness
Her sins to her Saviour."
—*Harper's Weekly*, March 12, 1859, p. 163

These pyrotechnics may have impressed the jury, but they got Stanton nowhere with Judge Crawford, who ruled that Wooldridge's communication to Sickles about Teresa's adultery was also inadmissible as evidence. This made little practical difference to the defense counsels, who had plenty of other ways to exploit the juicier aspects of the case. Witnesses testified to seeing Key waving his handkerchief in Lafayette Park for the better part of two hours— suggesting that he was one of the most indiscreet adulterers in history. Other witnesses recounted efforts made by Key's relatives and friends to padlock the house on 15th Street and remove any damaging evidence. Next came Nancy Brown, wife of President Buchanan's Negro gardener, who said that she lived on 15th Street and knew Key well by sight: "I saw him on the Wednesday before he was shot."

"Where did you see him?"

"I saw him going into a house on 15th Street ..."

Carlisle leaped to his feet in a vain attempt to suppress the answer. Desperately he cried out that once more "they were sliding along in the direction of giving evidence of adultery." For once and for all he demanded that Judge Crawford rule on whether any evidence of this past adultery could be rightfully admitted. He declared that Judge Crawford was being given a chance to establish a "new era in the administration of justice in cases of homicide." In a long résumé of the defense's intentions as gleaned from the evidence presented thus far, Carlisle decried the tactic of painting the murdered Key and Sickles' wife in the blackest possible hues in order to justify the Congressman's crime. The whole concept of civilized law was at stake here, Carlisle insisted. Adultery was a crime under the laws of the District. Sickles had a legal recourse, as Judge Crawford would be the first to admit, since he himself had tried several cases of adultery in this very court.

Carlisle spoke for almost an hour. Brady then coolly rose and exploded his plea with a single question. "Was the case of adultery to which you refer as being tried here an indictment under the statute?"

"Yes, under the statute of Maryland."

Now Sickles' use of local attorneys paid off. Mr. Magruder made the point that under the statute of Maryland the punishment for that crime was a fine of a hundred pounds of tobacco.

"Then the only satisfaction an injured husband could have," snorted Brady, "would be a chew of tobacco." The courtroom exploded with laughter.

Despite the fact that more court time already had been devoted to Key's act of adultery than to Sickles' act of homicide, Judge Crawford had not yet explicitly conceded that evidence of the adultery had any legal bearing on the trial. For days this point was wrangled over by the lawyers on both sides, while the Judge, obviously harassed and puzzled, pondered the question. Then, on the thirteenth day of the trial—Monday, April 18—he announced his decision. Sickles' cry about his defiled bed, at the moment of the shooting, intoned His Honor, was reason enough to admit the evidence of adultery as an "explanation." There was, declared Felix G. Fontaine, who published a transcript of the trial, "a perceptible though silent expression of satisfaction" in the audience when Judge Crawford pronounced this decision.

Jubilation undoubtedly reigned at the defense table. Witness after witness now paraded to the stand, giving vivid details of Key and Teresa Sickles scuttling down 15th Street to their love nest in the Negro slum known as Dark Town, or trysting in the Sickles study when the Congressman was away. Nancy Brown told how Key would hang a string from the upstairs shutters of the 15th Street house to signal to his mistress that the coast was clear. Everyone on the entire block, and every servant in Sickles' house, seemed to know what was going on, but not Dan Sickles.

By now it was hard to tell whether Sickles was on trial for murder or Key for adultery. But there was still one flaw in the case for the defense. Sickles had rushed into the street, loaded with lethal artillery, and shot down an apparently unarmed man. The next witness was designed

"An injured husband has but three ways of meeting the injury. He may laugh at it, or he may challenge his enemy; this is the French method. The first recourse affords but little consolation, and requires unusual philosophy; the second may superadd physical to moral injury. He may sue the adulterer for damages. This is the English plan. It involves patience, delay, exposure, disgrace.... Finally, the injured husband may take the life of him who has injured him. This is the American system.... Terrible as homicide is, this method must, on the whole, be admitted to be the most effectual, the wisest, and the most natural revenge....

"There can be no excuse for the adulterer. He commits a three-fold crime: a crime against the woman whom he misleads, a crime against the man whom he dishonors, a crime against society which he disorganizes.... In these latter days experience proves that in all such cases society will justify the infliction of the last penalty by the husband. Whatever may have been the character of Mr. Sickles, there is not a jury in the United States or in Europe which would convict him even of manslaughter. In the face of so decided a public sentiment, is it worth while to argue further on the question?"
—*Harper's Weekly,* March 12, 1859, p. 162

James Brady, for the defense

to remove this last potential element of sympathy for Key. A contractor named Albert A. Megaffey declared he was "tolerably intimate" with Key, and proceeded to recount a series of conversations he had had with the late district attorney about his attentions to Mrs. Sickles. Megaffey had warned Key that he might get into danger or difficulty about the matter. In reply, he said, Key laid his hand on the left breast of his coat and declared, "I am prepared for any emergency."

A new uproar ensued. Ould and Carlisle, almost wild with exasperation, cried that these conversations, the last of which took place twelve days before the murder, surely had no bearing on the case. They certainly did not tend to prove that Key was armed on the day of his death, or even that Sickles thought he was armed, since Mr. Megaffey never communicated anything about the conversation to the Congressman. The Judge emphatically agreed with the prosecution, and barred Megaffey's testimony. But the defense had scored another victory with the jury, who now saw at least the possibility that Key had had a gun in his pocket.

Throughout the long trial, Dan Sickles had sat silent in his prisoner's pen. It must have been a difficult feat for a man who found it almost impossible to ignore a fight. Equally tormenting must have been the sniggering testimony of his own servants recalling how they had referred to Key and Mrs. Sickles as Disgrace and Disgust and opining that more than once the clandestine couple "wasn't at no good work." Yet Sickles lost his composure only once, when Robert Walker, former senator from Mississippi and one-time Secretary of the Treasury, told of rushing to the Sickles house after the shooting and finding the Congressman on the edge of insanity. Walker described "unnatural and unearthly sounds. The most remarkable I ever heard —something like a scream interrupted by violent sobbing."

At this testimony Dan Sickles collapsed, and his sobs were audible throughout the courtroom. Judge Crawford ordered a recess, and the prisoner's friends, followed by his weeping father, helped him outside, where he regained his self-control. One reason for this breakdown, unknown at the time, may have been a correspondence that Sickles had opened with his wife while he was in jail awaiting trial. In the early days of the trial she had written him:

"You say that any object you have loved remains dear to you. Do I now stand upon a footing with the other women I know you have loved? I have long felt like asking you what your love affairs have been—love of the heart, or love of their superior qualities such as you have often informed me I did not possess, or attraction of face and form, or an infatuation? If during the first years we were married my good conduct did not keep you true to me, can I suppose for a moment the last year has? *Ask your own heart who sinned first, and then tell me, if you will.*"

J. M. Carlisle, bitter over his defeat on the adultery issue, no doubt would have given much for a copy of that letter. He was now more than ever determined to examine Sickles' amatory past. But he held his fire, meanwhile chipping away at the defense contention that Sickles was insane. Here once again District Attorney Ould was undone by the aggressive defense. When he asked Francis Doyle, who had been present when the dying Key was carried into the Washington Club, to give the court a description of Sickles' demeanor, Stanton protested, making the remarkable declaration that the burden of proof was on the *prosecution* to show that Sickles "was a person of sound memory and discretion at the time the act was committed." This produced more than a few splutterings from Judge Crawford, who hastened to declare that every man "is presumed to be sane till the contrary is proved; that is the normal condition of the human race, I hope."

Now, though his gentlemanly soul no doubt recoiled from it, Carlisle resolved to use his last weapon. In court was the proprietor of a Baltimore hotel with its register under his arm. He was prepared to show that on a date not too long before the day of the murder, Sickles had

....I have been in a house in 15ᵗʰ St. with Mr. Key; how many times I dont know...

Teresa Sickles' written confession made this nondescript house in a Negro section of Washington a notorious landmark.

visited that hotel with a lady who signed herself as Mrs. Sickles, though her handwriting clearly proved she was not.

But chunky Robert Ould, though he lacked fire, was a solid, well-trained lawyer; he knew that such evidence could not be introduced by the prosecution with the same reckless effrontery displayed by the defense. If Messrs. Graham, Brady, and Stanton objected to it as irrelevant and the judge sustained them, they would immediately move for a mistrial on the grounds that the jury's mind had been fatally prejudiced against the prisoner.

Thus Ould did the only thing a sensible prosecutor could do in such a situation. He submitted the incriminating ledger to the attorneys for the defense, before airing it publicly. Inevitably they objected, and the matter was referred to Judge Crawford for decision. *Sotto voce*, both sides argued before His Honor for several minutes. Then, wizened cheeks twitching, Crawford proceeded to declare: "For very obvious reasons the court will do no more than merely state his opinion on this point, and that opinion is that the evidence is *not* admissible."

There was nothing left now but the summation. In a long, passionate speech for the defense, Stanton covered much of the ground Graham had discussed in his opening oration. But his sarcasm was more biting, his denunciation of Key more intense. Again and again the courtroom burst into applause as he scored another sulphurous point against the adulterer whose deeds surpassed "all that has ever been written of cold, villainous, remorseless lust." Beside this Old Testament fury, the District Attorney seemed pale indeed, citing the New Testament example of Christ, who forgave the adulteress. Didn't the same argument, he pleaded, apply to Philip Barton Key? Then Ould touched, at the very last moment, on a theme that he might well have used effectively earlier: If Philip Barton Key were alive, he, and he alone, might be able to produce evidence that might show that he was more seduced than seducer; that he had yielded to "temptations repeated and continued until those higher moral bulwarks that should have supported his character gave way beneath repeated shocks."

James T. Brady tartly recalled a passage of previous testimony that had quoted Key himself to the effect that Mrs. Sickles was a mere child, and that he stood in parental relation to her.

Ould let the topic drop without another word.

The Judge's instructions to the jury caused the defense only mild alarm. He followed the traditional legal rule of thumb which held that the husband who killed an adulterer a day or even a half day after his act, rather than *flagrante delicto,* committed murder. But Crawford agreed with the main defense contention: "If the jury have any doubt as to the case, either in reference to the homicide or the question of sanity, Mr. Sickles should be acquitted."

Judge Crawford finished his instructions to the jury early on the twentieth and last day of the trial. Brady now rose for the defense and suggested that the case be submitted to the jury without additional summing up on either side. Robert Ould half rose from his seat and wearily concurred.

Friends crowded around the prisoner in his pen, assuring him it would all be over in five minutes. But the clock crept past the half-hour mark, and then the hour, with no sign of a forgiving jury. At the defense table, James Brady's face was by now pale and solemn. In the jury room, the wrangling was feverish. Only seven were for acquittal at the first vote; three were in doubt; two were firmly opposed. But the majority first convinced the doubters, and then went to work on the opposition. Both were intensely religious men, who obviously agreed with Ould's closing arguments. Finally one, a stern Presbyterian, yielded. The last suddenly broke away from the group, knelt in a corner, and prayed silently for guidance. Then he returned and said: "I have my answer. Let the prisoner go free."

When Foreman Arnold announced the verdict, the courtroom went berserk. Brady burst into tears. Edwin Stanton did a highly uncharacteristic jig and called for three cheers. Other friends rushed up to kiss and embrace Sickles. Outside in the streets an enormous crowd hurrahed wildly and tried to unhorse Sickles' carriage so they could pull him through the capital like a conquering hero.

Jury verdicts do not constitute precedents, in the American legal system, and no lawyer has ever urged a judge to remind a jury of Dan Sickles' acquittal. Strictly speaking the jury ruled against the proper interpretation of the law, and the law remained unchanged. Nevertheless, in years to come journalists frequently referred to the case as justifying the "unwritten law." Actually, as we have seen, Sickles' lawyers were too shrewd to rest their argument on a single plea, and utilized every possible argument from temporary insanity to justifiable homicide to save their client. The case did illustrate the wisdom of an adage at least as old as the jury system and as new as the latest murder trial in yesterday's headlines: when you're on trial for your life, hire the very best legal talent you can afford.

Later that year Sickles, in a gesture of generosity, took Teresa back as his wife—an act for which he was bitterly denounced by the same people who had acclaimed his "defense" of his bed and home. She never appeared with him in society again, however, and died eight years later, a wasted ghost of the young hostess who had charmed Washington. As for Congressman Sickles, another kind of gunfire along the Potomac soon converted him into a national hero of sorts. Wangling himself a major-generalship, he served courageously on a dozen Civil War battlefields. But even here, his genius for personal imbroglios made him a controversial figure. One school of thought, led by Sickles, argued that Dan really won the Battle of Gettysburg by taking a highly exposed position in a wheat field and orchard. Other military thinkers accused him of almost losing it, because his corps was torn to bits by a three-sided Southern assault, leaving a huge hole in the Union line. (Sickles lost a leg to a Confederate cannon ball.) But Dan insisted that the whole battle had gone exactly according to his plan: he had taken the position with clear foreknowledge that he was inviting the Southern onrush, which his brave boys blunted, enabling a reinforced second line to stop the Rebs for good. His powers of persuasion later inspired no less than James Longstreet, the Confederate general who had delivered the assault, to agree with him.

After the war Sickles served as minister to Spain under Grant, won himself a third term in Congress in 1893, and ended his days with another scandal—the New York State Monuments Commission, of which he was chairman, suddenly discovered it was some twenty-eight thousand dollars short of funds. Friends and relatives made up the difference, and Dan died at ninety-five, still one jump ahead of the bailiffs. Well into his eighties he continued to chase the girls, listing among his conquests ex-Queen Isabella of Spain—who, however, was easily his match in promiscuity. His second wife, whom he married in Spain, left him (after bearing two children) because he was habitually unfaithful. Perhaps George Templeton Strong summed up Daniel E. Sickles best when he wrote in his diary, "One might as well try to spoil a rotten egg as to damage Dan's character."

Mr. Key, after Mr. Sickles had taken "a husband's revenge"

The Girl in the Red Velvet Swing

A number of people who attended the opening of *Mamzelle Champagne* at the roof theatre of Madison Square Garden noted the arrival of Mr. and Mrs. Harry Kendall Thaw and their two male guests. Young Mrs. Thaw, the former show girl Evelyn Nesbit, was well known as one of the beauties of New York, and her husband, the thirty-five-year-old heir to a Pittsburgh rail and coke fortune, had achieved notoriety as an irresponsible playboy who was continually in the news: he once drove an automobile through a display window; he tried to ride a horse into an exclusive club that had blackballed him from membership; he reportedly gave an elaborate dinner in Paris at which the only guests were women of questionable reputation and the favors were pieces of jewelry; at another of his parties music had been provided by John Philip Sousa's entire band.

On that opening night—June 25, 1906—*Mamzelle Champagne* dragged badly (Mrs. Thaw described it as "putrid"), but no one seems to have observed Thaw leaving his table. When a member of the cast began singing "I Could Love a Million Girls," three pistol shots suddenly cracked, and the audience whirled around to see a man slump in his chair and slide to the floor, silver and glassware crashing about him. Standing beside him, Harry Thaw held a pistol in the air as if to signal the end of the deadly business; then he walked back and joined his wife and friends.

"Good God, Harry!" she cried, "What have you done?"

"It's all right, dear," he replied, kissing her. "I have probably saved your life."

At that, a fireman on duty at the Garden disarmed Thaw and a policeman led him to the elevator. Behind them the panicky crowd and the girls from the chorus clustered around the fallen man. Lying dead in a pool of blood, his face blackened beyond recognition by powder burns, was Stanford White, fifty-two-year-old man about town (a "voluptuary," some called him) and America's most famous architect, whose proudest achievement was Madison Square Garden.

Six months later the most sensational trial in the country's history began, a trial that revealed to plain people everywhere the hypocrisy of Victorian morality. Although Thaw was on trial for his life, the high moment of drama came when Evelyn Nesbit Thaw was called to testify. Ten thousand jammed the streets to see her—a twenty-two-year-old girl who looked sixteen ("the most exquisitely lovely human being I ever looked at," wrote Irvin S. Cobb)—and a shocked nation began to witness what one commentator called "the vivisection of a woman's soul."

Evelyn, it was clear, had come a long way from Tarentum,

Pennsylvania, where she was born. Detail by lurid detail, the prosecution took her through the story of how she had become an artist's model at fourteen, then a show girl with the hit musical *Florodora*. Along with other prominent New York men, Stanford White had arranged to meet her, and in his apartment one night, she said, he gave her drugged champagne and ravished her. After she became his mistress, White delighted in setting her naked on a red velvet swing and pushing her so high her feet touched a Japanese parasol that hung from the ceiling. In 1903 she left White for Thaw and went on the first of two premarital trips to Europe with him. She returned home alone, took up with White again, and revealed to him the sadistic brutality she had suffered at Thaw's hands after he learned of her relationship with White. Then—despite all she had discovered about the unbalanced Thaw—she left for Europe with him again. As most reporters perceived, it was Evelyn, not her husband, who was on trial: the prosecutor stated in his summation that she was a "tigress between two men, egging them on. To Thaw she said White had wronged her. To White she said Thaw had beaten her with a whip." Since White was married and could not give her respectability, she had decided in 1905 to marry Thaw. A year later her husband, who went into paroxysms of rage at the mention of White's name, could stand his jealous doubts no longer and killed the architect.

Three and a half months after the trial began it ended with a hung jury; so nine months later the whole sordid tale was recited before another jury, which concluded that the defendant was not guilty, on grounds of insanity. But the judge, declaring Thaw a manic-depressive and dangerous to the public safety, committed him to the Matteawan State Hospital for the Criminal Insane. Much of the next fifteen years he spent in asylums; in 1924 he was released and lived in semiseclusion, except for occasional colorful encounters with police and press, until his death in 1947.

For Evelyn, the years that followed the trial were all downhill: squabbles with Thaw and his family over money, affairs with other men, divorce, suicide attempts, night-club acts that took her into ever tawdrier cabarets, run-ins with the curious and the police. Through it all she made a living recalling her vicissitudes and the sensational trial in different versions of her "own true story." In 1934 she told it again in a book, *Prodigal Days,* and in 1955 she was hired as "technical consultant" for a motion picture, *The Girl in the Red Velvet Swing,* which purported to be her life story. Finally, at eighty-two, she died in a convalescent home, all too aware that for the lovely young girl life had ended that night sixty years ago at the roof garden. "Stanny White was killed," she said, "but my fate was worse. I lived."

—*Richard M. Ketchum*

The Lady-Killer

A tale of bigamous Johann Hoch (if that was his name), of the follies of wealthy

widows, and of the dreadful discoveries of a parson who suspected the worst

chas b slackman

By A. I. SCHUTZER

Just before dawn of a Monday early in July, 1895, a middle-aged man appeared on the bank of the Ohio River near Wheeling, West Virginia, and set a bulging gunny sack on the ground. His face boasted side whiskers, a chin beard, and a mustache. He wore a derby. Behind a pair of gold-rimmed spectacles stared light blue eyes, the left distinguished by a drooping lid. His teeth, as described by one of his admirers, were "large and well-kept."

The man removed his derby and looked around cautiously. Satisfied that he was alone, he began to undress. After stripping down to the bare skin, he made a neat pile of his clothes and placed a suicide note on top. Then, to make sure the police would know beyond any possible doubt who had done him-

self in, he put an old silver pocket watch of German make, with his photograph inside the lid, on top of the note and the clothes.

Now, gunny sack in hand, he walked barefoot into the river, leaving his footprints in the mud right down to the water's edge. He wanted the police to be absolutely certain that he had drowned himself.

Once in the water, however, he turned north and walked fifty yards upstream to a pile of rocks where he had previously cached a spare suit of clothes and a boat. He dropped the gunny sack into the boat, dressed, shoved the boat into the water, and started rowing across the Ohio River.

When he was halfway across, he shipped his oars and let the boat drift. Then he dumped the contents of his sack, letting—we must be blunt—the entrails of a human female, riddled with arsenic, slide beneath the surface of the dirty water to settle to the bottom.

Then he picked up his oars again, heading for a deserted stretch of bank above Martins Ferry, on the Ohio side of the river. As he disappeared into the mist, he was confident that he had successfully covered the tracks of still another of an astonishing number of murders, and that he had written off as a suicide another of the many personalities he had chosen to represent.

Who was the killer? He had been, in turn, Jacob Schmidt, Johann Hoch, Albert Buschberg, Count Otto von Kern, Jacob Erdorf, Henry Bartels, Dr. L. G. Hart, Martin Dotz, Jacob Duss, C. A. Meyer, H. Frick, Dr. James, C. A. Calford, Jacob Huff, DeWitt C. Cudney, Henry F. Hartman, John C. O. Schulze, Heinrich Valtzand, and many others besides. He was ultimately known to the police, the newspaper readers of his time, and the families of his victims, as Johann Hoch. He was the American Bluebeard—the equal of anything England, France, or Germany has produced in the highly specialized field of classic crime—right up to the moment when—but we will come to the climax later.

In his specialty, wife-murder, Hoch apparently never wasted time. On the very night (January 12, 1905) that his penultimate victim had breathed her last in an upstairs bedroom at 6034 Union Avenue in Chicago, the killer was downstairs in the kitchen courting her sister, whom he married four days later. The event was not unique in his career. Over a span of eighteen years he married between forty-three and fifty women, about a third of whom he murdered with systematic doses of arsenic. The exact number of his victims cannot be determined. His operations were too complex, his victims too many and too often permanently silenced, the trail he left too obscure, and his own version of his affairs too contradictory, for an exact total to be compiled.

In terms of technique, Johann Hoch was a German-American counterpart of Landru, the Frenchman who seduced and murdered lonely, middle-aged women who answered his matrimonial advertisements in Paris newspapers in the years 1915–19. In terms of his attitude toward the opposite sex, Hoch was a male Belle Gunness, as untouched by the dismal fate of his victims as Belle was by the sordid end of the string of husbands she slaughtered in her cellar abattoir at La Porte, Indiana, around 1905. In terms of number of victims, Hoch was almost a peer of H. H. Holmes, the dandy who asphyxiated or strangled an estimated fifty women in his multiroomed crematory and murder castle in Chicago in the years 1892–94.

For a little more than a decade Johann Hoch married, swindled, and either abandoned or murdered his victims with time-clock regularity—without arousing the curiosity or interest of anybody at all. The first man to peel back a few of the layers of fake personality and catch a glimpse of the killer underneath was, strangely enough, a mild-mannered clergyman, the pastor of St. Matthew's German Lutheran Church in Wheeling in 1895.

Early in February of that year the perambulating merchant of death turned up in Wheeling, posing as a wealthy man named Jacob Huff. He opened up a saloon at 4728 Jacobs Street, where he catered to the local German immigrant population with beer, spirited zither playing, and an old-country delivery of Heidelberg drinking songs. If he had stuck to saloon-keeping and *Heimatslieder*, Huff's path would no doubt never have crossed that of the Reverend Herman C. A. Haass, a local parson. What got the publican in trouble with the parson was his unconcealed talent with the ladies—especially with well-heeled German-speaking widows who were members of Haass' congregation.

Huff's romantic technique was of the scatter-shot variety. He proposed marriage to just about every wealthy widow in the neighborhood. "He wants to settle down," the minister later remembered one of his *Hausfrau* parishioners telling him. "He said he needs a woman to care for his home," she continued. "And he said he would be willing to provide for me."

To each of the widows who came to him for advice, Haass suggested caution. He distrusted Huff and urged delay until the stranger was better known. But in spite of the minister's opposition, Huff was a quick success. Mrs. Caroline Hoch, a widow with a nice house, $900 in the bank, an insurance policy for $2,500 on her life, and a mind of her own, decided to take the plunge. It was an old story, really. If she waited too long, Mrs. Hoch no doubt reasoned, she would lose her ardent suitor to one of the other widows of the congregation —and then where would she be?

On April 18, 1895, the Reverend Mr. Haass reluctantly performed the marriage ceremony. Huff moved into the widow's house right after the wedding. In short order the widow, who had been a plump, healthy beauty all her life, was stricken ill and took to her bed. She got worse fast.

On June 14, 1895, Haass was summoned to the sickroom, where he watched Huff dose his wife with a white powder. To his now suspicious mind it seemed that the widow was afraid of her husband and took the powdered medication with reluctance. By the time he left the sickroom, he was convinced that the saloon-keeper was poisoning his wife. But he needed proof.

How and where was he to get it before it was too late?

The pastor stewed over his problem for a few days. He considered going to the Wheeling police; but there was always the possibility he might be wrong. The widow's illness might be perfectly legitimate, and a false accusation would not only hurt the parson's reputation but would also be an unpardonable sin against an innocent man.

What he needed before he took any overt action was professional advice from somebody who could tell what was actually ailing the widow. Haass turned to a young local physician, Dr. Gregory Ackerman. He took the doctor back to the sickroom with him, only to run into resistance. Huff hovered over his wife like a jealous rooster. She was already under medical care, he maintained. "Dr. Ford is treating her," he said.

Ackerman hesitated, for there was a matter of professional ethics involved. He had no right to interfere in Dr. Ford's case without the specific request of that physician. Ackerman bowed himself out of the sickroom and out of the case. Ten years later, when he described his visit in an interview with the New York *American,* he made medical ethics look foolish in many eyes. The woman, he said, had been dying when he saw her. Her hands were swollen and her stomach was distended; she vomited continually. Either she had peritonitis or she had been poisoned—but Dr. Ford was the regular attending physician, and that meant Ackerman could not interfere.

At three o'clock in the morning following Ackerman's visit the widow died. Two hours later Haass was notified that Mrs. Huff was dead. When he reached the widow's house at 8 A.M. he found the body unattended. Thoroughly indignant, he scoured the town until he found Huff in a barbershop. The bereaved took one look at the furious parson and began to weep. But the minister's suspicions were not allayed.

By early afternoon of the following day, Mrs. Huff had been buried at Red Men's Cemetery on the outskirts of Wheeling, and shortly thereafter Haass began an investigation.

Soon he learned that Huff had been in financial trouble. The saloonkeeper was heavily in debt to a brewery, and the saloon had been shut down. Now Haass concentrated on the white-powder medication. Where did Huff get it? What was it? The pastor methodically visited all of the drugstores in Wheeling and found that Huff had brought in no prescriptions to be filled. Dr. H. T. Ford, the attending physician, had not written any; he had believed that the widow was suffering from nephritis, a disease of the kidneys, for which there was then no treatment.

Pastor Haass next made a surreptitious trip to the sickroom to see if he could get some of that white powder for analysis. He found that all traces of it had disappeared. For the first time it occurred to him that Huff was aware of his suspicions and was taking steps to cover up his trail.

At about this time the pastor fell ill, but by the second Sunday following Mrs. Huff's death, he was up and around again. That same day, while at dinner with his wife, he heard a noise in his bedroom, directly over the dining room. Rushing upstairs, he found Huff in his room. The pastor asked for an explanation of this strange visitation. Huff replied weakly that he had been looking for the pastor in order to have a talk with him, but it could wait. Why the bedroom? Why so furtive? Huff backed out of the room without saying—and that was the last Haass saw of him.

Fearing that Huff might have tampered with his own bottles of medicine, in open view over the fireplace in the bedroom, the minister emptied the bottles down the drain—and immediately regretted it. Of course it would have been wiser to have had their contents analyzed.

The next day Pastor Haass learned just how uncomfortably warm his investigation had been making it for the saloonkeeper. He was notified by the Wheeling police that they had found Huff's clothes, his derby, an old German silver pocket watch with his picture in it, and a suicide note he had written, on the banks of the Ohio. Footprints led down to the water. Evidently he had committed suicide, the police said, in a fit of depression over his wife's death.

For two days the police dragged the river at the point where Huff had left his clothes, but they found nothing. During this time it was discovered that Mrs. Huff's grave had been tampered with. Nobody could figure out why, and the matter was soon forgotten. The explanation for the opening and closing of the grave would not become apparent for almost three years.

Just one week after Huff's supposed suicide, a drummer in religious articles called on Haass and told the pastor that he had seen Huff—or Johann Hoch, as he was now calling himself—very much alive on the other side of the river, in Janesville, Ohio, with a middle-aged woman on his arm. The pastor sent a description of Hoch to the Janesville police and warned that he was dangerous and a swindler, but there was no reply. The use of the name Johann Hoch demonstrated a curious side of the killer's personality. He had a penchant for adopting as an alias the name of the deceased husband of the widow he had most recently married and murdered or abandoned.

From the moment when he knew that Huff-Hoch was still alive, the parson stuck to his trail like a bloodhound. Haass was a devoted reader of newspapers, both English and German. He was a fine-print man, and took a professional interest in those columns of a newspaper normally skipped over by the casual reader: the obituaries and routine birth and marriage notices. Thus, as time went by, he frequently thought he caught sight of his quarry, flitting in and out of the newspaper columns when he married under a recognizable name, when a former widow suddenly died and her husband disappeared, or when a husband abandoned his wife shortly after the marriage ceremony with all of her portable assets except for her whalebone corset.

In the course of his meticulous scanning of the many newspapers he subscribed to, the parson spotted an item about one Otto Hoch who had married a woman in Dayton, Ohio, and deserted her a few days later, taking her savings. In 1897 he scissored out a clipping describing the mysterious death in Cincinnati of a Mrs. Clara Bartels, who lasted for three months after her marriage to pudgy, zither-playing John Schmidt. Parson Haass next found a three-line item in a German-language newspaper, describing a Jacob Otto Hoch who married in Milwaukee. This time the minister fired off a letter to the police of that city, but Hoch had already absconded, leaving one wife dead and another swindled out of her savings.

It would have been difficult even for Scotland Yard to have kept a perfect score card on Johann Hoch in the years 1895–98. The parson missed a Mrs. Janet Spencer of Chicago, who married and lost $700 to C. A. Calford two months after the wedding late in 1895; he did not hear of Mrs. Minnie Rankin, who married a Mr. Warneke in January, 1896; no word reached him of Callie Charlotte Andrews, who was deserted two hours after the nuptial ceremony in 1897 by one DeWitt C. Cudney and $500. And there were many others.

In 1898 Haass' newspaper detective-work finally began to pay off. He found his man, or one just like him, in between wives, in Chicago. According to the newspaper accounts, the Chicago police had collared a man who claimed his name was Martin Dotz. He had been arrested on two counts, one of bigamy and the other of having swindled one F. J. Magerstadt, a Chicago used-furniture dealer, out of some merchandise. What caught the minister's sharp eye was the physical description of the culprit, his height, weight, beard, side whiskers, mustache, drooping left eyelid, and large teeth, all of which tallied exactly.

Haass now wrote at once to Captain Luke Colleran, chief of detectives of the Chicago police. The pastor said he believed the man the police were holding was the very same he suspected of murdering Mrs. Caroline Hoch in Wheeling. Would the police check their prisoner against the photograph he was enclosing? It was a copy of the picture the killer had left behind in his pocket watch.

The pastor's letter and the picture were turned over to Inspector George Shippy, who confronted Hoch with the photograph. Hoch admitted it was his picture without realizing he was incriminating himself. He denied, however, that he had ever been in Wheeling.

The inspector next visited the businessman who had brought charges against Hoch. Magerstadt had furnished Hoch's new flats after several of his marriages. His records went back to June, 1891, when Hoch had married under the name of H. Frick and furnished an apartment at 418 Franklin Street in Chicago for $115. There were two or three entries each year, and each time Hoch came in to the *Möbelhaus* with a new wife, his new name was the former married name of the widow he had most recently married and buried.

It was Magerstadt's unique role, according to his laborious explanation to the inspector, to be introduced to each one of the new wives, listen to her trill of her new romantic bliss, and help her select the furniture for the new love nest. In turn the doomed brides confided the intimate details of Hoch's courtship to Magerstadt—the musical background of Schubert on the zither, the groom's assurance that mutual loneliness would now be ended, the asserted need for the companionship of a woman, the old, old song. "With my money," one of the women had told Magerstadt, "and his brains, he'll make a fortune for both of us."

It once occurred to Magerstadt, who seems to have been rather slow on the uptake, to ask Hoch why he married under so many different names. "Women wouldn't like to marry a man," Hoch had replied logically, and with what may have been a mordant sense of humor, "if they knew he had been a widower so many times."

Magerstadt, out of curiosity, had actually gone to the funeral of one of Hoch's wives, a Mrs. Julia Steinbrecker, who had married Hoch in 1894 and lasted for two months after the wedding ceremony—about par for the course. There had been a fuss at the cemetery. The deceased's family turned up with the coroner and tried to stop the funeral. They claimed she swore on her deathbed that Hoch had poisoned her with a white powder. Hoch produced a death certificate, signed by the attending physician, which stated the woman had died of natural causes. He outbluffed the coroner, and his wife was buried.

In the course of his researches, Inspector Shippy interviewed Mrs. Martha Hertzfeldt, a German widow, who had been married in 1894 to Hoch, who was then posing as one Jacob Erdorf, a religious worker. He had told his wife that the bank where she had savings was about to fail. She withdrew her $1,800, and her sister withdrew $800 she had on deposit. Hoch took the money and said that he would put it in another bank under his own name in order to protect it. The sisters were still waiting, in 1898, for him to return from his trip to the bank.

Inspector Shippy's investigation alerted the Chicago police to the fact that they probably had a murderer on their hands. They believed, however, that too many years had passed for them to be able to dig up enough concrete evidence to convict the man of murder. The best chance of bringing the killer to book lay, it seemed, in Wheeling, and in the clergyman who had been on Hoch's trail.

On November 1, 1898, the Chicago police sent the following letter to Haass:

In reply to your letter relative to Jacob Adolph Hoch, serving a year's sentence here for bigamy under the name of Dotz or Doesing, I desire to inform you that I sent an officer with the photo you sent me to the Bridewell, and Hoch, or Doesing, acknowledged at once it was his, but denied knowing any person in Wheeling. Now we learn from a cousin of his deceased wife that he kept a saloon at No. 4728 Jacobs Street, your city, where he married his wife. Friends here are positive he poisoned his wife to get her money. He is said to have married several women to get their money. Lay the whole matter before your Chief of Police and have him hunt all criminal evidence in the matter. Obtain indictment, if possible, for murder. Forward papers to us and we will turn him over to the chief.

Yours truly,
L. P. COLLERAN, Chief of Detectives.

Pastor Haass now took his suspicions, his scrapbook dossier, and his correspondence with the Chicago police to State's Attorney William C. Meyer, Wheeling, West Virginia. The decision was made to exhume the body of Mrs. Caroline Hoch for autopsy.

On November 14, 1898, Mrs. Hoch's grave was opened. The coffin was hoisted out to ground level and its lid pried off. The men leaned over and peered into the pine box. Where the widow's mid-section should have been, there was a gaping hole. She had

been tidily cut open by a party or parties unknown, her vital organs removed, and along with them any poison they might have contained.

Some time before, the Reverend Mr. Haass had remembered that Hoch had claimed to have come from the town of Hoexter in Westphalia. The parson had written a letter of inquiry to the mayor of that city, and two weeks after the exhumation he got a reply from Herr Rung, the prosecuting attorney of Mainz, Germany:

Replying to your inquiry of the 4th November, 1898, to the Mayor of Hoexter, Westphalia, we return photo and answer you that the police of Hoexter, Brackel, and Driburg had no success in finding a man as described in your letter and photo. However the police of Bingen-on-the-Rhine are positive that it is that of merchant Jacob Schmidt from Herrweiler, near Bingen-on-the-Rhine. Schmidt was born there on November 10, 1862. He is the son of Adam and Anna Elizabeth Schmidt and he married Christine Phillippine Ramb, by whom he had four children. He left his home and country, January 5, 1895, and has since that time been pursued under a warrant charging him with being a fraudulent bankrupt.

This letter temporarily confused the chronology of killer Schmidt-Hoch's activities which the minister had been working out: the German authorities had the killer emigrating in 1895 to the United States, and the Chicago police, from information supplied by Magerstadt, the furniture dealer, had Hoch marrying and murdering at least four years earlier—in June, 1891, in Chicago. It remained for Haass, to whom Hoch had become an all-consuming obsession, to iron out any question as to where Hoch had been operating at any particular time. The minister's research, done entirely by correspondence, worked it out this way.

Hoch had been born the son of a German preacher.

This advice to ardent bachelors was boxed on the front page of the New York Evening Journal *after Hoch's arrest.*

Apprenticed as a metalworker, he had switched to the study of pharmacy and worked in several chemist's shops in Germany, where he got his knowledge of drugs and poisons. He married his first wife, name unknown, in Vienna in 1881 and buried her in 1883. Shortly thereafter he took wealthy Christine Ramb as his wife. He sired four children, and then skipped with Christine's savings to a neighboring town where he married again. He used the dowry obtained from this last marriage to finance his trip to America in 1888. (It must be reported that Pastor Haass missed a romance enjoyed by Hoch on the boat coming over. In 1905, Frank Weninzer, an employee of a brewery in Chicago, revealed that he came over on the same steamer with Schmidt-Hoch in 1888. Hoch courted an immigrant servant girl aboard ship, married her as soon as the boat landed in New York, absorbed her miserable savings, and buried her two months later.) Shortly after his arrival in Chicago, Hoch commenced work seriously on his marriages, murders, and swindles. Late in 1894, posing again as a religious worker, Jacob Erdorf, he swindled the Hertzfeldt sisters out of their $2,600 and used this money to finance a trip back to Germany. In Herrweiler he speculated in barley futures and lost heavily. When a note for 3,000 marks fell due, he fled the country a second time—in January, 1895. A little over a month later he turned up in Wheeling as Jacob Huff, opened the saloon and began the campaign that won him the Widow Hoch.

On June 30, 1900, this fantastic man was released from jail in Chicago and taken to Wheeling, to face a murder charge. Without the widow's vital organs, however, the situation was hopeless. Two weeks after his arrival in police custody, Hoch was freed for lack of evidence. The parson had brought him extremely close to the point of no return, but not all the way.

Immediately after his release Hoch journeyed to Argos, Indiana, where he introduced himself to a brand-new widow, Mrs. Mary Schultz, as Albert Buschberg, a millionaire Chicago druggist. He married the widow, collected the $2,000 insurance policy on her late husband's life, and prevailed upon the widow and her fifteen-year-old daughter, Nettie, to go back with him to Chicago where both mother and daughter disappeared, along with $1,500 in savings. This was the first in a new streak of murderous triumphs.

At this point, one question begs for an answer: why didn't Hoch give up his career in wife-murder after the law and the Reverend Mr. Haass came so close to fitting his neck for a noose in Wheeling?

One can only speculate. It seems doubtful Hoch possessed an arrogance so monumental that he be-

lieved he could murder without end and never run afoul of the law. More likely murder had become a habit. Wife-killing was his trade. He could make a living at nothing else.

Whatever the reason, Hoch plodded remorselessly on. In 1901 he had hardly buried a Widow Loughken in San Francisco when he began to court the young daughter who had inherited her baking establishment —and this while he was in correspondence with a woman in western New York, had become engaged to a St. Louis woman by mail, and was writing fervent love letters to a Mrs. Sophia Reichel in Chicago. Always the pot was kept boiling.

Late in 1901 Hoch took a mail-order course in hypnotism given by a "professor" in Jackson, Michigan. He stuck with the course long enough to earn a diploma certifying him as a "Graduate Hypnotist." He immediately went to work on a widow named Mrs. Marie Elizabeth Goerk, whom he met through a room-wanted advertisement he placed in the German-language *Abendpost* in Chicago. He married her in three weeks and tried to hypnotize her into taking out a large insurance policy on her life. The widow was a stubborn, strong-willed woman, one of the few in Hoch's career. When she fell ill she refused Hoch's offer to nurse her and medicate her with his white powder. Either she got well fast, the widow warned, or she was going into a hospital. Hoch took the hint. He packed his bags and left. There would be other prospects, he was sure.

And there were. As the Count Otto von Kern of Bavaria he swindled the widow Hulda Nagel out of $3,000 in St. Paul in May of 1902. As John Schultz, he married Mrs. Mary Becker, a widow, in St. Louis, insured her life, and attended the funeral two months later when she succumbed to a sudden illness of two days' duration.

On June 18, 1903, a strangely familiar and pudgy little man, travelling under the name of Dr. G. L. Hart, married Mabel Leichman, a burlesque queen of German extraction, in Milwaukee. He took her to a Minneapolis home he had rented and unsuccessfully attempted to chloroform her. After a quick getaway in the middle of the night, Dr. Hart, operating once more under the name of Johann Hoch, worked his way for the balance of 1903 and 1904 through a succession of widows that ranged the alphabet from Mrs. Ada Dodd to Mrs. Ida Zazuil, the former in Dayton and the latter in Milwaukee.

Then, late in November of 1904, Hoch returned to his old hunting grounds in Chicago. The move was to prove fatal for Mrs. Marie Welker, a widow who answered an advertisement that Hoch ran in the Chicago *Abendpost* on December 3, 1904. "MATRIMONIAL," the advertisement invited the unwary *Hausfrau,* "German, with his own income, own home, wishes acquaintance of widow without children. Object, matrimony."

Nine days after the ad appeared, Hoch led Mrs. Welker to the altar. The afternoon of the wedding he borrowed all of the blushing bride's ready capital, $475, to furnish their new rented home at 6034 Union Avenue. His own capital, he said, was all tied up in investments and real estate.

Overnight the widow fell ill. She was soon being treated in tandem, by a Dr. Reese, for what he diagnosed as nephritis, and by Hoch with a white powder for only he knew what. As the widow's condition rapidly became worse, a sister, Mrs. Emilie Fischer, who was a widow too, came to visit her. At first the sisters got along well, and Mrs. Fischer mentioned that she had a thousand dollars saved that could be used toward paying the medical expenses.

Hoch, having better things to do with a thousand dollars, rejected the offer. Somehow his sick wife got the idea that her sister had put the net out for Hoch and that a romance had begun. "I'll soon be dead," she told Emilie Fischer, "and then you can have him." A bitter argument developed, and it was midnight before it ended. It was too late for Emilie to go home, and she went down to make her bed on a couch in the kitchen, where Hoch came to visit her and apologize for his wife's accusations. By five thirty in the morning they were old friends, and Hoch slipped into his coat and went to fetch the doctor for his wife, whose imprecations seemed to be raining down on their heads with less and less strength.

Mrs. Welker was dead when Hoch and the doctor returned. The date was January 12, 1905, one month to the day after the marriage of Hoch and the widow. Hoch wept noisily in the kitchen, and Mrs. Fischer had her hands full comforting him. "Now I am a widower again," he cried, "and all alone in the world. I would have spent my entire fortune to have saved her life."

Hoch courted Mrs. Fischer through the funeral and steadily for the next four days. "If Marie had not insulted you with her accusations," he told her, "I would have mourned six weeks for her." Under the circumstances, he insisted, they should marry right away.

They would open a hotel together and make a fortune.

On January 16, 1905, four days after the death of her sister, Mrs. Fischer demurely consented to be Hoch's bride. The thousand dollars she had mentioned in her sister's sickroom was already burning a hole in Hoch's imagination. It would come in handy now, he said. He had an eighty-one-year-old father in Germany who was in feeble health and was about to leave him an estate of $15,000. Didn't Emilie think he should go over and protect *their* interests?

Less than a week after the ceremony Emilie advanced $750 to Hoch. That night he disappeared. Emilie thought it over for a couple of days and began to wonder if maybe there wasn't something odd about her sister's death after all. She went to the police, and by one of those remarkable coincidences that plague master criminals, was ushered into the office of Inspector George Shippy, who listened in complete fascination to her story. On January 22, 1905, a court order was obtained for the exhumation of Mrs. Marie Welker Hoch's body. An autopsy was performed, which showed that the unlucky woman was stuffed with enough arsenic to fell a brewery horse.

The search was now on in earnest. This time the Chicago police had a fresh corpse, and they intended to make the most of it. The case hit the newspapers, and overnight Hoch was a national sensation as more and more of his living ex-wives and the relatives of his dead ones suddenly learned about each other and began telling their stories to the police and reporters.

Hoch, however, had disappeared. Calling himself Henry Bartels, he turned up in Manhattan at a boardinghouse at 546 West Forty-seventh Street in answer to a room-for-rent advertisement in the German-language *Das Morgen Journal.* He rented a hall bedroom and commenced peeling potatoes for the landlady, Mrs. Catherine Kimmerle, a widow of German extraction, within twenty minutes of his arrival. The next day he proposed marriage in the kitchen while Mrs. Kimmerle was washing the breakfast dishes. Mrs. Kimmerle, not wishing to offend her new boarder, countered by offering to introduce him to the members of the three widows' clubs to which she belonged, some of whom were anxious to take the marital plunge.

On Monday morning, January 30, 1905, Mrs. Kimmerle took a trolley ride downtown. The man sitting opposite her was reading the New York *American.* On the page facing Mrs. Kimmerle was a picture of the "Bluebeard Murderer" all America was talking about. It was Mrs. Kimmerle's star boarder.

She notified the New York police. That night at ten, four detectives tiptoed up the stairs of Mrs. Kimmerle's boardinghouse and into Hoch's room, where they found him calmly rocking himself and smoking a cigar. He did not resist arrest. Among his possessions the police found six one-hundred-dollar bills, five fives, loose change in every pocket, a handkerchief that was heavily soaked in cologne, a wedding ring on his finger and a spare in his trunk with the inscription effaced, a dozen suits with the labels cut out plus one suit with a Cincinnati label and another with a San Francisco label, a loaded revolver, one empty new trunk and two suitcases, and a hollow fountain pen containing a white powder that turned out to be some fifty-eight grains of arsenic.

The prisoner was taken to the West Forty-seventh Street station house, where he was subjected to round-the-clock questioning. He denied emphatically that he was Johann Hoch, the wanted murderer, claiming that it was a case of mistaken identity. He insisted that he was Henry Bartels, a drummer in Rhine wines for a vintner with home offices in Frankfort on Main. This pose lasted until a Chicago newspaperwoman brought one of his living victims, Mrs. Anna Hendricks Schmidt, to New York to identify him. This was too much even for Hoch. He admitted his identity and unburdened himself of an extraordinary statement.

"I am Hoch," said the man who had married some fifty women and murdered at least a third of them, "and I am a much abused man."

Hoch-Bartels-Schmidt was extradited to Chicago for confrontation by those of his wives who were still among the living—an experience that left him un-moved. "Believe me," he told the newspaper reporters, "all those women married me, not because they loved me, but because they thought I was wealthy . . . they gave me their money because they thought they would receive it back with more."

One man who felt he had come to the end of a long trail with the arrest of Hoch was the Reverend Mr. Haass, who had left Wheeling to become pastor of St. Matthew's German Lutheran Church in Utica, New York. Mr. Haass, who was dubbed "Hoch's Nemesis" in the newspaper headlines, gave a lengthy interview to the Hearst papers, telling how the death of Mrs. Caroline Hoch in Wheeling had put him on the murderer's trail and how he had pursued the villain doggedly ever since. Pastor Haass closed his interview with this stern judgment on his long-time adversary: "No punishment that can be meted out to this man Hoch will be too severe. I have followed him for ten years and I know him to be the biggest scoundrel of the century. Certain it is, whatever may be proven, he is a murderer, and a multi-murderer. . . ."

Hoch went on trial for the murder of Mrs. Marie Welker Hoch on April 19, 1905, and was found guilty exactly one month later. The first words he uttered after getting the verdict were these: "It serves me right."

While awaiting execution Hoch actually received several proposals of marriage. Fortunately the inexorable processes of the law saved the authors from their own folly. The multiple murderer was hanged in Chicago's county jail on February 23, 1906. The legacy that Hoch left us, based on his travail as an experienced husband, was summed up in a terse bit of personal advice he gave to a reporter after his arrest. "Women are all right in their place," Hoch said, "but marry only one at a time."

Courtroom Scene by David Gilmore Blythe

COLLECTION OF MRS. SCREVEN LORILLARD

Continuing Arguments

No one who met him ever forgot him. His charm captivated beautiful women, his eloquence moved the United States Senate to tears, his political skills carried him to the very threshold of the White House. Yet while still Vice President he was indicted for murder, and was already dreaming the dreams of empire that would bring him to trial for treason. After a century and a half, historians still cannot decide whether he was a traitor, a con man, or a mere adventurer. Now, a distinguished writer enters the controversy with an account of

The Conspiracy and Trial of Aaron Burr

By JOHN DOS PASSOS

About eleven o'clock on the night of February 18 or 19, he never could remember which, in the year of our Lord 1807, a backwoods lawyer named Nicholas Perkins who headed the federal land office in Mississippi Territory left the group around the fire in Sheriff Theodore Brightwell's log tavern and went to the door for a breath of fresh air. It was a night of clear frosty moonlight. Perkins could see far down the rutted road. Though he was described as a fearless giant of a man, and a major in the territorial militia, Perkins was startled to see two horsemen come riding up out of the forest.

The smaller of the horsemen rode right past. He was a shabby-looking little fellow lost under a broad-brimmed beaver hat. His companion reined in his horse and asked Perkins the way to Major Hinson's. His name, it turned out, was Major Robert Ashley.

Perkins told Ashley that the major was away from home, and added that, on account of a freshet, the flooding of the creeks would make it hard for a stranger to reach the Hinson house that night. The sensible thing would be to put up at the tavern, where there was refreshment for man and beast. Ashley insisted they must push on, so Perkins told him the best places to ford the streams. While he was talking to Ashley, Perkins kept staring at the first traveller, who had pulled up his horse thirty or forty yards up the road. Something about the man aroused his suspicions.

Perkins had read President Jefferson's proclamation warning of a treasonous conspiracy on the Mississippi, and the territorial governor's proclamation that followed it offering a reward of two thousand dollars for the apprehension of the former Vice President of the United States, Colonel Aaron Burr. Colonel Burr was said to have jumped his bail at Natchez, 200 miles to the west, two weeks before. Perkins scratched his head as he walked to the fire. These men were up to no good. Mightn't the little man with the hatbrim flapped over his face be Aaron Burr himself?

Right away Perkins routed the sheriff, who was related to Mrs. Hinson, out of bed. They saddled their horses and rode off after the travellers. They found Ashley in the Hinsons' front room. When she heard voices she knew, Mrs. Hinson, who'd been hiding in the back of the house in a fright ever since the strangers walked in, let herself be seen, and started to fry up some supper for her visitors.

The small man sat warming himself beside the kitchen fire, his hat still pulled down over his face. Perkins observed him narrowly. He wore a boatman's ragged pantaloons and a coarse blanket wrap-around belted in by a strap. The hat that had once been white was stained and shabby, but the riding boots on his very small feet were elegant and new. Perkins caught

Vice President Aaron Burr, by John Vanderlyn. He had, a contemporary said, "a magnetism . . . few persons could resist."

Burr's principal confederates were Senator Jonathan Dayton of New Jersey (left), a college classmate and lifelong friend, and James Wilkinson (right), the Army's ranking general. Dayton, failing in land speculation at home, sought a new career in the West. Wilkinson, a secret pensioner of Spain, was a wily conspirator. His portrait was done by C. W. Peale in 1797; the engraving of Dayton, by Saint-Mémin in 1798.

one quick glance of his eyes from under the brim of the hat and was convinced that the man must be Colonel Burr. Everybody spoke of how Burr could look clear through you with his lustrous black eyes.

He took Ashley aside and asked him point-blank if his companion was Colonel Burr. Ashley became agitated and walked out of the house without a word.

Perkins began to feel the two thousand dollars almost in the palm of his hand, but he had to move with circumspection. The little colonel was held in great respect in the western country—and he was known to be a dead shot. Mumbling a misleading excuse, Perkins rode off in a hurry, borrowed a canoe, and went speeding down the flooding Tombigbee River to a palisade named Fort Stoddert, the last American fortification before the frontier of Spanish West Florida.

Arriving there about daybreak, he roused Lieutenant Edmund P. Gaines, commander of the federal detachment, and told him he had the traitor Burr in his grasp. Right at this moment Burr would be starting down the trail to Pensacola; there was no way to cross the river except at Mrs. Carson's ferry. The lieutenant ordered out a file of mounted soldiers, and they galloped off to intercept him.

They found Burr and his companion on the trail to the ferry. The sheriff, whom Burr seemed to have completely fascinated in a few minutes' conversation, was acting as their guide to the Spanish border. Colonel Burr pointed out to the young lieutenant the risk he took in making an arrest without a warrant. The lieutenant brought out the President's proclamation and that of the territorial governor. Burr declared both were illegal and unconstitutional. The lieutenant insisted that he was an officer in the United States Army and had to do his duty. Colonel Burr would be treated with all the respect due a former Vice President of the United States—if he made no effort to escape. The little

colonel was conducted back to the fort and shut up in a room. Dinner was served him in solitary state. Sentries were posted at the windows and doors. Ashley meanwhile had managed to disappear into the woods.

Lieutenant Gaines and Perkins started racking their brains as to how they could get their prisoner safely to Washington, D.C. The weather was freezing and drizzly. There were no roads yet through the enormous woodlands of Mississippi Territory. The country abounded in Indians of doubtful loyalty. Rumors had enormously magnified the size of Burr's expedition. For all Gaines and Perkins knew, the back country was full of partisans grouping to rescue their leader.

There was nothing for it but for Lieutenant Gaines to take the little colonel into his family under a sort of parole. Gaines' brother, who was government factor to the Choctaw nation, was ill in bed. Burr showed himself the soul of tact and courtesy. Explaining that he'd picked up a certain amount of medical information on his travels, he helped nurse the brother back to health. Meanwhile, he sat at his bedside keeping him amused with sprightly talk about Indian quirks and customs. At the table he fascinated the family with his knowledge of books and pictures and the great world. He fixed his black eyes on the ladies with respectful attention. He played chess with Mrs. Gaines. So long as he stayed at Fort Stoddert not a word passed his lips about the failure of his western project. or about his arrest or his plans.

Lieutenant Gaines was counting the hours until he should see the last of his charming prisoner, whose friends had spread the story that the aim of Burr's thwarted expedition was to drive the Spaniards out of West Florida. As that was the dearest wish of every settler in the Mississippi Territory, expressions of sympathy were heard on every hand. "A week longer," Gaines wrote to his commander, "[and] the consequences would have been of a most serious nature."

At last the floods subsided to the point where Gaines felt it would be safe to try to take his prisoner up the Alabama River. The party was rowed in a government boat. When they stopped at John Mills' house on the Tensaw River, the ladies of the family all wept over the sorrows of Colonel Burr. Indeed a certain Mrs. Johnson was so moved by his plight that when a boy was born to her some months later, she named him Aaron Burr. "When a lady does me the honor to name me the father of her child," Burr was wont to remark, "I trust I shall always be too gallant to show myself ungrateful for the favor."

At a boat yard at the head of navigation on the Alabama, Gaines turned his prisoner over to Perkins, Perkins' friend Thomas Malone, and a guard of six men, including two federal soldiers with muskets, to be conducted to Washington, D.C. Gaines sent them off under the strictest injunction not to speak to their prisoner or listen to his blandishments, and to shoot to kill at his first effort to escape.

The lieutenant had found them good horses. Riding thirty or forty miles a day, avoiding the settlements, they hurried their prisoner along Indian traces through drowned woodlands. It was a rainy March. The nights were cold. Wolves howled about their campfires. Half the time they were drenched to the skin. Burr's fortitude amazed his guards. Never a word of complaint. Never a sign of fatigue. He rode his fine horse with as much style, so one of the guards told his friends, as if he were at the head of his New York regiment.

They crossed the rivers in Indian canoes, swimming their horses alongside. At last, on the Oconee River in the state of Georgia, they found a ferry and an inn not far beyond. For the first time since leaving the Alabama country they slept under a roof. When they crossed into South Carolina, Perkins redoubled his precautions. He knew that Joseph Alston, the husband of Burr's beloved daughter, Theodosia, was a member of the legislature. Public sentiment there was supposed to be strong for Burr. Perkins arranged his cavalcade in a square with Burr in the middle. Two riders went ahead of him, two on either flank, and two behind. They passed through towns and villages at a brisk trot.

In the village of Chester, about fifty miles south of the North Carolina border, they rode past an inn. From inside came a sound of music and dancing, and a crowd had gathered to look in the windows. The prisoner suddenly jumped from his horse and cried out to the bystanders that he was Aaron Burr under military arrest, and must be taken to a magistrate. Perkins dismounted at one leap with a pistol in either hand and ordered Burr to remount.

"I will not," cried Burr.

Perkins, a man of enormous strength, dropped his pistols and, grabbing the little colonel round the waist, lifted him back on his horse as if he were a child. Malone grabbed Burr's reins, pulled them over his horse's head, and led him off as fast as he could while the guards formed up around him. Before the astonished villagers could open their mouths the cavalcade was lost in the dust. Aaron Burr broke into a flood of tears. Malone, who rode beside him, was so distressed at his prisoner's humiliation that he found tears streaming down his own face. It was the man's eyes that moved him so, Malone told his friends afterward: his eyes were like stars.

Aaron Burr, at fifty-one, had reached the end of his rope.

If ever a man was born to eminence it was Aaron Burr. On both sides of his family he was descended from clergymen, the aristocrats of colonial New England. Burr's father, though a Connecticut man, was the second president and virtual founder of the College of New Jersey, later Princeton University. His mother's father was the famous Jonathan Edwards, who preached predestined damnation so vividly that once a congregation ran out of the church in terror. On both sides there were strains of madness among the eminent divines. Burr early showed that he had inherited the family brains—and certain idiosyncrasies as well. He was only sixteen when he was graduated with honors from Princeton. While his classmates declaimed against taxation without representation, young Aaron graced the commencement with an Addisonian essay on building castles in the air.

After a winter's study of his grandfather's theology, he borrowed the best horse in his tutor's stable and rode off for Connecticut, declaring that predestined damnation was an unchristian doctrine. While a student at the Litchfield Law School, he put in more time piercing the hearts of the village girls with his intense black gaze than in memorizing Coke's Littleton. At the outbreak of the Revolutionary War he hurried to Cambridge in hopes of a commission. General Washington turned him down, so it was as a gentleman volunteer that in 1775 he joined Benedict Arnold's expedition against Quebec.

In view of his delicate frame his hardihood surprised his mates. He met privations fearlessly. Having at last procured a captain's commission from General Richard Montgomery, he walked beside the tall, laughing Irishman on the snowy night when they attempted to assault the lower city of Quebec. When the vanguard was cut down by a burst of grapeshot, Captain Burr distinguished himself by trying to drag the huge car-

The "Nags Head portrait," allegedly of Theodosia Burr Alston

Three Mysterious Portraits

Around almost everyone—and everything—connected with the Burr conspiracy, time and flourishing legend have drawn a cloak of mystery. This is particularly true of three supporting characters: Burr's beloved daughter, Theodosia, and Harman and Margaret Blennerhassett, the couple who were charmed into contributing much of their fortune to the little colonel's grandiose schemes. The mystery continues to cling even to the surviving portraits reproduced above and on the opposite page.

On December 30, 1812, the American privateer *Patriot* put out from Charleston, South Carolina, for New York, her guns and a rich cargo of booty concealed below decks under sacks of rice. In her cabin was a distinguished passenger, Theodosia Burr Alston —desperately ill and still grieving over the death of her little son—on her way to visit her father. To get the *Patriot* through the British blockade, Theodosia's husband, Governor Joseph Alston, had given the cap-

tain a letter addressed to the commander of the British fleet, calling upon his gentlemanly gallantry to let the lady pass. The ruse worked. On New Year's Day, 1813, when the privateer was stopped by a British warship off Cape Hatteras, the letter was produced and the *Patriot* was waved on her way. The Englishmen may have been the last to see her company alive: that night a violent storm blew up and the *Patriot* was never heard from again.

The scene shifts now to a dirty little shack in the hamlet of Nags Head on Cape Hatteras, that traditional graveyard of ships off the North Carolina coast. The year is 1869, and the shack's owner, a poor, sick old "banks" woman named Mrs. Mann, has called in Dr. William G. Pool of nearby Elizabeth City. Having no cash to pay his fee, she offers him an oil painting of a young and beautiful lady whose approximate age, auburn hair, and piercing eyes give her a strong resemblance to Theodosia Alston. With the portrait goes a story. The picture—and some dresses evidently made for a gentlewoman—had been given to Mrs. Mann many years before by her lover, a young Hatteras fisherman; they represented part of his share in the loot from a deserted sailing vessel found driving toward Nags Head one morning early in 1813, bunks made up and table laid, rudder set and sails drawing. No vessel other than the *Patriot* and no gentlewoman other than Theodosia were known to be missing as a result of the terrible storm. Was the lady in the picture Theodosia? Many, including Dr. John E. Stillwell, a long-time collector of Burr portraits, have thought so, and have speculated that she was taking the picture to New York as a present for her father. Others are not so sure.

But how did the lady meet her death? In the half century following the *Patriot*'s disappearance, there were at least seven reports of deathbed statements by sailors—in places as various as a death cell in Norfolk, Virginia, and a poorhouse in Cass County, Michigan—confessing that they had been among a crew of pirates who boarded the wallowing privateer off Hatteras and, having stripped her of everything valuable, forced her people to walk the plank. One even recalled that a beautiful lady passenger had asked for a moment's reprieve while she went below, changed into a long white dress, and got her Bible; then she walked to her death with seraphic calm. More sober historians are inclined to a more prosaic interpretation: storm, shipwreck, drowning at sea. No one knows.

No one really knew, either, why the wealthy, cultivated Blennerhassetts went to live on a nearly deserted island in the Ohio River a year after their arrival from England in 1796. Not until 1901, long after both were dead, was it revealed that Harman had married his own niece, and that the newlyweds had been ostracized by their families. Partly for that reason and partly in order to keep their secret from their children, they had crossed the seas and sought a remote abode where no one who knew them was likely to follow. Their two daughters died in infancy, their three sons turned out to be drunkards or ne'er-do-wells, and neither Harman nor Margaret ever recovered more than a fraction of the $50,000 their association with Burr had cost them. Harman died in much straitened circumstances on the island of Guernsey in 1831, his wife in New York in 1842. Ironically, her claim against the government for the damage done to her home on Blennerhassett Island by Ohio militiamen during the conspiracy was about to be honored; it was sponsored by Senator Henry Clay, who had once defended Aaron Burr.

In 1854, as Harman Blennerhassett, Jr., lay dying in an almshouse in New York City, he gave his few possessions to a merchant named Orlando D. McClain, who had befriended him. Among them were fine miniatures of his parents, each set in pearls. Before McClain could keep his promise to send the miniatures to a surviving Blennerhassett brother in St. Louis, a mysterious stranger came to the house. McClain was absent. To Mrs. McClain the man represented himself as a historian who wanted to have the miniatures daguerreotyped for a forthcoming book. He had already obtained Mr. McClain's consent, he said, and Mrs. McClain gave up the miniatures—much to the chagrin of her husband, who, it turned out, had never seen or heard of the stranger before. Several years later a package was left at the house containing good daguerreotype copies; the McClains never saw the original miniatures again. The daguerreotypes came into the possession of the same Dr. John Stillwell who spent so much time inquiring into the provenance of the Nags Head portrait of Theodosia Alston, and eventually became part of the collection of the New-York Historical Society, with whose permission they are reproduced below.
—*The Editors*

Margaret and Harman Blennerhassett

cass of his fallen chief back to the American lines. Before reaching twenty he was counted a national hero.

Washington invited him to join his staff. Young Burr made sport of his Commander in Chief's spelling, and criticized his handling of the New York campaign. At Valley Forge he was one of the grumblers, and, for all his services, the highest rank he attained was that of lieutenant colonel. At Monmouth he disobeyed orders and led his regiment into a British ambush. His horse was shot from under him. Shock and frustration brought on an illness which eventually caused him to resign from the service in the spring of 1779. If Colonel Burr did not appreciate General Washington, it had also become clear that General Washington did not appreciate Colonel Burr.

Burr was nursed back to health by a motherly lady named Theodosia Prevost. Though she was the wife of a British army officer, Mrs. Prevost entertained so charmingly during lulls in the war in the Jerseys that her stone house at Paramus became popular with George Washington and his staff. Her husband died in 1779. In July of 1782 Burr induced her to marry him, though she was ten years older than he. A year later they settled in New York, where he took up the law in earnest. The city was a paradise for young lawyers who had served in the Continental Army, since all Tory attorneys had been disbarred. Soon Burr had a practice rivalled only by Alexander Hamilton's.

The law led to politics. Burr climbed fast. He cast his lot with Jefferson's Democratic-Republicans when Governor Clinton made him attorney general of the state of New York. He served the Clinton faction so well they sent him to the United States Senate. During the years of the growth of the Jeffersonian party, he built himself a strong political machine in New York City. His wife died, leaving him a daughter he adored.

It was young Theodosia, hardly into her teens, who presided at Burr's great dinners at Richmond Hill, his country place on the outskirts of Greenwich Village, the same house which Washington had made his headquarters and which John Adams occupied as Vice President. Meanwhile Burr's ambitions became national. Though outwardly friends, Burr and Hamilton were now bitter rivals for the control of ward politics in the city. Gossip claimed they were rivals too for the favors of a young woman named Eliza Bowen, who was one of the city's better-known harlots. But setting the best table and pouring the choicest wines in New York cost a great deal, and Burr was dangerously in debt.

In the bitter presidential campaign of 1800, which brought about the defeat of Adams and the Federalists, Burr and his "Little Band"—a group of young hotspurs he had gathered around him—were instrumental in holding New York in the Republican column. By a fluke in the procedure, though nobody seems to have intended Burr for the Presidency, the vote in the Electoral College was a tie: seventy-three for Jefferson and seventy-three for Burr. After thirty-six ballots the House of Representatives finally chose Jefferson, and Burr was elected Vice President.

Just before the long stalemate in the House, Burr presided over the wedding of his darling Theodosia to Joseph Alston, member of a wealthy and powerful family of South Carolina planters. Friends of his daughter in New York wondered whether Aaron Burr had bartered Theodosia's hand for the eight votes from South Carolina that helped cause the tie. In any event, his connection with the wealthy Alstons certainly helped keep his creditors at bay.

Though Burr was an able presiding officer in the Senate, President Jefferson, like General Washington before him, soon began to show a lack of confidence in him. The New York Burrites were disappointed by the small share of federal patronage that went their way. The Louisiana Purchase, by threatening to upset the balance of power among the original states, stung some extreme Federalists in New England into agitating for secession and thereafter Burr's politics began to change. Jefferson's control of the Republican Party would bar his way to renomination. Plainly, Burr's future now lay with the Federalists.

Burr's ambitions began to build him a castle in the air. If he could get himself elected governor of New York, when the time was ripe he might swing that state into a New England federation. As scion of two great New England families, he would be in line for the presidency of a new government. The Little Band went to work with a will.

Hamilton, who had been instrumental in trying to swing votes away from Burr to Jefferson in the House of Representatives, again stood in the way. He was letting it be known he considered Burr "the Catiline of America." And Burr, having lost the support of the upstate Republicans, needed the Federalists to win. In the June, 1804, gubernatorial election he carried New York City, but upstate the various Republican factions combined to snow him under. In bitter frustration he challenged Hamilton to a duel.

The bullet that killed Alexander Hamilton that early July morning on the Weehawken shore put an end to Aaron Burr's political career. By a strange ricochet Hamilton's death also ruined the plans of the New England secessionists: Republicans and Federalists united to mourn the great man dead. Burr was denounced as a murderer. Proceedings were instituted to indict him in New York and New Jersey, and in spite of his office the Vice President became a fugitive from justice.

He made off to Philadelphia. From there he wrote Theodosia that he was retiring to a friend's plantation to the southward. Only the risk of crossing the lowlands in the malarial season kept him from paying her a visit. Already her little son, Aaron Burr Alston, was the center of his grandfather's ambitious dreams.

He kept her posted on his prospects of marrying a wealthy woman. "If any male friend of yours should be dying of ennui, recommend to him to engage in a duel and a courtship at the same time. . . ." She must ignore stories

of attempts to assassinate him: "Those who wish me dead prefer to keep at a very respectful distance. . . . I am very well and not without occupation and amusement."

The Plotters

The occupation Aaron Burr found so amusing in Philadelphia was plotting a dream castle even more breathtaking than the one that had just collapsed. He found a kindred spirit in his old friend Jonathan Dayton, U.S. Senator from New Jersey. The two dreamers turned their eyes far from Philadelphia, looking to exciting prospects both in Europe and the new American West.

Bonaparte's successes in Europe were tantalizing every ambitious schemer of the age. His victory over the Spanish Bourbons had knocked the props out from under the Spanish dominions in the New World. Out of the weakening of Spanish power in Mexico and the restless land hunger of the American settlers beyond the Alleghenies, men with a knack for leadership should be able to build themselves a Napoleonic empire on the Mississippi. Burr and Dayton would mask the early stages of their enterprise behind a perfectly reasonable project to build a canal around the falls of the Ohio opposite Louisville.

Since anyone who summered in Washington City was thought to be risking his life from malaria, most of the diplomatic corps spent the hot months in Philadelphia. Waiting on the British minister, Anthony Merry, was Colonel Charles Williamson, with whom Burr had been associated in land deals in upstate New York. Though Williamson had assumed American citizenship in order to take title to real estate, he was a retired British army officer and a long-term agent of the Foreign Office. Williamson had for years been urging on His Majesty's government a scheme to curb the growing power of the United States by spreading British influence down the Mississippi. The Louisiana Purchase had ruined these plans. When Burr let drop the suggestion that the settlers on the western waters might be induced to secede from the Union, Williamson caught fire.

Mr. Merry, who had nothing but scorn for President Jefferson and his levelling democratic tendencies, could hardly conceal his pleasurable astonishment when Burr declared to him outright that, given a naval force and financial backing, he would "effect the separation of the western part of the United States." Burr could speak with authority: after all, he was still Vice President.

On August 6, 1804, Merry urged consideration of Burr's plan in a dispatch to the Foreign Office. Colonel Williamson, soon to set sail for England, would explain the details. Though Merry admitted "the profligacy of Mr. Burr's character" and acknowledged that he had been "cast off as much by the democratic as by the Federal Party," he insisted that Burr "still preserves connections with some people of influence, added to his great ambition and a spirit of revenge against the present Administration." These factors, he wrote, "may possibly induce him to exert the talents and activity which he possesses with fidelity to his Employers."

With the Hamilton murder indictments still hanging over his head, Burr had to keep out of the way of the sheriff. He wangled an invitation from one of the Georgia senators to visit his plantation on St. Simon Island. With a follower named Sam Swartwout in attendance, he set out in high spirits on a coastal vessel. While the ship beat its way down the coast against light summer breezes, he had plenty of time to indulge himself with the glorious prospects of his great scheme.

First he would establish a government at New Orleans, and then he would launch a two-pronged expedition against Spanish Mexico. One army would advance overland while a naval expedition would disembark at Veracruz or the Rio Pánuco. All this would cost a great deal of money, but his interview with the British minister had opened up the prospect of a copious source of funds. With British help Burr would conquer Mexico. The Mexicans would flock to his standard. He was already counting all the fresh silver dollars that would flow from the Mexican mint.

The dream swelled to grand dimensions. There would be no more republican nonsense. Mexico would proclaim him emperor. He would govern with the aid of a council of worthies made up of the best brains in the land. Theodosia would be empress apparent, and little Gamp (Burr and his grandson each called the other Gamp) heir to the throne.

But by early December Burr was back in Washington presiding with his usual punctilious gravity over the Senate. Senator William Plumer of New Hampshire, the diarist of the session, found him changed. "He appears to have lost those easy graceful manners that beguiled the hours away last session—He is now uneasy, discontented & hurried.—So true it is 'great guilt ne'er knew great joy at heart.'" Plumer set to wondering what Burr's future would be. "He can never I think rise again. But surely he is a very extraordinary man & is an exception to all rules. . . . And considering of what materials the mass of men are formed—how easily they are gulled—& considering how little restraint laws human or divine have on his mind, it is impossible to say what he will attempt—or what he may obtain."

Burr's last appearance before Congress wound up all business on March 2, 1805, was impressive. He delivered the most effective address of his career. "This house is a sanctuary," he declaimed, "a citadel of law, of order, and of liberty; it is here—it is here in this exalted refuge, here, if anywhere, will resistance be made to the storms of political phrenzy and the silent arts of corruption; and if the Constitution be destined ever to perish by the sacrilegious hands of the demagogue or the usurper, which God avert, its expiring agonies will be witnessed on this floor."

When he walked out of the hushed chamber, many senators were in tears.

The Paths of Glory

Two weeks later Burr was back in Philadelphia telling Anthony Merry that the French inhabitants of Louisiana were ready to revolt against the United States and to ask for the protection of Great Britain. He suggested that the Foreign Office send as consul at New Orleans a confidential agent who spoke French, and arrange for a flotilla of two or three frigates and some smaller vessels to blockade the mouth of the river when Burr established his government there. For himself he requested an immediate loan of one hundred thousand pounds.

The same day that Mr. Merry transmitted this remarkable request for the consideration of his government, Burr wrote Theodosia that he was off for the West. He found the trip down the Ohio River a tonic to his spirits. Below Marietta he stopped at an island that was one of the showplaces of the region. A rich immigrant named Harman Blennerhassett had built himself a mansion there with gardens and parklands in the English style, almost ruining himself in the process. Blennerhassett, a graduate of Trinity College, Dublin, was a big, gangling, nearsighted man with some learning but not a trace of common sense. To the settlers up and down the Ohio he was known, half in affection, half in derision, as "Blanny." Blanny was away during Burr's first visit, but Burr was entertained by Mrs. Blennerhassett, described as an accomplished and well-educated woman who was pining for talk of music and books on that far frontier. Colonel Burr had at his tongue's tip all the fashionable conversation of the age. One contemporary historian claimed that Burr played Ulysses to Mrs. Blennerhassett's Calypso. Be that as it may, from that moment on, the Blennerhassetts, man and wife, were as fascinated by the little colonel as a pair of cuckoos by a snake.

By mid-May Burr was in Cincinnati, being entertained by Jonathan Dayton's colleague in the Senate, a busy Jack-of-all-trades named John Smith, who was storekeeper, land speculator, Baptist preacher, and politician. Dayton joined them. The three men put their heads together. The plan took shape.

Leaving his boat to follow the curves of the river, Burr rode briskly across country into Tennessee. The early summer weather was fine. He enjoyed the riding. No word in public of secession, only of a coming war with Spain; that was his posture. His progress became a personal triumph. Without quite saying so he managed to give the impression that his good friend Henry Dearborn, the Secretary of War, was only waiting for a declaration of war to put him in command of an expedition against the Spanish possessions. In Nashville he was tendered a public dinner. Andrew Jackson grasped him warmly by the hand and took him home to the Hermitage.

An enthusiastic duellist himself, Jackson considered the hue and cry against Burr over the death of Hamilton damnable persecution. And an expedition against the Dons had his hearty approval. General Jackson furnished Burr a boat to take him down the Cumberland River to Fort Massac, on the lower Ohio near present-day Cairo, Illinois, where he was to pick up his own boat again. There Burr at last caught up with an old acquaintance he had determined on as his second in command. This was Brigadier General James Wilkinson, General in Chief of the small Army of the United States.

The General in Chief

Wilkinson was then nearing fifty, short, red-faced, and corpulent from high living; grown gray before his time, so he liked to put it, in the service of his country. Like Burr he had served under Arnold in the botched Canadian expedition, but unlike Burr he had found promotion quick and easy.

Luck always seemed to be with young Wilkinson. By a series of fortunate chances he caught Washington's eye in a lucky moment at Trenton. General Horatio Gates, to whose headquarters staff he had transferred, found him pliable and sympathetic, a young officer adept at scrounging up a meal or a drink or a wench. In 1777 Wilkinson was promoted to deputy adjutant-general and brevetted brigadier general. In his memoirs he took credit for choosing General Gates' fine position on Bemis Heights and so bringing about Burgoyne's surrender.

Wilkinson had just turned twenty-one when he married Ann Biddle, the attractive daughter of a Quaker innkeeper rising in Philadelphia society. Because of some association with the discredited anti-Washington "Conway Cabal," Wilkinson had thought it prudent to resign from active service, but the young man had a way of ingratiating himself. Plump, popeyed, and convivial, he somehow slipped in and out of scrapes and scandals without leaving bad feelings behind. Finding a living hard to come by on the Bucks County farm he took over from a dispossessed Tory, he sold it in 1784, piled his wife and two children into a carriage and his household goods into a Conestoga wagon, and set out for Kentucky. As agent for the Philadelphia firm of Barclay, Moylan and Co., he opened a general store in Lexington.

In Kentucky he was in his element. Storekeepers were making fortunes. Speculation in military land grants held out prospects of wealth to every settler. Politics was a hive of intrigue. Not many months passed before young Wilkinson had outrun George Rogers Clark as the spokesman for the grievances of the frontiersmen along the Ohio.

When the Spanish attempted to close the Mississippi to American commerce in 1786, it could have meant ruin to the Kentuckians, especially Wilkinson, who invested in everything. He dealt in land. He speculated in cargoes for export. His livelihood depended on trade through New Orleans. Along with his business associate, Judge Harry Innes, he promoted the notion that the future of Kentucky depended on accommodation with the Spaniards, and he developed a real knack for dealing with them.

In the spring of 1787 he made his way down the Mississippi. His handsome gifts, such as the pair of blooded horses he presented to the commander at Natchez, opened every door. During the two months he spent in New Orleans, he and the Spanish governor, Don Esteban Miró, became thick as thieves. Wilkinson confided in Don Esteban that though he had a poor head for figures he had noticed that tobacco which could be bought for two dollars a hundredweight in Kentucky sold for nine and a half at the royal warehouse in New Orleans. Why not let him have the monopoly of the traffic down the Mississippi?

Don Esteban was no mean horse trader. Joining in the monopoly of the tobacco trade would require a somewhat hazardous interpretation of the royal regulations. He demanded a *quid pro quo*. Wilkinson intimated that there might be services he could perform for His Most Catholic Majesty.

Always an eager penman, Wilkinson set to work to draft a memorial setting forth for the Spanish officials the benefits that would accrue to them from a separation of the western settlements from the Atlantic states. Don Esteban was eager for news of disaffection in Kentucky. He pointed out that it would be a graceful gesture, as a mere formality between men of the world, if the General would sign an oath of allegiance to the Spanish sovereign. That grateful monarch furnished pensions to his retainers. Wilkinson signed, and his name was entered in the secret ledgers of the Ministry for the Colonies as Agent Number Thirteen. Two thousand silver dollars a year was mentioned as a suitable honorarium.

The tobacco monopoly failed to prove as lucrative as Wilkinson expected. His Spanish pension appeared intermittently. By 1790, high living and careless speculation had reduced him to bankruptcy. He applied for a commission in the new Army of the United States that President Washington was organizing to protect the frontier, and soon attained his old rank of brigadier. When Burr became Vice President, Wilkinson felt he had a friend at court. They had become intimate as young men in the days of the Conway Cabal, and occasionally corresponded in a private cipher. He had every reason for feeling cordial toward Burr, whose influence was thought by some to have brought Wilkinson the appointment, in 1805, as governor of the Territory of Louisiana. Furthermore, Burr's elimination of Hamilton left Wilkinson the ranking general officer in the United States Army.

Now, in June of 1805, the congenial pair spent four days together at Fort Massac tracing out the trails to Mexico on their maps. With Wilkinson's help, Burr believed, his project was certain of success.

The War Department, Tennessee, Kentucky, Ohio—all were in the palm of his hand. Now he must sound out the Creoles, the French-speaking natives of New Orleans, who were restive under the new regulations—and taxes—imposed by the Americans since the Louisiana Purchase. Wilkinson may have had his doubts, but if Burr did manage his coup, he wanted to be in on the loot. He offered Colonel Burr every civility.

"The general and his officers," Burr wrote Theodosia, "fitted me out with an elegant barge, sails, colours and ten oars, with a sergeant and ten able faithful hands."

In New Orleans Colonel Burr was soon the toast of the Vieux Carré. He was dined by the very Jeffersonian governor of Orleans Territory, W. C. C. Claiborne, and set up to grand turnouts by members of the Mexican Association, made up of buccaneering characters on fire to make their fortunes by promoting a new revolution in Mexico. He fluttered the hearts of the Creole beauties with his mysterious charm. He became fluent in bad French. He was attentive to the Catholic bishop, who like much of the local Spanish clergy was disgusted with the subjection of his homeland to the infidel French and eager for the independence of Mexico. As Burr told the story, the bishop sent off three Jesuit priests to prepare the Mexicans for Colonel Burr's expedition.

New Orleans seemed so ripe for Burr's plans that he felt he had to have fresh interviews with Andrew Jackson and General Wilkinson. After leaving New Orleans and spending a few days in Natchez ("and saw some tears of regret as I left it"—he kept boasting of his conquests in his letters to his daughter), he rode north along the Natchez Trace, "drinking the nasty puddle-water, covered with green scum, and full of animalculae—bah!" into the clear air of the Tennessee mountains.

From Nashville he wrote Theodosia: "For a week I have been lounging at the house of General Jackson, once a lawyer, after a judge, now a planter; a man of intelligence, and one of those prompt, frank, ardent souls I love to meet." To Andrew Jackson he said not a word about secession or funds from the British, but talked long of Santa Fe and his contacts with the Mexican patriots. He declared that the Mexican Association in New Orleans was behind him to a man.

A new project was rising on his horizon as a cover-up for his secret plan. While Louisiana was still under the control of the Dons, the Spanish governor had granted an enormous area—1,200,000 acres—of fertile land on the Ouachita River to a certain Baron de Bastrop. This tract was now, supposedly, on the market. Burr would find funds to buy it.

Burr's physical energy was inexhaustible. From Nashville he rode 250 miles to St. Louis for a second conference with General Wilkinson, who had now taken up his post as governor of the Louisiana Territory. As usual the two men enjoyed each other's company. Wilkinson was a great trencherman and amusing over his wine. Now Burr could report to him amid considerable merrymaking that General Jackson would march for Mexico at the drop of a hat. The Bastrop lands, which by this time Burr felt he virtually owned, would make them all rich, if everything else failed. They reached the point of drawing up lists of officers for their army.

By mid-November Burr was back in Washington, D.C., calling on Anthony Merry. Mr. Merry had disappointing news. His first dispatches had been lost at sea when a British packet was captured by the French. Duplicates had so far elicited no response from the Foreign Office. Jonathan Dayton, whom Burr had hoped would be on hand during the summer to fan Mr. Merry's enthusiasm for the scheme, had been delayed by illness and had only just arrived.

Though Merry wrote the Foreign Office on November 25, 1805, that Burr showed every sign of distress at the bad news, it didn't take the little colonel long to rally his spirits. He refused to be discouraged. He now demanded £110,000 and three ships of the line as well as the several frigates and smaller vessels to cruise off the mouth of the Mississippi. He set March of 1806 for the beginning of operations. The revolution in New Orleans would follow in April or May. He told Merry he had found a deposit there of ten thousand stand of arms and fifty-six pieces of artillery abandoned by the French. He must have "pecuniary aid" by February.

He held out a glittering prospect to the Foreign Office.

As a result of the *coup d'état* to set up a western federation, "the Eastern States will separate themselves immediately from the Southern:—and . . . thus the immense power which has risen up with such rapidity in the Western Hemisphere will, by such a division, be rendered at once informidable."

A few days later Colonel Burr dined with President Jefferson. It didn't take much conversation to discover another check to his plans. Jefferson believed his envoys in Paris were about to accomplish a deal through Talleyrand to purchase the Floridas. He had dropped any project for a war with Spain.

Burr Writes a Letter

News of Burr's goings and comings could hardly be kept out of the newspapers. For all his successful intriguing, Wilkinson was famous for his indiscretions when he'd had too much to drink, and that was almost every time the wine was uncorked after dinner. Burr too, usually enigmatic in his utterances, was so intoxicated by the prospects of grandeur that he allowed himself to be overheard making jeering remarks about the need for a change in Washington. Rumors circulated and multiplied.

On December 1, 1805, President Jefferson received an anonymous letter warning him against Burr's conspiracy. "You admit him to your table, and you held a long and private conference with him a few days ago *after dinner* at the very moment he is meditating the overthrow of your Administration. . . . Yes, Sir, his abberations through the Western states *had no other object*. . . . Watch his connections with Mr. M—y and you will find him a British pensioner and agent."

Actually, Burr's difficulties at that moment stemmed from the fact that he hadn't succeeded in becoming a British pensioner. It was only with the help of the Alstons that he paid his travelling expenses. Jonathan Dayton, too was flat broke; and despite extraordinary efforts, was able to raise only a few thousand dollars from the Spanish minister by selling him the details of a rival expedition against the Spanish dominions. For the moment, Theodosia's husband remained the conspirators' chief banker. Meanwhile, Burr was no more successful in his efforts to recruit prominent

R. M. DEVENS, *Our First Century*, 1879

American naval and military officers for his enterprise. He approached men he knew had some grievance against the Jefferson administration—Thomas Truxtun, Stephen Decatur, William Eaton—but they all thumbed him down when they realized the illicit character of Burr's plans. Still, Burr had Harman Blennerhassett under his spell.

Blanny proved even more credulous than Alston. He wrote Colonel Burr that his island estate was up for sale and that he was looking for a profitable way to invest his capital. He offered his services as a lawyer. Burr answered that he could offer Mr. Blennerhassett not only fortune but fame. He congratulated him on giving up "a vegetable existence" for a life of activity. He explained that he couldn't go into the details of his plans until they met face to face. His letter left Blanny panting to give his all.

Burr had gone too far now to turn back. He must act the part to the end. He recruited a German secretary and the services of a down-at-the-heels French officer named Julien de Pestre to act as chief of staff. Burr and Dayton were now dropping the fiction of the Ohio canal. The young men enlisted for service on the Mississippi were being told instead that in accordance with the secret policy of the administration they were to establish an armed settlement on Colonel Burr's lands up the Ouachita River. Each man was to have a hundred acres for his own.

Though many old Philadelphia friends turned Burr down, the famous Dr. Erich Bollman swallowed his scheme hook, line, and sinker. Bollman was the German physician who had been subsidized by Americans in London to try to free Lafayette from prison at Olmütz, in Austria. He was desperate for money. Burr told him he would send him to Europe as his diplomatic representative.

Somehow during the next few months he did scrape up funds to ship Bollman to New Orleans by sea, while Sam Swartwout and Peter Ogden of the Little Band started off across country to join forces with General Wilkinson. Each man carried a copy of a cipher letter that was soon to become famous. With its dispatch, Burr burned all his bridges.

". . . At length I have obtained funds and have actually commenced. The Eastern detachments, from different points and under different pretenses, will rendezvous on the Ohio 1st November. . . . Naval protection of England is secured. Truxtun is going to Jamaica to arrange with the [British] admiral on that station. It will meet us at the Mississippi. England, a navy of the United States, are ready to join, and final orders are given to my friends and followers. It will be a host of choice spirits. Wilkinson shall be second to Burr only. . . . Burr will proceed westward 1st August, never to return. With him goes his daughter; the husband will follow in October, with a corps of worthies. . . . Our object, my dear friend, is brought to a point so long desired. Burr guarantees the result with his life and honor, with the lives and honor and the fortunes of hundreds, the best blood of our country. Burr's plan of operation is to move down rapidly from the Falls [of the Ohio] on the 15th of November, with the first five hundred or a thousand men, in light boats now constructing for that purpose; to be at Natchez between the 5th and 15th of December, there

to meet you; there to determine whether it will be expedient to seize or pass by Baton Rouge. . . . The gods invite us to glory and fortune. . . ."

General Wilkinson Turns on a Friend

It is not till early October, 1806, that Sam Swartwout, after many hundreds of miles of weary riding, finds the General in camp at Natchitoches on the Red River, and delivers the cipher message. His companion, Ogden, hands Wilkinson an even more extravagant communication from Jonathan Dayton, warning him that he is to be put out of office by Jefferson at the next session of Congress: "You are not a man to despair, or even despond, especially when such prospects offer in another quarter. Are you ready? Are your numerous associates ready? Wealth and glory! Louisiana and Mexico!"

In the solitude of his tent, with the help of a pocket dictionary that furnishes the key, the General sits up half the night deciphering the hieroglyphics. Food for thought indeed. Wilkinson is a gentleman with the profoundest regard for the safety of his own skin. It strikes him at once that the conspiracy in its present form is crack-brained.

Burr is lying to him. Wilkinson knows that the administration has decided against war with Spain. His orders are to patch up a truce with the Spanish force which has advanced across Texas to meet a rumored American invasion, and to agree to the Sabine River as a provisional boundary.

Furthermore, even to this distant outpost news has come of Pitt's death and of the appointment of Charles James Fox, the most pro-American of British statesmen, as Foreign Minister. Wilkinson has no way of knowing that one of Fox's first acts in office was to recall the eager Mr. Merry, thereby putting a quietus on any hope of British help for Burr, but it is obvious that Fox is no man to back an insurrection against the United States. By now Wilkinson knows too that the western settlers are "bigotted for Jefferson," as he put it a few months later, and that the conspiracy has no backing among the people.

The General decides that the safest thing for him to do is to turn state's evidence on Dayton and Burr. Once that decision is made, he lashes himself up into a frenzy of righteous indignation. He writes the President in heroic vein: He will defend the Union with his life. He writes Governor Claiborne in New Orleans to be on his guard: "You are surrounded by dangers of which you dream not and the destruction of the American Union is seriously menaced. The Storm will probably burst on New Orleans, when I shall meet it & triumph or perish."

Not a word to Swartwout and Ogden; they must be deceived into believing that he is still one of them. But among his officers, in the privacy of the wine after dinner, he swells like a bullfrog. He is the man who will stamp out this foul conspiracy, so help him God. How better can he squelch the libellous rumors of his being on the Spanish payroll than by saving New Orleans for the Union? He and his little force will stand like the Spartans at Thermopylae.

After further cogitation the General hits on a scheme that he feels will not only keep him in good odor with the ad-

The island estate of Harman Blennerhassett

ministration in Washington but will produce a handsome bonus from his Spanish employers. He knows that President Jefferson is agog for exploration of the West. Wilkinson already has Lieutenant Zebulon Pike searching out the trails to Santa Fe. Now he sends off his aide, Walter Burling, to Mexico City—ostensibly to buy mules, but actually on a mission to the viceroy. For Washington his story will be that Burling is making a survey of roads and fortifications. For the viceroy he drafts a letter, picturing himself, again like Leonidas holding back the Persian hordes, as averting an attack on Mexico. He respectfully demands the sum of $121,000 in payment for these services.

Burr Sets the Plot in Motion

Never suspecting that his plans have been betrayed, Burr meanwhile is building his dream castle with the help of the doting Theodosia, Alston, and little Gampillo in the crisp air of Bedford Springs in the Pennsylvania mountains. They are already living in the imagined splendors of Montezuma's court under Aaron the First. They will put the Emperor Napoleon to shame. No title has yet been found for Joseph Alston. He announces that he will earn one by his deeds "in council and in the field."

Leaving the Alstons to follow by slow stages, Burr, attended by his secretary and chief of staff, rides off to Pittsburgh. There he sets up his headquarters at O'Hara's Tavern and starts recruiting young men of mettle. He contracts for twenty thousand barrels of flour and five thousand barrels of salt pork. He pays for everything with his own bills of exchange, guaranteed by the infatuated Alston.

Burr talks so big in Pittsburgh that a number of military men become alarmed and send warnings to Washington. Burr has already gone down river. On Blennerhassett's island he conquers all hearts. Poor nearsighted Blanny is transfigured by the prospect of glory. He sets to work collecting fowling pieces and muskets, and whiskey by the barrel. He has his hands build a kiln for drying Indian meal. They roll out tubs of salt pork and corned beef. Mrs. Blennerhassett packs her trunks, and when Theodosia ar-

rives, pronounces her the loveliest woman she has ever met.

Blanny mortgages what is left of his fortune to raise funds. Alston has told him he will guarantee every dollar. They sign a contract for fifteen boats with the Woodbridges at Belpre, across from the island. Blanny writes his name on every bill of exchange Burr puts under his nose. He retires to his study to prepare four articles for the *Ohio Gazette* advocating the secession of the western states.

Burr moves on in a fever of activity. He can't stay in one place long enough to complete his arrangements. Leaving Blennerhassett and Alston to recruit riflemen and to follow with the provisions when the boats are ready, he hurries to Cincinnati. On the way, at Wilmington, a mob denouncing disunion and treason surrounds Burr's lodgings. When fife and drum play "The Rogue's March," Colonel Burr declares coolly that there is nothing he enjoys more than martial music. The outcry can't refer to him because his plans are all for the honor and glory of the United States. His disclaimer is so plausible that he is tendered an apology and the mob goes home.

Mobs or senators, Burr pulls the wool over all eyes. John Adair, an old Indian fighter associated with Wilkinson in his wars against the Miamis, now a senator from Kentucky, joins Burr and lends a willing ear to his Mexican project. They ride through Kentucky in company.

Back in Nashville, Burr finds the Republican part of the population in a fever to march on the Spaniards. General Jackson has alerted his militia, but he still has occasional doubts. When he confronts Burr with rumors of secessionist talk drifting down river from Ohio, Burr is said to have shown him a blank commission signed by Jefferson. To cap that, he produces $3,500 in Kentucky banknotes to pay for the boats that Jackson's partner, John Coffee, is building at Clover Bottom. He has already paid five thousand (in his own paper) to a Colonel Lynch for his claims on the Bastrop lands. He draws sight drafts on all and sundry. According to the newspapers he is spending $200,000 on boats and provisions. Blanny's money flows like river water. Thoroughly reassured, Andrew Jackson puts on his best uniform to introduce Burr to the citizens of Nashville at a public ball.

To certain parties in Kentucky, this is all a red flag to a bull: the Spanish conspiracies all over again. Humphrey Marshall, Federalist brother-in-law of Jefferson's Chief Justice, has set up a newspaper named *The Western World* to expose the old Spanish intrigue to separate Kentucky from the Union; in it he charges that Wilkinson's old associate, Innes, is implicated. Joseph Daveiss, United States District Attorney, another brother-in-law of the Chief Justice, has been writing President Jefferson all summer warning him that Wilkinson and Burr are engaged in plots dangerous to the Union. On November 8, 1806, he presents an affidavit in federal court, charging Aaron Burr and John Adair with illegally promoting an expedition against Mexico. The presiding judge is none other than Harry Innes, under attack in *The Western World* as a pensioner of Spain. Motion dismissed.

Aaron Burr, ever eager to assume the role of injured innocence, rides back to Lexington and demands an inquiry.

Some of Burr's boats were captured at Marietta by Ohio militiamen alerted by a government agent. Meanwhile Burr, unaware of Wilkinson's treachery, was on his way down river.

Popular sentiment in Kentucky is still with him. He has induced a rising young lawyer named Henry Clay to act as his counsel. When a grand jury is impanelled to hear Daveiss' charges, Daveiss is unable to present them because his key witness is absent on business. Daveiss has to ask for a postponement. Burr makes an address to the court and walks out in triumph.

He is heard by a bystander to remark that Daveiss must think him a great fool if, supposing he did have an unlawful enterprise in view, he should conduct it in such a manner as to give anyone an opportunity of proving it.

Andrew Jackson is assailed by doubts again. On November 12 he writes his old friend Governor Claiborne in New Orleans one of his tempestuous epistles:

". . . I fear treachery is become the order of the day . . . Put your Town in a State of Defence organize your Militia, and defend your City as well against internal enemies as external . . . keep a watchful eye upon our General [Wilkinson]—and beware of an attack, as well from your own Country as Spain . . . your government I fear is in danger, I fear there are plans on foot inimical to the Union . . . —beware the month of December—I love my Country and Government, I hate the Dons—I would delight to see Mexico reduced, but I will die in the last ditch before I would yield a part to the Dons or see the Union disunited. This I write for your own eye and your own safety, profit by it and the Ides of March remember. . . ."

On November 25, in Frankfort this time, the District Attorney renews his motion for Burr's indictment. When Henry Clay demands an assurance from his client that Burr's expedition has no treasonable intent, Burr hands him the same written statement he has already sent to his old friend Senator Smith of Ohio, denying any intention of subverting the Union by force. Clay is convinced and declares to the court that he pledges his own honor on Burr's innocence. A second grand jury refuses to find a true bill. The Republicans of Frankfort honor the little colonel with another ball.

Meanwhile, President Jefferson and his Cabinet have been startled into activity by General Wilkinson's first warning of the conspiracy, which the General dispatched from Natchitoches some twelve days after he received Burr's cipher letter. Hitherto they seem to have discounted Daveiss' warnings as expressions of party spite by pestiferous Federalists. Now the Secretary of War and the Secretary of the Navy send out messengers to alert their forces, and on November 27 President Jefferson issues his proclamation that "sundry persons . . . are conspiring and confederating together to begin a military expedition or enterprise against

the dominions of Spain," and enjoining "all faithful citizens who have been led without due knowledge or consideration to participate in the said unlawful enterprises to withdraw from the same without delay. . . ."

During this period a private emissary of the President gives information he has collected about the conspiracy to Governor Edward Tiffin of Ohio. Tiffin informs the legislature, then in session in Chillicothe. A bill is rushed through authorizing the militia to seize Burr's boats and supplies.

Tatterdemalion troops take possession of the boats being built at Belpre. They descend on Harman Blennerhassett's island paradise, break into the wine cellar, plunder the kitchens, trample the flowerbeds, slaughter the sheep, and break up the fence rails for campfires. Blanny himself escapes by boat into a snowy night, while, according to one witness' story, the levelled muskets of his recruits hold off the militia officer come to arrest him.

Mrs. Blennerhassett follows in a big flatboat manned by a group of youngsters from Pittsburgh. From then on, the expedition is a race between the speed of the current and the couriers distributing the President's proclamation.

Almost two weeks go by before the Blennerhassetts get news of their leader. Taking refuge one late December evening from the chop and the storm in the mouth of the Cumberland, they are met by a skiff with a letter. Colonel Burr is anchored a couple of miles upstream and requests five hundred dollars in paper and fifty in silver. Next day the whole flotilla pushes off downstream.

For Burr it is just in time. A certain Colonel Hardin of South Carolina is already on his way down the Cumberland with the announced intention of shooting him on sight. The President's proclamation has thrown Nashville into a fury. The citizens have hardly read it before they get ready to burn Burr in effigy. General Jackson musters his militia. He almost breaks down with patriotic emotion when the elderly veterans of the Revolutionary War, who have formed a corps known as the Invincibles, ride up to tender their lives in defense of the Union. Days before, Jackson's man John Coffee has returned to Colonel Burr $1,725.62, which represents the unfinished boats that Burr had to abandon in his haste to depart. Accounts are closed between them, except for a note for $500 that Jackson unwisely put his name to, which eventually was to come back protested.

Unopposed except by cold rain and high winds and an occasional floating log, Burr's flotilla, amounting now to thirteen boats manned by some sixty men, drifts down the Ohio to Fort Massac. The lieutenant in command there, who has not heard of the proclamation or of orders to apprehend Burr, exchanges civilities with the little colonel, and, believing Burr to be leading a group of settlers to the Bastrop lands, gives one of his sergeants a furlough to go along as guide.

New Year's Day, 1807, finds the flotilla comfortably beached at New Madrid, on the Mississippi, in Louisiana Territory. According to one account, forty new recruits join Burr's party. Other witnesses were to speak of cannon, and of two gunboats building there. Some were to accuse Blennerhassett of trying to buy arms and ammunition from the army post. Next morning they push off. Still keeping ahead of the hue and cry, they are borne swiftly southward on the current of the enormous brown river. As they glide along, Blanny and Burr follow their boats' progress on their maps. Blanny is later to declare that it is when the boats sweep past what seems to him the logical landing from which they should have proceeded overland to the Bastrop lands that he first suspects an imposture.

Burr for his part seems to have forgotten all about the Bastrop settlement. His talk now is of Baton Rouge. This outpost of Spanish West Florida is supposedly so ill-defended that even the peaceable Governor Claiborne of Orleans Territory is said to have suggested jokingly over the wine after dinner that he and his guests drive up the levee in their carriages some evening and take it.

The weather has cleared. The little colonel is in high spirits. He appoints officers and noncoms. Muskets are brought out of a packing case, and he puts some of the boys through the manual of arms on one of the big flatboats as they drift down the river. At his friend Judge Peter Bruin's plantation some thirty miles above Natchez he is confidently expecting news from General Wilkinson, whom he believes to be waiting in New Orleans for the word.

Burr is so anxious to reach Judge Bruin that he has himself rowed ahead of the flotilla in a keelboat. He reaches Bayou Pierre the morning of January 10. Judge Bruin has the reputation of being a hard drinker. Burr finds him in a state. Burr is shown the President's proclamation. He is told that Acting Governor Cowles Mead of Mississippi has called out the militia with orders to arrest him. He is handed an issue of the *Mississippi Messenger* containing a transcription of his cipher message. For the first time Burr learns that Wilkinson has betrayed him.

He slips back into the role of injured innocence. Skillfully he fences for terms with Cowles Mead. Mead later declared that Burr's statements were so strange he doubted his sanity. After surrendering on terms to the civil authority, Burr lets himself be taken to Natchez. Friends stand bail.

Again Burr finds himself the toast of Federalist dinners. The ladies ply him with dainties. In Natchez he has a host of defenders. Another grand jury refuses to find him guilty of an indictable offense and furthermore issues a presentment against General Wilkinson's illegal arrests of suspected persons in New Orleans.

The presiding judge, Thomas Rodney, an administration supporter, has a different view. His son Caesar Augustus has just been appointed Attorney General of the United States. Judge Rodney refuses to lift Burr's bond.

News comes of the apprehension of Bollman and Swartwout. General Wilkinson has offered five thousand dollars for Burr's capture, living or dead. Burr knows the General well enough to be sure that, with all he knows, Wilkinson would much prefer to have him dead. Panic seizes the usually imperturbable conspirator. Nothing for it but to jump his bail and vanish into the wilderness.

From hiding, Burr tries to send a last message to his men. It is a note stitched into the Colonel's old overcoat worn by a slave boy. "If you are yet together keep together and

I will join you tomorrow night—in the mean time put *all* your arms in perfect order. Ask the bearer no questions but tell him all you may think I wish to know.—He does not know this is from me, nor where I am."

The boy is apprehended, the note discovered. Immediately Acting Governor Mead encircles Burr's camp with militia and arrests every man he can lay hands on.

Burr, with Major Robert Ashley for a guide, is already riding desperately off through the forest toward the Spanish border—and to capture at Carson's Ferry.

Attorney for the Defense

Theodosia had hurried back to South Carolina with her husband and little Gampillo as soon as it became clear that her father's castle in the air had collapsed. On March 27 Burr wrote her from Richmond: "My military escort having arrived at Fredericksburg on our way to Washington, there met a special messenger, with orders to convey me to this place. . . . I am to be surrendered to the civil authority tomorrow, when the question of bail is to be determined. In the mean time I remain at the Eagle Tavern."

While all Richmond buzzed with the excitement of his arrival, Burr was busy with a tailor rigging him more suitable apparel than the boatman's trousers and floppy felt hat that were already notorious. The consummate actor was preparing to play his greatest role. He managed somehow to secure funds and to get in touch with well-wishers willing to stand bail. Around noon on March 30, in a private room of the Eagle Tavern, he was brought before Chief Justice John Marshall for pre-trial examination.*

The government's case was in the hands of an ardent Republican, George Hay, United States District Attorney for Virginia, since Blennerhassett's island on the Ohio, the chief scene of the alleged crimes, was within the confines of that enormous commonwealth.

On behalf of Burr appeared two of the most esteemed members of the Richmond bar: portly Edmund Randolph, one-time governor of Virginia, and John Wickham, a Long Island man, accused by the Republicans of Tory antecedents.

George Hay presented a copy of the evidence on which the Attorney General had based his charges against Bollman and Swartwout when they appeared in Washington, shipped north under armed escort by General Wilkinson. Nicholas Perkins told a plain tale of Burr's arrest. Hay moved forthwith that the prisoner be committed on the charge of high misdemeanor in preparing a military expedition against the dominions of the king of Spain. Further, he contended that the prisoner had com-

* Until 1891, Justices of the Supreme Court, including the Chief Justice, regularly heard cases in the federal circuit courts as well.

Burr's men on the Mississippi, en route to New Orleans

mitted acts of treason in gathering a force of armed men with the intention of seizing the city of New Orleans, fomenting a revolt in the Orleans Territory, and separating the western states from the Union. Hay referred to the interpretation of treason promulgated by the Supreme Court in the Chief Justice's own words only a month before, when Bollman and Swartwout were freed on a writ of habeas corpus. This decision seemed to describe the assembling of armed men for a treasonable purpose as treason. Since argument by counsel would be necessary on this motion, all parties agreed to move the proceedings up the hill to the courtroom in the state's new Ionic capitol, designed by Thomas Jefferson.

Next morning the Chief Justice appeared betimes on the bench. William Wirt, who was himself soon to join the prosecution, had described John Marshall a couple of years before as "in person tall, meagre and emaciated. His head and face are small in proportion to his height, his complexion swarthy, the muscles of his face relaxed . . . his countenance has a faithful expression of great good humor and hilarity; while his black eyes . . . possess an irradiating spirit which proclaims the imperial powers of his mind. . . . His voice is hard and dry; his attitude . . . often extremely awkward; as it was not unusual for him to stand with his left foot in advance, while all his gesture proceeded from his right arm. . . . His eloquence consists in the apparently deep selfconviction, and emphatic earnestness of his manner."

Attorney General Rodney was waiting to address the court before leaving for Washington. Burr's lawyers were eager to begin the defense. The crowded courtroom waited, breathless. Colonel Burr appeared half an hour late, announcing with a debonair smile that he had mistaken the hour.

Since the stairways and lobbies were packed with Richmonders trying to get in, proceedings were adjourned to the hall of the House of Delegates. Burr's lawyers launched into their argument: intent was no basis for a charge of treason; according to the Constitution the crime of treason had to be an overt act, sworn to by two witnesses. Colonel Burr rose and in his most courtly manner pointed out that he had already been acquitted of all these charges in Kentucky and Mississippi; that in each case he himself had sought an investigation; that he had not forfeited his bond by fleeing the jurisdiction of any court, but had merely retired to avoid the illegal seizure of his person and property by a military force.

Burr had failed as a revolutionist, but he remained matchless as a courtroom lawyer. As the proceedings advanced, he regained all his aplomb. This was a world he knew how to deal with. Attack was the best defense. His safety depended on turning the case into a political wrangle between Federalists and Republicans. President Jefferson was personally directing the prosecution from Washington. The leading Federalists were rushing to Burr's defense. The prosecution's case must rest on Wilkinson. Burr now felt that the ranting Commanding General, whom a few weeks back he had relied on as his partner in high adventure, would be the easiest man in the world to discredit. Burr

knew that the Chief Justice hated Jefferson as hard as he himself did. If he could attack Jefferson through Wilkinson, he could not help winning John Marshall's sympathy. On the whole, in the crucial game that was about to be played, Burr held a good hand of cards.

The Chief Justice declared he preferred at this point not to commit Burr for treason, but that he felt the evidence sufficient to commit him for high misdemeanor. In explaining his decision, John Marshall pointed out what was to be the nub of the defense: As he interpreted the wording of the cipher letter, admitting that that document should turn out to be genuine, it pointed to an attack against the Spanish dominions instead of to a treasonable enterprise against New Orleans. Therefore, until the government presented more evidence he would hold Colonel Burr for misdemeanor only. Treason had to be proved by two witnesses. As to the proof of treason: "More than five weeks have elapsed since the opinion of the supreme court has declared the necessity of proving the fact if it exists. Why is it not proved?"

Treason would not have been a bailable charge, but misdemeanor was. Bail was set at ten thousand dollars, and later in the afternoon Colonel Burr presented five securities, entered into recognizance for that sum to appear before the circuit court on May 22, and walked out a free man.

Aaron Burr emerged from this first phase of his trial the hero of all the Federalist mansions scattered along the hilltops of Richmond, where detestation of Jefferson was becoming the password to social acceptance. Invitations poured in. The afternoon he dined with John Wickham in celebration of the initial victories of the defense, John Marshall was of the party. Wickham and the Chief Justice were warm and confidential friends. Wickham had been thoughtful enough to warn Marshall that the dinner was for Aaron Burr. Marshall, who loved a good dinner, said he'd come anyway. According to his friends he did sit at the other end of the table, had no direct communication with the accused man, and left early. But this incident did not pass unnoticed by the Republican press, which denounced the Chief Justice's conduct as "grossly indecent."

The President's Dilemma

Jefferson was anxiously studying every letter and newspaper that came in from Richmond. He could see right away that George Hay was no match for Burr's Federalist lawyers. Besides Randolph and Wickham, the little colonel had engaged two of the brightest of the younger Virginia attorneys, Benjamin Botts and John Baker. The President had heard too that Luther Martin, one of his bitter personal enemies, was on his way from Annapolis to join the defense counsel. The ablest lawyers, it seemed, tended to be Federalists. The President had to make do with what Republicans he could collect. He arranged to have Alexander McRae, a gruff Scot who was lieutenant governor of Virginia, assist in the prosecution, and got off an express to William Wirt, who was trying a case in Williamsburg, engaging him for the government. Young Wirt was generally thought of as a coming man.

Jefferson was exasperated by the difficulties the Chief Justice was putting in the way of the prosecution. From Monticello he wrote William B. Giles, the administration leader in the Senate, commenting testily on "the newborn zeal for the liberties of those whom we would not permit to overthrow the liberties of their country." Against Burr personally, he added, "I never had one hostile sentiment. I never indeed thought him an honest, frank-dealing man, but considered him as a crooked gun, or other perverted machine, whose aim or shot you could never be sure of."

Burr, on his side, was taking high ground in his letters to Theodosia: "Was there in Greece or Rome a man of virtue and independence, and supposed to possess great talents, who was not the object of vindictive and unrelenting persecution?"

Burr complained that the panel from which a grand jury was to be selected was composed of twenty Republicans and only four Federalists. A few days later William Wirt, still stoutly maintaining that John Marshall was a fair-minded man, was facing the fact that by insistence on a technicality the court had limited the number of grand jurors to sixteen, "and consequently the chance of the concurrence of 12 in finding a Bill was reduced to a minimum," as he explained when he got time to write an account of the trial to his foster brother Ninian Edwards in Kentucky. "Burr and his counsel were filled with triumph at the prospect that there would be no Bill found—they displayed their triumph very injudiciously."

After all challenges were exhausted, the list of grand jurors selected turned out to be a roster of some of the ablest men in Virginia. When the Chief Justice chose John Randolph of Roanoke as foreman, the Federalist dinner tables rocked with satisfaction. Nobody could accuse Marshall of bias; he had chosen a Republican; but of all Republicans, John Randolph was the least friendly to Jefferson. The erstwhile administration leader in the House was now making a career of opposition to the man he was coming to jeer at as "St. Thomas of Cantingbury."

As May wore on, Richmond filled to overflowing with curious visitors. The Burr trial was the greatest show in the history of the commonwealth. Every bed in every inn was taken. Every house was stuffed with guests sleeping on truckle beds in the attics. Every stable and shed had its complement of horses and gigs. Coaches and carriages encumbered the inn yards. Families of country people came in covered wagons and camped in the open lots. The streets were brilliant with uniforms of the Army and Navy and of various militia organizations. The ladies all wore their best.

Though many Republicans were wagering that Colonel Burr would jump his bail again, on the morning of May 22 the little colonel was seen flitting among his lawyers, cool as a cucumber, wearing a neat suit of black silk, with his hair carefully powdered and tied in a queue. Judge Cyrus Griffin, George Washington's appointee to the Virginia district court, joined the Chief Justice on the bench.

From day to day the crowds were disappointed. The trial marked time. The Chief Justice would not allow the grand jury to start examining witnesses until General Wilkinson arrived. Aaron Burr's friends scoffed loudly as May passed into June. The General would never dare show his face.

While the grand jurors sat idly deploring their wasted days, counsel for both sides entertained the courtroom with rambling arguments over the nature of treason and the amount of the prisoner's bail.

On May 28 the session was enlivened by the appearance of Luther Martin on behalf of Colonel Burr. Martin had been carrying on a vendetta with Thomas Jefferson for years. A great wassailer and brandy-drinker, fast drifting into helpless alcoholism, Luther Martin was a prey to violent hatreds and affections. But he was also the leading lawyer of his native Maryland, and he had taken a fancy to Aaron Burr.

When Burr, who never let an opportunity pass of playing up to the Chief Justice, did the handsome thing to end the dispute over bail by offering to raise his security to twenty thousand dollars "so that the court should not be embarrassed," Luther Martin stood up and offered himself as one of the sureties.

Confrontation at the Bar

On June 13, a Saturday, the news spread that General Wilkinson with a suite of witnesses had disembarked from a U.S. Navy schooner and was on his way to Richmond. George Hay reported to the court that only the fatigue of the journey prevented the General from presenting himself that very day.

The General in Chief had every reason to be fatigued. For three months Wilkinson had been charging about New Orleans in a state of frenzy. To clear his own skirts he had blown up such a bogey out of Burr's schemes that he ended by frightening himself. He kept the city under martial law. He set his troops to digging earthworks and building palisades. He sent out squads to arrest Burr's associates. Though Burr himself had slipped through his fingers, Wilkinson pounced on an old friend, John Adair, in town by prearrangement with the conspirators, and marched him off from his dinner table at the inn to the city prison. Wilkinson could not rest easy until every man jack who knew of his complicity in Burr's conspiracy was behind bars.

In February the General's wife died at the house of a hospitable Creole planter who was serving as the General's aide. Shattered with grief, Wilkinson lingered on in New Orleans in spite of insistent requests from Washington that he come north immediately to testify in Burr's trial. Meanwhile he tried to distract the administration from the clamor against his arbitrary acts by thundering letters about the torrent of Burrites that was about to descend on him.

Finally, with his son James for an aide and in company with a large band of witnesses under subpoena, he embarked May 20, 1807, for Hampton Roads.

As soon as the news of General Wilkinson's safe arrival was confirmed, the court began to swear witnesses for the grand jury. Two veterans of the naval war with France, Commodore Truxtun and Captain Decatur, led the way, along with Benjamin Stoddert, who had been John Adams' Secretary of the Navy. When Erich Bollman's turn came, George Hay tried rather clumsily to hand him the presidential pardon he had so eagerly sought in return for the information he gave during an interview with Jefferson and

Madison back in Washington. But Bollman had changed his mind. He had been feted by the Richmond Federalists as a minor hero of Burr's odyssey. Emboldened by the atmosphere of success in Burr's camp, he now refused to accept any pardon. Luther Martin hastily explained that Bollman preferred to rely on the constitutional guarantee that no man would be forced to testify against himself. The court sent him in to the grand jury anyway.

On Monday, June 15, the halls and lobbies of the capitol were jammed with people. General Wilkinson was on his way up the hill. Crowds stumbled panting after him. Men and boys hung from the window ledges and climbed the great trees on the eroded slope, craning their necks for a glimpse of the actors in the grand confrontation.

Men's accounts of the scene in the Hall of Delegates varied according to their political persuasions. Washington Irving, who reported the trial for a Burrite newspaper in New York, said Wilkinson "strutted into court . . . swelling like a turkey cock." David Robertson, the stenographer, described the General's countenance as "calm, dignified and commanding while that of Colonel Burr was marked by a haughty contempt."

Wirt's description in his letter to Ninian Edwards was possibly more discerning. "In the midst of all this hurly-burly came Wilkinson and his suite, like Pope's fame 'unlooked for' at least by Burr's partisans. It was curious to mark the interview between Burr and Wilkinson. There was no nature in it—they had anticipated the meeting and resolved on the countenance which they would wear—Wilkinson had been some time within the bar before Burr would look towards him affecting not to know he was there until Hay introduced him by saying to the court: 'It is my wish that General Wilkinson, who is now before the court, should be qualified and sent up to the Grand Jury.' At the words 'who is now before the court,' Burr started in his chair, turned quickly and fastened a look of scorn and contempt on Wilkinson—Wilkinson bowing to the court on his introduction did not receive Burr's first glance; but his bow finished, he turned his face down on Burr and looked with all the sullenness and protervity of a big black bull—Burr withdrew his eyes composedly and that was the end of it."

Wilkinson himself described the scene in a letter to President Jefferson in his own inimitable style. "I saluted the Bench & in spite of myself my eyes darted a flash of indignation at the little Traitor on whom they continued fixed until I was called to the Book—The Lyon hearted Eagle Eyed Hero, sinking under the weight of conscious guilt, with haggard Eye, made an Effort to meet the indignant salutation of outraged Honor, but it was in vain, his audacity failed Him, He averted his face, grew pale & affected passion to conceal his perturbation."

As soon as Wilkinson had taken the oath, he was sent to the grand jury. He had dressed in his best in the commanding general's uniform of his own devising. His enormous gold epaulets glittered in the light pouring through the tall windows. He wore his famous gold spurs, and his heavily encrusted sword trailed on the ground. John Randolph, the foreman, immediately piped up that the marshal must take

that man out and disarm him.

It was soon clear that the jurymen were set to give the General a hard time. John Randolph had discovered that the copies of Burr's and Dayton's cipher messages which had been in the General's hands had been tampered with. Phrases had been erased, words written in. The grand jurors kept asking the General why, since he claimed he'd first learned of Burr's plot from Swartwout in October, he had let a whole month go by before warning Governor Claiborne that an attack on New Orleans was imminent? In fact, wasn't Wilkinson guilty too? And when the grand jury came to vote its indictments, a motion to add Wilkinson's name to the list of defendants was just barely lost, seven to nine.

John Randolph was furious: "But the mammoth of iniquity escaped," he wrote a friend; "not that any man pretended to think him *innocent,* but upon certain wire-drawn distinctions that I will not pester you with. W——n is the only man that I ever saw who was from the bark to the very core a villain."

While the grand jury was closeted day after day in one part of the capitol, at the public sessions in the Hall of Delegates Burr and his lawyers hammered on a similar theme—that the true traitor of the piece was Wilkinson; instead of being a witness for the prosecution he should be in the prisoners' dock.

On Wednesday, June 24, Burr's attorneys brought in a motion for the attachment of the person of General Wilkinson. While this motion was being argued, word went around that the grand jury was about to bring in an indictment. Every man who could puffed up the hill to the capitol. At two o'clock that afternoon, as one of Burr's lawyers was arguing for the attachment of General Wilkinson (who, since he had emerged from his ordeal, was sitting brazen with self-righteousness among the government lawyers), John Randolph led his sober-faced jurors into court and laid several indictments on the clerk's table.

The clerk read out the endorsements: True bills against Burr and Blennerhassett for treason and misdemeanor.

In his letter to Ninian Edwards, Wirt described with relish the consternation in the camp of the defense: "When the grand-jury came down with the Bills against Burr and Blennerhassett, I never saw such a group of shocked faces. The chief justice, who is a very dark man, shrunk back with horror upon his seat and turned black. He kept his eyes fixed on Burr with an expression of sympathy so agonizing and horror so deep & overwhelming that he seemed for two or three seconds to have forgotten where & who he was. I observed him & saw him start from his reverie under the consciousness that he was giving away too much of his feelings and look around upon the multitude to see if he had been noticed. . . ."

The Chief Justice had no choice but to order Burr to the public jail, although he was moved the following day to a comfortable guarded room in a private house where Luther Martin lodged. Meanwhile the grand jury was deliberating further indictments, and John Randolph asked the court's assistance in obtaining a copy of a letter postmarked May 13, 1806, written by James Wilkinson, to which Burr's cipher letter was thought to be an answer. The members of the grand jury were aware that they could not ask the accused to present material which might incriminate him but hoped he would facilitate their inquiry into the facts. John Randolph was hinting that the letter might incriminate Wilkinson.

The Chief Justice replied dryly that the jurors were quite right in their opinion that the accused could not be required to incriminate himself.

Colonel Burr rose and in his most disarming manner declared that it would be impossible for him "to expose any letter which had been communicated to him confidentially." He added, with that suggestion of the steel claw under the velvet glove of which he was a master, that he was not then prepared to decide "how far the extremity of circumstances might impel him to such action."

Mr. McRae of the prosecution interposed that General Wilkinson had informed him that he wished to have the whole of the correspondence between Colonel Burr and himself exhibited before the court. Wilkinson was referring to other letters in his possession even more damaging to Burr.

Burr replied sarcastically that the General was "welcome to all the éclat which he may expect to derive from his challenge," but that the letter postmarked May 13 would not be produced. "The letter is not at this time in my possession and General Wilkinson knows it."

Even in their deadly grapple a curious intimacy persisted between the two men. Each knew how the other's mind worked. Each was telegraphing to the other that he held in his possession the evidence needed to convict him. Whoever produced any more damaging correspondence would do so at his own risk.

The grand jury promptly returned with a new set of indictments presenting ex-Senator Jonathan Dayton of New Jersey and Senator John Smith of Ohio, along with Comfort Tyler, Israel Smith, and Davis Floyd, who had been Burr's agents in organizing the expedition, as guilty of treason and of levying war against the United States on Blennerhassett's island in Wood County, Virginia, on December 13, 1806.

A few days later Burr was removed to the penitentiary which Benjamin Latrobe, the architect of the south wing of the U.S. Capitol, had designed and recently completed for the commonwealth of Virginia.

Burr seems to have been happy under the cool, vaulted ceilings of his new quarters. It was at least a protection from his creditors, who were getting ready to place Colonel Burr in debtors' prison whenever they could lay hands on him.

"I have three rooms in the third story of the penitentiary," Burr wrote Theodosia, "making an extent of a hundred feet. My jailer is quite a polite and civil man—altogether unlike the idea one would form of a jailer. You would have laughed to have heard our compliments last evening."

The jailer apologized for having to keep the door locked after dark. Burr replied that he would prefer it, to keep out intruders. When the jailer told him lights would have to be extinguished at nine, Colonel Burr said that was quite impossible because he never went to bed before midnight. "As you please, Sir," said the jailer.

Under the plea that travelling back and forth between the penitentiary and the capitol would be too great a tax on the accused and his lawyers during the sessions of the trial, Burr, accompanied by his seven guards, was again removed in the first days of August to a private house. His suite at the prison was promptly occupied by the chief victim of his impostures, Harman Blennerhassett.

Poor Blanny had been taken into custody by the federal marshal in Kentucky, where he had already fallen into the clutches of Burr's creditors, bent on attaching his person and property. He called in Henry Clay as his counsel and with Clay's help held off the bailiffs by producing a letter from Joseph Alston which promised to assume at least part of the indebtedness. Mrs. Blennerhassett meanwhile was struggling to exist with their two boys in Natchez.

When the Alstons arrived they took over Burr's old quarters in Luther Martin's house. "I want an independent and discerning witness to my conduct and to that of the government," Burr had written Theodosia. ". . . I should never invite anyone, much less those so dear to me, to witness my disgrace. I may be immured in dungeons, chained, murdered in legal form, but I cannot be humiliated or disgraced. If absent you will suffer much solicitude. In my presence you will feel none, whatever be the *malice* or the *power* of my enemies. . . ."

People were beginning to lose interest in Burr's machinations. It was the prospect of a war with England that worried them now. Late in June the British frigate *Leopard* had made an unprovoked attack on the American frigate *Chesapeake* off Cape Henry, and indignation was sweeping the country. The government witnesses had scattered to the hills.

The trial proper began on August 3. When Chief Justice Marshall appeared on the bench at noon, George Hay for the prosecution was forced shamefacedly to confess that he had not the witnesses on hand he needed to present his case. Again court was adjourned. It was not till the following Monday that enough government witnesses assembled to justify impanelling a jury. A number of jurors were rejected because they admitted having formed an opinion, like a certain Mr. Bucky, that whether treason were proved or not, Colonel Burr ought to be hung.

George Hay's prosecution never recovered its impetus, even though the people in general agreed with Mr. Bucky. In spite of William Wirt's flights of oratory, his fanciful description of the beauties of Blennerhassett's island before Burr arrived like the serpent in Eden, Burr and his lawyers retained the offensive.

President Jefferson could give only half his mind to the Burr trial. Yet the conviction of Burr had become an idea so fixed that it clouded his judgment. At one point he wrote Hay, after reading some particularly intemperate remarks by Luther Martin, that if "Old Brandy Bottle," as Martin was popularly called, was such a good friend of Burr's, maybe he should be indicted himself.

The administration was in a dilemma. To make a proper case against Burr they had to inculpate Wilkinson, and yet the President and his two advisers, Secretary of State James Madison and Secretary of the Treasury Albert Gallatin, had decided that the state of affairs in New Orleans demanded that, come what may, they support the General. The prosecution's case against Burr—though a procession of witnesses from the rank and file of those whom Burr had deceived produced evidence enough to convict him of all sorts of other crimes—depended on John Marshall's broad definition of treason as the assembling of armed men—the definition advanced by the Chief Justice in the habeas corpus proceedings against Bollman and Swartwout. George Hay made no effort to prove that Aaron Burr was present when the overt acts were committed by his armed forces assembled on Blennerhassett's island.

But on August 31, John Marshall seemed to shift his ground. Admitting that there were times when the Supreme Court might be called upon to reconsider its judgments, he explained away the phrases in his previous definition of treason which might imply that conspiracy to assemble armed men was sufficient to establish guilt. "The present indictment charges the prisoner with levying war against the United States, and alleges an overt act of levying war. That overt act must be proved, according to the mandates of the constitution and of the act of congress, by two witnesses. It is not proved by a single witness."

The Chief Justice furthermore ruled that since the overt act had not been proved, "corroborative or confirmatory testimony" was not admissible. This ruling by one scratch of the pen threw out all the testimony as to Burr's performances on the Mississippi and the Ohio which the prosecution had gone to such pains to collect. As was his wont, the Chief Justice presented his opinion in writing, and at great length.

The court adjourned to give District Attorney Hay time to read it over. Next morning he threw up the case. His swarm of witnesses had been ruled out unheard. He would leave it to the jury.

After twenty-five minutes the jury returned to the hall. The verdict was read by the foreman, this time the much-respected Colonel Edward Carrington. "We of the jury say that Aaron Burr is not proved to be guilty under this indictment by any evidence submitted to us."

Burr immediately objected to the form of the verdict. Luther Martin asked if the jury intended to censure the court for suppressing testimony. Members of the jury, as politely as they could, made it clear that that was exactly what they did intend. The Chief Justice, in his offhand manner, ended the imbroglio by suggesting that the verdict stand as written but that "Not guilty" be entered in the record.

The Case Falls Apart

The threat of the gallows was lifted, but the sun had not come out for Aaron Burr. He was no sooner freed of the indictment for treason than he found himself attached for debt in a civil suit. Somehow he managed to find surety to the amount of $36,000.

Emboldened by the favorable verdict in Burr's case, Jonathan Dayton emerged from hiding and appeared in court with an affidavit to the effect that he had not been on Blennerhassett's island in December, 1806. Hay entered a nolle prosequi. And when Harman Blennerhassett was brought into court the next day, his case was treated in the same way.

There was still the "misdemeanor" charge, the considerable misdemeanor of mounting an expedition against Spanish territories. Burr and the rest were admitted to bail on that. And while they waited, Blanny dogged Burr's footsteps; he kept writing the little colonel begging for an explanation. He and his family were penniless. Colonel Burr must propose some plan for repaying the money he owed him. Whenever he managed to see Burr, that gentleman was surrounded by friends and remarkably inattentive to talk of a financial settlement. Blennerhassett then sought out Alston. All Alston would talk about was how he himself was fifty thousand dollars in the hole. At last Burr granted Blanny a private interview. Burr wanted to know which influential men Blanny could introduce him to in England.

To his diary Blennerhassett confided his hopes that in exchange for letters to people of rank Burr might be induced to start repaying the money he owed, but when Blanny hinted at this *quid pro quo,* Burr would talk only of his projects. The new aggressive mood showing itself at the British Foreign Office would provide just the climate he needed for getting backing for his plan of disunion. "He is as gay as usual," Blanny noted, "and as busy in speculations on reorganizing his projects for action as if he had never suffered the least interruption."

The misdemeanor trial proved to be more of a trial of General Wilkinson than of Aaron Burr. The lawyers for the prosecution had lost heart. Important papers were mislaid. They had only the most perfunctory assistance from the Attorney General, and the result was another series of verdicts of Not Guilty. Other charges in Ohio were never pressed.

Aaron Burr departed for Philadelphia. Already he was trying to recruit young men to form his suite on his projected journey to England. Blennerhassett followed in his trail, still hopeful of a settlement of his claims.

A mob threatening tar and feathers caused them to hurry through Baltimore. In Philadelphia Blanny noted that the Colonel as usual moved in the best circles. Finding himself one of a crowd of creditors whom Burr always managed to avoid, Blanny gave up. Travelling under assumed names and under strange disguises, Aaron Burr managed to shake loose from his creditors long enough to get himself smuggled aboard a packet boat for England. One of his last acts in New York was to borrow a few dollars from his German cook, who, knowing his master, made him leave the deed to a trunkload of personal effects as security.

The Last Years

Burr's wanderings during his years of exile in Europe were as puzzling as his performances on the western waters. In England he ingratiated himself with Jeremy Bentham, the political economist whose utilitarian theories Burr claimed to find admirable. Bentham put him up and furnished him with funds while the little colonel tried to interest the government in the conquest of Mexico. When Lord Liverpool's administration turned his proposition down, and sought to expel him from Great Britain, Burr had the effrontery to claim that, having been born under King George, he was a British subject. He ran up so many bills that he had to take it on the run, nevertheless, to escape imprisonment for debt, and retired to Sweden. There he panhandled his way from nobleman's seat to nobleman's seat, keeping all the while, expressly for the eyes of Theodosia and little Gampillo, his grandson, one of the most extraordinary journals in the history of the human mind.

Using a curious code compounded of German and English and Swedish and French, he noted, for the edification of the only two people he loved in the world, every single detail of an existence dedicated to a conscienceless depravity without match in confessional literature. He noted every subterfuge he indulged in to cadge a meal or a handout; every time he drank too much; his efforts to ease the vacant spirit with opium; every success with a woman, were she duchess or chambermaid; the price he paid his harlots and whether they were worth it or not. Intermingled were sparkling descriptions of weather and places, shrewd estimates of people, philosophical disquisitions on the meaninglessness of life, but never a word or a phrase that betrayed a moment's escape from the strait jacket of self-worship.

When he wore out his welcome in Sweden and Germany, he made his way to Paris. There he presented to the Emperor Napoleon's foreign office a fanciful scheme involving the re-conquest of Louisiana and Canada for France. The response of Burr's old idol was to have him watched by the police.

In the end Burr somehow managed to shake down the French foreign office for his passage home. In June of 1812 he slipped back into New York in disguise and was sheltered by such members of the Little Band as still retained political influence. He even ventured to open a law office on Nassau Street. He had barely settled in practice before a distracted letter reached him from Theodosia. His grandson was dead. He would never see Gampillo again. Desperate with grief,

Theodosia could think only of rejoining her father. Too ill to travel by land, she tried to run the British blockade and was lost at sea on the pilot boat *Patriot*.

Friends remarked how nobly Burr bore his affliction. Stoicism amid total disaster fitted into his philosophy. He managed to make a living at the law, surrounded himself with a new family of outcasts, unfortunate women and foster children, some of whom were reputed to be his own bastards and whose education he supervised with pedantic care. He lived on for years as one of New York's minor notorieties. Men pointed him out on the street to their sons as the wickedest man alive.

To the end he protested that his strange schemes were never intended to be detrimental to the United States. In 1833, at the age of seventy-seven, he married a woman to whom his name had been linked by gossip forty years before. As Mme. Jumel, the wife of a successful French wine merchant for twenty-eight years, Eliza Bowen had attained a certain respectability. Now she was reputed to be one of the wealthiest widows in New York. They had been married barely a year before Mme. Jumel sued him for divorce on the charge of adultery. Burr had laid his hands on large sums of her money to invest in the Texas land schemes of a beautiful young woman named Jane McManus. The decree was granted, on the testimony of a housemaid, the day Burr died. The end had come, after a series of strokes, at a hotel on the Staten Island shore to which friends had carried him on a stretcher—partly becaues he loved the sea breezes and partly to escape the persecution of clergymen who wanted to take the credit for the deathbed conversion of the wickedest man alive.

In a batch of Burr papers that turned up recently in the possession of the New-York Historical Society appear the court records of a proceeding for perjury brought against the housemaid who testified to his adultery. With Aaron Burr, in small things as in great, one can never be quite sure.

The sketch above and painting at right are from a series by Ben Shahn on the trial and execution of Bartolomeo Vanzetti and Nicola Sacco. **The Passion of Sacco and Vanzetti** *reveals Shahn's attitude toward the legal system. He featured the Lowell Committee which affirmed the fairness of the trial and included an approving Judge Thayer in the background.*

104

Four years ago Mr. Russell claimed in our pages that the central figures in the famous trial at Dedham had been unjustly executed. Now he has restudied the long record, held new ballistic tests, and reached a dramatic new conclusion. Should not the verdict be, he asks:

SACCO *GUILTY,*
VANZETTI *INNOCENT?*

By FRANCIS RUSSELL

The murders for which Nicola Sacco and Bartolomeo Vanzetti were convicted and finally executed were quick, simple, and brutal. On the afternoon of April 15, 1920, in the small shoe manufacturing town of South Braintree, Massachusetts, a paymaster, Frederick Parmenter, and his guard, Alessandro Berardelli, were shot and robbed as they walked down Pearl Street with the Slater & Morrill Shoe Company payroll—some fifteen thousand dollars in two metal boxes.

The paymaster and the guard, each carrying a box, had crossed the railroad tracks near the front of the Rice & Hutchins factory when two strangers who had been leaning against the fence there suddenly stepped toward them. The strangers were short, dark men. One wore a felt hat and the other, a cap. In a flash the first man whipped a pistol from his pocket and fired several shots into Berardelli. The guard dropped to the ground. Parmenter, a step in advance, turned and when he saw what was happening, started to run across the street. Before he reached the other side he was shot twice. He dropped his box and collapsed in the gutter. Witnesses—of which there were a number in the factory windows and along Pearl Street—were afterward uncertain whether one man or two had done the shooting, but most thought there had been two.

With Parmenter and Berardelli lying in the gravel, one of their assailants fired a signal shot, and a Buick touring car that had been parked near the Slater & Morrill factory now started jerkily up the rise. As it slowed down, the two bandits picked up the money boxes and climbed into the back seat. Berardelli had managed to get to his hands and knees. Seeing him wavering, a third man sprang from the car and fired another shot into him. It was a death wound.

The Buick continued along Pearl Street with five men in it, a gunman in the front seat firing at random at the crowd drawn by the sound of the shots. No one was hit, although one bystander had his coat lapel singed. The car gathered speed, swung left at the top of Pearl Street, and one of the men in the rear seat threw out handfuls of tacks to hinder any pursuit. The speeding car was noticed at intervals along a ten-mile stretch of road; then it vanished. Two days later it was found abandoned in the woods near Brockton, a dozen miles away.

Berardelli died within a few minutes, the final bullet having severed the great artery issuing from his heart. Parmenter too had received a fatal wound, a bullet cutting his inferior vena cava, the body's largest vein. He died early the following morning. At the autopsy two bullets were found in Parmenter and four in Berardelli. The county medical examiner, Dr. George Burgess Magrath, removed the bullets from Berardelli's body, scratching the base of each with a Roman numeral. The bullet that had cut the artery and that, from the angle of its path, he determined must have been fired while Berardelli was down, he marked III. It had struck the hipbone obliquely and was slightly bent from this glancing contact.

Of the six bullets, five had been fired from a .32 caliber pistol or pistols with a right-hand twist to the rifling. These bullets were of varied manufacture—three Peters and two Remingtons. The remaining bullet, the one Dr. Magrath marked III, was a Winchester of an obsolete type having a cannelure, or milling around the edge. It had been fired from a .32 caliber pistol with a left-hand twist. Only a Colt, among American pistols, had such a reverse twist. Four spent cartridges of the same caliber as the bullets were picked up in the gravel near Berardelli's body. Two of these were Peters, one a Remington, and one a Winchester later known as Shell W.

No weapons were found on the bodies, although Berardelli customarily carried a revolver with him. On March 19, 1920, he had taken his gun to the Iver Johnson Company in Boston to have it repaired. According to his wife, it needed a new spring. Lincoln Wadsworth, in charge of the repair department, recorded that on that day he had received a .38 caliber Harrington & Richardson revolver from Alex Berardelli and had sent the gun upstairs to the workshop. There the foreman, George Fitzemeyer, for some reason marked it as a .32 caliber Harrington & Richardson requiring a new hammer and ticketed it with a repair number.

No one at Iver Johnson's recorded the revolver's serial number. The store manager testified a year later at the trial that the company did not keep a record of deliveries of repaired guns, but he was certain this particular revolver had been delivered. All weapons in the repair department not called for by the year's end were sold and a record made of each sale. Since Berardelli's revolver was no longer in the store, and there was no record of its being sold, the manager insisted it must have been called for.

Several witnesses of the shooting said at the inquest that they saw one of the bandits stoop over Berardelli. Peter McCullum, peering out of the first floor cutting room of Rice & Hutchins after he heard the shots, saw a man putting a money box into the Buick while holding a "white" revolver in his other hand. A Harrington & Richardson revolver was nickel-plated and might well have seemed white in the sunlight. This may have been Berardelli's. It seems unlikely that the guard would have accompanied the paymaster

without being armed. And if he had a revolver, it is possible that one of the men who shot him may have reached down and taken it.

Sacco and Vanzetti were arrested almost by chance on the night of May 5, 1920. They had met earlier in the evening at Sacco's bungalow in Stoughton—a half-dozen miles from South Braintree—with two anarchist comrades, Mike Boda and Ricardo Orciani, to arrange about gathering up incriminating literature from other comrades for fear of government "Red" raids. Until a few months before this, Boda had been living in West Bridgewater ten miles away with another anarchist, Ferruccio Coacci, who had been taken away for deportation on April 17. Not until Coacci was at sea did the police come to suspect that he and Boda might have been concerned in the South Braintree holdup. Boda had left an old Overland touring car in a West Bridgewater garage to be repaired, and the four men were planning to pick it up that evening. Orciani and Boda left Stoughton on Orciani's motorcycle. Sacco and Vanzetti went by streetcar. Once they had arrived, Boda was unable to get the car from the forewarned proprietor. As the men argued, the proprietor's wife telephoned the police.

Sacco and Vanzetti were arrested in Brockton while riding back to Stoughton on the streetcar. The police found a .32 caliber Colt automatic tucked in Sacco's waistband. In the gun's clip were eight cartridges, with another in the chamber. Sacco had twenty-three more loose cartridges in his pocket. These, though all .32 caliber, were of assorted makes—sixteen Peters, seven U.S., six Winchesters of the obsolete type, and three Remingtons. Vanzetti was found to be carrying a Harrington & Richardson .38 caliber revolver, its five chambers loaded with two Remington and three U.S. bullets.

The day following their arrest the two men were questioned at some length by the district attorney, Frederick Katzmann. Sacco told Katzmann he had bought his automatic two years before on Hanover Street in Boston under an assumed name. He had paid sixteen or seventeen dollars for it, and at the same time he had bought an unopened box of cartridges.

Vanzetti said he had bought his revolver four or five years before, also under an assumed name, at some shop on Hanover Street and had paid eighteen dollars for it. He had also bought an unopened box of cartridges, all but six of which he had fired off on the beach at Plymouth.

At their trial fourteen months later the two men told very different stories. They both admitted they had lied when they were first questioned, but explained that they then thought they were being held

PICTURE CREDITS: UPPER LEFT, BOSTON *Globe;* CENTER AND UPPER AND LOWER RIGHT, JET PHOTOGRAPHERS, 1962; AND LOWER LEFT, BOSTON *Globe,* BY ED JENNER

VANZETTI'S
.38 REVOLVER

SACCO'S .32
AUTOMATIC

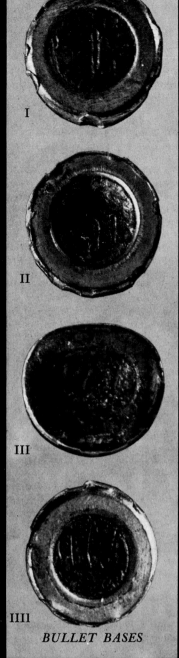

I

II

III

IIII

BULLET BASES

Among the key items which Mr. Russell dis-
cusses are the two pistols and the four bullets
taken from the body of the murdered guard.
The magnified base views show the numbers
scratched in them by the medical examiner;
much controversy once raged about whether
the "III" on the misshapen "mortal bullet"
differs in style from the other numbers. The
lead core of III is concave, whereas the others
are flat, for, as the side views show, the bullets
are of various makes. When Mr. Russell re-
examined them last year they were still in
sealed envelopes, ticketed (right) for ship-
ment to the Lowell Committee. He then made
new tests, one of which appears below, on October 11, 1961, as Colonel Frank Jury, New
Jersey firearms expert, fires Sacco's pistol into
wadded cotton at the Massachusetts Department of Public Safety ballistics laboratory.

18

Norfolk, ss.   Superior Court,

Nos. 5545 & 5546

Commonwealth

vs.

Sacco & Vanzetti

EXHIBIT 18

Mortal Bullet

"III"

From
Clerk of Courts
Dedham, Mass.

1927 JUN 9

SAME BULLETS: SIDE VIEWS

I   II   III   IIII

Vanzetti (left) and Sacco, in court before sentencing

because they were anarchists. They had lied, they said, partly because they were afraid and partly to protect their comrades. Indeed they had good reason to feel apprehensive about their anarchism, for there were rumors of new government Red raids, and only a few days before their arrest their comrade Salsedo had died mysteriously in New York while being held by federal agents.

Sacco's revised trial story was that he had bought the pistol in 1917 or 1918 in the small town where he was working. He had bought a box of cartridges on Hanover Street shortly afterward. The man who sold him the box filled it with various makes because of the wartime scarcity of cartridges.

Vanzetti now said that he had bought his revolver a few months before his arrest. Often he carried a hundred dollars or more with him from his fish business, and he felt he needed a gun to protect himself because of the many recent holdups. He had bought the revolver from a friend, Luigi Falzini. It was loaded when he bought it, and he had never fired it.

Falzini appeared in court, identified the revolver by certain rust spots and scratches as having belonged to him, and said he had bought it from Orciani. Another witness, Rexford Slater, testified that the revolver had originally belonged to him and that he had sold it to Orciani in the autumn of 1919.

Orciani had been arrested the day following the arrests of Sacco and Vanzetti. However, as he was able to provide a timecard alibi for his whereabouts on April 15, he was released. During the early part of the trial he acted as chauffeur for one of the defense attorneys, but although he was in the courthouse almost daily, he did not take the stand. Yet he was, as the district attorney pointed out in his summing up,

the missing link in the revolver's chain of ownership.

At the trial the prosecution contended that the automatic found on Sacco was the one that had fired Bullet III and that Vanzetti's revolver had been taken from the dying Berardelli. Several days before the ballistics testimony, two experts for the prosecution, Captain William Proctor of the Massachusetts State Police—then no more than a detective bureau—and Captain Charles Van Amburgh from the Remington Arms Company in Connecticut, fired a number of test shots from Sacco's automatic into oiled sawdust. Proctor and Van Amburgh were joined in these experiments by a defense expert, James Burns. After the test bullets were recovered they were then compared with Bullet III.

The trial testimony of the firearms experts on both sides was involved and confusing, "a wilderness of lands and grooves" as one reporter noted. In the opinion of the Gunther brothers, whose book on firearms identification has become a legal classic, all the ballistics evidence offered was so primitive as to be worthless.

Each tooled gun barrel, with its hundreds of minute striations, is unique. The one certain method of determining whether two separate bullets have been fired through any particular barrel is the use of a comparison microscope. Through this instrument the ends of the two bullets are brought together in one fused image. If the striations match, then it is practically certain that both bullets were fired from the same weapon.

Today the comparison microscope is the standard method of bullet identification. In 1920 it was just beginning to come into use, but it was not used in the Sacco-Vanzetti trial. There the experts attempted to measure the bullets with calipers and compare them with measurements made of a cast of the barrel of Sacco's pistol. It was a useless, haggling proceeding.

No one disputed that Bullet III had been fired from a Colt automatic, but Captain Proctor told District Attorney Katzmann before the trial that he did not believe it had been fired from Sacco's Colt. The prosecution was aware of Proctor's doubts when the captain was questioned in court. "My opinion is," Proctor said with a prearranged ambiguity that escaped the defense, "that it [Bullet III] is consistent with being fired by that pistol." The prosecution claimed that the Winchester cartridge among the four picked up near Berardelli had also been fired in Sacco's pistol. Comparing this cartridge with one fired on the test range, Proctor again used the word "consistent." Privately he had from the time of their arrest expressed doubt that Sacco and Vanzetti were guilty.

Two years after the trial he signed an affidavit saying that he had used the ambiguous phrase "consistent with" at Katzmann's request, but that if he had been asked directly in court whether he believed that Bullet III had been fired from Sacco's Colt, he would have replied No.

Captain Van Amburgh was scarcely more emphatic in his trial testimony: "I am inclined to believe," he said, "that the Number III bullet was fired from this Colt automatic pistol." Burns and a second defense expert, J. Henry Fitzgerald of the Colt Patent Firearms Company, denied this. In their opinion neither Bullet III nor Shell W, the Winchester cartridge, had any connection with Sacco's pistol.

Fitzemeyer, the Iver Johnson foreman, when handed Vanzetti's revolver on the witness stand and asked if it had been repaired recently, replied: "Well, a new hammer, I should call it, a new hammer."

In the summer of 1924 Captain Van Amburgh was appointed head of the newly formed ballistics laboratory of the Massachusetts State Police. Fortunately for his new career the repercussions of his blunder in the Harold Israel case had not yet reached Massachusetts. On February of that same year Father Dahme, a priest in Bridgeport, Connecticut, had been shot and killed as he was taking his customary evening walk. A week later a drifter by the name of Harold Israel was picked up by the police in nearby Norwalk. In Israel's pocket was a loaded .32 caliber revolver. Several witnesses identified him as the man they had seen shoot Father Dahme. Van Amburgh was called in to examine the ballistics evidence. He fired Israel's revolver and compared a test bullet with one taken from Father Dahme's body. Both bullets, he reported, had come from the same weapon. Later, however, five experts from the Remington Arms Company plus another from the New York Police Department examined the bullets and were of the unanimous opinion that the bullet that had killed Father Dahme could not have been fired from Israel's revolver. Israel was then released.

Captain Van Amburgh remained head of the state police laboratory until his retirement in 1946. During his earlier years there he developed a device called a spiralgraph with which he was able to make strip photographs of bullets as they revolved on a turntable. By comparing the strips of two bullets, he maintained he could determine whether or not they had been fired from the same gun. Later he made such comparative photographs of Bullet III and the test bullets of the Sacco-Vanzetti case. These photographs he used for demonstrations when he testified in the 1923 Hamilton-Proctor motion, one of the many filed requesting a new trial for Sacco and Vanzetti.

The Hamilton-Proctor motion was based in part on Captain Proctor's affidavit as to what he had really believed when he testified at the trial, although Proctor himself had died before the motion could be argued. In addition to his affidavit, there was further evidence offered by a post-trial defense expert, Dr. Albert Hamilton, that Bullet III could not have come from Sacco's Colt.

Dr. Hamilton would never have been engaged by the lawyers for Sacco and Vanzetti if they had known more about his background. His doctor's degree was self-awarded. He had started out in Auburn, New York, as a small-town druggist and concoctor of patent medicines. Over the years behind the counter he developed expertness at a second career, advertising himself in a publicity pamphlet as a qualified expert in chemistry, microscopy, handwriting, ink analysis, typewriting, photography, fingerprints, toxicology, gunshot wounds, guns and cartridges, bullet identifi-

The great funeral procession for Sacco and Vanzetti moves up Hanover Street in Boston after their execution in 1927. To thousands of the deeply committed it was a moment of sorrow and angry frustration; argument gave way to faith, and the dead anarchists were elevated into a kind of sainthood.

Even tests made back in the 1920's, before Sacco's execution, point to his gun as a murder weapon. This highly magnified composite picture brings together half of a test shell (top) fired from Sacco's pistol and half of Shell W (bottom), found near the murdered guard, so arranged as to show clearly how a pattern of vertical scratches, or markings, meet and match across the bases of the two shells. While the shells do not otherwise make a complete fit, having been fired on a different axis, these telltale markings prove to the satisfaction of experts that both shells struck the same breechblock. And each pistol's hand-finished breechblock is as individual as a man's fingerprint.

cation, gunpowder, nitroglycerine, dynamite, high explosives, blood and other stains, causes of death, embalming, and anatomy.

In 1915 Hamilton had come a cropper when he appeared as an expert for the prosecution in the New York trial of Charles Stielow, accused of murdering his housekeeper. According to Hamilton's testimony, a bullet taken from the housekeeper's body could only have come from Stielow's revolver. Principally because of this testimony Stielow was found guilty and sentenced to death. Yet later he was pardoned after it was shown by more competent experts that the death bullet could not have come from this revolver.

Hamilton's career survived even this devastating reverse. When he appeared in Boston to testify in the Proctor-Hamilton motion, he had the respectable assistance of Augustus Gill, a professor of chemical analysis at the Massachusetts Institute of Technology. Hamilton now claimed that by the measurements he had made under the microscope he was able to determine that the test bullets offered in evidence at the trial had been fired from Sacco's pistol but that Bullet III had not. Professor Gill corroborated this opinion. Hamilton also maintained that the hammer in Vanzetti's revolver was not new, since an essential screw did not show marks of having been removed.

In answering for the prosecution Captain Van Amburgh had become much more positive than he had been at the trial. He displayed his strip photographs, declaring that he was now "absolutely certain" that Bullet III and Shell W had been fired in Sacco's pistol.

Toward the close of the hearing, Hamilton appeared in court with two new .32 caliber Colt automatics that he said he wanted to compare with Sacco's pistol. Before Judge Webster Thayer and the lawyers for both sides, he disassembled all three pistols and placed their parts in three piles on a table in front of the judge's bench. Then, picking up various parts one by one, he explained their function and pointed out their interchangeability. Finally he reassembled the pistols, putting his own two back in his pocket and handing Sacco's to the clerk of court.

Just as Hamilton was leaving the courtroom Judge Thayer called him back and ordered him to hand over the two pistols in his pocket to be impounded. He did so. Two months later when Van Amburgh was again examining Sacco's pistol, he noticed that the barrel, previously fouled with rust, appeared bright and sparkling as if it were brand-new. At once he realized that there had been a substitution of barrels and that if the gun were now fired it would produce very different markings on the bullets. He notified Assistant District Attorney Williams, who went at once to Judge Thayer. After a private hearing Thayer ordered an

investigation. This was held in the following three weeks with only Van Amburgh, Hamilton, the district attorney, and a defense lawyer present.

At the opening of the investigation the three pistols were brought in. The briefest examination made it clear that Sacco's Colt had acquired a new barrel. Its original fouled barrel was now found to be in one of Hamilton's pistols. Everyone in the room was aware that Hamilton must have made the substitution when he disassembled the three guns in court, and the district attorney now accused him of trying to work up grounds for a new trial. Unabashed, Hamilton maintained that someone connected with the prosecution had made the switch. At the conclusion of the investigation Thayer passed no judgment as to who had switched the barrels but merely noted that the rusty barrel in the new pistol had come from Sacco's Colt. In concluding he ordered this barrel replaced and the three pistols delivered into the clerk's custody "without prejudice to either side." The prejudice, however, was not so easily erased. To the end Hamilton was a detriment, expensive, untrustworthy, and untrusted.

In the six years that had elapsed between the conviction of Sacco and Vanzetti and the passing of the death sentence on them in 1927, the case had expanded from its obscure beginnings to become an international issue of increasing turbulence. Finally in June, 1927, the governor of Massachusetts appointed a three-man committee headed by President A. Lawrence Lowell of Harvard to review the case.

The ballistics issue had remained dormant since Judge Thayer's rejection of the Proctor-Hamilton motion. Just before the Lowell Committee hearings, still another expert, Major Calvin Goddard, arrived in Boston with a comparison microscope, with which he offered to make without charge what he maintained would be conclusive tests on the Sacco-Vanzetti shells and bullets. The prosecution had no objections. William Thompson, the conservative Boston lawyer who had taken charge of the defense, would not approve of the tests but agreed not to try to prevent them.

Goddard made his tests June 3 before Professor Gill, a junior defense lawyer, an assistant district attorney, and several newsmen. His findings were:

1. That Shell W was fired in the Sacco pistol and could have been fired in no other.

2. That the so-called "mortal" bullet, Bullet III, was fired through the Sacco pistol and could have been fired through no other.

Professor Gill, after spending some time looking through the comparison microscope, became convinced of the parallel patterns of Bullet III and a test bullet, but felt that these would have shown more clearly if

Bullet III could have been cleaned of its encrusted grime. Thompson, for the defense, refused to give permission to have this done. Shortly afterward Gill wrote to Thompson that he now doubted his testimony at the Hamilton-Proctor motion and wished to sever all connection with the case. His disavowal was followed by another from the trial defense expert James Burns.

Goddard's findings, though unofficial, undoubtedly had much influence on the Lowell Committee. When Thompson later appeared before the committee, he made the novel accusation that the prosecution had juggled the evidence by substituting a test bullet and cartridge fired in Sacco's pistol for the original Shell W found in the gravel and Bullet III taken from Berardelli's body. As an indication of this he pointed out that the identifying scratches on Bullet III differed from those on the other bullets, being wider apart and uneven—as if made with a different instrument.

The year after Sacco and Vanzetti were executed, Thompson spoke out even more bluntly and emphatically, accusing Captain Proctor of having made the shell and bullet substitution just before the evidence was offered at the trial. After the substitution, according to Thompson, Proctor's conscience had bothered him to the point that he had just before his death signed the affidavit expressing his doubts.

The certainty that Goddard had hoped to bring to the ballistics evidence was made to seem less than certain in the autumn of 1927 by his findings in the Yorkell murder case in Cleveland. A few weeks after Yorkell, a bootlegger, had been shot down in the street, the police arrested a Frank Milazzo, who was found to be carrying a revolver similar in type to the one that killed Yorkell. Two bullets taken from Yorkell's body and several bullets test-fired from Milazzo's pistol were sent to Goddard for examination. After viewing the exhibits through his comparison microscope Goddard announced that one of the bullets found in Yorkell had been fired from Milazzo's revolver. In spite of Goddard's findings Milazzo was shortly afterward able to prove that he had bought the revolver new a month after the shooting. Goddard attributed the mistake to a mix-up of bullets at police headquarters. The Cleveland police denied this. Supporters of Sacco and Vanzetti have used the incident to question the infallibility of the comparison microscope. What apparently happened was that Goddard, instead of comparing a murder bullet and a test bullet, had compared the two Yorkell murder bullets with each other. They, of course, matched. Who was at fault it is impossible to say, but the comparison microscope itself was in no way discredited.

In July, 1927, the Sacco-Vanzetti guns and bullets were brought to Boston from the Dedham Courthouse, where they had been in the custody of the clerk of court since the trial, to be examined by the Lowell Committee. Then they disappeared. When in 1959 I tried to see them, they were nowhere to be found. The Dedham clerk of court had a record of their having been sent to Boston but no record of their return. The Massachusetts attorney general's office had no idea where they were, nor did the Commissioner of Public Safety at state police headquarters.

It took me six months of poking about before I finally managed to discover where they had gone. Apparently, after they had been examined by the Lowell Committee, they were sent to the ballistics laboratory of the state police and placed in the custody of Captain Van Amburgh. He put all the exhibits, each triple-sealed in its official court envelope, in a cardboard box and locked them away. The box remained there almost twenty years. Then when Van Amburgh retired he took several ballistics souvenirs with him, among them the box of Sacco-Vanzetti exhibits.

Van Amburgh—who died in 1949—was succeeded in the laboratory by his son. The son in turn retired in 1951 to Kingston, a small town near Plymouth, about forty miles from Boston. When I telephoned him to ask about the Sacco-Vanzetti exhibits, he refused at first to say whether he had them or not. But after I had persuaded the Boston *Globe* to run a feature article on the missing exhibits, he admitted to reporters that he did have them but regarded himself merely as their "custodian." The *Globe* story was a Sunday sensation. Among the paper's early readers was the Commissioner of Public Safety, J. Henry Goguen. The Commissioner at once sent two state troopers to Kingston to demand the surrender of the exhibits. The next day the guns and bullets, still in their box, were back in the state police laboratory.

When I at last saw the exhibits at the laboratory they were relatively free from corrosion, although the clips that fastened them in their triple envelopes had rusted into the paper. Apparently they had not been disturbed since 1927. What I first planned to do was to have comparison tests made of Bullet III and a bullet fired from Sacco's pistol, and similar comparisons made with Shell W. Then I hoped to determine whether or not the other bullets and shells had been fired from a single gun.

Yet I knew that even if Bullet III could be proved beyond dispute to have come from Sacco's pistol, there still remained the question raised by Thompson of bullet substitution. There was at least the possibility that the bullets might still test for blood. If it could

A Corroborative View

A quite similar view of the Sacco-Vanzetti case—concluding that Sacco was very probably guilty and Vanzetti probably innocent—is contained in James Grossman's stimulating article, "The Sacco-Vanzetti Case Reconsidered," in the January, 1962, issue of Commentary. After reviewing the facts of the crime and examining the ballistics evidence, Mr. Grossman goes on, in the excerpt reprinted below, to discuss the characters and beliefs of the principals.

Sacco and Vanzetti's defenders have always urged as their strongest argument that it is impossible for these two men to have committed this sordid crime; it is utterly inconsistent with their characters. . . . In part perhaps because it seems to fit in with their characters, Sacco and Vanzetti are often regarded as holding a harmless, mildly eccentric, utopian belief in the natural goodness of man and as being completely opposed to violence in all forms and under all circumstances. These views . . . are not the views they actually held. Sacco and Vanzetti were followers of Luigi Galleani ["the Nestor of the Massachusetts anarchists"], who approved not only of the traditional propaganda of the deed, killing kings and heads of state, which we associate with some anarchists, but who also justified robberies and thefts if they were committed for the cause. . . .

When we turn . . . to the conditions existing in 1920 we find that they are the very conditions which [Sacco and Vanzetti believed] would justify violence on behalf of themselves and their friends. The White Terror [their term for Attorney General Palmer's roundup of radicals during the Red Scare] was for them not a propaganda phrase but a reality. It was reported to them almost daily that their friends were being persecuted, arrested, held incommunicado . . . They had the right to defend themselves; and defense was bound to be expensive. . . .

While the Braintree murder is unthinkable as a personal theft of Sacco's, I am suggesting that it is possible to understand it as an act of war, a step in the raising of a defense fund. . . . The figure of speech, war, which taken fairly literally seems to be

© LOW, ALL COUNTRIES

the clue to the Braintree deed, may also explain how Sacco, if he was guilty of the deed, can be so sincere and convincing in his claim of innocence and never for a moment in his public statements in court or in his private letters seem to be a conscious murderer. For if he did commit the deed, he would no more feel guilty of murder than would a soldier defending his country. . . .

In the court proceedings, and in speaking to his supporters, Sacco, of course, did something more than assert innocence in general terms; he claimed he was in Boston and not in Braintree on the day of the murder. . . . [But] in writing to his comrades and his friends, publicly or privately, Sacco never in any letter that I have seen specifically denies the killing. . . . No word of his innocence was spoken at the solemn great moment of his death, when he cried out long life to anarchy and bade farewell to his wife, children, and friends . . .

Vanzetti's letters throughout, his statements on being sentenced and afterward, to the very moment of death, are startlingly different from Sacco's in the unmistakable explicitness of Vanzetti's assertions of innocence and denials of guilt. . . . When his words are general he excludes all possibility of revolutionary ambiguity: "I am utterly innocent in the whole sense of the word." And at the moment of death . . . he uses his most moving formulation; to those present he said, "I wish to tell you that I am an innocent man. I never committed any crime, but sometimes some sin." . . . The sense, whether true or false, of Vanzetti's innocence radiates so profusely through the pages of his fine letters and magnificent statements that we read Sacco's in their light. . . . Sacco has been parsimonious [in expressions of] innocence and generous only in the use of terms that do not necessarily imply it. . . .

Vanzetti's statements . . . seem to me affirmative proof of his innocence. But if we ignore them entirely, the evidence against him is not strong. . . . For in Vanzetti's case there is no strong evidence, like the bullet in Sacco's, requiring an almost irrefutable defense to overcome it.

now be demonstrated that all six bullets had traces of human blood on them, then the evidence would be overwhelming that there had been no bullet substitution. If on the other hand Bullet III showed no trace of blood, whereas the other five bullets did, the presumption would be strong that Proctor or someone connected with the prosecution had substituted one of the bullets fired into sawdust.

I thought there would be no difficulty in arranging these tests, but when I discussed the matter with Commissioner Goguen I found out otherwise. Even in 1959, it seemed, the Sacco-Vanzetti case was still an explosive political issue—as the spring legislative hearings requesting a posthumous pardon for the two men had demonstrated—and the Commissioner wanted to stay out of it. Each time I asked for permission to have properly qualified experts conduct ballistics tests, he postponed any definite answer, telling me to come back in a month or two. At last, after a year, he announced flatly that he would allow no tests.

Not until Goguen's term of office expired and his successor, Frank Giles, took over was I able to arrange for the tests. Finally on October 4, 1961, Professor William Boyd of the Boston University Medical School examined the six bullets for blood. Unfortunately, because of slight oxidization of the bullets, he was unable to determine whether any blood traces remained. However, after Bullet III had been washed I was able to examine the base under the microscope. Previously the bullet had been covered with some foreign substance that obscured the markings on the base. With this removed I could see the three scratched lines clearly. Although they were farther apart than the lines on the other bullets, this could have been because Bullet III had a concave base whereas the bases of the remaining bullets were flat. In any case as I looked through the microscope successively at Bullets I, II, III, and IIII, I could see no notable difference between the scratches on Bullet III and those on the rest.

A week after Professor Boyd had made his blood tests, two firearms consultants came to Boston to make the ballistics comparisons: Jac Weller, the honorary curator of the West Point Museum, and Lieutenant Colonel Frank Jury, formerly in charge of the Firearms Laboratory of the New Jersey State Police. On October 11, 1961, Weller and Jury conducted their tests in the laboratory of the Massachusetts State Police.

Sacco's pistol, they found, was still in condition to be used. After firing two shots to clear the rust from the barrel, Colonel Jury fired two more shots which he then used to match against Bullet III in the comparison microscope. Making independent examinations, Jury and Weller both concluded that "the bullet marked 'III' was fired in Sacco's pistol and in no other." They also agreed, after comparing the breech block markings of Shell W and a test shell (see picture on page 110), that Shell W must have been fired in Sacco's pistol. The other five bullets, they concluded, were fired from a single unknown gun, probably a semiautomatic pistol. It is to be presumed that the three shells, also from a single gun, came from the same weapon as did the five bullets—although this, as Jury and Weller pointed out, cannot be demonstrated.

I spent some time myself looking through the microscope at the cross-sections of Bullet III and the test bullet. The striations fitted into each other as if the two bullets were one. Here was a matter no longer open to question. But there still remained Thompson's question: was this Bullet III a substitution?

Even though nothing could be proved by blood tests, Jury and Weller felt that there had been no substitution. They maintained that a bullet fired into oiled sawdust would have shown characteristic marks on it. No such marks were on Bullet III. Theoretically, they pointed out, it would have been possible to have fired a test bullet into a side of beef, but this would have involved many problems, such as the purchase of the beef and keeping the experiment secret.

Besides the reasoning of Jury and Weller I had reasons of my own that made me feel there had been no bullet substitution, that the theory itself evolved out of Thompson's despair. There was, of course, the coincidence that Bullet III with its obsolete cannelure was duplicated by the six Winchester bullets found on Sacco when he was arrested. According to the autopsy report of April 17, 1920, Bullet III had been fired into Berardelli as he was in a prone position. Dr. Magrath identified Bullet III at the trial by the scratches he had originally made on it:

As I found it [he testified], it lay sideways against the flat surface of the hip bone, and in my opinion the flattening of the bullet was due to its striking that bone side on.

This peculiar flattening would have been almost impossible to duplicate in a substitute bullet. When Thompson in 1927 accused the prosecution of substituting Bullet III, the assistant district attorney offered to call Dr. Magrath before the Lowell Committee to reidentify the bullet he had marked, but the defense showed no interest in this.

Beyond the physical evidence of the bullet itself, the substitution theory breaks down when the trial record is examined. There Captain Van Amburgh on the stand had been most tentative in identifying Bullet III as having been fired from Sacco's pistol. Captain Proctor was even more ambiguous and later admitted that he never believed that Bullet III came from that particular Colt. If, however, Bullet III had been a substitution, the two captains would have *known* that it came from Sacco's Colt, since they themselves had fired it. Doubts they might have had as to their conduct, but none at all about the bullet.

When the case first came to trial, it was no earthshaking issue for District Attorney Katzmann or for the state police. Katzmann, if he had lost, would still have been re-elected district attorney. The case could not have been worth the risk of detection and disgrace to forge the evidence for a conviction.

In the light of the most recent ballistics evidence and after reviewing the inquest and autopsy reports, as well as the trial testimony, I felt I could come to no other conclusion than that the Colt automatic found on Sacco when he was picked up by the police was the one used to murder Berardelli three weeks earlier. About the gun found on Vanzetti there is too much uncertainty to come to any conclusion. Being of .38 caliber, it was obviously not used at South Braintree, where all the bullets fired were .32's. There is at least the possibility that it may have been taken from the dying Berardelli, but there is an equally strong if not stronger possibility that this is not so. A Harrington & Richardson was a cheap, common revolver, and there were several hundred thousand of them being carried at the time Vanzetti was arrested. No one today can be certain whether Berardelli's Harrington & Richardson was of .32 or .38 caliber, whether it had a broken spring or a broken hammer, whether it was ever called for at Iver Johnson's, whether in fact Berardelli had a gun with him the day he was murdered. Jury and Weller found it impossible to determine if the hammer of Vanzetti's revolver had been replaced.

Whether Sacco himself pulled the trigger of his automatic that day in South Braintree, whether he was even present, cannot be established definitely. But if he did not fire it, and if in fact he was not there, then one of his close associates must have been the murderer. The ballistics evidence leaves no alternative.

When a few years ago I wrote an article, "Tragedy in Dedham" (AMERICAN HERITAGE, October, 1958), I was convinced that the two men were innocent, victims if not of a judicial frame-up at least of an ironic fate. But after the ballistics tests of 1961 I felt that, at least in the case of Sacco, I could no longer hold to my opinion. It has been pointed out that Vanzetti, just before he died, solemnly proclaimed his innocence. Sacco, however, when he took his place in the electric chair, gave the traditional anarchist cry—"Long live anarchy!"

Whatever my altered views about Sacco, I still continue to feel that Vanzetti was innocent. Besides various subjective reasons, and convincing talks with Vanzetti's old friends, I found what seemed to me the clinching evidence in the statement of the New York anarchist leader, Carlo Tresca. Tresca, a luminous and vivid personality, became the most noted anarchist in the United States after the deportation of Luigi Galleani in 1919. He was the admired and trusted leader to whom the anarchists confidently turned when they were in trouble. It was he who had selected the original trial lawyer for Sacco and Vanzetti. His influence remained vast over the years, not only among the dwindling anarchists but throughout the whole New York Italian colony.

During World War II the anti-Soviet Tresca was so successful in keeping the Communists out of the government's overseas Italian broadcasts that a G.P.U. killer known as Enea Sormenti was imported to eliminate him. Tresca was shot down on a New York street in 1943. Several weeks before he died he happened to be talking with his long-time friend Max Eastman, who had earlier written a "Profile" of him for the *New Yorker*. The subject of Sacco and Vanzetti came up, and Eastman asked Tresca if he would feel free to tell him the truth about them.

Without hesitation Tresca replied: "Sacco was guilty, but Vanzetti was not." At that moment some people came into the room, interrupting the conversation, and Eastman never saw Tresca again. Yet the reasons for Tresca's answer must have been profound. He could easily have avoided the question or even denied his comrade's guilt. And if any man should have known the truth of the case, Tresca was the man.

To my mind the most that can be said against Vanzetti is that he must have known who did commit the Braintree crime. Sacco, if he was guilty, was so out of no personal motive. But anarchist deeds of robbery and violence for the sake of the cause were not unknown. If he actually participated in the South Braintree holdup, it was to get money to aid his imprisoned fellow anarchists, and he must then have seen himself not as a robber but as a soldier of the revolution. But if someone else of his group was guilty, someone from whom he had received the murder pistol, he would have preferred death to betraying a comrade.

As far as the guns and bullets in the Sacco-Vanzetti case are concerned, the evidence is in, no longer to be disputed. The human problem remains.

Matters of Principle

If he had never come across the Great Sea, if he had never founded his peaceful commonwealth, we would still be in debt to William Penn. At twenty-six, with all his better-known achievements before him, he performed an enduring service to the liberties of the English-speaking world. It was London in 1670, ten years after the overthrow of Cromwell's Puritans and the Restoration of the Stuarts. A new crusading faith was making its appearance (they are always annoying to the authorities), and young Penn, a Quaker agitator, was on trial for disturbing the peace.

Members of the court threatened the jury with fines ment of his peers, or by the Laws of the land." Now that pledge, so painfully wrung from King John, was being discarded by the courts. Three years before Penn's trial, the House of Commons had investigated Lord Chief Justice Keeling in connection with official misconduct, asserting that he had undervalued, vilified, and condemned Magna Charta, "the great preserver of our lives, freedom and property"; and on November 13, 1667, an entry was made in the Parliament Journal: "Resolved that the precedents and practice of fining or imprisoning jurors for verdicts is illegal." But this resolution had not stopped the practices of the judges.

THE ORDEAL OF WILLIAM PENN

Long before he founded his Quaker commonwealth in America, he stood up for religious freedom against the awesome power of the Crown—and put the entire English-speaking world in his debt

By FRANCIS BIDDLE

and hinted at torture if they did not bring in a verdict to the judge's taste—but they would not yield: "NOR WILL WE EVER DO IT!" their foreman shouted in answer to Penn's impassioned appeal, "Give not away your right!" The trial is a landmark in English and American history.

Less than 300 years ago these twelve men established the independence of English juries: they should make their own decisions, and must not be "led by the nose" by any court. The right they defended was embodied in Magna Charta, which provided: "No Freeman shall be taken, or imprisoned, nor be disseized of his Freehold or Liberties or Free-Customs or be Outlawed or Exiled, or any other ways destroyed; nor we shall not pass upon him nor condemn him, but by lawful judg-

What did stop them was the obstinate courage of an English jury who had faith in *their* law, and knew how to assert it, under the skillful leadership of the man whom they were trying.

The members of this jury were little, everyday men, none of them gentlemen, as Penn was described in the indictment, men of no importance. In ordinary circumstances a trial for disturbing the peace would have been held before only a single judge, who would quickly have sent the accused to jail, and the case would have been forgotten. But Penn had fired the Quakers with his dogged insistence that they had the right to worship their own God in their own way; to doff their headgear to no man, not even to any judge, for to God only was such obeisance due; and to meet

118

quietly to worship in the open air in Gracechurch Street (sometimes known as "Gracious Street"), in the parish of Bridgeward, London.

Penn was behind this "nuisance," and was causing all the trouble, claiming the rights of Englishmen—just as if Quakers could be thought of in those terms. So the Crown decided to put on a show; and summoned the Lord Mayor, Sir Samuel Starling, in his robes and his massive gold chain and his rather pitiful ignorance of the law, even if he could recognize a nuisance, especially when "rights" were being claimed to defend it. With him sat the Recorder, John Howel, the chief

And there was a goodly crowd of spectators who hated judges, and would not observe silence in court, and so strongly expressed their sympathy with the prisoners that now and then the Recorder had to call them to order.

. . . William's father, Sir William Penn, a Royalist at heart, was still a practical man and knew how to get along during the Protectorate. He advanced under Cromwell to become Rear Admiral of the Irish Seas and Vice Admiral in command of England's Third Fleet. After Sir William defeated the Dutch in 1652, when William was eight, the Protector appointed him

criminal judge of the City of London, equally un-learned in the law which he was supposed to administer, a stupid man with little to sustain him except a few worn-thin Latin proverbs which he took delight in misapplying. He was a dull, heavy man, who was soon angry when the trial came alive, and kept his hot temper simmering; he suspected that Penn was making fun of him—which indeed Penn was. Sir John Robinson, the prosecutor for the Crown, was Lieutenant of the Tower and had come to know this obstinate young Quaker agitator and pamphleteer when he had been sent to the Tower for nine months not long before to keep him out of mischief—"in safe custody," as the phrase went. Four aldermen also sat on the bench, all of them knights, and three knighted sheriffs.

General at Sea; many enemy ships, casualties, prisoners, and prizes lay to his credit. But in two or three years the Admiral was in the Tower, suspected of being too close to the exiled Charles II. Released in five weeks, he went to his castle at Macroon in Ireland, and it was there that William saw the "inner light" for the first time—the quickening of man's soul by direct mystical communication with its Creator. For, as we are informed by various Penn biographers, an itinerant and eloquent Quaker named Thomas Loe had been invited to Macroon, and when he preached, a black servant belonging to William's father wept aloud; William, watching his father with awe, saw the tears running down his cheeks, and he too was deeply moved. They were told of the new doctrine that men had the right to wait upon the Lord unaided by any kind of priest. Loe talked of the simplicity of honest, plain living, devoid of plumes and laces, and of the dignity of humility.

The Penns lived four years in Ireland. Oliver Cromwell died in 1658, when William was fourteen. "It was the joyfullest funerall that I ever saw," wrote the essayist and diarist, John Evelyn, "for there was none that Cried, but dogs, which the souldiers hooted away with a barbarous noise, drinking & taking tabacco in the streetes as they went." The Penns had returned from Ireland by 1660, when Charles II entered London in triumph, and the boy may have seen "the wayes

dents, Penn among them, in the Puritan tradition. They refused to wear surplices and would not go to chapel. For this beginning of nonconformity at the age of seventeen, Penn was finally expelled.

Samuel Pepys professed to be a friend of the Admiral, and though he could write in his diary: "Had Sir W. Pen, who I hate with all my heart . . . and his son, William . . . to dinner," the two were boon companions. Pepys found Penn "sociable, able, cunning" and full "of merry discourse," fond of gaudy dress and lewd plays. Sir William taught Pepys to take good drafts of sack in the morning to cure headaches caused by too much drinking the night before. We must take

ILLUSTRATED FOR AMERICAN HERITAGE BY MICHAEL BIDDLE

strew'd with flowers, the bells ringing, the streetes hung with tapissry, fountaines running with wine." Admiral Penn, who had helped in the Restoration, was knighted and made a Navy commissioner, with juicy emoluments in the form of commissions on purchases, which added to his already large landed fortune.

That same year William was sent to Christ Church College at Oxford and entered as a "gentleman commoner." His experience there was brief. He was shocked by the "Hellish Darkness and Debauchery" of the place, which was happily pro-Royalist. The persecution of the Puritan sects had already begun. His friend Thomas Loe was in jail in Oxford for teaching the Quaker faith; but John Owen, a famous Puritan preacher, dismissed as dean of Christ Church when the Restoration came, was exhorting nonconforming stu-

Pepys with a generous pinch of salt, but there is enough in this brief description to indicate the gulf between the father, with his genial sensuality, and the son, disgusted at the dissipation of Oxford. Apparently about this time there arose a severe misunderstanding between the two. William said that his father had administered him "bitter usage," whipping, beating, and turning him out of doors. The Admiral found a letter of Dr. Owen's to his son. Outraged but puzzled, he took it to Pepys, who thought that the Puritan preacher had "perverted" the boy, and now perceived what had put Sir William "so long off the hookes."

The father relented. He loved his son, but could not understand the lad's devotion to the Quakers, with their plain clothes and twaddle about the inner light. The Admiral was no mystic and knew he could do very much for his son if the boy would only let him. Forgiving him then, and changing his tactics, he sent William off to France with some persons of quality, among them Robert Spencer, later the Earl of Sunderland, who became William's lifelong friend. It was the summer of 1662; Penn was eighteen.

Penn wrote later that a man attacked him for not returning a salute and that he had disarmed his attacker but had not killed him. Instead of boasting, Penn philosophized, a bit solemnly, as was characteristic of his youth: "I ask any man of understanding or conscience if the whole ceremony were worth the life of a man, considering the dignity of the nature, and the importance of the life of man, both with respect to God, his Creator, himself, and the benefit of civil society?"

At the Académie Protestante de Saumur, Penn became a friend of the famous theologian and metaphysician Moïse Amyraut, the president of the college; lodged at his house; and imbibed his unflinching philosophy of toleration and religious liberty, learning in his classes to reject predestination and glory in personal liberty and to practice charity as well as piety.

Back in London in 1664 young Penn had become, according to Mrs. Pepys, "a most modish person, grown . . . a fine gentleman," with his athletic build and candid eyes. He studied law for a short time at Lincoln's Inn, and his curriculum included readings of Dryden and of Beaumont and Fletcher.

For a second time war was declared against Holland, and William joined his father for a few weeks on the *Royal Charles.* The Admiral, who had been made Great Captain Commander, sent his son as a personal messenger to the King, hoping that this would be the beginning of a brilliant career based on royal favor. From Harwich the boy wrote his father, whom he cherished: "I . . . firmly believe that if God has called you out to battle, He will cover your head in that smoky day . . . Your concerns are most dear to me. It's hard, meantime, to lose both a father and a friend." He had not yet made the choice between the kind of future his father wished for him and the way of life his instincts were reaching for, the way of the Quakers. He was moved by their persecutions and tortures—they would not meet in secret—and he saw dissenters in stocks, pelted and jeered at by the crowds.

The Great Plague had struck London. Lincoln's Inn, where Penn was again reading law, was deserted. Out of a population of half a million, nearly seventy thousand people died. Along the city's half-empty streets walked men to collect the corpses, crying, "Bring out your dead, bring out your dead!" Dr. Amyraut had said that man's responsibility to his brother was the ultimate morality, and Quakers worked to save the sick and helped carry out those who had died. Suffering increases nonconformity, and as unrest grew in the year of the Great Plague, the authorities took steps to suppress it. As usual, these had the opposite effect. The Quaker Act three years before had made it unlawful for five or more Quakers to assemble "under pretense of worship." The same year the Act of Uniformity required clergymen to follow exactly the established Prayer Book. And now the Five Mile Act forbade any nonconformist preacher to come within five miles of a corporate town. This suppression caused Catholics, Quakers, and Independents to protest by active disobedience.

Sir William meanwhile was triumphant over the Dutch at the battle of Lowestoft, and in September, 1665, brought home a host of prizes. It was his last battle, and his health began to fail. He sent his son to Ireland to settle the estates which the King had given him. Serving under the Earl of Arran, young Penn helped restore order, and was praised for his works. In Cork he went to hear Thomas Loe speak at a Quaker meeting, was singularly affected, and realized then that his decision had been made: "It was at this time that the Lord visited me with a certain sound and testimony of His eternal word." He knew himself to be a "seeker," and began regularly to go to meetings of the Friends. But he still loved a good fight.

At one of the meetings a soldier came in to break up the group. Penn took him by the neck and started to throw him downstairs, but more soldiers came and arrested the Quakers. When the mayor saw Penn among them, he ordered him released, but Penn insisted he be treated like the others. He always practiced what he preached. Then he acted as lawyer for his fellow prisoners. On what charge had they been arrested, he asked? By way of answer they were all sent to jail. Penn protested to the Earl of Orrery and was released. His father, who had evidently heard of William's association with the Quakers, wrote him to come to see him in England without delay—"unless for necessary rest or refreshment" on the road. William returned with a fellow Quaker, Josiah Coale, who had been persecuted "and dragged bareheaded under the spouts in time of rain," and took him to visit his father, a gesture hardly calculated to effect a reconciliation. After Coale withdrew, his father burst out—did he have to use *thee* and *thou?* William must use *you* in speaking to older people or persons of high rank. But William, fortified by his brief taste of martyrdom, refused. Quakers, he said, recognized no rank. His father suggested that he uncover before the King, the

Duke of York, *and* his father; but William, though he loved his father, would not. Exasperated, Sir William ordered his son from the house, saying he would dispose of his estates to those that pleased him better.

After this it was natural that William should throw himself without reserve into the Quaker cause, living with them, going to their meetings, protesting the increasing arrests, and writing religious tracts. He had not yet found his way of writing. *Truth Exalted* (1668), his first tract, was verbose and filled with the current exhortations. Another shaft, groaning under the title of *The Guide Mistaken and Temporizing Rebuked,* shortly followed. For writing *The Sandy Foundation Shaken,* in which he attacked the Trinity, Penn was arrested by the Privy Council on December 12, 1668, charged with failure to obtain a publishing license from the Bishop of London, and, as mentioned above, committed to the Tower for safe custody. John Evelyn was shocked and noted that "one of Sir William Pen's sons had published a blasphemous book against the Deity of our blessed Lord." But Pepys, who got his wife to read him Penn's book, found it "so well writ as, I think, it is too good for him ever to have writ it," and "a serious sort of book, and not fit for every body to read."

The warrant was issued by the Privy Council to Sir John Robinson, the Lord Lieutenant of the Tower, who would be Penn's prosecutor in the notorious trial two years later. The Bishop of London sent word to Penn that he could recant in Covent Garden at an appropriate time before the "Fair" of all the city or else be kept in prison for the rest of his life. Penn would not budge a jot; he said he owed his conscience to no mortal man; he had no need to fear; he valued not such threats. The King sent his chaplain, the Bishop of Worcester, to see him; the prospective life prisoner told Worcester that the Tower was the worst argument in the world to convince him. He also explained to the Bishop that he had not meant to deny the divinity of Christ, and agreed to write another pamphlet, clarifying his views. *Innocency With Her Open Face, Presented by Way of Apology for the Book Entitled, The Sandy Foundation Shaken,* was the result. In it Penn expounded his belief in Jesus Christ, despite his attack on the Trinity.

What could one do with a man like that? If you clapped him in the Tower he had time for his scandalous (and highly popular) attacks on the church, which were smuggled out of prison and sold everywhere—yet there was no doubt that he was a devout believer. If you let him out, at least he was more occupied with meetings and preachments, which were easier (perhaps) to handle. Besides, his father was a friend of the King, although the Admiral had recently been impeached

and tried for embezzling prize goods (he was not convicted); and the King still owed the Admiral some sixteen thousand pounds.

Whatever the reason, William Penn was discharged from the Tower on July 28, 1669.

Three weeks after his release his father, still hoping he could get the young man away from this crusading which got one nowhere, sent him to Ireland to transact some business affairs; perhaps the trip would divert his mind from such unbecoming missionary zeal. But even while attending to his father's business in such improbable places as Imokilly and Shanagarry, Penn spent a good part of his year in Ireland engaged in strenuous efforts to relieve the persecution of Irish Quakers. Having achieved much success in both ventures, he returned to London in August, 1670. The famous "tryal" was but a few days off.

During that year the persecution of both Quakers and Catholics was renewed. Laws were amended to provide more speedy remedies against these "dangerous practices of seditious sectaries," and particularly the assemblies. In order to test the law, George Fox, the founder of the Quakers and a dedicated expert in rousing popular emotion, went to the Friends Meeting House in Gracechurch Street, where he expected the storm was most likely to begin. A large crowd had gathered to see what would happen to the Quakers. A file of musketeers appeared. Fox and two others were dragged away, and someone shouted: "Have a care of him, he is a princely man!" Public opinion was turning against the excesses of the government. Moved by Fox's eloquence, the mayor, Sir Samuel Starling, the same official who would soon try to convict Penn under like circumstances, dismissed the charge. Later George Whitehead returned to the same spot, where some Friends were listening to a Catholic priest. After the sermon Whitehead preached peace and love, was committed to prison, and fined twenty pounds. The meeting place of the Quakers was boarded up and many of them sent to jail. Like Mahatma Gandhi, like Martin Luther King, like all men who will not fight but also will not yield, these quiet Quakers were a dangerous lot, particularly when they had leaders like Fox and Penn.

Penn's next opportunity to be tested and proven worthy of his God came on August 14. He was preaching outdoors in Gracechurch Street before the closed meetinghouse, with Friend William Mead acting as a kind of assistant. A crowd of a few hundred people had assembled, expecting trouble, but there had been no violence, certainly none until the sheriff and soldiers arrived. The speaker was arrested under a writ signed by the Lord Mayor, directing the sheriff to receive under his custody the body of William Penn, taken for preaching seditiously and causing a tumult of the people. Instead of being brought to the foul depths of Newgate, Penn, being a gentleman, was lodged at the Black Dog at Newgate Market, where one could buy comfort. The next day he wrote his father that he had told the Mayor he could bear harsh expressions about himself but not about his father; the Mayor had said that the Admiral had starved his seamen. "Be not displeased or grieved," the son

M. Biddle

continued. "What if this be designed of the Lord for an exercise of our patience?" Reading this, his father may have reflected how much and how often his own patience had been exercised by his son. "I am very well," the letter ended, "and have no trouble upon my spirits, besides my absence from thee." His heart seemed always to be light under adversity.

Two weeks later, on September 1, 1670, the trial against William Penn, gentleman, and William Mead, linen draper, began. The indictment was read. It charged the defendants and other unknown persons with assembling and congregating together to the "disturbance of the peace of the said Lord the King"; and recited that the defendant Penn by abetment with Mead did preach and speak, by reason whereof there followed "a great Concourse and Tumult of People," which remained and continued a long time in contempt of the King and his law "to the great disturbance of his Peace; to the great Terror and Disturbance of many of his Liege People and Subjects, to the ill Example of all others . . ."

"What say you, William Penn and William Mead, are you guilty or . . . not guilty?"

Penn demanded a copy of the indictment—how could he remember it verbatim?

The Recorder, presiding, answered that he must first plead.

Penn, assured that no advantage would be taken of him, pleaded "not guilty." The court very soon adjourned until the afternoon; and the anonymous "observer" to whom we are indebted for a lively account of the trial, and who was obviously outraged by the treatment that the prisoners received, suggests that it was the constant and unkind practice of the court to make prisoners "wait on the trials of Felons and Murderers, thereby designing in all probability, both to affront and tire them." When the adjournment ended late in the afternoon, there was an alter-

cation. The defendants were wearing their hats in court, having put them on when the Mayor asked who had ordered them off; now the court began to bait the prisoners—did they know the respect one showed to the court? If they did not pull off their hats they would be fined forty marks (about seventy-five dollars) apiece.

Penn now began his line of studied, polite insolence to the court, an attitude that lasted throughout the trial. He had tangled with Sir Samuel Starling before, and knew him for a man who stood on nothing but his dignity; and he quickly sized up the pompous Recorder as a bird of the same feather. The bench, said Penn, and not the defendants should be fined, since the bench had ordered the hats put on. Mead, backing up Penn's line a little cumbrously, called on all people to take notice of this injustice; and added, like some Greek chorus: "O fear the Lord, and dread his Power, and yield unto the Guidance of his Holy Spirit, for He is not far from every one of you."

Penn and Mead conducted their own case, without lawyers. The trial was in the Elizabethan manner, each side criticizing and contradicting the other, and speaking out of turn. Meanwhile the packed audience was applauding Penn, so that it had to be cautioned by the crier to keep silence upon pain of imprisonment.

Witnesses for the prosecution estimated the "great concourse" which the defendants had addressed at something between 300 and 500. The Recorder asked Mead what he thought the number was—had he been there? Mead quoted legal Latin back at him—"No man is bound to accuse himself . . . Why dost thou offer to ensnare me with such a question? . . . Doth not this show thy malice? Is this like unto a Judge that ought to be Counsel for the Prisoner at the Bar?"

The Recorder: "Sir, hold your tongue, I do not go about to ensnare you."

The room was in an uproar, and Penn suggested

that silence be demanded; and when this was done he briefly stated their case: They would not recant; they declined even to vindicate "the assembling of ourselves to preach, pray, or worship the Eternal, Holy, Just God . . ." It was "our indispensable duty to meet incessantly upon so good an account; nor shall all the powers upon Earth be able to divert us from reverencing and adoring our God who made us."

Alderman Brown interrupted to point out that Penn was not on trial for worshipping God, but for breaking the law.

Penn instantly affirmed that he had broken no law; and to the end that the bench, the jury, and himself, *"with those that hear us,"* might have a more direct understanding of the procedure, he desired to know by what law it was that he was prosecuted.

The Recorder, wary of a trap, answered "the Common Law"; and added, conscious that his reply sounded a little vague, that he could not be expected to "run up so many years, and over so many adjudged cases which we call Common Law," to answer Penn's curiosity.

Penn retorted that the answer was very short of his question; "if it be common, it should not be so hard to produce."

THE RECORDER (losing his temper): You are a saucy fellow, speak to the Indictment.

PENN: You are many mouths and ears against me . . . I say again, unless you show me *and the People* the law you ground your indictment upon [emphasis supplied—Penn never forgot his audience], I shall take it for granted your proceedings are merely arbitrary.

THE RECORDER (feeling himself cornered): The question is whether you are guilty of this indictment.

PENN: The question is not whether I am guilty of this indictment but whether this indictment be legal. . . . Where there is no law there is no transgression.

THE RECORDER (unable to answer this): You are an impertinent fellow. It's *lex non scripta* [law that is not written], that which many have studied thirty or forty years to know, and would you have me tell you in a moment?

Penn quoted the *Institutes* of Lord Coke (1552–1634), that implacable adherent of common law, referred to the privileges in Magna Charta, and cited statutes.

THE RECORDER (now thoroughly confused): Sir, you are a troublesome fellow, and it is not for the honour of the Court to suffer you to go on.

PENN: I have asked but one question, and you have not answered me; [then, doubtless, turning to the jury] though the rights and privileges of every Englishman be concerned in it.

THE RECORDER (his back against the wall): Sir, we must not stand to hear you talk all night.

PENN: If you deny me *oyer* [to be heard] of that law,

which you suggest I have broken, you do at once deny me an acknowledged right, and evidence to the whole World your resolution to sacrifice the privileges of Englishmen to your sinister and arbitrary views.

This was too much, and the Recorder, at the end of his rope, turned to the Mayor, crying: "Take him away. My Lord, if you take not some course with this pestilent Fellow, to stop his mouth, we shall not be able to do anything tonight."

The Mayor exclaimed, "Take him away, take him away, turn him into the bail-dock." (The bail-dock was a small room partitioned off in the corner of the courtroom.) Then Penn let himself go in grandiloquent speech to the jury: Was this justice? Must he be taken away because he pleaded the fundamental law of England? He left it to the conscience of the jury (his sole judge) that if these fundamental laws, which relate to liberty and property, be not maintained, "our liberties are to be openly invaded, our wives ravished, our children slaved, our families ruined, our estates led away in triumph by every sturdy beggar and malicious informer as their trophies . . . The Lord of Heaven and Earth will be judge between us in this matter." The word "informer" was a red rag to the crowd, who may have hissed when they heard it.

Penn was dragged to the bail-dock and Mead tried his hand at badgering their lordships, speaking directly to the jury: "You men of the jury, here I do now stand, to answer to an indictment against me, which is a Bundle of stuff, full of lies and falsehoods." He was accused of meeting illegally with force and arms. "Time was," he continued, "when I had freedom to use a carnal weapon, and then I thought I feared no

man; but now I fear the living God, and dare not make use thereof, nor hurt any man; nor do I know I demeaned myself as a tumultuous person . . . You men of the jury, who are my Judges, if the Recorder will not tell you what makes a riot, a rout, or an unlawful assembly—a riot is when three or more are met together to beat a man, or to enter forcibly into another man's land, to cut down his grass, his wood, or break down his poles . . ."

At this point the Recorder interrupted Mead, and said, pulling off his hat (a gesture he must have conceived to be biting sarcasm): "I thank you, Sir, that you will tell me what the law is."

To which Mead answered, disdainfully: "Thou may'est put on thy hat. I have never a fee for thee now."

Alderman Brown remarked that Mead talked at random, sometimes as an Independent, now as a Quaker, next as a Papist.

Mead answered impertinently in Latin, to the effect that the Alderman did not know what he was talking about.

THE MAYOR (losing his temper): You deserve to have your tongue cut out.

THE RECORDER: If you discourse in this manner, I shall take occasion against you.

MEAD: I am an Englishman, and you might be ashamed of this dealing.

RECORDER: I look upon you to be an enemy of the laws of England, which ought to be observed and kept, nor are you worthy of such privileges as others have.

MEAD: The Lord judge between me and thee in this matter.

That was again too much for the Recorder; and Mead also was placed in the bail-dock. In the absence of both defendants the Recorder charged the jury. Penn shouted his objection from the bail-dock "in a very raised voice," appealing to the jury, "who are my judges, and this great assembly." Were "the proceedings of the Court not most arbitrary, and void of all law in offering to give the jury their charge in the absence of the prisoners?" Again, citing chapter and verse from Coke, and from Magna Charta, he cried that he was thoroughly prepared to argue his own case. Whereupon the Recorder "being thus unexpectedly lashed for his extrajudicial procedure," said with a smug smile (according to the observer), "Why ye are present, ye do hear, do you not?"

"No thanks to the Court," Penn shouted; and continued: "You of the Jury take notice that I have not been heard." He had still at least ten or twelve material points to offer, he bellowed; and Mead added his objections to these "barbarous and unjust proceedings." The Recorder ordered them taken to the "hole,"

a sort of detention place in the Old Bailey, suggesting that it would not be to the honor of the court to hear them talk all night, "as they would."

The observer tells us that the jurors were commanded to agree upon their verdict, while the prisoners remained in the "stinking hole." After an hour and a half eight jurors came down, agreed on a verdict, and the court sent an officer to bring down the other four, who would not agree. They were Edward Bushell, John Hammond, Charles Milson, and John Baily. Edward Bushell was known to be their leader, and "the Bench [says the observer] used many unworthy threats on the four that dissented." The Recorder told Bushell that he was the cause of this "disturbance"; and added, "I shall set a mark [a fine] upon you, Sir." The prosecutor, Sir John Robinson, announced that he had known Bushell for fourteen years, and that he had thrust himself upon the jury: "I tell you, you deserve to be indicted more than any man that hath been brought to the Bar this day."

Bushell answered that he would willingly have avoided jury service, but had not been able to. Alderman Bludworth retorted that when he saw Mr. Bushell he knew that he would never yield: "Mr. Bushell, we know what you are." And the Mayor added: "Sirrah, you are an impudent fellow. I will put a mark upon you." According to the observer, the court used much menacing language, and behaved themselves imperiously toward the jury—all this because the four had refused to find Penn and Mead guilty. After this "barbarous language," the court sent the jurors out to reconsider the verdict.

After a considerable time the jury came back, stubborn as ever.

CLERK: Are you agreed in your verdict?
JURY: Yes.
CLERK: Who shall speak for you?
JURY: Our foreman.
CLERK: Look upon the prisoners at the Bar: Is William Penn Guilty of the matter whereof he stands indicted, in manner and form, or Not Guilty?
THE FOREMAN [Thomas Veer]: Guilty of speaking in Gracechurch Street.
THE COURT: *Is that all?*
THE FOREMAN: That is all I had in commission.
THE RECORDER: You had as good say nothing.
MAYOR: Was it not an Unlawful Assembly? You mean he was speaking to a tumult of people there?
FOREMAN (seeing the trap): My Lord, this is all I had in commission.

At this point, according to the observer, some of the jury seemed to "buckle" under the questions of the court, but the others would allow no such words as "unlawful assembly"; and the Recorder, the Mayor, the prosecutor, and Alderman Bludworth vilified them "with most opprobrious language." Finally the Mayor told them they had given no verdict, and that they should go and consider it again, so that an end might be made of this "troublesome business."

The jury had won the first two rounds, and Bushell must have harangued them during the half hour they were out. Their third verdict, signed by all twelve, was as queer, and as little satisfactory to the court, as the first. They found that William Penn was guilty of speaking or preaching to an assembly met together in Gracechurch Street on the fourteenth of August last, 1670. Obviously this was no "proper" verdict.

"This," says the observer, "the Mayor and Recorder resented at so high a rate, that they exceeded the bounds of all reason and civility." The Mayor asked them if they would be "led by such a silly fellow as Bushell." Then, addressing himself to the foreman: "I thought you had understood your place better"— meaning his duty to obey the court, and convict.

The court, the prisoners, the jury, and particularly the people knew what was at stake. The government was determined to stop forbidden religious assemblies, to break the spreading Quaker movement, and to use an instrument of the people, the jury, for such purposes. The Recorder said as much, frankly: "Gentlemen, you shall not be dismist till we have a Verdict that the Court will accept: and you shall be locked up without Meat, Drink, Fire, or tobacco; you shall not think thus to abuse the court; we will have a verdict, by the help of God, or you shall starve for it."

Penn, out of the bail-dock and back in court, objected: "The arbitrary resolves of the Bench may not be made the measure of my Jury's Verdict." The Recorder, again losing his temper, sputtered: "Stop that prating fellow's mouth, or put him out of the Court!"

As the court broke up, Penn continued to argue. The Quakers had made no tumult, as the Mayor claimed. Two soldiers with force and arms had closed the Friends' lawful meeting place. Now a verdict had been given, and Penn demanded, "I require the Clerk of the Court to record it, as he will answer it at his peril. And if the Jury bring in another Verdict contrary to this, I affirm they are perjured men in law."

As he was dragged out, Penn again appealed to the jury: "You are Englishmen, mind your privilege, give not away Your Right!" And Veer shouted back: "Nor will we ever do it." The jurors were sent out to spend the night without meat, drink, fire, or any other accommodation; and "they had not even so much as a chamber pot, tho' desired," as the observer sympathetically notes. The court adjourned to the next day, the fourth of the month at seven in the morning,

at which time the jury, as before, reported their finding—*guilty of speaking in Gracechurch Street*. Once more there were passages between jury and Mayor.

The jury, having received a fresh charge from the bench "to extort an unjust Verdict" (according to the observer), went up again, and for the third time the same colloquy took place on their return. Again the Recorder threatened Bushell: "You are a factious fellow, I will set a mark upon you; and whilst I have anything to do in the City, I will have an eye upon you"; and the Mayor, exasperated, lashed the others: "Have you no more wit than to be led by such a pitiful fellow? I will cut his nose!"

Here was another opening for Penn to pour out his angry eloquence. It was intolerable, he protested, that his jury should be thus menaced. Were these men not his judges under the Great Charter of England? What hope was there of ever having proper justice done when verdicts were rejected and juries were threatened with fines, starvation, and ruin to make them reach decisions contrary to their consciences?

In answer the Mayor, obviously hot and frightened as the faces of the crowd pressed against him, his self-control gone, could only cry out: "Stop his mouth, jailor, bring fetters and stake him to the ground!" The Recorder equally betrayed himself: "Till now I never understood the reason of the policy and prudence of the Spaniards, in suffering the Inquisition among them; and certainly it will never be well with us till something like the Spanish Inquisition be in England!"

This suggestion of the use of torture was no idle threat. Although torture was unknown in common law, it had been resorted to in England for several centuries as a means of obtaining evidence and for punishment. Torture could still be ordered by the Crown, the Privy Council, or by the Star Chamber, which was not bound by common law. *Peine forte et dure* might be used when the prisoner would not plead. He was "to be stretched upon his back, to have hot iron laid upon him as much as he could bear, and more, and so to continue, fed upon bad bread and stagnant water through alternate days until he pleaded or died." An instance of *peine* occurred as late as 1726, and was said to be common practice at the Old Bailey up to the eighteenth century.

The substance of this practice was doubtless known to Penn's jury. Half starved but wholly obstinate, they had not yet been broken. Being required to meet again to find another verdict, the observer says, they steadily refused. The Recorder, in great passion, was running off the bench, saying he would sit no longer to hear these things, when the Mayor made him stay, and told the jury to draw up another verdict that they might "bring it in special." The jury refused—they had set their hands to the verdict, they ought not to be returned to the hole. But the sheriffs were ordered to take the jury up again and sworn to keep them without any accommodation till they brought in their verdict; and the Recorder again threatened them: they should starve until a proper verdict was brought in; "I will have you carted about the city as in Edward the Third's time."

They returned once more from Newgate at seven the next morning, weak from such treatment but surely heartened by the angry murmuring of the spectators, who once more had to be silenced by the crier upon pain of imprisonment. On this fourth and final return the jury did bring in a proper verdict: the two prisoners were simply *not guilty*. The court ordered the jury to be polled, and each man answered "Not guilty," to the great and doubtless noisy satisfaction of the onlookers. Again the Recorder yielded to the stupidity of his instincts, saying to the jury that he was sorry they had followed *their own judgments and opinions* rather than *the good and wholesome advice which was given them;* and for this contempt the court fined them forty marks a man, and ordered them imprisoned till they paid.

Penn, sensing the drama of the moment, stepped in front of the bench. "I demand my Liberty," he said, "being freed by my Jury." The Mayor told him he must first pay his fine for contempt of court in not removing his hat during the trial.

"Take him away, take him away, take him out of the court," shouted the Recorder.

"I can never urge the fundamental laws of England," Penn answered, "but you cry 'take him away, take him away.' But it is no wonder, since the Spanish Inquisition hath so great place in the Recorder's heart. God Almighty, who is Just, will judge you for these things."

Eight of the jury, those who originally would have gone along with the Crown, paid their fines; but the four who had dissented, "phenatique jurymen" as they were dubbed, led by the "pertinaceous" Bushell, brought a writ of *habeas corpus* in the Court of Common Pleas. Twelve judges sat (showing that the government considered the case of great importance), and agreed without dissent that the prisoners should be discharged, since "there was not cause of fine or imprisonment."

The opinion was delivered by Sir John Vaughan, Lord Chief Justice. He carefully examined the functions of judges and of juries. A court cannot tell whether the evidence is full and manifest, or doubtful, lame and dark, he said. However manifest the evidence was,

if it were not manifest to the jury and they believed it not, it was not a finable fault, not deserving punishment. Why should a juror be imprisoned for abiding by his own oath and integrity? To say that a jury acquitted contrary to the instructions of the court in matter of law is not intelligible. "We must take off this vail and colour of words . . ." What use would a jury be otherwise? "The Judge's direction should be hypothetical and not positive . . . If you find the fact thus—then you are to find for the Plaintiff; but if you find the fact thus, then it is for the Defendant."

"If it be demanded," the Chief Justice continued, "what is the Fact? the Judge cannot answer it . . ." Juries like judges may differ as to the reasons for their result.

The learned justice cited a case where a juryman disagreed with his fellows for two days, and, being asked by the judges if he would agree, said he would die in prison first; whereupon he was committed and the verdict of the eleven was taken. But "upon better advice," the verdict was quashed, and the dissenting juror discharged without fine. The juror who disagreed in judgment only was not to be fined. To send such a man to prison seemed unworthy of a court. Accordingly, the prisoners were discharged.

Among the several pamphlets about the trial, one, very brief, published in 1719, purported to be written by Penn and Mead. It was now established, the pamphlet pointed out, that "Judges, how great soever they may be, have no right to fine, imprison or punish a jury for not finding a verdict according to the direction of the Court." "And this, I hope," the writer concluded, "is sufficient to prove that jurymen may see with their own eyes, hear with their own ears, and make use of their own consciences and understandings in judging the lives, liberties or estates of their fellow subjects"—a succinct yet eloquent summary of Vaughan's opinion.

The anonymously written reply, reflecting the point of view of the Crown, should be noticed. *The Answer to the Seditious and Scandalous Pamphlet, Entitled the Tryal of William Penn and William Mead,* by A Friend of Justice, written in the biassed language of a sycophant of the government, though addressed to "the impartial and ingenious reader," supported the prosecution. Penn, the anonymous author said, had blasphemed the Holy Trinity, and in his account of the trial had vilified and contemned the King's court, and reviled all methods of law and forms of indictments, calling them "detestable juggles." "Now, gentlemen of the Long Robe," the author warned the members of the legal profession, "look to yourselves and your Westminster Hall . . . Farewell then to your great acquisitions, your Yearbook will then be out of date. These are the Beasts of Ephesus that the late Lord Mayor, Recorder, and Bench of Justices have been contending withall . . . Justices are but cyphers if they cannot correct the corruption or misdemeanor of jurymen." That "Light" which the Quakers say is within them, is "the Spirit of the Devil, the Father of Lies."

Penn and Mead, like the four jurymen, had been sent to Newgate for nonpayment of their fines. Immediately Penn wrote his father, who was near death, that he and Mead had been declared not guilty, but that the Mayor and Recorder "might add to their malice, they fined us . . . for not pulling off our hats and kept us prisoners for the money, An injurious trifle which will blow over, or we shall bring it to the Common Pleas, because it was against law, and not by a jury sessed." He wanted his father not to worry, but, knowing the elder Penn would want to pay the fine, he could not help adding (in another letter): "I intreat thee not to purchase my liberty . . . I would rather perish than release myself by so indirect a course as to satiate their revengeful, avaricious appetites. The advantage of such freedom would fall very short of the trouble of accepting it." He ended, touchingly: "Let not this wicked world disturb thy mind, and whatever shall come to pass I hope in all

conditions to prove thy obedient son." But Sir William had already written to the King, who, along with the Duke of York, promised to continue their favor to young Penn. The Admiral paid the prisoners' fines, and they were released. At the end of his life Penn's father, knowing he was looking into the face of death, forgave his son and at last understood him. He was deeply moved by William's letter. "Son William," he wrote, "if you and your friends keep to your plain way of preaching, and keep to your plain way of living, you will make an end of the priests to the end of the world. . . . Bury me by my mother. Live all in love." Father and son at last had been reconciled.

The son was out in time to be present at his father's death on September 16, 1670. Sir William made him his residuary legatee and sole executor, and bequeathed to him the gold chain and medal that had been bestowed upon him by Cromwell.

William Penn left many memorials behind him: a reputation for fair dealing with all kinds and conditions of men, a clear call to religious liberty, and the "Holy Experiment" in America that became the great proprietorship, colony, and commonwealth of Pennsylvania. But not the least of his accomplishments was recorded in London, in a tablet erected in the Sessions House to the memory of two brave defendants, Penn and Mead, and two stout jurymen, Veer, the foreman, and Bushell. A hundred and fifty years after the trial, the Marquis de Lafayette gave a toast in Philadelphia to the memories of Penn and Franklin—"the one never greater than when arraigned before an English jury, or the other than before a British Parliament."

And so we leave William Penn, "the wild colt," who had just begun his long career of protest. A few months after the trial he would again be arrested for preaching and brought by the soldiers before a huddle of magistrates, this time without jury. Again he would be sent to the Tower. But now the soldiers were friendly and polite. "Send thy lackey," Penn said to the lieutenant, "I know the way to Newgate." There, as usual refusing to pay for special quarters, he wrote several tracts, among them *The Great Case of Liberty of Conscience,* discussing the recent trial; protested to Parliament with the other Quaker prisoners about the stiffening of the Conventicle Act; and dispatched a letter to the sheriffs of London giving them the details of their "common stinking jail."

He was out again in six months.

This charcoal portrait of William Penn by Englishman Francis Place dates from the 1690's and is believed to be the only authentic likeness of the Quaker idealist.

Fra'l Place delin

THE BOSTON MASSACRE

Even the worst offender, even the
lawyer. Our example is a passionate
Revolution, when John Adams
British soldiers who had fired into a
There are echoes of our own

"*The Jurors for the said Lord the King upon oath present that Thomas Preston, Esq.; William Wemms, laborer; James Hartegan, laborer; William McCauley, laborer; Hugh White, laborer; Matthew Killroy, laborer; William Warren, laborer; John Carroll, laborer and Hugh Montgomery, laborer, all now resident in Boston in the County of Suffolk, . . . not having the fear of God before their eyes, but being moved and seduced by the instigation of the devil and their own wicked hearts, did on the 5th day of this instant March, at Boston aforesaid within the county aforesaid with force and arms feloniously, willfully and of their malice aforethought assault one Crispus Attucks, then and there being in the peace of God and of the said Lord the King and that the said William Warren, with a certain handgun of the value of 20 shillings, which he the said William Warren then and there held in both his hands charged with gunpowder and two leaden bullets, then and there feloniously, willfully and of his malice aforethought, did shoot off and discharge at and against the said Crispus Attucks, and that the said William Warren, with the leaden bullets as aforesaid out of the said handgun then and there by force of the said gunpowder so shot off and discharged as aforesaid did then and there feloniously, willfully and of his malice aforethought, strike, penetrate and wound the said Crispus Attucks in and upon the right breast a little below the right pap of him the said Crispus and in and upon the left breast a little below the left pap . . . of which said mortal wounds the said Crispus Attucks then and there instantly died.*"

By THOMAS J. FLEMING

most unpopular cause, deserves a good
moment in Boston on the eve of the
undertook to defend the hated
Boston mob and created some "martyrs."
times in the trial that followed

Thus did the citizens of Boston indict nine British soldiers for murder. (The designation of the soldiers as "laborers" in the indictment emphasized that they were being tried as ordinary citizens—and also that they often eked out their pay by working for hire in and around Boston.) Never before in the history of Massachusetts had a trial aroused such intense, complex political and personal passion. Although his name stands alone in the indictment, Crispus Attucks was not the only victim. Four other Bostonians were also dead in what Samuel Adams, through his mouthpiece Benjamin Edes, publisher of the Boston *Gazette,* promptly called "a horrid massacre." For Adams and his friends in the Liberty party, the trial could have only one possible outcome. Paul Revere summed it up in the verse beneath his famous engraving of the scene.

> *But know, Fate summons to that awful Goal*
> *Where Justice strips the Murd'rer of his Soul:*
> *Should venal C[our]ts the scandal of the land*
> *Snatch the relentless Villain from her Hand*
> *Keen Execrations on this Plate inscrib'd*
> *Shall reach a Judge who never can be brib'd.*

The gist of what happened, whether baldly or passionately stated, was simple enough. Parliament's passage of the Townshend duties (import taxes on lead, paper, glass, tea) had inspired a series of riots and assaults on Royal officials which the magistrates and watchmen of Boston seemed helpless to prevent. On October 1, 1768, the Crown had landed two regiments

Paul Revere's famous engraving, from which these details come, gives a vivid if not quite detached view of the affray.

THE PROSECUTION: *Of the four principal lawyers who acted in the Boston Massacre trial, the one whose political sympathies leaned most toward the British soldiers was Samuel Quincy (left, as painted by John Singleton Copley). As solicitor general of Massachusetts, however, he was obliged to head the prosecution. When the Revolution came, he fled to the West Indies as a Loyalist. On the other hand, his associate counsellor, Robert Treat Paine (above), became a signer of the Declaration of Independence.*

of Royal troops to keep the peace. Relations between the townspeople and the soldiers had started poor and deteriorated steadily. After eighteen months, tempers on both sides were sputtering ominously.

Ironically, Parliament was about to repeal the Townshend duties, except for the tiny tax on tea, but the news had not reached Boston when the explosion occurred. At about eight o'clock on the moonlit night of March 5, 1770, a sentry on duty before the hated Custom House gave an impudent apprentice boy a knock on the ear with his gun. An unruly crowd gathered. Someone rang the bells in a nearby church. This signal, ordinarily a summons to fight fire, drew more people into the street. The frightened sentry called out the main guard. Seven men led by a corporal responded, and were shortly joined by Captain Thomas Preston. A few minutes later, a volley of shots left five "martyrs" dead or dying in the snow and six other men painfully wounded.

For a few hours Boston teetered on the brink of a blood bath. The well-armed Sons of Liberty outnumbered the British regiments ten to one, and the local militia was swiftly bolstered by hundreds of farmers who swarmed in from the countryside. Only a desperate speech by Lieutenant Governor Thomas Hutchinson, in which he promised to arrest the soldiers and charge them with murder, calmed the enraged city enough to restore an uneasy semblance of peace.

On the morning after the bloodshed, John Adams was in his office beside the Town House steps. Through the door came a tearful, wailing man, James Forest, known about Boston as a British toady and scornfully called "the Irish infant." The accused leader of the arrested British soldiers, Captain Preston, had begged him to find a lawyer posthaste. This had proved very difficult. Finally, young Josiah Quincy, Jr., from John Adams' home town of Braintree, had expressed a willingness on one condition—that John Adams join him in the defense. One other lawyer, Robert Auchmuty, a staunch conservative, had volunteered with the same proviso.

The challenge aroused all the latent conservatism in the thirty-four-year-old John Adams' pugnacious spirit. For a decade he had watched his distant cousin Samuel

THE DEFENSE: *The chief defending attorneys were both, ironically, American patriots—one of them destined for the Presidency after a uniquely distinguished career. John Adams (right, as painted by Benjamin Blyth in 1763) was a close friend of both prosecutors; his wife, Abigail, was a Quincy cousin. Josiah Quincy, Jr. (above), his assistant, was Samuel's younger brother. He too might have been one of the Founding Fathers; but his patriotic ardor was cut short by death from tuberculosis in 1775.*

construct a "political engine" in Boston, discovering under his tutelage "the wheels . . . cogs or pins, some of them dirty ones, which composed the machine and made it go." Though he wrote convincing defenses of the Liberty party position in the Boston *Gazette*, John often signed himself "Clarendon" (the British lord who had done his utmost to prevent Cromwell's excesses in the English civil war), and politely declined to harangue town meetings in the demagogic style of cousin Samuel and his friends Dr. Joseph Warren and James Otis. John took an even dimmer view of the violent tendencies of the Sons of Liberty—and obviously saw a direct connection between their terrorist tactics and the frightened state of the Boston bar.

Years later, John Adams recalled that he had "no hesitation" in accepting the case. He told Forest "that Council ought to be the very last thing that an accused person should want [*i.e.,* lack] in a free country. That the bar ought in my opinion to be independent and impartial at all times and in every circumstance."

This was a noble ideal, but John Adams knew that it was far from the reality of Boston in 1770. The city was ruthlessly divided into King's men and Liberty men. Doctors, lawyers, even clergymen, were chosen for their fiercely partisan political opinions. Adams himself had made his irrevocable choice in 1768, when he refused Thomas Hutchinson's offer to make him advocate general of the Court of Admiralty. Since that time the vast proportion of his law practice had come from Liberty clients.

Nevertheless Adams solemnly accepted a guinea from James Forest as a retainer to seal the agreement. He warned the overwrought Irishman that this would be "as important a cause as had ever been tried in any court or country of the world." Neither he nor Captain Preston could, of course, expect anything more than "fact, evidence and law would justify."

"Captain Preston," Forest answered, "requested and desired no more . . . as God Almighty is my judge I believe him an innocent man."

It was only a few days before the surprising news of Adams' decision had made a complete circuit of Boston and its environs. Rocks were flung through the windows of the Adams home. Boys jeered him on the

133

THE JUDGES: *Of the four justices presiding at the Massacre trials, the three most prominent were inclined toward the Loyalist side. Benjamin Lynde (left) was a moderate; but Peter Oliver (center) was a firm King's man who after 1776 resided in England; while Edmund Trowbridge (right), a famous jurist, remained neutral in the Revolution despite his views. THE JURY: John Adams managed to pack the jury with citizens sure to be unprejudiced against his clients. Loyalist Gilbert DeBlois (opposite page, in one of Copley's finer oil portraits) turned out to be a key man in Captain Preston's trial, in effect persuading the other jurors to vote for acquittal.*

streets. Josiah Quincy got a letter from his father in Braintree: "My Dear Son, I am under great affliction at hearing the bitterest reproaches uttered against you, for having become an advocate for those criminals who are charged with the murder of their fellow citizens. Good God! Is it possible? I will not believe it."

Young Quincy wrote his father a spirited defense of his decision. Tall and handsome, he was a fervent Liberty man, but above all an idealist. And he could afford to be reckless. He already knew he was suffering from tuberculosis, which was to cut short his brilliant career five years later. John Adams, with an established practice and a wife and three children to support, had no such motive. Nor was his temperament in the least inclined to enthusiasm. A worrier by nature, he sometimes expressed awed amazement at Sam Adams, who let the citizens of Boston pay his debts and lived "like the grasshopper" from day to day. John had always self-consciously planned his career. "The art of living," he once told Cousin Samuel, had cost him "much musing and pondering and anxiety."

Adams' morale did not improve when Cousin Samuel convened a town meeting of three thousand roaring adherents to demand the immediate expulsion of the two regiments. Lieutenant Governor Thomas Hutchinson yielded one regiment, then (literally trembling with anguish) yielded both, and the soldiers trudged through a barrage of derision to boats that took them to Castle William, far out in Boston Harbor.

Sam Adams' next move was a vigorous prosecution of a trial by newspaper. Ninety-six depositions from eyewitnesses were recorded by John Hodgson, the only shorthand writer in Boston, and solemnly sworn to before justices of the peace. They were attached to a twenty-two-page report compiled by the Boston selectmen and published and distributed throughout the province, but not in Boston. The Liberty men piously declared they did not want to prejudice anyone against the defendants.

As propaganda the book was a masterful document. The ninety-six witnesses were all but unanimous in their pro-Liberty description of the murder scene. Only one man had anything even faintly favorable to say for the soldiers, and editorial comments declared him to be a liar. The rest agreed that they were all in the streets of Boston that night on utterly peaceful errands —visiting friends, attending church meetings—when they were attacked by soldiers armed with bayonets, swords, and cutlasses.

But Samuel Adams was not the only person interested in compiling a version of what happened on the night of March 5. In New York, General Thomas Gage, commander in chief of all British troops in North America, wrote to Lieutenant Colonel Dalrymple, the commander of the Boston garrison.

It is absolutely necessary everything relating to the unhappy affair of the 5th of March should appear as full as it is possible upon Captain Preston's tryal. Not only what happened on the said night should be circumstantially made to appear, but also every insult and attack made upon the troops previous thereto with the pains taken by the military to prevent quarrels between the soldiers and inhabitants. If such things cannot be introduced at the tryal, affidavits should, however, be procured of these several circumstances and printed with the tryal which ought to be taken down for the purpose. . . .

Thus from the very start the trial became far more than a matter of determining the guilt or innocence of the arrested soldiers. The King's men were out to win a conviction against the mob-rule tactics of Samuel Adams. The Liberty men were as fiercely determined to pillory Parliament's use of armed force to suppress their political rights.

Between these two bitter, determined groups of men

stood the prisoners and their uneasy lawyers. Ironically, after the frantic search for defense attorneys, the Crown had almost as much trouble finding men willing to serve on the prosecution side. Jonathan Sewall, the colony's attorney general, handed up the indictment and disappeared from Boston, declaring that he would never appear in another court in that town. This may have been in part a maneuver to delay the trial. In the weeks succeeding the Massacre, Boston's inflamed state of mind made the possibility of an objective jury almost laughable.

But Samuel Adams was not to be easily put off. On the thirteenth of March, a town meeting resolved "That the selectmen be desired to employ one or more counsel to offer to the King's attorney as assistants to him in the trial of the murtherers now committed; and in case the King's attorney should refuse such assistance and the relatives of those persons who were murthered should apply for it, that then the town will bear the expense that may accrue thereby." The court soon appointed Samuel Quincy, Josiah Quincy's elder brother and a convinced Tory, to head the prosecution. Assisting him as the town's designee was attorney Robert Treat Paine, a staunch Liberty man.

On March 14, the day after the term opened, two of the judges declared themselves ill and announced a determination to adjourn to the second Tuesday in June. A committee of Liberty men swiftly appeared in court, with Samuel Adams and John Hancock as their spokesmen. In his quavering voice, gesturing with his palsied hands, Adams made what one observer called "a *very pathetic* [emotional] speech," calling on the court to proceed to the trial without delay. Governor Hutchinson described Adams as followed by "a vast concourse of people." The terrified judges, Hutchinson reported, "altered their determination and resolved to go on with the business. This, they assured me, was contrary to their inclination but they were under duress and afraid to offend the town."

A tax stamp

Captain Thomas Preston, meanwhile, tried to launch a small propaganda campaign on his own behalf. An Anglo-Irishman, forty years old with fifteen years of army service on his record, he was, compared to the other British soldiers in the garrison, well liked by the people of Boston. Various letters describe him as "amiable" and as being "a benevolent, humane man." Hoping no doubt to enlarge this image, he had the following "card" published in the Boston *Gazette*.

Messieurs Edes and Gill, permit me thro' the channel of your Paper, to return my Thanks in the most publick Manner to the Inhabitants in general of this Town—who throwing aside all *Party* and Prejudice, have with the utmost Humanity and Freedom stept forth Advocates for Truth in Defence of my injured Innocence, in the late unhappy Affair that happened on Monday Night last: and to assure them, that I shall ever have the highest Sense of the *Justice* they have done me, which will be ever gratefully remembered, by Their most obliged and most obedient humble Servant, Thomas Preston.

In New York, this gesture struck General Gage as the height of folly. "I can't be a proper judge at this distance," he wrote to Colonel Dalrymple, "but I wish he may not have been too premature in that measure; and if a legal proceedings are hereafter made use of against him, they will justify themselves by his own words."

Through late March and April, Samuel Adams kept his town meeting in almost continuous session by endlessly delaying matters of business. This gave him a perfectly legal device to maintain a relentless pressure on Governor Hutchinson and the judges.

The beleaguered Hutchinson decided that he would have to offer his enemies a sacrifice to allay their ferocity. Two weeks before the Massacre, a Custom House employee, Ebenezer Richardson, had gotten into a brawl with some boys who chased him home with a barrage of icy snowballs, stones, and brickbats. They continued the bombardment on his house, smashing most of the windows. The enraged Tory suddenly thrust a musket loaded with birdshot from an upstairs window. "By God," he shouted, "I'll make a lane through you." The gun boomed and most of the charge struck a twelve-year-old boy, who died that night. For Samuel Adams, Richardson was, of course, a very small fish. But his case did, in sequence of time, come first. Adams was therefore helpless to object when the judges moved to put Richardson in the dock.

Richardson had even more trouble procuring legal aid than Preston and his soldiers. Not a single attorney volunteered, and when the court appointed Samuel Fitch, he agreed to serve under violent protestations of duress, then became conveniently ill when the case went to trial. The court then appointed Josiah Quincy, Jr., an equally reluctant if more idealistic advocate. It is probable that in conducting Richardson's defense Quincy had the close advice of his friend John Adams. With Samuel Quincy and Robert Treat Paine handling the prosecution, Richardson's case became

136

almost a rehearsal for the Massacre trial.

"A vast concourse of rabble," as one Tory described his fellow Bostonians, packed the courtroom. They growled their disapproval when the three judges unanimously agreed that from the testimony of witnesses on both sides, the charge against Richardson could amount to no more than manslaughter. Justice Peter Oliver went even further and declared to the jury that in his opinion the case was justifiable homicide. Whereupon an improper Bostonian shouted from the crowd: "Damn that judge. If I was nigh him I would give it to him." When Oliver finished speaking, someone in the crowd roared out: "Remember, Jury, you are on oath. Blood requires blood."

The jury found Richardson guilty of first-degree murder, and only vigorous exertion by the sheriff and town constables prevented the mob from taking him outside and hanging him on the spot.

The judges, aghast at the jury's complete disregard of their charge, refused to sentence Richardson. He was remanded to jail, where he was to languish for another two years. His case, however, made it look certain that trying Preston and the soldiers right away would result in their conviction. "Procrastination is our only course as things are now situated," wrote Colonel Dalrymple to General Gage.

Samuel Adams and his friends continued to agitate for instant justice. Once more they appeared in the courtroom and harangued the judges, threatening to withhold their salaries if they delayed any longer. But Hutchinson, who had the courage of his convictions, finally won the seesaw battle. Under his direction, the court constantly met and adjourned, met and adjourned. Then Hutchinson shifted the next meeting of the judiciary to Cambridge, proclaiming it a necessity to avoid the threats of the Boston mob. This inspired (on June 1, 1770) what Hutchinson ironically called "a jovial celebration . . . at Boston in opposition to me," which involved roasting an ox whole on the Common and a great dinner at Faneuil Hall. While toasts were being drunk to liberty, the judges quietly adjourned the court *sine die* (without setting a day to reconvene), automatically continuing to the next term the question of the soldiers' fate. Hutchinson wrote proudly to Gage, describing how he had "procured without any tumult a continuance of the trial to the next term."

Through the hot Boston summer Preston and his men sat in their cells. Preston's fortunes, which seemed for a while to be rising, took a sharp downward turn when a Tory version of the Massacre, first published in England, appeared in the Boston *Gazette*. The Captain was soon writing Gage that he feared the mob was planning an attack on the jail to murder him and his men in their cells. Though nothing like that happened, the soldiers continued to sleep badly.

The menacing atmosphere meanwhile was working on the nervous judges. Twice that summer Chief Justice Benjamin Lynde, who was over seventy, tried to hand in his resignation. Justice Edmund Trowbridge was at least as terrified. Only Judge Peter Oliver stood firm, ignoring personal threats in the newspapers. It was also widely believed that the soldiers' attorneys would be intimidated and not defend their clients aggressively. And indeed, Robert Auchmuty told Hutchinson he did not see much hope for Preston.

Nevertheless, early in September, with Hutchinson's approval, Preston began to press for a trial. Actually Hutchinson was still certain Preston would be found guilty, but he wanted the matter settled early in the fall, with sentencing delayed until the opening of the March term. This might give him time to get a ship to England and back with a King's pardon to save Preston's neck.

The justices, however, reserved their own opinion of when they should risk their lives by bringing Preston to trial: they went on circuit into the country. First, however, they did bring the Captain and his eight soldiers into the courtroom for arraignment. Each pleaded "Not guilty," and "for trial put himself upon God and the country."

At this point John Adams played a surprise card, one he had been holding very close to his vest. He made a motion to try Captain Preston and the soldiers separately. The court granted it. The soldiers immediately decided they were to be the sacrificial lambs, and forwarded a plaintive petition to the court: "May it please Your Honors, we poor distressed prisoners beg that ye would be so good as to lett us have our trial at the same

The landing of British troops to garrison Boston in 1768 profoundly irritated most of the natives.

time with our Captain, for we did our Captain's orders and if we don't obey his command we should have been confined and shott for not doing it. . . ." This only confirmed defense fears that Preston and his men would each accuse the other if tried jointly, and in the confusion the jury would decide to hang them all. But as we shall soon see, this was not the only reason for Adams' unexpected motion.

Not until October 24, 1770, did the judges return and the lawyers assemble to impanel a jury to decide Captain Preston's fate. Almost immediately it became evident that the court and all the lawyers were involved in a curious kind of collusion. Adams, the acknowledged leader of the defense, challenged every juror who came from within the city limits of Boston, quickly rejecting the eighteen men who had been selected by the Boston town meeting of August 24, 1770. When the legally summoned jurors were used up, it was the custom of the day to allow the sheriff to contribute "talesmen." By no coincidence, every talesman produced by the sheriff for Preston's trial came from outside Boston.

These maneuvers must have been obvious to Samuel Adams. They were beyond all doubt known to John Adams and Josiah Quincy. Why did Samuel Adams by silence and inaction give tacit approval? A nod from him, and his well-disciplined bullyboys could have filled the courtroom as they did at Richardson's trial

NYPL

A failure in business, Sam Adams became one of the most successful politicians in American history. From 1764 until 1776 he bent all of his talents toward contesting British sovereignty.

and terrified the judges and jurors into submission. But there is no evidence of any disorder during Preston's trial, nor at the trial of the soldiers. The change of tactics is startling, and there is nothing in the written evidence of the Massacre story that explains it.

The answer must lie in the political struggle that surrounded the trials. By this time, John Adams and Josiah Quincy had, thanks to a liberal supply of sovereigns from General Gage, obtained depositions from dozens of people who had been witnesses to various aspects of the bloody deed. These statements conflicted so totally with the evidence advanced by the Liberty men in their ninety-six depositions that there was only one possible conclusion—someone was committing perjury. Worse, the evidence advanced by the witnesses Adams and Quincy uncovered put the town of Boston in a most unholy light. For the first time the Loyalists had a weapon with which they could smite Samuel Adams hard. But Sam on his side retained the weapon he knew and handled best: the Boston mob.

Even with the packed jury, Preston's case was by no means a sure thing. The prosecution attacked vigorously, parading witness after witness to the stand for the better part of two days; all of them agreed that the Captain gave the order to fire—and, equally important, that there was no provocation for it beyond name-calling and a few snowballs from the crowd gathered in King Street.

The defense attorneys did little to dispute these assertions in their cross-examination. But they did shake the believability of many witnesses by pointing out strange confusions in their testimony. Some swore the Captain stood in front of the men; others said he stood behind them. Several said that the Captain had on a "cloth color" surtout (a kind of overcoat); almost as many said they distinctly saw him in his bright red regimentals.

After a prosecution summation by Samuel Quincy, in which he accused Preston of "murder with malice aforethought," the defense produced their witnesses. The first few disputed the prosecution's claim that the crowd was small and peaceful, but said nothing that would stir an already tired jury. (It was the first time in Massachusetts' memory that a murder trial had lasted more than a day.) Then John Adams produced a merchant named Richard Palmes, and the courtroom came to life. Mr. Palmes was the real reason for the separate trials. He had earlier given a lengthy deposition supposedly supporting the Liberty side of the story. Even a cursory reading of this told a lawyer as keen as John Adams that detaching Preston from his men converted Palmes into a witness for the Captain.

Palmes knew it, and had desperately tried to decamp from Boston. John Adams had kept him in town by court order. On the stand, the reluctant Palmes was forced to repeat his sworn deposition. He told of stepping up to Preston as he joined his soldiers and asking: "Sir, I hope you don't intend the soldiers shall fire on the inhabitants."

"He said, 'by no means.' The instant he spoke I saw something resembling snow or ice strike the grenadier on the Captain's right hand, being the only one then at his right. [The grenadier] instantly stepped one foot back and fired the first gun. . . . The gun scorched the nap of my surtout at the elbow."

Other witnesses substantiated Palmes' statement. As a good lawyer, Adams also brought in a few people who bolstered the self-defense side of Preston's plea. But in his summation, he made it clear that Palmes was his key witness. Coolly, he noted that the mortified merchant was "an inhabitant of the town and therefore not prejudiced in favor of the soldiers." Robert Auchmuty, summing up after Adams, declared that Palmes' evidence "may be opposed to all the Crown's evidence." He went on to give an impressive speech, citing a wealth of precedents in the common law which permitted soldiers or other persons to kill rioters or even individuals who attacked them and threatened them with serious injury. Auchmuty's knowledge of the law was considered weak, but he sounded formidable as he cited case after case from Coke and other great authorities on English law. Undoubtedly he was using John Adams' research. But he put it together with an enthusiasm and flair that surprised and delighted Preston and the Tories who had been doubting him. His performance can probably be explained by a letter General Gage wrote to Colonel Dalrymple, "I am sorry," the British commander in chief said, "you doubt Mr. Auchmuty's zeal or good intentions. . . . If you find it necessary, you should encourage him, for very particular reports are to be made of every circumstance of the tryal." Caught between the threat of royal censure and his dread of the Boston mob, Auchmuty followed his Loyalist leanings and performed brilliantly.

Robert Treat Paine valiantly tried to rescue the prosecution's case. But he could not explain away Palmes. He called him "their principal witness" and admitted he was "a gentleman who I can by no means suppose would be guilty of a known falsehood." Paine could only maintain that this staunch Son of Liberty was "certainly mistaken," and fumble to an emotional peroration, calling on the jury to "find such a verdict as the laws of God, of nature and your own conscience will ever approve."

Now came the judges' charges to the jury. There were four sitting—Chief Justice Lynde and Justices John Cushing, Peter Oliver, and Edmund Trowbridge. Trowbridge was considered the best legal mind in

CULVER PICTURES

Thomas Hutchinson, lieutenant governor of Massachusetts at the time of the Massacre trial, was a thoroughbred New Englander, but also an arch-royalist who hated the idea of rebellion.

Massachusetts. Stately in their white wigs and long red (for a murder trial) robes, they proceeded to examine the evidence and the law. Trowbridge spoke first, pointing out the contradictory accounts given by the witnesses and declaring that it did not appear to him that the prisoner gave orders to fire. But even if the jury should think otherwise, they surely could not call his crime murder. The people assembled were "a riotous mob" who had murderously attacked the prisoner and his party. If Preston was guilty of any offense, it could only be excusable homicide. The other three judges concurred. Oliver added, "in a very nervous and pathetic manner," that he was resolved to do his duty to his God, his King, and his country, and despise both insults and threats.

The jury was then locked up for the night. Within three hours they voted to acquit Preston and so reported it to the assembled court the next morning. The Captain was immediately released from jail and rushed by boat to Castle William, where the guns of his regiment guaranteed his safety against possible revenge from the Boston mob. But Samuel Adams' obvious acquiescence in the choice of a packed jury made it clear that he had long since agreed to let Captain Preston go in peace. His men were another matter.

Thus far, John Adams, with Josiah Quincy's help, had maintained his perilous balancing act. At one point during the five days of Preston's trial, he had objected angrily when Auchmuty tried to advance more evidence of a Liberty conspiracy to incite a riot.

139

The Tories on the bench had stressed mob violence in their remarks to the jury; yet the violent side of the evidence had played only a minor role in Preston's trial. It had to be the heart of the soldiers' case. That they had fired their guns was beyond debating; five men were dead to prove it.

There was another hint of the way the local wind was blowing: Auchmuty now withdrew from the soldiers' defense, and another attorney, Sampson Salter Blowers, was appointed in his place. Like Quincy, he was young and comparatively inexperienced. Thus almost full responsibility for the soldiers' fate, both in a public and a private sense, fell on the stocky shoulders of John Adams.

If he had any illusions about the tactics of the opposition, they vanished when he picked up the Boston *Gazette* on the Monday before the trial began. "Is it then a dream—murder on the 5th of March with the dogs greedily licking human blood in King Street? Some say that righteous heaven will avenge it. And what says the Law of God? *Whoso sheddeth Man's Blood, by Man shall his Blood be shed!*" And the *Gazette* quoted at length from a sermon preached by the Reverend Doctor Chauncy, senior minister of Boston, declaring that should the soldiers be convicted of murder, Governor Hutchinson would never dare grant them a reprieve: "Surely he would not suffer the town and land to lie under the defilement of blood! Surely he would not make himself a partaker in the guilt of murder by putting a stop to the shedding of their blood, who have murderously spilt the blood of others."

On the day the second trial began, the audience was a good barometer of the local atmosphere. At Preston's trial the benches had been filled by Tories and army officers. Now the courtroom was jammed to the windows with townspeople. Shorthand-writer John Hodgson, who recorded the trial, complained that he did not have room to move his elbow. Outside, snow was falling, and the bailiffs had to light candles against the gloom. People shivered in winter clothes; the two small stoves in the room seemed to have no effect whatsoever on the pervading chill.

The prisoners were brought to the bar. Their blazing red coats set off their faces, drawn and pale from almost nine months in jail. The clerk of the court read an enlarged indictment to them. It accused them of murdering, besides Crispus Attucks, Samuel Maverick, a seventeen-year-old apprentice boy; Samuel Gray, a former employee of (but no relation to) the owner of Gray's rope works; James Caldwell, a sailor from a Massachusetts coasting vessel; and one Patrick Carr, known as "the Irish teague."

The jury was now chosen, and Adams and Quincy challenged and rejected no less than thirty prospects, forcing the sheriff to summon eight talesmen. As in Preston's case, the accepted jurymen were all from neighboring towns—Roxbury, Dedham, Milton, Hingham—and one, Isaiah Thayer, was from Adams' home town of Braintree. But there is no evidence that any had Tory leanings.

The prosecution opened with a brief, low-keyed talk by Samuel Quincy. He declared that the trial involved the "most melancholy event that has yet taken place on the continent of America, and perhaps of the greatest expectation of any that has yet come before a tribunal of civil justice in this part of the British dominions." He vowed to make no appeal to partiality or prejudice but to conduct himself "with decency and candor," with one object—"simply that of truth."

Whereupon he began summoning witnesses by the dozen. The first several (one was Jonathan W. Austin, John Adams' clerk) simply identified various soldiers and reported seeing one or two of the victims fall. Things heated up when Edward Langford, a town watchman, took the stand. He testified that Samuel Gray was standing beside him in the front rank of the crowd in the most peaceable manner, without any weapon, not even a snowball: "His hands were in his bosom." According to Langford, Gray asked him what was going on. Langford replied he did not know, and almost immediately Matthew Killroy's gun went off and Samuel Gray fell, striking Langford's left foot. A parade of succeeding witnesses repeatedly identified Killroy as Gray's assassin.

Richard Palmes returned to testify, for the prosecution this time, and was obviously much more comfortable about it. He identified bald-headed Hugh Montgomery, one of the sentries, and testified that he had knocked Montgomery down—but only *after* the grenadier had fired his gun, and was attempting to run Palmes through with his bayonet.

Subsequent testimony, notably by Nicholas Ferreter, supplied interesting background information for the "massacre." Ferreter was a worker at Gray's rope works. He reported that on Friday, March 2, during the lunch hour at Gray's, Samuel Gray hailed a passing soldier and asked him if he wanted work. "Yes," said the poorly paid redcoat, "I do, faith." Well, said Gray in pure Anglo-Saxon, he could go clean his outhouse. The soldier's temper exploded. He took a swing at Gray, and other ropemakers rushed to Gray's assistance. Ferreter described how he "knocked up his [the soldier's] heels, his coat flew open and out dropped a naked cutlass which I took up and carried off with me." The soldier was soon back with a dozen of his fellows, among them Matthew Killroy. A battle royal

On the Death of Five young Men who was Murthered, *March* 5th 1770. By the 29th Regiment.

Macabre coffin lids showing the victims' initials decorated the title page of this broadside published by Paul Revere.

ensued, until the ropewalk owner, John Gray, stopped it. That afternoon the soldiers returned in force, and this time the rope workers, in a furious brawl, drove them back to their barracks.

Ill feeling on the part of the British garrison toward the populace was thus well established. Another point in the prosecution's attack was the conduct of the soldiers on the night of the killing. There was, they argued, a plot afoot among the members of the 29th Regiment to attack anyone they caught on the street. Nathaniel Appleton told how a dozen soldiers with drawn bayonets had attacked him on the steps of his house and only fast footwork got him inside in time to bolt the door. John Appleton, "a young lad," told how he had been with his nine-year-old brother in King Street when twenty soldiers with cutlasses in their hands attacked him. He begged them to spare his life, he testified, and one said, "No, damn you, we will kill you all," and struck at his head with a sheathed cutlass. Thomas Marshall told how he saw "a party from the main guard, ten or twelve, come rushing out violently. I saw their arms glitter by the moonlight, hallooing, 'Damn them, where are they, by Jesus, let them come.'"

Finally, to certify the hideous and bloodthirsty character of the defendants, one Joseph Crosswell testified that the next morning he saw blood dried on five or six inches of Killroy's bayonet.

Samuel Quincy summed up the prosecution's evidence. He dwelt at length on testimony that accused Killroy of firing directly at Gray, and deduced that the private was guilty of murder with malice. He then deplored the conduct of the soldiers before the riot, maintaining that the church bells had rung because it was the soldiers who, rushing to the street, had cried the word "fire." "It is probable," declared Quincy darkly, "the word fire was the watchword. It appears to me that if we can believe the evidence, they had a design of attacking and slaughtering the inhabitants that night and they could have devised no better method to draw out the inhabitants unarmed than to cry fire!" Finally, he hammered again at Killroy, reminding the jury that it is "immaterial, where there are a number of persons concerned, who gave the mortal blow; all that are present are in the eye of the law principals. This is a rule settled by the judges of England upon solid argument."

To the bar now stepped young Josiah Quincy to open for the defense. After a vigorous speech, in which he reminded the jurors that a soldier's life was, from a legal standpoint, "as estimable as the life of any other citizen," he began summoning witnesses to bolster his assertion that the soldiers had fired in self-defense. This was the climax of the Adams-Quincy tightrope act. Could the defense prove a mob was at work without pricking the jury's civic pride and political animosity? One by one the witnesses paraded to the stand.

James Crawford told how on the way home he met "numbers of people" going downtown with sticks in their hands. The sticks were "not common walking canes but pretty large cudgels." Archibald Wilson told of sitting in a house near Dock Square when "a certain gentleman" came in and asked how "he came to be sitting there when there was such trouble betwixt the soldiers and inhabitants." Looking out the window, Wilson saw thirty or forty men from the North End make "two or three sundry attacks up that lane where the barracks which are called Murray's were."

"How were they armed that came from the North End?" Josiah Quincy asked.

"They had sticks or staves, I know not what they are called," Wilson said.

In Dock Square Wilson found some two hundred men gathered. They surged away as if on a signal giving "two or three cheers for [*i.e.*, challenging] the main guard." Wilson followed them and was in Royal Exchange Lane, leading into King Street, when the bells rang. He said he heard voices shouting fire and remarked it was "uncommon to go to a fire with bludgeons." Somebody told him, "they were uncommon bells."

William Hunter, the next witness, added another

Dr. John Jeffries, star witness for the defense, later moved to England as a Loyalist. In 1785 he became famous when, with a French partner, he made the first balloon crossing of the English Channel.

significant detail to the gathering in Dock Square. He told of seeing "a gentleman" with a red cloak around whom the crowd gathered. "He stood in the middle of them and they were all very quiet; he spoke to them a little while, and then he went off and they took off their hats and gave three cheers for the main guard."

"Was the man who spoke to these people a tall or short man?" Josiah Quincy asked.

"Pretty tall."

"How was he dressed?"

"He had a white wig and red cloak, and instantly after his talking a few minutes to them they made huzzas for the main guard."

It may well have been at this point that John Adams arose in distress to interrupt his colleague and declare that he would walk out of the case if Quincy insisted on cross-examining witnesses to such unnecessary lengths, thereby setting the town in a bad light. (The transcript of the trial does not show us exactly where this happened but we know it occurred.) William Gordon, the British historian of the Revolution, describes the incident but mistakenly places it in Preston's trial. We must be grateful to him, nonetheless, because in John Adams' personal copy of Gordon's book he wrote an explanatory marginal note: "Adams' motive is not here perceived. His clients' lives were

hazarded by Quincy's too youthful ardor." Could anything sum up more graphically the terrible pressure under which Quincy and Adams worked? If Quincy persuaded a witness to identify the tall, red-cloaked speaker in Dock Square (Samuel Adams was short, but Will Molineux, his right-hand man, was tall), the Liberty boys in wrathful self-defense would have almost certainly unleashed the mob, jammed the courtroom, and created the kind of atmosphere that had convicted Richardson.

The evidence Adams did tolerate was bad enough, from the Liberty viewpoint. Witness after witness confirmed that there had been mobs of Bostonians surging through the streets, armed with clubs. Doctor Richard Hirons gave some details of a scene before the barracks. As early as seven o'clock some twenty or thirty townspeople appeared there, he said, led by "a little man" who lectured four or five officers of the 29th Regiment on the conduct of their soldiers in the streets. The man then began making a speech, shouting, "We did not send for you. We will not have you here. We will get rid of you." The officers insisted they were doing their best to keep the soldiers in their barracks and urged the speechmaker to use "his interest" to disperse the people.

Next came Benjamin Davis, Jr., who shattered the prosecution's claim that Samuel Gray was "in the King's peace" on the night he died. Young Davis told of meeting Gray, who asked where the fire was. "I said there was no fire, it was the soldiers fighting. He said, 'Damn it, I am glad of it. I will knock some of them on the head.' He ran off. I said to him, take heed you do not get killed . . . He said, 'Do not you fear, damn their bloods.' "

"Had he a stick in his hand?"

"He had one under his arm."

Now Quincy concentrated his fire on the scene in Dock Square. Patrick Keaton saw "a tall mulatto fellow, the same that was killed; he had two clubs in his hand and he said, 'Here take one of them.' I did so." Nathaniel Russell, chairmaker, said he saw trouble coming and "intended to retreat as fast as I could. I had not got three yards before the guns were fired."

"How many people do you imagine were then gathered around the party?"

"Fifty or sixty able-bodied men."

"Did they crowd near the soldiers?"

"So near, that I think you could not get your hat betwixt them and the bayonets."

"How many people do you think there might be in the whole?"

"About two hundred."

"Did the soldiers say anything to the people?"

"They never opened their lips; they stood in a trem-

142

bling manner, as if they expected nothing but death."

This hit the prosecution so hard that they introduced a Crown witness, one John Cox, a bricklayer, who testified that he saw three soldiers threatening, earlier in the evening, to chop down or blow up Boston's sacred Liberty tree. They also threw in a future Revolutionary War general, Henry Knox, who said that Preston and his squad, while forcing their way through the crowd, behaved "in a very threatening" manner. "They said, 'Make way, damn you, make way,' and they pricked some of the people."

But the defense returned relentlessly to the evidence of riot. Benjamin Burdick admitted he stood in the front ranks of the crowd brandishing a highland broadsword. Newton Prince, a free Negro, told of watching people with sticks striking the guns of the soldiers at the right wing of the squad. Andrew, the Negro servant of Oliver Wendell, placed special emphasis on the conduct of Crispus Attucks. He told of seeing Attucks knock Killroy's gun away and strike him over the head. "The blow came either on the soldier's cheek or hat." Holding Killroy's bayonet with his left hand, Attucks tried to tear the gun loose, crying, "Kill the dogs. Knock them over." But Killroy wrenched his gun free, and Andrew, sensing imminent bloodshed, "turned to go off." He had gotten away "only about the length of a gun" when the first man fired.

"Did the soldiers of that party or any of them," Quincy asked, "step or move out of the rank in which they stood to push the people?"

"No," Andrew replied, "and if they had they might have killed me and many others with their bayonets."

Finally John Adams played his trump card, Doctor John Jeffries. Though he later became a Loyalist exile, Jeffries was one of Boston's most respected physicians. When Adams was representing America in London in the 1780's, he retained him as his family doctor. Jeffries told how he had been called to attend Patrick Carr, who had been mortally wounded in the firing. Carr lived nine days, and Jeffries conversed with him several times about the brawl. Carr told how he had been drawn from his boardinghouse by the ringing bells and had followed the crowd up Cornhill to King Street. Carr had not been in the front rank of the rioters. He was on the other side of the street circling the outer rim of the crowd when the guns began to fire, and obviously was hit by a wild bullet. Jeffries asked him whether he thought the soldiers would fire:

He told me that he thought that the soldiers would have fired long before. I then asked him if he thought the soldiers would have been hurt if they had not fired. He said he really thought they would, for he had heard many voices cry out "Kill them." I asked him then, meaning to close all, whether he thought they fired in self-defense or on purpose to destroy the people. He said he really thought they did fire to defend themselves; that he did not blame the man, whoever he was, who shot him. . . . He told me also that he was a native of Ireland, that he had frequently seen mobs and soldiers called upon to quell them: whenever he mentioned that he always called himself a fool, that he might have known better, that he had seen soldiers often fire on the people in Ireland, but had never seen them bear half so much before they fired in his life.

All by himself, Jeffries blew up ninety per cent of the prosecution's case. Proof of their consternation was the sudden production of additional witnesses at the very end of the trial. They were not particularly effective, merely reiterating what had been said before.

Josiah Quincy summed up for the defense. In a long, emotional speech he reviewed the evidence, urging the jurors to ask themselves crucial questions. "Was the sentinel insulted and attacked? Did he call for assistance, and did the party go to assist him? Was it lawful for them so to do? Were the soldiers when thus lawfully assembled, assaulted by a great number of people assembled? Was this last assembly lawful?" He closed with a moving appeal to mercy, quoting Shakespeare on the subject, asking the jurors to guarantee themselves "an absolving conscience" when the "agitations of the day" had subsided.

John Adams now took the floor to close for the defense. Thus far he had spoken little; Quincy had handled the interrogation of the witnesses. But everyone, jurors included, knew that Adams was the heart and head of the defense. His words would have a finality that Quincy, for all his emotion, could not convey.

Adams began with a direct and simple statement of his professional role: "I am for the prisoners at the bar." He would apologize for it, he said, only in the words of Cesare Beccaria, the eminent Italian jurist of the period: "If I can but be the instrument of preserving one life, his blessing and tears of transport shall be a sufficient consolation to me, for the contempt of all mankind."

In a quiet, matter-of-fact voice Adams proceeded to explain the law of homicide to the jury, and then applied the legal principle of self-defense to the situation of the soldiers in King Street, "with all the bells ringing to call the town together . . . [and] they knew by that time that there was no fire; the people shouting, huzzaing, and making the mob whistle . . . , which when a boy makes it in the street is no formidable thing, but when made by a multitude is a most hideous shriek, almost as terrible as an Indian yell; the people crying, 'Kill them! Kill them! Knock them over!' heaving snowballs, oyster shells, clubs, white birch sticks . . ." Consider, he asked the jury, whether any reasonable man in the soldiers' situation would not have concluded the mob was going to kill him.

Next he cited the law on riot: "Wheresoever more than three persons use force or violence, for the accomplishment of any design whatever, all concerned are rioters." Were there not more than three persons in Dock Square? Did they not agree to go to King Street and attack the main guard? Why hesitate then to call this so-called assembly a riot?

Perhaps at this point Adams saw the jurors' faces clouding. He swiftly led their emotions in the opposite direction by distinguishing between rioters and rebels. "I do not mean to apply the word rebel on this occasion: I have no reason to suppose that ever there was one in Boston, at least among the natives of the country; but rioters are in the same situation as far as my argument is concerned, and proper officers may suppress rioters and so may even private persons."

From 11 A.M. to 5 P.M. Adams examined the law and the evidence, frequently reading directly from authorities to bolster his arguments. The next morning he continued his summation, examining the testimony of various witnesses. He dismissed the Crown's attempt to prove Killroy's malice. "Admitting that this testimony is literally true and that he had all the malice they would wish to prove, yet if he was assaulted that night and his life in danger, he had a right to defend himself as well as another man."

The witnesses who had described Crispus Attucks' belligerent behavior were cited. Attucks was, said Adams, "a stout mulatto fellow whose very looks was enough to terrify any person . . . He had heartiness enough to fall in upon them [*i.e.*, the soldiers] and with one hand took hold of the bayonet and with the other knocked the man down." It was to Attucks' "mad behavior, in all probability, the dreadful carnage of that night is chiefly to be ascribed."

Proving he could play on the prejudices of the jurors as skillfully as he could cite the law, Adams added: "And it is in this manner this town has been often treated; a Carr from Ireland and an Attucks from Framingham, happening to be here, shall sally out upon their thoughtless enterprises, at the head of such a rabble of negroes, etcetera, as they can collect together, and then there are not wanting persons to ascribe all their doings to the good people of the town."

The law, Adams declared, was clear. The soldiers had a right to kill in their own defense. If the attack on them was not so severe as to endanger their lives, yet if they were assaulted at all, the law reduces their offense to manslaughter.

Finally came a soaring peroration.

To your candor and justice I submit the prisoners and their cause. The law, in all vicissitudes of government, fluctuations of the passions, or flights of enthusiasm, will preserve a steady, undeviating course. It will not bend to the uncertain wishes, imaginations, and wanton tempers of men . . . On the one hand it is inexorable to the cries and lamentations of the prisoners; on the other it is deaf, deaf as an adder, to the clamors of the populace.

Once more Robert Treat Paine strove to rescue the prosecution's collapsing case. But he was in retreat all the way. "I am sensible, gentlemen," he began, "I have got the severe side of the question to conduct." He wasted time trying to justify the presence of so many armed citizens on the streets, renewing the argument that the soldiers had started the trouble first. He had nothing whatsoever to say about Doctor Jeffries' report of Carr's words, insisting instead on his witnesses' versions of the conduct of Attucks and Gray: "Attucks, fifteen feet off leaning on his stick, Gray, twelve feet off with his hand in his bosom." He ended by concentrating his fire on Killroy, calling his deliberate murder of Gray "beyond dispute." He all but gave up on the other soldiers in his closing lines. "You must unavoidably find him [*i.e.*, Killroy] guilty of murder. What your judgement should think of the rest, though the evidence is undoubtedly the fullest against him, yet it is full enough against the rest."

The next morning, Justice Trowbridge charged the jury. It was a long and careful examination of the evidence and the law, most of which had already been covered by John Adams. But Adams must have stirred uneasily when he heard Trowbridge couple the words "riot and rebellion," and add a remark that the law in regard to treason should be "more generally known here than it seems to be." Judge Peter Oliver went even farther down this risky path. He declared that the riot had been perpetrated "by villains." As for the tall man in the red cloak and white wig, "that tall man is guilty in the sight of God of the murder of the five persons mentioned in the indictment."

Thus instructed, the jury withdrew. Two hours and a half dragged slowly by while the defense attorneys undoubtedly sat there fearing the worst. Finally, a door behind the bench opened, the twelve countrymen filed into their places, and the foreman, Joseph Mayo of Roxbury, arose to give the verdict. "William Wemms, James Hartegan, William McCauley, Hugh White, William Warren, and John Carroll: *Not guilty*. . . . Matthew Killroy and Hugh Montgomery, *Not guilty* of murder but *guilty* of manslaughter."

John Adams rose instantly and asked the benefit of clergy for Killroy and Montgomery. The judges dismissed the six acquitted men and quickly granted Adams' plea. ("Benefit of clergy," by 1770, had been interpreted to include anyone who was literate; and the "clergyman's" penalty for manslaughter was branding on the thumb.)

The sentence was carried out on December 14. Killroy and Montgomery first read a passage from the Bible to establish their literacy, and prepared for the shock of the glowing iron. Adams recalled later he "never pitied any men more . . . They were noble, fine-looking men; protested they had done nothing contrary to their duty as soldiers; and, when the sheriff approached to perform his office, they burst into tears."

For Preston and the soldiers, the ordeal was over. They went their various ways, and John Adams saw only one of them again. Years later, when he was ambassador of an independent America to the Court of St. James's, he recognized Preston as he passed by on a London street. For bearing his part of the ordeal with patience and dignity, Preston, retiring from the army almost immediately, received a pension of two hundred pounds a year from the King. The enlisted men, as was their lot in those days, received nothing.

In his diary and later letters, John Adams maintained that his "disinterested action" in defending the soldiers was "one of the best pieces of service I ever rendered my country." Samuel Adams did not think so, at least in public. Writing under the name *Vindex*, he denounced the jury's verdict and the defense arguments in a series of scathing articles in the Boston *Gazette*. But Samuel Adams was a very subtle man. Privately, his friendship with John became even more intimate; early in the following year, when John Adams took his family home to Braintree and became a commuter to his city law office, he frequently ate breakfast, lunch, and dinner at his "brother" Samuel's house.

Did Samuel Adams realize that without John at the defense table, the trials might well have sent him and other leaders of the Liberty party, such as the man in the red cloak, to London under arrest for treason? Did the trials enable John to convince his cousin that the Liberty policy of violence had come close to destroying the cause, and must be modified henceforth? Both conclusions seem almost inescapable. But two years later, patient Cousin Samuel revealed another reason for his friendship. He had organized an annual extravaganza to commemorate the death of the Massacre victims with prayers and fierce anti-British oratory. In 1772, Samuel asked John to make the principal address. It would have been a most satisfactory way of including him at last on the Boston side of the case. But John Adams was still his own man. He quietly declined, explaining that he felt "I should only expose myself to the lash of ignorant and malicious tongues on both sides of the question."

There the matter would have undoubtedly remained if Parliament had not foolishly reignited the quarrel with the colonies the following year. The dead rioters thereby became enshrined in American folklore as martyrs. And John Adams was able to stand beside his Cousin Samuel with a clear conscience in the struggle against British oppression. That John won the larger place in history should not be surprising to anyone who penetrates beyond the patriotic myth to the interior drama of this great but little-understood trial.

The principal sources used for this account of the Boston Massacre were Frederick Kidder's History of the Boston Massacre *(1870), which reprints important documents first published in 1770; Randolph G. Adams'* New Light on the Boston Massacre *(1938); Page Smith's* John Adams *(1962); and* Legal Papers of John Adams, *Vol. 3 (1965), edited by L. Kinvin Wroth and Hiller B. Zobel and published by the Belknap Press of Harvard University Press. This last is the most comprehensive scholarly study to date of the Boston Massacre and the ensuing trials.*

MARTYR FOR A FREE

Matthew Lyon did not like John Adam

There have been two downright attempts by government to curb freedom of the press in America since Plymouth Rock. The first took place when John Peter Zenger, a New York publisher, was jailed in 1735 for criticizing the British colonial governor, but through a brilliant defense by Andrew Hamilton, a salty old Philadelphia lawyer, was acquitted. In the second instance, 63 years later under our own young Constitution, the accused was less fortunate.

This latter case was an outcome of the first, last and only effort of the United States government to curb freedom of expression by statute; namely, the Sedition Law of 1798. This law was enacted when we were, as a government, young, amateurish and excitable; when, of our two parties, the Republican-Democrats suspected Alexander Hamilton and the Federalists of plotting a return to monarchy, while the Federalists regarded Jefferson, the Democratic leader and a frank admirer of the wild and bloody French Revolution, as a dangerous Communist. The victim in this case was an ebullient, red-headed Irishman named Matthew Lyon, who, as one might have known, would get into trouble of this sort sooner or later.

Among the many bizarre and colorful figures in

146

PRESS

By ALVIN HARLOW

nd insisted on his right to say so. He spent months in jail but he could not be silenced.

American history, none has been more distinctive than this indomitable son of Erin. Born in Wicklow in 1750, Matthew Lyon was not yet thirteen and had been in school two years in Dublin when his father was executed for plotting against the British Crown. For two years more the boy worked in a printer's shop in Dublin. Then at fifteen—here the versions differ—either he was inveigled into coming to America on a ship whose captain trickily sold him in New York for the remainder of his minority as an indentured servant, or he made the arrangement himself to get passage across the ocean. Anyhow, when the captain put the

sturdy, broad-shouldered lad on the block in New York, he represented him as aged eighteen, thereby shortening his possible servitude from six years to three. A Connecticut Yankee with the flavorous name of Jabez Bacon bought him for twelve pounds.

Mr. Bacon, a prosperous merchant of Litchfield County, liked to trade in cattle, and Matt, looking around for a way out of his thraldom, found a couple of likely-looking bulls which could be bought for something like $40 in later American money. Their owner, one Hannah, agreed to let him have them and work out their purchase price after he had obtained

147

his freedom. Mr. Bacon agreed to accept the animals in payment for Matt's remaining time, so the youth was free after only one year.

For two years thereafter he was in Hannah's store, working out his debt. Meanwhile, he was attracted to Ethan Allen—one of the few loud, flamboyant fellows who are also doers—who was mining coal nearby and had established a furnace and ironworks. Under him, young Lyon learned smelting and ironworking, and (a fast worker, Matt) at 21 he had acquired a small piece of property and married a young widow of one of Allen's nephews.

In 1769, the Allen tribe—Ethan, his brother Ira, and his sisters and his cousins and his aunts—moved en masse to the new wild country later known as Vermont, over whose possession New Hampshire and New York were squabbling. Connecticut's Litchfield County supplied it with such eminent founders as the Allens, Seth Warner, Matthew Lyon, and Thomas Chittenden, its first governor. In fact, Litchfield gave the young state four governors, three United States senators, seven congressmen and other honorables.

Lyon, like the other settlers, obtained his land title from New Hampshire, though New York was denying the legality of such grants and trying to invalidate them. In fact, Ethan Allen organized his Green Mountain Boys to protect their patents against attempts of New York and its claimants to oust them, and there were some rough doings in the course of the bickering. Lyon hadn't more than gotten a toe hold in the Vermont foothills—and joined the "Boys," of course—when the long-simmering Revolution boiled over, and Great Britain became the common enemy. On May 10, 1775, three weeks after Paul Revere rode, Allen and his 85 men, including Matthew Lyon, snatched Fort Ticonderoga from a sleepy, nightshirted British commander.

Lyon's private affairs must have been a secondary consideration that year, for he was on the Committee of Safety, watching and foiling the evil designs of Tories, and in the fall and early winter he invaded Canada as an officer under the brave but ill-fated General Montgomery, who was killed at Quebec. Off and on for the next two years, Lyon fought with militia or colonial troops, serving in the smashing victory of Bennington and in the final hammering of Burgoyne around Saratoga.

He then quitted army life, being far too busy with his civic duties to spare the time for soldiering. Vermont organized itself as an independent state in 1777, and elected Chittenden governor, whilst young Lyon became secretary to the governor and council, assistant treasurer and paymaster general of the state troops and militia. He also remained on the Committee of

Safety, was at various times a selectman, and in 1779 entered the legislature for the first of several terms.

In 1783, Lyon began to turn his flair for business to account. He founded the village of Fairhaven, where he created a sawmill, a gristmill and an ironworks. He cut ship timbers and sent them via nearby Lake Champlain to Canada and even to England. He essayed paper making from birch wood, and is said to have done creditably well with it. Naturally, the next tool was a printing press, with which he turned out not only job work, but at least two books, and presently a small periodical which he called *The Farmer's Library,* to which title, at a later date when he was running for Congress, he added *Scourge of Aristocracy and Repository of Important Political Truths.*

When Vermont was admitted to the Union in 1791, Lyon began itching for a seat in Congress, and he won election to it in 1796. His very first gesture in the House was not calculated to endear him to the new President, crusty old John Adams. Lyon objected to the custom, established in the previous Administration, of the representatives going in a body to the executive mansion to reply to the President's first message and ask whether he had any other wishes. To Lyon, the wine and cake served at the call could not overcome the unpleasantly obsequious odor of the affair, and he asked to be excused from attendance with the others. "I would be glad to see this custom done away," he added.

The year 1798 was when our bickering with France over comparatively small matters reached the point where French privateers were seizing our ships, and war talk was in the air. It would in essence have been a war between our Federalist and Democratic parties; the former, wearing black cockades, ardent partisans of England, hissing and hating France; the latter, singing "Ça ira" and the "Carmagnole," and topping "liberty poles" with the revolutionary Phrygian cap of chaotic France.

That summer Congress enacted the notorious "Alien and Sedition Laws," the first against "dangerous" foreigners, the second ordering that any person who should "write, utter or publish or shall cause . . . to be written, uttered or published or assist . . . in writing, uttering or publishing" any words calumniating the government or either House of Congress or the President, or calculated to bring either of them into disrepute or stir up sedition in the country, should be punished by a fine not exceeding $2,000 and imprisonment of not more than two years.

That this was in flat, seemingly impudent violation of the First Amendment to the Constitution merely proves the lightness of congressional thinking at the time, and the lack of that reverence for the Constitution which developed so strongly as time went on.

Matthew Lyon had not intensified the political editorializing in his *Scourge of Aristocracy,* etc., and saw things through the distorted lenses of an ardent partisan. A Vermont editor published a sharp criticism of him for his antagonism to President Adams, and Lyon sent him a reply which, according to the Sedition Law, had in it the makings of a crime. In the President he saw "every consideration of public welfare swallowed up in a continual grasp for power, an unbounded thirst for ridiculous pomp, foolish adulation and selfish avarice"; he saw "men of real merit daily turned out of office for no other cause but independency of spirit . . . men of firmness, merit, years, abilities and experience discarded in their applications for office, for fear they possess that independence, and men of meanness preferred, for the ease with which they can take up and advocate opinions, the consequences of which they know but little of."

His first group of charges was much exaggerated; the second had some basis in fact, and is the story of partisanship in government, even down to modern times. Worse charges have been made against many a President, and Lyon's diatribe would raise the blood pressure of a modern Chief Executive but little. But the Federalists' catchpolls were watching and listening for just such a malfeasance. Very shortly a grand jury

—packed against him, Lyon claimed, and not without a shadow of justification—in Rutland, a Federalist hotbed, found him "a wicked man of a depraved mind and a malicious and diabolical disposition . . . deceitfully, wickedly and maliciously contriving to defame the Government of the United States . . . and the said John Adams, Esq. . . ."

His letter was dated June 20, though for some reason it was not mailed, or at least not postmarked, until July 7. The Sedition Bill was passed by the Senate on July 4 and by the House of Representatives on July 10. It was therefore not yet a law when Lyon's letter was written and posted. By the time the Vermont editor had gotten the letter into type, the bill had become a statute.

To make matters worse, Lyon had published a letter from the poet Joel Barlow, then sojourning in Paris—where he prudently remained—expressing horror over a message of President Adams to Congress in which he said that there was no dependence to be put in any agreement with the French, "that their religion and morality were at an end, and that it would be necessary to be perpetually armed against them." Barlow was amazed "that the answer of both Houses had not been an order to send him [Adams] to a mad-house." Worse still, Lyon editorially urged Americans to prepare to resist the efforts of the Federalists to establish "a state of abject slavery and degrading subjection to a set of

Matthew Lyon was one of the Green Mountain Boys whom Ethan Allen led in the onslaught on Fort Ticonderoga.

assuming High Mightinesses in our own country, and a close connection with a corrupt, tottering monarchy in Europe."

Lyon's trial had some of the aspects of a cut-and-dried affair. His plea of the unconstitutionality of the act was brushed aside by the judge (Justice Paterson of the United States Supreme Court), another proof of the as yet unimpressive stature in the judicial mind of the Magna Carta of our being. Lyon hadn't the ghost of a chance. He hoped to show that the publication was innocuous and—his only defense under the law—to prove the truth of his allegations, which would have been well-nigh impossible, even by a horde of witnesses; the charges were too intangible.

The judge's charge to the jury was heavily weighted against the prisoner, and it is no wonder the verdict shortly brought in was one of Guilty. The judge complimented his own leniency in sentencing Lyon to no more than four months' imprisonment and a fine of $1,000 and costs for so heinous an offense. The marshal proposed to set out immediately with the convicted

man for Vergennes, forty miles away, where he was to be immured. Lyon asked permission to go to his lodgings to take care of some papers. "I was answered in a surly tone, No, and told to sit down. I stood up."

The cell into which Lyon was finally thrust was twelve by sixteen feet in size, with a "necessary" in one corner, "which afforded a stench about equal to that of the Philadelphia docks in August." There was little light and no heat, and his small, barred window had no glass in it, making his entombment there through most of the winter a pretty bleak prospect. He was at first denied writing materials, but presently the authorities realized that if he had them, he would undoubtedly violate the law again, so Lyon was given pen and paper, and the inevitable happened. He wrote:

"Every one who is not [in] favor of this mad war [with France] is branded with the epithets of Opposers of Government, Disorganizers, Jacobins, etc. It is quite a new kind of jargon to call a Representative of the people an opposer of the Government because he does not, as a Legislator, advocate and acquiesce in every proposition that comes from the Executive."

This was of course another violation, and another warrant was issued, to be served when the prison doors opened for him on February 6.

Lyon's term as congressman had expired, and just before his trial an election was held to fill the vacancy. He was the only Democratic candidate, and the Federalists, fearing his popularity, had nominated several men, not expecting that any of them might win, but hoping that they would draw enough votes from Lyon to prevent his winning. This negative strategy prevented his getting a majority, though he polled the largest vote, but checked him only momentarily. His stature as a persecuted hero was increasing. In December there was a second election, and this time the prisoner was re-elected overwhelmingly.

From the time of his incarceration, Lyon held frequent conferences with his loyal partisans through the little barred window of his cell. The Green Mountain Boys were all for shortening his term by demolishing the jail, but he dissuaded them. A petition signed by several thousand persons was presented to the President, asking for Lyon's release from a frigid and allegedly filthy cell. Mr. Adams declined unless the prisoner signed it, too. "Penitence before pardon," was the executive epigram. But Lyon was anything but penitent; he refused to sign and remained in his dungeon.

The question now arose: how was his fine to be paid when his prison term expired? He had property but little cash; his business had suffered from lack of his expert management until he was well-nigh in a state

Lyon's cell was cold and dimly lighted, with what he called "a stench about equal to that of the Philadelphia docks."

of bankruptcy. A lottery was proposed, with some of his property at Fairhaven as the prize. Anthony Haswell, publisher of the Vermont *Gazette*, a veteran of the Revolution and now state postmaster-general, willingly published an advertisement of the lottery—with a scorching reference to Revolutionary Tories now in government—and wrote an editorial beginning, "Our Representative is holden by the oppressive hand of usurped power in a loathsome prison, suffering all the indignities which can be heaped upon him by a hard-hearted savage." This was considered a libel upon the Vergennes jailer, and Haswell was sentenced to two months' imprisonment for it, plus a fine of $200.

Senator Stevens T. Mason of Virginia was another who took the matter of the fine into his own hands. He collected $1,060 in gold, the amount of the fine and costs—which must be paid in coin—from good Democratic party men in his own bailiwick, and with it in his saddlebags (and perhaps a pair of pistols), set forth on horseback shortly after the New Year to plod northward through mud, rain, snow, sleet and freezing cold to Vermont. We do not know when he reached Vergennes, but he was there by February 6, the day of Lyon's release, as were other messengers of relief.

The situation becomes a little confused as we hear of these others. There was of course a great crowd present, and it is reported that an appeal for small contributions had begun building a pile of quarters and half dollars on a stump when Apollos Austin—a name still eminent in Vermont—rode up with $1,060 in silver, the produce of the lottery. But before the prison door could be opened, Mrs. Lyon is said to have appeared in a sleigh and thanked the donors for their generosity. She pleaded that she and her husband would prefer to pay the penalty themselves, and hence she had sold some of his property to raise the money. Here there is a blank in the story, but a letter of thanks from the Democrats of Vermont to Senator Mason, appearing in the Vermont *Gazette* on March 28 following, seems to indicate that the gold which he had collected and ridden so far through bitter winter weather to deliver had been considered the worthiest of the proffered ransoms.

However that may be, the jail doors opened and the prisoner came forth, already wearing his greatcoat. As the officer reached into his inner pocket for the new warrant—we would not venture to suggest that anybody jostled him—Lyon leaped into the sleigh with his wife, cried out, "I'm on my way to Congress!" and they sped away. Someone must have told the marshal that Lyon, being a member of Congress, was immune to ordinary arrest, and he was not pursued.

His journey to Washington was a triumphal progress—cheers, flags waving, crowds thronging to applaud him. At the school at Tinmouth, little girls carried a banner on which was inscribed, "This day satisfies Federal vengeance. Our brave Representative, who has been suffering for us under an unjust sentence and the tyranny of a detested understrapper of despotism, this day rises superior to despotism." The little girls were not prosecuted.

Steadily the Federalist party tottered to its fall. In the election of 1800 two Democrats, Jefferson and Aaron Burr, were tied in the electoral college with 73 votes each. Adams could muster only 65 and C. C. Pinckney 64. This threw the election into the House of Representatives. Through 35 ballots Jefferson and Burr were deadlocked. Two states divided their votes between them, Maryland giving them four each and Vermont one each. Lyon was the steadfast Jeffersonian in Vermont. On the thirty-sixth ballot the Burrites weakened; their Maryland and Vermont members cast blank ballots, with the result that both states went for Jefferson and he became President.

Lyon did not seek re-election that year. His businesses had fallen into disorder, and a few bitter enemies were responsible for acts of sabotage and mysterious fires in his properties. Andrew Jackson urged him to move to a new frontier, and in 1801 he did so; he settled at a bend of the Cumberland River in western Kentucky, where he built up the town of Eddyville, in what was eventually to become Lyon County. Here he founded industries, as he had done in Vermont, and seemed on the way to a second manufacturing career. But he could not resist the call of politics. He entered the Kentucky legislature in 1802, and went back to the national House of Representatives in 1803, to serve another eight years.

The Embargo Act of 1807 and other trade curbs rapidly following hurt his businesses and drew him closer to his old Federalist opponents in New England, particularly with Josiah Quincy. Lyon tried to attend to business with one hand and politics with the other; both suffered. Neglect of his political "fences" and his opposition to the drift towards war with England combined to end his career in Congress.

He was growing old, and what with many distractions, he was losing his magic touch in business. The loss of a valuable cargo on its way to New Orleans was a staggering blow to his fortunes. In 1820 President Monroe appointed him factor to the Cherokee Indians, with headquarters at Spadra Bluff in western Arkansas. Here he toiled at his job with the nervous drive of a man forty years younger. Young Arkansas Territory elected him a delegate to Congress in 1822, but his overstrained heart gave way, and he died, "a hero of three frontiers," before he could take his seat.

"a scandalous, malicious and

MAD TOM in A RAGE

By THOMAS J. FLEMING

"At a Court of general Sessions of the Peace, holden at Claverack, in and for the county of Columbia, it is presented that Harry Croswell, late of the city of Hudson, in the county of Columbia aforesaid, Printer, being a malicious and seditious man, and of a depraved mind and wicked and diabolical disposition, and also deceitfully, wickedly and maliciously devising, contriving and intending, Thomas Jefferson, Esquire, President of the United States of America, to detract from, scandalize, traduce, and vilify, and to represent him, the said Thomas Jefferson, as unworthy of the confidence, respect and attachment of the People of the said United States, . . . and wickedly and seditiously to disturb the Peace and tranquility as well of the People of the State of New York as of the United States; . . . the said Harry Croswell did on the ninth day of September, in the year of our Lord 1802, with force and arms, at the said city of Hudson, in the said county of Columbia, wickedly, maliciously and seditiously print and publish and cause and procure to be printed and published, a certain scandalous, malicious and seditious libel, in a certain paper or publication entitled 'The Wasp.' . . ."

All history is a mingling of the great and small, of kings losing kingdoms for want of a horseshoe nail, of presidents assassinated because a guard needed a smoke. But seldom has there been a stranger concatenation of the petty and the magnificent, the comic and the tragic, the trivial and the profound, than in the case of the *People v. Croswell*, in 1803. By an odd blend of good and bad luck, an obscure twenty-four-year-old printer wrote himself into the *Dictionary of American Biography*, established the libel law on which contemporary press freedom still rests, jarred the political security of President Thomas Jefferson, and indirectly helped to involve Alexander Hamilton in his fatal duel with Aaron Burr.

In 1803 the infant American Republic was running a high political fever. The ferocity of the verbal warfare raging between the Federalists, the party created

seditious libel"

Is it libel to say that the President of the United States tried to seduce his neighbor's wife—even if he did? Thomas Jefferson tried to gag the venomous editor of upstate New York's *Wasp*; Alexander Hamilton argued brilliantly in defense of journalistic candor

by Alexander Hamilton, and the Democratic-Republicans, led by President Jefferson, has rarely been matched in American politics, even by the diatribes of today's New Left and Ultra Right.

The first fusillades had been fired during Washington's Presidency. The Jeffersonians, with not a little help from the Sage of Monticello himself, had set up journalists such as Philip Freneau and Benjamin Franklin Bache with one mission, to deflate and discredit an administration that was, in Jefferson's view, "galloping fast into monarchy." They soon had the Father of His Country in a state of near apoplexy. "That rascal Freneau," as Washington called him, insisted on sending his scurrilous *National Gazette,* published in Philadelphia, to the President's house even after he had cancelled his subscription. Freneau spent most of his abuse on Hamilton. Bache preferred Washington as a target, calling him "treacherous," "mischievous," "inefficient," and sneering at his "farce of disinterestedness" and his "stately journeyings through the American continent in search of personal incense."

These verbal guerrillas soon had imitators. Among the more savage was William Duane, Bache's successor as editor of the Philadelphia *Aurora.* Washington, he wrote, had "discharged the loathings of a sick mind." Even this was topped by an English newcomer, James T. Callender. In the Richmond *Examiner* he declared that "Mr. Washington has been twice a traitor."

The Federalists, the upholders of upper-class dignity, labored under a difficult handicap in such a war. They soon became afraid, in Washington's words, that "there seems to be no bounds to . . . attempts to destroy all confidence, that the People might, and . . . ought to have, in their government; thereby dissolving it, and producing a disunion of the States." The Alien and Sedition Acts of 1798 were an expression of this fear. Passed by a Federalist Congress with Washington's public approval, the Alien Act gave President John Adams the power to deport any foreigners he deemed

While less gentlemanly journalistic collaborators bludgeoned away at Thomas Jefferson in cartoons like the one opposite, Alexander Hamilton thrust a deft oratorical rapier at the Democratic-Republicans in the Croswell libel trial.

Harry Croswell—portrayed here as an Anglican priest a good many years after his trial for seditious libel—would have remained an obscure upstate New York citizen except for two things. As the young editor of the Wasp, *he had a wicked way with words; and he was attacking the Jeffersonians in the home county of New York's Jeffersonian attorney general, Ambrose Spencer. That was looking for trouble, and Croswell soon was in it right up to his stinger.*

dangerous to public peace. The Sedition Act empowered the federal judiciary to punish anyone convicted of false or malicious writing against the nation, the President, or Congress with a fine of not more than $2,000 and imprisonment for not more than two years.

Federalist judges immediately went to work and soon had indictments against Bache, Duane, Callender, and a dozen other Democratic-Republican editors. The Jeffersonians responded at the state level with the Kentucky and Virginia resolutions of 1798, which declared the Alien and Sedition Acts altogether void and introduced the doctrine of nullification into American constitutional thinking—a seed that would bear ominous fruit in a later era. Up and down the land, Jeffersonian editors bellowed mightily that the Federalists were attempting to erase the First Amendment and destroy the free press.

The Jeffersonian counterattack was beautifully executed: the Federalist judges retreated in disarray and all but abandoned the unpopular prosecutions after a mere ten convictions. The nation roared into the election of 1800 with both sides strenuously exercising their right of free speech. But except for a few slugging editors who sneered at "Massa Jefferson" the slave owner, most of the Federalist propaganda came from pulpits, where clergymen pictured the election of the pro-French and "atheistic" Jefferson as the beginning of a Jacobinical reign of terror against religion. In the print shops the Jeffersonians had the bigger, more vituperative guns. James Callender's pamphlet, *The Prospect Before Us,* slandered Washington and Adams with such recklessness that it achieved an unenviable literary fame. Although Federalist papers theoretically outnumbered the Jeffersonians 103 to 64, most of them maintained a tepid semineutrality that permitted the Democratic-Republicans to run away with public opinion and the election. Defeated John Adams wrote mournfully, "If we had been blessed

A much more prominent candidate for a libel suit on the part of the Jeffersonians against scurrilous Federalist editors was William Coleman, of the New York Evening Post. *A protégé of Hamilton's who translated his mentor's political views into inflammatory but scintillating satire on the Democratic-Republicans, he was widely read and quoted. But Hamilton was sure to leap to his aid; so the Jeffersonians picked on Croswell. Then Hamilton came to his aid.*

with common sense, we should not have been overthrown by Philip Freneau, Duane, Callender. . . . A group of foreign liars have discomfited the education, the talents, the virtues, and the property of the country."

But the Federalists were down, not out. Older leaders like John Jay might retire to their estates in dismay, but there were numerous young, vigorous Federalists in the prime of middle life, such as Hamilton and Fisher Ames of Massachusetts, who did not feel it was time for them to abandon politics. They decided Federalism was not dead, it had just been misrepresented, distorted, and smeared without rebuttal. It was time to junk the older Federalist ideas about the vulgarity of appealing to the people through the press. Ames suggested a Latin motto as a guide: *Fas est et ab hoste doceri* ("It is perfectly proper to be taught by one's enemy"). Up and down the Republic, Federalists began founding papers in which, Ames

declared, "wit and satire should flash like the electrical fire." At the same time, the paper he helped found, the *New England Palladium,* would, he predicted, be "fastidiously polite and well-bred. It should whip Jacobins as a gentleman would a chimney sweeper, at arms length, and keeping aloof from his soot."

In New York, Alexander Hamilton soon gathered a group of well-heeled Federalists who put up $10,000 for a daily to be called the *Evening Post* (still in business today, as the *New York Post*). Its editor, William Coleman, met Alexander Hamilton by night and took down his editorials from the very lips of the great man himself. Throughout the other states, similar papers suddenly blossomed: in Baltimore, for example, the *Republican, or, Anti-Democrat;* in South Carolina, the Charleston *Courier.* In Hudson, New York, another group of Federalists led by Elisha Williams, one of the state's most noted attorneys, backed Ezra Sampson as the editor of the *Balance and Columbian Re-*

155

pository. As a junior editor Sampson hired twenty-two-year-old Harry Croswell.

Connecticut born, this well-built, dignified young man had studied for a time in the household of Noah Webster, later of dictionary fame and a high Federalist of the old school. (Webster's solution for rampant Jeffersonianism was to raise the voting age to forty-five.) Temperamentally, Harry Croswell was a born Federalist. He was religious, had a natural deference for older, wiser, richer men, and tended to see political developments of the day as a clash between the forces of darkness and light.

Hudson at this time was not the somnolent little river town it is today. In the decade after the Revolution it carried more ships on its registers than the city of New York. Much of western Massachusetts and northern Connecticut used Hudson for a shipping center. One March day in 1802, a reporter counted 2,800 sleighs loaded with goods on Hudson's streets, creating a traffic jam of prodigious dimensions. At the

THE WASP.

By Robert Rufticoat, Efquire.

Vol. I.]   *" To lafh the Rafcals naked through the world."*   **[No. 6.**

HOLT fays, the burden of the Federal fong is, that Mr. Jefferfon paid Callender for writing againſt the late adminiſtration. This is wholly falfe. The charge is explicitly this :—Jefferfon paid Callender for calling Waſhington a traitor, a robber, and a perjurer— For calling Adams, a hoary headed incendiary ; and for moſt groſsly flandering the private charaſters of men, who, he well knew were virtuous. Thefe charges, not a democratic editor has yet dared, or ever will dare to meet in an open manly difcuffion.

Rhetorically quite mild, this passage still libelled Jefferson so "explicitly" as to count heavily against Croswell.

same time, with Albany, the state capital, a mere twenty-eight miles upriver, it was hardly surprising that Hudson and surrounding Columbia County were politically sensitive areas. Later in the century one local historian unabashedly claimed that the county had produced more distinguished politicians than any other comparable area in the entire country.

The Jeffersonians were strongly entrenched there. In 1802, the attorney general of the state of New York was sharp-eyed, hatchet-faced Ambrose Spencer, a native son of Columbia County. Morgan Lewis, chief justice of the state supreme court, was married to Gertrude Livingston, whose family's vast upstate hold-

ings included a large chunk of the southern portion of the county. The Livingstons were the most potent voice in the Jeffersonian party at that time.

It was hardly surprising, therefore, that the Jeffersonians decided to set up a rival to the Federalist *Balance*. For their printer they chose Charles Holt, former editor of the New London *Bee* and a Sedition Act martyr who had been convicted in 1800 for libel and spent several months in jail. Holt prepared to launch a *Bee* in Hudson and made it clear it would buzz impertinently in the face of the dignified *Balance*.

Young Harry Croswell forthwith saw an opportunity to prove his extreme devotion to Federalism. He persuaded his senior editor, Sampson, to let him publish in the garret of the *Balance* office a paper entitled the *Wasp*. As an editorial pseudonym, Croswell chose "Robert Rusticoat"; for a motto, "To lash the Rascals naked through the world." Down in New York, an observer in the *Evening Post* told the story in doggerel obviously modelled on "Yankee Doodle."

> *There's Charlie Holt is come to town*
>   *A proper lad with types, sir.*
> *The Democrats have fetched him here*
>   *To give the federals stripes, sir.*
>
> *The Balance-folks seem cruel 'fraid*
>   *That he'll pull down their scales, sir.*
> *And so they got a pokerish wasp,*
>   *To sting him with his tail, sir.*

Croswell's opening number was nothing less than a declaration of war:

Wherever the Bee ranges, the Wasp will follow over the same fields and on the same flowers—Without attempting to please his friends, the Wasp will only strive to displease, vex and torment his enemies... The Wasp has a dirty and disagreeable job to perform. He has undertaken the chastisement of a set of fellows who are entrenched in filth—who like lazy swine are wallowing in a puddle. He must therefore wade knee deep in smut before he can meet his enemies on their own ground.

At his opposite number, Holt, Croswell levelled the following blast:

It is well known that you was bro't here by virtue of $500 raised for that purpose by the leading Democrats in this city. That the public may know, therefore, with how much purity and independence you will conduct in your editorial labors, would you be kind enough to answer the following questions:

Did the contributors to the $500 purchase you, as they purchase Negroes in Virginia, or hire you as they hire servants in New England?

Are you not a mere automaton in the hands of your masters; pledged to publish whatever slanders or falsehoods they shall dictate? And by your contract with them if you refuse to pollute your sheets have they not a right to ship you back again to your 350 subscribers in New London?

Croswell soon made it clear that this was more than a local war. Down in Virginia, James Callender was demonstrating his lack of principle by turning on his former idol, Thomas Jefferson. After Jefferson became President, Callender, working on the assumption that his slanderous attack on Washington and Adams had done much to swing the election, coolly asked to be made postmaster of Richmond. Jefferson declined, whereupon Callender revealed in print that while he was working on *The Prospect Before Us,* Jefferson had sent him a hundred dollars and had even read part of the manuscript, returning it with the declaration, "Such papers cannot fail to produce the best affect. They inform the thinking part of the nation..."

This was sensational stuff, the kind of thing that could hurt Jefferson politically. Washington was now in his grave two years and already the process of canonization was in full swing. Federalist printers rushed to their presses to discuss Jefferson's rather lame explanation that he had sent Callender the hundred dollars out of charity, and because he was a Sedition Act victim. But few equalled the savagery with which the *Wasp* pilloried this explanation.

It amounts to this then. He [Jefferson] read the book and from that book inferred that Callender was an object of charity. Why! One who presented a face bloated with vices, a heart black as hell—one who could be guilty of such foul falsehoods, such vile aspersions of the best and greatest man the world has yet known—he an object of charity! No! He is the very man, that an aspiring mean and hollow hypocrite would press into the service of crime. He is precisely qualified to become a tool—to spit the venom and scatter the malicious, poisonous slanders of his employer. He, in short, is the very man that a dissembling patriot, pretended "man of the people" would employ to plunge for him the dagger, or administer the arsenic.

Again and again Croswell sank his stinger into this Jeffersonian blister.

Will the reader turn to that inaugural speech of 1801 and see how this incarnate [Jefferson] speaks of Washington. There he makes him a demigod—having already paid Callender for making him a devil...Will the word hypocrite describe this man? There is not strength enough in the term.

When Holt attempted to answer Croswell by impugning Callender's character, the young Federalist editor hoisted him with another petard.

About the time of Callender's trial, you [Holt] printed a paper in New London—in that paper Callender was

extolled to the skies. He was then an "excellent Republican," a "virtuous man," a "good citizen," a "suffering patriot."...If there is anything on earth to be pitied, it is a miser-"able editor" constantly tumbling into the mire; and whose every struggle but sinks him deeper.

The disarray of his antagonists emboldened Croswell to aim some shafts at local Democratic-Republicans. In the September 9, 1802, issue of the *Wasp* appeared the following poem:

Th' attorney general chanc'd one day to meet
A dirty, ragged fellow in the street
  A noisy swaggering beast
  With rum half drunk at least
Th' attorney, too, was drunk—but not with grog—
Power and pride had set his head agog.

The poem went on to describe how the attorney general, "madly frowning on the clown," asked him how he had the insolence to address him as a "fellow lab'rer for the common good."

"Why," said the fellow with a smile,
"You weekly in the paper toil,
"Condemn the old administration
"And do your best to 'save the nation'
"While I with just the same pretenses
"Chalk 'Damn the Feds' on gates and fences."

Croswell lampooned other leading local characters who were perfectly recognizable even when he named no names. One satire described a prominent judge who spent an evening eating and drinking at a nearby tavern and then refused to pay his bill. In a memoir that he attached to one of the few surviving complete sets of the *Wasp* (now at the New-York Historical Society), Croswell told how he was walking through the streets of Hudson, not long after publication of the latter tale, when up thundered a local justice of the peace, a big man named Hagedorn, who leaped off his wagon, shook his horsewhip under Croswell's nose, and vowed that he considered the tavern story slander and was going to extract instant revenge.

"I had no cane or other means of defense," Croswell wrote. "But I stood erect and dropping my hands to my sides looked him full in the face and in the most cool and collected manner apprised him that... neither he nor any other man could ever whip me and it was a mistake for him to talk so loud about it. He...broke out again in a tempest of oaths, turned shortly on his heel, mounted his wagon and drove off at a furious pace, his poor horse having received the rash intended for me."

Looking around him, Croswell noticed a staunch Federalist friend in a nearby doorway laughing heartily at the exchange. "Harry Croswell," said he, "how could you be so sure that he would not whip you?"

"Mainly," Croswell replied, "because I planned to run away if he had attempted it."

It never seemed to occur to Croswell that he was a David taking on a number of political Goliaths. One reason may have been the illusion created by the preponderance of Federalists in Hudson. Among his prominent contributors was a young attorney, Thomas Grosvenor, who was the brother-in-law of Elisha Williams. Williams did more than merely threaten Charlie Holt when the *Bee* turned some of its venom in his direction. He caught the small, thin Holt, described as a "cripple" by a Columbia County antiquarian, and with several supporters nearby, thrashed him thoroughly.

Meanwhile, Croswell broadened his attacks on Jefferson with other choice tidbits from Callender's pen. He quoted the erstwhile Jeffersonian as declaring that "Mr. Jefferson has for years past while his wife was living and does now since she is dead, keep a woolly headed concubine by the name of Sally—that by her he had had several children, and that one by the name of Tom has since his father's election taken upon himself many airs of importance, and boasted his extraction from a President." To this, Croswell added another noxious tale: how Jefferson, before his marriage, attempted to seduce Mrs. John Walker, the wife of a close friend.

Other extremist Federalist papers were printing the same stories. Publicly, Jefferson always maintained a philosopher's stance toward the abuse he was getting. In 1803 he wrote to a European friend, "[It] is so difficult to draw a line of separation between the abuse and the wholesome use of the press, that as yet we have found it better to trust the public judgment, rather than the magistrate, with the discrimination between truth and falsehood." But his actions in 1803 belied that view. One reason may have been that two out of the three stories the Federalists were spreading were uncomfortably close to the truth. The slave concubine would seem to be sheer slander, but three years later Jefferson admitted privately that the Walker story was essentially accurate; and even his most benevolent biographers find it hard to explain away his relations with Callender.

By private letter and personal messenger, in his wonted style, Jefferson passed the word to his state leaders. "[The] press ought to be restored to its credibility if possible," he told Thomas McKean, the governor of Pennsylvania. "... I have therefore long thought that a few prosecutions of the most prominent offenders would have a wholesome effect... Not a general prosecution, for that would look like persecution: but a selected one." For the already infuriated Jeffersonians in states where Federalists were most impudent, this was what they had been waiting for. Joseph Dennie, the arch-Federalist editor of the Philadelphia *Port Folio*, was promptly charged with seditious libel against the state and the United States. In New York, the selected victim was Harry Croswell.

Several historians have wondered why this obscure editor was singled out rather than the prestigious William Coleman of the *Evening Post*, who had also reprinted Callender's anti-Jefferson blasts. But even a rudimentary sketch of New York politics in 1802 makes it easy to see why Croswell was Attorney General Ambrose Spencer's number-one choice. There is nothing like smiting the enemy when he has had the effrontery to invade one of your most powerful bastions. To underscore this fact, Spencer himself appeared to prosecute the case, with the local district attorney, Ebenezer Foote, serving merely as an assistant.

Spencer was an ex-Federalist who had "gone over" to the other party, and seeing this turncoat undoubtedly made Harry Croswell seethe when he was brought on a bench warrant before three local judges at the Court of General Sessions sitting at Claverack, then the Columbia County seat. The fiery young editor was indicted for libel on two counts, which were duly read to him. One was based on the fourth issue of the *Wasp*, August 12, 1802, in which he had listed "a few 'squally' facts"—five executive acts by President Jefferson which, Croswell maintained, grossly

The only Federalist supreme court justice hearing the Croswell case, James Kent was still a match for his colleagues.

violated the federal Constitution. The second and more serious charge was based on a paragraph that had appeared in the *Wasp* on September 9, 1802:

Holt says, the burden of the Federal song is, that Mr. Jefferson paid Callender for writing against the late administration. This is wholly false. The charge is explicitly this:—Jefferson paid Callender for calling Washington a traitor, a robber, and a perjurer—. For calling Adams, a hoary headed incendiary; and for most grossly slandering the private characters of men, who, he well knew were virtuous. These charges, not a democratic editor has yet dared, or ever will dare to meet in an open manly discussion.

Croswell was not deserted by his Federalist friends. Standing beside him at the bar were Elisha Williams, Jacob Rutsen Van Rensselaer, and William W. Van Ness. Williams was already established as a legal giant. Oliver Wendell Holmes, in *The Poet at the Breakfast-Table*, wrote that he once asked a distinguished New Yorker, "Who on the whole seems the most considerable person you ever met?" Quite to Holmes's bemusement, the man replied without hesitation, "Elisha Williams." Van Rensselaer was a vigorous descendant of the great patroon family that had once owned 62,000 acres of land on the east side of the Hudson River, including the entire town of Claverack. Van Ness at twenty-seven was considered the most brilliant young attorney in Columbia County. His folksy courtroom manner was typical of the younger Federalists' new style. He often interrupted

BOTH: CULVER

Morgan Lewis, the Jeffersonian chief justice of New York's supreme court, went on to the governorship in 1805.

his speeches to ask the foreman of the jury for a chew of tobacco.

The tone of the trial was set from the very first defense motion. Croswell's counsel demanded copies of the indictments before entering a plea. The Attorney General objected and was sustained by the all-Republican bench, and Croswell pleaded not guilty. (In his *Wasp* memoir Croswell says that the Jefferson-Callender passage, which was to become the heart of the case, had actually been written by Thomas Grosvenor, but he declined to implicate this young man and took his chances before the court. This required courage. A sojourn in a crude county jail was no laughing matter in 1803.) The defense then requested a postponement until the next session of the circuit court. They argued that on an issue as legally complex as the law of libel, a state supreme court justice should sit. The Attorney General objected; he was promptly upheld.

The defense now made a most significant motion—a request for postponement in order to bring from Virginia James Callender himself, who would testify to the truth of the libel. Attorney General Spencer sprang to his feet, quivering like a wire. Under no circumstances would he tolerate such a procedure. They were trying this case according to the law of New York state. The truth or falsehood of the libel was irrelevant! All he had to prove to the twelve good men and true in the jury box was the question of fact. Did Harry Croswell publish these libelous statements against the President of the United States?

Thus in the small country courtroom before three farmer justices of the peace, the political-legal giants of the Empire State drew historic—and ironic—battle lines. Here was the Jeffersonian attorney general, backed by Jeffersonian justices, vociferously upholding the Royalist doctrine that had been brought to bear against John Peter Zenger at his famous trial in 1735.

But the Zenger case is by no means the landmark in the history of press freedom that has sometimes been supposed. The German printer's acquittal on charges of seditious libel against Governor William Cosby changed very little. The jury had simply disregarded the judge's admonition to disregard the question of the truth of the alleged libel, and the law remained as it was. Subsequent cases in New York and other colonies made it clear that American legislators and most voters were ready to support freedom of the press only when the press printed what they approved.

Essentially, in fact, what colonial and post-Revolutionary liberals meant by freedom of the press was a press free from licensing and prior censorship. When the framers wrote in the First Amendment, "Congress

159

shall make no law ... abridging the freedom of speech, or of the press," the key word to them was "Congress." The reason Jefferson had considered the Sedition Act null was not because it had muzzled his party's press, but because he was convinced that Congress, under the Constitution, had no power to enact such legislation. Writing to Abigail Adams in 1804, Jefferson would declare, "While we deny that Congress have a right to control the freedom of the press, we have ever asserted the right of the States, and their exclusive right, to do so."

Thus the Jeffersonians were not as inconsistent as they seemed to be in their stand on Harry Croswell. They rooted their opinion in the common-law tradition of England, best summed up by the great commentator Sir William Blackstone:

The liberty of the press is indeed essential to the nature of a free state; but this consists in laying no previous restraints upon publications and not in freedom from censure for criminal matter when published. Every free man has an undoubted right to lay what sentiments he pleases before the public; to forbid this is to destroy the freedom of the press; but if he publishes what is improper, mischievous or illegal, he must take the consequences of his own temerity.

But legal principles, even legal traditions, while they may be revered by lawyers and utilized in emergencies like the one in which Ambrose Spencer found himself, are not so sacred to the man in the street, and Croswell's trial soon made it clear that the Jeffersonians were riding a tiger of their own creation. The moment Spencer declared that "the truth cannot be given in evidence," Elisha Williams unlimbered his heaviest rhetorical artillery. Hitherto, he pointed out, it had been the first article in Spencer's political creed that the people possessed the sovereignty and that governors and Presidents were their servants; and that whenever the people should write on their ballots, "Turn them out. Turn them out," those whom they had rejected must fall. But how could this power, this sovereignty, be correctly exercised, how could the people "pluck down the vicious demagogue and raise and support the virtuous patriot unless their variant conduct could be faithfully represented? And what

Philip Freneau, now remembered chiefly as a poet, was also an anti-Federalist editor who stirred Hamilton's wrath.

printer would dare to represent such conduct if the truth of the fact so represented could not shield him from destruction?"

Almost immediately Spencer began to backwater. He first agreed to postpone trial of the indictment based on the *Wasp*'s claim that Jefferson had violated the Constitution. But he insisted on taking up the second indictment, the charge in regard to Callender, the next day.

Croswell's attorneys appeared in court the next evening and entered a formal affidavit stating that the Federalists intended and expected to prove the truth of the facts as stated in the *Wasp* in regard to Callender and President Jefferson. Like a shrewd fencer, the Attorney General returned an unexpected riposte. He wanted Croswell bound with $5,000 bail on each indictment "to keep the peace and be of good behavior." Croswell's attorneys exploded in a chorus of objections. Not only was such a demand illegal and a violation of Croswell's liberty as a free citizen of the United States—it was indirectly an attack upon the freedom of the press.

Elisha Williams and his confreres spent most of the next day debating this motion with Spencer. Again the political deficiencies of the Jeffersonian case were evident. Spencer, representative of the party that claimed to be the repository of the true spirit of the American Revolution, spent most of his time quoting cases out of English common law. The principal citation was a statute from the reign of Edward III which granted justices power to bind over "such as be not of good fame" to be of good behavior. Williams came back with a rain of English citations, including the still politically potent name of John Wilkes. When this erratic friend of the American Revolution had been arrested for libel in 1763 and the King's attorney attempted to have him bound, the Chief Justice of England dismissed the motion, "whereupon there was a loud huzzah in Westminster Hall."

The Attorney General rose with a rebuttal that the reporter for the *Balance* grudgingly admitted was, "with the exception of a few indecent expressions ... one of Mr. Spencer's most ingenious speeches." But in spite of his ingenuity, Spencer's motion to bind Croswell was denied. The Republican judges could not bring themselves to gag Croswell quite so flagrantly.

Six months of legal jousting followed. The Croswell attorneys fought to get the entire case transferred to the circuit court, under a New York supreme court justice, and Spencer struggled to retain it in the lower court, where he would have a local Jeffersonian bench and jury. In the interim, however, the Federalists scored a resounding electoral victory in Hudson and duplicated it in five other Columbia County towns.

The legal battle reached a climax on June 14, 1803, when Spencer and the Croswell legal trio once more clashed at Claverack. After a long and acrimonious debate, Spencer gave way and agreed that both indictments could be tried before a supreme court justice on the next circuit through the county. It soon became evident that Spencer had a good reason for accommodating his opponents. Chief Justice Morgan Lewis appeared as the circuit judge. A thorough Jeffersonian, Lewis interrupted Croswell's lawyers as they once more attempted to request a delay in order to obtain evidence from James Callender in Virginia. Such evidence, Lewis declared, concerned the truth of the charge for which the defendant was indicted and in his opinion the law was "settled, that the truth could not be given in evidence to the jury as a justification."

Croswell's lawyers argued manfully against this pre-judgment. They maintained that Croswell's case involved a public libel, which made the truth of vital consideration. On that ground, they requested a delay until a commission appointed by the court could examine Callender. (At this point in his career, Callender was on his way to becoming a hopeless drunkard, and Croswell's lawyers probably felt that he would be a sorry witness at best; hence the shift to a commission to examine him at a distance.)

Judge Lewis was unmoved by the Federalist eloquence. When the Attorney General rose to reply, the Chief Justice told him it was unnecessary. He said he was "astonished" at the application, and repeated his view that "the law is settled, that the truth of the matter published cannot be given in evidence." Then, suggesting the nervous state of the Jeffersonian position, his Honor hastened to add, "I very much regret that the law is not otherwise; but as I am to declare what the law is, I cannot on this ground put off the trial."

The outcome of the trial was easily predictable. The only thing that really mattered was the Chief Justice's charge to the jury, in which he instructed them that they had but one thing to decide: whether Harry Croswell did in fact publish the scurrilous statements in the *Wasp*. It was left to the court to weigh matters of truth or falsehood, and also of malice, in determining the sentence. The jury retired at "sunsetting" with nothing to debate. Nevertheless, they remained out the whole night, and not until eight o'clock the next morning did they come to the bar with a verdict of guilty.

Croswell's attorneys immediately moved for a new trial, arguing that Lewis had misdirected the jury, and reiterating that the truth should be given in evidence. The motion was granted and the case was carried over first to the November term of the New York supreme court, and finally to the January, 1804, term.

In the meantime, both sides regrouped for the climax of the battle. The Federalists sought out their chief intellect, Alexander Hamilton. As early as June 23, 1803, they had persuaded General Philip Schuyler, Hamilton's father-in-law, to write the brilliant former Secretary of the Treasury for help. (In a style that typified the primeval Federalist, the patrician Schuyler described the case as "a libel against that Jefferson, who disgraces not only the place he fills but produces immorality by his pernicious example.") There is some evidence that Hamilton advised Croswell's counsel before the circuit court trial. Now, with the proceedings at stage center, he agreed to appear in person, gratis.

Down in Virginia during the same months, fate put a dent in Croswell's cause. In the midst of a drunken spree his potential star witness, Callender, fell out of a boat to find a final resting place, as one writer put it, "in congenial mud" at the bottom of the James River. But he left behind him his published works, including letters Jefferson had written expressing his approval of *The Prospect Before Us,* so his dirty work was very much alive when the supreme court convened February 13, 1804, to hear the final round of *People v. Croswell.*

For Hamilton the case represented an opportunity for revenge against his great rival, who was riding high on the crest of political triumph. Some of it Jefferson owed to Hamilton, whose unwise attempt to dump John Adams as the Federalist candidate in 1800 had done much to hand Jefferson the election. Aaron Burr had in the same year destroyed Hamilton's political power base in New York, manipulating the votes of the Tammany Society to elect a Jeffersonian governor, George Clinton. Discredited with his own party, Hamilton had retreated to his law practice, where he had already established himself by his sheer brilliance as a thinker and speaker.

More than revenge may have stirred Hamilton in the Croswell case. This strange, often contradictory giant, who was considered by Talleyrand to be one of

Ambrose Spencer, Jeffersonian attorney general of New York, became one of the state's first political bosses.

161

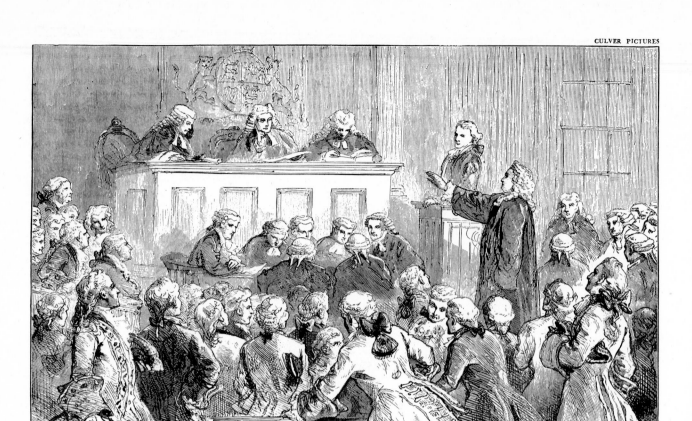

The trial of John Peter Zenger in 1735 for seditious libel is more famous than Croswell's, yet its effect on freedom of the press was less. Zenger was defended cogently by Andrew Hamilton (no relation to Alexander), here addressing the bench.

the three greatest men of the age along with Napoleon and Pitt, had a deep, instinctive love of liberty which was never extinguished by his vision of a compact organic society, organized and run by a natural aristocracy at the top. Now free from the inhibitions and necessities of party intrigue, which had prompted him to approve the Sedition Act, he flung himself wholeheartedly into Croswell's defense.

He brought with him from New York an old friend and staunch Federalist, Richard Harrison, who had shared Hamilton's mind and heart since their days together as Washington's aides-de-camp. With these two lawyers of the first rank was young William Van Ness, to provide continuity from the earlier court battles.

The opposition, meanwhile, had made a notable change. On February 3, 1804, Attorney General Ambrose Spencer had been nominated to the supreme court, but he properly abstained from sitting on the case, and summoned one of his political followers, George Caines, as his associate before the bar. Spencer's abstention left a four-man court: Chief Justice Lewis, who had already proved himself a devout Jeffersonian; Brockholst Livingston, who, true to his family reputation, was of a similar political faith; a third Jeffer-

sonian, Smith Thompson; and a lone Federalist, James Kent.

But in force of personality and weight of learning, Kent more than equalled the three Jeffersonian justices. "The American Blackstone," as he was later called for his *Commentaries on American Law,* the most influential legal volumes of the nineteenth century, had been converted to Federalism by listening to Alexander Hamilton's magnificent speeches in favor of the Constitution during the New York state ratifying convention in 1789, and by the still more cogent reasoning of the *Federalist Papers.* It was from a friendship with Hamilton begun in those days that he had acquired his conviction that the common-law tradition was essential to the nation's future. Not all lawyers agreed with this in 1804. In most states, the best legal minds were debating whether they should not scrap the common law and create a whole new code, as the French had done under Napoleon.

The problems—and the advantages—of the common law were all too evident in Croswell's case. All of the first day of the trial and most of the second were consumed by excursions far back into the mazes of English common law, with both sides endeavoring to show that the legal tradition of an earlier and sup-

162

posedly purer age upheld their view of the central question: whether the truth could be admitted as evidence in a case of seditious libel. It was something of a stand-off; but it did clear away legal debris and effectively set the stage for Alexander Hamilton.

By now the hearing was absorbing the attention of both the judicial and legislative wings of New York's state government. According to Charles Holt's *Bee,* almost the entire state senate and assembly poured into the supreme court chambers to hear the climax of the debate. They were there for more than the excitement of seeing Hamilton in action. Already a legislator had submitted a bill that would permit the truth to be heard in libel cases. The British Parliament had passed a similar bill in 1792.

No exact record of Hamilton's speeches in the Croswell case exists, but New York papers reported them quite fully and Justice James Kent kept ample notes. Hamilton began by emphasizing the importance of the subject and went on to examine what he called "the two Great Points"—the truth as evidence, and the jury's right to examine Croswell's intent. He insisted he was not arguing for "the pestilential Doctrine of an unchecked Press." The best man on earth (Washington) had had his great character besmirched by such a press. No, he was contending for the right to publish "the truth, with good motives, though the censure light on government or individuals." Above all he wanted to see "the check" on the press deposited not in a permanent body of magistrates, but in an "occasionally and fluctuating Body, the jury." He pointed out that in the American system judges were not as independent from the executive and legislative branches as they were in England. All the more reason, therefore, to anchor freedom of the press in the right of trial by jury.

Hamilton ranged up and down English legal history and even dipped into Roman law and scriptural texts, to prove that the common law had always maintained these rights, until it was corrupted by the Star Chamber courts, which only proved his point—"a permanent body of men without the wholesome check of a jury grows absolute." Then he turned and indirectly defended the Sedition Act, which despite its repressive intent had been directed against slander which could be proved to be "false." He declared that he "gloried in" the fact that the United States had "by act" established this doctrine.

From here Hamilton soared into a long paean to the juror's duties and rights. What if this were a "capital case" and the jury decided that it did not agree with the court's interpretation of the law? Everyone knew that jurors were bound by their oaths, in such a case, to vote according to their convictions. Were he himself

a juror, Hamilton declared, he would "die on the rack" before he would "immolate his convictions on the altar of power."

Throughout the afternoon, Hamilton all but hypnotized his audience with his dazzling oratory. Kent noted that he was *"sublimely eloquent."* The court adjourned at 5 P.M., and the next morning Hamilton took up the argument again. Once more he worked his way through an impressive number of citations to bolster his argument, but he soon got to the political meat in his morning's work, a digression that Judge Kent in his notes called *"impassioned & most eloquent,"* on the danger to American liberty, not from provisional armies but from *"dependent* Judges, from *selected* Juries, from *stifling* the Press & the voices of leaders & Patriots."

"We ought to resist, resist, resist, till we hurl the Demagogues & Tyrants from their imaginary Thrones," he cried. Never was there a libel case where the question of truth was more important. "It ought to be distinctly known," he thundered, "whether Mr. Jefferson be guilty or not of so foul an act as the one charged." This catapulted him into a eulogy of the dead Washington that in Kent's opinion was "never surpassed—never equalled."

Finally, he paid sarcastic tribute to the "other party" and especially to their "strange & unexpected compliments on the *Freedom* of the English nation." But, he reiterated, a country is free only where the people have a representation in the government, and where they have a trial by jury. If America abandoned the principles of the common law, a faction in power could construe the Constitution to make "any political Tenet or any Indiscretion a Crime." Sacrificing and crushing individuals "by the perverted Forms & mask of law" was the "most dangerous & destructive Tyranny."

As the stocky figure of the man whom Talleyrand said had "made the fortune of his country" bowed before the black-robed justices and retired to his seat, James Kent jotted a final note—"I never heard him so great." Thus inspired, Kent wrote a masterful opinion decreeing a new trial for Croswell. The power of his personality and his reasoning persuaded his fellow associate justices, Livingston and Thompson, to abandon their Jeffersonian principles and agree with him —at first. But Chief Justice Lewis, by now running hard for Governor, wrote a contrary opinion of his own. He also paid Justice Livingston a little visit, whereupon Livingston suddenly changed his mind. The court thus divided two and two, and the motion for a new trial was denied.

The prosecution could have moved immediately for

Hamilton's success at the Croswell trial may have prompted him to raise his political reputation further by accepting Aaron Burr's challenge to duel. It was a fatal mistake.

a judgment against Croswell, but no such motion was made. The Jeffersonians were already badly clawed by their ride on this legal tiger, and they had no penchant for further gouges. Moreover, the New York senators and assemblymen, having heard Hamilton's eloquence, had set to work on a truth-in-libel bill that was certain to pass; the Chief Justice was upholding a legal principle that was about to be officially invalidated. So the case was simply dropped. Its impact, however, was important: other states would soon follow New York's lead, transforming Harry Croswell's case from a *cause célèbre* into one of the bulwarks of our free press.

Croswell's personal troubles were not yet over. Ambrose Spencer returned to Hudson and brought a new suit against Croswell and his mentor, Sampson, for libel. Sampson settled out of court, but the stubborn Croswell refused to back away from the scathing comments he had made about both Spencer and his henchman, District Attorney Ebenezer Foote, in the farewell issue of the *Wasp*, which had appeared on January 26, 1803. Foote submitted a suit of his own. Spencer recovered $126 in damages; poor Foote, attempting to prove he was not a swindler and a blockhead, was ambushed by a host of witnesses who solemnly vowed they had seen him cheat at cards,

among other things. The jury awarded him damages of six cents. This final act of low comedy was gleefully reported in the *Balance*.

Croswell now became senior editor of the *Balance* and continued to do battle in the Federalist cause in Hudson until 1809, when he transferred his paper to Albany. This was a mistake. The Federalists there were in disarray, and his support was meager. Debts piled up; in 1811 a leading Federalist who had loaned him money obtained a judgment against him, and the harassed editor served a short sentence in a debtor's prison. It was one indication of the fatal deficiencies of the Federalists as a party. The "best people" were too interested in lining their own purses to make the sacrifices that a successful political machine demanded.

Totally disgusted, Croswell quit newspapering, took Episcopal orders, and after serving briefly as rector of Christ Church in Hudson, moved to Trinity Church in New Haven. He remained in this post, respected and eventually revered, for the next forty-three years. But he never attended another political meeting, or even exercised his rights as a voter. "His revulsion from Federalism was so entire," said one of his acquaintances after his death, "that in later life his tacit sympathy was evidently with the Democratic party."

Thus exit Harry Croswell. As for Alexander Hamilton, the sequel of the Croswell case was tragedy. During the hearings he had stayed at a friend's house near Albany, and in an evening's conversation, he delivered some scathing denunciations of Vice President Aaron Burr, who was soon to run against Chief Justice Lewis for the governorship of New York. In the course of the election campaign, the friend unwisely quoted Hamilton in a letter that got into the newspapers. Lewis won, finishing Burr politically in New York, and the embittered Vice President challenged Hamilton to a duel. The acclaim he won at Croswell's trial may well have played a part in persuading Hamilton to accept—in spite of his personal detestation of duelling, which had been redoubled by the death of his son Philip in a politically inspired duel two years before. Having regained not a little of the stature he had lost within his party, Hamilton may have been more inclined to risk the morning visit to Weehawken in the hope that it would be another step toward undoing his great rival in the White House, Jefferson. He guessed wrong, and paid for it with his life.

A letter from the President encouraged New York State Jeffersonians to launch their suit against Croswell. Rembrandt Peale completed this portrait of Jefferson in 1805.

164

THE TRIAL

In a dramatic but futile delaying tactic, a wounded John Brown lies before the jury in Horace Pippin's painting.

166

OF JOHN BROWN

By THOMAS J. FLEMING

"Judicial Circuit Court of Virginia, Jefferson County, to wit: The Jurors of the Commonwealth of Virginia, in and for the body of the County of Jefferson, duly impaneled, and attending upon the Circuit Court of said county, upon their oaths do present that John Brown, Aaron C. Stevens . . . , and Edwin Coppoc, white men, and Shields Green and John Copland, free negroes, together with divers other evil-minded and traitorous persons to the Jurors unknown, not having the fear of God before their eyes, but being moved and seduced by the false and malignant counsel of other evil and traitorous persons and the instigations of the devil, did, severally, on the sixteenth, seventeenth and eighteenth day of October, in the year of our Lord eighteen hundred and fifty-nine, and on divers other days before that time, within the Commonwealth of Virginia and the County of Jefferson aforesaid, and within the jurisdiction of this Court, with other confederates to the Jurors unknown, feloniously and traitorously make rebellion and levy war against the said Commonwealth of Virginia . . . ."

On droned the court clerk while the tall, bearded old man and his four confederates stood before the judge's bench. Few men, according to one reporter, could look John Brown in the eye more than a moment. But Judge Richard Parker, third in a judicial family that reached back to the American Revolution, was equally stern of eye and strong of jaw. Grimly he asked Brown how he pleaded to the grand jury's accusations of treason, servile insurrection, and murder. The gaunt old man replied, "Not guilty." Whereupon John Brown lay down on a crude cot, drew a blanket up to his chin, and closed his eyes; the bailiffs led Stevens, with five bullets in his body, and the others back to jail. The trial that would inflame a nation had begun.

The setting was a country courtroom with whitewashed walls smeared with haphazard fingerprints, the floor littered with peanut and chestnut shells, two wood stoves with ugly black pipes crooking their way to the ceiling, and high, dirty, curtainless windows. The benches on three sides of the judicial arena were crammed with five to six hundred spectators. Outside in the streets of Charlestown, Virginia, were several thousand more people, held at bay by lines of militiamen before the pillared courthouse.

At the lawyers' table sat portly Andrew Hunter, special counsel for the Commonwealth of Virginia, handsome, dignified, intelligent, the very model of a southern gentleman. Beside him sat the regular Jefferson County prosecutor, Charles Harding, his coat stained and dirty, his hair uncombed, a stubble of whiskers on his weak chin. Rarely was Harding sober two days in succession. At the defense tables sat lean, tense Lawson Botts, thirty-six, and hulking Thomas C. Green, thirty-nine, the mayor of Charlestown. But all eyes were on the bearded old man whose fanatic daring had created this epic drama.

An undeniable power could emanate from John Brown when he chose to unleash it. The spectators had gotten a glimpse of it the day before, when the sheriff brought Brown and his confederates into the courtroom to be arraigned before eight justices of the peace for the grand-jury hearing. That time Brown had walked from the nearby jail, head erect, stride steady. Prosecutor Harding was in charge of the arraignment, and he asked in a crude, peremptory tone if the defendants had counsel, or if they wished the court to assign them qualified lawyers. Brown transfixed the beak-nosed little alcoholic with a stare, then rose, and in a low, intense voice that reached every corner of the courtroom, proceeded to strike the first blow in his own defense:

Virginians, I did not ask for any quarter at the time I was taken. I did not ask to have my life spared. The Governor of the State of Virginia tendered me his assurance that I should have a fair trial; but, under no circumstances whatever will I be able to have a fair trial. If you seek my blood, you can have it at any moment, without this mockery of a trial. I have had no counsel; I have not been able to advise with any one. I know nothing about the feelings of my fellow prisoners, and am utterly unable to attend in any way to my own defense. My memory don't serve me: my

167

John Brown's body wasn't even in the grave when the New York Tribune marched into print with a report that Brown had kissed a Negro child on his way to the gallows. The northern public avidly accepted the tale. So did several artists. The Currier & Ives lithograph at left was based on a tear-jerking painting done the following year; both included a cruel guard uniformed as a Cossack. In 1867 T. S. Noble's John Brown's Blessing (below) depicted a benign patriarch caressing a slave child's head in a Bastille-like setting. Thomas Hovenden's The Last Moments of John Brown (right), painted in 1884, was more accurate in portraying the surroundings, but Hovenden too accepted the Tribune's story; curiously, the popularity of his picture touched off a debate that ultimately revealed the Negro baby as a reporter's invention: John Brown did kiss a baby, but it was the infant son of his friendly white jailer, John Avis.

John Brown:
The Enduring Myth

168

*The abiding power of the John Brown legend transcends time and
distance. To abolitionists he was an instant martyr; the poet Whittier
rhapsodized about how Brown had "stooped between the jeering ranks
and kissed the negro's child!" Three thousand miles away, Victor Hugo
was so moved by accounts of the execution that he drew the dark and
bitter sketch at left. Some eighty years later the metamorphosis from
tragic blunderer to avenging angel was achieved, in John Steuart Curry's
heroically powerful painting,* John Brown of Osawatomie *(above).*

169

health is insufficient, although improving. There are mitigating circumstances that I would urge in our favor, if a fair trial is to be allowed us: but if we are to be forced with a mere form—a trial for execution—you might spare yourselves that trouble. I am ready for my fate. I do not ask a trial. I beg for no mockery of a trial—no insult—nothing but that which conscience gives, or cowardice would drive you to practice. I ask again to be excused from the mockery of a trial. I do not even know what the special design of this examination is. I do not know what is to be the benefit of it to the Commonwealth. I have now little further to ask, other than that I may not be foolishly insulted only as cowardly barbarians insult those who fall into their power.

His plea was ignored, and shortly after noon the following day, October 26, 1859, Brown was summoned to hear his indictment. When he refused to rise from his jail bed, declaring he was too weak and disabled by his "wounds," which consisted mainly of cuts about the head, he was carried into the courtroom on a cot, a position he obviously found congenial. He had already demonstrated his skill at debating on his back when, a few hours after his capture, he had been confronted by Governor Henry A. Wise of Virginia, Congressman C. L. Vallandigham of Ohio, and Virginia's Senator James M. Mason, among others. It was then that Brown had begun his performance. For this was what the spectators in the small Virginia courtroom were watching—a performance that fanaticism and sectional hatred magnified into a terrible kind of truth.

John Brown was acting out a myth—"Old Brown of Osawatomie," the hero of the fight against slavery in Kansas. To play this part with a skill that combined desperation and grandeur, Brown was summoning every form and source of courage at his command. To win the only victory left for his fierce puritan soul, he was prepared to lie and dissemble again and again.

From boyhood Brown had dreamt grandiose dreams. Searching his Bible he had found quotation after quotation to support his conviction that God had destined his

righteous servant for great things. But through a long and intricate life, in which he had sired twenty children by two wives, success had perpetually eluded him. Before 1855 his life was a series of bankruptcies and lawsuits. Only a kind of faith that transcended reality could have sustained a man in the face of such a series of defeats.

Although he did little or nothing about it in a practical sense, a hatred of slavery ran like a dark thread through much of Brown's early life. In 1846, when he was working as a wool merchant, he was sufficiently well known as an abolitionist to receive a visit from Frederick Douglass, the ex-slave who had become a well-known lecturer in the North. As a believer in the peaceful abolition of slavery, Douglass was more than a little alarmed to hear Brown say: "No political action will ever abolish the system of slavery. It will have to go out in blood. Those men who hold slaves have even forfeited their right to live."

When the wool business failed, Brown persuaded philanthropist Gerrit Smith to give him a portion of the 120,000 acres of Smith's upstate New York patrimony which he had thrown open to refugee Negroes. There Brown lived as a farmer and stern paterfamilias to the handful of colored people who took advantage

The slave woman at right foreground turns away in horror as John Brown, bound and perched on his own coffin, is transported to the gallows, December 2, 1859. "This is a beautiful country," he told his jailer, John Avis, seated behind him. "I never truly had the pleasure of seeing it before." This painting, like the one on page 166, was done by Pippin, a Negro artist, whose mother said she had seen the execution.

of Smith's hospitality and braved the rigors of the cruel climate and the hostilities of the local whites.

But it was Kansas, whence five of his sons had gone in search of land and opportunity, that gave Brown his true mission. The doctrine of "squatter sovereignty" had made the fledgling state a cauldron of North-South animosity, and Brown had responded to his sons' call for help by abandoning the New York farm and joining them as "Captain" Brown, a title chosen in memory of his ancestor John Brown, who had died of illness in 1776 while serving in that rank in the Revolutionary Army.

Brown swiftly revealed a talent for guerrilla warfare in its vilest form. On May 24–25, 1856, he led his sons and a few followers in a raid on a handful of pro-southern settlers living on Pottawatomie Creek; the raiders dragged five defenseless victims, including the father and two oldest sons of the Doyle family, out of their homes and brutally murdered them. The slaughter—several of the victims were hacked almost to pieces by sabers—caused such a general revulsion of feeling that Brown and his sons had to flee like common criminals. But it was here that Brown first learned the technique of the big lie. James Redpath, an ardently abolitionist reporter, found Brown hiding out in a Kansas creek bed and published an extensive interview with him in which Brown piously declared that he had had nothing whatsoever to do with the Pottawatomie murders, although he "approved of them" as reprisal for murders committed by the pro-slavers.

The propaganda, plus his courage in several Kansas skirmishes, particularly his heroic battle at Osawatomie against proslavery forces, made John Brown a hero among a small circle of Boston abolitionists who advocated violence to overthrow slavery. From them and Smith, Brown raised several thousand dollars to finance a subsequent slave-and-horse-stealing expedition into Missouri and eventually to launch what was covertly referred to as "the well-matured plan."

This was the attack on Harpers Ferry, which Brown made on Sunday night, October 16, 1859. With twenty-one armed followers he seized the federal arsenal just across the Potomac River from Maryland and converted it into a fortress to which, Brown was confident, every Negro in the area would flee. Aroused Virginians the next day drove Brown and his band out of the arsenal and into the adjacent fire-engine house; a furious fire fight raged for the next day and a half, until all but seven of the raiders were killed, captured, or dispersed.

Brown tried to use ten local white hostages to guarantee a safe passage into the Maryland hills, but Colonel Robert E. Lee of the U. S. Cavalry, ordered

to the scene by President Buchanan, declined to bargain. When Brown refused a final demand to surrender, Lee sent a dozen Marines, led by Lieutenant Israel Green, to crash through the engine-room door with fixed bayonets. Green, according to his own account, caught Brown as he was reloading his gun and beat him to the ground with repeated blows on the head from his light dress sword. Such was the beginning and the end of "the well-matured plan."

On the same afternoon, as Brown lay on the floor of the office of the armory paymaster, he was confronted by Governor Wise and his party of distinguished interrogators. For more than three hours Brown sparred with them, laying the groundwork for his defense. His plan had failed, he insisted, because he had neglected tactics out of humane consideration for the hostages his men had rounded up after seizing the arsenal Sunday night. He went on to lament that his wounds were inflicted upon him "some minutes after I had ceased fighting and had consented to a surrender for the benefit of others, not for my own."

Brown blatantly maintained that he could have killed Lieutenant Green, "but I supposed he came in only to receive our surrender." When someone impatiently pointed out that the Lieutenant had scrambled headfirst through an opening battered in the door, with bullets whistling all around him, and that the first man to follow him had been killed and the second seriously wounded, Brown solemnly explained that the Marines had fired first. This was another lie. The Marines had been given strict orders to use only their bayonets lest they kill the hostages.

Meanwhile, the nation reverberated with the shock of John Brown's deed. The initial reports, based on rumors, trumpeted news of a military invasion and an uprising involving thousands of slaves. When the true dimensions of Brown's futile foray became visible, the first reaction was bewilderment. The Cleveland *Leader* thought the whole affair was "positively ridiculous." The New York *Tribune* called it "the work of a madman," and so did the Hartford *Evening Press* and the St. Louis *Evening News*. Even the *Liberator*, Boston's abolitionist organ, called Brown's raid a "misguided, wild and apparently insane, though disinterested and well-intended effort by insurrection to emancipate the slaves." Southern papers, of course, took a different point of view. The Richmond *Inquirer* echoed most of the South when it declared, "The Harpers Ferry invasion has advanced the cause of Disunion more than any other event that has happened since the formation of the Government...."

The reference in the indictment to "divers other evil-minded and traitorous persons to the Jurors unknown" echoed the southern conviction that Brown had not acted alone. On a Maryland farm a few miles from Harpers Ferry, where Brown had spent the summer planning the raid, searchers had found a carpet-bag full of correspondence between Brown and his backers. As for these gentlemen, the news of Harpers Ferry turned their blood to ice water. Smith had a mental collapse, which may have been real, and was confined to an asylum. Douglass and several others left for Canada, beyond the reach of federal warrants.

Within a week of his capture, Brown was on trial. The speed was in accordance with the Virginia statute which required, "when an indictment is found against a person for felony, in a court wherein he may be tried, the accused, if in custody, shall, unless good cause be shown for a continuance, be arraigned and tried in the same term." Governor Wise had already rejected the advice of some Virginians to declare martial law, convict Brown in a drumhead court, and hang him on the spot. He insisted that the honor and reputation of the South made it imperative to give Brown every benefit the law allowed. But Wise apparently could not bring himself to do more than yield the law's strict letter. Neither he nor his prosecutor could see that they were duelling John Brown for the minds and hearts of millions of neutral northerners.

Already Brown's tactics were having their effect beyond the borders of Virginia. The Lawrence, Kansas, *Republican* fulminated, "We defy an instance to be shown in a civilized community where a prisoner has been forced to trial for his life, when so disabled by sickness or ghastly wounds as to be unable even to sit up during the proceedings, and compelled to be carried to the judgment hall upon a litter. . . ." But Brown did not convince everyone. The reporter for the New York *Tribune* wrote, "The prisoner lay most of the time [during the reading of the indictment] with his eyes closed and the counterpane drawn close up to his chin. He is evidently not much injured, but is determined to resist the pushing of his trial by all the means in his power."

Brown's delaying tactics rose in part from his instinctive skill at putting his accusers on the defensive. But he also had more practical reasons. He had sent letters north to three prominent lawyers; as yet, none had responded. Moreover, if he managed to stall long enough, his supporters might have time to mount a rescue operation; freeing prisoners from well-guarded jails had been done more than once in Kansas.

When the news of Harpers Ferry reached Boston, abolitionist John W. Le Barnes hired George H. Hoyt, a fragile, pale, fledgling lawyer who was only twenty-one (and looked nineteen), to leave immediately for Charlestown. Hoyt's instructions were:

. . . first, to watch and be able to report proceedings, to see and talk with Brown, and be able to communicate with his friends anything Brown might want to say; and, second, to send me an accurate and detailed account of the military situation at Charlestown, the number and distribution of troops, the location and defenses of the jail, and nature of the approaches to the town and jail, the opportunities for a sudden attack, and the means of retreat, with the location and situation of the room in which Brown is confined, and all other particulars that might enable friends to consult as to some plan of attempt at rescue.

Hoyt was still riding a southbound train when Brown resumed his cot for the second day of his trial, which began with the defense presenting a telegram received late the previous night from Akron, Ohio, testifying that insanity was hereditary in the Brown family. Before either of the prosecuting attorneys could say a word, Brown rose from his cot to denounce such a plea in blazing terms:

I look upon it as a miserable artifice and pretext of those who ought to take a different course in regard to me, if they took any at all, and I view it with contempt more than otherwise. As I remarked to Mr. Green, insane persons, so far as my experience goes, have but little ability to judge of their own sanity; and if I am insane, of course I should think I know more than all the rest of the world. But I do not think so. I am perfectly unconscious of insanity, and I reject, so far as I am capable, any attempt to interfere in my behalf on that score.

The defendant's abashed lawyers dropped the plea. But they promptly presented the court with another document, a telegram from Judge Daniel Tilden, announcing he was en route from Ohio in response to Brown's letter. Botts and Green requested a delay until Tilden arrived. The prosecution objected strongly; Hunter asked tartly if Tilden was a lawyer or a leader of a band of desperadoes. The prosecutor insisted that if additional lawyers were coming, more than enough time had elapsed for them to reach Charlestown. What was there to debate, really? Brown had admitted and even gloried in his crimes.

This brought Green lumbering to his feet. In a rush of angry sentences whose "whar" and "thar" made northern reporters smile, he sharply rebutted Hunter. Treason, Green pointed out, could be confessed only in open court. What Brown had said to one or even a hundred persons outside the court was irrelevant. Equally "idle," Green said, were the prosecutor's fears of a rescue attempt. Earnestly Green asked Judge Parker for only one day's delay. Again the Judge insisted that time was of the essence and denied the motion.

Lawson Botts then rose to make the defense's opening statement to the jury. Urging the chosen farmers to remember that the burden of proof rested upon the commonwealth, he pointed out that in order to convict Brown of premeditated murder, the state must present evidence of malice; and Brown had gone to great lengths to guarantee the safety of the prisoners he had taken. More important, Botts contended that the prosecution could not possibly prove the charge of treason against Brown. According to the common-law tradition in the United States, treason could be committed only by a resident against his own state. Surely no stretch of logic could make Brown a citizen of Virginia. Finally there was the question of the court's jurisdiction over crimes committed on federal property such as an arsenal. With an eloquence that must have startled his fellow southerners, Botts argued that Virginia had no right whatsoever to try John Brown.

Hunter replied to Botts's claims. With obvious pride he pointed out that the Virginia law on treason was "more full" than the federal statute. A person was found guilty of treason against Virginia not only if he levied war against the commonwealth or gave aid and comfort to its enemies but also if he established without the authority of the legislature "any governments within its limits separate from the existing government." As for the jurisdiction, Hunter cited an 1830 case involving a murder committed on the arsenal grounds. The murderer had been tried, convicted, and executed under Virginia laws.

The prosecution now produced witnesses who narrated a blow-by-blow account of the assault on Harpers Ferry. Mr. Phelps, a Baltimore & Ohio conductor, told how, when his train had arrived at the bridge outside Harpers Ferry shortly after midnight Sunday, he was warned by the wounded bridge watchman that riflemen had seized the arsenal. For this reason, Phelps said, he refused to take his train into Harpers Ferry. When the baggagemaster of the station, a free Negro named Shephard Hayward, walked out on the railroad bridge to find out what was wrong, a gun barked and he staggered back to the station crying, "I am shot." The ball had entered Hayward's back and come out under his left nipple, Phelps reported. (Twelve hours later Hayward died in agony on the floor of the railroad station while the battle raged around the arsenal.)

"THE ARSENAL'S BEEN SEIZED!"

Until John Brown's fateful raid in October, 1859, few Americans were even aware of the existence of the federal arsenal, right, set in bucolic isolation in Harpers Ferry at the confluence of the Potomac and Shenandoah rivers. But as news of the audacious attack spread, public attention suddenly focused on the town, and the illustrators of the day rushed into print with drawings of the event. The story of the raid, as told by these artists, appears on the following pages.

Later in the night Brown had come to Phelps to guarantee personally the safety of the train, which then proceeded to Monocacy, Maryland, where Phelps telegraphed the first alarm. Phelps returned to Harpers Ferry on Tuesday and went with Governor Wise and others to interview Brown shortly after he was taken. The best way to ascertain his real purpose, Brown had told them, was to read the books in his trunk at his Maryland farm headquarters.

Colonel Lee had handed Wise one of these books, and Brown had explained that it was the constitution of a "provisional government" in which he was president and commander-in-chief. Brown said there was also a secretary of state, a secretary of war, and all the other officers for a general government, including a house of representatives which included "an intelligent colored man."

Green interrupted this sensational testimony to ask the court once more for a delay. He had received a message that counsel was arriving from Cleveland and would almost certainly be there by nightfall. Hunter had selected "only scraps" of the prisoner's long conversation with Governor Wise, Green explained, and the new counsel should have an opportunity to cross-question the witness. Hunter replied that there would be several other witnesses called the next day who would go over the same ground, and the new counsel could question them at that time—if he arrived. The court ordered the questioning of the witness to proceed, and the defense got Phelps to admit that Brown had said on Sunday night that "it was not his intention to harm anybody or anything. He was sorry men had been killed. It was not by his orders or with his approbation."

Colonel Lewis Washington now took the stand. The

173

most distinguished of Brown's hostages, he bore a striking resemblance to his famous great granduncle. Washington told how four of Brown's lieutenants had aroused him between one and two o'clock in the morning and, levelling rifles and a revolver at him, ordered him and his slaves to come with them to Harpers Ferry. On Brown's express orders, they forced the Colonel to hand over an old dress sword allegedly presented by Frederick the Great to George Washington. When the Colonel arrived at the arsenal, he was astonished to find the relic in Brown's hands. "I will take especial care of it and I shall endeavor to return it to you after you are released," Brown told him. Brown carried the sword throughout the battle on Monday and put it aside only when the Marines began to batter down the door.

Washington said Brown had advised each of the hostages that he could ransom himself by summoning a "stout Negro" to take his place. This Washington and the others steadfastly declined to do. The Colonel echoed the death knell of Brown's dream when he proudly testified, "No Negro from this neighborhood appeared to take arms voluntarily."

Not long after the court adjourned for the day, George Hoyt finally arrived from Boston. Hunter took one look at him and wrote to Governor Wise, "A beardless boy came in last night as Brown's counsel. I think he is a spy." The next morning when Hoyt appeared in court, Hunter demanded proof that he was a member of the Boston bar. Northern newspapers, unaware of Hoyt's real mission, were enraged. The embarrassed Hoyt could only murmur that he had brought no credentials. But Judge Parker, so unyielding when it came to granting delays, said he would be willing to accept "any citizen's evidence"

that Hoyt was indeed a qualified attorney. Green said he had read letters from Hoyt's fellow students alluding to him as a member of the bar, and the Judge permitted the young man to take the oath and assume a seat beside Botts and Green.

After some further cross-examination of conductor Phelps and Colonel Washington by the defense, Hunter laid before the jury the printed constitution and ordinance of Brown's provisional government. He also produced some fifty papers and letters captured in Brown's carpetbag at the Maryland farm linking Brown to Smith and his other abolitionist backers. Each document was handed to Brown, who identified it in a loud voice: "Yes, that is mine."

For the rest of the day Hunter paraded more witnesses to the stand. Armsted Ball, the master machinist of the Harpers Ferry armory, told how he had been seized by Brown's men when he went to the arsenal to investigate the disturbance. Ball had prevented one of Brown's men from firing at an old man named Guess, who was passing by; but he had been unable to stop him from killing Fontaine Beckham, the popular mayor of Harpers Ferry, who had ventured onto the railroad trestle to get a better look at the excitement in the arsenal below.

John Allstadt, who like Colonel Washington had been awakened and marched to the armory at rifle point with his seven slaves, said Brown's rifle was "cocked all the time." As for the Negroes, "they did nothing." The courtroom burst into laughter when Allstadt added, "Some of them were asleep nearly all the time." Not long after the afternoon session began, Hunter decided he had more than proved Brown guilty of treason, insurrection, and murder, and announced that the prosecution rested.

Harper's Weekly, NOVEMBER 5, 1859

With the arrival of the federal troops, Brown and his men attempted to defend their redoubt in the enginehouse.

When negotiations failed, Colonel Robert E. Lee gave the Marines the difficult assignment of breaking into the enginehouse and subduing its defenders.

The first defense witness was Joseph A. Brewer, one of the hostages, who described in vivid terms the strange mixture of murder and mercy that had characterized the bloodshed at Harpers Ferry. Brown had sent Stevens and hostage A. M. Kitzmiller out with a flag of truce to parley, and the maddened citizens of Harpers Ferry riddled Stevens. When Brewer realized that Stevens was still alive, he risked his life to venture out through the gunfire to carry the wounded man into a nearby building. Then, according to the pledge he had given to Brown, he returned to the enginehouse. Both he and Kitzmiller, who testified next, told how Brown had urged them to use their influence with the citizens to prevent unnecessary bloodshed.

Next the defense asked the court if it could introduce testimony about the death of Thompson, one of Brown's men who had been seized by the citizens when he left the enginehouse to parley under a flag of truce. Hunter objected; all this testimony about Brown's forbearance, he insisted, had no more to do with the legal realities of the case than the "dead languages." He could, moreover, see no point in introducing any testimony about how Thompson died after he was captured, unless the defense could show that John Brown knew about it and still exerted forbearance toward his prisoners. But Judge Parker ruled the evidence admissible, and Hunter had to sit stolidly while his own son, Harry, recited a grisly tale:

After Mr. Beckham, who was my granduncle, was shot, I was much exasperated and started with Mr. Chambers to the room where . . . Thompson was confined, with the purpose of shooting him. We found several persons in the room and had levelled our guns at him when Mrs. Foulke's sister threw herself before him and begged us to leave him to the laws. We then caught hold of him, and dragged him out by the throat, he saying, "though you may take my life, eighty thousand will rise up to avenge me and carry out my purpose of giving liberty to the slaves." We carried him out to the bridge and the two of us, levelling our guns in this moment of wild exasperation fired, and before he fell, a dozen or more balls were buried in him; we then threw his body off the trestlework . . . . I had just seen my loved uncle and best friend I ever had, shot down by those villainous Abolitionists, and felt justified in shooting any that I could find; I felt it my duty, and I have no regrets.

There was not a sound in the courtroom when this terrible story ended. But from the old man on the cot there came a long, low groan.

The defense now summoned several more witnesses. One name after another drew no response from the packed courtroom. Once more, without warning, Brown suddenly rose from his cot and electrified the court and the nation with a bitter protest:

May it please the Court: I discover that notwithstanding all the assurances I have received of a fair trial, nothing like a fair trial is to be given me, as it would seem. I gave the names, as soon as I could get them, of the persons I wished to have called as witnesses, and was assured that they would be subpoenaed. I wrote down a memorandum to that effect, saying where those parties were; but it appears they have not been subpoenaed as far as I can learn; and I now ask, if I am to have anything at all deserving the name and shadow of a fair trial, that this proceeding be deferred until tomorrow morning; for I have no counsel, as I before stated, in whom I feel that I can rely, but I am in hopes counsel may arrive who will attend to seeing that I get the witnesses who are necessary for my defense. I am myself unable to attend to it. I have given all the attention I possibly could to it, but am unable to see or know about them, and can't even find out their names; and I have nobody to do any errands, for my money was all taken

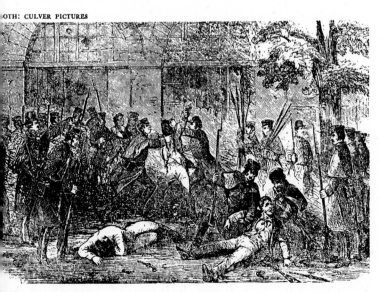

The attack was over in a few minutes. In this fanciful depiction, Brown is propped up, right foreground, by two of the Marines who captured him.

Shortly after capture, Brown and Aaron Stevens were interrogated by an official delegation headed by Governor Wise.

when I was sacked and stabbed, and I have not a dime. I had two hundred and fifty or sixty dollars in gold and silver taken from my pocket, and now I have no possible means of getting anybody to go my errands for me, and I have not had all the witnesses subpoenaed. They are not within reach, and are not here. I ask at least until tomorrow morning to have something done, if anything is designed; if not, I am ready for anything that may come up.

Reporting this outburst, the New York *Herald's* correspondent said that "the indignation of the citizens scarcely knew bounds. He [Brown] was stigmatized as an ungrateful villain, and some declared he deserved hanging for that act alone." The sheriff assured Judge Parker that all Brown's subpoenas had been served, and the courtroom seethed. John Brown lay down again, drew his blanket over him, and closing his eyes, "appeared to sink in tranquil slumber."

Young Hoyt now rose to make a new plea for delay. He knew that Brown's explosive repudiation of his court-appointed counsel meant that he was about to be left with the full responsibility for the defense. Hoyt told Judge Parker that he had not even read the indictment nor "got any idea of the line of the defense proposed and have no knowledge of the criminal code of Virginia and no time to read it." Botts offered Hoyt the full resources of his law office and declared he would "sit up with him all night to put him in possession of all the law and facts in relation to this case." Reluctantly, Judge Parker agreed to a limited postponement and adjourned at six o'clock.

Botts spent the night giving Hoyt a crash course in Virginia criminal law, only to discover in the morning that it was unnecessary. Two experienced lawyers had at last arrived in response to Brown's call for counsel. One was Hiram Griswold of Cleveland, sent as a substitute by Judge Tilden. The other was Samuel Chilton of Washington, D. C., a Virginian by birth and widely respected by fellow members of the bar. He had been hired (for a fee of one thousand dollars) by John A. Andrew, a leading Boston abolitionist. Chilton told Judge Parker he was totally unprepared and asked for a short delay of a few hours to make some preparation. But the Judge was weary of pleas for delay. He declared that Brown had no one to blame but himself for dismissing his previous counsel.

Hoyt then summoned more of the hostages John Brown had collected in the enginehouse. They repeated much of what had already been made clear before, adding only grim details to the over-all picture, such as seeing two of Brown's sons fatally wounded during the first day's fighting. Hunter replied that he could only regard this course as calculated to waste time. Hoyt replied that he was trying to "prove the absence of malicious intention," and

was besides acting in accordance "with the express commands" of his client. Hunter gave up and allowed the parade of witnesses to continue, but he did not even bother to cross-examine them.

By the time the court adjourned for a one-hour recess, the defense had run out of witnesses. It was Saturday, and Judge Parker was determined to end the trial before nightfall. But Brown was equally determined to prolong it until Monday. When the bailiffs summoned him to reappear in court, Brown again said he was too sick to rise from his jail bed. The Judge demanded a report from the doctor, who said Brown was malingering. Parker therefore ordered him carried into court once more. But by the time Brown arrived, another hour had been consumed.

Chilton then asked the court to compel the prosecution to elect one count of the indictment and abandon the others, arguing that it was unfair to force the prisoner to defend himself against three accusations simultaneously. After vigorous support for the indictment from prosecutor Hunter, Judge Parker ruled that the jury had been charged and sworn to try the prisoners on the indictment as drawn. The trial must go on, but Chilton could at its close ask for "an arrest of judgment."

Only the closing arguments from the prosecution and the defense now remained. It was after five o'clock and growing dark. Griswold rose to ask for an adjournment after the prosecution had completed its statements so that he and Chilton could make a more respectable defense on Monday morning. Once more there was a wrangle over this request for delay. Hunter blamed Brown for "dismissing his faithful, skillful, able and zealous counsel yesterday afternoon," and could see no reason why the jurors should be kept away from their families for the weekend, adding, somewhat irrelevantly, that there was not a "female in this county who was not trembling with anxiety and apprehension." Chilton replied that he hoped the court would not require a man on trial for his life to submit his case without an adequate argument.

With obvious reluctance, Judge Parker agreed to adjourn after hearing Harding's summation. Pulling himself out of his alcoholic fog, the county attorney declaimed for about forty minutes, while Hunter squirmed in his chair. "When Harding began to speak," recalled one of the spectators years later, "if you shut your eyes and listened, for the first few minutes you would think Patrick Henry had returned to earth; after that he dwindled away into ineptitudes." After enduring Harding's harangue, Judge Parker adjourned the court until 9:00 A.M. Monday.

The Judge and prosecutor Hunter could only glare in chagrin as John Brown, the moment the adjourning gavel fell, rose from his bed and without the least difficulty walked serenely back to his cell.

On Monday the contending attorneys met for the final round. Griswold and Chilton made vigorous orations in Brown's defense, but Botts had already made the best available arguments, and in essence the northern lawyers did little more than paraphrase him. They maintained that Brown was not a Virginia citizen, that the court did not have jurisdiction over the federal arsenal, and that Brown's consideration to his hostages proved his lack of malice and therefore his innocence of first-degree murder. They tried to use the slaves' failure to revolt as proof that Brown was equally innocent of insurrection, and did their best to dismiss Brown's provisional constitution as a "mere debating society . . . a wild chimerical production."

In reply, prosecutor Hunter underscored the irrelevance of the lack-of-malice argument by explaining to the jury that anyone who killed while committing a felony was *de facto* guilty of murder in the first degree. As for Brown's citizenship, Hunter argued that the Virginia code defined as citizens all those white persons born in any other state of this union who become residents. Brown, he maintained, was attempting to become a resident, albeit a most unwelcome one, when he seized the arsenal. He had come to stay "for the nefarious purpose of rallying forces into this Commonwealth and establishing himself at Harpers Ferry as a starting point for a new Government."

Whether one called it tragical or farcical or ridiculous, Hunter added, Brown's conduct showed clearly that his raid was not intended to carry off slaves. His provisional government was "a real thing and no debating society." It clearly showed that the property of slaveholders all over the South was to be confiscated and that any man found in arms was to be shot down.

Of course Brown had treated his prisoners well, Hunter pointed out. Why should he kill them and incite the country? He wanted to lull the citizens of Virginia into letting him "usurp the government, manumit our slaves, confiscate the property of slave holders and without drawing a trigger or shedding blood permit him to take possession of the Commonwealth. . . ." Brown's plan was "almost too abhorrent" to contemplate. Hunter asked that Brown be convicted in order that "the majesty of the laws" might be vindicated.

Throughout these orations Brown lay on his back with his eyes closed. Chilton now asked Judge Parker to instruct the jury that they could not convict Brown of treason, but Parker denied the motion. Chilton then asked the Judge to rule on the question of jurisdiction. Parker affirmed the court's jurisdiction, and the jury retired. For three-quarters of an hour the

court was in recess. Then the spectators swarmed back to hear the foreman of the jury announce that John Brown had been found guilty on all counts.

Reporters had expected whoops of elation, a storm of jeers, or at least wild applause, but there was not a sound in the hushed courtroom. Virginia was trying to prove with decorum the justice of John Brown's fate. No one, from the Governor to the lowliest groundling, seemed to understand that dignity was no match for John Brown's histrionics.

Chilton now moved for an arrest of judgment, citing the well-debated errors in the indictment. Judge Parker promised to hear arguments on it the following day, and the court adjourned after impanelling a jury to try Edwin Coppoc.

On Wednesday, November 2, everyone expected an early ruling by Judge Parker. But when Parker arrived in court he found the jury for the trial of Coppoc already in their seats. He therefore refrained from reading his opinion until Coppoc's guilt was confirmed by the jury that afternoon. Brown was summoned to the courtroom, and Parker ruled against the motion for an arrest of judgment. Then the clerk asked Brown, still prone on his cot, whether he wished to say anything before the sentence was pronounced.

Brown arose, flustered. He had not expected sentencing so soon. He was under the impression that he and his confederates would be sentenced in a body. "I have, may it please the court," he said hesitantly, "a few words to say." Then he braced himself and seemed to realize, fully and totally, that he was a dead man. The law had condemned him, and he no longer needed to worry about arguments that satisfied judge and jury. In a voice that was to echo down bitter decades, John Brown spoke to America:

In the first place, I deny everything but what I have all along admitted: the design on my part to free slaves. I

At the arraignment Brown asked for a trial delay on account of his wounds. Stevens had to be supported by attendants.

Harper's Weekly, NOVEMBER 12, 1859

intended certainly to have made a clean thing of that matter, as I did last winter, when I went into Missouri and there took slaves without the snapping of a gun on either side, moved them through the country and finally left them in Canada. I designed to have done the same thing again, on a larger scale. That was all I intended. I never did intend murder, or treason, or the destruction of property, or to excite or incite slaves to rebellion, or to make insurrection.

I have another objection; and that is, it is unjust that I should suffer such a penalty. Had I interfered in the manner which I admit, and which I admit has been fairly proved—for I admire the truthfulness and candor of the greater portion of the witnesses who have testified in this case—had I so interfered in behalf of the rich, the powerful, the intelligent, the so-called great, or in behalf of any of their friends, either father, mother, brother, sister, wife, or children, or any of that class, and suffered and sacrificed what I have in this interference, it would have been all right; and every man in this court would have deemed it an act worthy of reward rather than punishment.

This court acknowledges, as I suppose, the validity of the law of God. I see a book kissed here, which I suppose to be the Bible, or at least the New Testament, that teaches me that all things whatsoever I would that men should do to me, I should do even so to them. It teaches me, further, to "remember them that are in bonds, as bound with them." I endeavor to act up to that instruction. I say, I am yet too young to understand that God is any respecter of persons. I believe that to have interfered as I have done, as I have always freely admitted I have done, in behalf of His despised poor, was not wrong, but right. Now, if it is deemed necessary that I should forfeit my life for the furtherance of the ends of justice, and mingle my blood further with the blood of my children and with the blood of millions in this slave country whose rights are disregarded by wicked, cruel, and unjust enactments, I submit; so let it be done!

Let me say one word further.

I feel entirely satisfied with the treatment I have received on my trial. Considering all the circumstances, it has been more generous than I expected. But I feel no consciousness of guilt. I have stated from the first what was my intention, and what was not. I never had any design against the life of any person, nor any disposition to commit treason, or excite slaves to rebel, or make any general insurrection. I never encouraged any man to do so, but always discouraged any idea of that kind.

Let me say, also, a word in regard to the statements made by some of those connected with me. I hear it has been stated by some of them that I have induced them to join me. But the contrary is true. I do not say this to injure them, but as regretting their weakness. There is not one of them but joined me of his own accord, and the greater part of them at their own expense. A number of them I never saw, and never had a word of conversation with, till the day they came to me; and that was for the purpose I have stated.

Now, I have done.

Subtract the paragraphs on religion, and this speech, which Emerson was to compare to Lincoln's Gettysburg Address, was one long lie. Even the minor detail of his Missouri raid Brown distorted in the name of propaganda. His lieutenant, Stevens, had killed a slaveowner on that foray. But the larger lie concerned the intentions of his Harpers Ferry raid. A study of the correspondence of other members of the band and of the memoirs of those who knew Brown makes it clear that he never intended to repeat his Missouri raid "on a larger scale." His provisional constitution meant what it said.

Not for nothing had he insisted on confiscating George Washington's old sword; it was obviously intended for symbolic use. Two weeks before the attack, one of the younger raiders, William H. Leeman, wrote home: "I am now in a Southern *Slave State* and before I leave it, it will be a *free state,* Mother. . . ." Only a few days before the raid, another member of the band, Edward Kagi, wrote John Brown, Jr., in Ohio to send no more recruits "until we open the way clear up to the line (M. & D.'s) from the South." Douglass later recalled watching John Brown run his finger down a map of the Alleghenies from the border of New York into the southern states. "These mountains," Brown had said, "are the basis of my plan. God has given the strength of these hills to freedom; they were placed here to aid the emancipation of your race."

"With twenty-five picked men," Brown told Douglass, he would create an armed force in "the very heart of the South." These men were to gather recruits from the slave population, arm them and keep "the most restless and daring" in their ranks and send the others north. As his numbers grew, he planned to extend his operations to "more than one locality." Thus Brown's Harpers Ferry plan was the very opposite of his Missouri raid. His destination was south, not north. As for not inducing his followers to join him, he had, from the available evidence, cajoled all but one with promises of plunder far beyond anything they had seen in Kansas.

But few, north or south, were capable of analyzing or investigating John Brown's story. Even before he made his historic oration, newspapers were reporting the trial from a more and more partisan point of view. Virginia's conduct of the trial had lost the sympathy even of the conservative *New York Times,* which had deplored Brown's raid and castigated all those who supported him. The *Times* lamented Parker's refusal to grant delays and found particular fault with Hunter's Saturday night remarks about the jurors wanting to go home, and about Virginia's "trembling females."

It was on November 2 that Judge Parker sentenced

John Brown to death by hanging. The sentence was to be carried out on December 2, a month from the day. Now a new kind of contest began. From all over the nation men wrote to Governor Wise threatening, exhorting, and pleading with him not to hang John Brown. From Massachusetts, Amos Lawrence, who had given Brown money, warned the Governor, "From his blood would spring an army of martyrs." Fernando Wood, the pro-southern mayor of New York, thought the same way. "Dare you do a bold thing and temper 'justice with Mercy'?" he wrote Wise. "Have you nerve enough to send Brown to the State Prison instead of hanging him?"

On the other hand, bellicose types in the South were eager to see Brown die no matter what the consequences. "Though it convert the whole Northern people, without an exception, into furious armed abolition invaders," the Richmond *Whig* declared, *"yet old Brown will be hung!"*

The headstrong Wise did not need advice from any direction. Two days after Brown's sentence he wrote to Fernando Wood: "My mind is inflexibly made up." He rejected the argument that the hanging would make Brown a martyr. He could see no difference, so far as martyrdom was concerned, between the noose and a life sentence in a Virginia prison.

Some of John Brown's friends continued to foment desperate plans to free him. One involved a gathering of Kansas raiders and German immigrant volunteers who would storm the jail some propitious midnight. Another, even wilder scheme involved kidnapping Governor Wise and smuggling him aboard a seagoing tug, where he was to be held hostage until exchanged for Brown. None of these plots came close to fruition, in part because sensible men saw they were all but hopeless and declined to donate the thousands of dollars needed to set them in motion. But another, more powerful reason was the frank admission of the old man in the Charlestown prison cell that he did not want rescue, that he accepted and even gloried in "being worth infinitely more now to die than to live."

With magnificent courage, the fifty-nine-year-old Brown nerved himself for his final ordeal. He refused to see his wife until the day before his execution. In a letter to a cousin, he consoled himself that he had "never since I can remember required a great amount of sleep: so that I conclude that I have already enjoyed full an average amount of waking hours with those who reach their 'three scores and ten.' "

The best of Brown's letters were reprinted in newspapers throughout the North. They reportedly brought tears to the eyes of his southern jailer as he read and sealed them. To the numerous visitors and correspondents who discussed aspects of his past life Brown frequently vowed that he had had nothing to do with the Pottawatomie murders. But one letter was never answered by John Brown nor published by his admirers:

Altho' vengence is not mine I confess that I do feel gratified, to hear that you were stopped in your fiendish career at Harper's Ferry, with the loss of your two sons, you can now appreciate my distress in Kansas, when you then & there entered my house at midnight and arrested my Husband and two boys, and took them out of the yard and in cold blood shot them dead in my hearing, you cant say you done it to free slaves, we had none and never expected to own one, but has only made me a poor disconsolate widow with helpless children, while I feel for your folly I do hope & trust that you will meet your just reward, O how it pained my heart to hear the dying groans of my Husband & children, if this scrawl gives you any consolation you are welcome to it.

Mahala Doyle

Meanwhile, Brown's lawyers carried the exception they had taken to Jefferson County's jurisdiction to the Virginia court of appeals. They were turned down. Virginia's highest court was as disinclined to yield to the prerogatives of federal power as the lower one.

On December 2, John Brown, wearing a black frock coat and pants, a black slouch hat, and red slippers, was led into the street by his guards and saw some 1,500 armed men deployed. "I had no idea that Governor Wise considered my execution so important," Brown gasped. Wise had, in fact, yielded to hysteria. He told President Buchanan that "Devils . . . trained in all the Indian arts of predatory war" were massing in Kansas and Ohio to rescue Brown. He persuaded the President to send Colonel Lee and 264 artillerymen to guard Harpers Ferry, and during the first two

Frank Leslie's Illustrated Newspaper, DECEMBER 17, 1859

The day before his execution, Brown and his wife were permitted a four-hour, emotion-filled reunion in his jail cell.

days of December he clamped a security net around Charlestown which paralyzed the region. No person could travel on a train unless a station agent first issued him a certificate of good character. Numbers of people, including four congressmen, were jailed on suspicion the moment they reached Charlestown.

As he walked from the jail, John Brown handed to one of the guards a final, prophetic note, which probably revealed more of his real intentions at Harpers Ferry than anything else he said or wrote:

I, John Brown, am now quite *certain* that the crimes of this *guilty land: will* never be purged *away;* but with Blood. I had *as I now think: vainly* flattered myself that without *very much* bloodshed it might be done.

The day was exceptionally clear and warm, and as John Brown rode to the place of his execution, seated on his coffin in a wagon drawn by two white horses, he looked out at the Blue Ridge Mountains and said, "This *is* a beautiful country. I never truly had the pleasure of seeing it before." Around the gallows there were few civilians, for Governor Wise had issued a proclamation urging the citizens to stay home and guard their property.

Brown mounted the scaffold with unwavering steps, and throwing aside his slouch hat, permitted the sheriff to tie a white bag over his head. He was to stand waiting, the noose around his neck, for almost fifteen minutes while the untrained militia were marched to their prescribed positions. Colonel J. T. L. Preston of the Virginia Military Institute watched John Brown "narrowly" during this ordeal. "Once I thought I saw his knees tremble, but it was only the wind blowing his loose trousers," Preston said.

In the ranks of a Richmond militia company stood an unknown young private named John Wilkes Booth. Commanding a red-and-gray-clad unit of cadets from the Virginia Military Institute was Major Thomas Jackson, soon to be renamed Stonewall. In a letter to his wife that night he told how the sheriff, after the cruel delay, finally severed the rope that held the trap door and "Brown fell through about five inches, his knees falling on a level with the position occupied by his feet before the rope was cut. With the fall his arms, below the elbows, flew up horizontally, his hands clinched; and his arms gradually fell, but by spasmodic motions. . . . Soon the wind blew his lifeless body to and fro. . . . I sent up a petition that he might be saved." Colonel Preston advanced to the scaffold and thundered: "So perish all such enemies of Virginia! All such enemies of the Union! All such foes of the human race!"

Speaking in Kansas the same day, Abraham Lincoln said: "Old John Brown has been executed for treason against a State. We cannot object, even though he agreed with us in thinking slavery wrong. That cannot excuse violence, bloodshed and treason. It could avail him nothing that he might think himself right." But the voices of moderation were lost in the shouts of extremists south and north. Senator J. M. Mason of Virginia, author of the Fugitive Slave Act, fulminated: "John Brown's invasion was condemned [in the North] only because it failed." The Joint Committee of the General Assembly of Virginia declared, "The crimes of John Brown were neither more nor less than practical illustrations of the doctrines of the leaders of the Republican party. . . ."

A year and a half later, Governor Wise, out of office, inspired a detachment of Virginians to seize the same Harpers Ferry arsenal, an act of reckless violence which did much to help the secessionists carry the day in the Virginia Convention. Lawson Botts, who had defended John Brown so ably, died a Confederate colonel in the Second Battle of Bull Run. His fellow attorney, Thomas Green, served as a private in Botts' regiment. Prosecutor Andrew Hunter emerged from the war a ruined man, his fine house burned by northern troops. Charles Harding, dissipated as he was, volunteered to serve his native state with a musket on his shoulder and early in the war died of pneumonia after a freezing night on picket duty.

On July 18, 1861, the 12th Massachusetts Regiment marched through the streets of Boston singing an improvised song about John Brown's body. Men from Ohio sang other versions of it as the nation plunged into four mad years of war. In his poem in praise of Harriet Beecher Stowe, wry Oliver Wendell Holmes unintentionally best assayed John Brown's role in the holocaust when he wrote:

All through the conflict up and down
Marched Uncle Tom and Old John Brown,
 One ghost, one form ideal.
And which was false and which was true,
And which was mightier of the two,
 The wisest sybil never knew,
For both alike were real.

The Political Depths

"Let Us Prey" (Boss Tweed) by Thomas Nast

Today among the soaring buildings of lower Manhattan huddles a shabby, squat pile of Massachusetts marble. It is the old New York County courthouse, a forlorn little building just three stories high. Only a few offices within its dirty gray walls are still used. There is nothing about this grotesque relic to suggest a raucous past or a grand scandal. But in its old rooms and along its corridors there is, for the knowledgeable, a roar of history as loud as the sound of the sea in shells.

The courthouse was designed with great expectations. It was to be a heroic example of Renaissance architecture. But by the time the Tweed Ring finished with the building, it was heroic only in the amount of money spent on it, enough money, according to one re-

TWEED BUILT

By ALEXANDER B. CALLOW, JR.

former, to build sixteen courthouses. It cost more than the Erie Canal, said the *New York Times*. These and other complaints indicate the impact of one of the most brazen and grandiose feats of graft in American municipal history. The house that Tweed built was the Boss's legacy to New York, an Acropolis of graft, a shrine to boodle.

William Marcy Tweed looked like something that God had hacked out with a dull axe. His craggy hulk weighed nearly three hundred pounds. Everything about him was big: his brood of eight children; his fists; his shoulders; his head, with its reddish-brown hair carved into a mustache and beard; his eyes, foxy or "gritty," as the reformers called them; his diamond, which glittered like a planet in his shirt front; and, finally, his nose. "His nose is half-Brougham, half-Roman," said one observer, "and a man with a nose of that sort is not a man to be trifled with."

Born in New York in 1823, the son of a chairmaker, Tweed began his rise to ill fame in 1851 when he was elected an alderman and became the leader of a corrupt, predatory band of aldermen and assistant aldermen, aptly called the Forty Thieves. After two singularly undistinguished years as a congressman in the mid-fifties, Tweed began a ten-year struggle for power that resulted in making him the first man to bear the title of Boss of New York.

In these years he clawed his way upward until he became both the Grand Sachem of Tammany and the chairman of the powerful New York County Democratic central committee. His growing power was soon felt within the New York city government, and he collected sinecures—school commissioner, deputy street commissioner, supervisor—as a gunslinger would add notches to his gun.

By 1866 Boss Tweed was on the threshold of being the greatest political force in New York. In the same year he formed his notorious Ring by joining forces with three capital rogues: the district attorney, Abraham Oakey Hall, who was to serve as mayor from 1868 to 1872; Peter Barr Sweeny, a lobbyist and ex-district attorney whom Tweed made city chamberlain; and a man later to be city comptroller, Richard Connolly. For the next five years the Tweed Ring smothered New York in its political embrace. Like an invading Attila, Tweed stormed the four fortresses of power in New York State: City Hall, Tammany Hall, the Hall of Justice, and the Capitol in Albany. There were soon 12,000 Tammany men placed in key city jobs. From Tweed's Town—the lower part of New York, embracing Hell's Kitchen, Satan's Circus, the Bowery, Cat Alley, Cockroach Row, and the Five Points, with its spidery streets choked with garbage and the poor—came the votes of the floods of immigrants, in return for the Boss's bounty of jobs and food. And on election day Tammany braves of the "shiny-hat brigade," as they styled themselves, swooped down on election booths, early and often, their war whoops enlivened by firewater, to return to the wigwam that night with fresh political scalps. This political machine was run on strings of "wampum," as the Ring picturesquely called hard cash, and one of the main sources of this much-needed wampum turned out to be the new county courthouse building.

The house that Tweed built was actually begun years before the Ring was formed. In 1858, the distinguished architect John Kellum, who had designed the New York *Herald* building, completed the plans for the new courthouse amidst a great burst of civic pride. Here was to be a Renaissance marvel proclaiming the greatness of New York and the sanctity of the law. Except for providing a site in City Hall Park, little was done until 1862, when, by no coincidence, William Tweed became president of the Board of Supervisors. There had been a wrangle over who should appropriate funds for the new building, the state's Board of Commissioners or the city's Board of Supervisors. Tweed tipped the scale in favor of making the city pay the bill, and suddenly appropriations became brisk.

The enactment law of 1858 stated specifically that the building, with all its furnishings, should not cost more than $250,000. But this was hardly enough, Tweed argued, to build a fitting tribute to the city and to the law. The Board of Supervisors agreed, and

$1,000,000 more was authorized. In 1864 an additional $800,000 was granted. But even this was not enough. In 1865, $300,000 more was appropriated, yet the very next year still more money was needed, and Tweed lobbied successfully for an additional $300,000.

When a further half-million dollars was granted in 1866, a reform group sniffed the pungent odor of corruption. It seemed a bit odd that $3,150,000 of the taxpayers' money had been spent but that the courthouse still was not finished, except for one corner occupied by the court of appeals. The reformers indignantly demanded an investigation. The officials of the city and county of New York were obliging, but their feelings were somewhat ruffled. They pointed out that the Board of Supervisors had already set up a committee to investigate the courthouse contracts. Nevertheless, to serve justice, they established another committee, christening it the Special Committee to Investigate the Courthouse. This committee was to investigate the investigating committee set up by the Board of Supervisors that was investigating the courthouse. The Special Committee took a remarkably short time to declare that the investigating committee, the contracts, and everything else about the courthouse were free from fraud.

The tempo of appropriations for the courthouse increased as the Tweed Ring expanded its power. Boss Tweed demonstrated his unchallenged authority over the state legislature by having it contribute a large amount of money to the courthouse, and he completed a one-two punch by persuading the city at the same time to donate $6,997,893.24 more. "Just imagine," said a newspaper, "the untiring industry, the wear and tear of muscle, the anxiety of mind, the weary days and sleepless nights, that it must have cost the 'Boss' to procure all these sums of money." Thus, from 1858 to 1871, more than thirteen million dollars had been spent on the new courthouse.

When, in 1871, New Yorkers finally realized that their courthouse had been a gold mine of graft, one of the first questions asked was how this incredible swindle had been perpetrated. Such a colossal steal, it seemed, could be engineered only by a complicated and subtle stratagem. What astonished, angered, and perhaps embarrassed New Yorkers was the revelation that the Ring, confident of its power and contemptuous of detection, had employed such brazen tactics.

The scheme hinged upon each member of the Ring playing a role tailored to his particular talents and office. Boss Tweed's role was to operate exclusively in the area of top-level decision-making and to exercise his considerable charm—always enhanced by a bulging pocketbook—among his acquaintances in the New York

City and State governments. To assist him in the gentle art of political persuasion, Tweed, like most successful executives, had a resourceful and imaginative aide, Peter Barr Sweeny, the city chamberlain. Dark, brooding, mysterious, Sweeny seemed to some to be more shadow than man. Heavy-set, with a jet-black walrus mustache and a large head covered with a mass of thick black hair, he always wore black clothes and a high-crowned black hat. Sweeny, a behind-the-scenes manipulator, was painfully shy in public. In 1857, as district attorney, he broke down in his first speech before a jury and was so humiliated that he resigned and fled to Europe. His forte was to operate as Tweed's alter ego in party caucuses, private offices, and hotel corridors. This reputation for stealthy astuteness won him many nicknames—Brains Sweeny, Sly Sweeny, Spider Sweeny—but his friends called him Squire. It was Tweed and Sweeny who made all the initial arrangements between the Ring and the hand-picked courthouse contractors.

The third major figure in the operation was the city comptroller, Richard Connolly. His tall stovepipe hat, gold-rimmed spectacles, stately nose, clean-shaven face, and plump belly gave him a distinguished appearance, and he was called the Big Judge by his cronies. Connolly artfully feigned an innocence that led the uninitiated to think of him as a mere child in the game of politics. But the nickname given him by the reformers, Slippery Dick, was proved accurate when in 1871 he was shown to be worth six million dollars, although his salary had been only $3,600 in 1857. It was Connolly's job as the Ring's bookkeeper and financial expert to supervise the assault on the soft underbelly of the city treasury. After the contractors submitted the bills for their work, Connolly made certain that the Ring received sixty-five per cent of the amount due as its commission, with the remaining thirty-five per cent going to the contractors. He then drew up payments, or warrants, drawn from the city treasury, approved them as city comptroller, and turned them over to Boss Tweed, who in turn "persuaded" the Board of Supervisors to give its official approval to the warrants. The operation reached its final stage when the padded warrants were placed on the desk of the colorful "Elegant Oakey" Hall, the mayor of New York.

Abraham Oakey Hall, a nervous, sparkling little man who had a pool-shark's touch with the electorate, delighted New York with his purple rhetoric and his gaudy elegance. He was a politician, playwright (the heart-toaster, *Let Me Kiss Him for His Mother,* was one of his plays enjoyed by New York theatregoers), journalist, lawyer, poet, clubman, lecturer, humorist, and humbug. Oakey Hall had only one defect as mayor, one newspaper commented, "a lack of ability."

But there was one talent Hall did not lack: he could write his name. When, as the highest city officer, he signed the inflated warrants, the deed was done.

In this fashion, so crude and yet so straightforward, the taxpayers of New York were fleeced of thirteen million dollars. What made the building of the county courthouse a classic in the annals of American graft was the way in which money was spent. As the reformer Robert Roosevelt (Theodore Roosevelt's uncle) put it, the bills rendered by the Tweed contractors were not merely monstrous, "they [were] manifestly fabulous." For just three tables and forty chairs, for example, the city paid $179,729.60. Roscoe Conkling, the Republican senator from New York, complained that the money spent for furnishings was nearly three times as much as it cost the Grant administration to run the entire United States diplomatic corps for two years—and if one recalls the Grant administration, this was quite a feat. Conkling was referring to the cost of furniture, carpets, and shades supplied by a firm headed by an old boyhood chum of Boss Tweed's, James Ingersoll. The amount spent on these items was "the rather startling sum" of $5,691,144.26. Fascinated by the bill for $350,000 for carpets alone, the *New York Times* asked Ingersoll for an explanation. "There is one thing you people down in the *Times* don't seem to take into account," was the angry reply. "The carpets in these public buildings need to be changed a great deal oftener than in private houses." Even after this explanation the *Times* concluded that the city had been overcharged $336,821.31.

John Keyser, the plumbing contractor for the building, set a record to be envied even by his highly paid colleagues of today. He received nearly a million and a half dollars for "plumbing and gas light fixtures." It was estimated that in one year alone, Keyser made over a million dollars. Compared to Ingersoll and Keyser, Tweed's carpenter, "Lucky" George Miller, submitted puny bills. Lumber estimated to be worth not more than $48,000 cost the city only $460,000. As for the building's marble, it was supplied by a quarry owned by the Boss. The *New York Times,* always a pesky critic of Tweed, claimed it cost more to quarry the marble than it had cost to build the entire courthouse in Brooklyn.

The prices for safes and awnings suggested an obsession with security and shade. J. McBride Davidson, who maintained a private bar in his office for select politicians, charged over $400,000 for safes. James W. Smith charged $150 apiece for 160 awnings. Considering this, plus the charge for carpentry, a newspaper calculated that each courthouse window cost an astounding $8,000. Smith defended himself by saying that his bill for awnings included taking them down

THE HOUSE THAT SAM BUILT

Not far from the Capitol in Washington sits a brand-new fortress of granite and marble, the Rayburn House Office Building, a memorial to the late Speaker of the House of Representatives. Though we do not suggest that there was graft in its construction, the Rayburn Building is also a memorial to waste, which is always with us. Like the house that Tweed built, the Rayburn Building got off to a modest start when, in 1955, Sam Rayburn offered an amendment to a minor bill concerning planning for a new House office building. The amendment authorized construction of the building and appropriated $2,000,000 and "such additional sums as may be necessary." Authority for the building was put in the hands of the three-man House Office Building Commission and the Architect of the Capitol, J. George Stewart. It happens that the Architect of the Capitol is not an architect but a construction engineer, and that the Building Commission has a habit of meeting in executive session, which conveniently keeps out any nosy taxpayers.

The way the appropriations grew would have made Tweed green with envy. The first estimate of "such additional sums as may be necessary" was $63,000,000. But as construction continued, underestimated bids and the addition of such utter necessities as a swimming pool and tennis courts drove up the price to nearly $90,000,000, making this the most expensive United States government building in history. Quite a few of the expenditures that contributed to this grand sum sound almost as exorbitant as the costs of Tweedledom: it cost $10,000 to furnish each of the 169 office suites; a 700-foot subway to the Capitol had a $7.7 million price tag; the bill for each of the 1,600 parking spaces in the underground garage was $5,800. And as in Tweed's courthouse, there were lots of mistakes. For example, so that congressmen can reach their staffs without going through a crowded waiting room, doors will have to be cut through their office walls. The price for this will be $200,000. But the most striking similarity between the Tweed and Rayburn buildings is their mutual hideousness. The Rayburn Building has been called "Corrupt Classic," "the apotheosis of humdrum," and "the worst building for the most money in the history of the construction art." There have been demands for an investigation, but so far nothing has happened, and the Rayburn Building sits on Capitol Hill, a bloated dragon spawned by bureaucracy.—*David G. Lowe*

in the fall, putting them up again in the spring, and repairing them. Another manufacturer said that the awnings were worth not more than $12.50 apiece.

When a person is building a house he does not usually expect to receive a huge bill for repairs before the structure is completed. Yet the house that Tweed built cost the taxpayers of New York nearly two million dollars in repairs before it was finished. Here Andrew Garvey, a 240-pound ex-fireman, set a record which won for him the title "Prince of Plasterers." In one year Garvey charged the city $500,000 for plastering, and $1,000,000 for repairing the same work. His bill for the three-year plastering job in a supposedly marble building was $2,870,464.06—the *Times* suggested the six cents be donated to charity—and of this, $1,294,684.13 went for repairs! If Garvey was a prince, Tweed's carpenter rated at least an earldom. For "repairing and altering wood work," Lucky George was paid nearly $800,000. Compared to his colleagues, however, John Keyser was only a knight in tarnished armor. He received merely $51,481.74 for repairing his plumbing and lighting fixtures.

For all the shocking display of gluttony, there was sprinkled throughout the Ring's secret account books evidence of good humor, a certain dash, a feeling that here were men who really enjoyed their work. For example, a check was drawn to the order of Fillippo Donnoruma for $66,000. It was endorsed by "Phillip Dummy." Another check, for $64,000, was made out to "T. C. Cash." And wedged in among columns of massive figures was this tiny masterpiece of understatement: "Brooms, etc. . . . $41,190.95."

Then there was the charge for thermometers, which must be described as flippant. Tweed bought eleven thermometers for the new courthouse, each five feet long and one foot wide and encased in a gaudily carved frame. The faces were made of inexpensive paper, highly varnished and badly painted. Everything about them was cheap. The cost of the eleven thermometers was exactly $7,500. A reporter asked a reputable thermometer manufacturer how many thermometers he could supply for this amount. "For $7,500," he said, "I could line the courthouse." The New York Printing Company's charge of $186,495.61 for stationery was unique. It included the printing of all the reams of contractors' bills as well as the repair bills.

When the Tweed Ring was exposed in 1871, it became a favorite pastime to calculate how far, placed end to end, the furnishings and materials charged to the city for the courthouse would reach. One newspaper reckoned that there was carpeting enough to reach from New York almost to New Haven, or halfway to Albany. Another wag estimated that since Ingersoll was paid $170,729.60 for chairs alone, if each cost $5, the city had bought 34,145 chairs. Now if they were placed in a straight line, they would reach 85,363 feet, or nearly eighteen miles. What would happen, asked the *New York Times,* if the sum spent for cabinet work and furniture were spent in furnishing private houses? Allowing $10,000 per house, the paper estimated, it would furnish nearly 3,000 houses.

The revelations of the cost of the building inspired several New Yorkers to visit their new courthouse. Although they realized that corruption had been at work, they expected to see some kind of magnificence for their thirteen million dollars. Instead they found an unfinished waste of masonry—gloomy rooms, dark halls, and ugly, fake marble walls—resembling more an ancient tenement than a new public building. In 1871, after thirteen years of construction work, not all of the floors were occupied. One of the largest rooms, the Bureau of Arrears of Taxes, had no roof. The county clerk's office, sheriff's office, and office of the surrogate were not carpeted but were covered with oilcloth and grimy matting. The walls were filthy, and in many places large chunks of plaster had peeled off, leaving ugly blotches—a fitting tribute to the Prince of Plasterer's repair bills. One visitor counted 164 windows and shuddered at the cost of awnings and curtains, many of which had not yet been delivered. When the prominent reformer George C. Barrett made his pilgrimage, he came away shocked. His impression left no doubt that the city must long endure a reminder of the most audacious swindle in its history. "It might be considered," he said, "that the cornerstone of the temple was conceived in sin, and its dome, if ever finished, will be glazed all over with iniquity. The whole atmosphere was corrupt. You look up at its ceilings and find gaudy decorations; you wonder which is the greatest, the vulgarity or the corruptness of the place." As a final irony, the grand dome which had been planned to crown the county's temple of justice was never completed.

Boss Tweed and his friends reached the zenith of their power in July, 1871. On July 4, Tammany wildly celebrated the glories of Independence Day and the beneficent leadership of Grand Sachem William Marcy Tweed. Four days later came the beginning of the end. The *New York Times,* leading one of the greatest crusades against civic corruption in American history, began publishing the facts and figures on the Ring's adventures in graft. The *Times* was aided by *Harper's Weekly* with its acerbic cartoons by Thomas Nast, who drew the courthouse with "Thou Shalt Steal As Much As Thou Canst" over its portal. The evidence was turned over to the newspaper by an unhappy Tammany warrior, ex-Sheriff James O'Brien.

Furious because Tweed had not paid a fraudulent claim he had made against the city, O'Brien had hired a spy in Connolly's office to copy entries out of the Ring's secret account books.

While it was estimated that the Ring in all its various operations had stolen anywhere from twenty million to two hundred million dollars from the city and state, it was the courthouse that captured New York's attention and ignited its wrath. At first the Boss had magnificent poise. "Well," he said, "what are you going to do about it?" And Mayor Hall—or "Mayor Haul," as Nast labelled him—quipped, "Who's going to sue?" But as the *Times,* day by day, week by week, revealed the enormity of the courthouse scandal—the plaster, the carpets, the repair bills, the thermometers —the Forty Thieves panicked and Oakey Hall became a prophet: "We are likely to have what befell Adam," he said, "an early Fall." Tweed tried to bribe the *Times* into silence and failed, while Nast refused an offer of $500,000 to study art abroad rather than corruption at home. The Boss said of Thomas Nast, "I don't care a straw for your newspaper articles; my constituents don't know how to read, but they can't help seeing them damned pictures."

By the fall of 1871, the Ring was on the threshold of collapse. As new evidence of wrongdoing accumulated, a mass meeting of outraged New Yorkers was held at Cooper Union and a committee of seventy leading citizens was organized to bring about the fall of Tweed. Under the leadership of Samuel J. Tilden, who later became governor of New York and the Democratic nominee for President in 1876, a civil suit to recover the stolen money was brought against the Ring's leaders. In the November, 1871, election, one of the most exciting in New York history, the Ring was smashed when Tammany was crushed at the polls. New York now awaited expectantly the trials of all the culprits who had so boldly picked the civic purse, but the city was to be denied that satisfaction.

When Tweed was arrested in December, Connolly, Sweeny, and most of the other leading members of the Ring fled to Europe or to Canada and were never punished. Connolly wandered about Europe and died there, a man without a country, while Sweeny returned to New York in the eighteen eighties and lived out his years there in quiet respectability. One who did not flee was Mayor Oakey Hall. At his trial it was asked how the Mayor could have signed hundreds of padded courthouse warrants and not been aware of it. His attorney explained that the Elegant Oakey had "an ineradicable aversion to details." Hall was acquitted.

Only the Boss paid a price, a small price considering the crime. Tweed spent less than half his remaining years—from his downfall in 1871 until his death in 1878—in jail. In 1873 he was sentenced to twelve years in prison for fraud, but the court of appeals reduced the sentence to a year on a legal technicality. After his release in 1875 Tweed was arrested as the result of action brought by the state of New York to recover six million dollars he was accused of having stolen. While in prison awaiting trial the Boss was often allowed to visit his home under guard. During one such visit, in December of 1875, Tweed escaped to Cuba and then to Spain, only to be recognized from a Nast caricature. He was returned to New York in November, 1876, and was confined to the Ludlow Street Jail to await trial. He died there on April 12, 1878, at the age of fifty-five.

In the years after Tweed's death the horrendous scandals of his Ring softened into just another memory of old New York, but one which Tweed had made certain would not be forgotten. The shabby little building in City Hall Park, the house that Tweed built, was as unforgettable a memorial as a statue in Times Square. And Tweed had provided his own epitaph. When he arrived at the Blackwell's Island prison to begin his one-year sentence, the warden asked him what his profession was. The Boss, in a clear, strong voice, answered, "Statesman!"

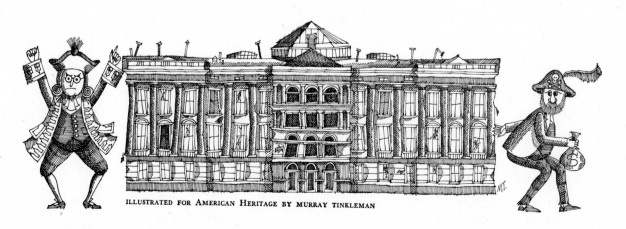

ILLUSTRATED FOR AMERICAN HERITAGE BY MURRAY TINKLEMAN

In November, 1901, the little town of Sonoma, California, a few miles north of San Francisco, lay dreaming in the haze of Indian summer. There were few guests in the town hotel, and only two were strangers. One of them was a small man with bright, beady eyes above a huge mustache; he looked like Ben Turpin with his eyes uncrossed. The other was big and broad-shouldered; he had a head of thick, curly black hair and a luxuriant mustache and Vandyke beard that, in pictures of him, give an irrepressible impression of being glued on.

These visitors seemed to be instructor and pupil. They had a single document with them, a copy of the San Francisco city charter, and hour after hour the little man could be heard through the thin walls of the hotel room explaining its provisions to the big one, quizzing him on its contents, expostulating when his companion got the answers wrong or didn't remember.

The people of Sonoma promptly recognized the pair, for their faces were well known in California. What the townsfolk did not realize was why they were there. The little man was Abraham Ruef, San Francisco's corrupt political boss who reaped the profits of bribery and corruption with unparalleled *sang-froid*. The big one was Eugene Schmitz, lately orchestra leader at San Francisco's fashionable Columbia Theater, whom Ruef had turned into a political figure only a few months earlier and, almost singlehandedly, had elected mayor. Now, in the Sonoma hideaway immediately after the election, Ruef was trying to teach his henchman the rudiments of public administration.

For Abraham Ruef's vivid imagination was already looking ahead to a dramatic future. Years later, from his cell in San Quentin Prison, he recalled those days in Sonoma in his autobiography, *The Road I Traveled:*

We were the only strangers in the little village. We had left our whereabouts unknown except to our immediate families. There, in undisturbed peace, we talked and planned day and night. There in the tranquil Sonoma hills I saw visions of political power; I saw the Union Labor Party [to which he and Schmitz belonged] a spark in California which would kindle the entire nation and make a Labor President; I saw the Union Labor Party a throne for Schmitz, as Mayor, as Governor—as President of the United States. Behind that throne, I saw myself its power, local, state—national . . . I saw myself United States Senator.

To understand how Ruef was able to put his grotesquely unqualified nominee into the mayor's chair, and how he himself could end up a few years later in a prison cell, it is necessary to glance briefly at San Francisco's earlier, turbulent history.

At the beginning of the twentieth century, the city could look back on a solid fifty years of sin, violence, and corruption. It had been a drowsy Mexican village of a thousand people when it was taken over by the Americans in 1846. Only five years later, the town having mushroomed following the discovery of gold, crimes of violence were so common and the local government so venal or spineless—or both—that the citizens organized the famous extralegal "vigilantes"— officially the Vigilance Committee—to restore order. Their method was simple and effective: hanging, after

The BOODLING BOSS

A corrupt lawyer and his complaisant all

until a crusading editor toppled their plot

By BRUC

Abraham Ruef, brilliant and ruthless, held the reins of power in turn-of-the-century San Francisco.

the briefest extemporaneous trials, some of the more conspicuous wrongdoers. The next few years saw the leading newspaper editor shot down by an indignant subscriber; a United States senator killed in a duel with the chief justice of the state supreme court; and howling mobs burning the houses of the Chinese, who were believed to be undercutting Americans in the labor market. For the whole half century, prostitution, gambling, and drunkenness raged through the town; its Barbary Coast was infamous for the public display of every sort of vice.

For a good part of that time, the venality of most municipal officials was duplicated in the capitol at Sacramento. The state was controlled politically—and to some extent economically—by the big corporations, especially the Southern Pacific Railroad, a situation dramatically and accurately described by Frank Norris in *The Octopus*. Distributor of money and favors for the Southern Pacific was its chief counsel, William F. Herrin, who, besides dispensing more serious bribes, saw to it that whenever the legislature was in session, a weekend round-trip ticket to San Francisco was dropped on the desk of every lawmaker every Friday.

When the twentieth century began, there was little evidence that very many people in the city objected to this state of affairs, and much evidence that most of them at least tacitly approved. They would have been dumfounded if they had been told that during the next decade San Francisco would be torn asunder by what was probably the greatest struggle in American history to end municipal corruption.

The forerunner of that struggle was a savage waterfront strike in the summer of 1901 that lasted about two months and left enduring scars. It was broken with the aid of the municipal authorities, who put city police on the drays to protect nonstriking drivers. Since the days of the gold rush, when labor was in desperately short supply and workers were able to dictate their own terms, San Francisco had always been a strong union town. With their defeat on the water front, the shocked and embittered workingmen turned to politics for revenge. They organized the Union Labor party and began to talk big about taking control of the city. This talk might easily have come to nothing but for the presence of Abraham Ruef.

The little boss, born of a prosperous Jewish mercantile family in San Francisco, had a fine mind and great personal ambition. He went through the University of California at Berkeley, studying classical languages. Graduated subsequently from San Francisco's Hastings College of Law, he began to practice and immediately went into politics as a Republican. He was successful in both careers from the first, aided by his native shrewdness and his unusual abilities as a writer and public speaker. In 1901 he was thirty-seven, and for more than ten years had already had many dubious underworld connections. He saw in the new Union Labor party an opportunity for himself, for power —and money. He needed a Trilby to whom he could play Svengali, and he soon found one. Like the original Trilby, his came from the world of music.

Eugene Schmitz, the orchestra leader, knew nothing

and the MUSICAL MAYOR

an San Francisco as their private preserve

nd schemes, and sent one of them to jail

BLIVEN

For three terms Eugene Schmitz, a former band leader, was Ruef's puppet as the city's mayor.

THE HUNTERS: *(Left to right) Francis J. Heney, the prosecutor; Detective William J. Burns; Editor Fremont Older; Rudolph Spreckels, a financial backer of the prosecution.*

of politics and did not want to run, but Ruef assured him victory was practically certain. "The psychology of the mass of voters," said Ruef, "is like that of a crowd of small boys or primitive men. Other things being equal, of two candidates they will almost invariably follow the strong, finely-built man." Ruef proved a good prophet. The Republican and Democratic opponents were weak, and every union man in the city was still smarting from the broken strike; Schmitz was elected.

After a few days of the Sonoma crammer's-course in the art of government, the two men returned to San Francisco, and soon thereafter Schmitz formally took office. Before very long, newspapermen and other knowledgeable people in the city began to hear that graft was on the increase, and that nearly all of it was channeling through Ruef. His method was admirably uncomplicated: he became attorney for any individual or group that had bribes to offer; the money was then paid to him as "legal fees," and he divided it with Schmitz and with anyone else who was entitled to a cut.

One of the important early sources of graft under this system was San Francisco's famous group of French "restaurants." Although owned by different people, these operated on a uniform and disreputable system. The ground floor was a respectable dining room, catering to the family trade and serving excellent food and wine at reasonable prices. There were always, however, several higher floors with private dining rooms and bedrooms, where prostitutes operated brazenly. These restaurants had to have city licenses, which came up for renewal from time to time, and before the Schmitz administration was very old the owners were

told, to their dismay, that their licenses were to be canceled. They promptly hired Ruef as their lawyer, paid him many thousands of dollars, and the threat of trouble faded away. Among the dozens of houses of prostitution which then flourished openly in San Francisco was one on Jackson Street, with seventy inmates, in which Mayor Schmitz was generally believed to have a heavy part-ownership. This was nicknamed "the Municipal Crib" and was so known throughout the city for years.

Other varieties of graft developed with great rapidity. The police in Chinatown were accused of collecting regular weekly immunity fees from gamblers. Various types of business had to pay for permission to do certain things, some of which were entirely legal and unobjectionable.

With the Republicans and Democrats still divided, and with the workers on the whole still behind the Union Labor party, Schmitz was re-elected in 1903 and again in 1905. He and Ruef had consolidated their power and gained experience, and in 1905, for the first time, nearly all eighteen members of the Board of Supervisors were their henchmen. Some came from the ranks of union labor, but others were variegated friends of Ruef, with backgrounds as dubious as his own. Almost at once it developed that most of them had heard that the city was full of easy money, and they intended to get their share; soon Ruef was told that individual supervisors were openly asking payment to vote in accordance with the wishes of various businessmen.

The boss saw that this would never do; with a number of men seeking bribes individually, open scandal could not be averted. Accordingly, he called an unofficial meeting of the board and made a short speech. His exact words have been lost to history, but of the substance there is no doubt. "You men owe your jobs to me," he said in effect. "You will do what I say, or you will be replaced. If anybody wants to make a gift to the supervisors in return for their consideration of his wishes and needs, this money will be collected and disbursed by me. You are not to know the name of the donor; you will simply vote as I tell you in all cases."

The supervisors saw that they were licked, and seventeen of them silently acquiesced. By some accident, however, one honest man had got on the board; he was not at the historic meeting, nor did he participate in the subsequent distribution of graft. Let his name be recorded for history: Louis A. Rea.

A typical example of how the Ruef system worked was the fight between two competing telephone companies. The Pacific States Telephone and Telegraph Company was already operating in San Francisco, while the Home Telephone Company wanted to set up a competing system there, as it had done in a number of other cities. Pacific States had for some time been paying Ruef $1,200 a month as "attorney's fees." Home Telephone now offered him a flat $125,000. (Ruef's custom was to share about half the money among the seventeen dishonest supervisors, and to divide the other half between himself and Schmitz in varying proportions, often equally.)

Pacific States now heard what was going on and proceeded to approach eleven of the supervisors directly, giving each of them about $5,000. When he learned of this, Ruef was furious; he told the supervisors that they would have to vote for the Home Company (which a majority did), and that they should give back at least part of the Pacific States bribes. The distribution of the Home Company money is interesting. According to Walton Bean in his authoritative book, *Boss Ruef's San Francisco,* Ruef kept about one fourth of the $125,000 and gave another fourth to Schmitz. The rest was distributed among the supervisors on a carefully graduated scale, according to whether or not they had accepted Pacific States bribes, and whether they had voted for or against the Home Company. Rea, the honest supervisor, of course got nothing. One other man, Patrick McGushin, also got nothing; in public speeches he had committed himself so thoroughly to municipal ownership that he did not dare vote for either corporation.

Many other companies and individuals at about this time felt it necessary to indulge in bribery, and found Ruef a willing recipient. The largest sum he received was $200,000 from the United Railroads, which controlled the city's streetcars. There was an agitation in San Francisco to have the overhead trolley wires put into underground conduits, and United Railroads paid the bribe to block this expensive project. Head of the United Railroads was Patrick Calhoun, an aggressive, able, and unscrupulous financier, grandson of John C. Calhoun, former Vice President and states' rights leader. Patrick Calhoun sent his chief counsel, Tirey L. Ford, to Ruef, who passed on part of the $200,000 to Schmitz and the seventeen supervisors.

On another occasion and from another source Ruef was promised a far larger bribe. San Francisco needed a supplementary supply of water from the Sierra Nevada, far across the state to the east, and owners of mountain land near Lake Tahoe proposed to build a water system there and sell it to the city at a profit of three million dollars; one third of this was to go to Ruef, who in turn would split with the supervisors. Before the plan could be carried out, however, the storm broke over the members of the graft ring.

The storm was created primarily by one individual,

Fremont Older, who in 1895, at the age of thirty-nine, had become managing editor of the San Francisco *Bulletin.* Older, generally considered by journalists to be one of the half-dozen top newspaper editors in American history, was a huge man, six feet two and broad-shouldered, with flashing eyes above a big beak of a nose, and a voice that rose to a roaring bellow when he was excited or angered, which was almost continuously. (I was a part-time cub reporter on the *Bulletin* for several years during the fight against the graft ring—while working my way through Stanford University as a campus correspondent—and I can testify to the equal amounts of terror, admiration, and passionate loyalty that Older inspired in every member of his staff.)

Why he possessed such a deep and burning zeal for municipal honesty is something that must be left to the psychiatrists. It was shared by few if any of the top executives of the other San Francisco newspapers, and certainly not by Older's boss, R. A. Crothers, part owner and active manager of the *Bulletin.* When Older came into the office the paper was moribund. It was also, as he relates in his fascinating autobiography, *My Own Story,* on the payroll of the Southern Pacific Railroad for $125 a month, the customary stipend paid at that time to all weak newspapers and many strong ones. During all the years of the fantastic struggle to expose the grafters, the *Bulletin* played a leading part. But Crothers, to put it mildly, dragged his feet. This, however, did not exempt him from the wrath of the graft ring. At one stage in the battle he was struck down in an alley behind his office, severely beaten, and left for dead.

Older, as the more aggressive fighter, ran even more serious risks. When in 1905 Schmitz was re-elected despite the opposition of the *Bulletin,* a riotous mob gathered in front of the newspaper, smashed all its windows, and followed Older and his wife, hooting and jeering at them, as they walked down the street

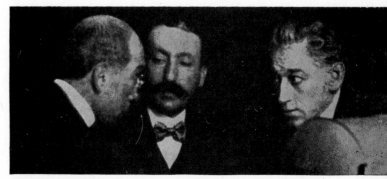

THE QUARRY: *A worried Boss Ruef (center) confers with two of his attorneys during his extortion trial. He was the only grafter who served any considerable time in prison.*

a few blocks to their home in the Palace Hotel.

One day in 1907, after two plots to kill him had misfired, Older was lured into a trap by an anonymous telephone call promising him "important information" if he would come to the Savoy Hotel on Van Ness Avenue. He could not resist the invitation, although he warned his colleagues at the *Bulletin* that it might be a trick. As he walked toward the hotel an automobile with four occupants stopped beside him. He was shown a Los Angeles warrant for his arrest, and was told to get into the car. A day or so earlier, a reporter for the *Bulletin* had, for one edition, confused the identity of two men named Brown, one of whom was head of the secret service for the United Railroads. This man had gone to an obscure justice of the peace in Los Angeles, 475 miles away, and obtained a warrant for Older's arrest on a charge of criminal libel. Of the four men in the automobile, two were private detectives representing the United Railroads; the other two were deputies representing the Los Angeles justice of the peace.

In the automobile, Older was told he would be taken to the chambers of a San Francisco judge, where he could arrange for bail. Instead, the car shot away out of the city at high speed, while one of his captors kept a gun pressed into the editor's ribs; in an accompanying car, Older recognized several employees of the United Railroads. By now he was really frightened, suspecting that they intended to kill him. He was right. Gangland had not yet learned to use the term, but Older was being "taken for a ride." The two Los Angeles men planned to take him aboard a train at a station a few miles down the coast, leave the train at another station in the early morning, and take Older up into wild mountain country. There he would be "shot while attempting to escape."

Older's life was saved by an extraordinary development. The Los Angeles men, since they were technically court officers, made no attempt to conceal Older's presence on the train, and took him into the dining car for dinner. A young San Francisco attorney happened to be on the same train, thought he recognized Older, and grew curious as to why he was traveling with such odd companions. When one of the Los Angeles deputies admitted Older's identity, the lawyer broke his journey, got off the train in the middle of the night at a way station, and telephoned the office of the San Francisco *Call*, owned by the brother of Rudolph Spreckels, who was working with the graft prosecution.

"Is Fremont Older missing, by any chance?" the attorney asked.

"My God, yes," came the answer. "The whole city is looking for him."

The attorney described Older's situation. A judge in Santa Barbara, a few miles north of Los Angeles, was routed out of bed by a long-distance telephone call, and a writ of habeas corpus was issued.

In spite of the early hour, word of what was happening spread through Santa Barbara, and when the train reached the city the station was thronged with interested citizens.

"Must be a wedding party," said one of the kidnappers as he looked out the compartment window. But he was wrong; a sheriff's posse boarded the train and took Older "into custody." A few hours later, in a Santa Barbara courtroom, he was set free. His four captors were subsequently arrested; the two from Los Angeles turned state's evidence and admitted the plot to kill Older. Of the other two, one jumped bail and was never recaptured; the fourth man, brought to trial a year later, was acquitted by a San Francisco jury presumably influenced by Ruef.

By 1905, Older and those working with him had realized that the grafters controlled nearly all the machinery of justice so completely that outside help would be necessary, and that this would be very expensive. Two prominent and wealthy citizens sympathized with Older and were helping him as much as possible. One was James D. Phelan, a millionaire businessman (and afterward United States senator) who had given San Francisco an honest and efficient government as mayor for three terms, just before Schmitz took office. The other was Spreckels, who came of a wealthy family but had quarreled with his father and made a fortune of his own before he was thirty.

Phelan and Spreckels promised to put up the money for an independent investigation and prosecution, which they thought would cost $100,000 (the final tab was about two and a half times that much). There was no doubt as to the man they wanted as prosecutor: he was Francis J. Heney, an attorney born in Lima, New York, but raised in San Francisco, a man of tremendous self-confidence, a bitter-end fighter, and a combined bloodhound and bulldog when he was on the trail of evil-doing. At the moment, Heney was being used by the United States government to prosecute a series of land-fraud cases in Oregon. Older went to Washington and easily obtained the promise of President Theodore Roosevelt to have Heney lent to the San Franciscans as soon as the Oregon cases were concluded. Since this was his home town, Heney gave his services without pay for a fight that was to last several years. He brought with him William J. Burns, a detective who had made a notable career in the Secret Service of the United States Treasury Department.

So intent were Older and his friends on tracking down the grafters that the great San Francisco earthquake and fire of April 18, 1906, which cost more than four hundred lives and almost completely destroyed all the important parts of the city, delayed them only temporarily. A few weeks later the prosecution was ready to proceed. With great audacity Ruef, well aware of what was going on, struck first.

The district attorney, William H. Langdon, had been appointed with Ruef's consent but had unexpectedly turned out to be honest, and had co-operated with the prosecution by appointing Heney as an assistant district attorney. Ruef responded by ordering Mayor Schmitz to dismiss Langdon and replace him by none other than Ruef himself! The prosecution succeeded in bringing the matter into court the next day, and the judge agreed to give his decision at 2 P.M. In the early morning, Older rushed out a special edition of the *Bulletin* telling what was happening, and distributed many thousands of free copies throughout the city. The paper invited honest residents of San Francisco to come at the zero hour and line up on the lawn outside the judge's chambers, which happened to be on the ground floor. Many hundreds of leading citizens responded, and as two o'clock approached, they stood packed together and silent, looking in at the judge. He ruled for Langdon.

The prosecution began its work with plenty of suspicion of bribery, but little solid evidence. Indeed, on several occasions both Older and Heney made public charges, which Older printed in the *Bulletin,* that went far beyond anything they were able to prove. The first break came, as it so often does, when the thieves fell out. Two minor members of the graft ring, joint owners of a skating rink, had reasons to dislike Ruef and to respect the power of Older and Heney. They now approached the prosecution with offers to help, and a trap was set for some of the dishonest supervisors.

The prosecution prepared an ordinance that would have crippled the operations of the skating rink by forbidding entrance to unchaperoned minors, and Mayor Schmitz was tricked into sponsoring it with the Board of Supervisors. Several members were then sounded out as to whether they would be willing to vote against it for a suitable sum of money. This was long before the days of dictaphones, but the trap was set efficiently, nonetheless. The first supervisor was approached in the office of the skating rink, and while Burns and two other men watched through holes bored in the wall,

he accepted $500 in marked bills. Another supervisor fell for the same ruse. A third was bribed in the home of one of the skating-rink owners while Burns, a stenographer, and another witness watched from a darkened adjoining room through folding doors left slightly ajar.

From the beginning, the prosecution wanted to reach the big businessmen who gave the bribes; Heney was willing to offer immunity to the lesser figures, including the supervisors. Such offers were not legally binding on the courts, but judges usually respected them. With the damaging evidence against the supervisors who had taken the money in the skating-rink affair, and with promises of immunity to their colleagues, Heney soon had detailed and documented confessions from almost all of the seventeen men.

The grand jury was known to be packed with henchmen of the graft ring, and a new one was clearly needed. District Attorney Langdon dismissed the old jury and had an honest one impaneled. Ruef and Schmitz were promptly indicted for mulcting the French "restaurants."

Both men exhausted every legal avenue to avoid trial, or to postpone it as long as possible. When Ruef's case came up, he did not appear in court, apparently believing that through a legal technicality he was not required to do so; he was promptly arrested. Since the sheriff was one of his own men, the duty of guarding him was transferred to the coroner. But he, also, was in the graft ring, and was not to be trusted. Ruef was therefore confined in a hotel under the care of William J. Biggy, a special officer called an elisor.

Heney, eager to reach the men higher up, now offered Ruef immunity if he would confess. For a long time the little boss refused; his story was that all the money paid him by everybody had been merely legal fees. But at last he broke down, after many appeals by two rabbis and a dramatic scene in the bedroom of his mother, who was gravely ill. He then made a complete confession, naming those who had bribed him and telling the amounts and where the money had gone. Describing the members of his own graft ring, he remarked that "They were so greedy they would eat the paint off the City Hall," leading the public to call them, for years thereafter, "the paint eaters."

Schmitz was now tried on the extortion indictment. Although he pursued the course that he followed to the day of his death—flatly denying every charge, no matter what anyone else might say—he was found guilty and sentenced to prison. Before this, the question had arisen as to whether the supervisors, nearly all of whom had now confessed to accepting bribes, should be turned out of office, and the prosecution had approved keeping them in their places temporarily, lest Ruef should furnish a new and worse set from his seemingly endless supply of underworld characters. As Lincoln Steffens pointed out at the time, this Board of Supervisors was "the best in America": they did not dare misbehave further, with their confessions of wrongdoing on record. With Schmitz in jail, and with no honest replacement in sight, the prosecution agreed to put one of the bribe-taking supervisors into the mayor's office temporarily.

As Heney began to tighten the noose on the big businessmen who were behind the corruption, a sudden turn appeared in San Francisco public opinion. As long as the quarry had been men from the lower social strata, the "best people" had heartily approved; but now Heney's detectives were getting close to important citizens, and the prosecution quickly became highly unpopular. Western rough-and-tumble mores still prevailed; the businessmen who were accused were, after all, self-made men and leaders of the community. As for trade-union members, they still thought of Schmitz as their spokesman. Since Ruef was a Jew, the prosecution was accused of anti-Semitism; since Patrick Calhoun, the streetcar tycoon, had come from Georgia, the bloody shirt was waved. Several of the other men who had taken bribes belonged to the Protestant Episcopal Church, and Heney and Older were attacked for prejudice against that institution.

Those allied with the prosecution were subjected to pressure both subtle and direct. Big advertisers withdrew from Older's *Bulletin,* and wealthy depositors took their money out of Rudolph Spreckels' First National Bank. The foreman of the honest grand jury, Bartley P. Oliver, was in the real-estate business; he was boycotted severely. (When it was all over, he had to move away from San Francisco and start life anew, as did Heney.)

Calhoun, while under indictment, was asked to a dinner at the fashionable Olympic Club, where he was warmly applauded and asked to make a speech; when one of the oldest members of the club, Dr. Charles A. Clinton, protested, he was expelled—and Calhoun was elected in his place. Mrs. Fremont Older described the social ostracism: "Members of the prosecution were not bidden to entertainments where people of fashion gathered . . . [where] women reserved their sweetest smiles for the candidates for state's prison . . . [and] to ask whether one believed in looting the city became a delicate personal question."

The *Bulletin* was the center of the storm, and the members of its staff worked under a tremendous strain; I myself saw plenty of evidence of this. Many reporters

and advertising solicitors habitually carried revolvers. Every setback for the prosecution—and there were many—became a personal tragedy to everybody who worked for Older.

The change in the city's moral climate was soon registered in the actions in the courts. Tirey L. Ford, who had bribed Ruef with $200,000 on behalf of Calhoun, was tried three times; in spite of ample evidence of his guilt, the jury disagreed once, and twice he was acquitted. (Each trial was for bribing a different supervisor; there were so many of these cases that the prosecution could have gone on for years.) The higher courts of the state, many of whose members were deeply respectful of men of property, also conspicuously sided against the prosecution. The district court of appeals soon freed Schmitz, on astonishing grounds: he was not guilty of extortion, it said, because the French "restaurants" were undoubtedly houses of pros-

This San Francisco Examiner *cartoon of May 16, 1907, shows Ruef offering up to Justice the heads of some of the powerful men he had implicated in his confession: Patrick Calhoun and Tirey L. Ford of the United Railroads; Louis Glass, vice president and general manager of the Pacific States Telephone Company; William F. Herrin, chief counsel for the Southern Pacific; and Ruef's puppet, Mayor Eugene Schmitz.*

194

titution, and their licenses could properly have been revoked; to threaten to do a legal act is not extortion. The state supreme court upheld this remarkable argument and added one of its own: that the whole trial of Schmitz was illegal anyway because the indictment had failed to mention that he was mayor of San Francisco, or that Ruef was a political boss!

In this atmosphere of mounting community disapproval, Ruef was finally tried for bribery. Because he had persisted, in trial after trial, in partly repudiating his confession and in insisting that all payments made to him had been merely legal fees, Heney canceled the promise of immunity; Ruef responded by pleading not guilty. The bitterness of San Francisco sentiment was shown by the fact that getting a jury took from August 27 until November 6, and used up a panel of almost fifteen hundred talesmen.

While examining prospective jurors Heney had publicly revealed the fact that one man on the panel, Morris Haas, was ineligible because he had many years earlier served a term in San Quentin Prison. Heney did not need to humiliate Haas publicly in this way; he did so in anger, believing that Ruef was trying to plant the man on the jury. Haas deeply resented Heney's action and brooded over it for many weeks. While the trial was in temporary recess, Haas approached Heney in the courtroom, whipped out a revolver, and shot the attorney in the head; the bullet lodged behind the jaw muscles, where a difference of a fraction of an inch in any direction would have produced a fatal wound. Heney was carried away on a stretcher, mumbling, "I'll get him [Ruef] yet." His place was taken by a bright young assistant named Hiram Johnson, and the trial went on.

Haas was placed in a prison cell with a policeman to guard him; but in spite of these precautions he was found dead the following evening, a small pistol beside him. Those who believed Haas had been hired by Ruef to murder Heney now believed, naturally, that some other gangster in Ruef's employ had done away with Haas so that he could not talk. The chief of police was deeply hurt by Heney's public criticism of him for negligence in the Haas case, so much so that some time later he committed suicide by jumping overboard from a launch during a nighttime crossing of San Francisco Bay.

Heney did not die, as he had been expected to, and some days later the trial was concluded. Detective Burns had given Johnson the names of four jurors who, Burns said, had been bribed, and in his summation Johnson called each of them by name, pointed a forefinger at him, and shouted: "You—you dare not acquit this man!" Nevertheless, when the jury retired for its deliberations everyone expected that it would let

Ruef go, or would disagree, as had happened in almost every other case growing out of the graft prosecution.

While the jury was out Heney telephoned Older to say that he was much recovered, and proposed to come down and pay his respects to the judge. Older, with his usual flair for the dramatic, told Heney not to come until the editor gave the signal. While most of the community was by now against the prosecution, there was a minority on the side of honesty, which had organized a League of Justice pledged to help at a moment's notice. Older now hastily sent word to dozens of these men, who came and crowded into the courtroom, which was directly under the chamber in which the jury was deliberating. Evelyn Wells, in her biography of Older, tells what happened when Heney entered the courtroom on Older's arm:

The "minutemen" raised a shout of welcome. Older himself trumpeted like a bull elephant. The rest of the crowd joined in. . . . It was a cheer of welcome, but to the scared jury on the floor above it sounded like a bellowed demand for lynching. A few minutes later twelve good men and true filed hurriedly into the courtroom. They had hastily made up their minds. All were deathly white. Some trembled. A few were weeping.

But their verdict was "Guilty," and Ruef was sentenced to fourteen years in prison. Of all the sentences meted out to leading figures in the whole course of the prosecution, it was the only one that was made to stick.

Another municipal election was approaching, and Langdon, the weary and battered district attorney, refused to run again. He was discouraged, with good reason: a key witness, the supervisor who had paid off his fellows on Ruef's behalf, had fled the country. In desperation, Heney himself ran for district attorney, and was defeated by a football hero from Stanford University, Charles M. Fickert, whose liaison with the grafters was notorious.

Fickert promptly and contemptuously refused to go on with any of the pending cases against the big businessmen. He pretended not to know the whereabouts of the supervisor who had fled, although everyone else knew that he was rusticating in Vancouver, British Columbia. William P. Lawlor, the honest judge who had presided in several of the cases, excoriated Fickert and ordered the others to trial; but he was overruled by the court of appeals, which decided that all of the large number of remaining indictments should be quashed.

The graft prosecution was over, having ended in almost total failure, with only Ruef in prison.

Or so it seemed. But the future was in fact brighter than any member of Older's group could have dared to hope. Even in the middle of the fight, a new mayor had been elected, Dr. Edward Robeson Taylor, who was not only a leading physician but a leading attorney as well; although he had stood aloof from the graft prosecution, he was a man of unquestioned probity who could be relied upon to put an end to the thieving. Moreover, the proceedings in the various cases had been watched not only in San Francisco but throughout the state, where many people did not share the San Franciscans' laissez-faire attitude toward crime. Hiram Johnson had become a hero by taking Heney's place; he now ran for governor, with the blessing of Older and his friends, on a platform of "turn the rascals out"—the rascals including not only the San Francisco bribers but the fixers for the Southern Pacific Railroad and other great business organizations that were not above stooping to corruption.

Johnson was overwhelmingly elected governor, and re-elected four years later, going from that office to the United States Senate. As governor he put through a series of reforms, including changes in the electoral system, that ended forever most of the worst practices of the graft ring. Today, San Francisco has an honest government, and the business organizations (or their successors) that handed out bribes half a century ago would look with proper horror on any suggestion that they should now resort to the old tactics.

Having finally put Ruef into prison, Older began to have qualms of conscience. He felt that the promise of immunity had been too cavalierly broken, that perhaps the community was more guilty than the little

boss, and that Ruef had been made a scapegoat for many worse men. The editor now began a campaign in the *Bulletin* for Ruef's release, but no one in a position of power shared his new-found Tolstoian attitude, and Ruef was not paroled until he had served a full half of his "net" sentence of nine years (after deductions for good behavior and for time in prison awaiting trial). His release came one month after it was legally possible—after four years and seven months.

In some other cases, Nemesis seemed to be at work. Fickert, a few years later, was discovered to have used a perjured witness to send Tom Mooney to prison, and his career ended in disgrace. One of the members of the state supreme court, who cast the deciding vote in some three-to-four decisions, was proved to have accepted a bribe of $410,000 a few years earlier in an important case involving the estate of a wealthy Californian, James G. Fair. Patrick Calhoun lost his fortune in land speculation, though many years later he partially recouped his losses in another city. Ruef, released from prison, went into the real-estate business and after some successes, went downhill into deepening poverty until he died bankrupt, a quarter of a century after he had gone to prison.

Ex-Mayor Eugene Schmitz fared better than any of his associates. He brazened it out in San Francisco for almost two decades; the city, perhaps remembering Steffens' advice that the best possible official is one who has already been proved dishonest, elected him to several successive terms—on the Board of Supervisors!

When the wheeling and dealing of some of President Harding's closest friends was revealed, the mud spattered Cabinet members, the heads of oil companies, the chairman of the Republican party, and eventually the President himself

Tempest Over Teapot

By BRUCE BLIVEN

In the spring of 1920, very few realistic Democrats expected to win that autumn's presidential election. Their party had been in power for nearly eight years, including the World War, and had accumulated all the assorted resentments invariably incurred in wartime. Their situation was not helped by the fact that President Wilson lay ill and and incapacitated in the White House while his wife and his doctor ran the Executive branch of the government.

The Republicans were correspondingly optimistic, as I knew better than most people. In that year I was managing editor of the liberal New York afternoon newspaper, *The Globe,* and naturally, as an editor who really preferred to write, I assigned myself the juicy job of interviewing all the potential presidential candidates of both parties, asking them identical questions so that their answers could be compared. I found most of the possible Democratic candidates lukewarm indeed. When I went to Miami to talk to Governor James M. Cox of Ohio, the cold-faced, weary, hard-driven man who finally got the Democratic nod, he breathed fire for public quotation; privately, he was pessimistic. He considered the nomination as hardly more than a plaque presented for meritorious past service, to be hung on the wall of his den along with the gilded golf ball with which he had once made a hole-in-one.

This impression was confirmed when I went out to San Francisco to cover the Democratic national convention. The delegates fell in love with the city—who doesn't?—and they were happy with the excellent connections with bootleggers that their hosts had provided; but I found nobody who felt that the party had any real chance of winning. Having picked Cox to head the ticket, the delegates rather casually chose as his running mate a tall, athletic young unknown with a good political name—Franklin D. Roosevelt.

But there had been a very different attitude when I made my rounds among the GOP possibilities. General Leonard Wood, Governor Frank Lowden of Illinois, Herbert Hoover, and Senator Warren G. Harding of Ohio all took the hope of nomination very seriously indeed, and none more so than the last.

I interviewed him in his suite in the Senate Office Building, and like everyone else I instantly perceived that this man, who talked like somebody invented by Sinclair Lewis, looked more like a President than any President who ever lived, with the possible exception of George Washington. With his leonine head of white hair, his large, mobile, frank and friendly face, and his portly dignity, it was hard to see why Harding

Senator ***Thomas J. Walsh,*** *left, whose investigations as a member of the Senate Public Lands and Surveys Committee lifted the lid on the complex Teapot Dome scandal.*

had not been chosen by acclamation years earlier.

Two of his remarks in that interview stand out in my memory. The first was his answer to my stock question as to what he would do, if elected, about the American tariff system that was holding back the restoration of Europe and making it harder for the Allies to pay their war debts—even if they had wanted to. His reply startled me so that I asked him to repeat it, and wrote it down verbatim.

"The United States," he said earnestly, "should adopt a protective tariff of such a character as will best help the struggling industries of Europe to get on their feet."

The other memorable remark came when he was talking about the general tendency of people to spend more money than they could afford. He lumbered from his chair, opened the door a crack, and pointed to the back of a young woman sitting at a desk twenty feet away. "That girl," he told me in a conspiratorial whisper, "owns a five-hundred-dollar fur coat. That's twice as much, by George, as I can afford to spend on a coat for Mrs. Harding." I have often wondered since if, with a touch of pixieish humor, he was pointing to Nan Britton, mother of a baby whose father, she claimed long afterward, was Harding himself.

Not long thereafter, following a deadlock between Wood and Lowden, Harding was nominated and went on to win the election handily, sixteen million votes to nine million. Then the country settled back to enjoy itself. "Normalcy," as Harding called it, with characteristic ineptitude in the use of language, was the new order of the day, but it took almost a decade for the country to learn all the chief facts of what really happened during the Harding administration. He had brought with him to Washington one of the most astonishing collections of crooks, grafters, and blackmailers ever assembled. They came to be known as "the Ohio Gang," though not all of them were from that state.

The key figure was Harry Micajah Daugherty, whom Harding made Attorney General. A corporation lawyer from Columbus who already had an unsavory reputation as a lobbyist and fixer, he had managed his friend's presidential campaign. He had come from the little Ohio crossroads of Washington Court House, where his brother was president of a bank, and had brought with him a devoted henchman, Jess (or Jesse) Smith, who had owned a dry-goods store there. Smith, though he had no title, promptly commandeered an office in the Department of Justice near that of Daugherty and began issuing orders, orally or in writing, in the Attorney General's name.

Smith and another man from Ohio rented what came to be known as "the Little Green House" at 1625 K Street, and it soon was a center of revelry almost twenty-four hours a day. For the right people, good liquor was available in unlimited amounts; much of it had been confiscated by the government, and sometimes it was delivered in official vehicles by armed guards in uniform. The Ohio Gang eagerly solicited bribes from bootleggers seeking immunity, men in jail who wanted to be released, men under indictment who wanted the proceedings dropped, and German owners of property sequestered during the war. Nobody knows what the take amounted to in the thirty months or so that the Ohio Gang was in the saddle, but it has been estimated that, in graft and waste, this group cost the country about two billion dollars.

What was the President's role in all this? At the beginning, he certainly did not know what was going on. Harding did not frequent the Little Green House on K Street, where he would have met bootleggers, dope peddlers or their agents, women of easy virtue, professional gamblers, and other sordid types. He did, however, spend much time in a similar establishment on H Street. One of his cronies was Ned McLean, young multimillionaire playboy, whose family had come from Cincinnati; Ned obligingly rented this second refuge. If some underworld character proved hard to convince that a few hundred thousand dollars put into the right hands would give him a license to break the law, Jess Smith or one of his colleagues would take the doubting Thomas over to stand near the door of "the House on H Street," to see Daugherty or some other high-level crook emerge from a presidential limousine and enter the house arm in arm with the President and his lady. This usually worked.

Just how much Harding knew of what was going on is not certain; but it is clear that he had some information about it. In the summer of 1923, just a few weeks before his death in San Francisco of a cerebral hemorrhage, he was visibly worried and depressed; he kept asking those about him what a President should do when he was betrayed by his friends.

The most famous and in some ways the most important of the scandals that came to light after Harding's death had to do with oil, and is commonly known as "Teapot Dome," from the name of one of the naval oil reserve areas involved.

In those days before nuclear power, there was concern lest our Navy in time of emergency might run out of its precious fuel. As early as 1910, Congress began setting aside special oil fields. Two of them, Elk Hills and Buena Vista, were only a few miles apart, near Bakersfield, California; the third, Teapot Dome, was not far from Casper, Wyoming. (Geologists speak of a "dome" when the earth strata curve upward and then down again, a situation that may bring oil close to the surface.)

There were commercial fields nearby, and supposedly there was some danger that the government oil might be drained off. Accordingly, in 1920 Congress gave the Secretary of the Navy almost unlimited power to save it. He might drill new wells anywhere within any reserve, pump out the oil, and store it. He might permit private operators to drill inside these areas, but only on condition that a certain proportion of the oil be turned over to the Navy for storage.

One of Harding's best friends while in the Senate had been Senator Albert B. Fall, of Three Rivers, New Mexico. With his western clothes, his luxuriant, drooping mustache, and his weather-beaten face, he looked like a movie sheriff. Fall had a terrible temper, which he made no effort to control; there were rumors that as a youth he had "killed his man," though he denied this. He had studied law, and President Cleveland had once put him on the Supreme Court bench of New Mexico Territory. But he had to be removed when he abruptly left the courtroom one day to join the pursuit of a fleeing bandit. Harding actually wanted to make him Secretary of State—which would not have suited Fall's plans at all. He persuaded the President to make him Secretary of the Interior instead.

Three months after the Cabinet was sworn in, Fall got Harding to transfer all the oil reserves from the Navy to the Interior Department, on the grounds that they would thus be better protected from depletion through private drilling nearby. Many people thought the transfer was unwise. Senator Robert M. La Follette of Wisconsin made a vigorous objection on the floor of the Senate; though he later gave his reluctant approval, Secretary of the Navy Edwin Denby protested to the President, but his letter mysteriously disappeared in transit.

Secretary Fall—promptly, secretly, and without the competitive bidding the law required—leased two rich oil reserves to two wealthy men. Elk Hills in California went to his friend of forty years, Edward L. Doheny, who had started with nothing and had accumulated about one hundred million dollars in oil holdings in the United States and Mexico. (Oddly enough, Doheny looked like a much warmer version of Fall, with the same ragged white mustache and weather-beaten face.) Teapot Dome went to Harry Sinclair, reputed to be more than three times as rich as Doheny. The Sinclair lease was for a minimum of twenty years and was to continue indefinitely as long as oil and gas could be produced at a profit. The government was to get a royalty of around sixteen per cent, and Sinclair was required to build some storage tanks and a pipeline. Doheny's lease required him to build, without profit

to himself, a pipeline and a refinery in California and storage tanks at Pearl Harbor. Doheny and Sinclair expected to make at least one hundred million dollars each; since there was much more oil in the ground than anyone then knew, their profits might have been larger still. If the oil lands had been leased under competitive bidding, the government's share would have been much more than sixteen per cent; M. R. Werner and John Starr, in their book, *Teapot Dome,* estimate that it might have been worth as much as fifty million dollars.

News of the secret leases leaked out in a few days, and the Senate Committee on Public Lands and Surveys attempted to investigate. Fall brushed its members off contemptuously, saying that he had taken his action in the interest of national security, which required him to suppress all the details. But the Senate was not satisfied, and in the fall of 1923 there began the long series of investigations and civil and criminal court actions that was to last almost a decade and to reveal the most shocking state of corruption since the Grant administration.

I spent a good deal of time in Washington during these investigations, writing a series of articles on the Ohio Gang for *The New Republic,* of which I was then managing editor. The reek of corruption hung over the city, apparent to anybody whose nostrils were reasonably sensitive. The spearheads of the Senate investigations were the two able senators from Montana, Thomas J. Walsh and Burton K. Wheeler. I sat in the committee rooms day after day and saw these men put together a jigsaw puzzle, many of whose pieces had been hidden by others with ingenuity and foresight.

Walsh was austere and carefully groomed, impeccable, soft-voiced, polite; he carried a formidable amount of information in his head. Wheeler was more the rough frontier type, with tousled hair and a truculent attitude toward a squirming witness. Both of them had superlative abilities as detective-prosecutors. On the theory that the investigations were just a Democratic plot, Republican members of the committees did what they could to impede proceedings. The small importance that Washington attached to the investigations in the beginning is shown by the fact that the senators were unceremoniously thrown out of an excellent room into an inferior one because the ladies of the Senate wanted the good one for a tea party.

The members of the Ohio Gang closed ranks against the attack and tried hard to thwart the investigation, in spite of the fact that Fall had repeatedly refused to let Attorney General Daugherty give an official ruling that his actions were legal; Fall had a well-founded fear that Daugherty would want a big share of the loot.

Harry Sinclair, whose Mammoth Oil Co. was secretly given a lease to Teapot Dome reserve.

Albert B. Fall, Secretary of the Interior, who for a bribe gave Sinclair the rights to government oil worth more than one hundred million dollars.

Harry M. Daugherty, Attorney General, knew "the whole sordid story of the oil leases," Walsh said, and might have profited thereby.

Edward Doheny, head of Pan-American Petroleum and friend of Fall, who got leases on California oil reserves and "loaned" Fall $100,000.

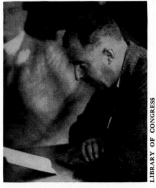

Edward B. McLean, millionaire newspaper publisher who tried to conceal from the Senate investigators the source of Fall's sudden wealth.

William J. Burns had been brought from New York, where he was head of the Burns Detective Agency (today thoroughly respectable), to head the Bureau of Investigation, which was wholeheartedly on the side of the Ohio Gang. Any member of Congress who expressed public criticism was subject to harassment. Senator La Follette's office was rifled; a detective went to Montana to investigate Senator Wheeler with the hope, as he openly admitted to one or two people, of finding something there that could be used to blackmail him. Senator Walsh was called a scandalmonger and a character assassin; his past life was investigated, his phones tapped, his mail opened; and anonymous letters threatened his life. His daughter, wheeling his three-year-old granddaughter along the street, was intercepted by a stranger who threatened her with harm if she did not force her father to drop the investigation. Female detectives hung around the ladies' room used by Senator Walsh's secretaries, hoping to pick up some valuable gossip.

The members of the Senate who were engaged in the investigation refused to be intimidated and went ahead with their work. Their first big break came with news from New Mexico that Secretary Fall's cattle ranch was showing remarkable prosperity, though his neighbors, because of depression and drought, were turning their cattle loose to survive as best they could.

There was a crusading journalist in New Mexico, Carl Magee, owner of the Albuquerque *Journal,* who had been having trouble with Secretary Fall for some time. Magee had exposed various ways in which the power of the Department of the Interior was being used for the benefit of private interests in New Mexico, which enjoyed such privileges as the improper use of public land. Secretary Fall responded by trying to ruin Magee, and he almost succeeded. Banks, under Fall's influence, called Magee's loans without warning; he was harassed with successive suits for criminal libel; people who feared Fall's power were afraid to entertain Magee and his wife socially, or to be entertained by them. In one of the criminal-libel cases, Magee was sentenced to a year in jail, though he was pardoned by the Governor of New Mexico, a Democrat.

Magee now came to Washington and told his story. In 1920, he reported, Fall had been practically bankrupt and thinking of resigning from the Senate for that reason. He had paid no taxes on his property for the past eight years. Yet now, only a few months later, he was buying additional land worth $124,000, paying his debts (often with $100 bills), building new fences, pouring expensive concrete gutters.

Senator Walsh was interested in where the money had come from. Fall, pleading illness, did not appear on the witness stand, but sent a sworn statement that

gave a ready explanation: He had with some difficulty persuaded Ned McLean to lend him $100,000. Senator Walsh decided to check this statement.

McLean was in a dilemma. He didn't want to lie, but he didn't want to tell the truth either. He was in Palm Beach, trying desperately to avoid returning to Washington and sending back coded messages to his aides. Finally, he sent Walsh a report saying that he had indeed lent $100,000 to his dear friend, Secretary Fall.

Walsh came near to accepting his word, but then the touch of the bloodhound in him made him decide to go to Palm Beach and see McLean. Face to face, the young playboy wilted and told the truth. At Fall's request he had in fact written checks totalling $100,000, but it was understood that these were never to be cashed and they had actually been returned to him uncancelled. Fall could not have paid for his new land with them; where did the money come from?

It came from me, said Doheny, hurrying across the country to save Fall's neck. He had loaned his old friend $100,000 in cash. He had sent the money by his son, Edward L. Doheny, Jr., who had carried a small black satchel full of greenbacks from New York to Washington. Was this not a large amount to be handled so cavalierly? "Not to me," said Croesus, with a grand wave. "A bagatelle to me . . . no more than twenty-five or fifty dollars to the ordinary individual." And had he demanded no security? Certainly not; but after long thought he remembered that Fall had given an unsecured note for the amount. Where was the note? Days later it was produced, but with the signature torn off. Why no signature? Doheny explained that he feared he might die suddenly and that his hardhearted executors might press Fall for the money at an embarrassing moment.

Doheny might have been able to bribe Fall out of cash on hand, but, as the investigating committee soon discovered, Harry Sinclair's approach to this problem was different. He had decided to raise the needed money, and a great deal more, through a shady transaction at the expense of the stockholders in two oil companies, one of which was his own. On November 17, 1921, a group of wealthy oilmen met in a hotel room in New York City. Besides Sinclair they included Colonel A. E. Humphreys, who owned a rich oil field of his own in East Texas; Colonel Robert W. Stewart, chairman of the board of the Standard Oil Company of Indiana; James E. O'Neil of the Prairie Oil and Gas Company; and Henry M. Blackmer of the Midwest Refining Company.

All except Humphreys were cronies and were in on

a simple scheme. A dummy corporation, the Continental Trading Company, Ltd., had been set up in Canada for the sole purpose of buying 33,333,333⅓ barrels of oil from Colonel Humphreys at the going rate of $1.50 a barrel, and instantly reselling it at an unwarranted profit of twenty-five cents a barrel to the companies of Sinclair and O'Neil. It was Colonel Humphreys who had decided upon the unusual number of barrels; the reason, he later sheepishly explained, was that this made the transaction come to a round fifty million dollars, the largest in his career.

With a profit of twenty-five cents a barrel, Continental stood to make over eight million dollars, which was more than ample for the illicit purposes for which the company had been formed. It actually did collect somewhat more than three million dollars. Then the Senate investigators began to get too hot on the trail: the company was liquidated, and all its records were destroyed. This money was turned into Liberty Bonds —an incredible blunder, since the bonds and their coupons were numbered, and the latter could be traced after they had been cashed. The law said that the Treasury Department must destroy these coupons after holding them a specified length of time; some of those that figured in the oil scandals were actually rescued by investigators only forty-eight hours before this would have been done.

The illicit profit was divided among the four oil men: Sinclair took about $750,000, Stewart $760,000, Blackmer $763,000, and O'Neil $800,000. (Humphreys got no cut, but of course he had made a neat—and legitimate—profit on the oil he sold to Continental.) At the time, none of them told the directors of their respective companies what was going on. Blackmer put his bonds into a safe-deposit vault; O'Neil kept his for four years and then turned them over to his company. In strict secrecy Stewart handed over his share to an employee of his firm, who hid the bonds in a far corner of a company safe. Sinclair took his money home. It was finally proved that he had given Fall a total of $304,000.

When the heat was really on, all these men left the country. Blackmer and O'Neil went to Europe and stayed there. Stewart went to Cuba, but finally came back to bully and berate the Senate committee investigators, refusing to answer their questions. In 1928 he was tried for contempt of the Senate and for perjury and was acquitted both times.

The Rockefeller family, of which John D. Rockefeller, Jr., was now the active head, owned nearly fifteen per cent of the stock of the Standard Oil Company of Indiana. John D., Jr., had tried unsuccessfully to get Stewart to make a clean breast of everything, and after his refusal, managed to get the stockholders to oust him at the next annual meeting. Stewart lost his job, with its $125,000 annual salary, and was forced thenceforth to scrape along on a pension of $75,000.

In January, 1924, after inconclusive testimony before the Senate committee, Sinclair had hurried off to Europe under an assumed name. But he came back some months later, for several reasons. His far-flung business enterprises demanded his presence; he believed his tracks had been well covered; and finally, he thought with some reason that he was too important an individual to be made to suffer seriously at the hands of the law.

In the meantime, the Senate committee had dug up some interesting evidence. Sinclair's secretary had remarked casually to Archie Roosevelt, who was then a Sinclair employee, that Sinclair had turned over $68,000 to the manager of Fall's ranch. Archie, after resigning his position, told the Senate committee about the money, and the secretary was summoned. All a mistake, this gentleman explained. He had not said "sixty-eight thou'." He had said "six or eight cows"—which anyone knows sounds much the same. Sinclair had in fact given Fall six heifers and a bull, and thrown in a horse and six hogs for good measure.

Since the committee still seemed skeptical, the secretary tried a new tack. He had indeed mentioned $68,000, but it was not money intended for the manager of Fall's ranch. He had been talking about the transmission of money to the manager of Sinclair's own farm—his celebrated racing stable.

But by now too much was known to keep the story bottled up. With the utmost difficulty, Coolidge was finally persuaded to authorize court proceedings. He announced that he would appoint a prominent Republican and a prominent Democrat to act jointly in carrying through the investigation, and in prosecuting whatever cases seemed to justify it. His Republican was Owen J. Roberts, a little-known but reputable attorney from Philadelphia who had tried cases for the government during the war under the Espionage Act. Roberts' Democratic colleague was former Senator Atlee Pomerene, who was now practicing law in Cincinnati. They had two able assistants, George Chandler and Ulrich J. Mengert, and four skilled members of the Secret Service, led by William H. Moran.

Roberts and Pomerene asked the courts to appoint temporary receivers to take charge of operations at Teapot Dome and the fields in California leased to Doheny, and to impound all the oil produced, until the cases had been decided in which the government was asking cancellation of the leases. This was done.

The two presidential appointees and their staff now began a monumental task of detective work, interviewing hundreds of people and checking bank records, brokerage accounts, and other files in half a dozen states and Canada. Finally, when they thought they had airtight evidence, they brought a group of civil and criminal actions, which were prosecuted with great skill. It was not the fault of Roberts and Pomerene that the results were rather disappointing as far as sending people to jail was concerned.*

Nothing could be more characteristic of the sickly moral atmosphere of the times than what happened when the three chief figures in the oil scandals were brought into court. Fall and Doheny were tried jointly for conspiracy, and were acquitted. The Washington jury, composed of average middle-class Americans, had no intention of sending a multimillionaire and a fine gentleman like Doheny to jail. Then Fall and Sinclair were also tried jointly for conspiracy, since the two crimes were substantially identical. They were also acquitted. Doheny was tried alone for giving the satchelful of money to Fall, and acquitted. Fall was tried for accepting the satchelful of money, but he was not a multimillionaire or a fine gentleman: he was found guilty and sentenced to a year in prison.

When Sinclair came back from Europe he had re-

Fall, Sinclair, and Denby maintained their innocence in the Teapot Dome scandals to the end of their days.

---

* The national attention Roberts received was to be a factor in his appointment as Associate Justice of the United States Supreme Court in 1930 by President Hoover. Pomerene was considered for the Democratic presidential nomination in 1928, and later was chairman of the Reconstruction Finance Corporation.

fused to answer questions by the Senate, but he made the bad mistake of failing to take refuge behind the Fifth Amendment, saying only that he intended to reserve his testimony until later. He was judged to be in contempt of the Senate.

There were other charges against him. During his trial for conspiracy, it was discovered that one juror had been bribed to vote for acquittal. This man indiscreetly told a friend that he had been promised, in a phrase that became famous, "a car as long as this block." He also hinted darkly that he was to get some cash. The friend knew a reporter on one of the Washington newspapers, told him about it, and arranged a meeting between the juror and the reporter. They met in a saloon, the reporter's occupation being concealed, and the juror repeated the substance of the story. The reporter promptly informed a representative of the prosecution.

Roberts and Pomerene also learned that at the beginning of the trial a horde of private detectives had been sent down from New York and assigned to shadow each member of the jury to learn all that could be learned about them. These agents, employees of the Burns Detective Agency, assumed new identities and worked with military precision, turning in daily reports that were co-ordinated at a central headquarters in a Washington hotel room.

One of the detectives, William J. McMullin, was ordered to assist in a frame-up that would involve

As the Senate investigations unfolded, Republican leaders began to realize they were in for some unpleasant medicine.

Norman Glasscock, one of the jurors, and Horace Lamb, a lawyer in the Department of Justice. The spies knew the license numbers of the automobiles of Glasscock and Lamb; McMullin was to swear that he had seen these two cars parked side by side on a given day at the Potomac Flying Field, and the occupants conferring. This was of course entirely false. The plan was that if the trial seemed likely to produce a verdict of guilty, McMullin was to come forward with the charge of improper contact between a juror and a Department of Justice lawyer, which would force a mistrial.

But Sinclair's forces had picked a poor choice for skulduggery in McMullin. A former New Jersey state trooper, he was sickened by what he had been asked to do. He made contact with former Governor Gifford Pinchot of Pennsylvania, his home state, and told him the story. Pinchot took it to representatives of the prosecution, who promptly made McMullin a double agent. He was to do everything that Sinclair's representatives told him to do, but he was to make a secret daily report to the prosecution of what was going on.

Armed with this information, representatives of Roberts and Pomerene raided the headquarters of Sinclair's detectives and seized carbon copies of a mass of field agents' reports. As a result, they were able to subpoena scores of individuals who had knowledge of, or who had participated in, the spying on the jurors.

Under orders from the prosecution, McMullin executed the false affidavit about Glasscock and Lamb. Before it could be used, however, the government men told the judge about the bribery of the juror. There was indeed a mistrial, though not under the circumstances Sinclair had anticipated.

The oilman's attorneys, seeking to turn public opinion against Roberts and Pomerene, produced McMullin's affidavit. The prosecution promptly revealed that he had been a double agent and released the evidence showing that the affidavit was false. Sinclair's attorneys now tried desperately to smear McMullin, digging up and publishing every unfavorable fact they could find about his past, but with little success. Fearing for his safety, the government gave him a bodyguard.

Some time later Sinclair was tried again, and found guilty of contempt of court. He was given six months in jail, in addition to the $500 fine and three months in jail he had received for contempt of the Senate.

But this was not the end of the tale of the Liberty Bonds, the profits from the only business deal ever made by the fabulous Continental Trading Company.

Will Hays, a smiling chipmunk of a man, had been Republican National Chairman in 1920, and had rashly promised that campaign contributions would be limited to $1,000 from any individual; the result was a deficit of $1,200,000. After he had made his deal with Fall, but before it was exposed, Sinclair felt it would be politic for him to make a substantial contribution toward erasing the deficit. Yet it was obviously undesirable for a single individual to give a large sum, especially an oilman who was in a position to get favors from Republican government officials.

Senator Walsh somehow picked up a rumor that Sinclair had made a very large contribution. Will Hays, who had been made Postmaster General by Harding, and then had become czar of movie morals, was summoned to the witness stand. Unluckily, Walsh's information was wrong in one detail. It said that Hays had been given not Liberty Bonds, which was a fact, but bonds of the Sinclair Consolidated Oil Corporation. This enabled Hays to deny the whole transaction. Asked whether Sinclair had made a private loan to Hays himself, he refused to answer on the ground that this was a personal matter.

What had happened was this: Sinclair had turned over to Hays $260,000 in bonds, part of his profits from the Continental Trading Company; $75,000 of this was supposed to be a contribution, and $185,000 (in theory) a loan. Hays had then approached several wealthy men and asked each of them to turn over a substantial sum of cash to the Republican National Committee. Each man would in turn be given Liberty Bonds in the same amount to hold as security. If and when the loan was repaid, he would give back the bonds. As far as Hays was concerned, there was of course little or no intention of ever repaying the "loans"; they were simply a device to conceal the large gift from Sinclair. T. Coleman Du Pont, who had been treasurer of the national committee, received bonds worth $75,000; John T. Pratt, a wealthy New Yorker, $50,000; John W. Weeks, a millionaire Bostonian and Harding's Secretary of War, $25,000. Fred Upham of Chicago, who was treasurer of the Republican National Committee in 1923, took $60,000 worth and sold them to various rich Chicagoans for cash.

On the witness stand in 1924, Hays mentioned only the $75,000 Sinclair contribution. In 1928, when the government knew more about the transaction, he was summoned again and confessed to the $185,000. And why had he kept silent four years earlier? "Nobody," said the moralist indignantly, "asked me about any Liberty Bonds."

Another man who figured in this episode was Andrew Mellon, Secretary of the Treasury. A multimillionaire Pittsburgh banker, he had inherited a fortune, greatly expanded it, and while in office had reduced the national debt by one third, from the gigantic sum of twenty-four billion dollars to sixteen billion dollars.

An investigator for the Senate committee found in the personal files of John T. Pratt, who had died some time earlier, small slips of paper that had on them in microscopic writing the names of several wealthy men, with a sum of money written after each one. In the 1928 investigation, the cashier for Pratt's estate, V. E. Hommel, was asked to look at these names and read them aloud to the committee. He read the first one clearly enough; it was "Weeks." The next name he professed to be unable to read. He thought it was the word "Candy." When Senator Gerald P. Nye asked whether the word might not be "Andy," Hommel admitted it might be, but had no idea who that could be. The spectators in the committee room laughed; there was only one famous Andy in the whole country. Mr. Mellon was now put on the stand and admitted that Hays had indeed sent him $50,000 in Liberty Bonds, suggesting that he regard them as security for a loan by himself of the same amount to the Republican National Committee. Mr. Mellon smelled something disreputable about this proposal, and instantly sent back the bonds, at the same time making an independent contribution of $50,000 of his own to reduce the Republican deficit. And why had he waited so long to tell about this? Like Hays, he was indignant; nobody had asked him.

Year after year, the government went on fighting to unravel the harm that Fall's greed had produced. Case after case was fought through to the Supreme Court. The oil leases were at last vacated on the ground that fraud and corruption had been employed. Sinclair had to return to the government more than twelve million dollars, and Doheny, almost thirty-five million. (Doheny had spent about eleven million on storage tanks at Pearl Harbor, for which he was not reimbursed.) Sinclair had also obligated himself to pay large sums to a group of blackmailers who had learned early in the game that there was something fishy about Teapot Dome. These blackmailers included the two notorious owners of the Denver *Post*, Frederick G. Bonfils and H. H. Tammen, who softened up Sinclair by publishing many articles raising questions about the Teapot Dome lease; after he had agreed to pay them off, the articles stopped. The blackmail, most of which was to come out of the profits of Teapot Dome, amounted in all to more than two million dollars.

Doheny died in 1935 at seventy-nine and Sinclair in 1956 at eighty; neither man ever publicly admitted his guilt, nor did Fall, who died in 1944 at eighty-three. Blackmer finally came home from Europe in 1949, at the age of eighty, to face the music; he was immediately arraigned on charges of tax evasion and perjury. He was fined $60,000, and he owed nearly $8,500,000 in unpaid back taxes, penalties, and interest. He finally settled with the government for about $3,600,000, and the charge of perjury was dropped.

O'Neil died in France in 1932 at sixty-four. Seven years earlier a doctor had told him, erroneously, that he had only a year or two to live, and he therefore made a secret trip to Canada. There he told two officials of his company about the bonds he was holding, and turned over the bulk of them; he had cashed a few —by inadvertence, so he said. Ned McLean, who became an alcoholic, was declared incompetent and was put into a mental institution, where he died in 1941 at the age of fifty-five. Colonel Stewart died in 1927 at eighty.

Little by little over the late nineteen twenties other scandals of the Harding regime became known. One of the worst of them centered around Charles R. Forbes, whom the President had made head of the Veterans' Bureau. The price of each new veterans' hospital planned under his regime was to be padded by $150,000, of which Forbes took $50,000 while the contractors split the rest. Sites were bought at four or five times their actual value, and Forbes demanded and got his cut. He also bought staggering quantities of supplies at inflated prices, with the understanding that he receive a kickback. Finally brought to trial, Forbes got two years in prison and was fined $10,000. Will Irwin, who made a careful study of the episode, said he had cost the United States not less than 200 million dollars.

Another notorious figure was Harding's brother-in-law, Heber Votaw, an ex-missionary from Burma, whom the President made Director of Federal Prisons. In his regime there was a huge increase in the bootlegging of narcotics to prisoners; Votaw's office tried to hamper efforts to investigate and remedy the situation. When the director of the Atlanta Penitentiary complained, he was fired. With the death of Harding, his protector, Votaw's days in office were numbered. There was insufficient evidence against him to impress a jury, and he was presently allowed to slip back into obscurity.

Of all the Ohio Gang, Harry Daugherty was the most brazen. With scandals exploding all around his head, he refused after the death of Harding to resign his post. Coolidge, characteristically, sent somebody else—Chief Justice William Howard Taft—to suggest this; the idea was coldly rebuffed. Finally, the odor of scandal became too strong, and Daugherty was forced out. When he came to trial at last, he refused to take the stand and invoked the Fifth Amendment.

It developed that a year earlier, Harry had gone to Washington Court House and had burned many records, some of them going back as far as 1916. The theory he circulated was that he did this to protect the good name of the dead President, since the records would tell both of financial irregularities by Harding and of his clandestine love life. Senate investigators were able, however, to discover that $75,000, its source unexplained, had been deposited to Daugherty's account at a time when he swore on his income-tax return that he had no property. Also on deposit in the bank was $63,000 for Jess Smith, $50,000 for Mal Daugherty, and smaller sums for other members of the Ohio Gang. This bank had been for them what the cave was for Ali Baba's forty thieves.

When the Senate committee tried to subpoena brother Mal, he fought all the way to the United States Supreme Court to avoid testifying. When he was cited for contempt of the Senate, an obliging judge, sitting in Ohio, set him free. His bank later failed with a loss of 2.6 million dollars, ruining a large proportion of the people around Washington Court House. (This was of course before the days of the Federal Bank Deposit Insurance Corporation.)

Harry Daugherty had been indicted with Thomas W. Miller, Alien Property Custodian, for having accepted bribes to turn back to a dummy Swiss corporation a large part of the assets of the American Metals Company, a German-owned firm in the United States, and I covered the trial for *The New Republic*. Daugherty looked, as always, shifty, squirming, and oily. Miller was thin-faced and sober, with, as I remember, a pince-nez like that of Woodrow Wilson; he sat bemused, as though wondering what in the world he was doing in the prisoner's dock. Well he might: He was a Yale graduate, from a good Philadelphia family, with an impeccable record until he went to Washington and came under the evil spell of the Ohio Gang.

The dummy Swiss corporation had paid $441,000 in bribes, of which Miller got $49,000 and Daugherty at least $40,000; where the rest went was never made clear. Miller was sentenced to prison, served some time, and was pardoned. More than fifty million dollars in German assets illegally released by his office was eventually returned to the U.S. government. In Harry Daugherty's case, two successive juries disagreed, and he was able to boast that he had never been convicted. In 1924, after being forced to resign from the Cabinet, he retired to a pleasant life in Ohio and Florida. He died, unrepentant, in 1944.

Two members of the Ohio Gang had committed suicide even before Harding's death. Charles F. Cramer, legal adviser to the Veterans' Bureau, wrote a letter to the President and then shot himself. (Harding refused even to look at the letter, and it later disappeared without any revelation of its contents.) Jesse Smith, Daugherty's shadow, was found dead one day in 1923 with a revolver beside him. Though cynics argued that he had been murdered, there is no doubt that he had been deeply depressed because both Harding and Daugherty had cooled toward him, had in fact exiled him back to Ohio.

Could we have a repetition of the Harding or Grant scandals today? It seems to me unlikely. The Grant and Harding administrations had several elements in common, and I feel that all of them, in combination, are essential for wholesale corruption. First, you must have a period of moral relaxation such as is common after a big war. Second, you must have a President in the White House who is complacent, ill-informed, and a poor judge of the integrity of his close friends. Third, and perhaps most important, the country must be un-aware, before electing him, of these aspects of a nominee's character.

Today, every serious candidate for the Presidency lives under intense scrutiny by magazines and newspapers, which in general do an enormously better job than they did forty-five (or ninety-seven) years ago. He also lives under the fierce white light of the television cameras, which have an uncanny way of revealing the things about a man that he would prefer to have concealed. If the media for mass communication do their work properly, we ought to be secure against the possibility of another Ohio Gang.

Bad Actors & Jolly Swindlers

SAY IT AIN'T

BROWN BROTHERS

One of baseball's legendary remarks was addressed to the great outfielder "Shoeless Joe" Jackson after he confessed having a part in the "Black Sox" scandal.

Foul was fair, and fair foul, when

eight players of the championship

White Sox conspired with gamblers

to throw the 1919 World Series

On November 6, 1920, a grand jury in Cook County, Illinois, issued to an aroused public a statement of reassurance on a question that seemed to eclipse in significance even the landslide presidential victory of Warren Gamaliel Harding just four days earlier. In spite of the jury's recent disclosures, the game of baseball was "clean."

Only five weeks before, this same jury had disclosed that the 1919 World Series had been fixed; eight players of the Chicago White Sox team of the American League had been indicted for accepting bribes. The grand jury had exposed what soon came to be celebrated as the "Black Sox" scandal—in the public mind, the most brazen conspiracy in the annals of American sports.

The outcry at this revelation was universal. Newspaper editorials thundered imprecations. In the Philadelphia *Bulletin,* for example, the disgraced players were compared with "the soldier or sailor who would sell out his country and its flag in time of war." More poignant was the plea of one or more small boys to their idol, "Shoeless Joe" Jackson, as he left the building where the grand jury met. It has come down to us, one of the most pitiful fragments of the American idiom: "Say it ain't so, Joe!"

The proprietors of baseball have watchfully guarded the integrity of the game ever since the Black Sox scandal; that a similar conspiracy could take place today seems quite improbable. It is unlikely that the public reaction would be so emotionally charged as in 1920. Though baseball is still our national pastime, it is regarded with a diminished sense of reverence. The notion that it is a big business, run for profit, is now widely embraced.

In contrast to the enormous publicity of the scandal, exact documentation of it is slight, and based almost entirely on circumstantial evidence. Those involved in the conspiracy were understandably reticent at the time, and have remained so ever since. After the case was closed, Shoeless Joe Jackson and his teammate, George "Buck" Weaver, spoke openly about their roles —to insist that they were innocent as the lilies of the field. In 1956, a third player, Chick Gandil, told his version of the inside story in a sports magazine, admitting a guilty part but only further confusing an already confused picture.

SO, JOE!

By LEWIS THOMPSON *and* CHARLES BOSWELL

There is no doubt, however, that once a fix had been arranged between eight of the White Sox players and a group of gamblers, it was one of the worst-kept secrets of all time. The first game of the Series was played on October 1, 1919, at Redland Park, the home grounds of the Cincinnati Reds, winners of the National League pennant. Among the sports writers who covered it were Hugh Fullerton and the baseball great, Christy Mathewson, who had been commissioned by a syndicate to write interpretative articles on the fine points of the Series play. Before the first game, the two compared notes. What was this talk about the Series being in the bag? Both had heard rumors. Both agreed that the possibility was too monstrous to believe. But others in the reporting fraternity, as well as an indeterminate number of ordinary citizens, had heard the same rumors.

One significant fact did give credence to the reports: the betting odds. These had started out overwhelmingly in favor of the White Sox, but by October 1 they were virtually even. It was curious that a heavy influx of Cincinnati cash into betting channels had brought about the change, for almost everyone agreed that the Sox were vastly superior to the Reds.

The 1919 White Sox were one of the notable teams in the history of baseball. Owned by Charles A. Comiskey—nicknamed the Old Roman—the team had Eddie Collins at second base and Ray Schalk as catcher. It would be risky to say they were the greatest ever at their positions; but there have been none better.

No less outstanding was the left fielder, Shoeless Joe Jackson. This back-country boy from South Carolina who could neither read nor write was one of the most colorful and idolized players the game has ever known. Described by some as the "greatest natural batsman that ever played," Jackson compiled a batting average of .356 during ten years in the majors.

There were other fine players on the team: "Shineball" Eddie Cicotte, an accomplished spitball pitcher; Claude "Lefty" Williams, a marvel of control on the mound; Oscar "Happy" Felsch in center field; and a great infield that, in addition to Collins, included Gandil at first, Charles "Swede" Risberg at shortstop, and Weaver at third. Under the management of William

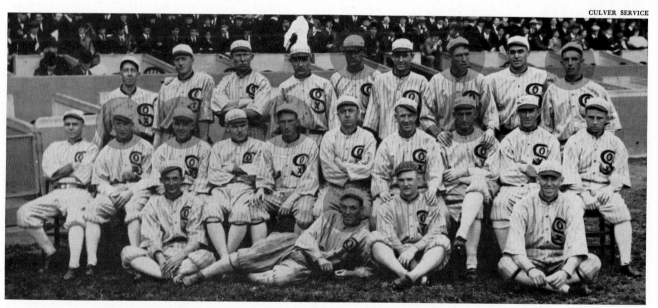

The eight guilty players have been circled in this team picture of the World Champion White Sox of 1917. From left to right, the so-called "Black Sox" are: front row, Weaver; seated, Felsch, Cicotte, McMullin, and Jackson; standing, Gandil, Risberg, and Williams.

"Kid" Gleason, the Sox had romped through the American League that season; with the pennant clinched, the only question seemed to be how quickly they would win the required five-out-of-nine games of which the Series then consisted. By contrast the Reds, who had beaten seven listless, ineffectual teams to win their first National League pennant, were at best a competent outfit.

The result of the first game amazed everyone—except, as it later developed, eight of the Sox and certain other shadowy figures. As *The New York Times* said in its page one story: "Never before in the history of America's biggest baseball spectacle has a pennant-winning club received such a disastrous drubbing in an opening game as the far-famed White Sox got this afternoon. . . . The heralded White Sox looked like bush leaguers."

These were not irresponsible words. In the bottom of the first inning, Eddie Cicotte took the mound to pitch against the Reds. He hit the first batter, lobbed up an easy single to the second, and twice sent Heinie Groh, the third Cincinnati hitter, into the dirt with beanballs. Cicotte's control seemed to have deserted him, and when the inning was over, the Reds were ahead, one to nothing.

In the bottom of the fourth, Cicotte blew up completely. The first batter flied out. The second singled, but then was thrown out on a fielder's choice.

Dapper Abe Attell, gambler and ex-pugilist, was involved in the Series fix.

There were two out and one on. Two singles followed, which brought in a run and put men on second and third. Up to the plate stepped Dutch Ruether, the Reds' pitcher but an above-average hitter for this traditionally weak-hitting position. Ruether leaned into a slow, easy pitch and whacked it for a triple. A double and a single followed, and when the third man was finally out, the Reds had enjoyed a five-run inning. The final score was nine to one.

As soon as the game was over, talk of a fix grew louder. Much of it was bruited about the lobby of

the Hotel Sinton, quarters for the visiting Sox and hence a natural gathering place for Series-minded sportsmen and gamblers. Presently, the gist of the rumor reached Kid Gleason; he in turn told Comiskey what he had heard—namely, that gamblers had bribed some members of the team.

Gleason was of two minds about the truth of the rumor. On the one hand, he knew that it would take a large number of players to throw a game, a possibility which seemed as unlikely as it was painful. On the other, Gleason was impressed by the peculiar gyrations of the betting odds, and he had heard that well-known gamblers had made a killing on the opening game. Then, Cicotte *had* pitched an extraordinarily bad game, and many of the Sox big bats had been remarkably ineffectual.

Comiskey was not so vacillating. Having seen his players' performance on the field, he felt there was something wrong.

Yet, what could he and Gleason do? The Series had to go on. They had no actual proof of wrongdoing, and without it, they could not very well suspend any of the players. Comiskey worried through the night, and the next morning approached an old friend, John A. Heydler, president of the rival National League. The natural person for Comiskey to have consulted was Byron Bancroft "Ban" Johnson, the president of Comiskey's own league; but the two were not on speaking terms.

In Heydler's view, Comiskey's concern was unwarranted. He believed that the White Sox had simply been taken "unawares" in the first game, and that they would quickly revert to form. Sometime during that day, however, Heydler sought out Ban Johnson and repeated what he had heard. Heydler later quoted Johnson as saying that the bribery explanation for the loss of the first game was like the "crying of a whipped cur." There Heydler let the matter rest.

The course of the second game, played on October 2, did nothing to reassure Gleason and Comiskey. Lefty Williams pitched for the Sox and performed well for three innings. But in the fourth, he walked three men and allowed two hits, for a total of three runs. The final score was four to two. Even the Sox's two runs were tainted, for they had scored on a wild pitch.

The teams moved to Chicago for the third, fourth, and fifth games at the home stadium of the Sox, Comiskey Park. For Gleason and Comiskey, it was a gloomy trip. By now, the manager was certain that some of his men were throwing the Series, but like Comiskey he realized there was no practical move he could make at the moment.

Then, on October 3, "Wee Dickie" Kerr shut out

the Reds, three to nothing. Gleason and Comiskey felt better. Perhaps the bribery talk was so much nonsense, and the Sox were at last finding themselves. Yet, in Chicago hotel lobbies there was talk of a double cross between the gamblers and the players involved, of a double-double cross; and talk that all was well between the conspiring parties, that the third game had been won in order to bring the betting odds into a more reasonable alignment.

It was Cicotte's turn to pitch the fourth game, and if Gleason hesitated to start him, the manager's doubts were allayed when Shineball made an earnest appeal for the starting assignment. Perhaps this reflected a change of heart—if indeed there had been dirty work. Perhaps the men involved were now determined to play to win.

The Sox were shut out in that fourth game, two

Cicotte was at his best, while Felsch and Joe Jackson led a batting attack which placed the Sox on the long end of a four to one score.

The Series now stood at four games to three, and the teams returned to Chicago for what the White Sox adherents hoped would be the final *two* games. The American League team needed both to win the Series. But in the eighth game, played on October 9, the Reds jumped on Lefty Williams for four runs in the first inning, and went on to a ten to five victory —and the world championship.

Although Charles Comiskey was deeply suspicious of his team's integrity, he could not make any invidious public admission without proof. Pressed for comment on the still-persisting fix rumors, he was quoted as being "sure of the fidelity of the players. I believe my boys fought the battle of the recent World Series

White Sox owner Charles A. Comiskey initiated an investigation of his own players.

National League president John A. Heydler at first discounted Comiskey's worries.

Ban Johnson, president of the American League, prompted several witnesses to testify.

As a result of the scandal, Kenesaw Mountain Landis was made baseball commissioner.

to nothing. The Cincinnati runs were largely made possible by two glaring fielding errors committed by Cicotte in the fifth inning. Regarded in the best light, these errors were singular examples of maladroitness by an experienced pitcher; at worst, they were highly suspicious. In any case, the Reds were now ahead in the Series, three games to one.

The fifth game, scheduled for Sunday, October 5, was postponed until the next day because of rain; when it was over the Reds had won again and the world championship seemed virtually clinched. The Sox had been shut out again, in a contest marked by the ragged fielding of Felsch and Risberg, and a disastrous four-run sixth inning. Lefty Williams, Chicago's starting pitcher, had lost again.

Back in Cincinnati for the next two games, the White Sox electrified the sports world by taking both. In the first, Wee Dickie Kerr pitched skillfully for ten innings for a five to four victory; in the second,

on the level as they have always done, and I would be the first to want information to the contrary." In the same breath, he offered $20,000 for evidence of any thrown games, and soon after, he visited Maclay Hoyne, state's attorney for Cook County. He told Hoyne he believed he had been "jobbed" in the Series, asked for help, and expressed willingness to foot the investigative bill.

Two months later, on December 10, Comiskey admitted to reporters that an inquiry was in progress. No evidence had been found, but he vowed that "if we land the goods on any of my players, I will see that there is no place in organized baseball for them."

By this time, Comiskey had heard a great deal more than he admitted publicly. Yet what he knew was still based largely on tip and rumor. He believed the Series had been thrown, and thought he knew the players involved. There were eight suspects: Cicotte, Williams, Gandil, Risberg, Felsch, Jackson, Weaver, and

Fred McMullin, a utility infielder. Detectives had reported to Comiskey a remark Cicotte allegedly had made to a relative who commiserated with him after the Series. "Don't worry," Cicotte had said, "I got mine." And, too, there was the wire Gandil reportedly sent to his wife before the Series began. "I have bet my shoes," it read. After the Series was over, Gandil seemed to be spending freely, and it was argued that if he had bet his shoes on his own team, he would have been in no position to throw his money around. Sketchy as this evidence appeared, Comiskey felt justified in holding up the World Series checks of the suspected players, each of whom had more than $3,000 coming to him. But on the advice of his lawyers, and after much pressure from the players, he finally released the payments.

The identity of the gamblers involved was even more uncertain; and in a sense it still is. No one able to speak with complete authority has ever publicly named all the persons, aside from the players, who manipulated the fix, or has explained the complexities of their interrelationships. Perhaps this authoritative voice does not exist, and never did, for there is reason to believe that some of the dozen or so gamblers whose names hover over the scandal were not even aware of the involvement of others. The higher echelons of the fraternity kept quiet; what we do know of the elaborate maneuvers and brisk footwork that went on (and the information, so far as it goes, is probably accurate enough) has come from the lesser ranks of those concerned.

In the early stages of Comiskey's investigation, specific emphasis fell on certain personalities. The most notorious was Arnold Rothstein, the gambler and manipulator whose name is synonymous with the shady aspects of the twenties. Equally as suspect was Abe Attell, the onetime featherweight boxing champion of the world. Then there was a former big-league pitcher, William "Sleepy" Burns, who had played for the White Sox and the Cincinnati Reds before going on to more lucrative endeavors in the Texas oil fields. Allied with Burns was one William Maharg, a Philadelphian who, like Attell, was an ex-prizefighter. Supposedly, these were the principal gamblers in the World Series fix; but others—in Boston, Des Moines, St. Louis, and elsewhere—were mentioned as accomplices.

Early in the new year, 1920, Comiskey sent out season contracts to his players, including—in spite of his doubts—the eight suspects. In the bargaining that ensued, Gandil's demands were too high for Comiskey, and the first baseman retired from big-league baseball; but after some maneuvering, the others signed.

The White Sox of 1920 were virtually the same team that had won the pennant the year before; and as the season drew to a close in September, they were in a hot race for the flag with the Cleveland Indians. Quite suddenly the scandal was exposed—in a curiously indirect manner.

All that summer, there had been disquieting speculation about the integrity of baseball; early in September, it centered on a game played on August 31 between the Chicago Cubs and the Philadelphia Phillies of the National League. Before the game there had been rumors that it would be thrown by the Cubs, and in a countermove, the Cub management decided not to start the pitcher previously announced. Instead, the great Grover Cleveland Alexander was named to pitch, and he was offered a bonus of $500 if he won. Nevertheless, the Cubs lost.

The fix rumors eventually came to the attention of Charles A. McDonald, Chief Justice of the Criminal Court of Cook County. McDonald wondered what action, if any, should be taken, and conferred with Ban Johnson. Johnson advised that a grand jury look into the matter, and McDonald followed his suggestion.

The jury opened its hearings on September 7; for two weeks a parade of witnesses marched through its chambers. These included ballplayers, owners, managers, officials of both leagues, and sports writers. Speculation about their testimony grew intense, especially when it became known that the 1919 Series had replaced the Cub-Phillies game as the focal point of the inquiry.

On September 22, Assistant State's Attorney Hartley Replogle asserted bluntly that the 1919 World Series had been fixed and that the grand jury had heard the testimony implicating eight of the White Sox. The eight, whom he named, were those on Comiskey's list.

Comiskey acknowledged that he had been suspicious of the Series, that he had spent $20,000 in investigating it, and had been unable to prove a thing. For that matter, he declared, he was *still* without proof. But if he received any, he swore to "ruin the evil-doers."

Meanwhile, in Philadelphia, Billy Maharg, the friend of Sleepy Bill Burns, had decided to talk. He told his story to Jimmy Isaminger, a sports writer for the Philadelphia *North American,* and what Isaminger wrote became a national sensation.

Maharg declared that in September, 1919, he had received a wire from Burns, inviting him to go hunting at the latter's New Mexico ranch. To make further arrangements, Maharg met Burns at the Hotel Ansonia in New York. There it developed that Burns had gambling, not hunting, on his mind. He introduced Maharg to Eddie Cicotte and Chick Gandil, who were in town with the White Sox to play the Yankees. The two players indicated that they could "deliver" the Series—for a price. The price was $100,000, to be paid in installments of $20,000 before each game and split among the eight players involved.

After this meeting, Burns asked Maharg if he knew of any gamblers who would underwrite the proposition. Maharg said he would go to Philadelphia and try to interest some men he knew there. His Philadelphia contacts refused the proposal, but suggested that Rothstein was the man to see. Back in New York, Maharg and Burns met with Rothstein, who declined the deal. According to Maharg, "Rothstein said he did not think such a frame-up could be possible."

Maharg returned to Philadelphia, just before the World Series was scheduled to start, and there he received a wire from Burns that "Arnold R. has gone through with everything. Got eight [players] in, leaving for Cinn." The next day, Maharg went to Cincinnati, where he met Burns, who told him he had run into Abe Attell in New York and that Attell had persuaded Rothstein to finance the deal.

On the morning of the first Series game, Maharg and Burns visited Attell at the Hotel Sinton, and asked him for the $100,000 to parcel out among the eight players. Attell told them he needed all the cash he could muster for betting; he proposed instead that the players be given $20,000 *after* each losing game. Burns talked to the players, who agreed to it.

The following morning, Maharg and Burns again called on Attell in his room; they were impressed by the great stacks of currency in evidence. Once again Attell demurred at paying off the players. Maharg and Burns were now suspicious, and pointedly questioned Attell as to whether Rothstein was actually backing him. As proof, Attell flashed a telegram which

A newspaper cartoon of 1920 commented on Comiskey's suspension of the players involved in the World Series fix.

read: "Abe Attell, Sinton Hotel, Cinn. Have wired you twenty grand and waived identification. A. R." Later, said Maharg, he became convinced the wire was spurious, and that Rothstein had not been involved.

At the moment, however, Burns was angry because there was no money for the players. He told Maharg that he would turn over to them $110,000 worth of oil leases. Maharg dissuaded Burns "and thereby saved him that money."

After the second game—and the second Sox loss—Maharg and Burns saw Attell and demanded the players' payoff. Attell stalled, but finally handed over $10,000. Burns gave this to one of the players (whom Maharg did not name), and afterward told Maharg that the eight White Sox were restless and might not go through with their agreement. On the other hand, Burns did not believe they would try to win for Dickie Kerr, the third-game pitcher, who was not in on the plot, and who had been referred to by those who were as a "busher." Consequently, Maharg and Burns bet their roll, including their winnings from the first two games, on the third—and lost everything when Kerr shut out the Reds.

For all its sensationalism and aura of authenticity, Maharg's story must be regarded as the account of one who was only a peripheral participant in what *The New York Times* characterized as "one of the most amazing and tangled tales of graft and bribery and interlocking 'double-crossing.'" Bill Burns and certain of the eight players were to affirm that Maharg's story was, in general, accurate; but others in the plot offered emendations and additions which suggested that his knowledge was limited.

A somewhat different story, for instance, was told by Chick Gandil in the magazine *Sports Illustrated* almost forty years later. Although it conflicts with Maharg's account, Gandil's version is probably just as accurate—and just as limited in its perspective.

According to Gandil, the 1919 White Sox were ripe for trouble. The players quarreled among themselves, and the one common bond among them seemed to be their dislike for Comiskey, who paid his pennant-winning team the lowest salaries in the league. "I would like to blame the trouble we got into on Comiskey's cheapness," Gandil commented, "but my conscience won't let me."

Gandil claimed that the plot originated in Boston, in September, 1919, when he and Cicotte were approached by a gambler named "Sport" Sullivan, who suggested that they get together seven or eight players to throw the Series. The pair consulted with the others, and the group decided to accept the offer—cash in advance. Sullivan, however, explained that it was difficult to raise so much money quickly, and made arrangements to meet the players again in Chicago.

Not long after, Cicotte introduced Gandil to Sleepy Bill Burns. Burns had heard of Sullivan's offer, and asked for a chance to interest a gambler in Montreal, who might make a better one. At a meeting, the players decided to consider Burns's terms.

A few days later, Sullivan and a friend from New York joined the players at the Hotel Warner in Chicago. The friend was introduced as "Mr. Ryan," but, said Gandil, "having met this man two years before in New York, I recognized him as Arnold Rothstein."

Rothstein's plan was to *win* the first game, in order to raise the odds on the White Sox; then the players could lose the Series as they wished. When it came to paying the players the promised $80,000, Rothstein demurred; he finally handed over ten $1,000 bills, with a promise to pay the rest in installments. "When the gamblers left," Gandil recalled, "we entrusted the money to Cicotte until it could be changed inconspicuously. He put the bills under his pillow." Gandil claimed that he never received a cent of the money.

By the time of the first game, talk of a fix was so prevalent that the players were reluctant to go through with it. According to Gandil their intention was to double-cross Rothstein by keeping his money and playing to win; in effect, this is what they did. But it was a demoralized White Sox team which took the field against their National League opponents—and the Reds played much better than anyone expected.

After the third game, which the White Sox won, Gandil received a visit from Burns, who was panicky. "He and some other gamblers, going on the assumption that the Series was fixed, had bet heavily on the Reds. Now they had their doubts." Burns offered Gandil $20,000 personally if he could guarantee that the Sox would lose the Series; but Gandil turned him down.

At any rate, it was Maharg's story that broke the Black Sox scandal. In Chicago, its publication set off a limited chain reaction. On the morning of September 28, 1920, the pressure became too much for Eddie Cicotte. Troubled by his conscience, he went to Comiskey's house to say that he wished to get something off his chest. The Old Roman told him that the proper place for any confession was the grand jury room, and that morning Cicotte appeared there, to testify that Maharg's story was substantially correct and that he was one of the ring. Later in the day, Shoeless Joe Jackson and Lefty Williams visited the grand jury chambers to add their *mea culpas*. Before the day was over, the grand jury had indicted the seven players still on the team, together with the now-retired Gandil, for "conspiracy to commit an illegal act." The crime carried with it a penalty of from one to five years in jail and/or a maximum fine of $10,000.

Comiskey at once suspended the tainted players, and in so doing ruined any chance of wresting the pennant from the Indians, who at the moment were leading the league by only one game, with three left to play. Yet outwardly he maintained his composure. "Thank God it did happen," he declared. "Forty-four years of baseball endeavor have convinced me more than ever that it is a wonderful game and a game worth keeping clean."

The stories told by Cicotte, Jackson, and Williams to the grand jury, as reported in the press, were the first embellishments of Maharg's account. Cicotte, for example, said:

The eight of us got together in my room three or four days before the [first] game started. Gandil was the master of ceremonies. We talked about "throwing" the Series. Decided we could get away with it. We agreed to do it.

I was thinking of the wife and kids and how I needed the money. I told them I had to have the cash in advance. I didn't want any checks. I didn't want any promise, as I wanted the money in bills. I wanted it before I pitched a ball.

The day before I went to Cincinnati, I put it up to them

The Chicago Daily Tribune.
THE WORLD'S GREATEST NEWSPAPER

THURSDAY, OCTOBER 2, 1919.   ★ 21

WHITE SOX LOSE IN OPENER, 9 TO 1

ALL CINCINNATI HAILS RUETHER | MORAN'S "BIG GUNS" WHO CRIPPLED CICOTTE, ACE OF THE SOX HURLING CORPS
"Dutch" Ruether Not Only Stilled the Hose Artillery but Let Loose Two Triples, Which with Hits by Daubert, Rath and Neale—Yes and a Few Others Wrecked Kid Gleason's Forces. | REDS DRIVE CICOTTE TO DUGOUT; RUETHER HOLDS FOE HELPLESS

WORLD SERIES SCORE | Five Run Assault in Fourth Inning Cinches Game.

2 CENTS PAY NO MORE

THE WORLD'S GREATEST NEWSPAPER

FINAL EDITION

VOLUME LXXIX.—NO. 234. C. WEDNESDAY, SEPTEMBER 29, 1920.—32 PAGES. **** PRICE TWO CENTS

TWO SOX CONFESS; EIGHT INDICTED; INQUIRY GOES ON

GRAND AND MANDATES

Eight Fired

"WE THREW WORLD SERIES." CICOTTE, JACKSON, ADMIT

squarely for the last time, that there would be nothing doing unless I had the money.

That night, I found the money under my pillow. There was ten thousand dollars. I counted it. I don't know who put it there, but it was there. It was my price. I had sold out "Commy"; I had sold out the other boys; sold them for ten thousand dollars to pay off a mortgage on a farm. . . .

After receiving the money, according to a statement later made by Burns, Cicotte vowed to lose the first game if he had "to throw the baseball clean out of the Cincinnati park."

Williams asserted that he and Jackson had been promised $20,000 each, but received only $5,000. According to Williams, Gandil had approached him at the Hotel Ansonia in New York with the fix proposition. Later, in Chicago, he met with Cicotte, Gandil, Weaver, Felsch, and two gamblers, Joseph Sullivan of Boston and Rachael Brown of New York. Williams said the group bargained over price. At the end of the *fourth* game, Gandil handed him $10,000 and said: "Five for you, five for Jackson. The rest has been called off." After that, nothing further was said.

One other player made momentary public acknowledgment of complicity. This was Happy Felsch, who told reporters the day after the indictments were handed down that he had received $5,000 for his part in the plot.

On September 29, *The New York Times* reported that when Shoeless Joe Jackson left the grand jury room the previous day, "a crowd of small boys gathered round their idol and asked: 'It isn't true, is it, Joe?' Shoeless Joe replied: 'Yes, boys, I'm afraid it is.'" Other newspapers and two wire services reported the same basic story, and the only question that remains is one of grammar. The version that has passed into popular mythology cannot be documented, but perhaps it is reasonable to assume that small boys are not overly sensitive to niceties of phraseology; perhaps the words actually were: "Say it ain't so, Joe!"

At this point Arnold Rothstein was subpoenaed by the Chicago grand jury. Protesting that he had long ago renounced gambling for an honest career in the real-estate business, Rothstein nevertheless took the precaution of hiring one of the slickest trial lawyers of the day, William J. Fallon. Rothstein emerged "exonerated completely from complicity in the conspiracy." In fact, the jury even acknowledged that his testimony had strengthened the case against some of those already indicted.

Although Rothstein was cleared, other gamblers were not. Before the case ultimately came to trial, in the summer of 1921, Attell, Burns, Sullivan, Brown, Hal Chase (a former Giant player who had been fired by John McGraw in 1918 for "shady playing"), and others had been indicted.

Meanwhile, organized baseball had taken a step that was greatly to affect the destinies of the indicted players. At the time the Black Sox scandal broke, baseball's top authority was vested in a three-man committee; but the club owners felt that a single executive with wide powers would better serve the game. On November 12, 1920, they appointed Federal Judge Kenesaw Mountain Landis as baseball's first commissioner. His first important act occurred on March 12, 1921, when he banned the eight guilty players from organized baseball by placing them on the ineligible list.

On June 27, 1921, the long-delayed trial finally got under way, with seven of the eight Black Sox present. Fred McMullin, who was not there, was said to be hurrying to Chicago from the West. Other notable absentees were Abe Attell (whose lawyer had wangled his freedom on a *habeas corpus* writ), Hal Chase, Joseph Sullivan, and Rachael Brown.

The proceedings attracted feverish interest on the part of the public. The courtroom was jammed daily to its capacity of five hundred, including many small boys, and special guards were needed to hold back those who could not be accommodated. Most of the

217

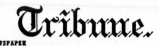

JURY FREES BASEBALL MEN

Trace Spurgin Mexico; Near **ALL BLACK SOX ACQUITTED ON SINGLE BALLOT**

spectators sweltered in their shirtsleeves, and collars were conspicuously absent.

A hard fight was expected, since it was no secret that Jackson, Cicotte, and Williams had repudiated their confessions; the admissibility of these statements as evidence would be briskly debated. At the same time, there was an air of near-joviality. The "clean" White Sox players, who were called into court by the defense, talked easily and with humor to their former teammates. And Joe Jackson, much impressed by the zealous infighting of the battery of defense attorneys, brought a laugh when he remarked: "Those are certainly smart men, and that lawyer of mine is one lawyerin' bird. They better not get him riled up." But always, the vocabulary of baseball prevailed. One exchange, involving the confessions, went as follows:

Michael Ahern, a defense attorney: "You won't get to first base with those confessions."

George E. Gorman, assistant state's attorney: "We'll make a home run with them."

Ahern: "You may make a long hit, but you'll be thrown out at the plate."

After the selection of a jury, which took over two weeks, the prosecution presented its case—which rested mainly on the testimony of Sleepy Bill Burns. The presence of Burns as a witness was due, it was said, to the persistence of Ban Johnson, who had tracked him to Mexico and persuaded him to testify. A representative of the state's attorney had met Burns at the border town of Del Rio, Texas, and there, "in the middle of the night," had discussed the implications of his giving evidence. One implication, of course, was that Burns would be spared prosecution.

His testimony was quite consistent with Maharg's earlier story; he insisted that the only money the players received was the $10,000 which he had conveyed to them from Attell before the third game. And on one point Burns was emphatic: the players, and not the gamblers, had conceived the idea of throwing the Series.

A sensational loss was revealed on July 22, following Burns's testimony, when it became known that the

waivers of immunity signed by Cicotte, Jackson, and Williams, as well as the original transcripts of their statements, had disappeared. Ban Johnson immediately came forward to charge that Arnold Rothstein had paid $10,000 to have the confessions stolen soon after they had been obtained and, after satisfying himself that he was not implicated, had turned them over to a newspaperman. What ultimately happened to the confessions and the waivers remains one of the unsolved mysteries of the case.

The trial ended on August 2, after the prosecutor, asking for conviction, had asserted that "the crime strikes at the heart of every red-blooded citizen and every kid who plays on a sand lot." The defense of course, called for acquittal.

The jury deliberated for two hours and forty-seven minutes, and then came in with a verdict of "Not Guilty." The outcome was not surprising, in view of the judge's charge that for conviction "the law required proof of intent of the players not merely to throw baseball games, but to defraud the public and others."

The verdict was greeted in the courtroom with a wild demonstration of approval. The spectators cheered, and the judge congratulated the jury, whose members responded by carrying the vindicated players from the courtroom on their shoulders.

To Buck Weaver and Happy Felsch, the acquittal may have seemed unnecessary, for before the case went to the jury, the judge had announced that, on the basis of the evidence, he would not let a verdict against them stand. Chick Gandil seasoned *his* joy with a dash of gloating. He said: "I guess that will learn Ban Johnson that he can't frame an honest bunch of players."

The press and organized baseball were hardly as jubilant. The Associated Press reported that the news was received with "surprise, disappointment and chagrin" by sports editors and writers. The outcome of the trial was a "travesty" as "stunning and disturbing as the original disclosures." The New York *World* asserted that "if the crooks who were acquitted try to show their faces in decent sporting circles, they should be boycotted and blackballed."

As a matter of fact, Commissioner Landis had precisely that in mind. On the day after the verdict, the eight were suspended for life. Landis stated:

Regardless of the verdict of juries, no player that undertakes or promises to throw a ball game; no player that sits in a conference with a bunch of crooked players and gamblers where the ways and means of throwing games are planned and discussed and does not promptly tell his club about it, will ever play professional baseball.

From that day on, organized baseball never retreated from this position.

It is no exaggeration to say that every one of the Black Sox bitterly regretted his role in the scandal. Although they had been held legally guiltless, they were nevertheless cut off from their livelihood—a livelihood that, at best, could offer relatively few working years. For a while, some of the Black Sox played exhibition baseball, but they found the public indifferent and their existence harassed by the hostility of the game's rulers. Ball parks were closed to them, and other obstacles appeared in their path. Gradually, most of them turned to other fields.

In the years immediately following the scandal, several of them tried to obtain through the courts what they considered equitable redress. None succeeded. Perhaps the most persistent protester of his own innocence was Buck Weaver, who, while admitting that he knew of the plot, was adamant in asserting that he had had no part in it. From time to time he addressed appeals to Landis. They were never answered. From time to time, too, baseball fans signed petitions for the reinstatement of various of the players—particularly Jackson—but none was ever effective.

It is doubtful if the ultimate truth will ever be known. Some of those concerned—like Rothstein, Jackson, McMullin, Weaver, and Williams—are dead, and those who survive are at the mercy of their memories and their pride. Chick Gandil's comment on his banishment may perhaps serve as a last word. "I felt it was unjust," he said, "but I truthfully never resented it because, even though the series wasn't thrown, we were guilty of a serious offense, and we knew it."

FRAUDERE EST VIVERE

DON JOSE NEMECIO GOMEZ DE SILVA
Grandfather of First Baron

DOÑA FRANCISCA ANA MARIA
Countess of Cordoba
Mother of First Baron

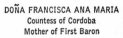

DON JOSE GASTON GOMEZ DE SILVA
Father of First Baron

DOÑA SOFIA ANA MARIA SANCHEZ
First Baroness

QUAESE MUSCAM IN UNGUENTO

DON JOSE ANTONIO SANCHEZ
Father of First Baroness

Age 30 years

Age
3½ years

Age 35 years

DON MIGUEL NEMECIO GOMEZ DE SILVA
DE PERALTA Y GARCIA DE LA CORDOBA
First Baron of Arizona

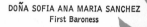

Age 70 years

DOÑA PETRA
ANTONIO GARCIA
Mother of First
Baroness

Age
100 years

DOÑA ANA LAURA ESCO
Mother of Second Baron

DOÑA JUANA
LAURA YBARRA
Second Baroness

DON MIGUEL DE PERALTA DE
LA CORDOBA Y SANCHEZ
Second Baron of Arizona

DON JOSE JUAN YBARR
Father of Second Barones

PERALTA AD ASPERA

NEMO INSIDIAS DETEXIT

DOÑA SOFIA LORETO MICAELA MASO
Y PERALTA DE LA CORDOBA
Third Baroness of Arizona

JAMES ADDISON PERALTA-REAVIS
Husband of Third Baroness

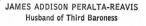

JOHN A. TREADWAY
Important relation of the Third Baroness

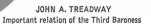

THE PRINCE
OF SWINDLERS

James Addison Reavis got rich—for a time, anyway—

on his Peralta land fraud. But in the end he went to jail.

By JOHN MYERS MYERS

The power of the imagination to triumph over the world of practicality has so far found its chief American exemplar not in any creative artist, philosophical visionary, or religious zealot but in a gold brick salesman. His name was James Addison Reavis. He lent the full range of his talents to only one undertaking, but in so doing he accomplished what neither Indian tribes nor foreign nations were ever able to achieve. For twelve years he held the upper hand in a struggle with the United States over a major slice of its continental territory.

The man who became architect of this gaudy and complex crime had an otherwise undistinguished history. Born in Henry County, Missouri, on August 20, 1841, he was brought up on a farm. Following service in the Confederate Army during the Civil War, he drove a streetcar in the days when such vehicles had whiffletrees. Like another famous Missourian, he peddled haberdashery. After a brief look at South America, he drifted into the real-estate business in St. Louis, still a shark waiting for its pilot fish.

These are the elegant Peraltas, claimants to 16,875 square miles of Arizona, as the family tree can be reconstructed from portraits produced by Reavis. He did not show the generation between the Second Baron and his grandchild, Sofia, since he outlived his twin children and the "title" passed direct. Nor did Reavis plan to appear wearing stripes.

It was not until 1871 that Dr. George M. Willing, Jr., entered his office. Willing, a Californian, was only a minor swindler; but he was to Reavis what the hack who wrote the original play about Hamlet was to Shakespeare. Dr. Willing's pet racket, when he was ready to talk, turned out to be Spanish land-grant claims. Under certain conditions these were recognized by United States courts, and there were just enough valid ones to make the fakes plausible.

With these facts as an initial point Willing had mapped out a monstrous land grant. The locus of this hornswoggler's mirage was in sketchily charted Arizona. Out of it the doctor planned to claim an area thirty leagues wide and ten leagues deep, something larger than the sovereign state of Delaware. This grant was supposed to have been given to a Spanish nobleman named Don Miguel de Peralta, whose last lineal descendant had passed it on to Willing.

Now, except that it was located in central Arizona, the grant wasn't nailed down. What the doctor had in mind was then called a "floater," a claim whose indefinite boundaries made it valuable as a legal nuisance, though not for much else. By moving a floater in where settlers had taken land, a con man could count on finding some who would get nervous about the validity of their own titles and would pay off.

Reavis was interested, but he wanted to see the general site of the claim before he committed himself. He took that look in 1876, and while he was making the

221

survey inspiration paid him its first tentative visit.

What he envisioned was the possibility of having the doctor's huge floater established as an actual land grant, to have and to hold. According to his own subsequent statement, though, he did not confide as much to Willing, nor the fact that he planned sole possession for himself.

Meanwhile Dr. Willing had gone to Prescott, the territorial capital, to file a claim on the property. Its basis was a deed which purported to show that he had been given the land by a certain Miguel Peralta of San Diego, heir of the original grantee, in 1864. It had been foreseen that the claim would be contested, however, and that was where James Addison Reavis came in. He was scheduled to show up later and be retained by Willing as an expert on the intricacies of real-estate law.

What Dr. Willing, at least, had not foreseen was that he would die in Prescott before Reavis got there. While it is obvious that two con men could not profitably pass as possessors of the same imaginary grant, this fatality is one of the mysteries of the case. Death was supposedly due to poison, but no one was charged with giving it. The most that can be said with assurance is that it happened because it had to happen. A petty craftsman was moved out of the way, leaving genius a free hand.

After a suitable interval Reavis also reached Prescott, where he represented himself as a correspondent of the old San Francisco *Alta Californian*. Having learned that a prominent California citizen had died in Arizona, the newspaper's editor had, Reavis announced, commissioned him to investigate the circumstances.

What he wanted and what he got was a piece of Willing's luggage. In it was a deed to the grant, made over to a third party whose name had been left blank. This had been the cautious doctor's way of leaving himself a quick out in case a storm arose.

Having pocketed this document, Reavis then set about determining what it would entitle him to claim. What he staked out was an empire of a magnitude which even the eloquence of a seasoned real-estate barker could not exaggerate.

After a late start, central Arizona was booming, once irrigation had proved that the Salt and Gila river valleys were fantastically fertile. The towns of Phoenix, Tempe, and Florence had sprung up, and many more were inevitable. The mighty bonanza of the Silver King mine had been discovered, to name only one of many glory holes. Some of the finest cattle country in the world was there, and the beef would be on it as soon as growing railroads could run their tracks across the territory.

Not wishing to leave out anything of value, Reavis had to stretch the claim. The grant to Don Miguel de Peralta, given him by the king of Spain in 1748, allowed him 300 square leagues, but the league was a measurement which varied in different countries and at different periods. Reading the dead king of Spain's mind, Reavis decided that what His Majesty had intended was a league of five miles. For a claim about the size of Delaware he thus substituted one which was nearly the size of New Jersey.

He placed his western border a little east of the junction of the Gila and the Salt. Running 49½ miles from north to south, it bracketed the richest section of both valleys, which were encompassed by lines stretching east for 149½ miles. They included millions of acres Reavis counted on making his own by a right of tenure, which would enable him to deal with the United States in the capacity of a sovereign power. For backing he could point to a provision of the Treaty of Guadalupe Hidalgo, later echoed by the Gadsden Purchase agreement, which pledged Uncle Sam to honor all land grants made while the territory which Mexico was turning over to the United States was under Mexican or Spanish dominion.

The American diplomats who had conceded such a point had done so with the thought that only a few square miles, scattered here and there, would be involved. They had not envisaged the generosity of the king of Spain, as conceived by Dr. Willing and enlarged by Reavis; but the principle would hold good if the validity of the title could be established.

Once that had been done, cities would have to pay James Addison Reavis for the right to continue on location. The pioneers who had fought the Indians and the wilderness in the course of developing their ranches would not be freeholders but tenants. The mining companies engaged in gouging gold and silver from the area would have to pay or go out of business.

As Reavis once admitted, the possible stakes were so enormous as to stagger even his imperial imagination. He readily saw that in order to have his claim honored he must know as much about land grants and all that pertained to them as the combined experts whom the United States would pit against him. He had to be an authority on international law. He had to be thoroughly at home in the Spanish of the Eighteenth Century. He had to have a flawless knowledge of Spanish legal jargon and to know the ins and outs of Spanish colonial procedure. He had to inform himself as to just how Spanish and Mexican records were preserved.

In 1881 and again in 1883 he was in Guadalajara,

Mexico, seeing to it that the proper documents in the case of the Peralta land grant did exist. What is more, he obtained statements from Mexican notaries vouching for the fact that papers in his possession were accurate copies of state papers which they themselves had seen, filed just where Reavis said they were.

First, of course, it had been necessary for him to identify the man whom a monarch had rewarded with an estate in Arizona, to show why the king of Spain had delighted to honor him and to trace the steps by which the grant had finally come into the hands of an American physician. The first tentative version demonstrating this sequence of fortunate events was a relatively simple matter.

In 1742 Don Miguel de Peralta de la Cordoba, a native of that city and a captain of dragoons, was sent to Mexico on a confidential mission by King Philip V. Skulduggery was afoot in this distant province, and the King was not receiving his proper slice of the revenues. Looking around for complete loyalty, unfailing courage, and a closed mouth, all in one package, Philip picked out Don Miguel. In spite of the hazards confronting him, the latter finally succeeded in straightening out the revenue tangle; and Ferdinand VI made him a grandee of Spain with the title of Baron of the Colorados.

That was in 1748, and somewhat later in the same year Ferdinand told the vice-regent of New Spain that he ought to fix the new grandee up with a piece of property to be baron of. Another man might have had Don Miguel in Arizona by Christmas, but Reavis had observed the deliberation with which vice-regents of New Spain moved, even when carrying out a royal order. The Baron was therefore handed 300 square leagues or 19,200,000,000 square varas of Pimeria Alta in 1757, with authority from the government of New Spain to occupy it as of January of the following year.

Although his main estate was in Arizona, Don Miguel preferred to live nearer to civilization. He had property in Hermosillo, Sonora, and he eventually married a lady of that city. For nineteen years there was no fruit of this union, but when the Baron was in his seventies Don Miguel de Peralta de la Cordoba y Sanchez was born. It was this Second Baron, finding himself without an heir in his old age, who had deeded his Arizona estate over to his friend and physician, Dr. Willing.

So far so good; but there was then the problem of how the grant passed from the hands of Willing to those of Reavis. As far as the deed was concerned, it was simple, for the space left blank by the doctor had long been adorned with James Addison Reavis' name. To make this post-mortem transfer credible was not so easy, however.

Reavis' solution was to find a man called Florin Masol, a former business associate of Willing's, whom he endowed with power of attorney for the doctor. Exercising his prerogative, Masol had turned the deed over to Reavis a couple of years before Willing died.

Commencing to press his claim on that basis, Reavis decided for himself that there was a hole in it big enough for the Peralta grant to drop through. This was his inability to give a satisfactory reason why the property of a married man should have been left to a friend instead of the deceased's relict. Reavis therefore looked up the woman whose widowhood had been his first necessity and obtained from her a bill of sale for the property, one of the few genuine documents in the case.

By that time he had spent seven years in study and the forging of testimony; but now at last he felt ready to take on the so far unsuspecting United States government. In 1883, following his second trip to Mexico, he filed his claim in the office of the surveyor-general of Arizona Territory. Significant of his confidence was the name he had adopted, which was James Addison Peralta-Reavis.

Manifest Destiny never received such a setback. The entire program of settlement in central Arizona faced destruction through a wholesale revoking of land grants to the region's pioneers. As Reavis himself stated the case, the United States could not dispose of territory to which it had no legal title.

Hired publicity men as well as newspapers spread the tidings among the anguished settlers of the Salt and Gila river valleys. The title to the great Peralta grant was ironclad, and it included all mineral and water rights. Ferdinand VI of Spain had been a foresighted fellow, and he had specifically mentioned them when awarding the grant to the Baron of the Colorados.

There were roars of protest from the pioneers, but they received little comfort from any direction. Local representatives of the federal government reported that, although naturally the matter of title would be thoroughly investigated, the claim had every appearance of being valid.

It was then that Reavis began to harvest where he had so patiently and dexterously sowed. Many were anxious to have the status of their property settled right away and came forward with offers to buy, lease, or pay for operational franchises. Reavis skimmed off $50,000 worth of cream in one easy motion when he charged the Southern Pacific that much for having run tracks across his property.

After that the panic was on in earnest. The railroad companies of the period were better known as rapacious predators than as easy marks. Many reasoned that if a railroad could be induced to pay off there

223

was no use in trying to fight the case. Some promptly abandoned their houses, barns, irrigation ditches and cultivated fields. Others who had previously held out called on agents of the new owner to see what they would have to pay in order to be permitted to stay where they were. Mine operating companies did the same thing, the Silver King alone handing over $25,000 as an initial payment.

How Reavis had financed himself in the beginning is not clear. As his knowledge and confidence increased, however, he had begun to test his claims to title by submitting them to prominent West Coast attorneys. When these opined that his legal position was very sound, he had started to prosper. Next to wealth in the pocket the rich admire the promise of wealth, and big business soon put funds at the disposal of a man who looked as though he would soon be able to reciprocate handsomely.

One effect of this bounty was that—a year or so before he filed his claim—Reavis found it possible to take over the guardianship of a pretty half-breed girl called Sophia Treadway. An orphan, she did not know the nature of her ancestry until Reavis broke the news to her. Although she had been reared as a house servant, she was really the great-granddaughter of that Spanish grandee, Don Miguel de Peralta de la Cordoba.

This was Reavis' deepest game, and it took some years for it to mature. For one thing, the waif had to be given an education and schooling in the social graces suitable to the lineal descendant of a baron.

That was still being attended to when Reavis finally pressed his claim and learned the joys of baronial estate at first hand. Money was rolling in, and he was a glad exponent of the theory that cash should be kept in circulation.

The headquarters of his domain was Hacienda Peralta at Arizola, a now vanished town near Casa Grande, but he was seldom there. In part this was due to prudence, for he knew enough about pioneers to realize that many would make no bones about shooting him. In the main, however, he eschewed Arizona because it was on the frontier, and his tastes were all for the opulence which only centers of civilization afford.

In proof of his own opulence he leased a mansion near New York, another in San Francisco, and a third in St. Louis, where he had once been a streetcar jockey. In these he entertained the wealthy and politically influential; and wherever he went the same ingredients of society gave him a 21-gun salute.

Yet while he was enjoying himself, he never forgot that his duel with the federal government was still going on. After many months of trying, the United States

had not found a way to save its threatened territory, but Reavis knew that its representatives had not given up. Day after day dogged employees of the State Department were looking for an excuse to thwart him. Like a chess master who plays dozens of opponents, he had to ponder the possible moves of each, so that he could outmaneuver them.

What he had long realized, for instance, was that the weakest link in the chain of his claims to title was none other than the originator of the basic scheme, Dr. Willing. The king of Spain had given land to a loyal subject, whose legitimate heirs could own it without doing violence to the ratifying clause in the Treaty of Guadalupe Hidalgo; but the transfer of the property to a California physician was something which might well be disallowed on a point of order. Reavis had had to use Willing at first, for the doctor had formed the only explanation as to how the Peralta grant could have wound up as his own. What he now felt ready to do was to keep the land without switching the chain of title away from old Don Miguel's descendants.

It was then that he introduced Doña Sofia Loreto Micaela Maso y Peralta de la Cordoba, his pretty ward, to eastern society.

New York's Four Hundred were delighted to have such aristocracy in their midst, though they did not have much time to enjoy it. Doña Sofia's guardian was anxious to carry her off to the land where her ancestors had flourished for countless generations.

In Spain, where she was presented at court by right of being a daughter of a noble house, Doña Sofia was also feted. Meanwhile her studious guardian haunted repositories of old records in Madrid and Seville. He also studied Spanish genealogy, finding much to interest him.

Thus enjoying themselves in their separate ways, they spent a couple of winters, but in July of 1887 they presented themselves before Edward H. Strobel, secretary of the United States Legation at Madrid. To him Reavis showed a contract of marriage between himself and his ward which dated back to 1882. Actually Reavis had just prepared it, but the secretary of the legation formally recognized it as binding.

The girl clearly accepted the situation because she found James Addison Reavis himself the most wonderful thing in the world he had created for her. As for her husband, he had his own motives for wedding. To his claim of having acquired the Peralta grant by purchase he could now add ownership through having married the woman who was rightfully entitled to inherit the land. Upon his return to America he filed this supporting claim, together with documents giving the history of Doña Sofia.

What had happened was that in the course of seeking to justify Dr. Willing's claims to title he had discovered that the second Miguel de Peralta had sired children, contrary to his original belief. There had been twins, of which the son had died in infancy. The other child, Doña Sofia Laura Micaela Silva de Peralta de la Cordoba de Sanchez de Ybarra de Escobeda had survived, however, to marry a wealthy Spanish gentleman named Maso, among a great many other things, and bore him twins, of whom the boy also perished in infancy. The girl, born on March 4, 1862, was now the wife of James Addison Peralta-Reavis. She was also the Third Baroness, the sole rightful owner of the Peralta grant, of which actual possession had been denied her through a chain of adverse circumstances.

The birth of this heiress had taken place on an estate called the Bandina Ranch near San Bernardino while her family was en route from Sonora to San Francisco. The mother died shortly afterward, and the child was an orphan before she could talk. Both her father (Maso) and her grandfather, who was Don Miguel the younger, left for Spain within the year, and there death separately overtook them. The baby girl and her grandmother, Doña Carmelita, of the house of Maso, had been left meanwhile at the home of a man called Alfred E. Sherwood. The death of Doña Carmelita eventually left the child without a natural guardian. She had thus been raised in ignorance of her due position until Reavis had run across a record of her birth and succeeded in locating her.

As usual Reavis was able to produce evidence in support of his statements. There were parish records of both the birth and baptism, and anybody who wanted to could go to a certain church and read of these matters himself. Reavis also had affidavits from people who had been associated with the Peralta and Maso families while they were in the States.

For four years Reavis had enjoyed the financial and social emoluments derived from his unshaken claim to the Peralta grant, previous to filling in his wife's name in 1887. Having staggered government officials with that blow, he went unchallenged for three years more. Meanwhile he had developed a fine new racket. In three states and territories he organized Peralta grant development companies, selling stock in them which was eagerly bought.

Finally, in 1890, the United States made its first countermove. Royal A. Johnson, surveyor-general of Arizona Territory, responded to the pleas of desperate settlers by publishing *An Adverse Report on the Alleged Peralta Grant*.

In it, Johnson noted that Reavis had shifted his ground, throwing up a new smoke screen when the old one had seemed in danger of being penetrated. The original documents which Reavis had exhibited were not as old as they purported to be, either. A newspaper editor had pointed out that the type on one allegedly ancient state paper had not been invented in the Eighteenth Century, while the stock had a watermark indicating it had been made in Minnesota. Adding these and a few other facts together, the surveyor-general pronounced the claim a fraudulent one.

A lesser thief would have taken that report as a cue to run for cover, but for James Addison Reavis crisis created the finest hour. He responded to Johnson's charges by suing the United States for $10,000,000. The grounds for this test case were that the federal government had wrongfully given to others property which belonged to his wife.

The United States had to gird itself to meet this new attack, and its operatives were far from confident. On the other hand, Reavis was; nor had he lost the confidence of the influential men with whom he now regularly consorted. Numbered among them were some of the best legal and financial minds in the nation, including that of one of this country's most famous skeptics.

Colonel Robert Ingersoll, able as a lawyer as well as an iconoclast, looked over what Reavis had to offer and pronounced his case airtight. John W. Mackay, launcher of the Postal Telegraph Company, was another who so believed, while Charles Crocker, one of the founders of the Southern Pacific, had died in that faith a couple of years earlier. Henry M. Porter, of the American Bank Note Company, was in Reavis' camp, and so was Edward S. Stokes, who had killed Jim Fisk over Josie Mansfield. It was said that Roscoe Conkling was on the Peralta team, while W. E. D. Stokes and other Wall Street wolves certainly were.

They had no choice but to believe, once Reavis had revealed to them the full fruits of his studies in Spain. The documents he had found there, and of which he had copies notarized as being true to the existing originals, not only supported the proofs he had found in the old colonial archives in Mexico but went far beyond them.

To begin with the original grantee, his full name was Don Miguel Nemecio Gomez de Silva de Peralta y Garcia de la Cordoba. Genealogical tables clearly traced his lineage back to men distinguished for mighty deeds as well as noble blood. The honors bestowed on Don Miguel were also revealed in full, for in documents signed by three different kings he had been cited as an aide-de-camp and ensign of the royal house, a gentleman of the king's chamber, and a knight of the orders of the Golden Fleece and Our Lady of Montesa, not to mention his membership in the Royal Order of Carlos III and the equally regal College of Our Lady of Guadalupe. Royal documents showed now that, although Don Miguel had been referred to as the Baron of the Colorados in Mexican documents, this was a mistake. What King Ferdinand had conferred, when making him a grandee, was the honorary title of the Caballero de los Colorados; but after he came into possession of his estate he was the Baron of Arizona, sometimes called Arizonaca.

One other thing, and that of the first importance, was also made clear by this new array of evidence. When the barony of Arizona had been given to Don Miguel its included total of so many square leagues and varas of land had been particularly specified as "ancient" leagues and varas, which were half again as big as those which Reavis had first mistakenly used in his computations. The dimensions of the barony were not a mere 49½ by 149½ miles; the correct measurements were 75 miles deep by 225 wide. To use easily locatable map points, it stretched from the Four Peaks to Picacho Pass, and from just east of the confluence of the Gila and the Salt to just west of Silver City, New Mexico. As for its area, instead of being about that of New Jersey, it was roughly that of New Jersey and New Hampshire combined.

Reavis thoroughly understood that a lie gains face if it is backed by another lie. Don Miguel had asked two successors of the original royal donor to confirm his title to the barony, thus furnishing an excuse for more substantiating documents. Reavis carried out this theory with respect to the two wills which he forged.

The First Baron of Arizona had lived to the unusual age of 116, giving him ample time to leave a codicil which repeated his original intention of leaving the barony to his son. The latter also attached a codicil to his will, just before he died in Madrid. In this he reiterated that the infant Doña Sofia was to get every square vara of the baronial estate.

With the area of threatened territory more than doubled, the defensive energy of the United States increased in proportion. Correspondence with Spain and Mexico had served only to confirm the seriousness of the situation. Every copy which Reavis exhibited found recognition in a duly filed original. In desperation the State Department dispatched a trio of special agents to study this material at first hand. William H. Tipton and Severo Mallet-Prevost were hustled off to Madrid, while Levi A. Hughes was entrusted with studying the Mexican records.

Reavis, in the meantime, was making the government collect testimony in his own favor in the Court of Private Land Claims, Chief Justice Joseph R. Reed presiding. Beginning in San Francisco in October of 1890, he had produced numerous witnesses who supported every statement he had made relative to the birth of Doña Sofia, the departure of the Second Baron of Arizona for Spain, and his speedy death there.

As these and other witnesses, examined in May of 1893, had been very well paid, it is not surprising that they vouched for statements previously made by Reavis. What is remarkable, however, is that they made such good witnesses. Or rather it would have been astonishing if they had been coached by anybody else. Only a master swindler could have schooled them to hit the right note between remembering distant events too carefully and not being uncertain about the principal points at issue.

Finally Reavis pulled a skillful bilingual act; in Mexico he had all the royal decrees pertaining to the Peralta grant printed in Spanish, complete with all the notarized statements swearing to their authenticity, later published in San Francisco under the name of *Muniments of Title*.

During that same year of 1893 the suit to collect $10,000,000 from the United States of America was formally pressed in the Court of Private Land Claims, this time in Santa Fe. By then Reavis had been seigneur of his barony for ten years, and far from gaining anything in the long struggle against him, the federal government had lost ground, both figuratively and literally.

Reavis expected to go on winning, wherefore he pressed plans for developing his property on a heroic scale. It is interesting to note, incidentally, that he was miles ahead of the government in this respect too. For example, he had planned to provide power as well as irrigation water by damming the Tonto Basin. The Roosevelt Dam, which serves both of these purposes, was not started until 1906.

But while building his empire up with one hand, Reavis was using the other to bombard the government with his unending series of proofs, of which the two most ingenious had not so far been noticed. Having exhausted the resources of law, history, genealogy, and international diplomacy, he turned to the arts. He produced ancient Spanish poems which recited the glories of the Peraltas and the allied house of Garcia. Moving from poetry to painting, he published reproductions of portraits, showing how several generations of the Peralta clan had looked to various Spanish painters.

It was the special agents of the State Department,

operating in Spain and Mexico, who at last proved a match for Reavis. They found the ancient documents in the ancient volumes in the ancient repositories, but, not content with that, they subjected them to minute scrutiny and a careful comparison with similar Eighteenth-Century papers. They furthermore enlisted the aid of government officials of the other two nations, as well as specialists in the fields of Hispanic history, law, and language of the period in question.

Reavis had wrought wonderfully, but his manifold forgeries could not all stand up against all the tests to which they were subjected. First a few discrepancies were observed, and these showed where to look for

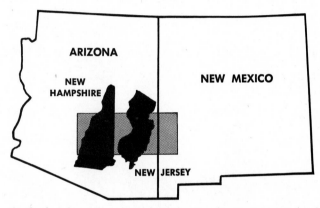

At the height of Reavis' vision, the Peralta Grant contained nearly 17,000 square miles of the best land in the Southwest —the size of New Jersey and New Hampshire combined.

others. With a few foundation stones pulled out from under, the whole marvelous edifice collapsed.

Actually what took the collaborating representatives of three governments so long was that they could not believe that Reavis had had no help whatever from fact. They could not believe that all the documents were absolute fiction as well as daring forgeries. They could not believe that old Don Miguel, complete with his genealogy, descendants, and vast Arizona estate, *had never lived at all,* and that the grandees and their ladies in the portraits were sheer invention. Only after many months of studying the pooled information at their disposal were the special agents able to comprehend that for more than a decade the United States had been waging a losing war with a man whose only weapons were his brains and effrontery.

William H. Tipton undertook to present the find-

ings of himself and his associates in 1895. The occasion was the $10,000,000 damage suit which Reavis was then pressing, with every prospect of success, in the Court of Special Land Claims in Santa Fe. Tipton's testimony made it plain at last that the claims made by Reavis had never had the slightest connection with actuality at any time. The test case which Reavis had come so near winning was thus lost, and so was his empire.

The long reign of America's peerless peer (1883-1895) ended with the adverse verdict of the Court of Private Land Claims, with the piper yet to be paid. Having at last regained control of the territory included in the Peralta grant, the government wanted blood as well.

It wasn't easy to get. Tried for conspiracy, Reavis handled his own case; and in spite of all that the government's representatives had on him, he made the prosecution sweat to win a conviction. What federal counsel found especially difficult to break down was the skein of court testimony which had established the birth and family ties of Doña Sofia.

That poor woman, who had borne Reavis twin sons, was eventually proved to be the posthumous daughter of a squaw man named John A. Treadway. Officially deposed as Third Baroness of Arizona by the court decision which convicted Reavis in 1896, she eventually got a divorce from the man who had ennobled her, on the grounds of nonsupport.

To do him justice, Reavis was in no position to support anybody from July 18, 1896, to April 18, 1898, as he spent that much of his six-year sentence in jail. Light as his punishment was, however, he emerged from it as fallen grandeur without the power to rise again. During the score of years which remained to him he tried other promotional schemes; but the strength of his genius had apparently been exhausted on his one master scheme, for he was never again successful.

Meanwhile all that remained of the barony of Arizona was the crumbling brick hacienda in the dying town of Arizola and the sore hearts of Reavis' grand army of dupes. Time has by now taken care of their sufferings, leaving the prince of hornswogglers a solitary monument. This is a rock at the western end of the Maricopa Mountains, which was used as the initial point of survey for the Peralta land grant. Before the wrath of defrauded pioneers played havoc with it, there was a map scratched on this rock which plainly showed the territory with which the king of Spain rewarded the unswerving devotion to duty of the nonexistent Don Miguel Nemecio Gomez de Silva de Peralta y Garcia de la Cordoba, Knight of the Colorados and First Baron of Arizona.

In the entire history of the turf there has probably never been anything remotely resembling the 1891 spring and fall horse-racing seasons at the old Gravesend track at Sheepshead Bay in Brooklyn, New York. The extraordinary events that attended the meetings resulted from an economic squeeze play on the part of the Brooklyn Jockey Club, which operated Gravesend. Then, as now, off-track betting was illegal in New York state, but then, as now, it was a popular form of gambling. To keep local betting parlors aware of all the pertinent racing data—post odds, scratches, jockey selections, weights, and results—the Poolsellers Association, a syndicate of Manhattan bookmakers, telegraphed the information direct from the various tracks to the "poolrooms"; for this privilege, the association paid the management of each track $1,000 a day. When in the spring of 1891 the Brooklyn Jockey Club suddenly decided to quadruple the rate, the bookies refused to pay. Somehow they would bootleg the information out of the track; the Jockey Club could go hang.

Thus began a spectacular running battle between Pinkerton's Race Track Police, representing the Jockey Club, and members of New York's remarkably picturesque Gay Nineties underworld, allies of the poolsellers' syndicate. The gamblers were also supported by the Western Union Telegraph Company, which, counting the bookmakers'

association a valued patron, threw into the fray several dozen highly imaginative telegraphers.

The ensuing trackside scrimmages went on for weeks, and became so lively and exhilarating that the racing seemed dull by comparison. Indeed, the sports editors of New York's newspapers became so preoccupied detailing Gravesend's warlike side show that a racing fan was often hard put to find on the sports pages the simple facts about which horse had won each race. Each day at the track Pinkerton men, some in uniform, others in plain clothes, guarded the gates, locking them once the crowd was inside. But this was a little like latching the hen-house door after the fox had slipped through. For undetected in the crowd, dis-

The bookies had to get racing data from paddock to betting parlor. All at once some very shady characters began showing up at the entrance to the track

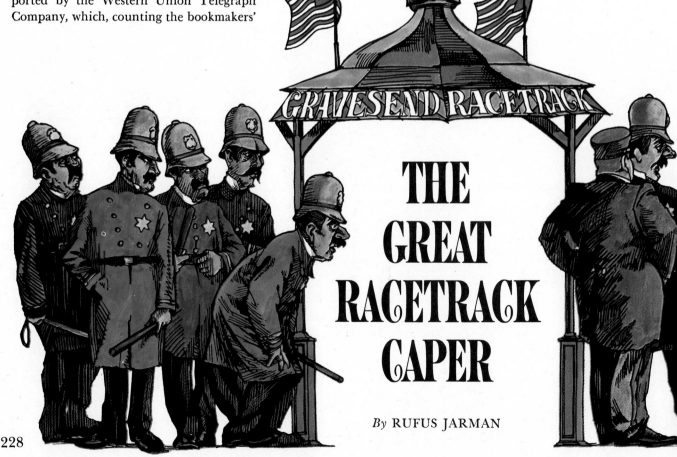

GRAVESEND RACETRACK

THE GREAT RACETRACK CAPER

By RUFUS JARMAN

228

guised as pregnant women, ladies of fashion, gentle-men, or country bumpkins, were a number of gamblers, thieves, dips, touts, and ladies of the evening, allied with the bookmakers and loaded down with all manner of exotic signalling equipment.

As post times neared, they wigwagged semaphores and flags, waved umbrellas, walking canes, and hand-kerchiefs—one woman even waved a baby—to convey racing data to confederates outside the fences; these in turn passed the information on to telegraphers, who relayed it to the poolrooms in Manhattan, several miles away. Shoplifters brought carrier pigeons into the grounds, concealed in the secret pockets of their professional costumes; released with racing data tied to their legs, the birds took wing and headed for the betting emporiums. But beyond the fences, under the birds' line of flight, marksmen lurked. The Pinkerton detectives were resourceful, too: they captured some of the pigeons inside the park, loaded the birds with incorrect results, and released them. Soon passionate cries of anguish were heard in the betting houses as operators realized they had been paying off the wrong people, sometimes on horses that had run last.

Out at the track, meanwhile, clubbings, fights, and assorted strife swirled about the beleaguered gates. Frequently the crowd was treated to the stirring spectacle of a squad of sweating Pinkertons in full uniform flashing past the grandstand in pursuit of a fleeing poolroom suspect. All this added zest to the sport of kings; the Gravesend track was something like a castle under siege, with the Marx Brothers in the roles of invaders and the Keystone Kops manning the ramparts.

The conflict stemmed indirectly from the Ives Law, passed in 1877, which restricted legal betting in New York state to racetracks. Naturally, the law made betting with bookies more popular. In 1877 Manhattan had only four or five poolrooms, which operated behind barricaded doors equipped with peepholes. By 1891, however, about sixty betting joints were running wide open. A few of them were pretentious and elegant, with mahogany furniture, gilt mirrors, and thick rugs. But most were big, barnlike places with dirty walls, cracked ceilings, and dusty windows. They ran three to the block in the Bowery as adjuncts to saloons, with dollar bets accounting for the bulk of business. All were packed with bettors six hours a day.

So popular had the poolrooms become, in fact, that the crowds at the tracks declined sharply; by 1891, the daily fee the tracks collected from the Pool-sellers Association did not make up for the loss in attendance.

The Brooklyn Jockey Club was controlled by Philip J. Dwyer and his brother, Michael, former butchers who had become interested in swift horses when they operated "the fastest meat delivery wagons in New York." Now they owned a celebrated stable of race horses. Phil Dwyer, the club's president, had a droopy mustache and a greater interest in money than in sport. Operating a racetrack in the red made no sense to him, and so, shortly before Gravesend opened its

ILLUSTRATED FOR AMERICAN HERITAGE BY GERRY GERSTEN

1891 spring season, he met with poolroom representatives and upped the daily fee to $4,000. The syndicate would not go higher than $1,600.

"The Poolroom King," Peter De Lacy, a top gambler who dressed like a banker, said he considered all betting evil, but if people were going to gamble, it was no worse to do it in poolrooms than at racetracks. "If Phil Dwyer bars Western Union's operators from the track, as he threatens to do," De Lacy told the press, "we'll send in messengers to bring out news of each race. But I don't take any stock in Dwyer's bluff. We defy the Dwyers."

Dwyer was not bluffing. As the spring meeting began, he disconnected all telegraph wires out of Gravesend except one that served the newspapers.

Western Union then rented the old Sleight's Hotel just outside Gravesend's entrance and strung in lines. Once a well-known inn, Sleight's was now a rickety, three-story shell with an old-fashioned cupola overlooking Gravesend's starting post and home stretch. With what they could see from this vantage point, supplemented by the reports of De Lacy's messengers shuttling in and out of the gates, Western Union telegraphers managed to meet their clients' needs with few delays.

The Jockey Club president countered by transforming the track into a fortress garrisoned by 130 private policemen under the personal command of Robert A. Pinkerton, who with his brother, "Big Bill," headed Pinkerton's National Detective Agency. Until now,

newspaper accounts had featured fleecy prose hailing Gravesend's racing as "spirited," "delightful," "splendid," "positively brilliant." Then, on the season's fifth day, the news from the track shifted dramatically from the sports pages to page one. "TRACK A PRISON," screamed the New York *World*. "THOUSANDS PENNED UP ON BROOKLYN RACE COURSE. PINKERTON SLUGGERS CLUB INOFFENSIVE CITIZENS."

The Pinkertons locked the gates, according to the *World*, after some eight thousand people had passed in "as guileless as the wide-mouthed shad which the Spring tides sweep into the fishermen's nets." The *World* and the *Herald* castigated the Jockey Club president as "King Philip, The First" and called the Pinkertons "hybrid policemen" and "chuckle-heads." Both newspapers recounted in horrendous detail the pitiful appeals of patrons to be let out of the track. "I must get to New York," one old gentleman shouted. "I have an important engagement."

"I don't care a damn about your engagement. Nobody can leave this track," said the guard. "Them's my orders."

The *Herald* quoted one "big fellow" who begged, "I am ill; I need a doctor. I've just had a hemorrhage." The Pinkertons were unmoved. A woman with a sick baby pleaded to get out, "but the guards were merciless."

Said an outraged Englishman to an American friend: "You call this a free country, do you? And yet I'm told when I come in here that I can't leave

until a certain hour. That's not liberty. It's tyranny. We wouldn't stand it on the other side." The *World* told of a Kentuckian who drew a big horse pistol and walked out grandly while "every Pinkerton in sight sought shelter." The newspaper added that "the hammering of Pinkerton clubs on other men's heads sounded like the popping of firecrackers on the Fourth of July."

The *New York Times* and the *Sun*, which were against gambling, called these charges "absurd." The persons most eager to leave the track, the *Times* said, "were almost without exception employees of the gambling syndicate or Western Union," which company "ought to be called to account for violating anti-gambling laws."

When the locked gates halted direct smuggling of information, the syndicate undertook fancier measures. Its telegraphers in the hotel cupola had a clear view of the paddock but not of the finish line, so operatives inside the gates performed as "horses": each one held a placard bearing a number corresponding to an entry in each race; after the official results were posted, they galloped across the paddock in the order in which the horses had finished. The watching telegraphers duly transmitted the results. The Pinkertons soon

began chasing the horses, who in their scramble to escape were not always able to flee in the proper sequence; transmitting correct results was a problem. Some poolroom agents now equipped themselves with hollow wooden balls; they stuffed these with papers on which were scribbled odds, jockeys, and results; then they flung the balls over the fences, hoping that associates outside would retrieve them. But the Pinkertons patrolled so vigilantly that few balls fell into the hands for which they were intended; some of them struck bystanders on the head, the *Times* reported, and at least one man was knocked insensible.

The track remained in a state of siege during the rest of the spring meeting. Fighting flared now and then at the gates. The Pinkertons roped off the paddock and continued to chase ball throwers. When the gamblers' telegraph lines suddenly went dead, the bookmakers claimed sabotage and offered a $5,000 reward for capture of the saboteur.

During that summer, while the track was idle, Dwyer had a sixty-five-foot-high wooden fence built, which completely blocked the view from the hotel's cupola. The fall meeting was due to open on September 15. A day or so before the opening, the *Herald*

reported a rumor that the syndicate would fly a balloon over Gravesend on each race day, with observers, operators, and a telegraph station in its basket. The poolsellers never actually used the balloon, but the strategy they did employ was perhaps even more spectacular.

At 3 A.M. on opening day, heavy wagons loaded with lumber, men, and tools rolled up to Sleight's Hotel. The lumber was carried to the hotel's cupola and the carpenters went to work. The *World* described their efforts:

No circus tent ever went up faster. Ten feet into the air, then a staircase and a landing. Ten feet higher, another staircase, another landing. Another ten feet, another staircase and landing. The carpenters paused for breath.

It was daylight now and the Dwyer forces rallied in a hurry. A group of carpenters set to work to raise the fence still higher. Ten feet more, and the huge structure began to tremble with the weight of the workers. A breeze blew in from the bay and the men's hats flew off. They climbed down, glad to be on earth again. They looked across at the Western Union tower.

"Give her another story," commanded the [tower] foreman. The carpenters hammered and knocked together another staircase and ten more feet of altitude. The tower was now forty-two feet above the cupola and its top platform seventy-seven feet from the ground.

Western Union installed four wires and a half dozen operators in the new tower, the *World* reported, and stationed a guard at the door. In the gamblers'

camp an air of triumph prevailed. Peter De Lacy walked about "with a quiet smile and remarked that he was content." He magnanimously handed a ten-dollar bill to some Gravesend employees and told them to "go blow it" on pie and milk. Racing Manager M. J. McKenna of Western Union "looked pleased," the *Sun* recounted, as did "Little Abe" Hummel of Howe & Hummel, lawyers for the Poolsellers Association. From Manhattan, reports were arriving that De Lacy's own poolroom was packed and that business was booming in all the betting places. Racing information was said to be coming in fine.

"The Brooklyn Jockey Club owns the racecourse," De Lacy declared, "and has the right to withhold its news if it can. But I don't think the effort will be a success. We need that information and we're bound to get it."

But Sleight's Hotel was so situated that, even from their tower, telegraphers could not see the track's finish line; in close races they had to guess the winners. Nor could they observe odds and scratches, which the management was now posting under the judge's stand. When Western Union offered twenty-five dollars to the first person to get the information for each race through to the hotel, racegoers having no connection with either the syndicate or the telegraph company began to fling rubber balls filled with racing data over the fences. But the patrolling Pinkertons foiled most of these efforts.

The detectives also increased their vigilance over those admitted to the track. One day they noticed a tall young man in a close-fitting gray coat behaving strangely near the betting ring. He would button and unbutton his coat, raise and lower his hat, hold his pink sporting sheet at various angles, mop his brow, and bow in different directions. Sure enough, he was signalling post odds to a man seated in a tree outside the grounds who was apparently cooling himself vigorously with a palm-leaf fan. Actually he too was signalling, in Morse code, to observers in the tower. At about that time, the *Sun* reported, a carrier pigeon fluttered out of the grandstand's second tier; catching sight of it, the crowd roared, "There it goes!" "There it goes!" Unfortunately, the message it bore had been insecurely fastened to its leg; as the bird circled overhead before streaking for its coop, the paper dropped into the paddock.

By the time the second day's racing began, telegraph lines had been strung from barns and trees, with sending stations on some flat-topped stumps. The syndicate was reportedly paying $100 a day to a farmer named Young for the use of his two big locust trees as observation posts.

That night the Jockey Club's carpenters increased

the height of the fence that stood in front of Farmer Young's trees. Next day the telegraphers climbed still higher, and the Gravesend carpenters appeared with more lumber. Lowering his binoculars, the man in the nearest tree shouted down to his telegrapher, "The horses are going to the post for the second race, and the Dwyers are building another fence!"

The *World* reported that one tree sitter received his signals from a baby, in the care of the "most innocent-looking woman in the grandstand."

The woman did not look like a regular, and certainly the baby didn't. It was a golden-haired, chubby little thing. When its mother—or alleged mother—secured the scratches and betting odds for the second race, she went down to within a few feet of the track, spread her shawl upon the ground and proceeded to amuse the baby.

While the little one kicked its heels in the air, filled its little mouth with tiny fingers and said "goo-goo" the young woman waved a green parasol up and down before its delighted eyes. It didn't make any difference to the baby that each motion of the parasol was a Morse Code dot or dash. And Mr. Dwyer and Mr. Pinkerton stood twenty feet away at the judge's stand and didn't suspect a thing. This little by-play was repeated after the second and third races. Then the new fence and a rainstorm broke up the combination.

Meanwhile, at one entrance the gatemen were challenging a woman. One grabbed at her clothes and a pigeon squawked. "Why," said a detective, "she's got enough pigeons on her to stock a good-sized loft. That dress has pockets all the way down. We know too much about shop-lifters to be fooled by a game like that."

Nevertheless, the poolsellers' lawyers estimated that fully a hundred pigeons were smuggled into the track that day. The Jockey Club reportedly hired "Snapper" Garrison, an unemployed jockey with a reputation as a champion pigeon shot.

Despite such efforts, signallers continued to infest the grounds. Red, white, blue, yellow, and green handkerchiefs fluttered from many points. The Pinkertons hustled a half dozen men out the gate for twirling their mustaches and walking sticks in a "suspicious" manner. One of them charged that he had been degraded when paraded in custody before the grandstand, and announced that he would sue.

The track management further confounded the poolroom forces by concealing the names of entries until twenty minutes before post time for each race. A printer named Eagan was employed to run the information off on slips of paper, using a portable press set up at the track. "The crowd lay in wait for the messengers who distributed the slips and rushed upon them with much scrambling," the *Herald* reported.

Gradually, it seemed, the cops were beating the robbers. Conditions at the betting places in Manhattan were dismal. Crowds melted, and the bettors who did come complained loudly of the poor service. At De Lacy's own place, the announcer said at 2:42 P.M., "They're at the post at Brooklyn." It was thirty-two minutes later when he got the word, "They're off at Brooklyn!" One place had the horses running in the stretch for two minutes. Some betting rooms posted signs, "Not Responsible For Errors In Weights And Jockeys." All this encouraged the antigambling *Times* to headline its lead story: "POOL MEN BEATEN AT LAST."

But the poolroom forces had a few tricks left. The next afternoon a pole was set up near Gravesend's lower turn, its top poking above the fence like the head of a great serpent. A telegrapher climbed on spikes to the crossarm near the top, took off his hat, and bowed solemnly in the direction of President Dwyer's box. Then he hauled up a telegraph key and fastened it to the pole. "In three minutes," the *Herald* reported, "he had a little telegraph office in operation, ninety feet in the air. He was a facetious little man as well as a bold one. No sooner was his shop in order than he pulled a national flag from his pocket and nailed it bravely to the top of the pole."

That night workmen planted another pole in a yard east of the track. It stood 120 feet high. When its telegrapher reached the top the following day, he was greeted by his colleague atop the shorter pole on the lower turn, who snatched his flag from the mast and waved it around his head.

At this point, the Pinkertons began to raise their own poles within the grounds. Each carried a great spread of canvas, like the mast of a sailing ship, which effectively blocked the views from the poles outside. Even so, the pole sitters returned to their perches on the days that followed, although the Pinkertons were certain they could see nothing of value. Pigeons had been cleared from the grounds, ball-throwing had ceased, and no signallers were in sight.

Still there was a leak somewhere. "By some mysterious means," said the *World*, "whether by necromancy, juggling or what, the 'pool rooms' yesterday seemed in their normal condition. Betting was in full swing on all the events at Brooklyn. Jockeys, with the exception of the first race, were listed. No one seemed to know how the information from Brooklyn had been obtained."

Robert Pinkerton and his men managed to unravel the mystery before the fall meeting ended. What they discovered was proclaimed in these *World* headlines: "ELECTRICITY IN THE HAT. THE MOST INGENIOUS SCHEME YET FOR OBTAINING RACING NEWS."

"Every afternoon," the *Herald* explained the next day, a "handsome barouche, drawn by a pair of spirited horses, whirled a party of ladies and gentlemen to the lawn just above the betting ring. The driver parked his vehicle at a spot near the track, and the party seemingly turned themselves to enjoying a holiday. They had lunch and wine and cigars in plenty and seemed bent on nothing but enjoying the sweets of life. . . ."

Had the Pinkertons scrutinized the barouche more carefully, they might have noticed that the coachman wore an unusually tall silk hat and that he kept his seat on the box while members of the party visited the betting ring or viewed the races. They returned to the carriage now and then, ostensibly to refresh themselves. This continued daily until five days before the season ended, when Pinkerton and his men raided the coach. The picnicking group was headed by Joseph W. Frost, an electrician and president of the Automatic Fire Alarm Company, 317 Broadway. He was accompanied by his wife, Eliza, and their ten-year-old son; Frost's brother, a onetime Indian agent and now manager of a Washington, D.C., hotel; a Mrs. C. A. LaVille; and the coachman, C. S. Pearsall, who, not entirely by coincidence, was a telegrapher.

It developed that Joseph Frost had arranged with the syndicate to supply complete racing information from Gravesend to Western Union for $1,000 a day, and he had succeeded in doing so for six days. Pearsall's tall coachman's hat had a hole in the center of its top the size of a half dollar. Inside the hat was a small electric light powered by batteries concealed in the coach. Under his clothing Pearsall wore a network of wires that connected the light with the batteries and with a telegraph key hidden on the coach floor.

Members of the party brought him information on odds, jockeys, and the like from the betting ring. The finishes Pearsall observed himself, simply by standing up in the carriage. He sent a running story by operating the key with his foot, causing the light in his hat to go on and off in Morse code. The telegraph operator in the hotel tower could not see the finish line or the posted odds, but he had a fine view of the top of the coachman's hat. Somehow or other the Pinkertons were tipped off, and suddenly one afternoon Robert Pinkerton himself leaped into the carriage and dragged Frost from it. During the struggle, Mrs. Frost screamed, "Turn that man loose!" and hit Pinkerton (he said later) on the head with her parasol. She claimed that Pinkerton had grabbed her by the throat and choked her. As the party was led away, Frost bellowed, "You'll suffer for this, as I have the Western Union Telegraph Company and ten million dollars at my back." The bookmakers left their stands and shouted in excitement. Bettors abandoned the ring and shouted encouragement to the Frosts. One man jumped over the fence, snatched off his coat, and, directing his ire at the Pinkertons, yelled, "Come on and hang 'em!" The crowd in the ring shouted, "Lynch 'em!" "Lynch 'em!"

Fortunately, nobody was lynched, and the carriage episode became the final act of "the Great Battle of Gravesend" as public spectacle. Thereafter, De Lacy and his cohorts resorted to more subtle strategems.

By instituting or backing a number of lawsuits during the decade following 1891, De Lacy secured several lower court decisions holding the Ives Law unconstitutional. Since that law had declared that the only place a man could get down a legal bet was at a racetrack, these findings had the effect, temporarily, of making *all* betting a crime in the state. Thus, in 1893, De Lacy secured the arrest of Phil Dwyer, by then a millionaire who controlled most of the racing in the metropolitan area, but the charges were dismissed in the higher courts. Meanwhile, track managements were bringing pressure on the police to close the poolrooms. De Lacy's own place was closed in 1893, but at the turn of the century the tenacious "Poolroom King" was still plaguing racetrack managements with arrests and lawsuits.

The man who came close to wrecking thoroughbred racing in New York state was not De Lacy, however, but the reform governor—and future presidential candidate, Secretary of State, and Chief Justice—Charles Evans Hughes. His administration outlawed all racetrack betting, and that closed every established track in the state after the end of the 1910 season. But racing interests got this law repealed in time to resume in 1913, and the sport of kings has thrived ever since.

Not, however, in Brooklyn: old Gravesend Racetrack, which closed with the others, failed to re-open in 1913. Brooklyn was changing from a center of sport to a "city of homes," and the land was later sold for real-estate development.

In the past few years, urged on mainly by New York City, which hopes for increased tax revenues, some members of the state legislature have made serious attempts to legalize off-track betting. They have not succeeded to date, but the idea refuses to die. It is possible that after all this time Peter De Lacy may eventually win his point.

Bubble, bubble— no toil, no trouble

By FRANCIS RUSSELL

The brisk little Italian immigrant promised you 100 per cent interest in ninety days. Some people actually got it

Seen from the high oval windows of Boston's City Hall on that sultry June morning in 1920, the line of stiff-brimmed straw hats bobbing along School Street resembled a roiled, wheat-colored stream. Among the straws were dark blotches of cloth caps, women's brighter hats, and even the official visors of the police. On the honky-tonk outskirts of Scollay Square the stream grew denser and contracted into the cleft of Pi Alley. Then it flooded left down City Hall Avenue past the blank, rusticated side of City Hall and left again beyond the pigeon-spattered statue of Mayor Josiah Quincy. The stream dissolved into a jabber of individuals who stormed up the dark stairway of Twenty-seven School Street, just below City Hall, to wedge themselves, seething and shoving, along the corridor and into the office of the Securities and Exchange Company.

For all its imposing name the Securities and Exchange Company consisted of one man, the dapper, dynamic five-foot three-inch Italian immigrant and financial wizard known as Charles Ponzi, who, it seemed in that Boston summer, had conjured up the secret of perpetual money. He had started the Securities and Exchange Company with a few hundred dollars borrowed from two discreetly silent partners, Louis Casullo and John Dondero. Lend me your cash, he promised in the prospectuses that he mailed out, and in forty-five days you will get it back with 50 per cent interest; in ninety days you will get it back doubled. And since the previous December, when fifteen investors lent him $870 and the following month happily drew out $1,218, he had been keeping his promise. In December Ponzi had paid only 40 per cent interest. By February he had raised the rate to 50 per cent for forty-five days, 100 per cent for ninety. Seventeen new investors paid him $5,290 that month. The good news spread, and in March, 110

Bostonians left $28,724 at the unpretentious office on School Street. April brought 471 hopefuls with $141,671. Four times that number paid almost a half million dollars in May, and during June, 7,824 persons trudged up the stairs to the Securities and Exchange Company to pay in $2.5 million in cash and receive forty-five- or ninety-day notes in return. In the latter part of the month Ponzi claimed to be receiving $500,000 and paying out $200,000 a day, and traffic in School Street had come to a standstill.

It was all very simple, the money wizard explained, merely a matter of knowing how to take advantage of the various and varying exchange rates in different parts of the world. He had conceived his scheme, so he said, when he received a business letter

Charles Ponzi in 1920, oozing confidence

from Spain enclosing a reply coupon —issued as a convenience by international postal agreement—which was exchangeable at any United States post office for a six-cent stamp. Ponzi was struck by the fact that the coupon in Spain had cost the buyer only the equivalent of one cent. As he told a Boston *Post* reporter interviewing him in his lush Lexington mansion at the height of his dollar-checkered career, "I looked the coupon over. I thought about its value on this side of the Atlantic and its value on the other side. I said to myself: 'If I can buy one of these stamps in Spain for one cent and cash it for six cents in the United States just because the rate of money exchange is higher here, why can't I buy hundreds, thousands, millions of these coupons? I'll make five cents on every one—of this particular kind—so why not?' Then . . . I investigated

the rate of exchange in many of the other foreign countries. My original theory, 'Why can't I make money this way?' grew more real. Then it became a fact."

Ponzi explained to the reporter that his operations were being conducted in nine unspecified foreign countries. His agents were bundling international reply coupons in massive quantities back and forth among these countries, although he had now stopped redeeming foreign coupons in the United States. The scheme might not, he admitted, be considered ethical, but it was positively legal. And the idea was foolproof. He said he had just set up thirty new branch offices throughout New England and was preparing to open an office in New York.

Each morning at eight o'clock his Japanese chauffeur brought him

from Lexington in a cream-colored Locomobile limousine to his School Street office. Each morning an ever larger crowd was waiting for the cocky little man with the bouncing step and elegant manner. Police cleared the way for his car. Men cheered him, and office girls blew him kisses. He smiled and bowed, tipped his hat, and sometimes on getting out of his car made a little speech. He exuded jauntiness, from his pointed shoes to his wide, pointed lapels, from the razor-sharp crease of his trousers and his sleeves to the pearl stickpin in his striped moiré tie. Nonchalantly he swung a gold-headed Malacca cane and smoked a Turkish cigarette in an ivory and gold holder. His manner and his manners never failed. "A born aristocrat," his young wife said of him. For his thirty-eight years and certainly for the hard rows he had al-

Patiently awaiting their turn to hand their life's savings over to Ponzi, investors line up outside his office in Boston in July, 1920.

READY TO BURST

THE
PONZI
GET RICH QUICK
BUBBLE

FEDERAL PROBERS

STATE PROBERS

Having investigated carefully, the Boston Post *cartooned Ponzi's imminent collapse.*
THE BOSTON *Post*

ready hoed in life, he looked amazingly fresh. There was no sign of a wrinkle on his high forehead. He had a wide mouth above a jaw of almost Mussolini set. His eyes were genial and sympathetic. His voice was soft and convincing, with just a trace of an Italian accent. Face and voice inspired trust and among some a permanent devotion.

Ponzi was born in Parma in 1882. His family was upper-class and his father a general in the Italian army (or so he said). As a boy he attended a boarding school founded by Napoleon's ex-empress, Marie Louise. When he was eighteen, he became a student at the University of Rome, but spent more time in cafés and at theatres and fashionable parties than in libraries and at lectures. In November, 1903, after three years of this gay nocturnal existence, his Roman uncle sent him to America with a one-way ticket and a thousand lire (then worth about two hundred dollars).

Having lost all but two and a half dollars to a cardsharp on the voyage over, Ponzi wandered from Boston to Pittsburgh, New York, Providence, Montreal, and various points in the South, passing fourteen years in such employments (when he was working at all) as dishwasher, waiter, clothes presser, shop clerk, and Italian interpreter. His English had become almost glib by the time he turned up in Massachusetts again in 1917.

In Boston he took a job typing and answering foreign mail for the J. R. Poole Company, merchant brokers, at sixteen dollars a week. On February 4, 1918, he married Rose Marie Guecco of Somerville, a second-generation Italian-American half his age, the daughter of one of the Guecco brothers, fruit dealers in Boston's Italian North End. He quit his job with Poole in September to go to work for his father-in-law. But in January of 1919 the fruit firm went bankrupt, with liabilities of eleven thousand dollars and assets of six thousand dollars. Ponzi tried to convince the Gueccos that if he could have the use of the six-thousand-dollar assets, with his knowledge of importing and exporting he could double the money and more than pay all their debts in a year. The dubious Gueccos refused. Ponzi at that time had a little upstairs back room in the School Street building of the Tremont Trust Company, where he liked to tuck himself away and scheme his schemes. There it was, in August, 1919, that he received his letter from Spain and evolved his Great Idea.

As the summer of 1920 wore on, the lines to School Street lengthened. The persistent and impatient crowd that blocked off School Street traffic all day long was made up of people from the city fringes—the Italian North End, the lodging-house South End, and the small suburbs. Periodically Ponzi distributed free coffee and doughnuts to them. Whenever he saw a pregnant woman or an elderly one in the hot sun, he would take her inside ahead of the others through a side door. Tucked visibly behind the twin-pointed handkerchief in his coat

pocket he carried a certified check for a million dollars. With that sum, he told people, he could live in all the comfort he wanted for the rest of his life. Anything he got above that million he intended to use to "do good in the world." The money now came into his office so fast that it filled all the desk drawers and spilled over into a dozen wastebaskets. Sixteen clerks, hired to do nothing but sort out the cash, tallied it and stacked it in closets until it reached the ceiling. When Police Commissioner Edwin U. Curtis sent three inspectors down to Twenty-seven School Street to investigate, Ponzi talked two of them into buying his notes. Others were investigating, too: the chief post-office inspector, state and federal attorneys, and Suffolk County's District Attorney Joseph C. Pelletier, who was later disbarred for his part in a blackmailing scandal. Ponzi welcomed them all, and none could see anything illegal in the Security and Exchange Company.

Ponzi now brought his mother,

COURTESY OF THE BOSTON *Globe*

Obviously a family man, Ponzi posed with his wife and mother at his mansion, 1920.

Imelda, over from Italy and provided her with a French maid. As his finances expanded he bought into the Hanover Trust Company, where he had first deposited his money, and became a director. As an ironic reminder of his clerical days he took over the J. R. Poole Company. He invited a group of New York financiers to the Copley Plaza at his expense and conferred with them about his newest plan to organize a $200-million corporation with a chain of "profit-sharing banks" in which depositors would share with stockholders in the net profits. His earnestness was convincing, contagious. A highly respected judge, Frank Leveroni of the Boston juvenile court, became his lawyer. With what would seem redundancy he hired a long-time Boston advertising man, William H. McMasters, as a publicity agent.

The bubble expanded, glittering, iridescent, irresistible now even to the covetous from State Street and Beacon Hill. Some plungers put down as much as $25,000, though most people bought a few hundred dollars' worth of Ponzi notes in return for handfuls of small bills. By the last week in July Ponzi was taking in several hundred thousand dollars a day. His name was in headlines in newspapers all over the country; he became something of a national hero. Newsreel cameramen flocked to his Lexington home and recorded him strolling across the lawn with his wife and his mother. There were armed guards at the mansion entrances and rumors of millions locked away in vaults in the cellar.

Although city, state, and federal officials in their overlapping investigations had turned up nothing against Ponzi, a less official but much more efficient investigation was being carried on in the editorial office of the Boston Post. Young Richard Grozier, the assistant editor and publisher, was convinced that Ponzi had never bought so much as a dime's worth of international reply coupons and that he was merely taking in money at one wicket to pay it out at the next. If nobody else was able to show Ponzi up, Grozier determined the Post would.

On Sunday, July 25, Grozier discussed Ponzi and his scheme with Clarence W. Barron, the Boston financier and publisher of the financial daily The Boston News Bureau (later Barron's Weekly). Barron admitted that it was theoretically possible to make money by manipulating international reply coupons, but said he was sure it would be impossible to turn over more than a few thousand dollars that way. To talk of running them up to Ponzi's ten million dollars was, Barron said, ridiculous. He added that it was odd for Ponzi to put his own funds into banks paying only around 5 per cent when he was offering 50 per cent to other people. Not even if Rockefeller made an offer like Ponzi's would anyone with any financial sense put his money into it. The wizard of School Street was, in Barron's opinion, just another goldbrick salesman.

Monday morning the Post headlined Barron's views on the front page. The result was a run on the Securities and Exchange Company. A line of a different temper and intent soon choked School Street, but Ponzi, jaunty and self-assured as ever, saw to it that everyone in the line who wanted his notes cashed got his money back. By afternoon he had turned the run into a stampede of new investors. Meanwhile, he calmly admitted that his story of the coupons was just a blind. Its purpose, he said, was to keep Wall Street speculators from catching on to his moneymaking methods, which were his secret. He told Grozier that no investigation could hurt him, that he had money enough to pay off his investors in full any time. In spite of Grozier's warning columns in the Post, Ponzi continued to prosper. Crowds welcomed him as he walked down Washington Street along Newspaper Row past the Post building. When someone shouted, "Three cheers for Ponzi,"

they were given with a roar; and as they died down he shouted back, to their laughter, "Three groans for the Post!" "Who's the greatest Italian that ever lived?" someone else called out to him. "Columbus," Ponzi called back, "because he discovered America." "But you discovered money!" came the reply, with many cheers. McMasters, the advertising man retained by Ponzi, told reporters that Ponzi was planning to give the city an Italian hospital and had already pledged $100,000 for an Italian orphanage. Ponzi himself said he was considering running for mayor or governor, not stressing the fact that he was still an alien.

Late Monday afternoon, July 26, 1920, District Attorney Pelletier announced that Ponzi had agreed to suspend accepting any more investment money until his books could be audited. The district attorney did not hint at any fraud and was careful to say that there was no charge against Ponzi; it was just that his operations had become so vast that an audit was in the public interest. Meanwhile Ponzi, unperturbed, continued to pay any notes that fell due and to

Temporarily out of jail in 1924, the little manipulator strolls with a big sheriff.
COURTESY OF THE BOSTON *Globe*

238

The most likely place for Ponzi in 1925 was Florida, where the great land boom was under way—and that's where he was.
U.P.I.

redeem later notes at face value.

By the time the deposits closed on Monday at Twenty-seven School Street, 30,195 persons had paid in $9,582,591 since December, 1919, for a promised return of $14,374,818. The average investor had put down $300. Some of those from the little streets, however, had turned in their life's savings. The confidence record seems to have gone to a Quincy woman who sold all her real estate and invested $33,000. Richard Engstrom, who had sold Ponzi his Lexington house, turned in $20,000. Judge Leveroni proved his faith, if not his acuity, by investing $5,400.

Even after the deposit wickets of the Securities and Exchange Company had been battened down, Ponzi was still a hero to the man in the street, the more so now because he seemed to have the bankers and the big people arrayed against him. He still continued to pay off any notes due, still drove into Boston daily in his Locomobile, as fresh and confident as ever.

One day, to relax, he went for a plane ride at the Lynnway Airport. It cost him thirty dollars for thirty minutes, and he gave the pilot a ten-dollar tip and said he planned to buy a plane of his own. However, he had by this time become something less than a hero to his publicity agent. A disillusioned McMasters went around the corner to Grozier to tell him that Ponzi was "as crooked as a winding staircase" and agreed to write the whole story for the *Post*. It appeared under McMasters' name in a special edition on the second of August. Ponzi was, according to McMasters, "hopelessly insolvent"; his debts were now between $2 million and $4.5 million.

McMasters' article started another and more persistent run on the Securities and Exchange Company offices. Again School Street was a bobbing mass of straw hats. Yet even now the little investor kept his faith in Ponzi, the man of the people, the one man who dared stand up to the big bankers and show he could beat them at their own game. Ponzi protested that if only the authorities would let him alone, he would pay 100 per cent interest in ninety days on all the money he had accepted. His supporters passed out handbills up and down School Street, defending their man and denouncing the "unscrupulous bankers" who were attacking him. Speculators edged up and down the lines of those waiting to get their money, offering to buy the notes on the spot at a discount. Ponzi followed, radiating reassurance, warning the impatient that anyone selling his notes then was giving up his certain profits. An employee of a Boston brokerage house declared that his firm had asked an Italian bank if Ponzi had credit, and the reply had come: "To any amount." That story spread and grew.

By passing out hundreds of thousands of dollars without a tremor Ponzi kept the crowd with him. He paid with checks on the Hanover Trust Company, to which he was now indebted for a quarter of a million. About the same time he acquired a personal poet laureate, one James Francis Morelli, a sometime vaudeville hoofer with a knack for making rhymes. Morelli had a desk at the Securities and Exchange Company and an alleged salary of three hundred dollars a week. One of his efforts advised:

> If they should ask you to sell
>   your notes,
> Step forward and exclaim:
> "No indeed, I'm sorry, lad,
> 'Cause my notes bear Ponzi's name."
> Just step in line, and wait
>   with ease,
> And avoid all sorts of commotion
> For Ponzi has as many dollars as
> There are ripples in the ocean.

Ponzi thumbed his nose at Grozier's office as he walked by on his way to the courthouse to bring a five-million-dollar libel suit against the *Post*. But the clouds were gathering. Early in August Massachusetts Bank Commissioner Joseph C. Allen closed down the Hanover Trust Company over the protest of the bank's officers. Ponzi supporters, undaunted, reviled the commissioner. In spite of the *Post* and McMasters and the commissioner, Ponzi was still the poor man's Midas, who could trounce the bankers at their own game.

Abruptly, predictably, and astonishingly—like John Law's Mississippi Scheme and the South Sea Bubble before it—the Ponzi bubble burst. Grozier, after receiving an anonymous tip that Ponzi had once been jailed in Quebec, sent a reporter, Herbert L. Baldwin, to Montreal. After two days of poking about in the Italian district and then checking his information at police headquarters Baldwin discovered that the Boston financier was none other than an ex-convict, Charles Bianchi, alias Ponsi, who in 1908 had been sentenced to twenty months in the St. Vincent de Paul Prison for forgery.

On August 11 the *Post* broke the

Looking older but little wiser, the fallen Midas takes center stage at his own deportation to Italy on October 7, 1934.

story in banner headlines. In 1908 Charles Ponsi had arrived in Montreal to organize a financial operation much like his later Boston scheme. With Joseph Zarrossi, the owner of a small cigar factory in a settlement of Italian immigrants, he had set up the banking office of Zarrossi & Company. Ponsi, as manager, announced that the company would pay depositors the highest rate of interest in the city. Immigrants flocked to the new bank with their savings. Ponsi paid the interest with the capital of the newest depositors. Zarrossi & Company also accepted remittances to be forwarded to Italy—money that somehow never arrived. When the police and the bank examiners finally closed in, Zarrossi decamped to Mexico. But Ponsi was so successful in placing the blame on his absent partner that he might have gone free if he had not lightheartedly borrowed a blank check from the Canadian Warehousing Company, traced the manager's signature on it, and filled it out to the plausible figure of $423.68. It was this minor feat of penmanship that sent him to St. Vincent de Paul.

The *Post*'s account of Charles Ponsi's Canadian career was flanked by a Montreal rogues'-gallery pho-

tograph of a mustached Ponsi and a photograph of Boston's Ponzi with a mustache painted on. The two looked almost identical. Before running the article Grozier sent two reporters to Lexington to show it to Ponzi, who laughed and said it was all false. The Montreal convict was somebody else, he assured the reporters. He himself had never been to Montreal, had never been arrested, and would bankrupt the *Post* with libel suits if any such story came out. Nevertheless Grozier, after a telephone talk with his reporter, who was still in Montreal, decided to go ahead and print.

Laggard city and state and federal officials now began to bestir themselves. Everyone, it seemed, wanted custody of Ponzi at once. He was arrested by a United States marshal on August 13 at his Lexington home. The house itself was impounded and searched in vain for hidden vaults and the bookcase shelves that, according to common talk, were stacked with Liberty Bonds. Before the examination of Ponzi's company books was finished, the School Street office had been shut down, but the auditor estimated there were liabilities of over seven million dollars and assets of less than four million. His estimate was optimistic. Few of the investors in the Securities and Exchange Company ever saw more than a fraction of their money again.

Ponzi's fall brought about one of the most tangled legal situations Massachusetts had ever known: criminal trials and civil trials; bankruptcy hearings; hearings before bank examiners; suits by Ponzi and suits against Ponzi. The Hanover Trust never again opened its doors; its president, Henry Chmielinski, a leader of Boston's Polish community and founder of the Polish *Daily Courier*, was ruined. Another bank that had lent Ponzi money, the Tremont Trust, collapsed later, as four other banks eventually did. More of Ponzi's past began to leak out. After he had served his time in Montreal, he had

gone to Georgia. It seemed that there, in 1910, he had been sentenced to two years in the federal penitentiary for smuggling alien Italians into the country.

Now, on November 30, 1920, Ponzi was indicted in Boston's federal court for using the mails to defraud. Massachusetts wanted to try him for larceny. At a retaining fee of $100,000 he engaged Daniel H. Coakley, one of the deftest and least scrupulous lawyers in Massachusetts (Coakley was disbarred a couple of years later as a result of the same scandal that brought down Joseph Pelletier).

In spite of the fee and in spite of a reputation for slipping his clients out of apparently impossible situations, Coakley advised this client to try to avoid further state prosecution by pleading guilty to the federal charge. Ponzi's face was livid and his voice high-pitched as he stood up in court to admit his guilt. Rose, among the spectators, fainted twice. Her husband was sentenced to five years in the Plymouth County Jail, used by the federal government because it had no jail of its own in Massachusetts. Ponzi became the most famous prisoner the old brick county jail had ever held. At times he seemed more a commuter than an inmate, travelling back and forth to Boston with the sheriff to attend innumerable bankruptcy proceedings, hearings of receivers, and various civil suits brought against him. For some months he was in the Massachusetts General Hospital, recuperating from a stomach operation. In the jail he was a model prisoner, spending his spare time studying law. For all Coakley's scheming, Ponzi while still at Plymouth was indicted by the Commonwealth of Massachusetts on twenty-two counts of conspiracy and larceny. During his long state trial he defended himself with considerable ability, maintaining that often persons who had the means took a chance because they heard of large profits. "But," he told the jury, "the promise of a profit is not larceny; it is merely a promise, and a promise may or may not be kept according to the circumstances." Acquitting him on four counts, the jury disagreed on the rest, making another trial necessary.

Of the fifteen million dollars that Ponzi had taken in, eight, at least, were never accounted for. When his assets were finally distributed, his noteholders received twelve cents on the dollar. Yet even while he was in jail, many of those he had bilked remained loyal to him, still believing that if the authorities and politicians had let him alone, he would have paid all the money he had promised.

Apparently Ponzi himself did not regard his Securities and Exchange Company wholly as a swindle. Carried away by euphoria as the wave of green bills surged over the counters, he had come to think that once he had accumulated sufficient capital to buy his way into the international financial world, he could make enough to pay off his investors. One of the silent

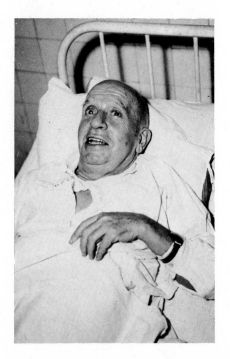

His last check cashed, a sick and tired Ponzi spent months as a charity patient in Rio de Janeiro before his death in 1949.

partners, Louis Casullo, had taken a prudent trip to Italy with over a million dollars, and the other, John Dondero, had disappeared with a trunkful of money. But Ponzi had stayed on to the end, confident that he could overcome any crisis, hypnotized by his own wizardry. Just before the debacle he was negotiating for a merger —or so he thought—with the Bank of America in California.

After three and a half years at Plymouth Ponzi was released on parole and at once rearrested by the Massachusetts authorities. He was tried again in February, 1925, convicted as a "common and notorious thief" (in the quaint phraseology of the Massachusetts statutes), and sentenced to seven to nine years in a state prison. Pending his appeal he was released on $14,000 bail. A month later he disappeared.

He turned up in Florida in the middle of the land bubble. Using the name Charpon—a partial anagram of his name—he organized the Charpon Land Syndicate and was soon selling underwater lots at ten dollars an acre, sight unseen, to buyers who in that hectic mid-twenties summer of pyramiding trades needed no more assurance than a blueprint. After this swamp went down the drain, Ponzi was indicted for fraud. The court in Jacksonville, Florida, found him guilty and sentenced him to a year. On June 3, 1926, he jumped his bail.

The trail led to Texas. Five days after he left Florida, he dodged the waiting authorities at Houston and shipped as a common seaman aboard an Italian freighter bound for Genoa. On June 28, 1926, when the freighter touched at New Orleans, a Houston deputy sheriff was waiting for him. Florida and Massachusetts both wanted him, but the Texas governor sent him back to Boston.

In February, 1927, he began his term for larceny at the Charlestown State Prison, across the river from Beacon Hill, where his compatriot, Bartolomeo Vanzetti, was undergo-

ing the final year of his imprisonment. While at Charlestown Ponzi continued to study law. He spent much of his time writing vain appeals to the governor for commutation of sentence in order to escape deportation. In 1934 his seven years' minimum was up, and as his behavior had been excellent, he was freed. Florida had forgotten about him.

Ponzi was now fifty-two years old. Charlestown prison had aged him. What was left of his hair was turning white. His face had sagged, and his dapper figure had grown pudgy, though he still carried himself in the grand manner. Rose was still waiting for him. Through all the years, even the Florida interlude, she had stood by him. Together they went to see the new governor, Joseph B. Ely, to plead against the deportation threat that was now beginning to loom large over Ponzi's head. While his wife worked as secretary for the owner of the Cocoanut Grove nightclub he spent his days in the law library of the Federal Building, trying to discover some legalism that would let him stay in the country. Meanwhile, he paid a visit to the city room of the *Post*. There he shook hands with the city editor, talked of old times with some nostalgia but no resentment, and then left. On the way out he walked past the Pulitzer Prize plaque the *Post* had won for exposing him.

There were no conjuring paragraphs to be found in the law library, and Governor Ely was as adamant as his predecessor had been. On October 7, 1934, the U.S. Immigration Service put Ponzi aboard the *Vulcania* in Boston Harbor for a single passage to Italy. He still had enough friends to give him a rousing sendoff from the dock. As he went up the gangplank, he raised his arm in the Fascist salute.

Back in Italy he became an English translator for a small export house in Rome. He revisited the cafés of his student days; his photograph, showing him at ease over an apéritif, appeared in the American press.

In his spare time he began writing his autobiography and apologia. Rose had expected that after he found work in Rome he would send for her, but he never did. After two years of waiting she at last lost patience and divorced him. She never remarried.

Shortly after Ponzi's divorce Mussolini offered him a job in Brazil with Italy's new airline. From 1939 to 1942 he served as branch manager in Rio de Janeiro. In 1942 he lost his job because, he claimed, of his protests against "wide departures from the organization's original, strictly honest commercial operations." A group of airline officials had, in fact, been smuggling currency. They had not included him in their group, and when he found out what they were doing, he tipped off the Brazilian government with the expectation of getting 25 per cent of the fines. Then as an afterthought he offered to come to America to tell the government what he knew about the operation.

The United States government did not want him. As the tide of war turned against Italy the airline closed down. No money came to Ponzi from any fines. For a while he tried unsuccessfully to run a lodging house in Rio de Janeiro. Through the war years he made a meager living giving English lessons while he drew a pittance from the Brazilian unemployment fund.

The year 1949 found him, semi-paralyzed and partly blind, in the charity ward of a Rio hospital. Flanked by an old man with a hacking cough and a quiet, senile black man who spent his days staring at the ceiling, he still tried to work on his autobiography. Somehow he had saved up seventy-five dollars, enough to keep his body from potter's field. He died in January, 1949, leaving behind him his unfinished manuscript, "The Fall of Mister Ponzi."

The Lawless West

When Guns Speak, Death Settles Dispute by Charles M. Russell

Nathan Meeker

Even when death struck suddenly,

the starry-eyed Indian agent was

still dreaming of turning his

Ute wards into white men overnight

Arvilla Delight Meeker

THE BLOODY END OF
MEEKER'S UTOPIA

By MARSHALL SPRAGUE

On September 29, 1879, a small band of Ute Indians went wild on the Western Slope of Colorado and murdered their Indian agent and all his employees at the remote Ute Agency on White River. A few hours earlier, another small Ute band ambushed a relief force of soldiers at Milk Creek 25 miles away. All told, the White River Utes, who had never hurt anybody before, killed 30 white men and wounded 44 more.

The murdered agent, Nathan Meeker, did not resemble the average second-rater sent out by the Indian Office as a political favor. Meeker was a newspaper editor and a writer of wide repute, and his violent death in the romantic Rocky Mountain wilderness shocked and thrilled the whole nation. In addition, the White River massacre gave Coloradans the pretext they had sought for a decade to take from the Utes their vast hunting paradise of 12,000,000 acres.

The hideous climax of Meeker's career derived from starry-eyed idealism, which he had cultivated all his life. He was born in 1817 on a breezy Ohio homestead overlooking Lake Erie. At seventeen he ran away from home to become a poet, starved a while as a young intellectual on MacDougal Street in New York and returned prosaically to Ohio to run a general store. He married a sea captain's gray-eyed daughter, Arvilla Delight Smith, who bore him three daughters and two sons. She was a plain, pious girl, always a little embarrassed about her fecundity and apprehensive about her husband who theorized brilliantly but disliked manual labor and talked of Jesus Christ as though He were a fairly sound but not entirely respectable neighbor down the street.

Meeker was often broke and twice bankrupt during the first twenty nomadic years of their marriage. In Ohio, and later in Illinois, Arvilla and the children often tended his store while he dabbled in Fourier socialism, Phalangist economics, planned parenthood, Brook Farm Transcendentalism, a Buddhist sort of Christianity, and the practice of nibbling carrots for better vision at night.

His yearning to improve the world expressed itself at last in his first novel, *The Adventures of Captain Armstrong,* the hero of which was tall, handsome, cool-headed, plausible, and indestructibly hopeful like himself. The captain was shipwrecked on a Polynesian atoll and in jig time created among the naked savages a co-operative Utopia of modern industries and crafts. Meeker was a great admirer of Horace Greeley, the famous editor of the New York *Tribune.* He mailed his novel to Greeley, who found a publisher for it. Later, Greeley made Meeker his war correspondent to cover for the *Tribune* Grant's Mississippi campaign.

Then he brought him to New York to be his agricultural editor.

Meeker was a persuasive columnist and he became a national oracle on farm problems. But in 1869 his Utopian dreams crystallized in a plan for a co-operative farm colony near Denver in semi-arid Colorado Territory. Horace Greeley approved the plan and gave him free space in the *Tribune* to promote it. Members of this Union Colony (Meeker called his new town "Greeley") had to be temperate, industrious, moral, and tolerant in their religious outlook.

The founder visited the Cache la Poudre region northeast of Denver and chose a flat, wind-swept tract which was to become the most successful co-operative venture in the Rockies. The tract, like the rest of the Great Plains, had no rainfall to speak of. Meeker's colonists watered their new farms by an elaborate system of ditches which distributed the snow water flowing down from the mountains seventy miles away. Their irrigation methods were copied widely. Their success made it possible to grow crops and livestock in quantity on small acreages. Colorado villages began expanding into cities, the mining districts swarmed with new people, and homesteaders poured into Colorado Territory, enabling it to win statehood in 1876.

Meanwhile the fates conspired to destroy Meeker. He was not a good executor of his own theories (his first irrigation ditch at Greeley cost Union Colony $25,000 and watered less than 200 acres, including the basements of several business establishments). He frittered away his small capital on his Utopia and on his newspaper, the Greeley *Tribune*. He went deeply in debt to Horace Greeley, himself, before the great editor died in 1872. By degrees, his colonists watered down his idealistic aims and eased him out of power. As his frustrations accumulated, he grew brusque and opinionated. He denounced traveling theatricals and dancing and picking wildflowers. He blackballed from membership in the Greeley Farmers' Club all those who opposed his views.

In 1877 the executors of Horace Greeley's estate demanded the money which he owed to it. Desperately

All was peaceful for the Utes when this picture was taken in Washington about 1874. Chief Ouray is second from right, front row; Jack and Johnson, later massacre leaders, are second and third from right, back row. Among their white friends is Otto Mears (right), *the fabulous western capitalist.*

Meeker sought and failed to get a postmastership. He applied for but was not accepted for duty at the Paris Exposition. Then he heard that an Indian agent was needed at the White River Ute Agency in northwest Colorado. He had no special interest in Indians as yet, but the job paid $1,500 a year. To get it, he sought the aid of old newspaper friends back East and some influential Coloradans like Senator Teller. Because of their recommendations, Carl Schurz, secretary of the interior under President Hayes, assigned him to the White River Ute Agency.

The assignment transformed the harried Utopian. He was only 61, but the bitter disappointments at Greeley had given him a defeated look. He had grown thin and stooped, as though bent by the burden of his own despair. As hope returned, his imagination resumed its extravagant soaring. His blue eyes sparkled. His stoop vanished. His shoulders swung confidently when he walked, like the swinging, confident shoulders of his fictional superman, Captain Armstrong.

As he applied his idealism to the problems of the Utes, he began telling himself that maybe he wasn't through yet. Maybe he could achieve Captain Arm-

strong's Utopia after all. And perhaps, after he had taught the wonders of modern society to these simple White River savages, a grateful President Hayes might ask him to perform the same miracle for the Sioux and Apaches and all the other suffering red men!

Leaving the Greeley *Tribune* in the hands of a friend, Meeker set out for his new post early in May, 1878. Arvilla and his youngest daughter Josie were to follow him there in mid-summer. The other two girls agreed to run the family home as a boarding house. The new Indian agent was hardly aware of the explosive situation into which he stepped during his five-day trek to White River. The seeds of bitter conflict over possession of Colorado's Western Slope had been a long time sprouting. The Colorado Utes, anciently of Aztec breeding, had endured centuries of misery as pariahs until the seventeenth century, when they became among the first, if not the very first, Indians to adopt the horse from Spanish colonists on the Rio Grande. This magical creature so inspired them as to completely change their tribal personality. They developed into superb horsemen and found themselves able to hold the Colorado highlands for their exclu-

NEW YORK *Illustrated Times*, FROM CULVER SERVICE

Eastern tabloids reported the White River massacre with considerable license, as this drawing indicates. That Josie Meeker wielded a rifle against the attackers is pure fantasy.

sive use. Thereafter their reverence was boundless for the divine beast which had raised them from the depths of human degradation to great happiness, prosperity, and dignity.

Eventually some 3,500 of these Utes divided into six loosely allied Colorado bands, led by an extraordinary man named Chief Ouray. He was 45 in 1878 and had a mind as spacious as his mountains. He had risen to power in 1863 and had set his political policy then. The Utes, he decreed, must live in peace with white men. They must modify their wasteful hunting economy, sell off bits of land as required by events, and learn to prosper on the reduced acreage as white men prospered.

Ouray's masterpiece was the Treaty of 1868 by which the U.S. Senate gave his six bands most of Colorado's Western Slope forever (4,500 acres for each Ute man, woman, and child). In 1873 he had to release the 4,000,000-acre San Juan silver region but the Utes had a 12,000,000-acre reservation left. They were still the richest Indian landed gentry in the nation. And they were the pets of the whites, befriending settlers and doing a big buckskin business with traders.

But Ouray played a losing game. By 1878 the tenfold increase in the state's white population had created a huge demand for more land. Politically, the demand was expressed in an outcry for the removal of the Colorado Utes and the liquidation of their vast Western Slope estate. Senator Teller and the land grabbers around him dreamed of herding them off to army-guarded desert camps. But the Teller crowd had to move with caution because of the good reputation of Ouray's people. Their strategy was to try to destroy this reputation by accusing the Utes falsely of all kinds of outrage, arson, theft, and murder.

The Utes were deeply disturbed by the charges, the resentment being highest among the two White River bands under the aging Chief Douglas and Chief Jack. This Jack was a young, forceful leader and he reacted to the white campaign of slander by urging an end to Ouray's peace policy. He wanted the Utes to fight for their homeland, though Ouray warned him that he was playing into Senator Teller's hands. Ouray added that if the Utes went on the warpath, they would abrogate their treaty rights and lose all they possessed.

Chief Jack was not convinced. The government, he said, had always mistaken Ouray's peace policy for weakness and was preparing to dispossess the Utes anyway. He stressed that Interior Secretary Schurz had just dismissed the White River agent who had protected their rights for years. Schurz had replaced this good agent with a Teller appointee named Nathan Meeker. In Jack's opinion, such an appointee could

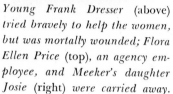

Young Frank Dresser (above) *tried bravely to help the women, but was mortally wounded; Flora Ellen Price* (top), *an agency employee, and Meeker's daughter Josie* (right) *were carried away.*

have but two aims; to steal Ute land and destroy the Ute way of life.

On May 10, 1878, the new agent arrived blithesomely at the cluster of tumble-down log buildings in White River valley at the utter end of the 185-mile road south from Rawlins, Wyoming. The bleak agency setting did not resemble Captain Armstrong's charming atoll in the South Seas, but Meeker did not care. He was abloom with love for and faith in his Utes and had high hopes of easing their presumed misery. He was not worried about the hostility which greeted him at first. He placated many Indians soon by his success in obtaining better rations and distributing annuities on time. They were pleased too with his agency staff— eight good-natured young men hand-picked by Meeker from the best families in Greeley.

The agent outlined his Utopian dream to the principal chiefs, Douglas and Jack, and to the head medicine man, Johnson, a distinguished horseman who was also Ouray's brother-in-law. Meeker explained how he would teach them modern farming and irrigation so that they could all be rich, live in houses, ride in carriages, use privies, sleep in beds, wear underwear, and send their children to the agency school. He described plans for associated industries to raise their living standard still higher—saw mills, orchards, wool plants, coal mines, and a railroad to Rawlins.

He observed that Douglas and Johnson were mildly intrigued by his dream. But Jack had an irritating way of asking loaded questions. He asked whether or not white men would allow Utes to compete in business with them. He wanted to know if the high living standard of the whites was worth all the work and worry they had to put into it. He asked if white men enjoyed working as much as the Utes enjoyed their lordly leisure of hunting and fishing and riding their ponies about their Colorado estate.

That fall agent Meeker discovered a perfect site for his model Ute farm at Powell Park a dozen miles down White River. He was sure of its value because the Utes pastured thousands of ponies on it in winter. To Meeker's surprise, Douglas objected heatedly to moving the agency there.

Meeker thought it over and concluded that this pony business did indeed present an obstacle to his whole bright plan for Ute salvation. The Utes, he perceived, were obsessed with these confounded ponies. They could never achieve the happiness which he held out to them as long as they had so many ponies to care for. It was a ticklish matter. And yet he was sure that Captain Armstrong had more than enough persuasive power to make the Indians see that the ponies were millstones around their necks.

And, sure enough, in the ensuing winter months, Douglas and Johnson let him have his way. The agency buildings were moved downstream to the richest part of Powell Park. Neat streets were laid out, ditches were dug, and forty acres of pony pasture were plowed, fenced, and planted to wheat. The young employees from Greeley built a nice house for Johnson and put cook stoves in the tepees of four families. Meeker's gentle daughter Josie induced three children to attend her agency school.

But serious trouble from outside the reservation came in the spring of 1879, and Meeker watched with mounting anguish as his dream faded. Colorado's new governor, Frederick W. Pitkin, had been elected on a Utes-Must-Go platform which he was trying hard to implement. The Denver papers were full of incendiary anti-Ute propaganda. Senator Teller forced Chief

Douglas, chief of the White River Utes.

Ouray's Uncompahgre band to sell 10,000 acres of prime farm land for $10,000—and failed to produce the promised money. It was a terribly dry spring. By mid-June the state's forests burned in hundreds of places, and the Teller crowd charged that the Utes had deliberately set all the fires.

At White River Agency the Indians took out their anger at all this unfairness toward them by ceasing to co-operate with Meeker further. And, as his dream collapsed, the agent's optimism faltered. His all-embracing love for his charges turned rapidly to hate. He spent much time alone nursing grudges against Douglas, against Johnson, against the ponies, even against his agency staff and his daughter Josie, who sided often with the Indians.

A particular irritation to him was the attitude of Arvilla Meeker's Ute housemaid, Jane. To say that this tall, pretty, bilingual girl of 22 disturbed Meeker is to understate probabilities. He had done everything he could to please her, including weeding her garden for six weeks in 1878 while she was off hunting. When she had returned, she had rewarded him with a sort of smile and nine beets out of a total crop of thirty bushels. In that tense spring of 1879, Meeker decided to coddle Jane no longer. He summoned her to his office one morning and began the conversation in a gentle kindly vein:

MEEKER: Now Jane, you will be planting your garden soon. I just want to warn you that last summer's style of gardening is played out.

JANE: Played out? How so?

MEEKER: Well, I'll tell you. After the things are planted, it will not do for you to run off and leave me to plow, hoe and pull weeds. You or some of your family must stay here all three moons and work your crops, for no one will touch them, and in that case you

will have nothing. Or they will be given to some other Indian to work and he will have all.

JANE: You say we must stay three moons? What for? Hoeing the things once is enough.

MEEKER: You must hoe them three or four times, and must keep watch of them and you need not undertake to tell me how the work is to be done.

JANE: But we never done so before and we had heaps.

MEEKER (warming up): But I tell you the thing is played out. If you get anything you must work for it.

JANE: Why can't white men do the work as before? They understand it. We don't.

MEEKER: It won't do. Now I worked your garden last year. I carried hundreds of pails of water to it. You had a nice garden and got lots of money. But this year we have a big ditch and plenty of water. You must attend to things yourself.

JANE (sweetly): But, Mr. Meeker, ain't you paid for working?

MEEKER: No. Not to work for you.

JANE: Well, what are you paid money for if not to work for us?

MEEKER (momentarily stumped): Yes, I see how it is. . . . I'll put it this way. I am paid to show you how to work.

JANE: But the Utes have a heap of money. What is the money for if it is not to have work done for us?

MEEKER (coming to a boil): I'll tell you, Jane. This money is to hire me and the rest of us to teach you to help yourselves so that you can be like white folks and get rich as they are rich—by work. You are not to be waited upon and supported in idleness all your lives. You have got to take hold and support yourselves or you will have trouble.

JANE (black eyes wide): Ain't all these cattle ours, and all this land?

MEEKER: The cattle, yes. The land, no.

JANE: Well, whose land is it, and whose is the money?

MEEKER (almost yelling): The land belongs to the government and is for your use, if you use it. If you won't use it and won't work, and if you expect me to weed your garden for you, white men away off will come in and by and by you will have nothing. This thing can't go on forever. As to money, it is to be used to make you helpful. It is time you turn to and take care of yourselves and have houses and stoves and chairs and beds and crockery and heaps of things. Do you understand?

JANE (very quiet): Yes. But I can't tell you, Mr. Meeker, how bad you make me feel.

She left the office and Meeker watched her straight proud form as she walked across the office porch, past his hitching rack and down the street which ended at Douglas' lodge on White River. She walked stiffly and rapidly, keeping her handsome head straight ahead.

We may guess that the agent was aware that he had said too much. He had asserted not only that the Utes didn't own White River valley, but that they couldn't even stay there if they didn't do what Meeker ordered them to do. And to make matters still worse, Meeker sat down now and wrote out the entire conversation verbatim for publication in the next issue of the Greeley *Tribune*.

Tension at the agency became so unbearable by early September that Meeker feared for the safety of Arvilla and Josie Meeker. But he would not call for troops from Fort Steele in Wyoming 200 miles away. The agent knew that to ask for soldiers would be to accept final defeat.

On the morning of September 8 he mailed a list of complaints to the Indian Office. Also, he called in the medicine man Johnson and accused him of stealing water for his ponies from Josie's school water barrel. Ponies! Always the ponies! Meeker was becoming psychopathic about them. Johnson denied stealing any water and left Meeker's office muttering. After lunch he returned and stood before the agent talking fast and loud. Meeker leaned easily back in his office chair, his pale blue eyes cold and a set smile on his weary face. He did not catch all that Johnson said, but it seemed to concern the plowing up of pony pasture and his suspicion that the agent was sending lies about the Utes to Washington.

Suddenly Meeker decided that he had heard enough. He raised an imperious hand and said, very deliberately, "The trouble is this, Johnson. You have too many ponies. You had better shoot some of them."

Johnson stared at the agent for a long moment, utterly dumfounded. Then his brown eyes blazed with the fire of a reasonable man who had just heard the consummation of blasphemy. He moved slowly toward Meeker, grasped his shoulders, lifted his long spare body from the chair and hustled him across the office and on to the porch. There, two employees ran up and grabbed Johnson as he flung Meeker hard against the hitching rack.

That was all. Johnson did not touch Meeker again. The agent tottered back to his chair, felt himself over and found that he was not badly hurt. Next day, he penned a telegraphic request to Washington for troops, stating that his life and those of his employees were in danger. As his courier rode north toward the Western Union office in Rawlins, Meeker must have known that his life's dream went with him.

In Washington the Indian Office passed Meeker's wire on to General Sherman who ordered a force of 153 soldiers and 25 civilians under Major Thomas T. Thornburgh to go to White River from Rawlins. Presumably the Major did not care for the task. As an army officer he detested the Indian Office and all its works. The Ute Agency was not even in his military department. He had no decent maps, no proper guides. He had had fighting experience only with Plains Indians. He knew nothing about these Utes, with whom he tended to sympathize.

The Major took his time. On Monday morning, September 29, his force reached the Ute Reservation line at Milk Creek, 25 miles north of White River. Thornburgh had exchanged messages earlier with Meeker and had agreed to ride alone over Yellowjacket Pass to the agency for talks with Douglas and Jack, leaving his soldiers outside the reservation. But he found that Milk Creek was almost dry because of the record drought. He had to have fresh water for his men and for his 400 animals. Therefore he ordered his force to move some miles into the reservation to a spot where water was available.

From the sage ridges above Milk Creek valley, Chief Jack and his band watched this unexpected movement with enraged astonishment. Suddenly the soldiers spied the Indians. Someone fired a gun. Then everyone was firing. Men began falling to earth. After some minutes Jack's courier leaped on his pony and galloped southward to bring the awful news to Douglas' band at the agency. Before noon Major Thornburgh, eleven of his troopers, and many Utes lay dead. Forty-odd white men were wounded. Nearly 300 army horses and mules were out of action. Without the use of these animals, the army survivors were completely trapped. They forted up behind their wagons and dead horses and barely managed to hold Jack's warriors off until relief troops arrived from Rawlins six days later.

On that same fateful Monday morning, everything seemed peaceful at White River Agency. The tension of recent weeks was as bad as ever, but the boys from Greeley and Douglas' men and the white women did their best to ignore it. Several young Utes loitered about begging biscuits at the big agency kitchen which Josie Meeker ran for the nine employees. She was helped by Flora Ellen Price, the plump, blond, teen-aged wife of Meeker's plowman. The agent, preoccupied and wan, spent all morning describing his difficulties in his September report. Soon after lunch he appeared at Josie's kitchen window to get from her the key to the government gun closet. He walked with a stoop again as in his unhappiest Greeley days. There was a grim smile on his strained face. And still he re-

tained enough of his old spirit to ask Josie if she knew what day September 29 was. When she shook her head, he said jauntily: "On this day in 1066, William the Conqueror landed in England!"

At 1:30 P.M. Josie, Arvilla, and Flora Ellen were still in the kitchen, washing and wiping the dinner dishes in the Indian summer heat. A small Ute boy stopped to borrow matches, announcing proudly, "Now I go smoke." Flora Ellen stepped outside to fetch her two small children. She saw some Greeley boys spreading dirt on the roof of a new building. Beyond them, on the street down to White River, she saw Douglas and a dozen of his men. Then she saw an Indian on a sweat-flecked pony galloping up to Douglas from the direction of Milk Creek.

The Indian said something to the old chief and immediately after that, Flora Ellen saw doom come. It came without signal, like the spontaneous firing at Milk Creek. Some of Douglas' men simply raised their Winchesters and began shooting at their white friends, the unarmed Greeley boys. Flora Ellen watched one boy fall from the new roof. She watched another as he begged the Utes not to shoot him. She saw her husband collapse holding his stomach. She snatched her crying children, joined the other women, and went with them and Frank Dresser, a Greeley boy, to the adobe milk house while the Indians fired some of the log buildings.

The three women, two children, and Dresser sat in the milk house for four hours, too stunned, too helpless, too hopeless to entirely comprehend the horror which was upon them. Arvilla Meeker picked at her faded calico dress, wept and stopped weeping, and prayed for her husband's safety. Josie was mixed sorrow and gentle compassion for the Utes, whom she had learned to understand. Flora Ellen was pure terror, dying the deaths of all the Indian-ravished heroines she had met in fiction.

At last they left the milk house in the cooling twi-

The Utes ambushed the troops sent to aid Meeker, an action that set off the agency attack. It was six days before a relief column lifted the siege.

250

light and ran back to Meeker's unburned house. In the agent's office, peaceful as a church, Josie stood a moment, a tall, slender, white-faced girl of 22, her lips parted in anguished query. She was staring at Pepys' Diary lying open on her father's desk where he had left it, apparently, just before stepping outside to investigate the firing. Through the window she saw Utes looting the agency storehouse. She said to the others, "Let's try to escape north while they are busy."

They went through the gate into Meeker's wheat field. Frank Dresser ran like a deer and disappeared in the sage, but later was wounded and died before he could reach help. The Utes saw the three women and the children and came for them. Arvilla fell when a bullet grazed her thigh and lay still on the ground. A young Ute named Thompson reached her and helped her to rise. "I am sorry," he said. "I am heap much sorry. Can you walk?"

Arvilla whispered, "Yes, sir."

The young Ute offered her his arm politely and led her toward White River. Near the agent's house, he asked if she had money inside.

"Very little."

"Please go and get money."

She limped into the quiet house calling "Papa! Papa!" and somehow found twenty-six dollars in bills and four dollars in silver. Then Thompson helped her to walk to Douglas near his tepee and she gave him the money. Near him was Josie on a pile of blankets holding little May Price on her lap. Further away were Flora Ellen and her son.

Arvilla limped from Ute captor to captor. Where, she asked, was the agent? The Utes shrugged. As night came on she watched the great full moon yellowing in the east. She began to shiver and she spoke to Douglas about the thin dresses she and the girls were wearing. Douglas told Thompson to take her back with a horse and lantern to get some things.

Meeker's house was burning at one end. Entering, Arvilla called, "Nathan!" but low and sorrowfully now, almost to herself. Then she loaded Thompson with warm clothes, towels, blankets, and a medicine box. She donned her hat and shawl, put a handkerchief and a needle packet in her pocket, and limped out hugging her big volume of *Pilgrim's Progress*.

A hundred yards south of the house she came suddenly on a man's dead body, startlingly white in the moonlight, and clad only in a shirt. It was Meeker. He had been shot in the side of his handsome head and a little blood trickled still from his mouth. But he lay entirely composed, straight as he had stood in life, his arms tranquil beside him as though he were about to tell Arvilla what had happened to William the Conqueror on September 29, 1066.

She cried softly and knelt to kiss him. But she did not actually kiss him. Young Thompson was beside her and she realized that he would not understand the gesture. Then she stood up and left the body, hop-

Frank Leslie's Illustrated Newspaper, FROM CULVER SERVICE

ing that Nathan Meeker s Utopia would be easier for him to come by in the land where he was now.

The massacre of Meeker and his eight young men by Douglas' band, the "ambush" of Thornburgh's soldiers by Jack's band, and the holding of the three white women as hostages for 23 days by both bands caused as much consternation as the Custer massacre in 1876. Millions of people were especially upset when the women testified after their rescue that Josie's person had been outraged repeatedly during their captivity, that Flora Ellen had been forced twice to submit, and that even old Douglas had insisted on "having connection" with Mrs. Meeker once.

The punishment of the alleged guilty was all the landgrabbers could have asked. The two White River bands were branded as criminals en masse by a political commission without any judicial powers whatever. Though only twenty White River Utes had staged the massacre, all 700 were penalized in that money owed to them by the government was paid instead to relatives of victims. Chief Ouray's Uncompahgre Utes, who had had nothing to do with the massacre or the "ambush," were held equally responsible. The 1868 treaty rights of all three bands were canceled. Their rights to be Americans as set forth in the Fourteenth Amendment were ignored. Title to their ancient Colorado homeland was extinguished and they were moved at gun point to barren lands in Utah. By these means the last and largest chunk of desirable Indian real estate was thrown open to white settlement.

And still, the year 1879 marked a happier turning point. It was the beginning of the end of indefensible white attitudes toward red men. Interior Secretary Carl Schurz was only one of many people who probed beneath the surface causes of the White River tragedy and then had the courage to say, and to keep on saying, that it would not have happened if the Utes had lived under the same laws as other Americans.

This novel notion took root and the roots spread far and wide. Before another decade passed, white men generally were agreeing that perhaps Indians were human beings too. Though the living Nathan Meeker failed to build his Utopia, in dying he made a contribution of far more value to his country than persuading an outdoor people to sleep in beds.

The Sioux were among the last to give up the unequal struggle with the white man. The 1862 uprising by the Santee Sioux in Minnesota—depicted in the scenes from a panorama by John Stevens on the opposite page—marked the beginning of the end. Minnesotans demanded and received vengeance—38 Indians were hanged from one scaffold, the largest legal execution in American history. Fighting ended for the Sioux at Wounded Knee in 1890.

AT LAST

for the discriminating reader

An unvarnished, straight-shooting, and instructive account of

THE WILD, WILD WEST

containing the irreducible, rock-bottom, and unadorned

about such **DESPERADOES, SHERIFFS, GUN SLINGERS, COWTOWN MARSHALS,** and assorted *RIFFRAFF* as

WILD BILL HICKOK, BAT MASTERSON, WYATT EARP, BILLY THE KID, AND JESSE JAMES

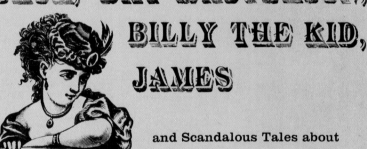

together with
various Moral Lessons

and Scandalous Tales about

Their fair
but frail
COM-
PANIONS

CALAMITY JANE

AND BELLE STARR

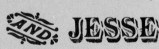

not forbearing to include certain **REVOLTING REVELATIONS**
concerning their conduct at the gaming table, low character,
tendency to shoot from behind, and fondness for

THE BOTTLE

to which are added Unavoidable Animadversions upon the Frauds and Fictions of the

SILVER SCREEN & ELECTRIC TELEVISION

All collected, elucidated, and certified to be in the public interest by

PETER LYON

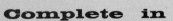**Complete in** **This Number**

The world of the Wild West is an odd world, internally consistent in its own cockeyed way, and complete with a history, an ethic, a language, wars, a geography, a code, and a costume. The history is compounded of lies, the ethic was based on evil, the language was composed largely of argot and cant, the wars were fought by gangs of greedy gunmen, the geography was elastic, and the code and costume were both designed to accommodate violence. Yet this sinful world is, by any test, the most popular ever to be described to an American audience.

Thousands of books have been written about it, many of them purporting to be history or biography; all but a very few are fiction, and rubbish to boot. It has, of course, afforded wondrously rich pickings for the journeymen of the mass entertainments; scores of writers for pulp magazines, motion pictures, comic strips, radio, and television have hacked their way over its trails. Even artists of the first rank have drawn upon it. Mark Twain reported as fact some grisly rumors about one of its heroes; Aaron Copland composed the music for a ballet that glorified one of its most celebrated killers; Puccini wrote an opera about it; George Bernard Shaw confected an exceedingly silly play about it.

And it has not disappeared. It is still around, over thataway just a piece, bounded on three sides by credulity and on the fourth by the television screen. It will never disappear.

Any discussion of the conquest of the West may be likened to an animated gabble down the length of a long dinner table. At the head of it, where historians have gathered, the talk is thoughtful and focuses on events of weighty consequence. One man mentions the discovery of precious metals, which inspired adventurers by the scores of thousands. Another man tells of the Homestead Act of May, 1862, under the terms of which, within a generation, 350,000 hardy souls each carved a 160-acre farm out of raw prairie. A third speaks of the railroads that were a-building, four of them by 1884, to link the Mississippi Valley to the Pacific Coast. When it comes to the Indians, the historians all wag their heads dolefully, for they agree that the westward expansion came about only by virtue of treaties cynically violated and territory shamelessly seized.

The picture that emerges from their talk is one of grueling hard work; of explorers and trappers and bearded prospectors; of Chinese coolies toiling east and Irish immigrants toiling west, laying track across wilderness; of farmers with hands as hard as horn, sheltered from the blizzards and the northers only by sod huts; of ranchers and longhorn cattle and cowboys weary in the saddle. The quality evoked by their talk is of enduring courage, the greater because it is largely anonymous. The smell that hangs over their talk is of sweat.

But at the foot of the table, below the salt, where sit the chroniclers of the Wild West, the talk is shrill and excited, and the smell that hangs overhead is of gunpowder. For here the concern is with men of dash and derring-do, and the picture that emerges from the talk is of gaudy cowtowns and slambang mining camps: curious settlements in which the only structures are saloons, gambling hells, dance palaces, brothels, burlesque theaters, and jails; in which there are no people, but only heroes and villains, all made of pasteboard and buckram, all wearing six-guns, and all (except for the banker) with hearts of 22-carat gold.

In this never-never land, the superhero is the gunslinger, the man who can draw fastest and shoot straightest; in brief, the killer. Sometimes he swaggered along the wooden sidewalks with a silver star pinned to his shirt, a sheriff or a United States marshal, but whether he was outlaw or officer of the law, if he applied himself diligently to the smashing of the Ten Commandments, with special attention to the Sixth—that is, if he was a sufficiently ugly, evil, and murderous killer—he was in a way to become a storied American hero.

We propose to trundle five of these paragons—Billy the Kid and Jesse James, Wild Bill Hickok, Bat Masterson, and Wyatt Earp—up for inspection at close range. Nor will the ladies be ignored: we will ask Calamity Jane and Belle Starr, the Bandit Queen, to curtsy briefly. But before entering this gallery of Papier-Mâché Horribles, we may find it instructive to reflect upon the technique by which an uproariously bad man can acquire a reputation at once inflated, grisly, and prettified. This will require some small knowledge of the economics of the Wild West and a brief peek at the sources available to the chroniclers of this hazy world, this world so clouded by the black gunsmoke of all those Navy Colt .45's.

There were, broadly speaking, two ways of making money in the Wild West. One, as has been suggested, demanded hard, hard work of farmer, cowhand, railroader, or miner. But as always seems to be the case in this bad old world, there were some few men who did not care for hard work. Either they had tried it personally, for a day or two, and found it repugnant, or they had conceived a distaste for it by watching others try it, or perhaps they had simply heard about others who had tried it and so come to a bad end. In any case, these men determined never to work but to rely, rather, on their wits.

Now how could a quick-witted man get rich out on the bare, bleak plains? Clearly the first step was to head for those outposts of civilization, however malodorous to a discriminating rogue, where a little heap of wealth had been piled up through the labor of others. This meant the cowtowns, the mining camps, and the slowly shifting railroad settlements. Here he could gamble with the chumps: few professional gamblers starve. Here he could trade on women of easy virtue, or no virtue whatever, who were in even greater demand west of the Mississippi than east of it. Here he could buy a share of a dance hall or saloon: either enterprise was gilt-edged. Before long he would have found, as others have before and since, that these careers lead straight into politics. He might have concluded that it was cheaper to stand for office himself than to pay tribute to some stupider, lazier politician. So were marshals and sheriffs born.

But what of the dull-witted man who didn't choose to work? He had behind him a life of violence bred by the Civil War; often his thick skull held no learning whatever save how to ride, shoot, kill, burn, rob, rape, and run. With the end of the war he doffed his blue blouse—or, more often, his gray—and headed west toward a short, gory life of bank heists and train robberies. So were outlaws born.

For the man who was preternaturally active and had no objection to a day in the outdoors, there was a third, coarsening, semi-legal path to quick dollars: he could slaughter bison. Only the Indians would object, and who cared a hoot for the Indians? A treaty of 1867 guaranteed that no white man would hunt buffalo south of the Arkansas River; by 1870, when the army officer commanding at Fort Dodge was asked what he would do if this promise were broken, he laughed and said, "Boys, if I were hunting buffalo I would go where buffalo are"; in 1871 the massacre began in earnest. One hunter bagged 5,855 in two months. It has been estimated that 4,373,730 bison were killed in the three years 1872–74. To shoot the placid beasts was no easier than shooting fish in a barrel, but it was certainly no more difficult. And splendid practice, as safe as on a target range, for the marksman who might later choose to pot riskier game—a stagecoach driver or the leader of a posse. So were killers trained.

For the purposes of American myth, it remained only to make over all these sheriffs, outlaws, killers, and assorted villains into heroes. Considering the material on hand to work with, this transfiguration is on the order of a major miracle. It was brought about in two ways. First, whilst the assorted plug-uglies were still alive, hosannas were raised in their honor (a) by the "National Police Gazette," a lively weekly edited from 1877 to 1922 by Richard K. Fox and commanding a circulation that reached into every self-respecting barbershop, billiard parlor, barroom, and bagnio throughout the Republic; and (b) by each impressionable journalist, from the more gen-

teel eastern magazines, who had wangled enough expense money out of his publisher to waft him west of Wichita. Fox required no authentication and desired none; his staff writers simply pitched their stuff out by the forkful, to be engorged by yokels from Fifth Avenue to Horner's Corners. The aforesaid round-eyed journalists, on the other hand, got their stuff straight from the gun fighters themselves, so naturally it was deemed wholly reliable.

Second, after the assorted plug-uglies had been gathered to their everlasting sleep, the latter-day chroniclers crept eagerly in. They (or at least a few of them) would be careful and scholarly; they would write nothing that was not verified either by a contemporary newspaper account or by an oldtimer who knew whereof he spoke from personal knowledge. Thus, whatever they printed would be the truth, the whole truth, &c.

One flaw in this admirable approach was that the contemporary newspaper accounts are not reliable. How could they be, when the newspapers themselves were flaring examples of the sort of personal journalism in which bias as to local politics and personalities customarily displaced respect for facts? Any halfway independent and intelligent reporter for the newspapers of the Wild West knew that, when he wrote about the gunmen of his community, he was describing an interconnected underworld, a brotherhood that embraced outlaw, politician, and sheriff quite as amicably as does the brotherhood of gangster and corrupt official in the cities of our own time. Such an insight normally flavored his copy.

The other flaw was that the stories of oldtimers came not from personal knowledge of what happened so much as from the files of the imaginative "National Police Gazette." Venerable nesters could be found all over the Southwest, fifty years after the timely deaths of Billy the Kid or Jesse James or Belle Starr, clamoring to testify to the boyish charm of the one, the selfless nobility of the other, and the amorous exploits of the third. Their memories were all faithful transcripts of the "Gazette's" nonsense. Its editor's classic formula for manufacturing heroes had so effectively retted the minds of his readers that they could never thereafter disentangle fiction from fact.

Analysis of this Fox formula for heroes reveals that it has ten ingredients, like a Chinese soup:

(1) The hero's accuracy with any weapon is prodigious.

(2) He is a nonpareil of bravery and courage.

(3) He is courteous to all women, regardless of rank, station, age, or physical charm.

(4) He is gentle, modest, and unassuming.

(5) He is handsome, sometimes even pretty, so that he seems even feminine in appearance; but withal he is of course very masculine, and exceedingly attractive to women.

(6) He is blue-eyed. His piercing blue eyes turn gray as steel when he is aroused; his associates would have been well advised to keep a color chart handy, so that they might have dived for a storm cellar when the blue turned to tattletale gray.

(7) He was driven to a life of outlawry and crime by having quite properly defended a loved one from an intolerable affront—with lethal consequences. Thereafter, however,

(8) He shields the widow and orphan, robbing only the banker or railroad monopolist.

(9) His death comes about by means of betrayal or treachery, but

(10) It is rarely a conclusive death, since he keeps on bobbing up later on, in other places, for many years. It is, indeed, arguable whether he is dead yet.

With these attributes in mind let us gather around the first exhibit—a man narrow-waisted and wide-hipped, with small hands and feet, whose long curly hair tumbles to his shoulders—in sum, a man who looks like a male impersonator. His label reads

WILD BILL HICKOK

James Butler (Wild Bill) Hickok was born on a farm in La Salle County, Illinois, on May 27, 1837. He died on the afternoon of August 2, 1876, in Saloon No. 10, on the main street of Deadwood, in the Dakota Territory, when a bullet fired by Jack McCall plowed through the back of his head, coming out through his cheek and smashing a bone in the left forearm of a Captain Massey, a river-boat pilot with whom Hickok had been playing poker. During his lifetime Hickok did some remarkable deeds, and they were even more remarkably embroidered by himself and by a corps of admiring tagtails and tuft-hunters. When he died, he held two pair—aces and eights—a legendary combination known ever since as "the dead man's hand." It is the least of the legends that has encrusted his reputation, like barnacles on an old hulk.

Was he brave? His most critical biographer, William E. Connelley, has said that fear "was simply a quality he lacked."

Was he handsome? He was "the handsomest man west of the Mississippi. His eyes were blue—but could freeze to a cruel steel-gray at threat of evil or danger."

Was he gallant? His morals were "much the same as those of Achilles, King David, Lancelot, and Chevalier Bayard, though his amours were hardly as frequent as David's or as inexcusable as Lancelot's."

Had he no minor vices? Very few: "Wild Bill found relaxation and enjoyment in cards but he seldom drank."

Could he shoot? Once in Solomon, Kansas, a pair of murderers fled from him. "One was running up the street and the other down the street in the opposite direction. Bill fired at both men simultaneously and killed them both." Presumably with his eyes closed. Again, in Topeka, in 1870, Buffalo Bill Cody threw his hat into the air as a target. "Wild Bill shot an evenly spaced row of holes along the outside of the rim as it was falling, and before it touched the ground." To appreciate fully this miracle of marksmanship, one must remember that Hickok was shooting black-powder cartridges. (Smokeless powder did not come into general use until about 1893.) Each time he fired, therefore, he put a puff of black smoke between himself and his target. After his first shot, he could not have seen his target. But then, nothing is impossible to the gun slinger of the Wild West.

But surely he was modest? Yes, indeed. "Faced with admirers, he blushed and stammered and fled."

Was he a sure-enough killer? Once he was asked how many white men he had killed, to his certain knowledge (Indians didn't count). Wild Bill reflected. "I suppose," he said at last, "I have killed considerably over a hundred." But this was in 1866: he would have another ten years to improve his record. To another reporter, he remarked: "As to killing men, I never think much about it. . . . The killing of a bad man shouldn't trouble one any more than killing a rat or an ugly cat or a vicious dog." Of course, it helps if one is as good a judge as Hickok of the badness of a man, or the ugliness of a cat.

But was a good man not obliged to kill a bad man, to tame the Wild West? And, after all, was Wild Bill not a pillar of righteousness in those sinful times? What about his lustrous reputation as marshal of the Kansas cowtowns?

Hickok was, perhaps, a United States deputy marshal operating out of Fort Riley in February, 1866, and charged with rounding up deserters and horse thieves; but the record of his tenure is fuzzy.

In mid-August, 1869, he was elected sheriff of Ellis County—of which Hays was the biggest town —to fill an unexpired term. He failed of re-election in November. A brief time in which to tame a tough town—nor does the record show any notable success. He may have killed a man named Jack (or Sam) Strawhorn (or Strawhan) who tried to get the drop on him; he may have killed two soldiers who talked tough at him; he may have thrashed Tom Custer, a brother of General George Custer; he may have killed three soldiers whom Custer had vengefully sicked on him—all the evidence bearing on these matters is likewise fuzzy. What is certain is that Hickok left Hays in a hurry one winter night, lest he be further beset by the Seventh Cavalry.

In April, 1871, Hickok was appointed marshal of Abilene, and now the picture grows sharper. It was an auspicious conjunction of man and town: each was at the height of notoriety. As for the town, which was all of five years old, 1871 would be its peak year as a cowtown; 600,000 cattle would pass through its yards on the way to eastern markets; and all summer, cowboys by the hundreds would jam its saloons and dance halls—the Alamo, the Bull's Head, the Mint, and the Gold Room—to squander a year's wages. As for the man, "Harper's Monthly" had published not long before a lurid account of Hickok's fatal skill in battle, as told to George Ward Nichols by Wild Bill himself. There was, for instance, Hickok's version of the McCanles affair. In truth, Hickok had shot down Dave Mc-Canles from behind a curtain, shot a second man from behind a door, and mortally wounded a third man who was running for his life. But as Wild Bill told the tale to the bug-eyed Nichols, he had been attacked by McCanles and a gang of nine "desperadoes, horsethieves, murderers, regular cut-throats," but had slain six men with six shots and dispatched the other four "blood-thirsty devils" with his knife.

A man whose fame rested on such fabulous fibs was just the sort needed to quell the frequent riots of a wicked cowtown. At least, so thought Joseph McCoy, the founder of Abilene and, in 1871, also the town's mayor. Moreover, McCoy knew where to find his man, for Hickok was right in town, gambling for a living at the Alamo. Wild Bill took the job. He slung two six-guns at his hips; he thrust a knife in the red sash he affected. In this fashion, he occasionally patrolled the streets.

But only occasionally. Most hours of most evenings he could be found at the Alamo, gambling with the cowboys. Most hours of most nights he had business in Abilene's red-light district. Meantime the taxpayers of Abilene chafed. Nor were the cowboys happy; for they were persuaded that Hickok wore the star only to protect the extortions of the professional gamblers, madames, and saloonkeepers.

Matters came to a head on the night of October 5. A bunch of cowboys had been hurrahing the town in their traditional and tiresome fashion—forcing merchants of clothing to outfit poorly clad strangers, obliging passers-by to stand drinks for all hands—and Hickok reportedly warned them to quiet down.

THE MAKING OF A LEGEND

The Wild Bill Hickok of real life (above), with his slicked-down ringlets and his satin lapels, has now become the clean-shaven paragon portrayed on television (below) by Guy Madison. Harper's New Monthly Magazine contributed to the process in 1867 (center) with an adulatory account of Wild Bill's prowess by George Ward Nichols.

Our hero, to be honest, was a dandy.

Wild Bill, said Harper's, "has killed hundreds of men."

For TV, he has changed to buckskins.

Calamity Jane (left) was also transformed, by way of the cover of Beadle's Pocket Library *(center), into the blonde tomboy played by Jean Arthur (right) in DeMille's* The Plainsman.

Back in the Alamo at his poker table, Wild Bill heard someone fire a shot. He plunged out into the darkness to confront a Texan named Phil Coe. Some say that Coe's gun was already back in its holster, some that it was dangling in his hand. Whichever the case, Hickok fired, felling Coe, and then, when he heard someone running toward him, at once wheeled and plugged his own deputy, one Mike Williams, in a typical exhibition of coolness, calm, and nerve. He was relieved of his official duties six weeks later.

After that there was nothing left but to exploit his celebrity in show business. He joined Buffalo Bill Cody's stock company, an ignoble enterprise, but quit before long. In June, 1876, a Kansas newspaper reported, from Fort Laramie, that Wild Bill "was arrested on several occasions as a vagrant, having no visible means of support."

Later that month he galloped into Deadwood with a retinue that included, of all people, Calamity Jane. He settled down to gambling, as was his wont; she to drinking, as was hers. A little more than a month later Jack McCall shot him from behind, for no particular reason.

Hickok had been a brave army scout and an able Indian scout; he had also been a liar, a frequenter of bawdy houses, a professional gambler, and a killer. His score, according to a conservative chronicler of his deeds, was thirty-six men killed, apart from his service in the Army and against the Indians. What more fitting, for such a man, than to enshrine him on television, during the children's hour?

There is a tale that tells of how Calamity Jane, furious when she hears of Wild Bill's death, pursues his killer and corners him in a butcher shop, where she has to be restrained from splitting his brisket with a cleaver. Alas! not true. There is another tale that tells of how Calamity, on her deathbed years later, whispers, "What's the date?" When she is told it is August 2, she smiles and murmurs, "It's the twenty-seventh anniversary of Bill's death." Then, while the violins sob a little in the background, she adds, "Bury me next to Bill." This is likewise horsefeathers. (She died on August 1, 1903.) Yet the legends persist in linking the two together.

Were they lovers? Wild Bill's adherents flatly deny it, claiming that their man was far too fastidious. What their denial lacks in gallantry, it makes up in logic. Calamity was the most celebrated female of the Wild West, but she was no rose.

She may have been born in 1852, in Missouri (or Illinois); her name may have been Mary Jane Canary (or Conarray). Her mother may have been a prostitute, and later a madame in Blackfoot, Montana, around 1866, managing a house that may have been called the Bird Cage. Notable citizens of the Wild West share an irritating nebulosity when it comes to recorded data.

There are seven different theories as to how she came by her name, none of them plausible enough to concern us here. This much is certain: Calamity Jane loved the company of men and, as time went on, she craved booze more and more.

Assuming that she was born in 1852, she was thirteen when she bobbed up in Montana, conjecturally an orphan; seventeen when, wearing men's clothes, she was consorting with the railroad section gangs in Piedmont and Cheyenne, Wyoming; twenty when, in Dodge City, she made a cowboy crooner called Darling Bob Mackay dance tenderfoot (i.e., obliged him to scamper about by firing bullets at his feet) because he had said something indelicate about her underwear; twenty-three, and the only female member, when she joined a geological expedition into the Black Hills; and twenty-four when, the only woman amongst 1,500 men, she left Fort Laramie with a bull train hauling supplies for General Crook's expedition against the Sioux.

Not long after, a scandalized colonel caught her swimming naked with some of her buddies in Hat Creek, near Sheridan, and promptly banished her. Undaunted, she got Grouard, Crook's chief of scouts, to appoint her an Indian scout under his command—or so it was said, but never proved.

By then the unfortunate woman was a seriously sick alcoholic, ready for any man's exploitation if only she could get a drink. Greedy showmen hired her for appearances in dime museums; her ghost-written memoirs appeared, published in a cheap pamphlet, and Calamity took to hawking copies for whatever she could get.

And then, long after Calamity was dead, a woman appeared who produced a paper certifying the marriage on September 1, 1870, of Martha Jane Cannary and James Butler Hickok; she claimed to be the daughter of Wild Bill and Calamity Jane. She claimed it right out loud, to an audience of several million persons, over a network of radio stations. But presently the document was characterized as a forgery by experts, and the chroniclers of the Wild West could return to their speculations.

And here let us leave Calamity and Bill.

For we have come to our second Horrible—a slope-shouldered man whose blue eyes blink incessantly (he has granulated eyelids), and whose short whiskers grow dark on his chin and lower lip. We are now in the presence of the bandit-hero. He is

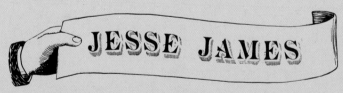

JESSE JAMES

Any study of Jesse Woodson James (September 5, 1847–April 3, 1882)—the celebrated Missouri ruffian, murderer, bank robber, train robber, and American demigod—is best prefaced by a quick glimpse at his mother, Zerelda E. Cole James Simms Samuel. She was, by all accounts, a notable woman.

After attending a Roman Catholic convent school in Lexington, Kentucky, she married a Baptist seminarian, Robert James. He left her to seek gold in California, where he died. Her second husband, Simms, having died as she was about to divorce him, she married a third, "a meek man." "She was, all her life, a religious woman," says one of Jesse's admiring biographers. "Love became her religion," says

another. "She was a woman thoroughly good and noble," the first biographer insists. Most certainly, the second agrees; and then informs us that, after her notorious son had been killed, she "boldly" showed tourists around Jesse's old farm, "extracting every dime she could from them." "This woman who had always been so upright," he adds, sold the tourists stones allegedly from Jesse's grave but actually from the creek. She also sold tourists enough shoes from the horses her two bandit sons had ridden "to fill a wagonbed."

But hear her cry out at Jesse's funeral, while two ministers lead the mourners in singing "We Will Wait Till Jesus Comes." * "Oh, my generous, noble-hearted Jesse," she moans, clearly enough to be heard by the reporters attending. "Oh, why did they kill my poor boy who never wronged anybody, but helped them and fed them with the bread that should go to his orphans?"

Her poor, generous, noble-hearted boy, who never wronged anybody, was the leader of a gang of comparably generous, noble-hearted thugs who, in fifteen years, held up eleven banks, seven trains, three stages, one county fair, and one payroll messenger, in the process looting some $200,000 and killing at least sixteen men. What the mothers of these sixteen said at their graves has unfortunately not been recorded.

Jesse's deification proceeded along the routine lines laid down by the "Police Gazette"—his prankish charm, his courteous behavior to women involved in his stick-ups, his protection of fictitious widows from villainous bankers seeking to foreclose fictitious mortgages, and all the rest—but in his case a unique attribute was added, one guaranteed to inflame the partisan passions bred of the Civil War. For Jesse symbolized the gallant Rebel, ground down beneath the boot of the victorious Yankee oppressor, and such was the potency of this bogus magic that his death kept the sovereign state of Missouri in an uproar for an entire decade.

Jesse grew up in an atmosphere of hate. Missouri men rode across the line into Kansas to cast fradulent votes they hoped would make Kansas a slave state; Kansas men resisted; Missouri men rode again to raid and kill; Kansas men rode back in vengeance. When the Civil War erupted, there was a whole generation of teen-age toughs living in the tier of Missouri counties that border on Kansas, all of them handy with guns and knives, all of them committed on the political issues of the day, all of them itching to start a rumble. To name just a handful of these hellions: there were Frank James, eighteen, and his brother Jesse, fourteen; Cole Younger, seventeen, Jim Younger, thirteen, and two

---

* Or, as it may have been, "What a Friend We Have in Jesus." As seems always to be the case in these histories of Wild West personages, the authorities cannot agree on anything, no matter how grave of import.

other brothers, Bob and John, who were still just children; Jim Reed, sixteen; Ed Shirley, about eighteen, and his sister Myra Belle, thirteen.

All these youngters (except Myra Belle) became bushwhackers—i.e., Confederate irregulars—most of them serving under the infamous William C. Quantrill, the psychopathic turncoat and killer who is justifiably remembered as "the bloodiest man known to the annals of America." Frank James and Cole Younger were with Quantrill when, in August, 1863, the town of Lawrence, Kansas, was sacked and 182 of its citizens murdered. Jesse James and Jim Younger were with Quantrill's lieutenant, Bloody Bill Anderson, at the Centralia massacre a year later, when more than two hundred Federal soldiers were shot down, many of them being prisoners.

themselves variously. When Cole Younger, for example, hid out in Texas in 1868, who should he find down there near Dallas but li'l ole Myra Belle Shirley! Why, the last time he saw Myra Belle, back in Jasper County, she was just a scrawny kid in pigtails! But before long she was the mother of his illegitimate daughter, a girl she named Pearl Younger. And when Jim Reed came south in 1870, also on the lam, Myra Belle took him also into her house, and she cleaved unto him and presented him also with an illegitimate child, a boy she named Ed Reed. For his part, Jim Younger whiled away the time between robberies by serving as deputy sheriff in Dallas.

But the acknowledged leader of "The Boys," as they were fondly called, had no use for such tom-

Jesse James (left) was handsomely revived by Tyrone Power (right), who ornamented the picture of the same name in 1939; yet his legend was already flourishing when Ford shot him (center).

Jesse is credited with killing the commander, Major Johnson. Jesse was then seventeen.

With the end of the war, most of the bushwhackers laid down their guns and went to work as decent citizens. Not, however, this handful.

The James and Younger brothers (and probably Jim Reed) hitched together a gang of like-minded hooligans that went right on robbing and killing. Their first score, at Liberty, Missouri, on February 14, 1866, was against the Clay County Savings Association Bank, an institution where, it may be presumed, many of their friends and neighbors kept their money. Frank and Jesse missed this caper, but their henchmen stole a sum estimated at from $62,-000 to $75,000; they killed one man. Why should they turn back after such a success?

In between robberies and murders, they occupied

foolery because, we are told, he was too pious. Jesse James was baptized and added to the strength of the Kearney Baptist Church near his home in 1868 (soon after he had killed a man in a bank robbery at Richmond, Missouri). He sang in church choirs; he even organized a group of the faithful and taught hymn-singing (a few months after murdering the cashier of a bank in Gallatin, Missouri). His Bible, we are assured, was well-thumbed; but apparently he skipped the chapters in Exodus where are listed the Ten Commandments, for he continued to kill and to steal, and at least twice he did not remember the Sabbath day, to keep it holy, but rather used it as the occasion for a train robbery.

By 1874 Jesse's crimes were a chief issue in Missouri's gubernatorial campaign: whether or not to suppress outlawry so that "capital and immigration can once again enter our state." But nothing was done; his raids continued.

By 1881 the baying was so close at Jesse's heels that pious or no, he likewise took off for Myra Belle's recherché resort for the criminally inclined. She had removed to a country place on the Canadian River in Oklahoma, which for nostalgic reasons she called Younger's Bend. Belle, having by now given the boot to such sometime outlaw-lovers as Jack Spaniard, Jim French, Jim July, John Middleton, and an Indian known as Blue Duck, had actually gotten married to a Cherokee named Sam Starr. She was in consequence now known as Belle Starr, and could Jesse have known that she would one day be celebrated all over the country as the Bandit Queen, or the Female Jesse James, he might have

his way into the affections of future generations.

Her old neighbor Jesse James lies under a small stone near the site of the Kearney Baptist Church. The stone is all that has been left by souvenir hunters of what was once a pretentious monument, on which had been carved this inscription:

In Loving Remembrance of My Beloved Son
JESSE JAMES
Died April 3, 1882
Aged 34 Years, 6 Months, 28 Days
Murdered by a Traitor and Coward Whose
Name Is Not Worthy to Appear Here.

His mother and stepfather lie in graves on either side of his. On her stone is carved MOTHER, and on his is carved PAPPY.

Belle Starr (left, with her paramour "Blue Duck") got a most touching tombstone (center). But what admirer could have foreseen her reincarnation as Gene Tierney (right) in the 1941 movie?

cursed a tiny curse, pious man that he may have been notwithstanding. But he was dead before then, shot in the back of the head by "the dirty little coward," Bob Ford.

Myra Belle Shirley, horse thief, cattle thief, suspected robber of stagecoaches, constant concubine and protector of desperate criminals, was shot in the back and killed near Eufaula, Oklahoma, on February 3, 1889. A neighbor, Edgar Watson, was accused of her murder, but the charges against him were dismissed. It was rumored that she was slain by her son, Ed Reed, with whom she had had incestuous relations. He was angry with his mother, for she had whipped him after he rode her favorite horse without her permission. So it went, out in the glamorous, romantic Wild West. Scarcely a day passed without some gay and gallant gun slinger shooting

But had Jesse really been killed in 1882? There were folk in Clay County—and elsewhere, too—who whispered that the murder had been staged, that Jesse still lived and would ride again. He "couldn't" have died. The flood of dime novels about him, the plays, the six motion pictures contrived by Hollywood, this was not enough: the gullible still swore that Jesse lived. Naturally, this being the case, men claiming to be Jesse began to appear one after another. But at length time ran out on them. The last claimant bobbed up in 1948, which meant that he had to act 101 years old, an irksome role. This scalawag at least had the wit to take an appropriate alias. He asserted that he had lived through the years as Frank Dalton, a name which, since it recalled the Dalton gang of the 1890's, fitly closed the circle of Wild West outlawry.

It is time to turn to our next exhibit. Here we have two men mounted on the same pedestal, standing shoulder to shoulder; pals, pards till hell freezes. Each is expressionless, poker-faced; each is clad in black broadcloth and white linen; each affects a handlebar moustache; each has hard blue-gray eyes; each wears a star; at each hip hangs a six-gun. Clearly we are now confronting the men who tamed the Wild West. Sure enough, for their labels read

WYATT EARP AND BAT MASTERSON

Here are two of the regnant superheroes of the televised Wild West. Once upon a time they faced the same foes in the same filmed fables, but times have changed; they have gone their separate sponsored ways. This is a pity, for in real life the two were thick as thieves.

Each week we are shown—in bland, bright little slices of televised entertainment—just how they scrubbed the Wild West clean, including the back of its neck and behind its ears. Clean-cut and clean-shaven, Wyatt romances Nellie Cashman, the "miners' angel," or he avenges the murder of some Indian friends, or he traps some mining executives who would thieve silver bullion. Elegant and clean-shaven, Bat foils a horse-race swindler, or he gallantly assists some ladies in their struggle for woman's rights, or by examining the brushwork he perceives that some oil paintings are spurious. All this is only so much ingenious fretwork on the Earp-Masterson legend, contrived by worthy successors to the staff writers of the "National Police Gazette." But the legend is itself such an imposing structure as to require no further embellishment.

The legend tells us that Marshal Earp cleaned up two Kansas cowtowns, Ellsworth and Wichita, singlehanded. He then joined forces with Bat Masterson to clean up Dodge City, "the wickedest little city in America." So much accomplished, Marshal Earp turned his attention to the featherweight task of pacifying Tombstone, Arizona, a hotbed of outlaws unparalleled in history, whilst Sheriff Masterson proceeded to stamp out sin in the mining camps of Colorado. Thereafter both men retired, breathing easily, having made the Wild West safe for the effete tenderfeet of the East.

Both men, the legend adds, were courteous to women, modest, handsome, and blue-eyed. We are also told that Earp was the Wild West's speediest and deadliest gun fighter. For his part, Masterson disdained to pull a gun, preferring to clout an ad-

versary senseless with his cane, whence his nickname. But he was quite willing to testify to his pal's prowess and so contribute to the legend. Earp, so Masterson has assured us, could kill a coyote with his Colt .45 at four hundred yards.*

Masterson himself, who was in truth a poor shot, killed at most four men throughout his career (not counting Indians). Indeed, these two differ sharply from other Wild West heroes in that they rarely fired their six-guns in anger. They were both sly, cunning, cautious men, who early learned that shooting might reap a bloody harvest. In consequence, they walked warily, carrying a big bluff. In their time, the Wild West killer and outlaw was dying out, to be replaced by the confidence man. Confidence men rarely kill; they are too artful. Both Earp and Masterson were, among other things, eager students of the technique of early confidence games.

They first met in 1872, when both were hunting buffalo on the Salt Fork of the Arkansas, in direct violation of the Indian treaty. Earp was twenty-four; Masterson was nineteen. They seem to have recognized that they were kindred souls, but they parted, not to come together again until the summer of 1876, in Dodge City. During those four years Bat was, so to say, preparing himself to be a peace officer. He stole forty ponies from some Indians and sold them for $1,200, he killed other Indians both as a free-lance buffalo hunter and as an army scout, and he got into a brawl with an army sergeant at Sweetwater, Texas, over a dance-hall girl. The girl was killed while trying to shield Masterson; Bat was wounded, but he killed the soldier.

Meantime Earp, by his own account, had engaged in even more impressive heroics. First there was his mettlesome exploit at Ellsworth in 1873. To hear him tell it, Earp stepped out of a crowd, unknown and unheralded, and stalked alone across that familiar sun-baked plaza to disarm an able and truculent gun fighter, the Texas gambler Ben Thompson. Not only that, but Thompson was backed up at the time by a hundred pugnacious cowboy friends. How could Earp ever have dared to do it? He would seem to have been cloaked in invisibility, for others who were present never saw him—not the reporter for the Ellsworth newspaper; not Thompson himself; not Deputy Sheriff Hogue, to whom Thompson voluntarily turned over his gun; and not Mayor

* Such skill calls for some respectful analysis. At four hundred yards a coyote cannot be seen against his natural background, so we shall assume the animal is silhouetted against the sky. Even so, an expert using a rifle with a globe sight would congratulate himself if he hit such a target with any regularity, much more if he killed it. A pistol, of course, will not carry so far directly; the marksman must use Kentucky windage—i.e., he must aim appreciably above his target so that his bullet will carry. Masterson admitted that "luck figures largely in such shooting." If, instead of "largely," he had said "completely," he would have come closer to that coyote.

James Miller, to whom Thompson gave bond for his appearance when he might be wanted later.

Is it possible Earp was not there at all?

In May, 1874, Earp arrived in Wichita, another rowdy cowtown, where, he said later, Mayor Jim Hope promptly made him the marshal. Let Earp speak: "In two years at Wichita my deputies and I arrested more than eight hundred men. In all that time I had to shoot but one man—and that only to disarm him. All he got was a flesh wound."

And now a look at the minutes of the Wichita city commission. They show that Earp was elected on April 21, 1875, as one of two policemen to serve under the marshal and assistant marshal. They show further that on April 19, 1876, the commission voted against rehiring him. A month later it was recommended that the vagrancy act be enforced against Earp and his brother Jim.

Judging from the Wichita newspapers, Earp seems not to have won much of a reputation during his one year as a policeman. They keep referring to him as "Policeman Erp," which makes him sound like a walking advertisement for Dr. Brown's Celery Tonic. Now and then he arrested a suspected horse thief; but the longest newspaper story about him describes how he was arrested, fined, and fired from the police force for violating the peace on April 5, 1876. All this resulted from an election-eve fracas in which Earp slugged an opposition candidate for city marshal. And so he turned up in Dodge City, another cowtown.

Dodge was run by a small clique of saloonkeepers who, as the years went on, took turns at being mayor. Most saloons were routinely outfitted with gambling layouts. In 1878 the town council enacted an ordinance against gambling. Had its members gone out of their minds? No: they were moved by sound common sense. For, with a law on the books prohibiting gambling, any chump who complained that he had been cheated could be forthwith walked Spanish to the hoosegow on the grounds that he had been breaking the law.

A town run along these lines clearly required something special in the way of a peace officer: a man who would know how and when to enforce the freakish laws, who would know how to wink at the artful ways in which cowpokes from Texas were mulcted. We are told that the saloonkeeper who was mayor in 1876 sent for Wyatt Earp.

Earp told his skillful biographer, Stuart Lake, that he appointed Bat Masterson as one of his deputies. Earp also asserted that he was paid $250 a month, plus a fee of $2.50 for each arrest; he and his deputies, he said, arrested some three hundred persons a month, or enough to bring in about $750 a month. (One month in 1877, he recalled, the fees reached almost $1,000 from nearly four hundred arrests; that was the peak.) Earp's share would have brought his income to more than $400 a month, nice money for the time and place.

And now to the town records. Earp was never marshal of Dodge. He served two terms as assistant marshal: from May, 1876, to September, 1876, and from May, 1878, to September, 1879. (During that month of 1877 when, by his own account, he and his deputies arrested nearly four hundred rowdy cowboys, Earp was not a peace officer at all. In fact, he was himself arrested that month for brawling with a dance-hall girl.) His salary as assistant marshal was $75 a month. The fee paid for an arrest (and conviction) was only $2. The docket of the police court shows that during 1878 there were only sixty-four arrests; during 1879 there were only twenty-nine arrests.

One interpretation of this remarkable decline in arrests—from three hundred or four hundred a month in 1876–77 to just four a month in 1878–79—is that lion-hearted Wyatt Earp had tamed the town. There is another interpretation.

At all events, it is clear that Earp's income in 1878 could not have been much more than $80 a month—not much money for the time and place. Bat Masterson's income was about the same. Both had to add to it. Both did: as professional gamblers.

It has been argued that professional gambling in the Wild West was honest. This is to impose on credulity. Obviously it was no more honest than professional gambling whenever and wherever—which is to say, no more honest than it had to be.

Earp was a professional gambler long before he got to Dodge; his reputation around Hays City, according to Dr. Floyd Streeter, a Kansas historian, was that of a card player who was "up to some dishonest trick every time he played."

Masterson, who left Dodge in July, 1876, to follow the gold rush to Deadwood, got no further than Cheyenne, Wyoming, where he did so well as a faro banker that he stuck. But he was back in Dodge for the cattle season of 1877. On June 6 he was arrested, jugged, and fined $25 and costs for an act of hooliganism. Then he returned to his faro bank.

However, he badly wanted a star. Every professional gambler needed a star; the badge of office permitted its wearer to carry a gun, which in turn provided just the psychological advantage necessary in a game of chance played for high stakes. (Only peace officers were permitted to carry guns in Dodge City; all others were obliged to check their weapons in racks provided for the purpose.) And so Bat decided to run for sheriff of Ford County.

His electioneering technique was simplicity itself: he bought an interest in the Lone Star Dance Hall. Only thus could a candidate convince the bizarre

Bat Masterson (standing, second from right) and Wyatt Earp (seated, second from left), now each rate a TV series of his own. Gene Barry (center) and Hugh O'Brian (right) play the partners who have gone their separate ways; in life, they were "thick as thieves."

electorate of Dodge City that he was a sound citizen and a responsible taxpayer. In November, 1877, Bat was elected by a three-vote margin. He took office in January, and what is more, he started off in high gear by catching some would-be train robbers. But as the months wore on, like Earp, and like Hickok before them both, he whiled away his evening hours as a professional gambler along with cronies like Doc Holliday, an alcoholic ex-dentist, and Luke Short, a dandiprat. Earp banked faro at the Long Branch Saloon for a percentage of the house's gross. He and Bat and the others spent so many nights in Dodge's brothels that they were nicknamed "the Fighting Pimps."

There was justification for the slur. Earp lived with a girl called Mattie Blaylock; since no record of any marriage has ever been found, she is presumed to have been his common-law wife. And Nyle Miller, director of the Kansas State Historical Society, and an authority on the dossiers of Earp and Masterson, has established that, according to the census of 1880, Bat Masterson was living with Annie Ladue, nineteen, described as his "concubine," whilst his younger brother, Jim Masterson, by then Dodge's marshal in his turn, was living with Minnie Roberts, sixteen, also a concubine. As Mr. Miller has commented acidly, "Maybe that was the way some of the officers in those days kept watch over juvenile delinquents. They just lived with them."

By that time Bat was no longer sheriff, having been walloped in his bid for re-election by George Hinkle, a bartender. Earp had also turned in his star. Dodge was not appreciably tamer, but the silver strike in the Arizona hills meant that there might be more money lying around loose in Tombstone; he followed his brother Virgil there in December, 1879.

With him came Mattie; with him too were other Earps, his brothers Jim and Morgan and their wives; and presently, tagging along after him, came Doc Holliday with his common-law wife, Big Nose Kate Fisher, a Dodge prostitute.

Tombstone, they soon found, was strangely unlike Dodge City. Four churches were going up. (Groton's future headmaster, Endicott Peabody, was the young Episcopalian clergyman.) There were carpets in the saloons, forsooth, and French phrases on the menus in restaurants. No doubt about it, the Wild West was running out of steam.

Dogged traditionalists, Wyatt Earp got a job as a shotgun messenger for Wells Fargo and his brother Jim caught on as a faro banker.

Wyatt was not, as the legend has it, a United States marshal at this time. His brother Virgil was appointed a deputy marshal for southern Arizona in November, 1879, and was appointed an assistant town marshal of Tombstone in October, 1880; but Wyatt, after a brief term as civil deputy sheriff of Pima County, went back to gambling at the Oriental Saloon.

A word about Doc Holliday. He was, from every account but Wyatt's, a mean and vicious man. He was Georgia-born, tubercular, and fond of killing. After killing two Negroes in Georgia, he fled; after killing a man in Dallas, he fled; after killing a soldier near Fort Richardson, he fled; after wounding a man in Denver, he fled. It was the pattern of his life. Then he met Earp. "Doc idolized him," Masterson said later. And Earp, for his part, found much to admire in Holliday.

"With all of Doc's shortcomings and his undeniably poor disposition," Earp told Stuart Lake, "I found him a loyal friend and good company. . . ."

Earp's trouble began on the night of March 15, 1881, when a stagecoach left Tombstone carrying eight passengers, and, we are told, $80,000 worth of bullion.* Bandits attempted to halt this miracle of transportation. They failed, but in the process they killed the driver and one passenger. The killer was, according to a statement by his wife, Doc Holliday; and the talk around town was that the brain behind the bungled holdup was Wyatt Earp's. Moving fast, the Earps persuaded Big Nose Kate to retract her statement and bundled her out of town lest she contradict the retraction. There remained the task of silencing forever Holliday's accomplices.

Wyatt went to one of their friends, Ike Clanton, and offered a deal. If Clanton would arrange to have those accomplices hold up another stage so that Earp and Holliday could ambush them, he, Earp, would guarantee that Clanton would be paid the reward for their capture. Clanton seems to have considered this offer seriously, but at length he refused. The rebuff was serious, for Ike was a blabbermouth who could not be trusted to keep the offer quiet.

Nor did he. Scared stiff that he would be shot for a stool pigeon, Clanton denied everything, so loudly and publicly that Doc Holliday overheard him and reported to Wyatt. That was in mid-October. Something would have to be done.

On October 26, Ike Clanton was back in Tombstone with his younger brother, Billy. With them were Frank and Tom McLowry and another youngster, Billy Claiborne. All these men were cattle rustlers or, at the very least, hard cases. That morning Virgil Earp, as town marshal, deputized his brothers Wyatt and Morgan, and thereafter the three prowled the streets, seeking to pick a quarrel with the Clantons or the McLowrys. Virgil Earp clubbed Ike Clanton with the barrel of his revolver. Wyatt Earp deliberately jostled Tom McLowry and then struck him. But despite the provocations, there was no fight.

That afternoon the Clanton brothers, the McLowry brothers, and Claiborne went to the O. K. Corral to pick up their horses and ride out of town. Wyatt, Virgil, and Morgan Earp, together with Doc Holliday, went after them. Sheriff John Behan tried to interfere, but he was brushed aside.

The Earps and Holliday marched into the corral. Somebody spoke; somebody started shooting. After a couple of minutes, Billy Clanton was dead, Frank and Tom McLowry were dead, and Ike Clanton and Billy Claiborne, having run for their lives, were safe. Morgan Earp was hit in the left shoulder; Virgil in the leg; Holliday in the left hip.

The Earp apologists have described these slayings as a triumph of law and order. In Tombstone

the reaction was somewhat different. A sign over the caskets of the dead proclaimed: MURDERED IN THE STREETS OF TOMBSTONE. A mining engineer named Lewis, who had witnessed what he called cold-blooded murder, was one of three men appointed by the Citizens' Safety Committee to tell the Earps that there should be no more killing inside the town's limits, and that, if there were, the committee would act without regain to law; finally, Virgil Earp was fired as town marshal on October 29.

In any case, friends of those slain took matters into their own hands. Virgil Earp was ambushed and wounded on December 29. In March, 1882, Morgan Earp was picked off in the middle of a billiard game, by a sharpshooter who fired through a window from an alley in back. By this time Wyatt Earp had apparently at long last managed to be deputized by a federal marshal. (No records exist in either the Department of Justice or the National Archives to show that he ever held a regular commission as U.S. marshal or deputy.) He in turn deputized such gunmen as Doc Holliday, Turkey Creek Jack Johnson, and Texas Jack Vermillion, and took off in pursuit of his brother's killers.

He rode and he rode, but he never came back. He rode north and east to Colorado where, he hoped, he would be safe. Behind him he left Mattie, his common-law wife, who had taken in sewing at a penny a yard when money was scarce. Behind him, too, he left a town so far from being tamed that President Chester Arthur was obliged, a few months later, to threaten martial law. It was left to a short-spoken, sawed-off, former Texas Ranger named John H. Slaughter to restore order to Cochise County.

And meanwhile, what of Bat Masterson? He had hustled back to Dodge City from Tombstone in April, 1881, in response to a hurry-up plea for help from his younger brother Jim. This worthy, still Dodge's marshal and also co-owner of a dance hall, had got into a scrape with his partner, A. J. Peacock, and the man they employed as bartender, Al Updegraff, but Jim Masterson was apparently too timid to do his own fighting. His big brother stepped off the train at noon on April 16. Peacock and Updegraff were there waiting, and once again the tiresome shooting commenced. It was laughable. They all fired their guns empty, without effect. Some unknown hero, using a rifle, wounded Updegraff from behind. Masterson was fined $8 for shooting his pistol on the street. The Ford County "Globe" commented, "The citizens are thoroughly aroused and will not stand any more foolishness," while the Jetmore "Republican" referred caustically to "the old gang." Bat and his brother were ordered out of town.

Like a cat, Bat landed on his feet in Trinidad, Colorado, where in addition to running a gambling concession he appears to have been appointed a peace officer. Certainly he had some political influ-

---

* It is always instructive to examine Wild Western estimates. At $1 per fine ounce, $80,000 worth of bullion would weigh two and a half tons, a load sure to snap the axles of any coach.

ence. For, when an Arizona sheriff came to Denver with a request for the extradition of Wyatt Earp and Doc Holliday, Masterson helped protect them. He got out a warrant for Holliday's arrest on the charge of running a confidence game. This superseded the request for extradition, after which the charges against Holliday were of course dropped. "I know him well," Bat told a reporter for the Denver "Republican," speaking of Holliday. "He was with me in Dodge, where he was known as an enemy of the lawless element."

But the trail led down from glory. In the 1890's Masterson ran a faro layout at the Arcade in Denver, then notoriously the crookedest town in the country. (Earp was dealing nearby, at the Central.) But around the turn of the century Bat was ordered to leave even Denver—it was like being told he was too low for the sewer. In 1902 he went to New York where he was at once arrested. On the train from Chicago he had, it seems, fleeced a Mormon elder of $16,000 by using marked cards in a faro game. No matter: New York was then also corrupt; Bat was bailed by John Considine, a partner of Big Tim Sullivan, who bossed the town. The elder was persuaded to mumble that he must have been mistaken when he identified Masterson. When Bat was again arrested, this time for illegally carrying a gun, his friends pulled on strings that led all the way to the White House; and such was the magic of the Wild West legend that President Theodore Roosevelt appointed Masterson a deputy U.S. marshal for the southern district of New York. The term of the appointment was brief. Then Bat was put out to pasture as a sports writer for the "Morning Telegraph." He died at his desk in 1921.

Meantime Earp had married a San Francisco woman named Josephine Marcus. As late as 1911 he was accused of complicity in a confidence game, but in the main he had retired to live off his investments. He died in Los Angeles in 1930. The ugliest bit of his past has been dug up, with some disgust, by Frank Waters. It concerns Mattie, the girl Earp deserted in Tombstone. Alone and friendless, Mattie drifted first to Globe and then to a mining camp near Willcox, Arizona. She was reduced to prostitution for a living. In July, 1888, she died of an overdose of laudanum, a suicide. The coroner who sent her few belongings back to her family in Iowa tucked into the package a letter in which he wrote that Mattie had been deserted by "a gambler, blackleg, and coward." Among her effects was a Bible that had been presented to Earp when he was in Dodge. The inscription read: "To Wyatt S. Earp as a slight recognition of his many Christian virtues and steady following in the footsteps of the meek and lowly Jesus."

Amen.

We have come at last to our fifth Horrible, a slight, short, buck-toothed, narrow-shouldered youth whose slouch adds to his unwholesome appearance.

He looks like a cretin, but this may be deceptive. As we crane cautiously forward, we can see that his label reads

This young outlaw is less interesting as a human being than as a sort of Rorschach ink blot by which one may elicit fantasies and so study their inventors. It is safe to say that at least a thousand writers have used Billy the Kid as a vessel into which to pour their passions, prejudices, and opinions; but it is likely that no two portraits of him jibe. He has been endowed with every imaginable personality; from the way he has been described one could conclude that he was the original Man With a Thousand Faces; his alleged backgrounds are as various; so even are his names.

The best guess is that he was born November 23, 1859, in New York City, and called Henry McCarty. There was a younger brother, Joe. Around 1863 the family went west to Kansas. The father may have died here; at all events Mrs. Catherine McCarty was married on March 1, 1873, with her two sons as witnesses, to William H. Antrim, in Santa Fé, New Mexico. The newlyweds settled in Silver City, near the Arizona border, and here Mrs. Antrim died on September 16, 1874. Henry McCarty was not yet fifteen.

He killed for the first time three years later: a blacksmith called Windy Cahill, in a saloon near Camp Grant, Arizona. There followed some gambling and some horse stealing. He was next a principal figure in the celebrated Lincoln County War, an affair which, including skirmishes and at least one pitched battle, went on for more than a year. The villains of this "war" were politicians, involved in their customary muttonheaded struggle for power, and guilty of their customary nonfeasance, misfeasance, and malfeasance. The Kid seems to have been caught up in it chiefly because he wasn't old enough to know any better. Several persons were killed in the course of this "war," and the Kid may have killed one or more of them; none can say for sure. In any case, his side lost, and for the rest of his brief life he was an outlaw, a hunted man.

He stole some more livestock. He killed a man named Joe Grant, who had thought to shoot first. He rode with some exceedingly case-hardened characters, including Hendry Brown, John Middleton, and Dave Rudabaugh. Sheriff Pat Garrett and a posse first caught the Kid near Stinking Springs. He stood trial for murder, was found guilty, and was sentenced to be hanged. There were two men guarding him in the jail at Lincoln, but the Kid managed to get hold of a gun, killed them both, and fled again, again a free man.

Garrett, implacable, continued his pursuit. One brightly moonlit night he shot and killed the Kid in Fort Sumner, New Mexico. It was July 14, 1881. Henry McCarty, alias William Bonney, alias The Kid, was not yet twenty-two.

And now the fun began.

The first book to follow the Kid's death appeared a month later and was subtitled, "The history of an outlaw who killed a man for every year in his life," a fiction which was seized upon and inflated by nine out of every ten writers who followed. The author of this book was a man named Fable, appropriately enough, and he described the Kid as wearing "a blue dragoon jacket of the finest broadcloth, heavily loaded down with gold embroidery, buckskin pants, dyed a jet black, with small tinkling bells sewed down the sides . . . drawers of fine scarlet broadcloth . . . and a hat covered with gold and jewels. . . ."

The "Police Gazette" published a biography too, as did Pat Garrett. Both poured gore liberally over the Kid. Garrett added a nice touch: he said that Billy, to show his skill, once shot the heads off several snowbirds, one after another. (J. Frank Dobie has remarked tartly, of this story, that it didn't happen because it couldn't happen.)

By 1889 a Frenchman, the Baron de Mandat-Grancey, had written a wondrous book called "La Brèche aux Buffles"—this was his way of saying Buffalo Gap—in which he reported how Billy the Kid killed his prison guard, a man named William Bonny. Other accounts appeared: the Kid had been a dishwasher in his youth; no, he had been a boot-black in New York City's Fourth Ward; no, he had gone to college in the East and was really an Ivy League type.

The number of his killings mounted steadily. Soon he had killed twenty-three men, one for each of his now twenty-three years, not counting seven Mexicans whom he shot "just to see them kick." A play about him opened in 1906 and ran for years. By 1918 its producers claimed it had been seen by ten million people. It was in 1906, too, that a dime novel appeared in which the Kid was described as an Apache who had been killed by Buffalo Bill, assisted by Wild Bill Hickok.

Then, oddly, the Kid dropped out of sight for a generation. When he reappeared, he had been twenty-four years old, and killed twenty-four men. Walter Noble Burns sentimentalized him so successfully that Hollywood brought out the first of some twenty movies about him. (Of these, the two best-known, perhaps, are those that starred Robert Taylor and Jane Russell.) Somebody made up the wonderful story that the gun Garrett had used to kill the Kid was the same gun worn by Wild Bill Hickok when he was shot in Deadwood. Somebody else wrote that the judge who sentenced the Kid ordered him to be hanged by the neck until "you are dead, dead, dead," to which Billy retorted, "You go to hell, hell, hell!"

The further away the mythmakers got from him, the more precisely they described him. He was "a boy of talent and exceptional intelligence," "good-natured and of a happy, carefree disposition," with "an unusually attractive personality." He was also "an adenoidal moron, both constitutionally and emotionally inadequate to a high degree." He killed forty-five men. He never killed anybody.

Billy the Kid (left), an "adenoidal moron," had not been dead a month when the Wide Awake Library *(center) published his "true life." In 1941 (right) he reappeared again as Robert Taylor.*

He was driven to a life of crime because, at the age of twelve, he killed a man who made a slurring remark to his mother. "His blue-gray eyes at times could turn cold and deadly." Pat Garrett never shot him at all, that night at Fort Sumner, for he was still alive in 1920, when he was known as Walk-Along Smith.

In one sense, it is, of course, perfectly true that Billy the Kid did not die. He is the most imperishable of our folk heroes. Under his name there will always appear, whenever appropriate, a figure freshly refurbished so as to embody the hero who appropriately symbolizes the need of the hour: brutal killer, avenging angel, mama's boy, slayer of capitalist dragons, bewildered cat's paw, or gay, gallant, carefree cowpoke. The face is blank, but it comes complete with a handy do-it-yourself kit so that the features may be easily filled in.

What, in summary, of the world of the Wild West? Manifestly, it was an underworld, corrupt and rotten. Its heroes, vaunted for their courage, in fact showed only the rashness of the alcoholic or the desperation of the cornered rat. They were popularly supposed to have honored the Wild West's so-called code, which forbade the shooting of an unarmed man and likewise the shooting of an armed man until he had been faced and warned of the peril in which he stood. But look at our five—the most celebrated heroes of all:

Hickok made his reputation by killing, from his hiding place, two unarmed men and then mortally wounding a third unarmed man who was running for his life.

Jesse James murdered at least two unarmed bank tellers, not because they had offered resistance, but when they were cowering at the bandit's feet.

Wyatt Earp and his brothers, shielded by police badges, provoked a fight, shot first, and killed men who, according to three eyewitnesses, were holding up their hands.

Bat Masterson is saved from any similar charge chiefly because he was such a poor shot.

Billy the Kid shot and killed from ambush, not once, but several times. Indeed, only the first of his authenticated killings seems to have come about in a man-to-man fight, and even on that occasion his opponent was unarmed.

What heroes, to be exalted by the Republic!

As outlaws, they were first adored because, it was argued, they robbed only the railroad monopolist and the banker, the men most heartily hated west of the Mississippi. As law officers, they were first adored because, it was argued, they enforced the peace in perilous circumstances, against overwhelming odds. Both propositions are cockeyed. Outlaw or law officer, it made little difference, they were one brutal brotherhood. The so-called law officers more often caused than quelled crime. Hendry Brown, an outlaw in New Mexico, could ride to Kansas and pin on a sheriff's star; Jim Younger, an outlaw in Missouri, could ride to Texas and pin on a deputy sheriff's star; even Billy the Kid rode for a time as a member of a bailiff's posse and, had his side won the Lincoln County War, might well have come down to us in folklore as a force for law and order. The whole boodle of them careened through lives of unredeemed violence and vulgarity, to fetch up—where else? In the Valhalla of the comics, the movies, and television.

But surely the producers of the popular entertainments do not pretend that they are purveying history? Surely they concede that their Wild West peep shows, especially on television, are at most so much embroidery basted onto the national folklore? Yet these entrepreneurs persist in using names of real people and real places. They cite dates of real occurrences—usually, to be sure, absurdly wrong. They lard their diversions with such sly phrases as "based on actual events" or "a colorful look at our American heritage." Speaking of Wyatt Earp, they describe him as "one of the real-life heroes of yesterday . . . one of the greatest marshals in the annals of history . . . this famous straight-shootin', fast-ridin', fair-playin', clean-livin' lawman. . . ." They transform vicious, alcoholic gun fighters like Johnny Ringo and Clay Allison into sheriffs, symbols of justice and peace. They portray Jesse James as an innocent youth unfairly forced into a career of crime, and Belle Starr as a winsome, dewy-eyed ingénue who looks for all the world like Miss Cream Puff of 1960.

And even granting the assumption that the purveyors of this sludge are concerned not with history but with legend, what a shameful and ghastly legend it is! to be despised, if not on the sufficient grounds of its ugly violence, then on the grounds of its even uglier vulgarity.

The moral, of course, is that crime, when commercially exploited, does pay, and the more sadistic the better. The Wild West—portrayed by irresponsible men who care not a hang for the truth of history so long as they can count their audiences in the scores of millions—has become a permanent industry and has created for the world an enduring image of America.

Over it there hangs the stink of evil.

THE END

On a blizzardy April morning in 1892, fifty armed men surrounded a cabin on Powder River in which two accused cattle rustlers had been spending the night. The first rustler was shot as he came down the path for the morning bucket of water; he was dragged over the doorstep by his companion, to die inside. The second man held out until afternoon, when the besiegers fired the house. Driven out by the flames, he went down with twenty-eight bullets in him. He was left on the bloodstained snow with a card pinned to his shirt, reading: "Cattle thieves, beware!"

So far the affair follows the standard pattern of frontier heroics, a pattern popularized by Owen Wister and justified to some extent by the facts of history if you don't look too closely: strong men on a far frontier, in the absence of law, make their own law for the protection of society, which generally approves.

Thus runs the cliché, but in Wyoming this time it went awry. In the first place the attackers were not crude frontiersmen taking the law into their own hands. They were men of means and education, predominantly eastern, who really should have known better; civilized men, at home in drawing rooms and familiar with Paris. Two were Harvard classmates of the year '78, the one a Boston blue blood, the other a member of a Wall Street banking family. Hubert E. Teschemacher and Fred DeBillier had come west after graduation to hunt elk, as so many gilded youths from both sides of the Atlantic were doing; had fallen in love with the country; and had remained as partners in a half-million-dollar ranching enterprise.

Our fifty vigilantes were truly a strange company to ride through the land slaughtering people. The instigators dominated the cattle business and the affairs of the former territory, which had recently been elevated to statehood, and more than half of them had served in the legislature. Their leader, Major Frank Wolcott, was a fierce little pouter pigeon of a man, a Kentuckian lately of the Union Army, whose brother was United States senator from Colorado. Accompanying the party as surgeon was a socially prominent Philadelphian, Dr. Charles Bingham Penrose, who had come to Wyoming for his health. It was not improved by his experiences.

These gentlemen had no thought of the danger to themselves as they set out, without benefit of the law, to liquidate their enemies. Convinced of their own righteousness, they expected nine-tenths of the people of Wyoming to be on their side, and they even looked for a popular uprising to assist them. Instead, thirty-six hours after their sanguinary victory on Powder River, they were surrounded in their turn by an enraged horde of citizens, and just missed being lynched

Enraged by losses from their herd.

took the law into their own hand.

THE JOHNSON

band of respectable cattle barons

—and barely escaped with their lives

COUNTY WAR

By HELENA HUNTINGTON SMITH

themselves. They were saved only by the intervention of the President of the United States, who ordered federal troops to their aid. But it wasn't quite the usual scene of the cavalry riding to the rescue at the end of the movie, for while the cattlemen were snatched from imminent death, they were also arrested for the murder of the two men and marched off in custody of the troops—the latter, from the commanding officer on down, making clear their personal opinion that they regretted the rescue.

So ended the Johnson County War—tragic, bizarre, unbelievable. It was all a sequel to the great beef bonanza, which began around 1880. The cattle boom combined the most familiar features of the South Sea Bubble and the 1929 bull market—such as forty per cent dividends that would never cease—with some special features of its own—such as a rash of adventuring English Lords and Honorables, free grass, and the blessings of "natural increase" provided by the prolific Texas cow. A man could grow rich without his lifting a finger.

Instead of the old-style cow outfit with its headquarters in a dugout and a boss who ate beef, bacon, and beans, there were cattle companies with offices in Wall Street, London, or Edinburgh; champagne parties; thoroughbred racing on the plains; and younger sons who were shipped out west to mismanage great ranches at fancy salaries. In a raw new city sprawled along the Union Pacific tracks, the Cheyenne Club boasted the best steward of any club in the United States, and its members were drawn from a roster of aristocracy on both sides of the Atlantic. Burke's Peerage and the Social Register mingled, though not intimately, with common cowhands from Texas, but only the latter knew anything about cattle.

To be sure, some of what they knew was a trifle shady: they knew how to handle a long rope and a running iron; how to brand a maverick right out from under the noses of the lords. But the mavericks, unbranded animals of uncertain ownership, were rather casually regarded anyhow; "finders keepers" was the unwritten rule which had governed their disposition in the early days, and they had been a source of controversy and bloodshed throughout the history of the West. While they were now claimed by the big cattle companies, the Texas cowboys were not impressed.

The boom crashed into ruin in the awful winter of 1886-87. Snow fell and drifted and thawed and froze and fell again, clothing the ground with an iron

A Necktie Party *was the title given to this sketch by Charles M. Russell of summary Far Western justice and its somber, deliberate executioners. At least one such lynching was a part of the prologue to the Johnson County War.*

271

sheath of white on which a stagecoach could travel and through which no bovine hoof could paw for grass; and since the plains were heavily overstocked and the previous summer had been hot and dry, there was no grass anyway. Moaning cattle wandered into the outskirts of towns, trying to eat frozen garbage and the tar paper off the eaves of the shacks; and when the hot sun of early summer uncovered the fetid carcasses piled in the creek bottoms, the bark of trees and brush was gnawed as high as a cow could reach. Herd losses averaged fifty per cent, with ninety per cent for unacclimated southern herds, and some moral revulsion set in, even the Cheyenne *Daily Sun* remarking that a man who turned animals out on a barren plain without food or shelter would suffer loss of respect of the community in which he lived.

Meanwhile there were gloomy faces at the Cheyenne Club. "Cheer up, boys," quipped the bartender across the street, setting out a row of glasses, "the books won't freeze."

In the heyday of the beef bonanza, herds had been bought and sold by "book count," based on a back-of-an-envelope calculation of "natural increase," with no pother about a tally on the range. As the day of reckoning dawned, it turned out that many big companies had fewer than half the number of cattle claimed on their books. Now the terrible winter cut this half down to small fractions; faraway directors, grown glacial as the weather, hinted that blizzards were the fault of their underlings in Cheyenne; while the few surviving cows, instead of giving birth to sextuplets as was their clear duty, produced a correspondingly diminished calf crop to fatten on the gorgeous grass that sprang up after the snows.

In their bitterness, the cattlemen believed that the damned thieves were to blame. Obsessed with this idea, they now proceeded to bring upon themselves an epidemic of stealing without parallel in the West. At least that was what they called it, though to a cool-headed observer from Nebraska it looked more like "the bitter conflict which has raged incessantly between large and small owners."

In fact it was even more. For Wyoming in the nineties shared the outlook of that decade everywhere else; a decade of economic and moral monopoly, when righteousness belonged exclusively to the upper class, along with the means of production; a decade when the best people simply could not be wrong. The best people in this case were the Wyoming Stock Growers Association and their several rich and prominent eastern friends, and the climate of opinion they breathed was startlingly revealed in the hanging of Jim Averill and Cattle Kate. When the cattlemen shed crocodile tears because thieves went unwhipped,

they forgot that thieves were not the worst to go free. At least six persons were shot or hanged in the years before the final flare-up, but not one person was ever brought to trial for the crimes—not even in the case of Jim Averill and the woman whose real name was Ella, who were hanged on the Sweetwater in 1889.

Averill and Ella ran a log-cabin saloon and road ranch up a desolate little valley off the Sweetwater, and they were nuisances. The man was articulate and a Populist of sorts, and had attacked the big cattlemen in a letter to the local press; the woman was a cowboys' prostitute who took her pay in stolen cattle. From this, aristocratic Dr. Penrose could argue later that "she had to die for the good of the country."

Die she did, with her paramour, at the end of a rope thrown over a tree limb and swung out over a gulch. There were three eyewitnesses to the abduction and one to the actual hanging, and a coroner's jury named four prominent cattlemen among the perpetrators. But before the case reached the grand jury three of the witnesses had vanished and the fourth had conveniently died. Afterward two of the men whose hands were filthy from this affair continued to rub elbows with the fastidious Teschemaker on the executive committee of the Stock Growers Association, and nauseating jokes about the last moments of Kate were applauded at the Cheyenne Club. Even Owen Wister joined in the applause, noting in his diary for October 12, 1889: "Sat yesterday in smoking car with one of the gentlemen indicted [sic] for lynching the man and the woman. He seemed a good solid citizen and I hope he'll get off."

The association tightened its blacklist. In a cattle

economy where cows were the only means of getting ahead, the cowboys had long been forbidden to own a brand or a head of stock on their own, lest they be tempted to brand a maverick. Now more and more of them were "blackballed" on suspicion from all lawful employment within the territory. Likewise the association made the rules of the range, ran the round-ups to suit itself, and kept out the increasing number of people it didn't like; hence many small stockmen, suspect of misbehavior by their very smallness, were also relegated to a shady no man's land outside the law.

If you call a man a thief, treat him like a thief, and deprive him of all chance to earn a living honestly, he will soon oblige you by becoming a thief.

By 1890 a thin colony of blackballed cowboys had settled on the rivers and creeks of Johnson County and were waging war with rope and running iron on the big outfits. Then early in 1892 a group calling themselves the Northern Wyoming Farmers' and Stockgrowers' Association announced in the press their intention of holding an independent roundup, in defiance of the state law and the Wyoming Stock Growers Association. This was provocative, insolent, outrageous if you like; it was hardly the furtive behavior of ordinary thieves.

Also announced in the press were the names of two foremen for what was now being called the "shotgun roundup." One was a Texan, known as a skilled cowhand, who was lightning with a gun. His name was Nathan D. Champion.

Meanwhile the storied walls of the Cheyenne Club beheld the amazing spectacle of nineteenth century gentlemen plotting wholesale murder. The declared object of their expedition was the "extermination"— not "arrest," but "extermination"—of various undesirable persons in the northern part of the state. The death list stood at seventy. In addition to a hard core of nineteen most-wanted rustlers, it almost certainly included a large number who were merely thought to be too close to the rustler faction, among them the sheriff of Johnson County and the three county commissioners.

This incredible project was fully known in advance to Acting Governor Amos W. Barber, to United States Senators Joseph M. Carey and Francis E. Warren, and to officials of the Union Pacific Railroad, whose consent to run a special train was obtained; and none of whom found anything questionable in the undertaking. Twenty-five hired gunfighters from Texas raised the manpower complement to fifty, since the local cowboys were thoroughly disaffected and would not have pulled a trigger for their employers. A smart Chicago newsman, Sam T. Clover, had heard about the impending necktie party and was in Cheyenne determined to get the story for the *Herald.* He and a local reporter were taken along just as though the expedition were legal; it apparently had not occurred to the planners that they were inviting witnesses to murder.

They got started the afternoon of April 5, on board a train loaded with men, arms, equipment, horses, and three supply wagons. An overnight run landed them in Casper, two hundred miles to the northwest, where they descended, saddled their horses, and were off before the townspeople were up—except for enough of the latter to start talk. Their objective was Buffalo, the county seat of Johnson County, but when they arrived at a friendly ranch on the second night, they received new intelligence which determined them to change their course: Nate Champion and possibly a good catch of other rustlers were at a cabin on the Middle Fork of Powder River, only twelve miles away. They decided to detour and finish this group off before proceeding to Buffalo.

Rumors have come down to us of the drinking and dissension that accompanied this decision: faced with the actuality of shooting trapped men in a cabin the next morning, stomachs began to turn over, and three members of the party pulled out, including the doctor and the local newsman. But that night the main body rode on to the attack, through one of the worst April

blizzards in memory. They plodded along without speaking, while beards and mustaches became coated with ice, and the wind lashed knife-edged snow in their faces. Halting before daybreak to thaw out around sagebrush fires, they went on until they looked down over a low bluff at the still-sleeping KC ranch.

Two innocent visitors, trappers, had been spending the night in the cabin. As first one and then the other sauntered forth into the gray morning air, he was recognized as not among the wanted men, and as soon as a corner of the barn hid him from the house, each was made prisoner. After a long wait Champion's friend Nick Ray finally appeared and was shot down. The door opened, and Champion himself faced a storm of bullets to drag Ray inside.

The fusillade went on for hour after hour. In the log shack Nate Champion was writing, with a cramped hand in a pocket notebook, the record of his last hours.

Me and Nick was getting breakfast when the attack took place. Two men was with us—Bill Jones and another man. The old man went after water and did not come back. His friend went to see what was the matter and he did not come back. Nick started out and I told him to look out, that I thought there was someone at the stable and would not let them come back.

Nick is shot but not dead yet. He is awful sick. I must go and wait on him.

It is now about two hours since the first shot. Nick is still alive.

They are still shooting and are all around the house, Boys, there is bullets coming in here like hail.

Them fellows is in such shape I can't get at them. They are shooting from the stable and river and back of the house.

Nick is dead. He died about 9 o'clock.

Hour after hour the hills crackled with rifle fire,

and such was the emptiness of the country that while the besiegers were on a main road, such as it was, connecting civilization with a little settlement at the back of beyond, they could bang away all day without fear of interruption. Or almost. As it happened there was a slight interruption in midafternoon.

Jack Flagg, a rustler intellectual of sorts, had left his ranch eighteen miles up the Red Fork of Powder River on this snowy morning of April 9, on his way to the Democratic state convention at Douglas, to which he was a delegate from Johnson County. It was one of the oddities of the situation that the thieves were all Democrats, and the murderers were all Republicans. A rancher, newspaper editor, and schoolteacher, Flagg was an accomplished demagogue who had twisted the tails of the big outfits by means fair and foul. He was very much on the wanted list.

He was riding about fifty yards or so behind a wagon driven by his seventeen-year-old stepson; and since the invaders had withdrawn into a strategy huddle and pulled in their pickets, there was no sound of firing to warn him as the wagon rattled downhill to the bridge by the KC. Flagg started over to the house to greet his friends, and was ordered to halt by someone who failed to recognize him.

"Don't shoot me, boys, I'm all right," he called gaily, taking it for a joke. Under the hail of bullets which disabused him, he fled back to the wagon and slashed the tugs holding one of the team, and he and the boy made their miraculous escape.

The wagon Flagg left behind was put to use by the invaders. Since hours of cannonading had failed to dislodge Champion, they loaded it with old hay and dry chips and pushed it up to the cabin, where they set it afire. Flames and smoke rolled skyward until they wondered if the man inside had cheated them by shooting himself. Champion, however, was still writing.

I heard them splitting wood. I guess they are going to fire the house to-night.

I think I will make a break when night comes if alive.

It's not night yet.

The house is all fired. Goodbye boys, if I never see you again.

Nathan D. Champion.

Finally, he broke through the roof at one end of the house and sprinted desperately for the cover of a little draw, which he never reached.

Pawing over the body, the invaders found and read the diary, after which it was presented to the Chicago newsman. Its contents survived, to become a classic of raw courage in the annals of the West.

Next day, Sunday, April 10, the invaders were approaching Buffalo when they were met by a rider on a lathered horse, who warned them that the town was in an uproar and they had better turn back if they valued their lives. They had just made a rest halt at the friendly TA ranch. Their only hope was to return there and dig in.

Sam Clover, ace reporter, was too smart for that trap. Deciding to take his chance with the aroused local population, he left the now deflated avengers and rode on into Buffalo, where he did some fast talking and finally got himself under the wing of his old friend Major Edmond G. Fechet of the 6th Cavalry, with whom he had campaigned during the Ghost Dance troubles in North Dakota. With the rest of the 6th, Fechet was now stationed at Fort McKinney, near Buffalo. So Clover rode off to the fort to luxuriate in hot baths and clean sheets and to write dispatches, while the wretched invaders prepared to stand siege for their lives.

They worked all night, and by morning of the eleventh were entrenched behind a very efficient set of fortifications at the TA ranch, where they were virtually impregnable except for a shortage of food supplies. By morning they were besieged by an impromptu army of hornet-mad cowboys and ranchmen, led by Sheriff "Red" Angus of Johnson County. The army numbered over three hundred on the day of surrender.

In Buffalo, churches and schools were turned into headquarters for the steadily arriving recruits; ladies baked cakes to send to Sheriff Angus' command post; the young Methodist preacher, who was possessed of no mean tongue, employed it to denounce this crime of the century. The leading merchant, a venerable Scotsman named Robert Foote, mounted his black horse and, with his long white beard flying in the breeze, dashed up and down the streets, calling the citizens to arms. More impressive still, he threw open his store, inviting them to help themselves to ammunition, slickers, blankets, flour—everything. He was said to be a heavy dealer in rustled beef, and on the invaders' list; but so was almost everyone of importance in Buffalo.

The telegraph wires had been cut repeatedly since the start of the invasion, but on April 12 they were working again momentarily, and a friend in Buffalo got a telegram through to the governor with the first definite word of the invaders' plight. From that time on, all the heavy artillery of influence, from Cheyenne to Washington and on up to the White House, was brought to bear to rescue the cattlemen from the consequences of their act.

Senators Carey and Warren called at the executive mansion late that night and got President Benjamin Harrison out of bed. He was urged to suppress an insurrection in Wyoming, though the question of just who was in insurrection against whom was not clarified. Telegrams flew back and forth. At 12:50 A.M. on April 13, Colonel J. J. Van Horn of the 6th Cavalry wired the commanding general of the Department of the Platte, acknowledging receipt of orders to proceed to the TA ranch.

Two hours later, three troops of the 6th filed out of Fort McKinney in the freezing dark, in a thoroughly disgusted frame of mind because (a) they had just come in that afternoon from chasing a band of marauding Crows back to the reservation and did not relish being ordered out again at three in the morning; and furthermore because (b) they were heartily on the side of Johnson County and would rather have left the invaders to their fate.

© THE LEADER CO.

They reached the TA at daybreak. Inside the beleaguered ranch house Major Wolcott and his men, their food exhausted, were preparing to make a break as soon as it was sufficiently light. They had eaten what they thought would be their last breakfast, and were awaiting the lookout's whistle which would call them to make that last desperate run—like so many Nate Champions—into the ring of hopelessly outnumbering rifles.

But hark! Instead of the suicide signal, a cavalry bugle! Major Wolcott crossed to a window.

"Gentlemen, it is the troops!"

From start to finish the Johnson County story reads like a parody of every Hollywood western ever filmed, and never more so than at this moment. Down the hill swept a line of seven horsemen abreast; between the fluttering pennons rode Colonel Van Horn, Major Fechet, Sheriff Angus; a representative of the governor, who would not have stuck his neck into northern Wyoming at this point for anything; and, of course, Sam T. Clover of the Chicago *Herald*. One of the guidon bearers carried a white handkerchief. An answering flutter of white appeared on the breastworks. Major Wolcott advanced stiffly and saluted Colonel Van Horn.

"I will surrender to you, but to that man"—indicating Sheriff Angus—"never!"

$27,000 to get the witnesses across Nebraska alone. The trappers had been promised a payoff of $2,500 each, and given postdated checks. When presented for cashing, the checks proved to be on a bank that had never existed.

Meanwhile the armor of self-pity remained undented. In their own eyes and those of their friends, the cattlemen were the innocent victims of an outrage. While awaiting a hearing at Fort Russell, they were kept in the lightest of durance, coming and going freely to Cheyenne. Major Wolcott was permitted a trip outside the state. When Fred DeBillier showed signs of cracking under the strain of captivity, raving and uttering strange outcries in the middle of the night, he was tenderly removed, first to a hotel and later to his home in New York, for rest and medical treatment.

Eventually the prisoners were transferred to the state penitentiary at Laramie, where the district judge who ordered the removal assured Governor Amos W. Barber that these important persons would by no means be required to mingle with ordinary convicts. They were then escorted to their new quarters by a guard of honor, which included Wyoming's adjutant general and acting secretary of state.

Public opinion was overwhelmingly against the prisoners, but it was poorly led and ineffective, and public wrath was dissipated into thin air. On their side, however, in the words of a newspaper correspondent, the cattlemen were "backed not only by the Republican machine from President Harrison on down to the state organization, but by at least twenty-five million dollars in invested capital. They have the President, the governor, the courts, their United States Senators, the state legislature and the army at their backs." It was enough.

Forty-four prisoners were marched off to the fort, not including the few defectors and two of the Texas mercenaries, who later died of wounds. Of the ringleaders, only one had received so much as a scratch.

"The cattlemen's war" was front-paged all over the nation for some three weeks, with the Boston *Transcript* putting tongue in cheek to remark on the everwidening activities of Harvard men. Then the rest of the country forgot it. Four days after the surrender, still guarded by unsympathetic troops, the prisoners were removed to Fort Russell, near Cheyenne. Here they were safely away from Johnson County, which had, however, been behaving with remarkable restraint. The weather was worse than ever and the march overland one of the most miserable on record. Apart from that, the killers got off at no heavier cost to themselves than minor inconvenience and some ignominy. They were never brought to justice.

They did, however, pay an admitted $100,000 as the price of the invasion, counting legal expenses and not mentioning the illegal. Of the sordid features of the Johnson County invasion which all but defy comment, the worst was the affair of the trappers. These two simple and unheroic men, who had been with Champion and Nick Ray in the cabin and had the bad luck to witness the KC slaughter, were hustled out of the state under an escort of gunmen in terror of their lives, and thence across Nebraska to Omaha, where they were piled onto a train, still under escort of gunmen and lawyers, and delivered at an eastern destination. The Johnson County authorities and their friends had been trying frantically to get them back, but no subpoenas could be issued because the cattlemen, still protected by the army, were not yet formally charged with anything. Counting bribes to federal officers and judges, legal fees, forfeited bail, and other expenses, it was said to have cost

One sequel to the episode was an attempt to muzzle the press. A small-town editor who criticized the cattlemen too violently was jailed on a charge of criminal libel and held for thirty days—long enough to silence his paper. A second editor was beaten. But the latter, whose name was A. S. Mercer, exacted an eye for an eye in his celebrated chronicle of the invasion, published two years later and resoundingly entitled: *The Banditti of the Plains, or The Cattlemen's Invasion of Wyoming. The Crowning Infamy of the Ages.*

Thereupon his print shop was burned to the ground, and another subservient judge ordered all copies of the book seized and burned. But while they were awaiting the bonfire, a wagonload of them was removed one night and drawn by galloping horses over the Colorado line. Thereafter copies on library shelves were stolen and mutilated as far away as the Library of Congress until only a few were left. But two new editions have since been published, and so—in the end—Mr. Mercer won.

The same judge who had shown himself so solicitous of the prisoners' comfort granted a change of venue from Johnson County, not to a neutral county but to the cattlemen's own stronghold in Cheyenne. The trial was set for January 2, 1893. Nineteen days later over a thousand veniremen had been examined and there were still only eleven men on the jury. The prolonged financial strain was too much for Johnson County; since there were no witnesses anyway, the prosecution tossed in the towel, and the case was dismissed.

The so-called rustlers came out with the cleaner hands. Good luck had saved them from spilling the blood of the invaders; and while there was one unsolved killing of a cattlemen's adherent afterward, this appears to have been an act of personal grudge, not of community vengeance. The chain reaction of retaliatory murders that could have started never did; and strife-torn Johnson County settled down to peace. The roundups became democratic, with big and little stockmen working side by side. Montagu sons married Capulet daughters; notorious rustlers turned into respectable ranchmen and hobnobbed with their former enemies. One was mentioned for governor, and another rose to high position in—of all things—the Wyoming Stock Growers Association.

Yet, if bitterness has mercifully subsided, a certain remnant of injustice remains. The ghosts of old wrongs unrighted still walk in Buffalo, and, with the law cheated of its due, the pleasant little town with its creek and its cottonwood trees can only wait for that earthly equivalent of the Last Judgment, the verdict of history.

Black Tragedy

By STEPHEN B. OATES

CHILDREN

OF

DARKNESS

SURE THAT HE WAS DIVINELY APPOINTED, NAT TURNER LED FELLOW SLAVES IN A BLOODY ATTEMPT TO OVERTHROW THEIR MASTERS

Until August, 1831, most Americans had never heard of Virginia's Southampton County, an isolated, impoverished neighborhood located along the border in the southeastern part of the state. It was mostly a small farming area, with cotton fields and apple orchards dotting the flat, wooded landscape. The farmers were singularly fond of their apple crops: from them they made a potent apple brandy, one of the major sources of pleasure in this hardscrabble region. The county seat, or "county town," was Jerusalem, a lethargic little community where pigs rooted in the streets and old-timers spat tobacco

that was nearly 60 per cent black. While most of the blacks were still enslaved, an unusual number—some seventeen hundred, in fact—were "free persons of color."

By southern white standards, enlightened benevolence did exist in Southampton County—and it existed in the rest of the state, too. Virginia whites allowed a few slave schools to operate—then a crime by state law—and almost without complaint permitted slaves to hold illegal religious meetings. Indeed, Virginians liked to boast that slavery was not so harsh in their "enlightened" state as it was in the brutal cotton plantations

FROM AN OLD PRINT PUBLISHED BY J. D. TORREY, N.Y.

In the depths of the woods near Cabin Pond, Nat and his henchmen work out their plans.

juice in the shade of the courthouse. Jerusalem lay on the bank of the Nottoway River some seventy miles south of Richmond. There had never been any large plantations in Southampton County, for the soil had always been too poor for extensive tobacco or cotton cultivation. Although one gentleman did own eighty slaves in 1830, the average was around three or four per family. A number of whites had moved on to new cotton lands in Georgia and Alabama, so that Southampton now had a population

in the Deep South. Still, this was a dark time for southern whites—a time of sporadic insurrection panics, especially in South Carolina, and of rising abolitionist militancy in the North—and Virginians were taking no chances. Even though their slaves, they contended, were too happy and too submissive to strike back, Virginia was nevertheless almost a military garrison, with a militia force of some hundred thousand men to guard against insurrection.

Southampton whites, of course,

280

were caught in the same paradox: most of the white males over twenty-one voluntarily belonged to the militia and turned out for the annual drills, yet none of them thought a slave revolt would happen here. *Their* blacks, they told themselves, had never been more content, more docile. True, they did get a bit carried away in their religious meetings these days, with much too much singing and clapping. And true, there were white preachers who punctuated their sermons with what a local observer called "ranting cant about equality" and who might inspire black exhorters to retail that doctrine to their congregations. But generally things were quiet and unchanged in this remote tidewater county, where time seemed to stand as still as a windless summer day.

It happened with shattering suddenness, an explosion of black rage that rocked Southampton County to its foundations. On August 22, 1831, a band of insurgent slaves, led by a black mystic called Nat Turner, rose up with axes and plunged southeastern Virginia—and much of the rest of the South—into convulsions of fear and racial violence. It turned out to be the bloodiest slave insurrection in southern history, one that was to have a profound and irrevocable impact on the destinies of southern whites and blacks alike.

Afterward, white authorities described him as a small man with "distinct African features." Though his shoulders were broad from work in the fields, he was short, slender, and a little knock-kneed, with thin hair, a complexion like black pearl, and large, deep-set eyes. He wore a mustache and cultivated a tuft of whiskers under his lower lip. Before that fateful August day whites who knew Nat Turner thought him harmless, even though he was intelligent and did gabble on about strange religious powers. Among the slaves, though, he enjoyed a powerful influence as an exhorter and self-proclaimed prophet.

He was born in 1800, the property of Benjamin Turner of Southampton County and the son of two strong-minded parents. Tradition has it that his African-born mother threatened to

kill him rather than see him grow up in bondage. His father eventually escaped to the North, but not before he had helped inculcate an enormous sense of self-importance in his son. Both parents praised Nat for his brilliance and extraordinary imagination; his mother even claimed that he could recall episodes that happened before his birth—a power that others insisted only the Almighty could have given him. His mother and father both told him that he was intended for some great purpose, that he would surely become a prophet. Nat was also influenced by his grandmother, who along with his white masters taught him to pray and to take pride in his superior intelligence. He learned to read and write with great ease, prompting those who knew him to remark that he had too much sense to be raised in bondage—he "would never be of any service to any one as a slave," one of them said.

In 1810 Benjamin Turner died, and Nat became the property of Turner's oldest son Samuel. Under Samuel Turner's permissive supervision Nat exploited every opportunity to improve his knowledge: he studied white children's school books and experimented in making paper and gunpowder. But it was religion that interested him the most. He attended Negro religious meetings, where the slaves cried out in ecstasy and sang hymns that expressed their longing for a better life. He listened transfixed as black exhorters preached from the Bible with stabbing gestures, singing out in a rhythmic language that was charged with emotion and vivid imagery. He studied the Bible, too, practically memorizing the books of the Old Testament, and grew to manhood with the words of the prophets roaring in his ears.

Evidently Nat came of age a bit confused if not resentful. Both whites and blacks had said he was too intelligent to be raised a slave; yet here he was, fully grown and still in bondage. Obviously he felt betrayed by false hopes. Obviously he thought he should be liberated like the large number of free blacks who lived in Southampton County and who were not nearly so gifted as he. Still en-

slaved as a man, he zealously cultivated his image as a prophet, aloof, austere, and mystical. As he said later in an oral autobiographical sketch, "Having soon discovered to be great, I must appear so, and therefore studiously avoided mixing in society, and wrapped myself in mystery, devoting myself to fasting and prayer."

Remote, introspective, Turner had religious fantasies in which the Holy Spirit seemed to speak to him as it had to the prophets of old. "Seek ye the kingdom of Heaven," the Spirit told him, "and all things shall be added unto you." Convinced that he "was ordained for some great purpose in the hands of the Almighty," Turner told his fellow slaves about his communion with the Spirit. "And they believed," Turner recalled, "and said my wisdom came from God." Pleased with their response, he began to prepare them for some unnamed mission. He also started preaching at black religious gatherings and soon rose to prominence as a leading exhorter in the slave church. Although never ordained and never officially a member of any church, he was accepted as a Baptist preacher in the slave community, and once he even baptized a white man in a swampy pond. There can be little doubt that the slave church nourished Turner's self-esteem and his desire for independence, for it was not only a center for underground slave plottings against the master class, but a focal point for an entire alternate culture—a subterranean culture that the slaves sought to construct beyond the white man's control. Moreover, Turner's status as a slave preacher gave him considerable freedom of movement, so that he came to know most of Southampton County intimately.

Sometime around 1821 Turner disappeared. His master had put him under an overseer, who may have whipped him, and he fled for his freedom as his father had done. But thirty days later he voluntarily returned. The other slaves were astonished. No fugitive ever came back on his own. "And the negroes found fault, and murmured against me," Turner recounted later, "saying that if they had my sense they would not serve any master in the world." But in his mind Turner did not serve any earthly master. His master was Jehovah—the angry and vengeful God of ancient Israel—and it was Jehovah, he insisted, who had chastened him and brought him back to bondage.

At about this time Nat married. Evidently his wife was a young slave named Cherry who lived on Samuel Turner's place. But in 1822 Samuel Turner died, and they were sold to different masters—Cherry to Giles Reese and Nat to Thomas Moore. Although they were not far apart and still saw each other from time to time, their separation was nevertheless a painful example of the wretched privations that slavery placed on black people, even here in mellowed Southampton County.

As a perceptive man with a prodigious knowledge of the Bible, Turner was more than aware of the hypocrisies and contradictions loose in this Christian area, where whites gloried in the teachings of Jesus and yet discriminated against the "free coloreds" and kept the other blacks in chains. Here slave owners bragged about their benevolence (in Virginia they took care of their "niggers") and yet broke up families, sold Negroes off to whip-happy slave traders when money was scarce, and denied intelligent and skilled blacks something even the most debauched and useless poor whites enjoyed: freedom. Increasingly embittered about his condition and that of his people, his imagination fired to incandescence by prolonged fasting and Old Testament prayers, Turner began to have apocalyptic visions and bloody fantasies in the fields and woods southwest of Jerusalem. "I saw white spirits and black spirits engaged in battle," he declared later, "and the sun was darkened—the thunder rolled in the heavens, and blood flowed in streams—and I heard a voice saying, 'Such is your luck, such you are called to see, and let it come rough or smooth, you must surely bare it.'" He was awestruck, he recalled, but what did the voice mean? What must he bare? He withdrew from his fellow slaves and prayed for a revelation; and one day when he was plowing in the field, he

thought the Spirit called out, "Behold me as I stand in the Heavens," and Turner looked up and saw forms of men there in a variety of attitudes, "and there were lights in the sky to which the children of darkness gave other names than what they really were—for they were the lights of the Saviour's hands, stretched forth from east to west, even as they extended on the cross on Calvary for the redemption of sinners."

Certain that Judgment Day was fast approaching, Turner strove to attain "true holiness" and "the true knowledge of faith." And once he had them, once he was "made perfect,"

No actual likeness of Nat Turner is known to exist. This sketch, based on descriptions, is by black artist William Braxton.

then the Spirit showed him other miracles. While working in the field, he said, he discovered drops of blood on the corn. In the woods he found leaves with hieroglyphic characters and numbers etched on them; other leaves contained forms of men—some drawn in blood—like the figures in the sky. He told his fellow slaves about these signs —they were simply astounded—and claimed that the Spirit had endowed him with a special knowledge of the seasons, the rotation of the planets, and the operation of the tides. He ac-

quired an even greater reputation among the county's slaves, many of whom thought he could control the weather and heal disease. He told his followers that clearly something large was about to happen, that he was soon to fulfill "the great promise that had been made to me."

But he still did not know what his mission was. Then on May 12, 1828, "I heard a loud noise in the heavens," Turner remembered, "and the Spirit instantly appeared to me and said the Serpent was loosened, and Christ had laid down the yoke he had borne for the sins of men, and that I should take it on and fight against the Serpent." Now at last it was clear. By signs in the heavens Jehovah would show him when to commence the great work, whereupon "I should arise and prepare myself, and slay my enemies with their own weapons." Until then he should keep his lips sealed.

But his work was too momentous for him to remain entirely silent. He announced to Thomas Moore that the slaves ought to be free and would be "one day or other." Moore, of course, regarded this as dangerous talk from a slave and gave Turner a thrashing.

In 1829 a convention met in Virginia to draft a new state constitution, and there was talk among the slaves—who communicated along a slave grapevine—that they might be liberated. Their hopes were crushed, though, when the convention emphatically rejected emancipation and restricted suffrage to whites only. There was also a strong backlash against antislavery publications thought to be infiltrating from the North, one of which—David Walker's *Appeal*—actually called on the slaves to revolt. In reaction the Virginia legislature enacted a law against teaching slaves to read and write. True, it was not yet rigorously enforced, but from the blacks' viewpoint slavery seemed more entrenched in "enlightened" Virginia than ever.

There is no evidence that Turner ever read antislavery publications, but he was certainly sensitive to the despair of his people. Still, Jehovah gave him no further signs, and he was carried along in the ebb and flow of ordinary life. Moore had died in 1828, and Turner had become the legal property of Moore's nine-year-old son —something that must have humiliated him. In 1829 a local wheelwright, Joseph Travis, married Moore's widow and soon moved into her house near the Cross Keys, a village located southwest of Jerusalem. Still known as Nat Turner even though he had changed owners several times, Nat considered Travis "a kind master" and later said that Travis "placed the greatest confidence in me."

In February, 1831, there was an eclipse of the sun. The sign Turner had been waiting for—could there be any doubt? Removing the seal from his lips, he gathered around him four slaves in whom he had complete trust —Hark, Henry, Nelson, and Sam— and confided what he was called to do. They would commence "the work of death" on July 4, whose connotation Turner clearly understood. But they formed and rejected so many plans that his mind was affected. He was seized with dread. He fell sick, and Independence Day came and passed.

On August 13 there was another sign. Because of some atmospheric disturbance the sun grew so dim that it could be looked at directly. Then it seemed to change colors—now pale green, now blue, now white—and there was much excitement and consternation in many parts of the eastern United States. By afternoon the sun was like an immense ball of polished silver, and the air was moist and hazy. Then a black spot could be seen, apparently on the sun's surface—a phenomenon that greatly aroused the slaves in southeastern Virginia. For Turner the black spot was unmistakable proof that God wanted him to move. With awakened resolution he told his men that "as the black spot passed over the sun, so shall the blacks pass over the earth."

It was Sunday, August 21, deep in the woods near the Travis house at a place called Cabin Pond. Around a crackling fire Turner's confederates feasted on roast pig and apple brandy. With them were two new recruits— Jack, one of Hark's cronies, and Will, a powerful man who intended to gain his freedom or die in the attempt. Around midafternoon Turner himself made a dramatic appearance, and in the glare of pine-knot torches they finally made their plans. They would rise that night and "kill all the white people." It was a propitious time to begin, because many whites of the militia were away at a camp meeting. The revolt would be so swift and so terrible that the whites would be too panic-stricken to fight back. Until they had sufficient recruits and equipment, the insurgents would annihilate everybody in their path—women and children included. When one of the slaves complained about their small number (there were only seven of them, after all), Turner was quick to reassure him. He had deliberately avoided an extensive plot involving a lot of slaves. He knew that blacks had "frequently attempted similar things," but their plans had "leaked out." Turner intended for his revolt to happen completely without warning. The "march of destruction," he explained, "should be the first news of the insurrection," whereupon slaves and free blacks alike would rise up and join him. He did not say what their ultimate objective was, but possibly he wanted to fight his way into the Great Dismal Swamp some twenty miles to the east. This immense, snake-filled quagmire had long been a haven for fugitives, and Turner may have planned to establish a slave stronghold there from which to launch punitive raids against Virginia and North Carolina. On the other hand, he may well have had nothing in mind beyond the extermination of every white on the ten-mile route to Jerusalem. There are indications that he thought God would guide him after the revolt began, just as He had directed Gideon against the Midianites. Certainly Turner's command of unremitting carnage was that of the Almighty, who had said through his prophet Ezekiel: "Slay utterly old and young, both maids and little children, and women. . . ."

The slaves talked and schemed through the evening. Night came on. Around two in the morning of August 22 they left the woods, by-passed Giles Reese's farm, where Cherry lived, and headed for the Travis homestead, the first target in their crusade.

All was still at the Travis house. In the darkness the insurgents gathered about the cider press, and all drank except Turner, who never touched liquor. Then they moved across the yard with their axes. Hark placed a ladder against the house, and Turner, armed with a hatchet, climbed up and disappeared through a second-story window. In a moment he unbarred the door, and the slaves spread through the house without a sound. The others wanted Turner the prophet, Turner the black messiah, to strike the first blow and kill Joseph Travis. With Will close behind, Turner entered Travis' bedroom and made his way to the white man's bed. Turner swung his hatchet—a wild blow that glanced off Travis' head and brought him out of bed yelling for his wife. But with a sure killer's instinct Will moved in and hacked Travis to death with his axe. In minutes Will and the others had slaughtered the four whites they found in the house, including Mrs. Travis and young Putnam Moore, Turner's legal owner. With Putnam's death Turner felt that at last, after thirty years in bondage, he was free.

The rebels gathered up a handful of old muskets and followed "General Nat" out to the barn. There Turner paraded his men about, leading them through every military maneuver he knew. Not all of them, however, were proud of their work. Jack sank to his knees with his head in his hands and said he was sick. But Hark made him get up and forced him along as they set out across the field to the next farm. Along the way somebody remembered the Travis baby. Will and Henry returned and killed it in its cradle.

And so it went throughout that malignant night, as the rebels took farm after farm by surprise. They used no firearms, in order not to arouse the countryside, instead stabbing and decapitating their victims. Although they confiscated horses, weapons, and brandy, they took only what was necessary to continue the struggle, and they committed no rapes. They even spared a few homesteads, one because Turner believed the poor white inhabitants "thought no better of themselves than they did of negroes." By dawn on Monday there were fifteen insurgents —nine on horses—and they were armed with a motley assortment of guns, clubs, swords, and axes. Turner himself now carried a light dress sword, but for some mysterious reason (a fatal irresolution? the dread again?) he had killed nobody yet.

At Elizabeth Turner's place, which the slaves stormed at sunrise, the prophet tried once again to kill. They broke into the house, and there, in the middle of the room, too frightened to move or cry out, stood Mrs. Turner and a neighbor named Mrs. Newsome. Nat knew Elizabeth Turner very well, for she was the widow of his second master, Samuel Turner. While Will attacked her with his axe the prophet took Mrs. Newsome's hand and hit her over the head with his sword. But evidently he could not bring himself to kill her. Finally Will moved him aside and chopped her to death as methodically as though he were cutting wood.

With the sun low in the east, Turner sent a group on foot to another farm while he and Will led the horsemen at a gallop to Caty Whitehead's place. They surrounded the house in a rush, but not before several people fled into the garden. Turner chased after somebody, but it turned out to be a slave girl, as terrified as the whites, and he let her go. All around him, all over the Whitehead farm, there were scenes of unspeakable violence. He saw Will drag Mrs. Whitehead kicking and screaming out of the house and almost sever her head from her body. Running around the house, Turner came upon young Margaret Whitehead hiding under a cellar cap between two chimneys. She ran crying for her life, and Turner set out after her—a wild chase against the hot August sun. He overtook the girl in a field and hit her again and again with his sword, but she would not die. In desperation he picked up a fence rail and beat her to death. Finally he had killed someone. He was to kill no one else.

After the Whitehead massacre the insurgents united briefly and then divided again, those on foot moving in one direction and Turner and the mounted slaves in another. The riders moved across the fields, kicking their

horses and mules faster and faster, until at last they raced down the lane to Richard Porter's house, scattering dogs and chickens as they went. But the Porters had fled—forewarned by their own slaves that a revolt was under way. Turner knew that the alarm was spreading now, knew that the militia would soon be mobilizing, so he set out alone to retrieve the other column. While he was gone Will took the cavalry and raided Nathaniel Francis' homestead. Young Francis was Will's owner, but he could not have been a harsh master: several free blacks voluntarily lived on his farm. Francis was not home, and his pregnant young wife survived Will's onslaught only because a slave concealed her in the attic. After killing the overseer and Francis' two nephews Will and his men raced on to another farm, and another, and then overran John Barrow's place on the Barrow Road. Old man Barrow fought back manfully while his wife escaped in the woods, but the insurgents overwhelmed him and slit his throat. As a tribute to his courage they wrapped his body in a quilt and left a plug of tobacco on his chest.

Meanwhile Turner rode chaotically around the countryside, chasing after one column and then the other, almost always reaching the farms after his scattered troops had done the killing and gone. Eventually he found both columns waiting for him at another pillaged homestead, took charge again, and sent them down the Barrow Road, which intersected the main highway to Jerusalem. They were forty strong now and all mounted. Many of the new recruits had joined up eager "to kill all the white people." But others had been forced to come along as though they were hostages. A Negro later testified that several slaves —among them three teen-age boys— "were constantly guarded by negroes with guns who were ordered to shoot them if they attempted to escape."

On the Barrow Road, Turner's strategy was to put his twenty most dependable men in front and send them galloping down on the homesteads before anybody could escape. But the cry of insurrection had preceded them, and many families had already escaped to nearby Jerusalem, throwing

the village into pandemonium. By midmorning church bells were tolling the terrible news—insurrection, insurrection—and shouting men were riding through the countryside in a desperate effort to get the militia together before the slaves overran Jerusalem itself.

As Turner's column moved relentlessly toward Jerusalem one Levi Waller, having heard that the blacks had risen, summoned his children from a nearby schoolhouse (some of the other children came running too) and tried to load his guns. But before he could do so, Turner's advance horsemen swept into his yard, a whirlwind of axes and swords, and chased Waller into some tall weeds. Waller managed to escape, but not before he saw the blacks cut down his wife and children. One small girl also escaped by crawling up a dirt chimney, scarcely daring to breathe as the insurgents decapitated the other children—ten in all—and threw their bodies in a pile.

Turner had stationed himself at the rear of his little army and did not participate in these or any other killings along the Barrow Road. He never explained why. He had been fasting for several days and may well have been too weak to try any more killing himself. Or maybe as God's prophet he preferred to let Will and the eight or nine other lieutenants do the slaughtering. All he said about it afterward was that he "sometimes got in sight in time to see the work of death completed" and that he paused to view the bodies "in silent satisfaction" before riding on.

Around noon on Monday the insurgents reached the Jerusalem highway, and Turner soon joined them. Behind them lay a zigzag path of unredeemable destruction: some fifteen homesteads sacked and approximately sixty whites slain. By now the rebels amounted to fifty or sixty—including three or four free blacks. But even at its zenith Turner's army showed signs of disintegration. A few reluctant slaves had already escaped or deserted. And many others were roaring drunk, so drunk they could scarcely ride their horses, let alone do any fighting. To make matters worse, many of the confiscated muskets were broken or too rusty to fire.

Turner resolved to march on Jerusalem at once and seize all the guns and powder he could find there. But a half mile up the road he stopped at the Parker farm, because some of his men had relatives and friends there. When the insurgents did not return, Turner went after them—and found his men not in the slave quarters but down in Parker's brandy cellar. He ordered them back to the highway at once.

On the way back they met a party of armed men—whites. There were about eighteen of them, as far as Turner could make out. They had already routed his small guard at the gate and were now advancing toward the Parker house. With renewed zeal Turner rallied his remaining troops and ordered an attack. Yelling at the top of their lungs, wielding axes, clubs, and gun butts, the Negroes drove the whites back into Parker's cornfield. But their advantage was short-lived.

White reinforcements arrived, and more were on the way from nearby Jerusalem. Regrouping in the cornfield, the whites counterattacked, throwing the rebels back in confusion. In the fighting some of Turner's best men fell wounded, though none of them died. Several insurgents, too drunk to fight any more, fled pell-mell into the woods.

If Turner had often seemed irresolute earlier in the revolt, he was now undaunted. Even though his force was considerably reduced, he still wanted to storm Jerusalem. He led his men away from the main highway, which was blocked with militia, and took them along a back road, planning to cross the Cypress Bridge and strike the village from the rear. But the bridge was crawling with armed whites. In desperation the blacks set out to find reinforcements: they fell back to the south and then veered north again, picking up new recruits as they moved. They raided a few more farms, too, only to find them

deserted, and finally encamped for the night near the slave quarters on Ridley's plantation.

All Monday night news of the revolt spread beyond Southampton County as express riders carried the alarm up to Petersburg and from there to the capitol in Richmond. Governor John Floyd, fearing a statewide uprising, alerted the militia and sent cavalry, infantry, and artillery units to the stricken county. Federal troops from Fortress Monroe were on the way, too, and other volunteers and militia outfits were marching from contiguous counties in Virginia and North Carolina. Soon over three thousand armed whites were in Southampton County, and hundreds more were mobilizing.

With whites swarming the countryside, Turner and his lieutenants did not know what to do. During the night an alarm had stampeded their new recruits, so that by Tuesday morning they had only twenty men left. Frantically they set out for Dr. Simon Blunt's farm to get volunteers—and

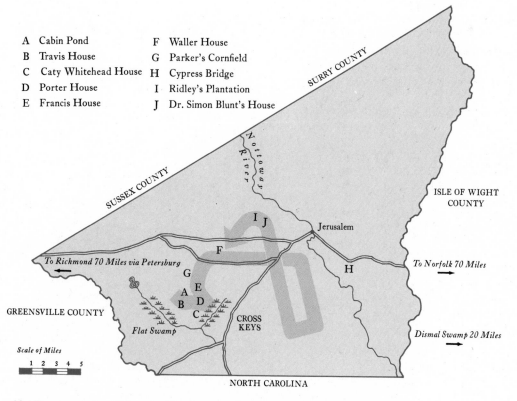

A Cabin Pond
B Travis House
C Caty Whitehead House
D Porter House
E Francis House
F Waller House
G Parker's Cornfield
H Cypress Bridge
I Ridley's Plantation
J Dr. Simon Blunt's House

Nat Turner country: This map of Southampton County, Virginia, shows the places mentioned in the story as well as the path (shaded arrow) of his campaign of destruction.

MAP BY CAL SACKS, ADAPTED FROM *The Southampton Slave Revolt of 1831* (RANDOM HOUSE, 1973)

The extensive manhunt for Nat Turner ended when a lone white man named Benjamin Phipps accidentally discovered him near Cabin Pond.

rode straight into an ambush. Whites barricaded in the house opened fire on them at pointblank range, killing one or more insurgents and capturing several others—among them Hark Travis. Blunt's own slaves, armed with farm tools, helped in the defense and captured a few rebels themselves.

Repulsed at Blunt's farm, Turner led a handful of the faithful back toward the Cross Keys, still hoping to gather reinforcements. But the signs were truly ominous, for armed whites were everywhere. At last the militia overtook Turner's little band and in a final, desperate skirmish killed Will and scattered the rest. Turner himself, alone and in deep anguish, escaped to the vicinity of the Travis farm and hid in a hole under some fence rails.

By Tuesday evening a full-scale manhunt was under way in southeastern Virginia and North Carolina as armed whites prowled the woods and swamps in search of fugitive rebels and alleged collaborators. They chased the blacks down with howling dogs, killing those who resisted—and many of them resisted zealously—and dragging others back to Jerusalem to stand trial in the county court. One free black insurgent committed suicide rather than be taken by white men. Within a week nearly all the bona fide rebels except Turner had either been executed or imprisoned, but not before white vigilantes—and some militiamen—had perpetrated barbarities on more than a score of innocent blacks. Outraged by the atrocities committed on whites, vigilantes rounded up Negroes in the Cross Keys and decapitated them. Another vigilante gang in North Carolina not only beheaded several blacks but placed their skulls on poles, where they remained for days. In all directions whites took Negroes from their shacks and tortured, shot, and burned them to death and then mutilated their corpses in ways that witnesses refused to describe. No one knows how many innocent Negroes died in this reign of terror—at least a hundred twenty, probably more. Finally the militia commander of Southampton County issued a proclamation that any further outrages would be dealt with according to the articles of war. Many whites publicly regretted these atrocities but argued that they were the inevitable results of slave insurrection. Another revolt, they said, would end with the extermination of every black in the region.

Although Turner's uprising ended on Tuesday, August 24, reports of additional insurrections swept over the South long afterward, and dozens of communities from Virginia to Alabama were seized with hysteria. In North Carolina rumors flew that slave armies had been seen on the highways, that one—maybe led by Turner himself—had burned Wilmington, butchered all the inhabitants, and was now marching on the state capital. The hysteria was even worse in Virginia, where reports of concerted slave rebellions and demands for men and guns swamped the governor's office. For a time it seemed that thousands of slaves had risen, that Virginia and perhaps the entire South would soon be ablaze. But Governor Floyd kept his head, examined the reports carefully, and concluded that no such widespread insurrection had taken place. Actually no additional uprisings had happened anywhere. Out of blind panic whites in many parts of the South had mobilized the militia, chased after imaginary insurgents, and jailed or executed still more innocent blacks. Working in cooperation with other political and military authorities in Virginia and North Carolina, Floyd did all he could to quell the excitement, to reassure the public that the slaves were quiet now. Still, the governor did not think the Turner revolt was the work of a solitary fanatic. Behind it, he believed, was a conspiracy of Yankee agitators and black preachers—especially black preachers. "The whole of that massacre in Southampton is the work of these Preachers," he declared, and demanded that they be suppressed.

Meanwhile the "great bandit chieftain," as the newspapers called him, was still at large. For more than two

286

months Turner managed to elude white patrols, hiding out most of the time near Cabin Pond where the revolt had begun. Hunted by a host of aroused whites (there were various rewards totalling eleven hundred dollars on his head), Turner considered giving himself up and once got within two miles of Jerusalem before turning back. Finally on Sunday, October 30, a white named Benjamin Phipps accidentally discovered him in another hideout near Cabin Pond. Since the man had a loaded shotgun, Turner had no choice but to throw down his sword.

The next day, with lynch mobs crying for his head, a white guard hurried Turner up to Jerusalem to stand trial. By now he was resigned to his fate as the will of Almighty God and was entirely fearless and unrepentant. When a couple of court justices examined him that day, he stated emphatically that *he* had conceived and directed the slaughter of all those white people (even though he had killed only Margaret Whitehead) and announced that God had endowed him with extraordinary powers. The justices ordered this "fanatic" locked up in the same small wooden jail where the other captured rebels had been incarcerated.

On November 1 one Thomas Gray, an elderly Jerusalem lawyer and slaveholder, came to interrogate Turner as he lay in his cell "clothed with rags and covered with chains." In Gray's opinion the public was anxious to learn the facts about the insurrection—for whites in Southampton could not fathom why their slaves would revolt. What Gray wanted was to take down and publish a confession from Turner that would tell the public the truth about why the rebellion had happened. It appears that Gray had already gathered a wealth of information about the outbreak from other prisoners, some of whom he had defended as a court-appointed counsel. Evidently he had also written unsigned newspaper accounts of the affair, reporting in one that whites had located Turner's wife and lashed her until she surrendered his papers (remarkable papers, papers with hieroglyphics on them and sketches

of the Crucifixion and the sun). According to Gray and to other sources as well, Turner over a period of three days gave him a voluntary and authentic confession about the genesis and execution of the revolt, recounting his religious visions in graphic detail and contending again that he was a prophet of Almighty God. "Do you not find yourself mistaken now?" Gray asked. Turner replied testily, "Was not Christ crucified?" Turner insisted that the uprising was local in origin but warned that other slaves might see signs and act as he had done. By the end of the confession Turner was in high spirits, perfectly "willing to suffer the fate that awaits me." Although Gray considered him "a gloomy fanatic," he thought Turner was one of the most articulate men he had ever met. And Turner could be frightening. When, in a burst of enthusiasm, he spoke of the killings and raised his manacled hands toward heaven, "I looked on him," Gray said, "and my blood curdled in my veins."

On November 5, with William C. Parker acting as his counsel, Turner

came to trial in Jerusalem. The court, of course, found him guilty of committing insurrection and sentenced him to hang. Turner, though, insisted that he was not guilty because he did not feel so. On November 11 he went to his death in resolute silence. In addition to Turner, the county court tried some forty-eight other Negroes on various charges of conspiracy, insurrection, and treason. In all, eighteen blacks—including one woman—were convicted and hanged. Ten others were convicted and "transported"—presumably out of the United States.

But the consequences of the Turner revolt did not end with public hangings in Jerusalem. For southern whites the uprising seemed a monstrous climax to a whole decade of ominous events, a decade of abominable tariffs and economic panics, of obstreperous antislavery activities, and of growing slave unrest and insurrection plots, beginning with the Denmark Vesey conspiracy in Charleston in 1822 and culminating now in the worst insurrection Southerners had ever known. Desperately needing

Nat Turner was incarcerated in the Old Southampton County Jail.

to blame somebody besides themselves for Nat Turner, Southerners linked the revolt to some sinister Yankee-abolitionist plot to destroy their cherished way of life. Southern zealots declared that the antislavery movement, gathering momentum in the North throughout the 1820's, had now burst into a full-blown crusade against the South. In January, 1831, William Lloyd Garrison had started publishing *The Liberator* in Boston, demanding in bold, strident language that the slaves be immediately and unconditionally emancipated. If Garrison's rhetoric shocked Southerners, even more disturbing was the fact that about eight months after the appearance of *The Liberator* Nat Turner embarked on his bloody crusade—something southern politicians and newspapers refused to accept as mere coincidence. They charged that Garrison was behind the insurrection, that it was his "bloodthirsty" invective that had incited Turner to violence. Never mind that there was no evidence that Turner had ever heard of *The Liberator;* never mind that Garrison categorically denied any connection with the revolt, saying that he and his abolitionist followers were Christian pacifists who wanted to free the slaves through moral suasion. From 1831 on, northern abolitionism and slave rebellion were inextricably associated in the southern mind.

But if Virginians blamed the insurrection on northern abolitionism, many of them defended emancipation itself as the only way to prevent further violence. In fact, for several months in late 1831 and early 1832 Virginians engaged in a momentous public debate over the feasibility of manumission. Out of the western part of the state, where antislavery and anti-Negro sentiment had long been smoldering, came petitions demanding that Virginia eradicate the "accursed," "evil" slave system and colonize all blacks at state expense. Only by removing the entire black population, the petitions argued, could future revolts be avoided. Newspapers also discussed the idea of emancipation and colonization, prompting one to announce that "Nat Turner and the blood of his innocent victims have

conquered the silence of fifty years." The debate moved into the Virginia legislature, too, and early in 1832 proslavery and antislavery orators harangued one another in an unprecedented legislative struggle over emancipation. In the end most delegates concluded that colonization was too costly and too complicated to carry out. And since they were not about to manumit the blacks and leave them as free men in a white man's country,

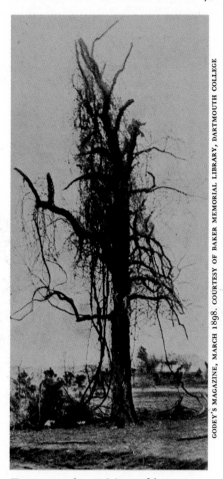

GODEY'S MAGAZINE, MARCH 1898. COURTESY OF BAKER MEMORIAL LIBRARY, DARTMOUTH COLLEGE

Turner was hanged from this tree.

they rejected emancipation. Indeed, they went on to revise and implement the slave codes in order to restrict blacks so stringently that they could never mount another revolt. The modified codes not only strengthened the patrol and militia systems, but sharply curtailed the rights of free blacks and all but eliminated slave schools, slave religious meetings, and slave preachers. For Turner had taught white Virginians a hard lesson

about what might happen if they gave slaves enough education and religion to think for themselves.

In the wake of the Turner revolt, the rise of the abolitionists, and the Virginia debates over slavery, the other southern states also expanded their patrol and militia systems and increased the severity of their slave codes. What followed was the Great Reaction of the 1830's and 1840's, during which the South, threatened it seemed by internal and external enemies, became a closed, martial society determined to preserve its slave-based civilization at whatever cost. If Southerners had once apologized for slavery as a necessary evil, they now trumpeted that institution as a positive good—"the greatest of all the great blessings," as James H. Hammond phrased it, "which a kind providence has bestowed." Southern postmasters set about confiscating abolitionist literature, lest these "incendiary" tracts invite the slaves to violence. Some states actually passed sedition laws and other restrictive measures that prohibited Negroes and whites alike from criticizing slavery. And slave owners all across the South tightened up slave discipline, refusing to let blacks visit other plantations and threatening to hang any slave who even looked rebellious. By the 1840's the Old South had devised such an oppressive slave system that organized insurrection was all but impossible.

Even so, southern whites in the antebellum period never escaped the haunting fear that somewhere, maybe even in their own slave quarters, another Nat Turner was plotting to rise up and slit their throats. They never forgot him. His name became for them a symbol of terror and violent retribution.

But for ante-bellum blacks—and for their descendants—the name of Nat Turner took on a profoundly different connotation. He became a legendary black hero who broke his chains and murdered white people because slavery had murdered Negroes. Turner, said an elderly black man in Southampton County only a few years ago, was "God's man. He was a man for war, and for legal rights, and for freedom."

Nat Turner remains an enigmatic and controversial figure in our own time, thanks largely to the furor generated by William Styron's novel The Confessions of Nat Turner (Random House, 1967). Although principally based on Turner's Confessions as given to Thomas Gray, the novel portrayed Turner as a celibate bachelor afflicted with masturbation fantasies about Margaret Whitehead—a psychosexual supposition unsupported by any known evidence. Styron also violated the historical record in many other details, so that from the point of view of historical scholarship his novel must be regarded as an inaccurate and unacceptable re-creation of Turner and his insurrection.

These shortcomings were emphatically brought to public attention in a volume called William Styron's Nat Turner: Ten Black Writers Respond (Beacon Press, 1968). Unfortunately, although the book included trenchant essays by Mike Thelwell and Vincent Harding that subjected Styron's novel to valid historical criticism, most of the other selections were mere diatribes, filled with their own inaccuracies and attempting to enshrine the figure of Nat Turner as a flawless black god—a military genius and inflexible white-hater with whom today's blacks ought to identify.

In reconstructing the Nat Turner story for my own narrative, I made extensive use of Henry Irving Tragle's The Southampton Slave Revolt of 1831 (Random House, 1973), a valuable collection of documents about virtually all aspects of the rebellion. It includes a detailed, annotated chronology of Turner's life and the revolt itself, numerous contemporary newspaper reports, a verbatim record of the slave trials, Governor Floyd's diary and correspondence, and most of the previously published accounts, including the original Confessions to Thomas Gray as published in Baltimore in 1831. I am also indebted to Eric Foner, whose Nat Turner (Prentice-Hall, 1971), another compilation of source materials, includes a great deal about the role of the slave church in the genesis of the Turner insurrection.

—S.B.O.

DRED SCOTT v. SANDFORD | *Black Pawn*

Dred Scott was nobody in particular. A slave born of slave parents, unable to read or write, physically frail, he was a man without energy, who for a full decade drifted about in St. Louis as an errand boy and general odd-jobs factotum, an unremarkable bondsman on whom the burden of servitude rested rather lightly. Nobody directly concerned with him wanted him as a slave. As a chattel he was a liability rather than an asset, and in any case his various owners seem to have been antislavery people. Yet his unsuccessful legal battle to become free left an enduring shadow on the history of the United States and was an important factor in the coming of the Civil War.

He is remembered because in March, 1857, the Supreme Court of the United States handed down its decision in the case of *Dred Scott v. Sandford*. (That last name, by the way, was misspelled and should be Sanford: one minor mistake in a case clouded by larger errors.) The Chief Justice asserted that Scott and all men like him neither were nor ever could be citizens. This opinion was upset a few years later by marching armies, at the cost of much bloodshed, but the reversal came too late to be of any help to Dred Scott because he died before the Civil War began.

It is hard to feel that Scott was the prime mover in this momentous case that shook the entire nation. He unquestionably wanted very much to be free, and as his struggle progressed he appears to have enjoyed the backhanded sort of fame which it brought to him, but his part was chiefly that of a pawn. He was a counter played in a tense and ominous game, and the fact that this particular counter was played just when and as it was played was one of the reasons why the game at last broke up in a furious fight. Yet the whole of it touched Scott himself only indirectly.

Dred Scott was born in Southampton County, Virginia, somewhere around 1795, the property of a man named Peter Blow. In 1827, Blow moved to St. Louis, taking his family and his chattels with him. Four years later Peter Blow died, and Scott became the property of Blow's daughter Elizabeth, who in 1833 sold him to Dr. John Emerson, an army surgeon. In 1834 Dr. Emerson was transferred to duty at Rock Island, Illinois,

and some time after that he was transferred again to Fort Snelling, which lay farther up the Mississippi River in what was then Wisconsin Territory. Dr. Emerson took Scott with him as a body servant during all of this time, so that for approximately five years Scott lived on free soil. At the end of 1838 Dr. Emerson returned to St. Louis, taking Scott along, and soon after this Dr. Emerson died, leaving Scott to his widow, Mrs. Irene Sanford Emerson.

For some time Mrs. Emerson did what many slaveowners did in those days—hired her chattel out to various families who needed servants. Then, in the mid-1840's, she moved to New York, and she did not take Dred Scott with her. Instead she left him in St. Louis in the charge of the two sons of Scott's original owner, Henry and Taylor Blow. It was at about this time that the seeds of what was to become one of America's most famous court cases were planted.

Henry Blow was then in his thirties, a lawyer and businessman of some wealth and prominence. He was head of a railroad, active in developing lead-mining properties in southwestern Missouri; active also in the Whig party, beginning to be known as an opponent of the extension of slavery. (A few years later Henry Blow helped organize the Free Soil movement in Missouri, and eventually he became a Republican.) As an antislavery man, Blow wanted Scott freed, and in 1846 he helped finance a suit in the Missouri courts to have Scott declared free. Scott himself appears to have been a little hazy as to what this was all about, but he willingly signed his mark to the necessary papers, and the lawsuit was on.

At this point it becomes obvious that the real point to this proceeding was not so much to win freedom for Scott personally as to win a legal point in the broad fight against slavery as an institution. Mrs. Emerson obviously did not want to retain Scott as her slave, and she apparently was no believer in slavery—a few years later she became the wife of Calvin Clifford Chaffee, a radical antislavery congressman from Massachusetts. When she moved to New York she could easily have executed papers of manumission to give Scott his freedom. She did not do that; instead, she

on a Field of Peril

BRUCE CATTON

left him with the Blows, and when his lawsuit began she was technically the defendant—the case was listed formally as "Scott, a Man of Color, v. Emerson." The case is just a little mysterious, but it seems clear that what everyone wanted was a definite ruling about the status of a slave whose master took him into free territory.

This was beginning to be an important point. The western country was opening up for settlement, and the law said that north of the Missouri Compromise line of 36 degrees, 30 minutes, the new territory was free soil. Exactly what would happen if a slaveowner took his slaves with him when he moved into such territory?

Lawyers for Dred Scott argued that his five-year sojourn on free soil had ended his bondage and that on his return to Missouri the state court should make formal declaration of his freedom. The lower court ruled in Scott's favor, but an appeal was taken—what everybody wanted, obviously, was a high-level finding that would stand as some sort of landmark—and the state supreme court eventually reversed the lower court, holding that Missouri law still applied and that Scott, as a resident of Missouri, must remain a slave.

The law's delays were as notorious then as they are now, and the case dragged on for six years; the ruling of the state supreme court was not handed down until 1852. During this time Scott remained under the nominal control of the county sheriff, who hired him out here and there for five dollars a month. Scott was in limbo, everybody's slave and nobody's slave; if he had any thoughts about this interminable process of determining his future, they were never recorded.

Meanwhile, things had been happening—not to Scott, but to the country that countenanced the institution that held him in slavery. The Mexican War had been fought and won, and the United States came into possession of a vast new area running all the way to the golden shores of California, one of the immediate results being that the whole slavery controversy became a dominant issue in national politics. Until now there had been a slightly unstable equilibrium, with the Missouri Compromise decreeing that new ter-

MISSOURI HISTORICAL SOCIETY

For Dred Scott, an innocent Negro caught in the storm, the case was a "heap o' trouble." He was amazed at all "de fuss dey made dar in Washington."

291

ritories created from Louisiana Purchase lands lying north of the line that marked the southern boundary of Missouri should be free soil. This equilibrium vanished when the immense acquisitions of the Mexican War made it obvious that sooner or later many new states would be created, and the issue was pointed up when Congressman David Wilmot of Pennsylvania unsuccessfully tried to get Congress to pass a law providing that slavery be excluded from all the land that had been taken from Mexico. The question of slavery in the territories, by the early 1850's, had become the great, engrossing question in American politics.

It became important because the way this issue was settled would determine whether the institution of slavery could continue to expand or must be limited to the areas where it already existed. On the surface, it might seem to make very little difference to a planter in Alabama or a farmer in Ohio whether slaves could or could not be held in some such faraway place as New Mexico; actually, the future of slavery itself was at stake, and everybody knew it.

The Compromise of 1850 brought a temporary easing of the tension. Under this arrangement, California came in as a free state, a stronger fugitive slave law was enacted, and it was agreed that when new territories were organized out of the empty lands that had been taken from Mexico the inhabitants of those territories would themselves decide whether slavery was to be permitted or prohibited. This was the famous principle of popular sovereignty; it looked like a fair, democratic way to settle things, and for a short time the nation relaxed.

It did not relax very long. Senator Stephen A. Douglas of Illinois in 1854 brought in his Kansas-Nebraska Act, a measure to organize the new territories of Kansas and Nebraska. This area had been acquired through the Louisiana Purchase, and it lay north of the Missouri Compromise line of 36 degrees, 30 minutes, and hence these territories must be free soil. But Douglas was a Democrat, in a Democratic Congress, and the Democratic party was largely dominated by southerners, who were most unlikely to consent to the creation of two new free territories which would presently become free states. So Douglas, a firm believer in the principle of popular sovereignty, decided to extend that principle to Kansas and Nebraska. His act, which passed Congress after most heated debate, wiped out the Missouri Compromise line and provided that the settlers of Kansas and Nebraska could say whether slavery might exist there. Meanwhile, slaveowners and their chattels were free to move in.

When he introduced this bill Douglas commented that it would "raise [a] hell of a storm." He was entirely right. It did; and the slavery controversy returned to the center of the stage, never to leave it until the papers were signed at Appomattox Courthouse.

Of all of this Dred Scott knew nothing. He continued to shift back and forth on the little jobs for which he was now and then farmed out, totally unaware of the new currents that were swirling about him. But he suddenly became an important person because of that old lawsuit. Missouri slaveowners were moving into Kansas, taking their slaves with them; antislavery people from the North were also moving in, taking their antislavery convictions with them; and there were bitter clashes, with bloodshed and gunfire to focus national attention on the situation. The old question about the status of a slave whose owner took him into an area which the old Missouri Compromise called free soil had become a matter of vast consequence.

It was time, in other words, to get a ruling from the Supreme Court of the United States. The original lawsuit was revived. Mrs. Emerson transferred title to Scott to her brother, John F. A. Sanford of New York, and in 1854 the case, now known as *Dred Scott v. Sandford,* got on the docket in the federal circuit court for Missouri.

It was a bit complicated. If Scott was to sue Sanford in a federal court he had to show that he was a citizen of Missouri—that is, a federal case had to involve an action between citizens of different states. Sanford's lawyers argued that as a Negro slave Scott was not a citizen of Missouri and that the federal court therefore lacked jurisdiction. The circuit court eventually ruled that way, and Scott's lawyers took the case to the Supreme Court on a writ of error. In 1856 the Supreme Court heard the arguments.

Bear in mind, again, that what happened to Scott in all of this was of no especial importance to anybody except Scott himself. What everybody wanted was a final ruling from the highest court in the land—a finding which (it was innocently hoped) would settle once and for all the disturbing question of slavery in the territories.

Three issues were involved. Was Scott actually a citizen of Missouri and so entitled to sue in a federal court? Did his residence on free soil give him a title to freedom which Missouri was bound to respect? Finally, was the Missouri Compromise itself, which had made Wisconsin Territory free soil, constitutional? (That is, did Congress actually have the power to prohibit slavery in a territory?) A final ruling on all of these points might have much to do with the question of slavery in Kansas.

So the Supreme Court had been given a very hot potato to handle, and the rising tumult in Kansas made it all the hotter. So did the presidential election of 1856, in which the new Republican party—a sectional northern party, dedicated chiefly to the theory that slavery must not be allowed to expand—showed enormous growth and came respectably close to electing John C. Frémont President of the United States. The whole argument over slavery, which was fast becoming too explosive for American political machinery to handle, had come to center on this question of slavery in the territories, and the Dred Scott case brought the question into sharp relief.

The Supreme Court could have avoided most of the thorns in this case simply by declaring that it lacked jurisdiction. A somewhat similar case had been handled so in 1850, and in the beginning most of the justices seem to have been disposed to follow that precedent. Justice Samuel Nelson prepared such an opinion: Missouri law controlled Scott's status, Missouri law said that he was still a slave, and as a slave he could not sue in the federal courts. Yet the pressures were too great for such an easy solution. The justices at last concluded to handle all of the issues. A brief glance at the make-up of the Court is in order.

Of the nine justices, five came from slave states: Chief Justice Roger B. Taney of Maryland, and Justices James M. Wayne of Georgia, John Catron of Tennessee, Peter V. Daniel of Virginia, and John A. Campbell of Alabama. Seven of the nine were Democrats—these five plus two northerners, Justices Samuel Nelson of New York and Robert C. Grier of Pennsylvania. Justice John McLean of Ohio was a Republican, and Justice Benjamin R. Curtis of Massachusetts was a Whig. All nine were men of integrity and repute, but everything considered, it might be hard for them to be completely objective about the issues that were presented to them.

It might be hard; and indeed it proved quite impossible for these men to limit themselves to the basic question about Scott's actual status. They had to say something, not just about one slave, but about all slaves.

To begin with, it soon became apparent that Justices McLean and Curtis were prepared to write dissenting opinions setting forth their views about the Missouri Compromise and the power of Congress to legislate about slavery in the territories. (They held that Scott had properly been made free by his sojourn on free soil, and that Congress had a constitutional right to outlaw slavery in the territories.) If these two dissenters were going to air their views on this latter point, those who disagreed with them would obviously do the same. In addition, many of the justices honestly believed that it was necessary to hand down a broad, definitive ruling that would stand as a landmark, settling the

Henry Blow, son of Scott's original owner, was an antislavery man who, to strike at the "peculiar institution," helped finance the case which split the nation.

293

territorial problem once and for all. Finally, Mr. James Buchanan exerted a little pressure of his own.

James Buchanan was elected President in the fall of 1856, and during the following winter—after the arguments had been heard, but before the Court had handed down its opinion—he was composing the address which he would deliver when he took the oath of office on March 4. He was bound to say something about popular sovereignty, and the issue was a tough one for a brand-new President to discuss, especially a President who owed his nomination and election largely to the fact that he had never been directly involved in the furious arguments over the territorial question. It occurred to him that it would be excellent if, in his inaugural, he could say that the question of Congress' constitutional power to legislate on slavery in the territories would very shortly be decided by the Supreme Court and that all good citizens might well stop agitating the issue and prepare to abide by the Court's ruling.

In February the President-elect wrote a letter to Justice Catron, setting forth his desire to say that the Supreme Court would presently settle this question. A bit later he wrote to Justice Grier in the same vein. Mr. Buchanan, clearly, was skirting the edge of outright impropriety; he was not exactly telling the justices what he wanted the Court to say, but. he was making it clear that he wanted the Court to say *something,* and Justice Catron finally assured him that the Court would handle the matter and that Buchanan could safely say that the country ought to wait for its decision.

This Mr. Buchanan proceeded to do. In his inaugural address he remarked that the whole question of legalizing or prohibiting slavery in the territories was "a judicial question, which legitimately belongs to the Supreme Court of the United States, before whom it is now pending and will, it is understood, be speedily and finally settled. To their decision, in common with all good citizens, I shall cheerfully submit, whatever this may be."

This set the stage. Two days later—on March 6, 1857—the Court handed down its decision, the gist of which was that Dred Scott was a slave and not a citizen, and hence could not sue in federal court, and that the Missouri Compromise was unconstitutional because Congress had no power to prohibit slavery in the territories. To these basic findings there were just two dissents, those of Justices McLean and Curtis.

Thus the Supreme Court had (to use a police-court colloquialism) thrown the book at Dred Scott. But the case was most complicated. Each of the nine justices wrote an opinion; and although the majority agreed on the basic findings, they gave different reasons for their beliefs, and some of them remained silent on points which others considered highly important. In effect, the Court went beyond both Scott and the authority of Congress and discussed the whole rationale of slavery and the status of the Negro, and in all of this the sectional and political backgrounds of the justices were sharply emphasized. As Allan Nevins sums it up in his book, *The Emergence of Lincoln:*

Three Southern judges declared that no Negro of slave ancestry could be entitled to citizenship; five Southern judges, with Nelson of New York, decided that Dred's status depended upon the laws of Missouri; five Southern judges, with Grier of Pennsylvania, maintained that any law excluding slavery from a territory was unconstitutional; and two Northern judges, McLean and Curtis, held that Dred was a citizen, that Missouri law did not control his status, and that Congress had a constitutional right to pass laws debarring slavery from any Territory.

It was Taney's opinion that went across the land like a thunderclap. Not only was Taney the Chief Justice; he was a man of immense prestige and learning, a veteran of Andrew Jackson's famous fight with the Bank of the United States, named Chief Justice by Jackson in 1835 as successor to John Marshall, one of the most impressive figures in American life. Taney was eighty now, shrunken, wispy, with a heavy shock of iron-gray hair framing a deeply lined face. Fires burned in him, but he was physically frail, and as he read his momentous opinion his voice was so low that many of the people in the courtroom could not catch his words. Nevertheless, what he said was heard all across the country.

The Chief Justice addressed himself to the question of the constitutional power of Congress over the territories. It had been argued, he noted, that federal authority over the territories came from a clause permitting Congress to make rules and regulations for the government of the territories; but this, he held, was a mere emergency provision applying only to the lands ceded to the Confederation by the original states and did not apply to lands acquired after 1789. Properly, Congress had only those powers associated with the right to acquire territory and prepare it for statehood; it had no internal police authority, and while it might organize local territorial government it could not "infringe upon local rights of person or rights of property."

The right to hold slaves was a property right; since Congress could not interfere with a man's property rights, it could not prohibit slavery in the territories: "And no word can be found in the Constitution which gives Congress a greater power over slave property, or which entitles property of that kind to less protection, than property of any other description." To exclude slavery would violate the due process clause of the Fifth Amendment. Congress had nothing more than the power—"coupled with the duty"—to protect the owner in his property rights. Thus all territorial restrictions on slavery were dead.

Therefore the Missouri Compromise was unconstitutional. Its provision prohibiting slavery north of the 36 degree, 30 minute line was "not warranted by the Constitution" and was void. It was idle to argue that Dred Scott's residence on free soil had made him a free man, because slavery had not lawfully been excluded from Wisconsin Territory in the first place.

But that was not all. As a Negro of slave origins (said Taney) Scott could not be a citizen of the United States anyway. He and all people like him were simply ineligible. The Founding Fathers who wrote the Declaration of Independence and framed the Constitution had been thinking only of white men. At the time the Constitution was adopted, and for a long time before that, there was general agreement that Negroes were "beings of an inferior order, and altogether unfit to associate with the white race, either in social or political relations; and so far inferior that they had no rights which the white man was bound to respect."

It is clear enough now that in making this remark the Chief Justice was in no sense laying down a rule of law for his own day; he was simply expressing what he believed was the prevailing opinion of Americans in the latter part of the eighteenth century. But his use of these words, embedded in an opinion which antislavery people were going to object to in any case, was in the highest degree unfortunate. To many people in the North it seemed that the Chief Justice had officially declared that the colored man had no rights which the white man was bound to respect. President Buchanan's pious hope that all good citizens would willingly accept the Court's finding in the Dred Scott case was bound to run onto this reef if on no other.

Only two other justices, Wayne and Daniel, joined with Taney in the opinion that no Negro could be a citizen. Justices Curtis and McLean dissented vigorously, and the remainder kept silent on this particular question. This made very little difference. The Missouri Compromise was unconstitutional—the first act of Congress to be declared unconstitutional since the famous *Marbury v. Madison* case in 1803 (see "The Case of the 'Missing' Commissions" in the June, 1963, AMERICAN HERITAGE)—and Dred Scott was still a slave; the net effect of the decision was to give an immense impetus to the furious arguments over slavery and to help materially to make this issue so acute and so emotion-laden that it was too explosive for political settlement.

Chief Justice Roger Taney's decision was excoriated in the North. "It is a singular . . . fact in nature," the New York Tribune *said, "that the body to some extent intimates the character of the soul that inhabits it. [Taney] walks with inverted and hesitating steps. His forehead is contracted, his eyes sunken and his visage has a sinister expression."*

To the rising Republican party the ruling was simply a challenge to renewed struggle. This party was dedicated to the conviction that slavery must not be allowed to expand; now the High Court was formally saying that there was no legal way by which it could be excluded from the territories. Congress could not do it; a territorial legislature, as a creature of Congress, could not do it either. Only when the people of a territory drafted a constitution and prepared to enter the Union as a state could they adopt an effective antislavery law. To many northerners it seemed that, logically, the next step would be for the Court to declare that no state could outlaw slavery and that the institution must be legalized all across the country.

Free-soil adherents in the North promptly accepted the challenge which they found implicit in the decision. They expressed profound contempt for the Court itself, asserting that it was wholly biased in favor of the southern sectional interest and that its decision in the Dred Scott case had no moral substance and could not be permanently binding. For the moment, to be sure, the ruling was legally valid, but in effect the antislavery people of the North defied the Court. Seeking to take the territorial issue out of politics, the Court had instead put itself squarely and disastrously into politics. Never before had there been such a profound and widespread revulsion against a finding of the nation's highest judicial tribunal.

To the northern wing of the Democratic party—the wing that followed Senator Douglas—the ruling was equally disturbing, because it knocked the props out from under the doctrine of popular sovereignty. Douglas, to be sure, defended the Court against Republican criticism, declaring that "whoever resists the final decision of the highest judicial tribunal aims a deadly blow at our whole republican system of government," and expressed the conviction that the decision must not be made a political issue. But he was breaking with the Buchanan administration on the Kansas issue—the administration was accepting a rigged election which would give Kansas a constitution permitting slavery even though a majority of the voters obviously were antislavery. Douglas was fighting hard for popular sovereignty, and the Dred Scott decision simply accentuated this issue by splitting the northern and southern wings of the Democratic party farther and farther apart.

For while the Douglas Democrats in the North continued to rely on popular sovereignty as the answer to the territorial problem, the southern Democrats were led by this decision to press forward in complete opposition to popular sovereignty. Now they demanded positive protection of the slaveowner's right to take his chattels with him when he moved into a territory. The decision said that nobody could outlaw slavery in a territory: the southerners felt it was only logical that the federal government act to protect slavery there by formal legislation. The northern and southern wings of the party could never agree on any such formula. In substance, the Court's decision was a weighty factor in determining that no Democrat who had any chance to carry the North could also carry the South, which meant that the presidential election of 1860 would be won by the Republicans, after which the discordant sections would find themselves at the parting of the ways. The irreconcilable sectionalism which would bring the country to civil war was accentuated by this ruling of the High Court.

Perhaps the real trouble with the decision was that the general trend of events was moving in the other direction. The New York *Herald,* on March 9, 1857, summed it up:

The Washington politicians who believe that it [the Dred Scott decision] settles anything must be afflicted with very severe ophthalmia indeed. For while these venerable judges are discoursing on theoretical expansions of slavery to North and West, free labor is marching with a very tangible step into the heart of the strongest slaveholds of slavery. Chief Justice Taney lays out on paper an infinitude of new slave states and territories; he makes all the states in a measure slave states; but while the old gentleman is thus diverting his slippered leisure, free carpenters and blacksmiths and farmers with hoe, spade and plough are invading Missouri, Kentucky, Delaware, Maryland and Virginia, and quietly elbowing the slaves further South. It will take a good many Supreme Court decisions to reverse a law of nature such as we here see in operation.

All in all, the Dred Scott decision did the Court profound and lasting harm. Many years later Chief Justice Charles Evans Hughes remarked that it was a case in which the Court suffered from a self-inflicted wound, and characterized the ruling as a "public calamity." More than a century after the decision was handed down, a historian of the Court wrote of it as a "monumental indiscretion." The Court's prestige suffered immensely, and Justice Felix Frankfurter once remarked that after the Civil War, justices of the Supreme Court never mentioned the Dred Scott case, any more than a family in which a son had been hanged mentioned ropes and scaffolds.

In the end, the profound majority of people in the North, who, regardless of party labels, believed that slavery's expansion into the territories must be checked, agreed that while the Court's finding was binding it must eventually be reversed. A new administration would give the Court new justices and a new background, and in the course of time it would be shown that a nation whose majority did not want slavery to expand would be able to make its wish good. There was just one point on which Republicans, northern Democrats, and southern Democrats all agreed: the finding in respect to Dred Scott as a person remained good. He was still a slave.

Their legal efforts to have him declared free having failed, Dred Scott's owners manumitted him a few weeks later. On September 17, 1858, he died, in St. Louis, of tuberculosis. Henry Blow paid his funeral expenses.

Coatesville, Pennsylvania, dozed fitfully

in the oppressive heat of August. Then two shots rang out,

and set off an ugly train of racial violence

SUMMER
SUNDAY

By ERIC F. GOLDMAN

The grim and vivid account which follows may strike some of our readers as a frightful fantasy. Unfortunately it all took place, detail for detail, in the year 1911. Since we believe, as this magazine regularly testifies, that the good in our past generously outweighs the bad, we never shrink from chronicling cruelty and rascality. Yet we might hesitate, even so, to print this unusually ugly story of racial violence long ago if it did not lay bare so much that lies dangerously hidden in the folk memory of the white man and the black, if it did not help in some way to explain some of the bitterness and guilt which presently afflict the two races, if it did not admonish us so powerfully—if, in short, good did not sometimes spring out of evil.

Zachariah Walker had a few drinks of straight gin and felt good. He drank some more and felt even better. Now he poured the gin in quick spurts, his aim half missing the glass, and the world of here and now was racing away.

That evening, Saturday, August 12, 1911, everybody in Coatesville could use less of the here and now. The overgrown town, population about 11,000, lay thirty-eight miles west of Philadelphia in the trough of the Chester Valley, and the heat of the eastern seaboard hung over it dank and steaming. The discomforts nature did not bring, Coatesville managed itself. The town's life centered in two sprawling iron and steel corporations, the Lukens Iron and Steel Company and the Worth Brothers Company. Any day or night the furnaces sent up clouds of soot. This Saturday evening, like all Saturday evenings, was the time for blowing the waste boilers, and great billows of dirty smoke, stirred along by desultory tufts of wind, kept drifting through the valley.

Most of the well-to-do of Coatesville, the steel executives and the more prosperous merchants along Main Street, had chugged off to the Jersey Coast in their high-fendered automobiles. The clerks and the skilled workers and the grocery-store keepers flocked to the nearby Pinto Kit's Wild West Show where "real cowboys," "absolutely guaranteed, money-back" real cowboys, did their fancy riding, lassoing, and shooting;

Coming into Coatesville on the Pennsylvania Railroad, one saw this homely panorama of a typical American industrial town.

or to Coatesville's three movie houses with the hard-working big propeller fans; or to Davy's Soda Garden, which offered oversize helpings of frosted fruit and Terry's Orchestra playing "Come Josephine in My Flying Machine" and "Dream Kisses" for the waltzing, and an occasional thumping march when the couples sat down, worked away with their bamboo fans, told each other fretfully that the hay fever had never been so bad and that something simply had to be done about the stray dogs.

Workingmen jammed Coatesville's five long rectangular bars on Main Street. (Liquor licenses in the town, kept limited by fervid prohibitionists, could bring as much as $100,000.) At some of the bars, customers had to shove their way in. At all of them the beer or whiskey, passed from the bartender to men in the back rows, splashed and spilled until the heavy sawdust on the floors could no longer absorb it and the liquor flowed, in dirty, caking rivulets, out to the sidewalks.

Up on the hill to the southeast, near the dingy black buildings of Lukens and Worth, thousands sweltered away with no money for the downtown bars or a Wild West Show. Rows of wooden shacks housed some 3,000 eastern European immigrants brought over for unskilled labor in the steel plants. Further up the hill, huts still more ramshackle were the quarters for about 2,000 Negro workers imported from the South.

Zachariah Walker, a lanky, tan-colored Negro brought up from Greene County, Virginia, and now working as a water-wagon driver in the Worth plant, took the last swig from his bottle and shambled off to a neighboring shack. A few more drinks, it was a boring eight o'clock or so, and Walker went back to his own place, stuck a hat on his head and a revolver in his pocket, and made off down Youngsburg Road, which ran alongside the shacks through a patch of woods toward central Coatesville.

Shortly before 9 P.M., two shots rang out from the woods. They were heard by Edgar Rice, a company policeman employed by Worth who had stopped into the grocery store of a Slovakian immigrant, Leon Miclcorck. Rice hurried toward the woods and met an immigrant fleeing from them. A Negro had tried to hold him up, the immigrant said, and when he ran, the Negro fired at him twice. The policeman went into the woods. Soon there was another shot, then two more.

Rice came staggering out, reeled along the road some sixty yards with his arms flung out before him, dropped face down near Miclcorck's grocery. The terrified storekeeper and other immigrants carried the policeman into the store. One bullet had torn through his shoulder and another was lodged in the left side of his head at the base of the brain. In a few minutes Rice stopped breathing.

The immigrants had scarcely realized that the policeman was dead when the August skies broke into a torrential rain. One of the immigrants, a Hungarian, went running into town, sloshing through the mud and shouting the news in a frenzy of broken syntax. Coatesville heard of the killing with a gasp. Edgar Rice was widely known and just about as popular as anyone in town. Middle-class Coatesville thought of him as the middle-class ideal, a hard-working, church-going man, good husband and good father to his five children, properly proud of his oldest boy, Thomas, who was serving on the U.S.S. *Chester*. Working-class Coatesville knew him as a highly unusual company cop, a friendly, good-humored fellow who rarely used his pistol or stick and was more likely to take a troublemaker home than to jail him. All kinds of people remembered Rice as the victim of highhanded politics. For six years he had been a member of the regular town police force but two years before, he had had the temerity to run for the office of chief of police and, worse still, to come within forty-four votes of winning. Rice was promptly fired and had to settle for the lower-paying job of company cop.

As the news of the killing raced through town, bars, movies, and homes emptied and angry groups gathered on the street corners. Everybody was soon agreeing on much the same story: Edgar Rice, always the brave man, had gone into the woods with his pistol in its holster. He found the Negro, grabbed him by the arm, started leading him to the nearby Worth lockup. The Negro wrenched himself free, tripped Rice, and as the policeman fell, shot him in the back. The more the story was told, the bigger and the more restless the crowds became. The largest number gathered on East Chestnut Street, just off Main Street, in front of the boxlike, two-story, red-brick building that functioned both as borough hall and borough jail but served above all as the headquarters of Charles E. Umsted, Elk, Mason, Eagle, leader in the Washington Hose Company and the United Sportsmen's Association,

pillar of the First Baptist Church, constable, high constable, and chief of police of the Borough of Coatesville.

Several years before, Chief Umsted had unceremoniously dumped a reporter from the Coatesville *Record* out of his office and the *Record*'s editor, William W. Long, replied with an editorial that compared the Chief to the elephant Jumbo, which P. T. Barnum had imported from England. Jumbo, the editorial explained, was so big he nearly sank the ship and so dumb he had trouble learning to eat peanuts. From that day on, to everybody in Coatesville Chief Umsted was "Jumbo" or "Jummy"—depending on the mood— and the nicknames were not without their appropriateness. A huge hulk of a man, six feet three inches in his flat policeman's shoes and sending the scales over 250 pounds when he was eating lightly, Umsted crunched his way through the jungle of Coatesville police life.

Everybody had stories of the Chief's mastodonic law enforcement. Was there word that three New York pickpockets were arriving on the morning train to work the local fair? Umsted met the men as they alighted, bundled them together like so many bags of potatoes, deposited them back on the train. Had a steelworker in the Speakman Bar pulled a knife? Umsted arrived with an impatient glower, knocked the knife out of the man's hand, removed him forthwith by the seat of his pants and the scruff of his neck.

But the roughhouse Chief also had his own deft sense of how to get along and get ahead. Starting out as a butcher, he had quickly tired of cleaving steaks and in election after election he kept winning the post of chief of police despite Coatesville's endlessly intricate politics. Among the town's steel executives, men used to smile and say, "Jummy knows what we want." Ladies' clubs passed more than a few glowing resolutions about the Chief; he managed to give his roughest manhandlings the aura of law and justice. Even the drunks of the town could find good words for Umsted. At the back of the borough jail was a square room, with concrete walls and narrow slits for a door and a window, that was known as "The Tank." The man who had had too many would be put in the Tank, doused by the Chief with a hose and permitted to sleep it off, then sent on his way the next morning with a friendly, if paralyzing, shake of the hand. "Jummy was the most lumbering man I ever saw," one Coatesville resident remembers, "but he always lumbered, clumsy as could be, to exactly where he wanted to get."

Now, as the crowd milled outside his office, the Chief lumbered into action once again. All the policemen in the town—the seven men of the borough force

ILLUSTRATED FOR AMERICAN HERITAGE BY BERNARD KRIGSTEIN

and the company policemen of Lukens and Worth—were reporting in for emergency duty and Umsted growled his instructions: Get the killer of Rice—"I don't care how you get him but get him." Identifying the murderer was hardly difficult. By midnight of Saturday all kinds of clues were pointing to Zachariah Walker. Loosely organized posses, made up of eager volunteers from the crowds and armed with revolvers, shotguns, pitchforks, and sticks, were already fanning out in a farm area to the south of the scene of the killing. The problem was the darkness and the unremitting rain. At daybreak the posses were back, bedraggled and muttering that they would get some sleep and wait for tomorrow. The Chief sank into the big swivel chair in his office with a tremendous sigh. "More of it," he groaned to a friend. "Always more of it. Nigger kills. Nigger gets chased. Well, it's my job."

About 10 o'clock Sunday morning the telephone jolted Umsted out of his sleep. A farmer who lived three-quarters of a mile from the murder spot was calling to say that he had just seen Walker running across his field. Once again the posses assembled and this time they were better organized. Of course one was led by Umsted; another by Alfred S. Jackson, chief of the Lukens company police; a third by Alfred A. Berry, who had recently come to Coatesville from Philadelphia and was making a living doing balloon ascensions and running dances at a nearby Negro amusement place, the 20th Century Park. Early Sunday afternoon word came from a second farm. A fourteen-year-old boy, Lewis Townsend, had gone out to the barn looking for eggs and had seen a tan-colored leg showing from beneath a loose pile of hay.

The three posses closed in, shotguns ready. Suddenly, from a cherry tree, came the sound of two shots and Zachariah Walker tumbled down. The closest posse leader was Berry and he, wondering whether the Negro had really tried to commit suicide or was attempting a ruse, approached cautiously. There was no doubt about the suicide attempt. Walker was unconscious and bleeding profusely from his lower jaw. Berry and his group improvised a stretcher by placing coats across the barrels of three shotguns and carried the Negro to an automobile.

As the car approached town it had to fight its way through increasingly large crowds. Four to five hundred men and women churned in the narrow street in front of the police station. Everyone assumed that Walker was all but dead and people squeezed a path for him to be carried into the building. Once inside, he regained a degree of consciousness. He refused to say anything; instead he made frantic motions to the policemen to kill him. Dr. Artemus Carmichael examined the Negro and ordered him to the hospital. The crowd made way again as Walker was brought out. "Well, that nigger sure saved us the trouble," said one man, swishing his hands in a that's-that motion.

About 4 P.M. the automobile carrying Walker, Chief Umsted, and several policemen reached the hill to the southwest on which stood the two-and-a-half story, red-brick Coatesville Hospital, a gift of the owners of Lukens and Worth. Dr. Carmichael arrived in his own car and immediately operated on Walker to remove the bullet. The Negro was placed in a private room at the right front of the building, his body strapped to the bed by a canvas restraint sheet, his right leg attached to the foot of the iron bedstead by a chain. Umsted assigned one of his patrolmen, Stanley Howe, to stand guard and he, Dr. Carmichael, and the rest of the policemen left.

Soon people began arriving at the hospital room, individually and in family groups. Mostly the visitors would stare at the Negro, whisper behind their hands, and ask Officer Howe the same question: Was there any chance Walker would recover? The Negro's head was swathed in thick bandages but he gave every appearance of a man who was going to live. He had now regained full consciousness and was breathing normally and returning stare for stare.

During the supper hour Umsted returned to the hospital and started questioning Walker. The Negro agreed to make a confession but his admissions were decidedly limited. Stanley Howe took down the words: Walker had made no attempt to rob "a foreigner" or anyone else. He was simply "feeling pretty good" and when he saw a "Hunkey" in the woods, he fired into the air to whoop things up. Walker had killed Rice but in self-defense. The policeman "came over and placed me under arrest. I knew if he would take me I would serve time for carrying concealed weapons, and I resisted him. Rice told me to quit . . . , and if I didn't he would hit me over the head with a club. I told him that if he did I would kill him. Rice then made a plunge at me with the club, and he dropped the stick and reached for his revolver. I was too quick for him. I had my gun out first and fired two shots into him. . . ."

When the posses closed in, the Negro gave up hope.

301

"I saw you, Umsted, in your uniform, come down the road in the automobile and heard the crowds say they were going to surround the place, and I knew it was all up with me. . . . When some of the men surrounded me, I thought I would end it all, and sent a bullet into the back of my head. . . ." Walker added: "I wish I had finished the job."

As dusk fell, the news was all over Coatesville that the Negro was recovering and the town was stirring again. One crowd of men, women, and children milled fretfully on the long sloping green in front of the hospital. Another gathered closer to Main Street, at the Ashley & Bailey Silk Mill on Strode Avenue. The largest crowd, composed almost exclusively of men, formed on Main Street, outside the Brandywine Fire Company, which had long been a political and social center of the town and of which Edgar Rice had been a member. In all of the groups, middle-class people and old-stock workers predominated; there were few if any immigrants. In all of the groups, the talk ran rampant: "Let's lynch that nigger."

Before long the word was going out to the towns and farm areas surrounding Coatesville. Hundreds were in the same mood as Ambrose Boyd, a conductor for the Conestoga Traction Company on the five-mile run from Coatesville to Parkesburg. When Boyd reached Parkesburg shortly after 8 P.M., he went to the house of his crony, Joseph Schofield, a master mechanic and company policeman for Conestoga.

"Joe, come on along. We are going to Coatesville. There's a big crowd down there talking about lynching that nigger." The two men took the next streetcar back.

In Coatesville, Umsted had returned from the hospital and joined the crowd at the Brandywine Firehouse, where he kept talking about Walker's confession. Mordecai P. Markward, assistant chief of the Brandywine, was worried by the mood of the men and tactfully hinted to the police chief that he ought to get off the subject. "I must be drawing flies," Umsted chuckled and continued to go on about the confession. The crowd kept growing. It clogged the pavement and street outside the firehouse, overflowed in front of Braunstein's furniture store and around First Avenue. Men would break off into little groups and hold whispered conferences, then mill back into the general throng.

After a while Umsted wandered catercorner across Main Street to the office of his old friend, Justice of the Peace George G. Myer, who had a habit of being in his office at all kinds of hours. One part of the Brandywine crowd, some fifty men, started to move too, west on Main Street toward Strode Avenue, which

led to the hospital. At first they walked silently. Then yells began going up, some of them so loud they could be clearly heard above the Salvation Army band blaring hymns up the street. "Anything's too good for that nigger." "No ten niggers are worth an Ed Rice." "The beasts are getting too uppity anyhow." After a few blocks the crowd got to arguing whether they had enough men to "fix" Walker, stopped, drifted back to the firehouse.

There the enthusiastic buttonholed the reluctant, shook fingers in their faces, demanded, "Are you or aren't you a man?" About 8:30 a much larger crowd started toward the hospital. Along the way men, women, and children joined the shouting, jostling

mob. The evening services of the churches were letting out now and whole families moved along with the throng, some asking what was going on and then drifting off, more falling into line. As the crowd poured down Strode Avenue it met the group at the Ashley-Bailey Silk Mill, which promptly joined forces.

On and on the mob swept, into the hundreds already on the hospital grounds, into more hundreds converging on the lawn in all directions from neighboring regions. Soon some three thousand people were at the hospital. A scattering of the men were the local toughs and here and there somebody plainly had observed the Sabbath with a bottle. But for the most part the crowd was made up of the respectable of the Coatesville area, a mass of neat shirt sleeves and starched gingham and cotton wilting in the heat.

A horse-drawn ambulance drove up bringing Dr. E. A. Graves, a Coatesville physician, with an accident case from the Pennsylvania Railroad station. The crowd opened a way for the vehicle to pull up to the emergency entrance. When it started down the hospital drive determined-faced men, thinking it was taking

Walker away, grabbed the bridles of the horses, told the frightened driver to mind his own business, and thoroughly searched the ambulance. Finding no one, the men ran back up the grounds, shouted and beckoned, and some of the crowd edged toward the steps leading to the porch of the hospital.

Inside Miss Lena Gray Townsend, the spinsterish superintendent who had taken over the post only the previous November, was decidedly nervous. "What is all that crowd doing down there?" she asked anyone who came by, and she was not reassured when told that the crowd would leave as soon as it discovered that Walker was not being taken away.

Now, with men moving toward the hospital steps, Miss Townsend turned in panic to Officer Howe. "Oh, what must I do?" she screamed.

Call up 19, Police Headquarters, said Howe.

Miss Townsend called 19. She called the Brandywine Firehouse and all other likely places and she reached no policeman. She begged Central to keep trying, to get her somebody, anybody, and she ran from the phone to lock the two tall screen doors leading from the porch into the hospital.

In Coatesville, Chief of Police Umsted was sitting in Magistrate Myer's office, his feet on the table, swapping stories. About the time the Brandywine crowd started for the hospital, Mordecai Markward hurried into the office and told Umsted: "Things look desperate. . . . They are going to lynch that man sure."

The Chief waved his hand impatiently. "That is all hot air; there is no danger."

Umsted remained for twenty minutes or so and then ambled up Main Street. Across the street from the Stephenson Hotel he ran into Dr. Carmichael, who had stopped his car to chat with Jesse Shallcross, burgess of Coatesville, and two policemen, Robert Allison and Thomas Nafe. The Doctor showed the group a bullet he had taken from the body of Rice, and while they looked at it, Dr. Graves drove up in the ambulance.

The men who had searched the ambulance, Dr. Graves told the police chief, were in a violent mood. There was going to be trouble and Umsted had better get policemen over there.

The Chief's face flushed with irritation. He was sick of all this gabble. He had been up the whole night before, he was tired, and to hell with it. Burgess Shallcross and Officer Nafe drifted off.

A few more minutes and the central telephone operator, still trying to reach somebody, got Richard D. Gibney, a livery stable owner who was a member of the borough City Council and chairman of its Police Committee. Gibney called Umsted's office and reached Harry Downing, a friend of the police chief, who was

sitting there.

Get Umsted, Gibney ordered. Tell him police are needed immediately at the hospital. And tell him that he has permission to call out the sixteen volunteer firemen.

Downing found Umsted still talking with Dr. Carmichael and this time the Chief was furious. He had heard just about enough of this business, Umsted exploded. He wanted to hear no more.

At the hospital several men were on the front steps. But no one joined them and the crowd churned without moving forward for a long few minutes. Just after 9 P.M. a neatly dressed man with a mask over the top part of his face ran up the stairs, turned, fired a shot into the air. People remembered his words differently. Some thought they were: "Men of Coatesville, will you allow a drunken nigger to do up such a white man as Ed Rice?" Others thought they heard: "Men, are you going to allow a white man to be downed by a nigger?" Or, "You are all cowards—will you let niggers ride over the whites?"

Whatever the exact words, they did it. "No-o-o," the crowd chorused back. In seconds twelve to fifteen more men, some in half masks, some with handkerchiefs tied in triangles below their eyes, some with no covering, were up the steps and on the porch, wildly ringing the bell, rattling the screen doors, pushing and yelling.

Miss Townsend pleaded through the screen: "Oh, go away men and leave this man alone. There are very sick people in this house, some at the point of death; there are mothers and sisters here, and if your mother or your sister was here you would not do this thing."

"You open up this door quietly and we will go in quietly," one of the men replied, "but if you don't we will batter the doors down."

Miss Townsend checked the lock on the door. Then she hurried inside to try to rally her panicking nurses and to quiet her eighteen patients, most of whom were out of bed, shrieking and sobbing as they struggled to make their way upstairs.

Stanley Howe took over at the screen door, telling the men they ought to go away. Somebody hollered: "The nigger or Howe." Another said: "Stanley, you might as well open the door. We'll get him anyhow." Suddenly a foot went through the window on the left side of the porch and Howe ran over to close the door leading from that room into the vestibule. Then the screen doors went crashing in and the mob leaders careened into the hospital. They turned toward Walker's room at the right, pushing Howe ahead of them. The powerfully built officer went jostling along, unresisting, his Colt revolver, fully loaded, in its holster.

In Walker's room eager hands tore at the canvas restraint jacket on the Negro's body. A nurse started to intervene. She was pushed into a corner and stood there, frozen in terror. As the jacket loosened, Walker, fighting back ferociously, was hammered down by fists on all sides. The bandages came off his head and blood spattered everything. Outside the crowd roared impatiently: "Why don't you get him? Bring him out!" Stones clattered through windows of the hospital and more of the mob poured through the front doors.

The men in Walker's room yanked at the chain binding the Negro's leg to the foot of the iron bedstead. Where are the keys? they demanded of Howe.

The officer, standing very much aside, said he did not have the keys. They were with Umsted.

Someone yelled, "To hell with the keys. Cut his leg off." Instead, feet smashed against the bedstead. The men picked up Walker, chain, and foot of the bedstead, and carried, pulled, and dragged them pell-mell. They brought the Negro out on the porch a bleeding, flailing, shrieking mass of flesh.

At the sight of Walker a tremendous noise went up from the crowd. Now and again a chant broke through the bedlam: "Lynch him! Lynch him! Lynch him!" The sounds rolled down the hospital hill, all through the sultry air of the valley.

Some fifteen to twenty men, as many as could lay hands on Walker, half carried, half dragged him down the hospital lawn and along the cinder path leading to Strode Avenue and to central Coatesville. The mob kept closing in on the Negro, then making way, torn between its zest to get Walker done with and its urge to curse and to jab at him. A female voice screeched above the din: "Niggers, you have been good but you are done for now." A man broke to the head of the crowd, held a lantern high, led a response: "Right, right, right. Niggers you have been good but you are done for now."

At the intersection of Strode Avenue, three arc lights overhead cut through the night with a purplish haze. Everything paused. Walker was dumped on the ground, a rope was looped around his feet, and he writhed and begged at the end of the rope while the leaders argued. Some said he ought to be weighted down and thrown in the Brandywine Creek. Others wanted to take him the few hundred yards to the Ashley-Bailey Silk Mill and hang him from the electric pole there. One man cried out: "Burn him! Burn him! Burn him!"

The cry produced an instant decision. Hands reached forward to get Walker, chain, and foot of the bedstead moving again, the opposite way from Coatesville, up the extension of Strode Avenue known as Ercildoun Road and leading to farms and woods. The decision went out to the crowd in the special, sure language of a mob. Most received it with a roar of approval. Little groups drew back, milling about uncertainly.

One person with no hesitancy at all was a woman who came running down Strode Avenue still adjusting her hood. The wispish, mild-mannered Mrs. Edgar Rice was now a tigress, fighting her way into the crowd. Men grabbed her and pulled her aside, insisting she could not go along.

Her laughter was shrill. Not going? she screamed. I'm going and I'm going to light the fire.

Four men seized her tightly by the arms and pulled her, struggling and weeping, toward her house on West Main Street. "I pleaded, I begged, I implored . . . [I] begged them on my knees . . . ," Anna Rice remembered the next day. "Why would they stop me from avenging Ed? They took me back to the house and thrust me inside and slammed the door. Two of the men stayed there for a few minutes to see that I did not get away. But when I saw the men depart I sort of lost my nerve and fell into a chair. I was all unstrung and could only pray that he died in terrible agony."

Further up Main Street a messenger from the Stephenson Hotel ran across the street to Chief Umsted and told him that there was an emergency call. Umsted went to the phone and a frantic voice sobbed that Walker was about to be taken out of the hospital. He rejoined Dr. Carmichael and Officer Allison and the three went in the Doctor's car to the hospital.

When they arrived, the mob taking the Negro up Ercildoun Road could be plainly seen and heard. The chief of police made his decision. He ordered Allison to tell the people still on the hospital grounds that they were trespassing and to go home. He went inside the hospital, elaborately interviewed Stanley Howe and others, painstakingly examined the lock on the hospital door and the room in which Walker had been. Then Chief of Police Umsted emerged from the hospital—and went home.

The mob continued its way along the muddy ruts of Ercildoun Road, shouting, subsiding, shouting still more loudly. A heavy gray fog was moving in from the Brandywine Creek; the hundreds of lanterns came through with a dim, yellowish light. Shifting groups of men, some with masks, carried Walker by his arms and legs, swung between them like a bag of potatoes, the chain and the foot of the bedstead dragging along crazily. The leaders had their own rules of restraint. In the words of a local reporter who was with the crowd, "men in every walk of life, staid citizens and the town loafers, joined in heaping blows and execrations upon [Walker]. . . . though every precaution was taken by those having him in charge to prevent him from receiving a wound which would make him insensible to the flames. . . ."

Most of the route was uphill. Often the Negro was dumped in the road and men and boys forced him to crawl by kicks and the jabs of shotguns, pitchforks, and poles. When he collapsed, more kicks and jabs brought him to his hands and knees again. Walker resisted little now. Most of the time he moaned and begged to be shot. Occasionally, when being carried, he lay quietly, his lips moving in what seemed to be a prayer.

With every passing minute the mob increased in size. Men, women, and children—the total crowd was almost half female—came running from the hesitant group at the hospital, from Coatesville, and from surrounding areas. As the number mounted close to five thousand, the noise tore through the mists in great snarling waves. "Burn the nigger!" "Lynch the beast!" "Burn him! Burn him! Burn him!" Along the way somebody gave the mob its favorite. A voice rang out: "Last night you were in Coatesville and you murdered a policeman. Tonight you will be in a fiery furnace and tomorrow you will be in hell." Over and over again the crowd chanted: "Tonight you'll be in a fiery furnace, tomorrow you'll be in hell."

At the end of about half a mile, the leaders stopped. Here the farm lands of Mrs. Sarah Jane Newlin stretched on both sides of Ercildoun Road. A lane with a fence made of chestnut rails cut diagonally across the public road. Walker, the chain, and the foot of the bedstead were dragged left on the lane, about fifty yards in, and thrown across the fence into an adjoining field. A ring of men, with guns drawn, closed around the Negro. The crowd shuffled for positions behind the circle and most had to make their way up the hilly meadows rolling back from either side of Ercildoun Road.

For seconds—perhaps a minute—nothing happened. The mob hushed, the leaders stood silent, Walker lay still, very still. A flock of birds, fluttering away, sounded weirdly loud.

Then the cries went up: "Let's finish him." Men and boys tore fence rails loose and piled them griddle-wise. The leaders, now mostly in masks, picked up Walker and heaved him on the pile. He groaned as the bedstead gouged into his body but he made no outcry and lay limp. Kindling was stuffed between the logs. Matches came out. Everything was still damp and the kindling did not ignite.

The mob stirred irritably. "Get straw! Get hay! Burn him!" Scores ran to the Newlin barn for dry forage. More fence rails were torn off and logs six to seven feet long were heaped around and over the Negro. At the touch of match to the straw and hay the fire caught on and Zachariah Walker found his voice.

"For God's sake, give a man a chance. I killed Rice in self-defense." A storm of jeers obliterated his words except for those close by. "Don't give me a crooked death because I'm not white."

The flames leaped up. The fierce glow made the masks of the leaders seem blood-red. They broke into a dance around the fire, whooping and flinging their hands up and down. The mob went into its own frenzy, backslapping, swinging lanterns wildly aloft, roaring a new chant: "Niggers, *now* you'll learn. Niggers, *now* you'll learn."

As the flames crackled seven and ten feet high, the mood relaxed. The dance around the fire turned into a laughing caper, joined in by small boys and girls. There were cheers, pleasant cheers, like the cheering at "a baseball game," people remembered. "Very much of a social affair," "resembling a big carnival," others said. On the outer fringes of the crowd, where farm roads cut in, automobiles pulled up with trimly

dressed men and women, most of the women demurely holding motor veils over the lower part of their faces. The thousands just stood, chatting, pointing out this or that happening around the flaming mound, reaching across to shake hands with a friend.

There was camaraderie and thoughtfulness and chivalry too. Near the fire, the reporter of the Coatesville *Record* observed, "there was no loud talking, no profanity," and the "utmost deference" was shown to women. The leaders would stop stoking the flames to doff their hats to some female friend they recognized. In the crowd men stepped aside to provide women a better position or led them to a place of vantage. Fathers and mothers hoisted children on their shoulders.

Suddenly there was a commotion down Ercildoun Road: "Police automobile! The police are coming!" People ran helter-skelter but soon everything relaxed again. The auto, a large touring car, was filled with young men and women arriving to join the occasion. "Hurrah for Coatesville!" the couples shouted to the crowd. "Hurrah for Coatesville!" the crowd shouted back.

With a desperate heave, Zachariah Walker burst up through the wood and started to drag himself off the pile. Charred flesh hung from his body; the foot of the bedstead had somehow come loose but the iron chain, glowing red, clung to his right leg. Pitchforks, poles, and shotguns jabbed him back. The crowd cheered.

Again Walker tried. This time the leaders let him get completely off the logs, work himself to the lane, and start fumbling to get over a broken part of the fence. Then, with hoots of derision, they looped a rope around his neck, half pulled and half threw him back on the flames. The cheers were louder than ever.

With a superhuman heave and a terrible scream, the Negro hurled himself to the edge of the pyre. Fence rails and gun butts went into action. Men bashed him in the face and across the body, and he fell back into the center of the fire. The cheers were thunderous.

Zachariah Walker was barely visible now. He lay a flaming crumple, shrieking. Soon the shrieks softened to moans. Then the moans stopped. Some twenty minutes after the first straw was lit, about 10:30 this summer Sunday evening, all was quiet on the pyre except the softening crackle of the flames.

EPILOGUE

Late Sunday night, officials began arriving from West Chester, the county seat of Chester County, in which Coatesville was located. Soon the arrests came. In all, twelve men from Coatesville or neighboring areas were indicted for murder in varying degrees. Police Chief Charles E. Umsted and Officer Stanley Howe were indicted for involuntary manslaughter. The governor of Pennsylvania, John K. Tener, took the unusual step of sending his attorney general and his deputy attorney general to aid in the prosecutions.

In quick succession six of the cases came to trial in the West Chester Court House. One after another the men were acquitted. Usually the juries deliberated only for brief periods. Most of the defendants left the courtroom heroes, cheered by crowds in their home areas.

Then the state brought to trial what it believed was its strongest case, that against Lewis Denithorne, who had signed a confession that he helped tear the restraint jacket off Walker and drag him out of the hospital. The jury got the case shortly before bedtime. The next morning, fifteen minutes after court convened, the foreman delivered the verdict: not guilty.

Late that morning the spokesman for the Commonwealth of Pennsylvania rose in court to announce that the state was dropping all the remaining cases, including the ones against Chief Umsted and Officer Howe. It was useless to go on, he said, and further prosecutions would simply serve to bring the processes of justice into disrepute. Judge William Butler, Jr., who had presided over most of the trials, agreed. The Judge added that when the lynching first occurred, he thought it would be difficult to secure justice for the accused. The community would be up in arms against men charged with a crime that "we had been accustomed to look upon . . . as peculiar to people of a different character from ourselves, as something that could not happen in our midst. . . ." Now he was "absolutely convinced" that there was, "for some reason that I am entirely unable to understand, a sentiment in this County, a general sentiment, utterly opposed to the prosecution and conviction of anybody and of everybody who took part in this horrible affair."

Judge Butler's puzzlement was understandable. Chester County and Coatesville were part of a North where a few decades before such a lynching would have been highly unlikely and such a public reaction, still more improbable. But this was 1911 and things had been happening that were none too visible to the aging, high-minded jurist.

The early 1900's were a curious period in the life of the North. "Progressivism," with its summons to greater opportunities for ordinary men, dominated the region and the lanterns of reform were lighting up a hundred areas of living. But the lanterns brought little glow into the Negro ghettos of New York, Chicago, or Coatesville. The Negro in the North was not only the outsider; he was further outside than he had been in previous, less reformist decades. The abolitionist fervor of the Civil War and the Reconstruction periods had burned itself out. The pell-mell industrialization, with its unremitting demand for cheap labor, was sucking unskilled Negroes into situations which neither they nor the whites could manage. All the while, the beginnings of a significant migration of southern Negroes to the North was exacerbating a peculiarly emotional concern.

The general outlook of many northerners included a mounting defensiveness, a sense almost of beleaguerment, a feeling that the sensible and decent way of life —the way of the white "Anglo-Saxons"—was being threatened by all kinds of people in and outside the United States. There were the "hordes" of "Slavs" pouring through Ellis Island; there was the "yellow peril" from the Far East. Perhaps most worrisome to a considerable section of northern opinion, there were the black men coming up from Alabama or Virginia with habits and attitudes "fit only for a cottonfield," as people said, and the northern Negroes themselves, now starting to talk a weird doctrine of equality, even founding the dangerously "uppity" National Association for the Advancement of Colored People.

In the year that Walker was lynched, one of the more moderate Negro newspapers, the New York *Age,* spoke of "a crisis in the Northern and Western states," marked by a "perfervid sensitiveness" of the whites on the color question. The newspaper was hardly exaggerating. These were the years when the hero of northern progressives, President Woodrow Wilson, looked the other way while subordinates Jim Crowed offices, lunchrooms, and lavatories in federal buildings which had been unsegregated since the Civil War; when the fact that the black Jack Johnson knocked out the white Jim Jeffries in a prize fight produced a nationwide outcry for a "white hope" and brought on rioting, North and South, that killed nineteen and injured scores; when farmers in Kansas, aghast that a Negro postman had been appointed to their R.F.D. route, tore down their boxes and announced that they would rather travel to town for their mail; when Booker T. Washington, apostle of Negro patience and optimism, could only sigh, "I have never seen the colored people so discouraged as they are at the present time."

Somehow—and just how is a long, tangled story— the North surmounted the crisis. The open clash between Negro and white did not come. Gradually the general trend toward greater opportunities for ordinary men came to include less hostility toward the Negro. In this critically important development, Zachariah Walker, who amounted to so little in life, was not without significance by the manner of his death. The brutal lynching served as an alarm bell—heeded by more than a few in the North—as to just where the mounting racism of the early 1900's could lead.

In time the alarm was hearkened to in Coatesville itself. On June 3, 1938, a nineteen-year-old white girl was criminally attacked on South Hill in the city. Once again the posses fanned out from Coatesville and seized a young Negro; once again a crowd milled outside the jail crying, "Lynch him! Lynch him!" But this time the man in Umsted's old post, Chief of Police Ralph E. Williams, stood up in front of the mob and told them to remember that justice required a fair trial. He added: Coatesville does not want "another blot on its fair name." The crowd grew quiet, and began to drift away. The Negro was taken to another city.

Things had changed indeed—in Coatesville and in America.—*E. F. G.*

"We are going to do away with these boys ..."

The black laborers on John Williams' plantation never seemed

to leave or complain. It took some digging to find out why

By PETE DANIEL

Out of the ashes and ruins of the Civil War the shadow of slavery once more crept over the South. Even while some southern Negroes tried to achieve political power, civil rights, and personal security during Reconstruction, many laborers became mired in the quicksand of debt. Booker T. Washington, usually soft-spoken on economic and social issues, observed in 1888 that black share-croppers "are held in a kind of slavery that is in one sense as bad as the slavery of antebellum days." Washington referred to the system of debt that oppressed the black laborer, that "binds him, robs him of independence, allures him and winds him deeper and deeper in its meshes each year till he is lost and bewildered." Blacks were forced to work without compensation to pay off obligations that somehow became never ending. At the turn of the twentieth century the Justice Department, seeking to end this new form of slavery, discovered that an 1867 federal statute outlawing peonage—forced servitude to creditors—could be used to free laborers who were held involuntarily because of debt.

Booker T. Washington secretly joined in the campaign to eliminate this complicated and often invisible practice that blended into the customs and laws of the South. Yet neither his efforts nor those of the Justice Department ended peonage. It clung to poor workers like a disease. An experienced investigator estimated in 1907 that one third of the large planters "are holding their negro employees to a condition of peonage, and arresting and returning those that leave before alleged indebtedness is paid."

Periodically throughout the twentieth century, the Justice Department would announce that peonage had been stricken, that only the vestiges of the system remained, but complaints of the practice continued. It was most prevalent during the first dozen years of the twentieth century, but a rash of cases broke out in the 1920's and again in the late 1930's, and even during the 1960's the Justice Department continued to receive some fifty complaints of peonage each year. Among those thousands of complaints and cases, one story emerged that drastically illustrated

both the dreadfulness of the system and the halting inadequacy of federal officials in controlling it. The tale unfolded in rural Georgia in 1921.

On February 18 of that year federal agents George W. Brown and A. J. Wismer investigated the two-thousand-acre plantation of John S. Williams in Jasper County. Finding the owner briefly away that Friday afternoon, they talked to several of his black workers before he returned, and were especially interested in questioning twenty-seven-year-old Clyde Manning, Williams' black foreman. They asked him if he and Williams had once caught a Negro laborer named Gus Chapman who had fled from the plantation. Manning said No.

When Williams, a fifty-four-year-old man who one observer said was a "giant in stature," got back, he learned that the agents were investigating a complaint that he held men in peonage. The planter quickly offered to show the agents anything they wished; then he asked the terms of the law. Wismer and the other agent told him if he "paid a nigger out of the stockade, paid his fine, and kept him working on his plantation . . . he would be guilty of peonage, since he worked the nigger against his will." Williams expressed amazement and declared that "I and most all of the farmers in this county must be guilty of peonage." Then the agents asked Williams, as they had Manning, whether he had caught and returned to his farm Gus Chapman. The planter admitted that he had, claiming that Chapman had assaulted Clyde Manning's wife and that they had thought of prosecuting him. Brown turned to Manning. "You lied to us about that," he said.

Williams, at this point, escorted the visitors to his sons' two farms five miles away and allowed them to talk with any of the hands. Before the federal men left, Williams asked if they had found conditions that would lead to prosecution. Getting no specific commitment, he assured the departing agents that though he might technically be guilty of peonage, he would never break the law again.

Less than a month later a small white boy named Cash spied the foot of a human body near the surface of a stream near Allen's Bridge in neighboring Newton County. He immediately went for help, and before nightfall on March 13 two Negro bodies had been brought up from the Yellow River. The coroner ruled that the men had been murdered and postulated that they had been bound and weighted and thrown from the bridge alive.

The large crowd gathered at the bridge soon buzzed with speculation about the slain men's identity. They surmised that Jasper County, rather than their own, would be the place to look for the murderer, because it had a history of racial turmoil. Thus county pride, plus the zeal of a group of conscientious local officers, combined to launch an investigation that led back to the Williams plantation. Within a few days Clyde Manning was arrested on suspicion of murder.

On March 24—after being promised protection by officials—Manning confessed that he and John Williams had murdered eleven men. Two days later, with hundreds of local citizens flocking behind, he led law-enforcement officers on a gruesome trip about the county, pointing out the graves of nine other victims.

Williams, never caught without an alibi, claimed that he had been framed by a neighbor who had a feud with him. Nevertheless, he was immediately arrested. The tale that unfolded in the following weeks of trial and testimony revealed a grotesque murder story, a vivid picture of peonage, and a good deal of information that cast doubt on the effectiveness of the federal machinery for investigating southern labor practices.

John S. Williams began his peonage operation while his four older sons were fighting in World War I. To secure labor, he (or, later, one of his sons) would travel to Atlanta, to Macon, or to some nearby jail, pay the fine of a black who had run afoul of the law, and take him back to Jasper County. Indebted to Williams for his bond, the man theoretically worked only until he repaid that sum. Actually, he stayed for as long as Williams could hold him; he moved from peonage to slavery. And Williams was no easy man to escape from. Once the victim reached the farm, he went through a seasoning process. "When we got down there that night," explained one laborer, "he told me to go in there and stay with the other boys, and when I went in there I just laid down on the floor, I didn't have any cover and I begun to work the next day, they took me out to work on new ground and I got a whipping that Saturday."

Williams gave two trusted black men, Clyde Manning and Claude Freeman, authority over the "stockade" (or jail) Negroes. Freeman remembered that Williams gave them both pistols. "He said if any of the hands got away or tried to get away, or did anything to me to kill them, and he said if I let any one get away I would know what was coming then to me." Manning claimed that he did not relish his job, but having observed Williams for thirteen years, "I was there long enough to find out you had to go ahead and do what he said."

While Manning managed the peons on the Williams home place, Freeman helped Huland, Marvin, and Leroy Williams on farms five miles away. The house on Huland Williams' farm had a hall running through it, and Williams stayed on one side of the hall and the blacks on the other. "They had a cleat across there and they had it fastened on the outside of the door and they had a hole through and a big wire run through the hole and there was a bolt in the door, and a hook on the outside," Freeman recalled. As many as eighteen prisoners slept there at one time.

To enforce discipline on the Williams plantations, the overseers often administered beatings, not only to the stockade men, but also to the free blacks who lived on the place. Freeman's wife, Emma, stated that she had been whipped "a heap of times" so severely that "the whelps come." Huland Williams had also hit her with his pistol; she still bore the scar years later. Twenty-seven-year-old Lessie May Whitlow, who cooked for the hands, revealed that the peons were whipped at least once a week. She, too, was once struck on the head with a pistol by Huland, for not having the evening meal ready on time. Nearly all the hands remembered savage assaults, often for trivial or imagined offenses.

Though John S. Williams and his sons had warned the laborers that they would catch and kill them if they tried to escape, several peons attempted to run away. Sixteen-year-old Frank Dozier, who had been arrested for vagrancy (for merely sitting down at the Macon depot), successfully made it, though Huland Williams spotted him in Covington, twenty miles away, and chased him with a bloodhound. Dozier fled up a creek "and lay in the water all night, under the bridge." Gus Chapman, whose successful escape and complaint led the special agents to the Williams plantations, tried once earlier and failed. After his recapture, "Mr. Williams took me back and took me down in the wagon shelter and made me pull down my clothes and said he would kill me, but as I was a kind of an old son of a bitch he would let me go that time but if I ever did it again he would sure kill me.... He whipped me with a buggy trace."

Despite the warnings, beatings, and the bloodhound, the black peons continued to trouble the Williams family. When threats and beatings failed, the atmosphere of the farm became more macabre, more unreal. The Williams men carried pistols and often shot at the peons when their work did not suit the overseers. One, James Strickland, said they "didn't shoot just to scare me because one time they shot at me and the bullet went through my hat and knocked my hat off." Another time, John Williams "snapped his pistol" at a worker named Jake "three times and it didn't fire because it didn't have nothing in it." The Williams family knew how to keep men insecure and ready to perform any task at a trot. And unlike slaves, the peons had no monetary value. They could be replaced at the nearest jail.

When all else failed to keep the peons cowed, the Williamses resorted to murder. According to a statement of an old man who had once worked on the Williams place, three laborers had been killed there as early as 1911. The deaths were random, bizarre, unpredictable, without reason. In 1919, as near as determinable, Long John Singleton "went to the goat

THE PLANTER: *John S. Williams*

pasture and never come back." Rumor around the plantation said that Marvin Williams shot him. Claude Freeman only knew that about a week after Long John vanished "me and Mr. Marvin and Barber was pulling corn, and the buzzards was flying around." So Marvin went to investigate and returned saying that "John Singleton had come to the top" of a pond on the farm. Freeman testified that Williams got ropes and wire "and took the body out there and put some rock to it and sunk it again."

In the spring of 1920 Leroy Williams shot Iron Jaw, a stockade

Negro. Freeman said that he was "rolling some wire, he was not rolling the wire straight and they whipped him." When Iron Jaw said he had rather be dead than treated that way, "Mr. Leroy pulled out his pistol and shot him." In the same year, Nathaniel Wade, nicknamed Blackstrap, was killed for running away— reputedly by one of the other hands on the farm at the orders of Huland Williams. At hog-killing time in the winter of 1920–21, Will Napeer was shot by Huland. Three doctors, including still another of Williams' sons, tended the wounded man in an unexplained display of concern, but

THE OVERSEER: *Clyde Manning*

he died that night of abdominal injuries. The doctors failed both to inquire how the shooting occurred and to report it to the authorities. What a white man did to his black laborers was his own business.

By the spring of 1921, then, three of Williams' sons had committed murder, and virtual slavery existed on the family's plantations. Williams stated only that he took the men from the jails and worked them just until they repaid him for their fines, but he never said what the wage rate was or how long he kept them. There remains no record of his allowing a man to leave, however, and

some of the fines were as little as five dollars. Yet all the blacks on the plantations agreed that they were afraid to leave, afraid to disobey the Williamses, afraid for their lives. These acts of terror took place within several miles of houses and a store. Incredibly, the neighbors seemed unaware of the atrocities, or they were intimidated by the savage reputation of the family.

The Williamses thus seemed secure in their stronghold until the autumn of 1920. Then, on Labor Day, James Strickland escaped. On Thanksgiving, Gus Chapman also took his chance and fled a second time. Both

went to Atlanta, where they complained to the Justice Department and spoke of their imprisonment and the murders. The visit of agents Wismer and Brown to Williams' lands in February, 1921, was the result.

Though Williams had counted on his brand of terror to keep the blacks quiet about his crimes, he must have thought he had reason to fear prosecution. Sometime during the week after the agents' visit, Williams evidently had a serious talk with his sons about their chances before a federal court. About the twenty-fourth or twenty-fifth of February, Huland, Marvin, and Leroy Williams left for some unannounced destination. If federal charges emerged, the old man decided, he would face them alone. After the sons were gone, Williams talked to Manning. "Clyde," he told him, "we are going to do away with these boys and I want you to help." Manning said he did not want to do that. "Well, by God, it is all right with me, if you don't want to, it means your neck or theirs," Williams told him. "If you think more of their necks than you do of your own it is all right." Manning knew of the earlier killings, and the memory frightened him. His statement to jurors later was: "It was against my will to do it, but it was against my power not to do it and live."

The killings began within a week of the agents' call. Ironically, the first to die bore the name of Johnny Williams. Manning and John S. Williams went to the pasture where this peon was working, and the planter ordered Manning to kill him with an axe. The doomed man "kept backing around," Manning related, and "I didn't want to hit him, he was beggin' and going on, and I didn't want to kill him." But when Williams himself demanded the axe, Manning was afraid to hand it over, so he swung at the peon, "hit him one lick on the back of the head, sort of side of the head with the back of the ax, and then we dug a hole there." Three other men, "Big John," Johnnie Green, and Willie Givens, were also murdered with an axe. For six others, death came by water. Manning remembered vividly how it came to Lindsey Peterson, Will Preston, and Harry Price. On February 26 Williams told these three stockade laborers on his sons' farms that he would take them to the train that night. After supper he loaded them in a car along with Manning and Charlie Chisholm, a peon whose bond had been paid three or four years earlier. After driving a few miles, they stopped the car, and Manning and Chisholm bound the other three blacks with trace chains and hung hundred-pound sacks filled with rocks around their necks. The three submitted, possibly in ignorance of what was coming. "Lindsey Peterson and Will Preston, they didn't think we were going to do anything to them, until we got to the river." But when they were hoisted to the railing of a bridge where they were next taken, "they were scuffling and trying to keep back, to keep from going over, and he told us to push them over . . . and we throwed them over." Williams now drove several miles to another bridge, over the South River, and it was Price's turn. He begged Manning: "Don't throw me over, I will get over." Then he "crawled up on the bannister, set up on the bannister, he set there just a little while, and he says 'Don't throw me.' He says, 'Lord, have mercy' and went right on over."

Two other peons known only as Little Bit and Red were tossed, bound and weighted, into the Alcovy River. And so was Charlie Chisholm, only a week after he helped to drown three of his fellow victims. Two blacks, Artis Freeman and Fred Favors, were apparently dealt with by Williams alone. He drove Freeman away and returned without him, while Favors, after being spoken to by Williams, left for Huland Wil-

liams' farm and was never seen by Manning again. Finally, Williams shot Fletcher Smith with a shotgun, and Manning assisted in burying him. That brought the total of certain dead to eleven. "After we got him covered up we plowed over him again." Williams now made a final threat: "Clyde, I don't want to hear nothing from this. There is nobody knows about this but just me and you. If I ever hear it come out I will know where it come from." Manning assured him: "I ain't going to say nothing about it to nobody."

But under the pressure of arrest and interrogation, Clyde Manning confessed. Sheriff B. L. Johnson, of Newton County, thereupon promised that he would get the full story of the murders and would not sidestep his responsibility. Though he was the one who led the investigation, he took occasion, on March 26, to praise Sheriff W. F. Persons, of Jasper County, of whom he said there was not "a man in Jasper or Newton county more determined than he is to bring the whole truth to the surface." Sheriff Persons needed public-relations help, for he was a cousin of John S. Williams. Moreover, he himself had only recently received one of the rare indictments in Georgia for holding workers in bondage.

Two days after Manning disclosed the location of the remaining bodies, rumors spread throughout the area that the blacks of Jasper County were gathering along the river bank. There were reports of black insurrection. Suddenly, the roads were clogged with automobiles bearing armed white men, racing toward the river. There, they discovered the blacks holding a prayer meeting, and sheepishly returned home. Later, looking into the murders, the grand jury learned that anonymous letters had been sent to white planters in the area warning them of "black vengeance." Further probing revealed that the notes actually had

been sent by three of Williams' sons. The jury concluded that the Williams menfolk had sought to bring about a race war in order to shift attention from their father and create a climate of opinion that would discredit Clyde Manning's testimony. Such was also the view of James Weldon Johnson, executive secretary of the National Association for the Advancement of Colored People, who editorialized in the Negro newspaper, the New York Age, that in the entire history of peonage the Williams affair was "the most flagrant and savage case."

The general reaction of disgust at the grotesqueness of the crimes was not restricted to northern whites and blacks but was also felt among many Southerners. Georgia's Governor Hugh M. Dorsey, for example, deplored the killings, and a white Georgia church organization declared that "Christ . . . is using the murder of the eleven negroes . . . to wake Georgia to the need for justice to the negro." Even rural Georgia whites, who were usually reluctant to admit the existence of sin in their midst, were shocked. It was the brutal nature of the drownings, the publicity, the vivid confession of Manning, and the apparent lack of provocation such as an assault by the victims on white people ("There wasn't even a remote phase of the 'usual crime' involved," one southern newspaper admitted) that led to Williams' murder indictment.

The trial of Williams opened in Covington, Georgia, on April 5; the specific indictment was for the murder of Lindsey Peterson, one of the three men chained and then drowned on February 26. The county courthouse was packed with observers and numerous law officers to preserve order, as blacks and whites mingled in the overflow crowd or strained to catch each word from their segregated vantage points. Williams would be judged by his peers; seven farmers, four merchants, and one druggist were on the jury.

The state claimed that Williams' motive for murder was to silence his victims in case he was tried for peonage. His defense attorneys countered by attempting to show that the agents had not discovered peonage on the Williams plantations and that Williams therefore did not need to murder the men for fear of prosecution.

Over the objection of Williams' lawyers, Judge John B. Hutcheson allowed the two federal agents to testify on this point. George W. Brown took the stand first. He told of Williams' openness and earnestness. He said he had examined the partitioned houses and admitted that they could have been used for keeping prisoners. Williams had explained that he "worked some stockade negroes on his place and . . . instructed them that they must not leave . . . until they had paid him back what he had paid out for them." Brown stated it as his impression that most of the stockade Negroes had left by the time of the investigation. At this point his testimony began to blur and fragment. He would only say of his conversations with the peons that he "didn't go into details" with them. When cross-examined, the special agent denied that he told a state official, Doyle Campbell, solicitor of the Ocmulgee circuit, that he found nothing objectionable at Williams' place. Then, the prosecution asked, if there *was* something objectionable, why had Williams not been arrested? "I don't make cases," Brown replied. He added that he had reported to the United States Attorney General and to the district attorney in Atlanta. "I found enough there to issue a warrant on," he added. "As to why I did not swear one out, Mr. Williams stated that he might have technically violated the law, but he was doing better and [besides] the case was still under investigation." But this statement conflicted with a report in the New York *World* that

appeared just before the trial began. A correspondent reported that the federal agents had been impressed with Williams' "frankness" and desire to reform, and they "returned to Atlanta convinced of his innocence."

Whether the agents glossed over the nature of Williams' operations, or the district attorney and the Justice Department ignored the report remains a mystery, for the department will not yet make its investigatory files available to researchers.

Agent Wismer gave much the same testimony as Brown, excusing his failure to prosecute Williams with the identical words that Brown used: "I don't make cases." He described a house with locks on windows and doors, Manning's lies, and his own talk with Williams about the meaning of peonage. He said he had told Williams that the fact that his son Leroy was carrying a gun looked bad. But not until two months later, at Clyde Manning's trial—after Williams' fate was decided—did the agents go into more detail. By then Brown no longer worked for the government. Wismer then admitted that a conversation with Johnny Williams (the first peon to be killed in the grisly week) substantiated the complaints. "Johnny Williams told us," said Wismer, "that Clyde Manning acted as guard over the hands on the John S. Williams place, he looked after them at night and he was made to tote a pistol." He added that from the "general attitude" of the blacks he concluded that "they were afraid to tell anything for fear they would tell the wrong thing and would get into trouble and be punished."

The cooperative attitude of Williams, the agents testified, offset Johnny Williams' complaints, the barracks with locks, and Leroy's gun. Nevertheless, they had made complete reports to the authorities. But John S. Williams testified that they told him: "[We] don't think you need to have any fear of any case before the Federal Grand Jury."

And though Williams' word was not to be trusted, the fact remains that no charges were brought prior to the finding of the bodies.

Clyde Manning took the stand next. Sitting in the splint-bottomed witness chair, he calmly told of each murder in gory detail. The "coal black, short, stockily built man" impressed a newspaper reporter with his iciness. His voice did not show any emotion nor did he "twiddle a finger of those folded black hands, or shuffle a foot." Williams "listened with an inscrutable face."

The two made a grim pair. Williams' lawyer tried to shake Manning's testimony by implying that the black was trying to place the entire blame on Williams in order to ease his own sentence. Manning denied that. "As to my expecting to get off lighter," he said, "I just expect to tell the truth, and take it just as it comes. I ain't putting no more on Mr. Williams than his part and I ain't telling any more on myself than my part."

In such a case, Georgia law permitted the defendant to give a statement, not under oath or subject to cross-examination. Williams began his statement next day by saying that he had "never had any kind of crime charged against me in my life." Four of his twelve children had served in World War I. "I have always tried to do the best that I could for my fellow man," he went on. Newspapers had exaggerated the size of his properties. "Niggers, boll weevil and low price of cotton just about cleaned me up," was his plaint. Admitting that "like most farmers that I know" he had bonded blacks out of jail and worked them, he stressed that "in many instances" he paid them. Finally, he asserted that following the departure of the agents, he called all his help together and told them they could leave. He gave them five dollars each; and when none appeared next day, he asked

Manning where they were. "They went on off last night," he quoted Manning as saying.

Throughout his testimony Williams tried to make it appear that Manning alone had killed the peons. He, Williams, had offended Manning, he said, when he admitted to the agents that Gus Chapman had been chased, a confession which made a liar out of the black man. Manning had therefore proved willing when the sheriff and other officials "insisted on him telling something on me." Finally, Williams charged: "He is a very cruel nigger to the niggers, the whole Manning crowd is." No witnesses spoke up in Williams' defense. Except for the planter's own statement, the prosecution's testimony stood unchallenged.

Williams and his attorneys knew that it was rare for a jury to convict a white man for the murder of a black, especially when the sole witness to the slaying was also black. In fact, Williams was—though he could hardly have known it—the first southern white man since 1877 even to be indicted for the first-degree murder of a Negro, and he would be the last until 1966. On April 8 the jury was locked up, and Williams, "smiling and unconcerned, chatted with those around him." He had every reason, it seemed, to be confident, as he "joined his family in a picnic lunch spread on [the] counsel's table inside the bar."

The next day the jury returned with the verdict of guilty and asked for life imprisonment. They might have requested the death sentence, a southern newspaper reported, but "there were some who felt rather strongly opposed to hanging a white man based upon the statement of a negro."

If it was the guilty verdict against a white killer of blacks that made the Williams case unusual, it was the ordeal of Clyde Manning that was most instructive in the ways of peonage, and in how a man could become completely encased in a brutal system. Manning stood trial for murder in May, 1921, and the jury found him guilty and sentenced him to life imprisonment. But his case was appealed successfully on a technicality. At his second trial, on July 26 and 27, 1922, his defense was based on the nature of the compulsion that Williams used. There was no denial that Manning had murdered the men, only the claim that he had been compelled to do so by fear.

The witnesses, those black men and women who had survived, revealed the hopeless desperation, the terror, and the ignorance that characterized the vertiginous world of peonage. They knew little of the country beyond the Williams acres. The farms were twenty miles from Covington, seven miles from Monticello, and only five miles from a place referred to as "Polk's store." Yet Claude Freeman, an overseer,

testified that he did not even know where that nearby landmark was. Lessie May Whitlow, the cook, made much the same statement: "I don't know, sir, where Polk's store is at." Except for the stockade Negroes, who came from the outer world, most of the blacks had spent their lives on the Williams farms. They knew vaguely that some white people lived nearby, but they had no dealings with them. When the state attempted to show that Clyde Manning could have fled at any time and reported the murders, Emma Freeman answered: "I mean to say he couldn't get away. I was there, we couldn't get away." For the men and women there, the situation was hopeless; peonage on the Williams place was the only life they knew.

Williams' revealing statement that most of the neighboring planters were also guilty of peonage perhaps explained why no whites complained. His neighbors evidently approved or acquiesced. Those sparsely settled river bottoms were still frontierlike in their customs and seclusion, and strong men were their own law.

Like Williams, Manning made an unsworn statement to the jury. "The crime what I have done, I done to save my own life," the illiterate Negro began. Following the murders, all the fear born of the farms' harrowing history encompassed him, for he, better than others, knew the nature of John S. Williams. "After these killings started, he would call me all through the night," Manning related. "He would call me during the night to see if the cows were in the wheat or in the oats and he would say he heard a noise with the mules . . . and I figured it he was calling me to see if I was off the place." Had he fled, Williams would have "found me and he would have brought me back there, and would have killed me."

Manning said he wanted to flee nonetheless and tell someone of the murders, but he was unfamiliar with the surrounding countryside. "I was

Scenes in Jasper Tragedy

Top: The home of John S. Williams, Jasper county farmer, now held in Fulton county jail under indictment for murder in connection with the killing of eleven negroes on or near his farm, and who will be placed on trial in the Newton county superior court next Tuesday. The residence is located twenty miles from Covington on the Covington-Monticello highway. Bottom: This picture shows the large iron cotton mill screw, which was tied with chains and wires to the bound-together bodies of "Little Bit" and John Brown and the stones and sack used to weight the body of Charlie Chisholm, all of which were found in the Alcovy river. Clyde Manning declared in his confession that he and Charlie Chisholm help down the first named blacks and, later, he and John S. Williams, prominent Jasper county farmer, drowned Charlie. The cap in the picture was removed from the head of one of the dead negroes.

314

raised around there . . . never had been but a little ways from the farm. . . . I didn't know anything about going nowhere." He also had his family to think of—wife, baby, mother, sister, brothers; "I couldn't run off with my whole family." And if he did steal away alone to tell his tale, "my wife and sister and mother would all have been killed right there." He asked the jury to understand that he had no choice. "Anybody on that place, white folks, that he said to do it . . . they would have done it." Manning maintained the same natural, unaffected manner in making this last statement as he had throughout his ordeal. "I am not crying for mercy, just give me justice," he concluded. And the jury sentenced him to life imprisonment.

The case was closed. Williams and Manning were punished—but not for holding men in bondage, simply for murdering them. Moreover, Manning's ignorance, Williams' intimidation of his workers, and the apathy of the federal investigative personnel were not unique; they were typical of the factors that allowed peonage to exist—and these were grim facts of life in the isolated South; nor was there any sweeping investigation into them as an aftermath of the case. The opportunity was lost.

Consequently, peonage continued beyond the 1920's. Much of its constitutional history emerged in Supreme Court decisions, spurred by numerous complaints, in the 1940's. In ensuing years, despite the civil-rights movement and communications developments that seemingly would not permit such a cruel anachronism to survive, peonage occasionally endured in one form or another. The United States Com-

mission on Civil Rights complained in 1961 that between January 1, 1958, and June 30, 1960, sixty-seven accusations were brought to the Justice Department, but no prosecutions followed because none of the charges was deemed valid. Another analysis showed that between 1961 and 1963, the Department dropped 92 out of 104 complaints without even an investigation, and followed up only two with prosecution. And in July of 1969, the *New Republic* revealed peonagelike conditions among migratory workers in Florida, but Justice Department lawyers denied that the institution any longer existed.

Against this background of governmental inaction, the attitude of the Justice Department toward completing prosecutions in the Williams case appears consistent with the larger pattern. Three of Williams' sons remained fugitives for several years, facing federal peonage and state murder charges. By 1927 Huland, Marvin, and Leroy Williams had surrendered and made bond. Yet they never stood trial for either state or federal offenses. A United States attorney explained in 1930 that "less than half the witnesses could be located." Further excusing his failure to bring the culprits to trial, he noted that John S. Williams had been "the real moving spirit of the offense." The three sons had moved to Florida where "each of them is running a store and filling station and is no longer employing or working labor of any kind." This seeming good behavior apparently convinced the government lawyer that a trial was unnecessary. Though surviving witnesses would have certainly linked the three brothers to the peonage system, it was the attorney's belief that such a trial would

be a "hopeless task," and he persuaded the Attorney General to drop the case.

What of the two men who were sent to jail for the murders? For Clyde Manning, his life sentence turned out to be short. One reason offered by the federal government for not trying the three Williams brothers was that Manning, obviously the key witness, had died on the chain gang several years before—presumably of natural causes. And John S. Williams himself furnished the final ironic twist to the case. Years after the trials, on a Georgia prison farm where he had earned the position of trusty, he was killed while attempting to prevent a jailbreak.

The charge was rape.
The accuser was a
southern white
woman, the accused
were Negroes. But
what kind of
woman was
Victoria Price?
And what had
really happened
aboard that freight   train?

A
Reasonable
Doubt

By DAN T. CARTER

The Scottsboro Case—an infamous series of litigations which was to inflame both the North and the South for many years—began inconspicuously on March 25, 1931, as white and Negro hobos brawled aboard a freight train moving across northeastern Alabama. One of the white youths thrown from the train reported the fight to the nearest stationmaster, and a Jackson County posse stopped the train at the rural village of Paint Rock. When deputies removed the nine Negro teenagers on board they also discovered two young white girls, aged seventeen and twenty-one, who were hitching a ride from Chattanooga, Tennessee, back to their home in Huntsville, Alabama. In the first confusing minutes after the arrests, Ruby Bates whispered to officials that she and her friend, Victoria Price, had been raped by the nine Negroes, who ranged in age from twelve to nineteen. A hasty medical examination revealed evidence of sexual intercourse.

That night, sheriff's deputies, strengthened by the Alabama National Guard, averted a mass lynching after a sullen mob gathered outside the Jackson County jailhouse in the little town of Scottsboro. Two weeks later, while a crowd of eight to ten thousand filled Scottsboro's streets, two court-appointed attorneys half-heartedly defended the frightened boys. Four juries convicted and sentenced eight to death; the trial of Leroy Wright, aged twelve, for whom the state had asked a life sentence, ended in a hung jury.

Cases similar to the Scottsboro one had been largely unnoticed outside the South. But the number of defendants, their extreme youth, the stunning rapidity of the trials, and the harsh sentences the boys received attracted the attention of national newspapers. In April, the International Labor Defense, a close affiliate of the Communist party, launched a propaganda campaign to expose what it called "the Alabama frame-up." Although the N.A.A.C.P. belatedly offered legal support to the convicted youths, the I.L.D. swiftly gained the backing of the boys and their parents. In late December of 1931, N.A.A.C.P. attorneys withdrew from the case.

The United States Supreme Court accepted the I.L.D.'s contention that the youths had had inadequate legal counsel at Scottsboro and overturned the convictions in 1932. But the rallies, pamphlets, and flamboyant accusations of the International Labor Defense and the Communist party only stiffened the resolve of Alabamians to repel the accusations of "outsiders" and see the Scottsboro defendants put to death. As the new trials approached in the spring of 1933, the International Labor Defense reluctantly turned to one of the nation's most brilliant criminal attorneys, Samuel S. Leibowitz of Brooklyn, New York. Leibowitz did not subscribe to the I.L.D. ideology, but he felt that the boys' basic civil rights had been violated, and when the I.L.D.'s executive secretary promised to shelve temporarily his organization's revolutionary rhetoric, Leibowitz agreed to defend the youths without fee.

He began the case with a plea for a change of venue, and the presiding judge agreed to transfer the trials fifty miles west of Scottsboro to Decatur, the seat of Morgan County. There, with a National Guard unit on duty to keep order, the second series of trials began in late March. The first defendant to be tried was Haywood Patterson, nineteen.

March 27, the opening day, was warm and clear in Decatur. Before 7 A.M. a large and cheerful crowd had gathered outside the two-story yellow brick courthouse. Even the announcement that there would be a half-day's delay in the proceedings did not seem to dispel the spectators' good nature. Throughout the morning they sunned lazily on the wide lawn or gossiped around the two courthouse statues, one honoring justice and the other paying tribute to those Confederate soldiers "who gave their lives for a just cause—State's Rights." There was some talk about the trial, but mostly the relaxed crowd discussed the Depression. Three and a half years after the crash of 1929, these Alabamians—like most Americans—were optimistically looking to Mr. Roosevelt and his New Deal for relief. For as the cotton mills and railroad shops had closed or curtailed their operations, hard times had come to Decatur. The spring foliage and flowers camouflaged, but they could not conceal, the empty, dilapidated stores downtown and the peeling paint on the outlying houses.

Samuel Leibowitz had been apprehensive when he first arrived in Decatur. He was keenly aware that he and his fellow defense attorney, Joseph Brodsky, were outsiders. Worse, they were New York Jews. To his relief, however, the townspeople greeted him with unaffected hospitality. "[They] . . . impress me as being honest, God-fearing people who want to see justice done," he told reporters.

After lunch, as officials announced that the court would soon convene, an irregular line formed, stretching through the courthouse corridors and past the brass spittoons resting on their tobacco-stained rubber pads. Within minutes, the 425 seats were filled—whites in three sections, Negroes in the fourth. At 2 P.M., Judge James Edwin Horton, Jr., settled into the raised judge's chair, adjusted his tortoise-shell spectacles, and nodded to the prosecutor to begin reading the indictment.

Lank, raw-boned and more than six feet tall, Horton strongly resembled photographs of the young and beardless Lincoln. His family had served prominently in the political life of the ante-bellum South, and the fifty-five-year-old judge spoke without self-consciousness of his obligation to uphold the integrity of the family name. His views on the Negro, like those of the traditionally conservative southerner, were kindly and well-meaning, with a trace of *noblesse oblige*, yet when one of the two Negro reporters present introduced himself on the first day of the trial, Horton, in the presence of disapproving townspeople, unhesitatingly offered a firm handshake. In the Decatur courtroom he was easygoing and lenient, unbothered by the clatter of reporters' noisy typewriters. During the two-week trial he had to rule upon many questions of law that he had accepted without question throughout his legal career; generally he remained calm

BOTH: BROWN BROTHERS

Flanked by National Guardsmen, the nine "Scottsboro boys" pose with defense attorney Samuel Leibowitz in a narrow prison corridor. Seated on a box at the lawyer's left is Haywood Patterson.

and unruffled, his voice at an even, conversational level.

To the disappointment of the spectators, the sensational testimony that they expected to hear did not begin right away. In fact, the whole first week of the trial was taken up with a complex constitutional duel between defense and state attorneys over the question of Negro jurors, and the crowd quickly lost interest. Leibowitz argued that Alabama officials had defied the Fourteenth Amendment by excluding Negroes from the Jackson County juries which had originally convicted the nine youths, and from the Morgan County venire from which a new jury would now be chosen to retry the first defendant, Haywood Patter-

"The vaginal examination showed . . . [the spermatozoa] were nonmotile."
—Dr. R. R. Bridges

son. The absence of Negro jurors was incontestable; a courtroom official said he could not recall seeing black men in the jury box since before the turn of the century. But a Scottsboro civic leader explained on the witness stand that the absence of Negro jurors was not a matter of racial prejudice. It was simply that Negroes had not been "trained for jury duty in our county . . . and I don't think their judgment—you could depend on it altogether." Besides, he added as the spectators chuckled, "they will nearly all steal." One jury commissioner told Leibowitz that Negroes were not excluded for any particular reason; "Negroes was never discussed."

Thomas Knight, Jr., Alabama's thirty-four-year-old attorney general, was present to handle the prosecution. Affable and charming, he ordinarily conveyed the image of well-bred southern gentility. In the courtroom, however, he was a fierce antagonist. Nervously pacing across the courtroom, he alternately cajoled and threatened the apprehensive Negro leaders from Scottsboro and Decatur who testified on the jury question. The nineteen witnesses included a Pullman porter, the owner of a dry-cleaning shop, a dentist, a seminary-trained minister, and a doctor educated at Phillips Exeter Academy in New Hampshire and the University of Illinois. Knight succeeded in showing that some of them were unaware of the intricate details of the jury selection system and that others did not know all the legal requirements for jury duty. He was not able to conceal, however, what Leibowitz wanted to prove: that the Negro wit-

"My God, Doctor, is this whole thing a horrible mistake?"
—Judge James Horton

nesses were completely qualified to serve as jurors yet that, because of their race, none had ever been called.

After four days of testimony and argument, Horton denied Leibowitz's motions to quash the Jackson County indictment and set aside the Morgan County venire. Significantly, however, he also ruled that the jury rolls of both counties contained only the names of whites. A smiling Leibowitz perfunctorily objected to the court's decision; privately he told friends he was confident no conviction could now withstand the scrutiny of the United States Supreme Court.

Despite Leibowitz's pleasure at the progress of the trial, reporters had sensed a shift of local mood from geniality to distrust and then to anger. However well-intentioned Morgan County citizens might be, their ultimate loyalty was to preserving the racial status quo. Still buried in the walls of several of the town's buildings were bullets fired during the Civil War; the entire area had been a center of Ku Klux Klan strength during the Reconstruction era and again in the Klan resurgence

"I told it just like Victoria Price told it."
—Surprise witness Ruby Bates

of the 1920's. Leibowitz's insistence on referring to Negro witnesses as "Mr." had perplexed the spectators, but when he pressed his demand for Negro jurors, grim hostility appeared on the faces of the overalled farmers. Leibowitz, warned a Black Belt newspaper, had "thrown down the challenge to . . . white supremacy."

Judge Horton's brief remarks to the venire of jurors on Friday afternoon referred obliquely to the rising hostility. "Now, gentlemen," he said, "under our law when it comes to the courts we know neither black nor white. . . . It is our duty to mete out even-handed justice. . . . No other course is open to you"—his voice suddenly became stern and harsh—"and let no one think they can act otherwise." The judge's implicit warning ended the open threats which had been heard on Decatur's streets, but resentment smouldered beneath the surface, a resentment bolstered by the presence of "outside radicals" who had come to observe the proceedings.

The jury was selected in one afternoon. Leibowitz was not altogether satisfied, since the state had used its challenges to exclude younger men who might have had "liberal" ideas, but at least he felt he had managed to keep the most obvious "red-neck" types off the jury.

When the actual taking of testimony began the following Monday, the seats were jammed for the first time since the opening day. Although it was cool in the building when the courtroom doors opened at 8:30 A.M., within an hour the spectators had begun to shed their

"I hung my hat on a little limb and went to having intercourse with the girl."
—*Defense witness Lester Carter*

coats, and by noon courthouse officials were forced to turn on the overhead fans to dispel the oppressive stuffiness caused by constant smoking in the crowded courtroom. Just before 9 A.M. Victoria Price, the older of the two complainants, took the stand. (The other girl, Ruby Bates, was absent; although she had testified at the trials two years before in Scottsboro, state officials said that she had recently disappeared.) Mrs. Price wore a blue straw hat and a black dress with a fichu of white lace at the throat. Her stylish costume was quite unlike the bedraggled outfit she had worn at Scottsboro, and in keeping with her new mien, she restrained her habit of chewing snuff, which at earlier hearings had necessitated frequent spitting. She seemed nervous in the witness chair, crossing and uncrossing her legs and fingering her long necklace of glass beads. When Attorney General Knight began his questioning, however, she spoke in a clear, firm voice that carried to the back of the courtroom.

Mrs. Price began her story from the time she and her friend Ruby boarded the train at Chattanooga to return to their home in Huntsville. Just south of Stevenson, Alabama, she said, about a dozen Negro youths leaped from the top of an adjacent boxcar into the gondola that she and Ruby were sharing with seven white hobos. After a brief scuffle, all but one of the outnumbered white boys were thrown from the train. The only remaining white, Orville Gilley, was forced to watch the brutal assaults that followed. Thrusting her finger toward Haywood Patterson, Mrs. Price identified him as one of the rapists. Knight asked her if Patterson's "private parts penetrated your private parts." "Yes sir, they did," she replied. Suddenly Knight pulled a torn cotton undergarment from his briefcase, and asked Victoria Price to state whether these were the step-ins she was wearing at the time of the assault. Leibowitz leaped to his feet. "This is the first time in two years any such step-ins have ever been shown" in connection with the case, he objected. "They are here now," Knight answered, grinning, and tossed them into the lap of one of the bewildered jurors. The courtroom exploded into

"If you acquit this Negro, put a garland of roses around his neck . . ."
—*Prosecutor Thomas Knight, Jr.*

"What [the prosecution] is saying is 'Come on, boys! We can lick this Jew from New York!'"
—*Defense attorney Samuel Leibowitz*

laughter, and Judge Horton had to gavel for quiet. In less than twenty minutes the Alabama attorney general completed his direct examination and, with a gracious smile toward the defense table, abandoned his star witness to Leibowitz.

The balding lawyer, younger than most spectators had anticipated, exuded confidence. During his career he had reduced even honest witnesses to incoherent confusion, and he was convinced that Victoria Price was lying. Leibowitz had all the skills of a good trial lawyer: an actor's sense of timing, a flair for the dramatic, and a clear, forceful voice. But his main strength was an almost infallible memory for detail and, above all, for contradictions. "I am not a great lawyer," he had once said in response to a compliment. "I'm only thorough." He began his cross-examination gently, almost kindly: "Miss Price . . . shall I call you Miss Price or Mrs. Price?" "Mrs. Price," answered the witness sullenly. She looked at her interrogator as though he were a poisonous snake circling her chair.

For more than three hours Leibowitz put her through a grueling cross-examination. First, he sought to discredit her testimony by proving she was a known prostitute and thus unworthy of belief. Second, by confusing her in cross-examination he hoped to convince the jury that she was lying. Finally, he planned to reveal what had really happened during the forty-eight hours preceding the alleged assault.

It was easy enough to discredit Mrs. Price's claim to be a "southern lady." In Huntsville, with the nickname of Big Leg Price, she was a well-known streetwalker. Leibowitz introduced arrest and conviction records showing she had been found guilty of "adultery and fornication" on January 26, 1931, with a Huntsville married man, L. J. "Jack" Tiller. But Mrs. Price proved unexpectedly difficult to entangle in cross-examination. Using a model of the freight train, Leibowitz tried to illustrate the sequence of events. Mrs. Price adamantly refused to agree that the model looked like the train she had ridden. What were the differences? asked Leibowitz. "That is not the train I was on," she snapped. "It was bigger, lots bigger, that is a toy." No amount of cajoling from Leibowitz could force from her an admission that it was a suitable replica.

During the trials in Scottsboro, Mrs. Price had been colorful and inventive in her account of the assault. At

Decatur she stuck to a plain, unembroidered story, as lacking in specific details as possible. She and Leibowitz often shouted back and forth at each other, but whenever the attorney uncovered contradictions in her testimony, she would retreat into vagueness: "I can't remember," or "I ain't sure, that has been two years ago."

"When you got to the doctor's office, were you not crying in any way?" Leibowitz asked. "I had just hushed crying, the best I remember I was crying—I won't say, I ain't positive," Victoria said crossly. To the attentive courtroom, Leibowitz recalled Mrs. Price's story in the original trials: that she and Ruby had gone to Chattanooga looking for work and on the night of March 24 had stayed at Mrs. Callie Brochie's boardinghouse on Seventh Street. The next morning, both girls had testified, they fruitlessly searched for a job in the city's cotton mills before boarding the Huntsville-bound freight at 11 A.M.

Leibowitz pointed out that Mrs. Price had said Mrs. Brochie's house was three or four blocks from the train yards. Wouldn't you rather say it was two miles? asked Leibowitz. "No sir, I wouldn't say two miles," she replied. "Suppose I told you that Seventh Street in Chattanooga, the nearest point . . . to the railroad yards of the Southern Railroad is two miles and show you the map, would that refresh your recollection?" he asked sarcastically. "I don't know," retorted an equally sarcastic Victoria, "I haven't got a good enough education." When he challenged her entire account of the overnight stay in Chattanooga, she broke in, shouting, "That's some of Ruby Bates's dope," and added: "I do know one thing, those Negroes and this Haywood Patterson raped me." Leibowitz stood and stared at her for a moment. She was, he told her, "a little bit of an actress." "You're a pretty good actor yourself," she quickly replied.

After a few questions about her activities on the day before the alleged incident, the tone of Leibowitz's voice suddenly changed. Gravely, he asked Mrs. Price: "Do you know a man by the name of Lester Carter?" She thought he was one of the white boys thrown from the train, she replied. "Mrs. Price, I . . . want to ask you that question again and give you an opportunity to change your answer if you want to," said Leibowitz. "Did you know Lester Carter before that day, Yes or No?" By his intense expression, spectators in the courtroom knew the question was crucial; they leaned forward to hear her answer. Mrs. Price, losing her composure for the first time, mumbled: "Before in

Scottsboro—he—was on the train." "I didn't ask you that," said Leibowitz. "Before this day on the train did you know Lester Carter?" "I never did know him," she said firmly.

He continued in the same low voice. Had she asked a companion of hers "to pose as your brother, since you didn't want the authorities to know you were travelling across the state line from Chattanooga . . . [with] somebody with you?" Mrs. Price looked to the table where Knight sat and then back at Leibowitz. "If I said that I must have been out of my mind." "Did you say it?" he asked firmly. Shouting, she clenched the arms of her chair. "If I said it I must have been out of my mind!"

Leibowitz questioned Mrs. Price about Jack Tiller, the married man with whom she had been convicted of adultery. "Did you have intercourse with Tiller a short time before you left Huntsville [for Chattanooga]?" She shook her head emphatically. "In the railroad yards?" he asked, still in the same quiet voice. "I have told you three times, and I am not telling you any more—no, sir, I didn't." Leibowitz returned to Carter. He asked her again if she had arranged with Carter, or "whatever man that was with you, [that] he wasn't supposed to know you on the train because you were afraid to cross the state line and [were afraid of] being locked up for the Mann Act?" She turned angrily to Judge Horton: "I haven't heard no such stuff," she shouted. "That is some of Ruby's dope he has got."

Relentlessly the chief defense attorney continued to probe. He asked Mrs. Price once more where she had spent the night before the alleged assault. Perhaps in a hobo jungle? he asked slyly. Victoria stared at him, her eyes filled with hatred. Columnist Mary Heaton Vorse, one of only two women in the courtroom, found it impossible to describe her "appalling hardness." Only two years before, reporters had described Mrs. Price as "pretty and vivacious." Now, with her hair tightly curled in a new permanent and her face heavily rouged, she seemed more than "tough," Miss Vorse wrote. She was "terrifying in her depravity." Through clenched teeth Mrs. Price repeated again the account of how she had stayed with Mrs. Brochie while she looked for work. Leibowitz asked her if she didn't want to change her story. She shook her head. "By the way, Mrs. Price," said Leibowitz with open disgust, "as a matter of fact, the name of Mrs. Callie [Brochie] you apply to this boardinghouse lady is the name of a boardinghouse lady used by Octavius Roy Cohn in the *Saturday Evening Post* stories—Sis Callie, isn't that where you got the name?" Knight jumped to his feet in protest and Judge Horton sustained his objection. Leibowitz, however, had dramatically made his point;

he was pleased with the results of his cross-examination.

The prosecution, concerned about the damaging effects of Leibowitz's questions, re-examined Mrs. Price in order to impress upon the jurors the gravity of the charge. Without the "flutter of an eyelash and in a voice that carried to the furthest corner of the courtroom" (wrote one reporter), she related in the most specific Anglo-Saxon terms the sexual demands made upon her by the defendants. Leibowitz knew the only purpose of the re-examination was to inflame the emotions of the jurors. In a voice shaking with anger he sarcastically asked Mrs. Price: "You are not embarrassed before this huge crowd when you utter these words?" "We object," exclaimed Knight, while Mrs. Price looked at Leibowitz with such venom that one reporter thought she was going to strike him. Suspecting that Victoria's fear of the Mann Act had led her to accuse the Negroes, Leibowitz explained that he had only one more question. "I want to ask you if you have ever heard of any single white woman ever being locked up in jail when she is the complaining witness against Negroes in the history of the State of Alabama?" Without waiting for her answer or Knight's objection, Leibowitz angrily took his seat at the defense table.

New York Times, APRIL 4, 1933

GIRL REPEATS STORY
IN SCOTTSBORO CASE

State's Witness at Decatur
Trial Screams Denial of 'Framing' Negro Defendants.

MORAL ATTACK RULED OUT

Judge Rejects Court Records as
Not Affecting the Credibility
of Her Testimony.

The last witness for the state on Monday was Dr. R. R. Bridges, one of the doctors who had examined the girls shortly after the alleged rape. Bridges' testimony and that of his younger colleague, Dr. M. W. Lynch, had been crucial for the state's case at Scottsboro. Under cross-examination, however, Leibowitz brought out facts that made the doctor a stronger witness for the defense than for the state. Bridges admitted that less than two hours after the alleged rape both girls were completely composed and calm, with normal pulse and respiration rates, and no pupil dilation. Even though Mrs. Price claimed she had been brutally raped six times, the doctor testified that there was no vaginal bleeding and that he and Dr. Lynch had had great difficulty finding enough semen to make a smear slide. The semen they did find was completely nonmotile. Bridges readily admitted that this was unusual: spermatozoa normally live from twelve hours to two days in the vagina.

The following morning, Attorney General Knight explained to Judge Horton that the state did not intend to call Dr. Lynch, since his testimony would be repetitious. After Horton's consent, however, a bailiff whispered to the judge that the young doctor urgently wanted to speak to him—in private. The only room available in the crowded building was one of the courthouse restrooms, and there the two men talked. Lynch, visibly unnerved, went straight to the point. Contrary to Knight's explanation, said Lynch, his testimony would not be a repetition of Dr. Bridges', because Lynch did not believe the girls had been raped. From the very beginning, said the Scottsboro physician, he was convinced the girls were lying. Even Dr. Bridges had noted at the examination that the vaginal areas of the two women were "not even red." "My God, Doctor, is this whole thing a horrible mistake?" asked the stunned Horton. "Judge, I looked at both the women and told them they were lying, that they knew they had not been raped," replied the doctor, "and they just laughed at me."*

Horton sent for Knight and confronted him with Lynch's statement. Knight was adamant. It was only the opinion of one doctor, he insisted, and the state was committed to the prosecution of the nine boys.

Judge Horton, now doubting that any rape had occurred, faced a painful dilemma. He could force Dr. Lynch to take the stand or he could himself, by Alabama statute, end the trial. In either case, Lynch—because of his courageous act—would be ruined. In his mind, Horton went over the twelve jurors who sat on his left. He knew more than half of them personally and—in spite of their conventional southern attitude toward Negroes—he believed that the weight of the evidence presented by the defense would convince them of Patterson's innocence. With many misgivings, he decided to allow the trial to continue.

Before the state rested its case on Tuesday afternoon, Knight called to the stand five additional witnesses. Their testimony was inconclusive, and it became clear that the case would stand or fall on the testimony of Victoria Price.

In planning his defense, Leibowitz realized that normal legal assumptions could not be made at this trial. Usually a defense lawyer has only to prove that there is reasonable doubt of his client's guilt. In Decatur, Leibowitz knew he would have to prove beyond a reasonable doubt that Patterson was innocent.

His first witness was Dallas Ramsey, a Negro who

---

* This account, based upon recent interviews and correspondence with former Judge Horton—and carefully checked by him in manuscript form—has been emphatically denied by Dr. Lynch, who wrote to the author on October 16, 1967, that as "far as I can recall, no such statements were ever made to Judge James E. Horton or anyone else regarding the trial of Haywood Patterson versus Alabama. Of course, it has been 35 years and better since this incident happened; and as far as I can recall, I was never put on the stand as a witness in this case."

lived near the hobo jungle in Chattanooga. He testified he had seen and talked with two white girls and two white men on the evening of March 24 and the morning of March 25, 1931. Ramsey picked Mrs. Price from the courtroom as one of the women; from a photograph he identified Ruby Bates. The four had apparently stayed the night in the wooded vagrant's refuge near his home.

George W. Chamlee, a prominent white Chattanooga attorney, took the stand next. He told the jury he had made dozens of personal inquiries and examined city directories in an effort to locate Mrs. Price's "boardinghouse friend," Callie Brochie. He was convinced, he said, that Mrs. Brochie was a figment of Victoria's imagination. No woman by that name had lived in Chattanooga between 1930 and 1933.

Then Leibowitz took a calculated risk. One by one he put six of the Scottsboro boys on the stand. The jury, he knew, would surely discount their insistence that they were innocent; and, if they made an unfavorable impression, Patterson's conviction would be assured. But Leibowitz had to dispel the state's image of the youths as malevolent conspirators acting coldly and methodically to throw the white boys from the train and then rape the two defenseless white girls.

The first two boys who testified were tragic representatives of a society's deprivation and neglect. Homeless, unemployed, illiterate, they had wandered across the South since their early teens. Willie Roberson, short and stocky and with a wild shock of hair, sat quietly in the courtroom with a vacuous stare. Syphilitic since birth, he spoke with a severe speech impediment. At the time of his arrest, he was in great pain from open venereal sores, and walked with a cane. (Four years later a psychiatric examination disclosed a mental age of nine and an intelligence quotient of sixty-four.) Olen Montgomery was blind in his left eye; with his right he could see "good enough not to get hurt, that is all." Yet Victoria Price had identified them "positively" as two of the defendants who had run across the top of a moving boxcar, leaped into the gondola where she sat, fought a pitched battle with the white boys, and then brutally raped her. Montgomery and Roberson told the courtroom they had been riding back toward the rear of the train and had not even known of the disturbance until they were arrested at Paint Rock.

On the witness stand Ozie Powell, Eugene Williams, Andrew Wright, and Haywood Patterson readily admitted participating in the fight. Williams and Patterson, who were travelling with the two Wright brothers (Andy and his twelve-year-old brother, Leroy), explained that somewhere between Chattanooga and Stevenson several whites had begun throwing rocks at them and shouting, "Black son-of-a-bitches." Patterson said that he had rounded up the other Negroes who were hitching on the train to "have it out." Most of the white youths leaped from the gondola before actually being hit. After the fight, the victorious blacks scattered across the train. Unanimously the Scottsboro boys insisted they had not even seen, let alone molested, the two white girls. Patterson in particular, tall, black, and ostentatiously unservile, held his own during Knight's stormy questioning. When the Attorney General made some reference to Patterson's having been tried at Scottsboro, he was bluntly corrected. "I was framed at Scottsboro," declared the young Negro. Knight, flushed with anger, demanded, "Who told you to say you were framed?" Patterson retorted: "I told myself to say it."

It is doubtful whether the testimony of the Scottsboro boys had any effect, one way or the other, on the deliberations of the jurors, for it was Leibowitz's scathing cross-examination of Mrs. Price that preoccupied Alabamians. Anyone "possessed of that old Southern chivalry," said the Sylacauga News, could not read of the "brutal" harassment of Mrs. Price without "reaching for his gun while his blood boils to the nth degree." Within hours after Victoria stepped from the witness stand, reporters overheard angry threats on the streets of Decatur. On Wednesday, Judge Horton learned that a "mass indignation rally" had been held the night before in the local Masonic hall. Several of the two hundred men at the meeting bluntly demanded that the "New York Jew lawyers" be tarred, feathered, and ridden out of Decatur on a rail. For the Scottsboro boys, the prescription was summary justice from the nearest tree.

A grim-faced Judge Horton ordered the jury removed from the courtroom, and then, in a voice betraying deep emotion, he told the spectators that the guilt or innocence of Haywood Patterson and his fellows was for the jury alone to decide. He wanted to make it absolutely clear, he said, that the court intended to protect the prisoners and their attorneys. "I say this much, that the man who would engage in anything that would cause the death of any of these prisoners is a murderer; he is not only a murderer, but a cowardly murderer." For the first time in the trial Horton raised his voice. Anyone who attempted to take the lives of the prisoners "may expect that his own life be forfeited," he sternly told the silent courtroom. "I believe I am as gentle as any man . . . I don't believe I would harm anyone wrongfully." But he added, emphasizing every word, that there would be no compromise with mob violence. "Now, gentlemen, I have spoken . . . harsh words, but every word I say is true and I hope we will have no more of any such conduct. Let the jury return."

Horton's stern warning ended the open threats of violence. But according to reporters, it also seemed to intensify the community's bitter hostility.

Now under round-the-clock protection by National Guardsmen, Leibowitz continued doggedly to hammer away at the state's case. To intensify the impact for the defense of Dr. Bridges' testimony, he called to the stand Edward A. Reisman, a Chattanooga gynecologist who had spent all his life in Alabama and Tennessee. After reviewing all the medical evidence, Dr. Reisman declared that in his professional opinion it was "inconceivable" that Mrs. Price had been raped six times, as she claimed. But the spectators completely distrusted Dr. Reisman. As one Decatur resident told the *New York Times* reporter, "When a nigger has expert witnesses, we have a right to ask who is paying for them." On Thursday morning Leibowitz presented his most damaging witness. Lester Carter, a twenty-three-year-old hobo, had been on the train when the fight began; it was his name that had so startled Mrs. Price during Leibowitz's cross-examination. Now, wearing a new gabardine suit and a brightly flowered tie, Carter added graphic details to the story Leibowitz had previously sketched. In January of 1931, Carter testified, a Huntsville police court had convicted him of vagrancy and sentenced him to sixty days in the county workhouse. There he met Victoria Price and her boyfriend, Jack Tiller, who were serving time for adultery. When the three were released in March, Tiller invited Carter to stay around Huntsville for a few days. The hospitable Mrs. Price even offered to arrange a date for Carter with her best girl friend, Ruby Bates. On the night of March 23, approximately forty hours before the alleged rape, Tiller and Carter met the two girls outside the gates of a local mill. Talking and giggling, they walked to the Huntsville hobo jungles.

"What occurred in the jungles that night?" asked Leibowitz. "I hung my hat on a little limb and went to having intercourse with the girl [Ruby]," replied Carter. Less than three feet away, Tiller and Victoria also were "having intercourse." When a light rain

began to fall, the four got up from the honeysuckle bushes where they had been lying and crawled into an empty boxcar pulled onto a sidetrack. During the night, in the intervals between love-making, they "talked and started planning this hobo trip," he said. The girls complained that they were sick of Huntsville; perhaps they could go to Chattanooga and "hustle" while the two men got temporary jobs. Tiller explained that he did not want to risk another adultery conviction, but he promised vaguely to meet the other three in Chattanooga if they did not return in a few days. Just before daybreak, the girls went home and collected a change of clothes. They agreed to meet Carter in the freight yards that afternoon.

On the way to Chattanooga, Carter explained, he pretended he did not know the girls; they rejoined each other only after leaving the train. Just beyond the railroad yards, they met Orville Gilley, a slender, self-styled "hobo poet." After Gilley introduced himself, they walked together to Chattanooga's hobo jungle, built a small fire, and shared a meager meal of chili and coffee. During the night, Carter told the court, he once again had sexual relations with Ruby Bates. He could not say for certain about Victoria and their new friend.

The next morning, the four decided they had seen enough of Chattanooga. Tired and hungry, they boarded the 11 A.M. freight for Huntsville. Five white hobos sat in the next car toward the caboose. Just south of Stevenson, Alabama, Carter said, he heard several shouts above the noise of the train. He investigated and saw white and Negro boys fighting in the adjoining car. By the time he and Gilley could get there, however, most of the white youths had jumped or been shoved from the train. Without striking a single blow, Carter "climbed down where the couplings are" and got off. Gilley remained behind. In Scottsboro several hours later, Gilley denied there had been any rape, said Carter.

Although Carter testified persuasively and was unshakable in cross-examination, the jury and spectators listened with open skepticism. His eagerness to testify, his frequent nervous gestures, and his immaculate appearance, one observer said, gave the impression that the defense had "carefully schooled" him. Carter's most damaging mannerism was his insistence on saying "Negro," instead of the typical white southern pronunciation, "Nigra." In cross-examination, Morgan County Solicitor Wade Wright, who was assisting Knight, drew from Carter an admission that the defense had paid his room and board for almost a month and had even bought him the "fancy" new eleven-dollar suit he was wearing.

Shortly after noon on Thursday, the defense rested

"with reservations," but Leibowitz had scarcely taken his seat when a messenger brought a note to his table. Walking over to the bench, Leibowitz whispered to Judge Horton, who then announced a brief recess. The courtroom remained quiet but visibly excited. Ten minutes later, National Guardsmen opened the back doors of the room. A heavy-set, perspiring woman in her forties came down the aisle; Ruby Bates walked behind, her eyes fixed on the floor. The spectators leaned forward with an audible gasp; at the prosecution table there was open consternation. Miss Bates's chaperone, a social worker from the Church of the Advent in Birmingham, explained that the church rector had asked her to bring the young woman to Decatur. The chaperone knew nothing about the case.

Ruby was dressed in a smart gray coat with matching cloche. In 1931 an investigator for the American Civil Liberties Union had described her as a "large, fresh, good-looking girl" with soft "calflike" eyes. But the freshness now was gone. Unlike the spirited Victoria, Ruby seldom raised her eyes from the floor as she mumbled her testimony. Leibowitz asked few questions in his direct examination. On the night of March 23, 1931, "did you have intercourse with Lester Carter . . . ?" "I certainly did," Ruby replied softly. "Did Victoria Price have intercourse with Jack Tiller . . . in your presence?" he asked. "She certainly did," said Ruby. Judge Horton, who had been sitting behind the bench throughout the trial, got up and moved down to a seat in front of the spectators facing Miss Bates.

Did any rape take place on the Chattanooga-to-Huntsville freight train? continued Leibowitz. Not that she knew of, Ruby replied, and she had been with Victoria Price for the entire trip. While the jury and spectators strained to hear her low voice, she explained why she had decided to testify for the defense. Five weeks before, she said, she had left Huntsville with a boyfriend to avoid any involvement in the new Decatur trials. First she had gone to Montgomery; from there she had hitched a ride to New York, where she had worked for a "Jewish lady" for several weeks. But her conscience bothered her, and after reading about a famous New York minister, Dr. Harry Emerson Fosdick ("Dr. Fostick," she called him), she visited him in his study one evening late in March. He arranged for her to go to the Birmingham Church of the Advent and from there to Decatur. Leibowitz completed his questioning in less than fifteen minutes.

For a moment, the Attorney General stared silently at Ruby, who sat with her eyes downcast. "Where did you get that coat?" he finally asked. She hesitated for a moment, and then whispered, "I bought it." "Who gave you the money to buy it?" Knight asked. "Well, I don't know," she replied evasively, her eyes still fixed on the floor. "You don't know?" Knight repeated sarcastically. "Where did you get that hat? Who was the beneficent donor?" There was a long pause as Ruby sat biting nervously at her lower lip. From his seat inside the spectators' rail, Judge Horton leaned forward and gently asked her, "Do you know?" Almost inaudibly she murmured, "Dr. Fostick of New York."

Whenever Knight questioned her about her testimony at Scottsboro, she repeated over and over: "I told it just like Victoria Price told it," or "I said it, but Victoria told me to." The majority of the Attorney General's questions were not, however, about her earlier allegations at Scottsboro. He seemed more intent on proving to the jury that Ruby had been bribed by the defense. Knight suspected that her conscience had been given an assist by representatives of the International Labor Defense. Firing his questions rapidly at the subdued witness, he asked her about her finances. How much money was she making when she left Huntsville? How had she paid for the trip from Montgomery to New York? Who gave her funds for the trip back to Alabama? Although she talked vaguely of loans from her employer in New York, her obvious lack of candor brought smirks and open laughter from the packed courtroom. The Attorney General also drew from Ruby an admission that she was suffering from syphilis and gonorrhea in May of 1931 and had told a Huntsville doctor who treated her that she had contracted it from Negroes who had raped her.

The main testimony in the trial ended when Ruby Bates meekly stepped from the witness stand late Thursday afternoon. Her story caused "an immediate and bitter reaction among the residents of . . . [Morgan] and neighboring counties," said the New York Times correspondent. Citizens of the area were convinced she had "sold out" to the defense. Although Attorney General Knight expressed confidence that the "mob spirit" would exhaust itself in harmless talk, reporters noticed that Miss Bates was hustled away from the courtroom and taken to a secret hiding place by a detachment of National Guardsmen. Knight also strengthened the National Guard unit guarding Leibowitz and Brodsky.

On the following afternoon County Solicitor Wright began the state's summation. Renowned among local all-day singers, Wright bellowed his remarks in the singsong chant of a sawdust-trail evangelist. At first he rambled on about the "fancy New York clothes" of the defense's chief witnesses, Lester Carter and Ruby Bates. But soon he was ringing the changes on all the fears and hatreds that had been aroused in the two weeks of the trial. In summarizing the testimony of Carter, he said with mincing sarcasm: "What does Mr. Carter tell you, maybe it is Carterinsky now! If he had a-been with Brodsky another two weeks he would have been down here with a pack on his back a-trying to sell you goods. Are you going to countenance that sort of thing?" From a front-row seat, an excited spectator exclaimed "No!" with the fervor of an "Amen" in church.

As Wright's anti-Semitic tirade poured out, Leibowitz sat at the defense table with a look of stunned disbelief. Attorney General Knight stared fixedly at the floor, his face flushed with embarrassment. The faces of several jurors betrayed their excitement. Horton sharply reprimanded the solicitor, but Wright went tumbling on, almost lost in his own rhetorical fervor. He turned and pointed a finger at the counsel table where Leibowitz and Brodsky sat. "Show them," he paused for effect, "show them that Alabama justice cannot be bought and sold with Jew money from New York." Leibowitz leaped to his feet, slamming his hand on the defense table. "I move for a mistrial," he said. "I submit a conviction in this case won't be worth a pinch of snuff in view of what this man just said." Horton scolded Wright for his "improper statements" but refused to end the trial.

Leibowitz, facing the unenviable task of restoring calm to the feverish courtroom, began his closing remarks late in the afternoon. "Let us assume the prosecution is prejudiced," he began. "Let us assume the defense is also prejudiced. Let us assume both sides are trying to prove their points." He looked squarely into the face of each juror. "It is the sworn duty of each of you," he told them, to convict only upon "hard evidence," not emotion. He summarized the four days of testimony and emphasized what several state officials were admitting privately: that the prosecution's case rested solely on the testimony of Victoria Price. And her story, he said, was the "foul, contemptible, outrageous lie . . . [of] an abandoned, brazen woman."

The defense attorney continued his summation the next morning. By ten o'clock his voice had begun to crack with fatigue. Several times he took a few sips of water, pausing as if to gather his strength. He recalled Wade Wright's tirade, referring to it as a "hangman's speech." "What is it but an appeal to prejudice, to

New York Times, APRIL 10, 1933

NEGRO FOUND GUILTY IN SCOTTSBORO CASE; JURY OUT 22 HOURS

Verdict Carries Sentence of Death After One Juror Had Held Out for Life Term.

DEFENSE SCORES FINDING

Leibowitz Terms It a Mockery of Justice While Lauding Fairness of Judge.

sectionalism, to bigotry?" Wright, he maintained, was simply saying: "Come on, boys! We can lick this Jew from New York!" The jury's verdict, he concluded, would show whether Alabamians would give even this "poor scrap of colored humanity" a "fair, square deal."

When the weary Leibowitz took his seat, Attorney General Knight began the final arguments for the state. In an obvious reference to Wright's tirade, he shouted: "I do not want a verdict based on racial prejudice or a religious creed. I want a verdict on the merits of this case." Knight exhorted the jurors to stand up for Alabama; he expressed his confidence that they were not "cowards." Referring scornfully to the almost forgotten Patterson as "that thing," he told the jury in a tone of unveiled contempt: "If you acquit this Negro, put a garland of roses around his neck, give him a supper, and send him to New York City." There, he said, "Dr. Harry Fosdick [will] dress him up in a high hat and morning coat, gray-striped trousers, and spats." Only one verdict was possible: death in the electric chair.

Horton delivered his charge to the jury before noon. He began with a pointed reference to the state's star witness, Victoria Price. The law was designed to protect all classes of people, he said, but the law also had a "stern duty to perform when women of the underworld come before it." It was the obligation of the jury, in evaluating Mrs. Price's testimony, to weigh her background of promiscuity and prostitution. In an effort to calm the emotionally charged courtroom, the judge concluded with a plea for the jury to put aside extraneous matters. "We are not trying lawyers," he said. "We are not trying state lines. We are not trying whether the defendant is black or white." The only duty of the jury was to ascertain whether there was a reasonable doubt about the guilt of Haywood Patterson. If there was a reasonable doubt, he emphasized, then they should return a verdict of not guilty. Horton, visibly exhausted from the wearing two-week trial, gave the case to the jury just before one o'clock.

The courtroom was soon empty except for lawyers and newspapermen. Patterson and the other Scottsboro boys sat in their cells and played cards or sang gospel songs to pass the time. When the jury still had not reached a decision at 11:30 P.M., Horton ordered them locked up for the night, and told them to resume their deliberations the following morning, Sunday, at 8:30 A.M.

They reached a verdict at 10 A.M. Leibowitz and Brodsky hurried over to the courthouse. There they found Patterson—guarded by two militiamen—sprawled in a chair and smoking a cigarette. Across the room, Knight sat at the prosecution table, the muscles of his face twitching nervously. When Judge

Horton arrived at 11 A.M., he called for the jury; the court stenographer opened his notebook to take down the last words of the trial. As the jurors filed in they were still laughing from a joke; they became solemn when they saw the tense courtroom.

"Have you agreed upon a verdict?" Horton asked the foreman. He replied, "We have, your honor," and handed a heavily creased slip of paper to the bailiff, who laid it on the judge's bench. Horton unfolded the slip of paper and read the large pencilled letters: "We find the defendant guilty as charged and fix the punishment at death in the electric chair." There was not a sound in the courtroom as spectators craned to see the defense table. That night a shaking Haywood Patterson would clutch a prison Bible in fear, but he had decided beforehand he would never show his inner terror to the gawking white spectators. His face did not change expression. Leibowitz looked as though he had been struck; he leaned back slackly in his chair.

After the jury had been dismissed and a postponement of further trials announced, Leibowitz walked to the bench and grasped Horton's hand. The judge warmly returned the handshake. "I am taking back to New York with me a picture of one of the finest jurists I have ever met," said Leibowitz, his voice shaking with emotion. "I am sorry I cannot say as much for the jury which has decided this case against the evidence."

Later, reporters learned from several jurors that they had not even discussed, much less considered, the testimony of Ruby Bates. The twelve men had taken their first ballot five minutes after the judge gave them the case. The vote was: guilty 12, not guilty 0. The rest of their deliberation time had been taken up with the question of the sentence. Eleven jurors had voted immediately to send Patterson to the electric chair. One, the foreman, had held out until Sunday morning for life imprisonment.

On June 22, 1933, ignoring a warning that he was jeopardizing his own chances for re-election, Judge Horton granted a defense motion and overturned Haywood Patterson's conviction. In a devastating indictment of the state's case, he concluded that Victoria Price's testimony was not only uncorroborated, but also improbable and contradicted by evidence which "greatly preponderates in favor of the defendant." To reporters, Horton implied he would also reverse any

future convictions based upon her testimony.

Defense attorneys hoped that Horton's meticulous and persuasively written decision would cause a shift in public opinion in the state. It did not. At the instigation of Attorney General Knight, Horton was removed from the case and another jurist more amenable to the state's position was appointed. (The warning to Judge Horton was not just a threat: in the 1934 Democratic primary he lost his seat on the bench, despite a vigorous campaign. That same year, Attorney General Knight was elected lieutenant governor.) When Patterson and Clarence Norris, another of the Scottsboro boys, were tried again in December of 1933, both received the death sentence. In 1934, the United States Supreme Court accepted the defense contention that Negroes were systematically excluded from Alabama's juries and gave Patterson and Norris another trial. But in 1936, Patterson was convicted for the fourth time and received a sentence of seventy-five years.

The following year, the state began prosecution of the remaining eight defendants, and in rapid succession juries convicted Clarence Norris, Charley Weems, Andrew Wright, and Ozie Powell. But Lieutenant Governor Knight was dead by this time, and the state was in a mood to compromise. Instead of death, the assistant attorney general had asked only for life imprisonment. In the midst of the trials, it was suddenly announced that the state would dismiss the charges against the remaining four defendants. Although Willie Roberson and Olen Montgomery had already spent six years in jail, it was admitted that they were "unquestionably innocent." Since Leroy Wright and Eugene Williams had been only twelve and thirteen years of age in 1931, "the State thinks that the ends of justice would be met . . . by releasing these two juveniles on condition that they leave the State never to return." On this grotesque note, the public story of Scottsboro came to an end.

Of the five who remained in jail, Patterson successfully escaped to Detroit years later, and eventually died of cancer in a Michigan jail. The other four were finally paroled. Andrew Wright, the last of the parolees, left prison nineteen years after he had been taken from the freight train in Paint Rock.

In 1939, Victoria Price offered to recant—for a substantial fee. No one cared to pay it. She and Ruby Bates both died in the same year, 1961, in towns thirty miles apart.

SECTION IX

The Assassins

LIBRARY OF CONGRESS

327

ASSASSINATION

By DOROTHY MESERVE KUNHARDT *and* PHILIP B. KUNHARDT, JR.

Had there been a Warren Commission exactly a century ago, when Abraham Lincoln was shot, its report might have read like the somber, moving, and impressively researched book from which the following narrative is taken

At about ten thirty on the black night of April 14, 1865, a man signalled with a lighted candle from the stoop of Petersen's boardinghouse in Washington, D.C., and shouted four ordinary words, "Bring him in here!" Opposite, across the street, something far out of the ordinary began to move. Monstrous and many-legged like a centipede, it had just squeezed itself out through the doorway of Ford's Theatre and now began to crawl in agonizingly slow motion toward the candle's flame, its many feet moving in weirdly unrelated, out-of-time steps, all struggling for stances in the wheel-rutted and hoof-chopped dirt.

Viewed close up, its true nature became apparent and even more horrifying, for it represented twenty-five soldiers and doctors and bystanders carrying the body of Abraham Lincoln, sixteenth President of the United States and the first ever to be struck down by an assassin, to the nearest bed. An officer's sword had opened a path in the crowd that stood transfixed with shock, eyes straining beyond the short flare of three gas jets to glimpse the familiar face. They saw it, wax pale. The President was naked to the waist, but flung lopsidedly over his chest was his overcoat, its collar sticky with new blood.

Twice in Mr. Lincoln's journey across Tenth Street there was a halt while the surgeon in charge plucked blood clots from down near the roots of hair at the back of the head, opening the mouth of the wound for free bleeding. Whenever the hole became plugged and the red trickle stopped, so did the breathing, almost.

At last, clumsily inching their way by multiple finicky steps up the Petersen stoop, humping their burden and narrowing file to flow through the tight entrance, the bearers vanished from the crowd's view.

Even as fifty mud-caked boots moved over the oil-cloth floor-covering toward the end of the hall where the candle led—entering and filling the modest living quarters of the young soldier who kept them in such apple-pie order—twenty-five stories were born. Twenty-five men would describe and redescribe throughout their days this high point in all their existences—they had helped bear the Union's martyr from the place

Lincoln Borne by Loving Hands was painted by Carl Bersch from on-the-spot sketches drawn moments after the shooting. "All Washington was celebrating, delirious with joy," the artist remembered; earlier in the evening he himself, from the balcony of his house opposite Ford's Theatre, had been making sketches of a victory parade (lower right corner) proceeding down Tenth Street. Suddenly someone in the crowd shouted, "The President has been shot!" As the body was carried toward the Petersen house next door, Bersch hurriedly made new sketches; his final painting—now owned by his granddaughter, Mrs. E. A. Vey, and here reproduced in color for the first time—combined both sets of sketches.

329

of assassination to his deathbed. Out of a life's ending came the beginnings of a host of conflicting stories, unimportant but persistent, of remembrances both strange and muddled, and of events impressive and much stranger.

The knowledge that he might very easily be assassinated was something Lincoln had lived with for four years before the night he was finally murdered. By the beginning of his second term the threats to his life had increased, and so had the warnings from his friends to be more prudent, not to go about alone.

In 1861 his Secretary of State, William Henry Seward, had declared confidently, "Assassination is not an American habit or practice," but with Lee's final defeat he changed his mind, pointed out to Attorney General James Speed that certain individuals among the Southern people would be in a mood of absolute madness and that the President might indeed be killed. He advised Speed to go to City Point, where Lincoln was visiting Grant's army, and warn him to be careful.

When the Attorney General arrived, the President had already walked several miles through the still-burning city of Richmond; its white residents were invisible inside their houses and only a crowd of Negroes followed Lincoln, trying to kneel in his path and bless him for their emancipation. He made an inviting target, but no one even called out a bad name.

Lincoln was saying in one breath, of his excursion, "I was not scared about myself one bit," and in another, that it had occurred to him as he walked that a gun could have been aimed from any window along the route. But then, he had said the same of his daily situation back in Washington. "If anyone wanted to kill me, he could shoot me from a window on Seventh Street any day when I am riding out to the Soldiers' Home. I do not believe it is my fate to die in this way."

Speed tried to talk to the President about Seward's fear for him, but reported, "He stopped me at once, saying he had rather be dead than live in continual dread. Any precautions against assassination would be to him perpetual reminders of danger."

It was not just the Attorney General, it was every caller. No one ever let him forget the subject, and though the President sometimes met it with light banter, at other times his eyes showed his deep depression and betrayed the fact that the continual talk about his possible sudden death had become a torture.

The Secret Service detective La Fayette C. Baker said that whenever he began to bring Lincoln up to date on the latest plots and threats, the President's manner became playful. "Well, Baker," he would say, "what do they want to kill me for? If they kill me, they will run the risk of getting a worse man."

It was the same with his best friend and self-appointed bodyguard, Ward Hill Lamon, who had gone off to Richmond on a mission three days before the tragedy at Ford's Theatre. He tried to make Lincoln promise not to expose himself in crowds and especially not to go to the theatre while Lamon was away.

The President just laughed and remarked to Secretary of the Interior Usher, "This boy is a monomaniac on the subject of my safety." Lamon was crazy, he said. He wanted Lincoln to sit in his lap all day.

He kept giving people his answers on the touchy subject. "I have received a great many threatening letters but I have no fear of them." "If they kill me, I shall never die another death." "I determined when I first came here I should not be dying all the while." "If anyone is willing to give his life for mine, there is nothing that can prevent it."

He didn't believe the knife was yet made or the bullet run that would end his life. "I shall live till my work is done and no earthly power can prevent it. And then, it doesn't matter, so that I am ready, and that I ever mean to be."

A black mood could fall upon him without warning and bring remarks like, "I shall never live out the four years of my term. When the rebellion is crushed, my work is done." In a cubbyhole of his office desk, in fact, Lincoln had two letters which he had tied together and labelled "Assassination." One purported to be written to a man who had drawn the lot to kill "the monster" and was meant to bolster the killer's courage. The assassin was to get into the monster's office, "congratulate him, listen to his stories. . . ." "Abe must die and now. You can choose your weapons—the cup, the knife, the bullet."

The President had already barely escaped a bullet. During the summer of 1864, just as he entered the grounds of the Soldiers' Home, riding alone and at night, a hidden marksman had fired at him, but the ball had whizzed through his high hat. He asked that no mention of it be made. "It was probably an accident and might worry my family."

There was talk around Washington that the cup had been tried too—that castor oil ordered from a pharmacy had arrived deadly with poison, but had had too queer a taste to be swallowed.

In the same category of whispered rumor was the trunk of old clothes taken from yellow-fever victims in Cuba that had been delivered to the White House in the hope that the Lincolns would come down with the disease and that it would be fatal.

A man kept coming to see the President to say he positively knew that a small, square package was being mailed to Mr. Lincoln which would explode when it was unwrapped. Lincoln told him each time, "No package yet, and I promise never to open any small square packages."

Though the mailed bomb proved a myth, the President regularly received photographs and drawings of himself spattered suggestively with red ink. Usually there was a rope around the neck, stretching up to the branch of a tree. These he minded chiefly because they upset Mrs. Lincoln. She worried constantly over his safety, and he agreed, if it would comfort her, to carry a particularly sturdy cane. But even if he wore a shirt of mail, it would do no good: there were a thousand ways, he remarked, to get at a man if you wanted to assassinate him. He would have to shut himself up in an iron box if he wanted to be really safe.

Explosives had always been prominent in the Lincoln plot scares. Right now, at the war's end, it was known that an infernal machine was ready to be fastened on crossbars under the presidential carriage—the same one in which Lincoln rode to Ford's Theatre on the night of the assassination. The train carrying him from Springfield to his first inauguration was to have been blown up as it travelled over a bridge. If by any chance Lincoln was still alive, hand grenades were to have been tossed into his carriage at Baltimore. The President-elect made the last lap of his journey secretly, ahead of schedule, and arrived safely.

On March 4, 1861, came the first swearing-in of an American President under heavy military protection. There were sharpshooters stationed in every window of the two Capitol wings, with their guns trained on the small temporary platform on the steps of the east front. There had been a report that a bomb was set to go off under this platform, but a search revealed nothing, and Lincoln rose and made his appeal that the country choose peace instead of war.

All the side streets were full of troops, and old General Winfield Scott, who had worked out the plan to guard the President-elect, was only a block away as Lincoln took the oath and kissed the Bible. Scott had expressed himself as determined that Abraham Lincoln should live to be inaugurated, and he considered this the most momentous hour of his long career.

Cavalry officers who escorted the carriage taking Lincoln and Buchanan to the Capitol and afterward to the White House were ordered to spur their animals with pretended clumsiness so that there would be constant unpredictable movement and any bullet fired at the head of the new Chief Magistrate would be apt merely to drill a hole in a horse's stomach.

No horse was injured on that first inauguration day, but finally, after four interminable years of threats that would have left most mortals raw-nerved, there had been a hole drilled in the head of the man who was, as he had promised to be, ready.

To a generation in whose memory the murder of a President is still tragically vivid, an account of the assassination of President Lincoln reads like a bit of current history. We know from our own experience the shock and horror such an act of madness evokes, and the story of what happened in Washington on the night of April 14, 1865, has a new impact when it is read in the living awareness of what happened in Dallas on November 22, 1963.

The story has been told many times, but never with the wealth of detail contained in *Twenty Days*, a book by Dorothy Meserve Kunhardt and her son, Philip B. Kunhardt, Jr., which is being prepared by Harper & Row for publication later this year. In the pages that follow, AMERICAN HERITAGE presents a long excerpt from the first half of *Twenty Days*.

Working in a field made familiar by the extensive researches of her father, the late Frederick Hill Meserve, who compiled and left in her care the greatest private collection of Lincoln and Civil War photographs in existence, Mrs. Kunhardt, with her son, spent years gathering firsthand accounts of that terrible evening. Here are Lincoln's last hours, described by the people who played the important parts in them—a presentation of the true stories, the garbled stories, the maybe-so stories, and the outright legends that grew out of the greatest single tragedy in American history. In a sense, the Kunhardts' book does what a Warren Commission would have done if the dazed government in 1865 had set up such a group. Here is the deeply moving record, as far as a record can be established at this late date.

To this presentation, AMERICAN HERITAGE devotes much more space than it ordinarily gives to any single subject—both because the record is fascinating in its own right and because today's reader is especially and unhappily fitted to understand it. We have all seen how an event of this kind brings a wealth of stories that just do not add up to anything very coherent. One bit of evidence contradicts another, the weight of it all seems at first to prove one thing and ends by proving something different, and in the end the tragedy is all the more terrible because it does not fit into any orderly historic pattern. The story told in *Twenty Days* is hauntingly like the story that came out of Dallas.

—*Bruce Catton*

"I've never been so happy in my life"

Twelve feet above the Ford's Theatre stage, set for Act III, Scene 2 of Our American Cousin, *is Lincoln's box. In this photograph, taken later by Mathew Brady, the Treasury Guards flag—on which Booth caught his spur—hangs from a staff against the center pillar. On the fatal night the flag, staffless, was draped below the framed portrait of George Washington.*

Lee had surrendered at Appomattox on Palm Sunday, April 9. In the five days of the week of peace, the President relaxed and watched the shooting fireworks, laughing when mischievous Tad took time out to wave a Rebel flag behind his father's back. At meals in the White House Mr. Lincoln was the cordial host to the guests whom his wife delighted to summon with her meticulously written invitations.

A circumspect ordained minister, the Reverend George Buzelle from Bangor, Maine, summed up everyone's feelings when he wrote his family a letter postmarked City Point, Virginia, April 9, 1865:

"Evening

Great News!! Lee's army of Northern Virginia is surrendered—Lee has surrendered—so goes the news. Guns—drums—yells—cheers—shaking hands, general confusion and wildness—hip! hip! hurrah! Bully! Yi! Ge whoop! Keee-ih! Then—just then—our dog Jack came into the tent and I told him to holler but he wouldn't and I grabbed him by the throat and choked him until he gave a half strangled Yakerwakrrr and I threw him off and knocked the table and upset the lamp and smashed the chimney and set the table in a blaze—whowray!! Yi keeoo Yeep! Keweew!!

Good! Well good night and thank God.

George"

The President's reaction was more sedate, but his joy was no less real. "I've never been so happy in my life," Abraham Lincoln said in that first week of peace. Long careworn under the burden of the war, suddenly he was erect and buoyant—the President looked grand, absolutely grand, people said. Those who knew him best said that he was not merely happy, he was transfigured with joy over the ending of the war. There were those who looked at Lincoln and looked again and swore they could see a radiance shining from him that was almost physical.

That week after the surrender, Lincoln asked every band he met parading the avenues to play "Dixie" for him; it was, he said, a wonderful song rightfully captured. Now Lincoln could let himself start thinking again of Springfield, of his little brown house out West—there was a good chance he would be going home in four years.

Mrs. Lincoln said his very happiness frightened her, that the only other time he had said, "I have never been so happy in my life," they had lost their three-year-old Eddie the next day. Besides, Mary Lincoln had examined the verses in the Bible which had been used at her husband's second swearing-in on March 4 and studied the words at the exact spot where he had kissed the page on taking the oath. It was in Isaiah 5, and the prophet was speaking of the enemies of Israel: "None shall be weary nor stumble among them . . . Whose arrows are sharp, and all their bows bent, their horses' hoofs shall be counted like flint, and their wheels like a whirlwind . . ."

To Mary Lincoln the words were clearly a warning of danger—she must be vigilant and on guard to protect the President; how cruel it was, with all the care she had taken of him, to have this worry now, in peacetime.

The President was anxious for her to get over her nervousness. He felt that close involvement in war was probably too great a strain for any woman. "We must both," he told Mary, "be more cheerful in the future . . . we have both been very miserable."

She would try. She would begin by dwelling on the blessed word *peace*. That Bible warning might have been helpful five weeks ago, but who would want to commit an act of violence now?

At eleven thirty that Good Friday morning of April 14, 1865, less than eight hours before curtain time, a White House messenger arrived at Ford's Theatre with the welcome news that the President accepted the management's invitation to attend that evening's performance of *Our American Cousin*. The news was received by James Ford, the business manager. His twenty-one-year-old brother Harry, realizing that a presidential visit during the week of national victory was an occasion, personally set about furnishing and decorating the ample space provided by throwing boxes seven and eight together. He used flags, a framed engraving of George Washington, and a set of furniture—a sofa, two stuffed chairs on casters, and a rocking chair that he thought the President would find comfortable. He added six straight-legged chairs for extra guests. The rocking chair (lower right) was placed where its long rockers exactly fitted, in the left-hand corner.

The President and Mrs. Lincoln had a hard time assembling guests for their theatre party. That very morning their oldest son, twenty-one-year-old Captain Robert Todd Lincoln, had arrived home from the war, and even at breakfast he was so sleepy he could barely keep his eyes open. After dinner, his father sought him out in his room and said the few words that Robert would never forget all his life.

"Son," he said, "we want for you to come to the theatre with us tonight."

Robert explained that he was too sleepy, that he was longing to lie down in a real bed between sheets.

"All right, son," said the President, "run along to bed."

Besides Robert, the Lincolns had invited at least twelve people to go with them, including General and Mrs. U. S. Grant, Secretary of War Edwin M. Stanton and his wife, Speaker of the House Schuyler Colfax, Illinois Governor Richard Oglesby, and Senator Richard Yates (who had been Illinois' wartime governor). Almost everyone had begged off, for one reason or another, and at the end there were just two ac-

Theatre guests who didn't come (from left): Robert Lincoln, just home from the front, told his father he was tired and went to bed. Major Thomas T. Eckert, head of the military telegraph and a physically powerful man, had reason to be suspicious of Booth and would have recognized him at once, but the Secretary of War said he had other duties for Eckert that evening. Speaker Schuyler Colfax was leaving the next day for California, he explained, and wanted to retire early. General Grant and his wife also declined the President's invitation: Julia Grant could not abide Mary Lincoln's haughty airs.

ceptances. The Lincolns picked up their guests—Major Henry Reed Rathbone and his stepsister and fiancée, Clara Harris, daughter of a New York senator—at the Harris home and drove them in their carriage to the theatre. Major Rathbone was twenty-eight years old and had only recently been appointed by the President as assistant adjutant general of Volunteers. Obviously he had not had it impressed upon him that he was to watch out for the President's safety, for he sat on the sofa in the far front of the box, slightly behind Clara but nowhere near Mr. Lincoln.

The presidential party was so late that evening that the curtain had to go up without the Lincolns and their guests. In about half an hour they were seen in the dress circle approaching their box; the play stopped, the audience rose and applauded, and the orchestra struck up "Hail to the Chief." The First Lady was all smiles, but Mr. Lincoln seemed weary and his face was serious. The audience had settled down for an evening of laughter at a silly play, and now the President's melancholy mood would be a poor match for the high spirits of the crowd.

It was true that Lincoln had experienced one of his swift changes from confident hope to depression. Late that afternoon he had walked to the War Department with his guard William Crook, as he had done so many times before, and had said something that he had never said before.

"Crook, do you know," he said, "I believe there are men who want to take my life." Then he lowered his voice, as though talking to himself. "And I have no doubt they will do it."

"Why do you think so, Mr. President?" asked Crook.

"Other men have been assassinated," Lincoln answered. "I know no one could do it and escape alive. But if it is to be done, it is impossible to prevent it."

And the guard remembered afterward that a little later, when the President left for the theatre in his carriage, Lincoln had said, for the first time, "Good-by, Crook," instead of the usual "Good night."

As the performance of *Our American Cousin* resumed, Mrs. Lincoln laughed openly and heartily at every joke; but her husband frequently leaned forward and rested his chin in one hand, seemingly thinking of something not present. The First Lady was oblivious to the fact that the President's thoughts were straying from the performance. She was to be questioned closely as to what Mr. Lincoln's exact last words had been, and she would ultimately take refuge in remembering two completely opposite versions, which she told alternately.

First, she recalled that her hand had been on Mr. Lincoln's knee and that she had been leaning across the arm of his chair, over very close to him, so close that she had asked rather apologetically, with a look at the engaged couple in the front of the box, "What will Miss Harris think of my hanging on to you so?" The President's last words were, "She won't think anything about it."

But then later Mrs. Lincoln was sure the President had turned to her just before Booth's shot and remarked earnestly, "How I should like to visit Jerusalem some time!" This was an odd sequence of thought, as the play had been following a less than spiritual course, convulsing the audience as a wildly caricatured American backwoodsman arrived to visit his English cousins. The Lincolns had heard Binny the butler ask the backwoodsman, Asa Trenchard, if he would like to have a "baath," heard Asa tell Binny to "absquatulate—vamose!"—that he was a "tarnal fat critter, swelling out his bosom like an old turkey cock in laying time." The actual last speech before the assassination was by the American cousin in answer to the scheming English mother who had just found out he was not a rich catch for her daughter and called out angrily that Asa did not know the manners of good society. Harry Hawk, playing Asa, was alone on the stage, and for the final time Mr. Lincoln heard the sound of a human voice. "Don't know the manners of good society, eh? Well, I guess I know enough to turn you inside out, old gal—you sockdologizing old man-trap."

Only Mary Lincoln and two young guests went to the theatre with the President. During the play the First Lady laughed at the old jokes and rested her hand on Lincoln's knee. This fine likeness is from an original Mathew Brady negative.

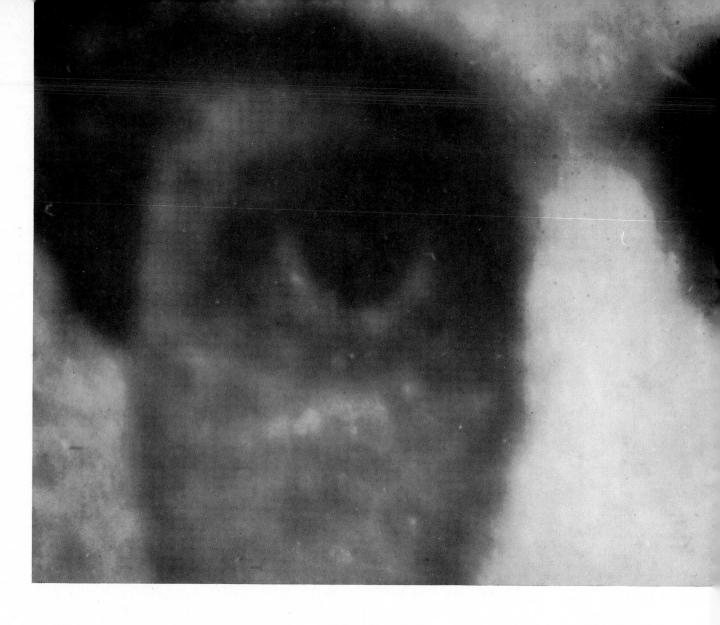

The eyes of an assassin, filled with a strange, wild fire

If Abraham Lincoln had been given time to turn around in his rocking chair, he would have recognized his assassin instantly. Twenty-six-year-old John Wilkes Booth was one of the country's promising actors, though no one expected him to come near the genius of his father, Junius Brutus Booth, or his incomparable brother, Edwin. Lincoln had seen him perform, seen that handsome, pale face, the thick raven hair, the deep-set eyes, black as ink and filled with a strange, wild fire. Only a few months before, the President had been at Ford's Theatre in his usual box watching Booth play the part of a villain; whenever the Maryland actor had had anything ugly and threatening to say, he had stepped up near the presidential box, shaken his finger toward Lincoln, and said the lines directly to him. "He looks as if he meant that for you," the President's companion said, and Lincoln replied, "Well, he does look pretty sharp at me, doesn't he?"

For six months Booth had been working on plans to kidnap Lincoln with the band of conspirators he had gathered together—among them a Maryland coach painter and blockade-runner, an unstable twenty-three-year-old drugstore clerk, and a former Confederate soldier. At first they had planned to spirit Lincoln away to Richmond and demand that all Southern prisoners be freed and the war ended. One scheme was to throw Lincoln from a theatre box to the stage below, rush him out the back door, and drive him away, tied up, before the audience knew what had happened. On March 4, during Lincoln's second inauguration, Booth and his men had been in the crowd quite close to the President, and had had a perfect opportunity to strike. Later in March the conspirators had surrounded and stopped the President's carriage, only to find another man inside. By April, Booth had decided that kidnapping would not do, that Lincoln must die. "Our country owed all her troubles to him, and God simply made me the instrument of His punishment," Booth wrote in his diary.

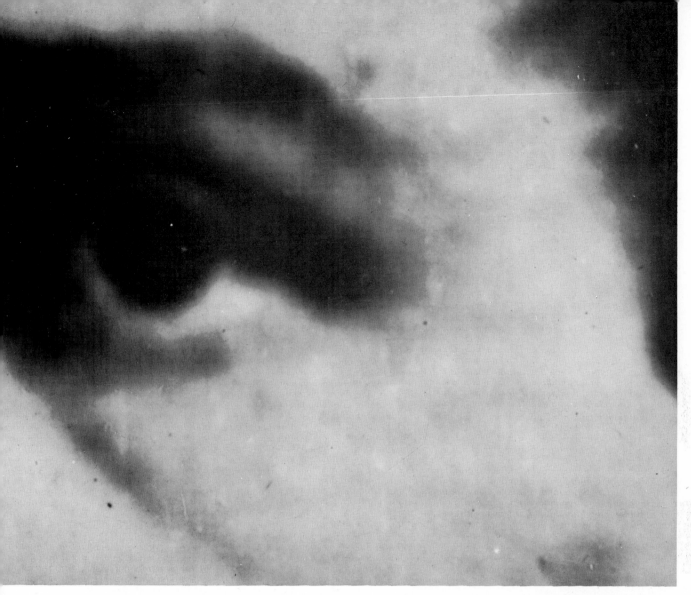

At eleven thirty on the morning of April 14 the actor arrived at Ford's Theatre to pick up his mail, and learned of the President's planned attendance that evening. He seemed casual as he sat down on the theatre steps to read his letter, but everyone who saw him from that moment on noticed that he was deathly pale—thought he looked sick. He left soon to begin a day of frenzied preparation.

No one has ever pinpointed the hour at which Booth stole back into the theatre, made a hole in the wall for a bar to jam the door in the corridor leading to the President's box, and bored a peephole in the door to the box itself, grinding through the wood with a large iron-handled gimlet, then using a penknife to enlarge the hole to the size of a finger. Through it he had a deadeye view of the back of the rocking chair.

Dressed in high silk hat and dark suit, he went straight from the theatre to Pumphrey's Livery Stable. There he hired a swift little bay mare with a white star on her fore-

Here, in a much enlarged photograph, is the peephole which Booth, sometime during an earlier visit to Ford's Theatre on the day

head and black tail and mane, saying he would call for her about four. At the appointed time Booth returned, now wearing a soft dark hat and high riding boots. Pumphrey warned him not to tie the mare if he left her; he must get someone to hold her, for she was high-spirited and would break her halter. Booth mentioned that he was going to Grover's Theatre to write a letter, that he intended stopping for a drink somewhere, and indicated that he might take a pleasure ride.

Instead of going to Grover's, Booth went to the National Hotel, where he was staying, to do his writing and walked into the office there, looking for privacy it seemed. He appeared dazed and asked the clerk in charge, Mr. Merrick, what year it was. Merrick said surely he was joking, and Booth said no, he wasn't. On Pennsylvania Avenue at about four thirty Booth met John Matthews, a fellow actor who

was playing the part of an attorney in *Our American Cousin,* handed Matthews the letter he had just written, and asked him to give it to the editor of the *National Intelligencer* the following day. Ten minutes later he spotted a carriage with General and Mrs. Grant in it proceeding to the station on their way to New Jersey. Booth galloped after the carriage and made them uncomfortable by peering into it.

Sometime that afternoon—the clerk did not remember exactly when—Booth appeared at the desk of the Kirkwood House with a card, addressed to no one, on which was written, "Don't wish to disturb you. Are you at home? J. Wilkes Booth." The clerk thought he heard Booth say the name Johnson, and he put the card into the box of Vice President Andrew Johnson's private secretary.

At six thirty that evening Booth had supper at the National Hotel. At about eight he met his accomplices at the

This is the wooden bar, prepared in advance, with which Booth blocked the outer door to the box after he entered. A souvenir hunter took it home, later sawed off a piece for a man who asked for a relic, then decided he didn't want it.

of the assassination, bored in the inner door to Lincoln's box. It gave him a perfect view of the back of the President's head.

Herndon House and went over the plans for them to kill Secretary of State Seward and Vice President Johnson that evening.

It was about nine thirty when Booth rode into the alley behind Ford's Theatre. With "Peanuts," a messenger boy, holding his mare's bridle and the horse already stamping in protest, he entered the back door and asked if he could cross the stage. He was told no, the dairy scene was playing, which took the full depth. In a few moments he went down under the stage and through a special stage door to another alley that led to the front of the theatre. The ticket seller, John Buckingham, saw him leaving and entering the theatre lobby five times. Booth seemed very nervous. He took hold of two of Buckingham's fingers and asked him the time. Buckingham told him there was a clock in the lobby. It was after ten. When Buckingham went into the saloon next

door for a drink, Booth was there drinking brandy. At about ten fifteen Booth went into the back of the house and stood looking at the audience. Then he walked up the stairs leading to the dress circle, humming a tune. He was still wearing his dark slouch hat and riding clothes—high boots and spurs. He approached John Parker, the special policeman who was supposed to be sitting outside the door of the President's box but who had gone down into one of the dress circle seats to watch the play. Booth tapped a card out from his card case, showed it to Parker, and a moment later entered the outer door of the little hall leading to the presidential box and closed it behind him. He barred the door so that no one could follow. In the narrow darkness between the doors he drew his pistol. Then he opened the second door and stepped into the box directly behind President Lincoln.

"The President has been shot!"

It was an instant in history the world would never forget. Lincoln was leaning forward, looking over the rail down into the audience, when the tiny derringer pistol was fired just behind his head. The enormous handmade lead bullet struck the President behind the left ear, flattened out as it drove through his skull, tunnelled into the brain, and came to rest behind the right eye.

For a split second no one spoke, no one moved. Mrs. Lincoln and Clara Harris sat frozen in their seats. A dense smoke enveloped the President and curled upward; suddenly the assassin appeared within the smoke, as though materialized by some demon magician.

President Lincoln threw up his right arm at the impact of the shot and Mrs. Lincoln instinctively caught him around the neck, struggling to keep him upright. Now Rathbone lunged out of his seat and grabbed at Booth's arm. Booth had dropped the pistol and was brandishing a dagger which he tried to plunge into Rathbone's chest. The Major knocked the knife upward with his arm, and received a two-inch-deep slash just above the elbow.

Now, as Booth vaulted over the railing of the box, Rathbone clutched at him again and felt clothes tear as Booth wrenched himself free and leapt the twelve feet down to the stage. As he dropped, his spur caught in the Treasury flag draped on the railing of the box, and the off-balance landing shattered a small bone above his left ankle. "Stop that man!" Rathbone cried. Clara Harris screamed, "Stop that man, won't somebody stop that man!" Then Mrs. Lincoln was leaning over the box and shrieking, "Help! Help!" followed by a series of words that made no sense at all—gibberish, insane sounds that filled the stunned theatre. Standing on the stage all alone, Harry Hawk saw Booth coming for him, brandishing a large knife and calling out "Sic semper tyrannis!"—"Thus shall it ever be for tyrants!" Hawk turned and fled terrified into the wings and up a flight of stairs. Booth charged backstage and toward the back door. There was orchestra leader William Withers, and Booth slashed out at him and cut his clothes. A moment later Booth was outside, knocking over "Peanuts," who was still patiently holding the reins of his horse, kicking the

The Petersen house

boy to the ground, clumsily throwing himself onto the horse, which for a moment circled crazily in the alleyway, and then setting off at a gallop into the night.

"Hang him!" The shouts began from the audience. "Hang him!" Up in the box Clara Harris was screaming down for someone to bring water, and now there was pounding on the outer door, which Booth had barred shut. Rathbone, dripping blood from his arm, rushed to open it, to admit the world to the tragedy.

Dr. Charles Augustus Leale, twenty-three, by coincidence an avid student of gunshot wounds, was seated in the dress circle only forty feet away from the President's box. For a moment after the shot he sat transfixed as a man jumped from the box onto the stage, the knife in his hand shining like a diamond in the gaslight. Then, gathering his wits, Leale hurtled over the seats and got to the door of the box just as the bar was being removed inside by Rathbone, who showed Leale his bleeding arm and begged for help. The Doctor quickly saw that the real help was needed by the President. He was being supported now in his chair by Mrs. Lincoln, who cried, "Oh, Doctor, do what you can for my dear husband! Is he dead? Can he recover?"

The President was indeed almost dead—he was paralyzed, there was no pulse in his wrists, and he drew breaths only at long intervals. Leale laid him on the floor and with a penknife cut his collar and coat away around the shoulders and neck. He ran his fingers through the hair until he came upon a clot of blood behind the left ear. He removed the clot and inserted the little finger of his left hand into the smooth opening as far as it would go. With the hole open for blood to ooze from, the breathing became better.

At this moment a second doctor, Charles Sabin Taft, also twenty-three years old, arrived. Through the confusion that reigned in the theatre—the cries of "Kill him!" "Lynch him!" "Water!" "A surgeon!"—Taft had bounded out of his seat in the orchestra, leapt onto the stage, and half scrambled, half was lifted up over the railing into the box, where he joined Leale. Desperate, realizing he had perhaps only seconds now, Leale straddled the long, lean body, his knees on the floor on each side of the hips. He bent forward, opened the mouth, and firmly pressed down and forward the back of the tongue, which was blocking air from getting down the windpipe. He directed Dr. Taft to raise and lower the arms while he himself pushed upward with his hands against the diaphragm, putting all the strength of his fingers into massaging the chest above the silent heart. There was a sucking in of air, three gulps, then stillness again. Now Dr. Leale leaned down with his mouth sealed lip to lip against the President's. Again and again he drew in his own breath to the bursting point and forced it with all his might down into the paralyzed lungs. After mouth-to-mouth resuscitation, he tried mouth-to-nostrils and, working on like a straining athlete, aching and stubborn, once more mouth-to-mouth. All at once he realized that Mr. Lincoln was inhaling by himself. The heart was stirring, just barely, but there was a faint, irregular flutter.

Leale stood up. "His wound is mortal," he said. "It is impossible for him to recover." Then he added: "We must get him to the nearest bed." Now, before the move was attempted, a diluted spoonful of brandy was poured between the President's lips, and it was swallowed. This would be done three times more during the evening; thus it happened that the last sustenance that passed into Lincoln's stomach was alcohol, which he had avoided all his life, saying it made him feel flabby and undone. He was beyond any feelings now, nor could he see or hear in the slightest degree as Laura Keene, the play's leading lady, arrived in the box with a pitcher of water and begged emotionally to be allowed to hold the President's head in her lap and bathe his temples. Mrs. Lincoln, who was usually so jealous that she disliked seeing another woman engage her husband in conversation, was now so absorbed in her loud sobs that she made no objection. The actress sat on the floor, bending intimately over Lincoln's upturned face as, oblivious to the red stains spreading on the skirt of her elaborate satin dress, she tenderly and uselessly sprinkled and patted.

Two other doctors had been in the audience and had joined Leale and Taft in the box. They were Dr. Africanus F. A. King, twenty-four, so named because of his father's admiration for the Dark Continent, and Dr. Charles A. Gatch, who had served through the war with the armies of General Rosecrans. Now Dr. Leale directed Dr. King to lift the President's left shoulder, others raised the rest of the body, and Leale himself supported the head. Thus Abraham Lincoln began his final journey in life. Slowly, struggling, the group edged out of the never-to-be-forgotten box, past the dress circle, down the stairs, into the lobby of the theatre, and out onto Tenth Street. Now a passage through the stunned and staring crowd was being cleared by soldiers.

Young Henry Safford, who headed the property returns division in the War Department, had been out celebrating the war's end for five wild nights in a row, and tonight he was tired enough to stay home and doze in his stuffed chair over a good book. The nap turned out to be a short one. At about ten thirty a sudden noisiness across the street exploded into the angry yells of a riot. Jolted awake, Safford saw people streaming from the theatre doors, and it seemed to him they were acting peculiarly, hitting and even kicking each other. "Are they all mad?" he wondered. He threw open his window. He shouted, "What's the matter?" and got the immediate answer: "The President has been shot!"

Safford hurled himself down the narrow stairway, lighted a candle, and went to the front doorway. Halfway across the street a knot of men moved directly toward him. He heard a voice asking, "Where shall we take him?" and then heard what he realized was his own voice crying, "Bring him in here!"

He watched the bearers struggle to negotiate the stoop's abrupt right angle by giving the President a quick hoist to a higher level. The man in the lead climbed backward, reaching out with both hands to grasp his particular share of the attenuated, endlessly mounting figure—the head, it proved to be, by the candle's flicker. Obviously in authority, this first hunched climber gave the command, "Take me to your best room!" Henry Safford led the way to a small sleeping apartment straight back at the end of the first-floor hall and stood holding his candle up near the ceiling. It would be much harder in the dark, the trying not to let the President's arms dangle, the trying not to land him with a bump, the fumbling and feeling with so many fingers to get the overcoat spread quilted-satin-side down over the bare chest. Somehow, Henry Safford's tiny glow held, and he used it to light the single gas jet which was to provide not only the greenish illumination that intensified every horror of the night, but for good measure a furious hissing, maddening in its persistence.

The best room was a sort of shedlike extension with a roof that sloped from a high right-hand wall to a low window on the left. It was shabby, but Safford knew that the carpet was swept and that there were clean sheets on the low walnut cottage bed. William T. Clark, the young boarder whose modest room this was, took meticulous care of his few possessions.

The four doctors in the room dismissed the other twenty-one bearers, and again led by Safford, the men left with their lungs full of air almost druggingly sweet from lilacs blooming in the yard outside the window.

Once again Dr. Leale, the young surgeon who had carried Mr. Lincoln's head, spoke urgently to Safford, telling him to get wash boilers of water boiling on the cookstove in the kitchen and to search for bottles, any kind of bottles he could find that could be filled with hot water and put next to the President's legs.

The doctors now stood helpless beside the rumpled figure on the bed, gaining time to think by murmuring that they must let the President rest after the exertion of being carried across the street. They knew he had lost both blood and brain matter on the way; how much could never be measured, for the red dribble had been churned into the mud of Tenth Street by the half-hundred boots of his bearers. Their patient lay ominously still and out of kilter, exactly as he had been set down, knees bent and the soles of his high boots pressing hard against the footboard. Nothing was going to do any good, but it was unthinkable to do nothing, even while waiting for the messengers sent earlier from the theatre by horseback and on foot to nearby hospitals for mustard plasters, hot-water bottles, army blankets, and brandy.

Suddenly Dr. Leale had an unreasonable desire. He was a high-strung young man, and by virtue of having been the first to enter the theatre box after John Wilkes Booth's shot, he could give the orders now. He had just had the sickening experience of wiping from palms and fingers with a towel the blood and seeping brain matter that had stained his hands as they supported Lincoln's head, with its bullet wound down behind the left ear, in the interminable crossing of Tenth Street. Now, though he knew his patient was totally unconscious, like a fussy nurse he wanted to make everything nice, to get the President into a comfortable position lying exactly in the middle of the mattress, under sheets with no wrinkles. "Break off the end of that bed," he ordered, and the other doctors wrestled with the sturdily built spool-turned rungs. The walnut held like cast iron. The only alternative was to arrange the six-foot-four-inch body diagonally, with the feet sticking out over near the wall. The head was moved over next to the door and settled on two overhanging pillows which would soak up blood for several hours at least before they could take no more. Then the red puddle would begin to form on the worn Brussels carpet below, but right now the room was still immaculate.

The next step was obvious. Perhaps there was a stab wound somewhere on Mr. Lincoln's body, in addition to

the hole made by the bullet. Everyone in the theatre had seen the shining dagger that Booth had flourished back there on the stage. It was imperative that the doctors make an examination, immediately. But the four men seemed suggestive to the paralysis of their charge. They moved with such sluggish deliberation that they were still agreeing that they must act quickly when there was a burst of excitement at the front of the house.

Mrs. Lincoln was making the journey across Tenth Street, almost unrecognizable as the First Lady who had curtsied so happily two hours before at her husband's side when the audience rose, cheering and waving handkerchiefs, to the thrilling sound of "Hail to the Chief." All her delicate southern-belle femininity gone, she dug the heels of her evening slippers into the manure-spattered soil in exaggerated paces, whirled and pulled along her escort, Major Rathbone, as though he were weightless.

Once in the hallway she flounced away from hands outstretched to help her and cried wildly, "Where is my dear husband? Where is he?" She walked past two locked rooms on the left, to the bed where she saw him lying with his boots still on. The doctors asked her to leave while they made an examination, and she allowed herself to be led back toward the entrance.

Young, red-haired Major Rathbone was unexpectedly

342

Mr. Lincoln's trousers (with a thirty-two-inch waist), frock coat, and Brooks Brothers overcoat—slit by doctors' penknives—were sent to the White House, but his high boots were kept by Willie Clark, the young soldier in whose room the President died. His tall beaver hat, left at the theatre, was taken to police headquarters.

taking up most of the hallway space, extended full length on the floor and unconscious from loss of blood. The messy wound in his left arm had bled in livelier spurts after the punishment of being wrenched this way and that during the street crossing with Mrs. Lincoln. While Clara Harris made arrangements for a carriage to be brought through the crowd to drive her betrothed back to the Harris home, strenuous efforts were made to find somewhere for the First Lady to sit down.

There was no time to search for keys to the locked rooms, so their doors were broken open with heavy kicks and an onslaught of ramming shoulders. The front room that looked across at the theatre was chosen as Mary Lincoln's refuge during the long night. It was an exceptionally prim parlor, furnished with black horsehair-covered chairs and sofa, a slippery, unyielding sofa on which the wife—when morning came, the widow—lay and gave herself up to spasms of sobbing that reverted unpredictably to deafening screams.

In about twenty minutes now the Lincolns' family doctor and the Surgeon General of the United States—as well as members of the Cabinet, who were being sought out all over the city of Washington—would arrive. Soon after, there would come tiptoeing into the President's nine-by-seventeen-foot room more doctors, making sixteen in all, and a changing parade not only of chiefs of departments but senators,

congressmen, army officers, personal friends, the four other boarders in the Petersen house and their landlord, Mr. Lincoln's son Robert and his mother's circle of comforters, actors from the interrupted *Our American Cousin,* and just plain people who had slipped in somehow to watch Abraham Lincoln die. More than ninety individuals would pass in and out of the death room during the night, filling it to the choking point, pressing against the bed, weeping, kneeling to pray. Uncounted others, nameless, would slip into the confusion of the hallway like restless sleepwalkers, every so often escaping the delirium to let those keeping vigil out on Tenth Street know it would not be long now.

This was all in the future, as, in comparative peace in the cramped space provided—with only Mrs. Lincoln's lamentations in the front room and the snoring, jerky breathing of the patient to unnerve them—the four medical men began their futile ritual.

They undressed the President, beginning by pulling off his high party-going boots, size fourteen. Mr. Lincoln's shirt had been slashed into strips of white cotton and its collar hacked away completely. There was a cuff button bearing the graven letter *L.* Its link had been broken as the button was wrenched with urgency from its lost mate.

When Mr. Lincoln lay naked on the bed, the physicians jointly examined every inch of him. There was one old scar

343

on his left thumb, two small scars in his scalp, well hidden among the black locks. He was unharmed except for that brutal thrust through his head.

There would be disagreements among the four doctors as to the right treatment to pursue, and their versions of what happened on the death night would vary startlingly. There was total agreement always on the astonishment they all felt at that first sight of Mr. Lincoln's extraordinary physique.

They were familiar with the dark, brown face, weather-worn and crisscrossed with lines, and they knew that Old Abe's neck, too, was leathery and wrinkled: the "old" in his nickname was apt. The stunning surprise was that the fifty-six-year-old President's body was that of a much younger man and was unbelievably perfect. The beautiful proportions, the magnificent muscular development, and the clear, firm flesh were all the more astounding because the visible man had given no clue. Charlie Taft pointed out that there was not one ounce of fat on the entire frame. Charles Leale was something of a student of classical sculpture, and he remarked immediately that the President could have been the model for Michelangelo's *Moses:* he had the same massive grandeur.

A steward arrived from the hospitals with the bottles, which had been filled with hot water downstairs, and the mustard plasters. Henry Safford trudged up from the basement kitchen with his collection of bottles. The hot-water bottles were laid along the sides of the President's legs, which had grown cold to a point above the knees. Outsized mustard plasters, like clammy pies, were placed over the entire upper surface of the body from ankles to neck. When in a few minutes Dr. Leale raised the corner of a sinapism —he disliked the layman's term, plaster—and saw no slightest pink tinge in the parchment skin, he ordered that a stronger paste of mustard and flour be mixed downstairs, and that the army blankets brought from the hospitals be heated. Soon Mr. Lincoln lay between walls of bottles and under steaming layers of wool, and clinging to him as though a death mold were being made of his form was that hot yellow dough, enfolded in an assortment of cloths. There was no reaching the cold within him, though; just as he had always said during the war years, there was no way of reaching the tired spot that was inside.

Here is the evidence of that agonized night of dying one hundred years ago: a torn, fading death-room photograph taken by a boarder named Julius Ulke only minutes after Lincoln's body was removed. Since Stanton had given stringent orders that no photographs be taken of the dead President, Ulke hid his bloody death scene lest it fall into the forbidden category. But his family preserved it, and here is the rumpled bed, here one of the pillows soaked with the President's blood, here the chair in which Mary Lincoln sat, begging, "Oh, shoot me, Doctor, why don't you shoot me, too!"

345

Stanton ran the country singlehanded after the assassination. As Lincoln lay dying, the Secretary of War questioned every witness he could find. He later arrested some who were innocent, like the Ford brothers. Yet he allowed John Parker, who had been the President's only bodyguard and had strayed from his post, to return to White House guard duty. Stanton was after bigger fish: announcing that Booth had been the tool of Confederate leaders, he offered $100,000 reward for the capture of Jefferson Davis, thus helping turn the climate of mercy Lincoln had hoped to establish into the tragedy of hate again. Through that long night in the room next to Lincoln's, Stanton controlled himself only by a superhuman effort, for he had an unreasoning, morbid fear of death. In 1833, when a young girl in his boardinghouse died of cholera and was buried immediately, he went that evening to dig her up—he could not believe she was really dead, as she had served him lunch that very day. In 1841, when his little daughter Lucy died, he had her body exhumed and kept the coffin in his room for two years. When his first wife died in 1844, he dressed and redressed her in her wedding clothes, and after she was buried he walked about the house at night, asking, "Where is Mary?" This portrait and the one opposite are from Brady negatives.

That night the capital of the United States was completely stricken. Through it all the government was driven and directed by one man—Lincoln's dynamic, unpredictable, and emotionally unstable Secretary of War, Edwin McMasters Stanton.

Stanton had just begun to undress for bed when downstairs a frantic voice shouted the incredible—Secretary of State Seward had been murdered. "Humbug!" Stanton grunted. Hadn't he just left Seward a few minutes ago? But soon the night outside was filled with the terrible news, and Stanton was dressing and rushing across the square to Seward's house. The Secretary of State lay unconscious across his bed, his cheek laid back by a deep knife wound inflicted by Booth's confederate Lewis Paine. The President, they were saying, had been murdered, too, and who knew how many others. Now, through all the floundering and confusion and pain, Stanton assumed total power. And he did so swiftly, rushing by hack to the Petersen house and setting up an office in the room next to where Lincoln lay. Along with his Assistant Secretary of War, Charles A. Dana, Stanton began dictating orders and telegrams. The country had to be alerted, witnesses questioned, the assassins identified and captured. Road blocks were to be set up in Maryland, all passenger trains and ships heading south on the Potomac were to be stopped, the sixty-eight forts and batteries guarding Washington were to be alerted, any suspicious persons in Alexandria were to be arrested, the whole countryside round about the city was to be patrolled. The orders to all commanders: Find a man named John Wilkes Booth, "twenty-five years old [*sic*], five feet eight inches tall, dark hair and mustache. Use all efforts to secure him."

It was a frenzied night for Stanton, a pudgy, curt, rude, disobliging but dedicated man who worked with a kind of demon energy every day and far into the night in the crumbling old War Department building, just a short walk for Lincoln across the White House lawn.

Now, all night long, as Stanton issued his orders from the room next door, people moved endlessly in and out of the tiny chamber where the President lay dying. Here came Senator Charles Sumner, Boston Brahmin and impatient abolitionist, together with Robert Lincoln. Sumner sat down at the head of the bed and took the President's hand. A doctor said, "It's no use, Mr. Sumner. He can't hear you. He is dead." "No, he isn't dead," replied Sumner. "Look at his face, he's breathing." "It will never be anything more than this," came the answer. Then Robert broke down in tears and Sumner put his arm around Lincoln's eldest son and held him close and tried to comfort him.

Gideon Welles, Lincoln's efficient, garrulous Secretary of the Navy, had attended the Cabinet meeting held on the morning of the President's last day. Along with the others he had heard the President tell of his strange dream of the

Stanton takes command

night before—one that he always had before some important event—of being in a strange vessel, sailing rapidly toward a shadowy shore. Lincoln had turned to Welles and remarked, "It has to do with your element, Mr. Welles, the water."

That evening Secretary Welles went up to bed about ten thirty, and soon afterward a Navy Department messenger called up to the window the news about Lincoln and Seward. While Welles was dressing he did an unprecedented thing: swearing in front of his wife. "Damn the Rebels," he said, "this is their work!"

Through the night Welles sat quietly beside Lincoln's bed; later he described the scene in his extraordinary diary. "The giant sufferer lay extended diagonally across the bed," Welles began. ". . . His slow, full respiration lifted the clothes with each breath that he took. His features were calm and striking. I had never seen them appear to better advantage than for the first hour, perhaps, that I was there. After that, his right eye began to swell and that part of his face became discolored."

On the night of the assassination, Andrew Johnson was staying at the Kirkwood House, at Twelfth Street and Pennsylvania Avenue, and in the middle of the night Stanton sent for him because he thought the Vice President should make an appearance at the dying President's bedside. Johnson had been there only a very few minutes when word came from the front room that Mrs. Lincoln wanted to pay another visit to her husband. It was quickly agreed that Johnson must be got rid of first, as Mrs. Lincoln despised him so. The Vice President went back to his hotel with a guard and spent the rest of the night excitedly walking up and down his room saying, "They shall suffer for this! They shall suffer for this!" Mrs. Lincoln never stopped believing Johnson was somehow mixed up in the assassination plot. A year later she wrote in one of her violent letters: ". . . that miserable inebriate Johnson. He never wrote me a line of condolence and behaved in the most brutal way. . . . As sure as you and I live, Johnson had some hand in all this."

Lincoln's gay, witty assistant private secretary, John Hay, was another of Mary Lincoln's pet dislikes. Once she had questioned the cost of the grain that Lincoln's secretaries' horses were eating in the White House stables, and when she economized by getting rid of an employee, she wanted Hay to turn over to her for her personal use the money the employee would have been paid. "The Hell-cat," Hay said of her, "is getting more Hell-cattical day by day." But when the terrible news reached him this April evening, he hurried to the Petersen house and several times during the night attempted to comfort the distraught First Lady.

Benjamin B. French, the Commissioner of Public Buildings, first incurred Mrs. Lincoln's wrath on the same subject over which she had fought with Hay—money. French re-

No one looked to Andrew Johnson to make decisions. Only a month had passed since he had misjudged the amount of brandy needed to carry him through his inauguration as Vice President, and many distrusted him. Now rumors flew that he had been drunk all night after Lincoln was shot, and that it had taken both a doctor and a barber, working feverishly, to get him ready to take the presidential oath, which was administered by Chief Justice Salmon P. Chase in Johnson's hotel just three hours after Lincoln died. But Secretary of the Treasury Hugh McCulloch, who was present at the ceremony, said Mr. Johnson handled himself very creditably, seemed properly grief-stricken, and in quiet and dignified tones begged the Cabinet members to remain in office and support him in his burdens. In the first days of his administration, since Stanton actually ran the country, Johnson merely received delegations in his temporary office in the Treasury Building, and assured his visitors he would punish treason. Later, as Johnson began to make bitter, spur-of-the-moment denunciations of the South, Secretary McCulloch remarked that it would have been better if Johnson had been stricken dumb on assuming the Presidency—his written speeches were fine, but whenever he spoke without preparation he became so wild he could easily be mistaken for a drunkard.

347

fused to manipulate the White House expense account and cover up for her when she overran her decorating allowance by thousands of dollars. At the Petersen house French controlled his true feelings, sought out Mrs. Lincoln in her front room, and took her hand. But privately, in his diary, he set down in verse what he really thought of her. She

> . . . *moved in all the insolence of pride*
> *As if the world beneath her feet she trod;*
> *Her vulgar bearing, jewels could not hide,*
> *And gold's base glitter was her only god!*

As the visitors came and went, the doctors kept up their frantic fight to do something, anything—probing the wound to keep it bleeding, trying to warm the President's cold body, trying to remember to put clean towels over the blood-soaked pillows whenever Mrs. Lincoln appeared, to save her the horror that transfixed everyone else. At 11:30 P.M. a great protrusion of the President's right eye was noted, and for the next twenty minutes there was twitching on the left side of his face. At five minutes before one o'clock, Lincoln began making a struggling motion with his arms. His chest muscles stiffened, his breath held, and then finally exhaled as the spasm passed. Twice during the night the Lincolns' pastor, Dr. Phineas D. Gurley, prayed, and everyone in the room got down on his knees. At a quarter to two and again at three o'clock, Mrs. Lincoln made visits to the bedside. She wept piteously, throwing herself upon her husband's body, begging the doctors to kill her and let her join him. Putting her face close to Lin-

348

Hermann Faber, an artist who saw the death room just after the body was removed, made a fairly realistic sketch of it showing Robert Lincoln and Secretary Welles seated by the bed, and Stanton standing by Welles. Many ludicrous drawings soon appeared, however, typified by the tidy Currier and Ives below, in which Mary Lincoln behaves with dignity while the sorrowing statesmen (including Andrew Johnson) look on. It is all sadly false, even to little Tad, who was never there.

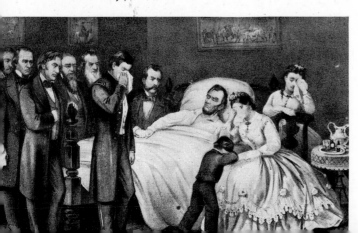

coln's, she pleaded, "Love, live but one moment to speak to our children—Oh, Oh that my little Taddy might see his father before he died." A spell of loud, rattling breathing by the President frightened her, and with a piercing shriek she fell fainting to the floor. Stanton ordered: "Take that woman out and do not let her in again!" As she was led down the hall, Mrs. Lincoln cried, "Oh, my God, and have I given my husband to die!" It was the last time she would see him alive.

Finally dawn came. It was Saturday morning, the fifteenth of April. As the end drew near Dr. Africanus King—a young Englishman with a flair for telling words—made notes. At 6:25, Lincoln's breaths were "jerking." At 6:40, "the expirations prolonged and groaning,—a deep, softly sonorous cooing sound at the end of each expiration." At 6:45, "respiration uneasy and grunting, lower jaw relaxed." Then, "a minute without a breath, face growing dark." At seven, "still breathing at long pauses." Now Dr. Gurley left Mrs. Lincoln in the front parlor and entered the death room.

At twenty-two minutes past seven o'clock Dr. Taft's hand, pressed upon Abraham Lincoln's chest, felt that great heart throb one last time and then go still. The Surgeon General, Dr. Joseph Barnes, touching the carotid artery, felt the last thrust of blood, as did Dr. Leale, who held the right wrist pulse. All night long Leale had held Lincoln's hand "so that in his darkness he would know he had a friend." Now the darkness was absolute.

The fullest account of that terribly sad, historic moment was made by James Tanner, a legless corporal who lived next door and who had been summoned to take down testimony through the night for Stanton. ". . . His stertorous breathing subsided a couple of minutes after 7 o'clock. From then till the end only the gentle rise and fall of his bosom gave indication that life remained. The Surgeon General was near the head of the bed, sometimes sitting on the edge, his finger on the pulse of the dying man. Occasionally he put his ear down to catch the lessening beats of his heart. . . . Dr. Gurley stood a little to the left of the bed. Mr. Stanton sat in a chair near the foot on the left . . . I stood quite near the head of the bed and from that position had full view of Mr. Stanton, across the president's body. At my right Robert Lincoln sobbed on the shoulder of Charles Sumner. Stanton's gaze was fixed intently on the countenance of his dying chief. The first indication that the dreaded end had come was at twenty-two minutes past seven, when the surgeon general gently crossed the pulseless hands of Lincoln across the motionless breast and rose to his feet. Rev. Dr. Gurley stepped forward and lifting his hands began 'Our Father and our God' . . . As 'Thy will be done, Amen' in subdued and tremulous tones floated through the little chamber, Mr. Stanton raised his head, the tears streaming down his face. A more agonized expression I never saw on a human countenance as he sobbed out the words: 'He belongs to the angels now.' "

While rumors fly, an autopsy is performed

As Mrs. Lincoln left the Petersen house to be driven back to the Executive Mansion, she stood a moment beside her carriage and cried, "That dreadful house! That dreadful house!" A few minutes later the body of her husband was carried out and placed in a hearse, the coffin wrapped in a star-spangled flag. Then, with measured tread and arms reversed, the little procession moved away—a lieutenant and ten privates. Slowly up Tenth Street to G the horses pulled the dead President back to the White House.

Meanwhile, far from regarding it as an honor to have Abraham Lincoln die in his boardinghouse, landlord William Petersen was in a black temper. Even before Mr. Lincoln's body had been removed, Petersen had advanced to the bed, seized one of the bloodstained pillows from beneath the head of the recently expired President, and hurled it angrily through the window into the yard. He soon made loud explanation. His house was a mess: all that blood and mud underfoot, unwashed basins and bottles piled up, and dozens of old leaking mustard plasters littering the hall. What was worse, he had read in the paper that the President had died in a tenement. He would let that paper know, and soon, that his was one of the most respectable dwelling houses in Washington.

For a few days after the murder, people talked a lot about what they had seen, and blew up scraps of information and guesswork, for the thrill of dabbling in a real-life mystery. There had been nearly two thousand people in the theatre, more than ninety over in the death room, and twenty-five who had borne the body. From all these conflicting accounts the story of that terrible night was emerging crazily.

Eight of the bearers insisted that theirs had been the honor of carrying the head. One, a New York grocer on a sight-seeing trip in Washington, announced that he had run up and supported an elbow, had moved along with his other hand on Lincoln's pulse, and recalled giving the weeping crowd the news that the injury would be fatal. Another bearer remembered that the President had sagged in the middle until two men were assigned to reach beneath him and push upward—he had been a pusher. As a third told it, the victim had made the trip extended perfectly flat on a shutter wrenched from a theatre window. One of the most positive recollections had Lincoln transported sitting upright in the rocking chair in which he had failed to rock out of range of John Wilkes Booth's huge bullet.

The picture of Booth's escape from Ford's Theatre was given earnestly, and with bewildering variations.

Booth had put one hand on the box rail, vaulted over it, and sailed through the air the twelve feet to the stage. As he jumped, his right spur had turned the framed engraving of Washington completely over and had snagged the blue Treasury Guards flag festooned around the front of the box; a shred of the blue material fluttered behind his heel all the way. Booth had risen, flourished his dagger, shouted "*Sic semper tyrannis!*" and strode out of sight.

Some said that the blue flag had not been draped around the box, but had been on a staff that stood straight up against the box's central pillar, and that Booth managed to flip his spurred heel up there and make the tear, then grasped the flagpole, slid down its length, and dropped to the stage. In another version, Booth rode the rail first as though it were a saddle, and his gait as he crossed the stage was a slow limp. He also coasted down the front of the box as though he were sledding, ran at top speed to the exit opposite, and didn't say a word. He landed on his hands first, he was hurt dreadfully, he went by moaning with pain. He soared fifteen feet from a crouched position, sauntered slowly to the footlights as though he were part of the troupe, flashed his knife blade in the gaslight, hissed "*Sic semper tyrannis!*" with deathly pale face and eyes glittering, almost emitting fire, turned and with defiantly unhurried gait stalked off the stage.

There were two especially far-out variations. In one, Booth hopped across the stage like a toad and the blue cloth hopped along just out of time behind him. In the other, he was so completely paralyzed from the fall that his helpers had to throw a rope to him and he was pulled off into the wings.

A young girl eyewitness contributed the fact that Booth had asked her just the day before whether *tyrannis* was spelled with two *r*'s or two *n*'s. She agreed with the versions of Booth's swift escape, but added an extra morsel—the maddened crowd had heaved her up on the stage, and in a half faint she realized the actor who played Lord Dundreary was fanning her with his wig.

The stories of the President's last moments in the death room over at the Petersen house were just as baffling and fuzzy. To some in the room Lincoln's breathing was a frightening thing—a deep snoring, a wild gurgling. To others, it had a musical quality—Stanton likened it to an Aeolian harp.

There were watchers by the bedside who heard not a sound of any kind; the President left the world after long, agonizing minutes of utter silence. The only way of knowing it was all over was to watch the doctors with their fingers over the heart, the big artery in the neck, and the two wrist pulses. When they darted looks at each other of question and then agreement, Dr. Barnes made the announcement.

Some said that Stanton rose from his knees, smoothed Lincoln's eyelids, and pulled down the window shades. Maunsell B. Field, Assistant Secretary of the Treasury, said convincingly that right at that time he noticed that Mr.

Lincoln's eyes were not quite closed, so he smoothed and closed them.

Now comes a real and fascinating conflict. Dr. Leale recounted, "Then I gently smoothed the President's contracted facial muscles, took two coins from my pocket, placed them over his eyelids, and drew a white cloth over the martyr's face."

Thomas McCurdy Vincent of the War Department claimed it was he who smoothed Lincoln's eyelids and placed the coins. He wrote, "Soon after eight the devoted War Minister had ordered all to be arranged for the removal of the body to the Executive Mansion and left me as his representative until the transfer should take place. It was about this time that pressing and smoothing the eyes of the dead President, I placed coins on them to close them for a last long slumber."

These two statements made Colonel George V. Rutherford angrily indignant, because it was he and he alone who had placed the coins on Lincoln's eyes. He resolved to produce as evidence something a little more convincing than the mere words of honorable men. He would get up an exhibit of the very coins themselves that he had placed, silver half dollars dated 1854 and 1861, and he would use sealing wax and impressive ribbon and get the signed certification of a man no one could question. The man was General Daniel H. Rucker of the Quartermaster's Department, whose soldiers escorted Lincoln's body home from the Petersen house; General Rucker officially received it into the White House, and ordered it placed for the autopsy.

As the claims and counterclaims flew, as the stories of that terrible night were told and retold, the President's body lay in the Guest Room at the northeast corner of the second floor of the White House, resting upon two boards laid across trestles. There, at eleven o'clock on Saturday morning, the autopsy was begun.

First, the top of the President's skull was sawed straight around on a line above his ears so that the top could be lifted off. Two pathologists from the Army Medical Museum did the actual work—Assistant Surgeon J. Janvier Woodward and Assistant Surgeon Edward Curtis. Young Curtis movingly described the scene.

". . . Dr. Woodward and I proceeded to open the head and remove the brain down to the track of the ball. The latter had entered a little to the left of the median line at the back of the head, had passed almost directly forwards through the center of the brain and lodged. Not finding it readily, we proceeded to remove the entire brain, when, as I was lifting the latter from the cavity of the skull, suddenly the bullet dropped out through my fingers and fell, breaking the solemn silence of the room with its clatter, into an empty basin that was standing beneath. There it lay

The fatal bullet— shown here slightly enlarged—was a half- inch lead ball that flattened on impact.

upon the white china, a little black mass no bigger than the end of my finger—dull, motionless and harmless, yet the cause of such mighty changes in the world's history as we may perhaps never realize."

Now, the autopsy done, undertaker Dr. Charles D. Brown of Brown and Alexander took over. (Three years before, Brown had prepared the body of little Willie Lincoln, doing such a handsome job that Lincoln twice had the coffin opened to look upon his son's face.) Andrew Johnson, who had just been sworn in as the new President of the United States by Chief Justice Chase at the Kirkwood House, entered the room and watched briefly. Brown and his assistant drained Lincoln's blood through the jugular vein. Then they made a cut on the inside of the thigh and through it force-pumped a chemical preparation which soon hardened the body like marble. The face was shaved except for a short tuft left at the chin. The eyes were closed, the eyebrows arched, the mouth reset in the slight smile that had been on the President's face when he died.

As the undertakers worked, Dr. Curtis suggested to Surgeon General Barnes, who was also in the room, that Lincoln's brain be weighed. Again Dr. Curtis describes the scene: ". . . silently, in one corner of the room, I prepared the brain for weighing. As I looked at the mass of soft gray and white substance that I was carefully washing, it was impossible to realize that it was that mere clay upon whose workings, but the day before, rested the hopes of the nation. I felt more profoundly impressed than ever with the mystery of that unknown something which may be named 'vital spark' as well as anything else, whose absence or presence makes all the immeasurable difference between an inert mass of matter owing obedience to no laws but those governing the physical and chemical forces of the universe, and on the other hand, a living brain by whose silent, subtle machinery a world may be ruled. The weighing of the brain . . . gave approximate results only, since there had been some loss of brain substance, in consequence of the wound, during the hours of life after the shooting. But the figures, as they were, seemed to show that the brain weight was not above the ordinary for a man of Lincoln's size."

Now Lincoln's body was covered with a white cloth, and a fine cambric handkerchief was spread over his face. Upon the pillow and over the breast were scattered white flowers and green leaves. Guards were posted at the door, and the doctors began to pack up and leave.

Later in the day Stanton supervised the clothing of the body—from the black suit Lincoln had worn at his second inauguration to a low collar and small bow tie and white kid gloves. Stanton decided that the dark putty color under Lincoln's eyes and down his cheeks would be left there for posterity. It was, he said, "part of the history of the event."

Twelve-year-old Thomas ("Tad") Lincoln—here seen a few weeks after the assassination, a mourning band on his hat—was his father's pet and the White House tyrant. After his older brother Willie died in 1862, Tad became even more tightly glued to the President's side. He was mercurial like his mother—mischievous, fun-loving, work-hating, destructive—and was known (behind his back) as a spoiled brat. But his naughtiness was ignored by his parents. He interrupted important state meetings; he once turned a hose on Secretary Stanton; he practiced his whittling on the White House furniture; he drove his team of goats through the East Room. If he saw his father walking down the hall, he would race to him, give him a tight, fierce hug, and dash away again. While Lincoln worked in his office until midnight, Tad would fall asleep on the floor under the President's table, and when the last paper was signed, Lincoln would carry the boy down the hall and put him to bed. Tad was allowed to run wild and just grow. "Let him run," said Lincoln, "there's time enough for him to learn his letters and get pokey." Tad never did learn in his father's lifetime; and at ten he still could not understand that a small gold dollar was the same in value as a handful of larger coins. But he was acquisitive: several times he bought out the supply of gingerbread and apples of an old woman who kept a stand a few blocks from the White House and set up in business for himself nearer its entrance, where he could pressure visitors to buy his wares. His father laughed and thought Tad was smart and enterprising, just as he laughed fondly when the boy, in anticipation of a national Fast Day, hid a succulent supply of goodies from the family kitchen in the coach house—where he could retire and munch while the nation went hungry. But Tad was also tenderhearted. On the night of April 11, as the President stood in the candle-lighted window above the White House portico to deliver what turned out to be his last speech, someone in the crowd below cried out, "What shall we do with the Rebels?" A voice answered, "Hang them!" and Tad said quickly, "Oh, no, we must hang on to them." "That's right, Tad," said Lincoln, "we must hang on to them."

The mantle of grief

While *Our American Cousin* was being performed at Ford's, a gala production of *Aladdin! or His Wonderful Lamp* was under way a few blocks away at Grover's Theatre. Just before a moment in the Aladdin extravaganza where a man was supposed to tumble to the stage from a balloon, the manager stepped to the footlights to announce that President Lincoln had been shot. For a moment there was silence, then a voice called out that it was a trick of pickpockets to set the audience in a panic. But suddenly a boy sprang from his seat and went shrieking—"like a wounded deer," the papers later said—to the theatre's door and out.

Twelve-year-old Tad Lincoln had been taken to Grover's Theatre that evening by White House doorkeeper Alphonso Donn, a great favorite with the Lincoln family. Now he was driven home, where his other doorman friend, Tom Pendel, tried to calm his fears and comfort him. About midnight Pendel got the boy up to his father's room, undressed him, and lay down on the trundle bed beside him till he dropped off to sleep.

When she returned to the White House the next morning, Mrs. Lincoln refused to enter either her own bedroom, in the southwest corner of the second floor, or Mr. Lincoln's, next to it. She finally chose a room with no memories which she had fitted up for the President so that he could do some writing there during the summer. The shades were lowered, and Mary Lincoln got into bed and began an endless tossing and sobbing. Tad had run weeping to meet her as she got out of the carriage and buried his face in the folds of her dress, and he now stood terrified at the foot of his mother's bed, watching her as she lay very near convulsions.

"Don't cry so, Mama, or you will make me cry too," said Tad. That was the only thing that stopped Mrs. Lincoln's hysterics: she could not bear to see little Tad cry.

No one could be hardhearted enough not to feel sorry for Mary Lincoln now. Her desolation was complete because she did not have the character to meet her grief with any dignity and fortitude. She had hidden herself away to rail against her fate, while the country prepared to bury her husband. All during the war years it had been a kind of sport to make fun of the President's wife from the West and let her read in print that she was a dumpy woman with no taste who wore overgorgeous, too-low-necked dresses, that she carried whole flower gardens on her head, that she didn't know any better than to wear her rings over her gloves. Now that kind of criticism was silenced, but pity could not bring liking.

The news that President Lincoln was dead spread like a prairie fire across the nation. The people heard the news and were stunned, and each in his own heart suffered alone and in his own way. The mantle of grief was like a bond, so that all of a sudden friends felt a terrible closeness and strangers passing in the street knew what was in each other's eyes and hearts and were brothers.

Her husband's murder was not the first grief Mary Lincoln had had to bear. She and the President had already lost two children. Eddie, the second son, who followed Robert, had died at three of consumption in 1850, while the Lincolns were still in Springfield. Sorrowfully his father ordered a marble slab (left above) carved with the name and date, a dove with outstretched wings, and the words, "Of such is the kingdom of Heaven." Then, eleven months later, appeared William Wallace Lincoln (right), a perfect, beautiful boy to be rocked in Eddie's cradle and dressed in Eddie's first clothes. Always, through Willie's twelve years of life, he was to be bound up in his parents' thoughts and love with the child they had lost, and when Willie had to die they felt they were losing Eddie all over again. Willie was a quiet, thoughtful boy who wanted to be good as much as Tad wanted to be naughty. Whereas Tad had no interest in learning, Willie studied faithfully, memorized long portions of the Bible for Sunday school, and told his mother and father he was going to be a preacher when he grew up. During the last days of January, 1862, he caught cold after riding his pony in a slushy half-snow. He got no better, and though one or the other of his parents was always at his bedside, and though consulting doctors were called in, he died on February 20. For a long time the President was inconsolable. "My poor boy," he said, "he was too good for this earth. God has called him home. I know that he is much better off in heaven, but then we loved him so. It is hard, hard to have him die!" The minister's eulogy revealed that the dying boy had given his savings—six dollars—to a missionary society. Father and son were to be reunited in death. After her husband's funeral, Mary Lincoln had Willie's little metal coffin removed from its resting place in Georgetown's Oak Hill Cemetery, enclosed in a new black walnut one, and taken to the depot where the presidential funeral train stood waiting. His father would join Willie soon for the long, slow trip back to Springfield.

Washington says good-by to Mr. Lincoln

The business of saying good-by to the President was to take the city of Washington almost a full week. The plan was for Lincoln to be carried downstairs to the East Room in his huge coffin on Monday night; there, starting Tuesday morning, he would be on view to the public and there, on Wednesday, his official funeral would be held. Afterward his body was to be taken in procession from the White House to the Capitol, where he would lie in state in the Rotunda until Friday morning. Finally, a special train would take him slowly north, then west through a country of sorrow toward Springfield, on almost the same route he had taken east four years before.

George A. Harrington, Assistant Secretary of the Treasury, was put in charge of the funeral preparations, and now he issued orders for the building of a catafalque in the East Room. Upstairs in her room Mrs. Lincoln was wracked day and night by the sound of nails being hammered as carpenters worked on the huge structure. She cowered and put her fingers to her ears, saying every blow sounded like a pistol shot. She sent a request to Secretary Harrington, begging him not to dismantle the catafalque until she had moved out of the White House, which meant it would stand there—the "Temple of Death" it came to be called—for five whole weeks, while souvenir-hunting citizens snipped away at it.

On Tuesday, Lincoln belonged to the people. Early that morning the line began forming outside the White House and was soon a mile long, six and seven abreast. Promptly at nine-thirty the west driveway gate was opened, and the crowds silently filed in through the heavily draped south portico. In the center of the East Room stood the catafalque. Since it reached up as high as eleven feet from the floor, the middle one of the three enormous, low-hanging crystal chandeliers had had to be removed and its gas pipe capped; the other two were completely shrouded in black bags, like giant bunches of grapes. The eight tall mirrors over the eight marble mantelpieces were swathed from top to bottom with black cloth over their frames and white cloth stretching the length of their glasses. From all the room's cornices hung black streamers, but it had been impossible to cover the blood-red and gold velvet wallpaper which Mrs. Lincoln had so extravagantly sent to France for—had actually dispatched a decorator on an ocean steamer to bring home.

The catafalque which bore Abraham Lincoln's coffin had been built at top speed and with no regard for economy. It had been designed by Benjamin B. French, Commissioner of Public Buildings, who was in charge of everything in the funeral that had directly to do with Lincoln's body. From the tops of four seven-foot-high posts rose an arched canopy to the height of eleven feet from the floor. Its upper side was made of black alpaca and the finest black velvet, which, in turn, was decorated with swooping festoons of black crape. The underside of the canopy was white fluted satin which

caught and reflected a little of what light there was in the room down on the face below.

The $1,500 coffin had been ready since late Sunday afternoon, after marathon work by the undertaker for more than twenty-four hours. It was the last glorious word in funeral trappings. The wood was walnut, but not an inch of it showed, for it was entirely covered with the finest black broadcloth. It was six feet six inches long on the outside and must have been a tight fit on the inside for its six-foot, four-inch tenant, for the white satin lining was quilted and lavishly stuffed to make the resting place a soft one.

Inside the walnut case was an extra heavy lining of lead. On each side were four massive silver handles, and on the center of the lid there was a shield outlined in silver tacks in the center of which was a silver plate with the inscription

Abraham Lincoln
16th President of the United States
Born February 12, 1809
Died April 15, 1865

The lid was hinged to fold back a third of the way down, so as to expose the President's face and shoulders. In the gloom of the great East Room the people who came to pay their last respects to Lincoln were directed by officers to the foot of the catafalque; there they divided into single lines on each side, mounted the step, and walked along beside the coffin, pausing to look down at the face for an average of one second each.

At 5:30 P.M. the public was shut out, and for the next two hours special privileged groups were admitted to the East Room. Then carpenters entered in force; they had a big job

to do before the funeral the next morning. They began to build a series of steps arranged like an amphitheatre, beginning low about five feet away from the catafalque and growing higher back to the East Room walls, so that everyone invited could have a clear view of the dead President and the clergymen conducting the funeral.

Extra trains, crowded to the platforms, had been running into the city of Washington for the last two days, and people had been driving in from towns and villages in carriages or buggies or even hay wagons—the authorities figured that 6,000 people slept Tuesday night on floors of houses or hotels (Willard's Hotel turned away 400 applicants) or in their vehicles or on blankets spread on whatever grass plots they could find. Washington was bursting—there were 100,000 human beings in the city, and 60,000 of them were prepared to watch a procession of 40,000 following the White House services on Wednesday.

At sunrise on the morning of the funeral the people who had been sleeping were waked by the booming of cannon in all the forts encircling the city, with a counterpoint of tolling bells in church towers and firehouses. It was a radiantly beautiful day—warm, cloudless, with a bright sun—and as early as eight o'clock there were throngs on Pennsylvania Avenue outside the White House and under the trees of Lafayette Square Park across the way. The heavy black draping all across the great front of the mansion contrasted with the spring gaiety of the bright green lawns and all the trees in blossom.

Every house and store in Washington was shut tight for the day. The rich had sent messengers to other cities to buy mourning decorations when the supply in the capital gave out, but even the poorest shanties had their bits of black

cloth tacked up, and it was these humble, fluttering shreds that made people choke up. The big displays only filled them with awe.

By eleven o'clock, tickets were being presented and the majority of those invited entered the funeral chamber through the Green Room. In the Blue Room, the adjoining oval parlor, appeared the great names. It was crowded almost full with the late President's personal cavalry guard from Ohio, who had ridden their matched black horses wherever Mr. Lincoln went. A path two and a half feet wide was opened in their midst, and along this path and through the Green Room passed General Grant, Admiral Farragut, the Supreme Court justices, and the diplomatic corps. At two minutes to twelve President Johnson and his friend Preston King entered, followed by former Vice President Hamlin and the Cabinet; for everyone, there was the shock of Seward's absence and the thought of how near they had come to standing beside two coffins today.

Lincoln's complexion had always been dark, but now, instead of being even darker, it was unpleasingly lighter, a grayish putty color. Around his mouth he still had the faintly happy expression that those who watched him die saw come over his face a few minutes after he stopped breathing. They said it resembled "an effort of life," as though he really had found peace. The trouble was that the smile was frozen on a face that was unfamiliar in its unresponsive stoniness. Gone was the mobility that so entranced anyone who had watched him in life: the magic lighting-up of the features that had made a plain man handsome when his mind struck sparks.

At each corner of the catafalque was an officer of a special guard of honor. At the foot of the coffin sat Robert Lincoln, along with Ninian W. Edwards and Clark M. Smith of Springfield, the husbands of his mother's two sisters, and two of his mother's first cousins, Dr. Lyman Beecher Todd and General John B. S. Todd. Lincoln's two young secretaries, John Nicolay and John Hay, stood beside Robert. Mrs. Lincoln would have been at the foot of the coffin, too, had she been there at all. Instead, she remained upstairs in bed the entire day.

General Grant, with tears in his eyes, sat alone at the President's head, facing a cross of lilies. Just a little over a year before, on March 8, 1864, he had paid his first visit to the White House after being made lieutenant general. It was the evening of a weekly reception, and Mr. Lincoln, surrounded by citizens in the oval Blue Room, spied the shy soldier and recognized him immediately from his photographs. The President stepped up the line to greet his new

No photograph exists of the catafalque built in the East Room for the President's funeral. Harper's Weekly's engraving showed the family minister offering a benediction. The artist included a heavily veiled Mrs. Lincoln; actually she did not attend, but remained prostrated upstairs.

head of the armies, took hold of him and moved him along to Mrs. Lincoln, saying, "Here is General Grant. What a surprise! What a delight!"

President Johnson stood at the east side of the coffin and behind him, the Cabinet. Standing neatly in their appointed squares were the clergy, the Supreme Court justices, governors of states, officers of the Army and Navy, a tremendous New York delegation, members of the Senate and House, members of the boards of the Christian and sanitary commissions, forty mourners from Kentucky and Illinois, the pallbearers, heads of bureaus, assistant secretaries, the diplomatic corps, and many others, such as the nurse who had taken care of Willie Lincoln in his last illness. At the time of the assassination she herself was ill in a hospital, of typhoid fever. But she was determined to look for a last time on Mr. Lincoln's face, and she was carried down the hospital stairs and brought to the White House.

Just before the first of the four ministers who were to conduct the service began speaking, Johnson and Preston King stepped up to the coffin, mounted the foot-high ledge at its side, looked down intently at the face for a moment, then retired to their places a few feet back. Johnson had been visited by many delegations in his office in the Treasury Building since Lincoln's death, and he was trying to show everyone that he was going to be a strong President. He began all his interviews by praising Lincoln, lamenting his loss, and saying that all his own efforts would go to carrying on the great work his predecessor had begun—Lincoln's policies would be his policies. This he invariably followed up by a statement that treason was the most vicious of all crimes, and those guilty of it must be punished. "Very vigorous," said some. "Vindictive," said others. "We will have no trouble now," said all those who had opposed Mr. Lincoln's gentle and forgiving attitude toward those who had rebelled.

At exactly ten minutes past twelve Dr. Hall began the Episcopal burial service: "I am the resurrection and the life, saith the Lord; he that believeth in me, though he were dead, yet shall he live, and whosoever liveth and believeth in me shall never die."

Bishop Simpson of the Methodist Episcopal Church delivered a prayer in which he likened Lincoln to Moses, who brought his people to the edge of the Promised Land but was not permitted to enter it. When he was done, all six hundred listeners were in tears.

Lincoln's pastor, Dr. Gurley, gave the funeral sermon, speaking of the "cruel, cruel hand, that dark hand of the assassin, which smote our honored, wise and noble President, and filled the land with sorrow. . . ."

While the funeral was going on, twenty-five million people all across the nation and even in Canada were hearing similar sermons and prayers in their churches, hearing that Lincoln's work on earth was finished and that God had removed him purposefully; hearing how regrettable it was

that Lincoln had died in such low surroundings; hearing him likened to Washington, the savior of his country; to Moses, deprived of his reward; even to Christ—for Lincoln had been murdered on the anniversary of the Crucifixion.

After the White House services the six hundred people went outside, blinking in the sudden strong sunlight. Twelve Veteran Reserve Corps sergeants, who were to be the only ones ever to lift the coffin until it reached the Springfield tomb, now carried it, lid closed, outdoors and placed it on the funeral car waiting behind its six white horses at the mansion's front door. The platform on which the coffin rested was eleven feet off the ground, high enough so that everyone in the crowd along the streets would see the object of greatest interest. Much of the height was accounted for by the wheels of the car (right), which were

A contemporary photograph shows the funeral procession moving down Pennsylvania Avenue toward its goal (top right): the Capitol. Not visible is the ornate, high-wheeled funeral car (below), drawn by six white horses.

LINCOLN MUSEUM, WASHINGTON, D.C.

enormous though seemingly frail, with spokes that looked too spindly for the important journey they were to make.

As the procession began to move, the minute guns took up their regular booming, and again the church and fire-house bells began to toll. Lincoln's old friend and body-guard, Ward Hill Lamon, had made the arrangements for the great procession, and he had done it well. Some of the units had been waiting for hours on side streets, and they joined the marching lines just as had been planned. Leading the procession and preceding the coffin on its high black car along Pennsylvania Avenue—full of ruts and potholes made from dragging heavy war supplies over it for four years—was a detachment of Negro troops. They had been the second unit to enter Richmond at its surrender. Officers of the Army, Navy, and Marine Corps followed. Then came the marshals, the clergymen who had conducted the funeral, the doctors who had attended the President on his death-bed, the twenty-two pallbearers, General Grant and Admiral Farragut, and finally the civilian mourners.

Just behind the hearse walked Mr. Lincoln's favorite horse, branded *U.S.,* bearing his master's boots reversed in the stirrups. Many people who had seen the President riding this horse now remembered the tall figure with the plug hat slipped back on his head, his feet in the long stirrups. Behind the hearse Robert Lincoln and Tad rode in a carriage together, with doorkeeper Tom Pendel up behind. The two brothers rode close enough to their father's body to see the men's hats in the crowds along the sidewalks being removed by the hundreds as the colossal coffin with all its silver ornaments shining in the bright sunlight passed by.

Many convalescent soldiers had left their beds in the Washington hospitals to march out of respect to their late Commander in Chief, and though some were too weak to go far, there were those on crutches who actually hobbled all the way to the Capitol. The colored citizens of Washington made one of the most impressive sights of all. They walked in lines of forty, straight across the avenue from curb to curb, four thousand of them. They wore high silk hats and white gloves and marched in dignified silence, holding hands.

The scene was solemn and impressive as the procession swept around into Pennsylvania Avenue from Fifteenth Street—and suddenly, movingly, the whole mile-and-a-half distance leading to the Capitol came into view. Every window, housetop, and tree was weighted down with silent watchers, the sidewalks were crowded, and there were many colored people with very young children. The grandeur and sadness of it all was indescribable. Every face in line was solemn—and most were streaked with tears. The measured tread of the marchers, the slow rolling of the wheels of the gun carriages over the cobblestones, the dirges of the thirty bands, the beat, beat, beat of the muffled drums—the sounds as well as the sights—made the day unforgettable.

357

"I knowed they'd kill him"

Amid the solemn pageantry of the funeral in Washington, one family was not represented—Mr. Lincoln's own people, those who had raised him and grown up with him. But they had received the heartbreaking news. Dennis Hanks, the cousin who had lived with Abe in a cabin in Indiana, took the news out to an old woman on the Illinois prairie. This was Sarah Bush Lincoln (opposite page), Abe's stepmother, born December 13, 1788, and twice a widow. No one knew the origins of the boy from the wilderness the way Sarah did, and his yearnings. And no one was more responsible for the paths he had taken. A widow with three children of her own, Sarah married Abe's father, Thomas Lincoln, after the boy's mother died of the "milksick"—drinking milk from cows that had eaten poison snakeroot.

When their new stepmother arrived, Abe and his sister Sarah liked her immediately. She was tall, slim, and curly-haired, with lovely white skin, blue-gray eyes, and a beautiful nature. She scrubbed Abe and his sister, made one family of all five children—six, with Dennis Hanks—cooked the good game with which the forest was filled, and made Thomas clear more land and raise vegetables. She also got him to put a wood floor in the cabin and stop the roof from leaking. Although she could not read or even sign her own name, Sarah brought with her three books—Webster's Speller, *Robinson Crusoe,* and *The Arabian Nights.* Abe already owned *Aesop's Fables* and *The Pilgrim's Progress,* and there was the family Bible which his own mother had read daily to him. The boy, "raised to farmwork," as he said of himself, spent long hours reading—borrowing every neighbor's book within walking distance. Sarah's greatest contribution to her stepson's life was persuading her husband not to disturb this reading time or force Abe to turn wholly to physical labor. She had felt immediate kinship with this boy. "His mind and mine," she said proudly, "what little I had, seemed to run together, move in the same channel."

Later, when Thomas and Sarah lived in their cabin in Illinois, Lincoln came as often as he could when he was practicing law in Springfield or riding the circuit. Mary Lincoln never went the seventy miles to see her husband's parents, nor did she ever invite Sarah to Springfield or allow her sons to meet such humble relatives. A few days before he went east to be inaugurated President of the United States, Lincoln made the trip once more to see the woman he wrote and spoke to as "Mother." He brought her a woolen shawl and a black wool dress. He took her in his arms and she cried over him. She told him she would never see him again and that he would be killed.

So when Dennis Hanks set out for Sarah's cabin with the dread news, the old lady knew before he spoke. "Aunt Sairy," Dennis said, "Abe's dead."

"Yes, I know, Denny, I knowed they'd kill him. I ben awaiting fur it."

Several weeks before this mournful day, the President and his wife were driving by horse and buggy along the James River in Virginia when they came to an old country graveyard. It was far from the busy world and had tall trees, and on the graves the buds of spring flowers were opening in the sunlight. They both wanted to stop and walk through it, and they did. Mr. Lincoln, said his wife, seemed thoughtful and impressed. He said, "Mary, you are younger than I. You will survive me. When I am gone, lay my remains in some quiet place like this."

Twenty days after the shooting at Ford's Theatre, the President got his wish. After twelve funerals in twelve cities as he was borne home to his prairie state, his long coffin was placed in a hillside tomb in Oak Ridge Cemetery in Springfield, Illinois,—with tender leaves of spring opening on all the trees and a little brook, brimming with April rains, dashing joyfully by.

Sarah Bush Lincoln (opposite page) heard the news of her stepson's assassination in the tiny Illinois cabin above, where she lived all during his Presidency. The sad tidings were brought by Dennis Hanks (left above), Lincoln's cousin, who had taught young Abe to write, using a buzzard's quill. In 1831 cousin John Hanks (right) had helped Abe build a flatboat on which they floated all the way down-river to New Orleans, with hogs to sell.

Two shots rang out in the railroad station, and the President of the United States slumped to the floor, mortally wounded

DRAWN BY W. A. ROGERS FOR *Harper's Weekly*, JULY 8, 1881

Charles Guiteau fires the second bullet from his .44 revolver, and the stricken Garfield starts to fall. Secretary of State James G. Blaine (foreground), who had been walking arm in arm with the President only seconds before, stands frozen in shocked horror.

"MURDER MOST FOUL"

By ARCHIE ROBERTSON

Early on the morning of July 2, 1881, President James A. Garfield was awakened in the White House by his two older sons, Harry, seventeen, and James, fifteen. Their mood was sportive, for they were all about to leave on a vacation together. They challenged their father to jump over the bed. Garfield, whom Thomas Wolfe included in that procession of "gravely vacant and bewhiskered faces" between Lincoln and McKinley, was indeed bewhiskered. But he was not a stuffed shirt: he jumped over the bed.

Others of the President's five children were with their mother at Elberon, New Jersey. Here Lucretia Garfield, to whom he had been happily married for almost a quarter of a century, was recuperating by the seashore from a month-long siege of malaria that had proved nearly fatal. Her recovery was yet another reason for rejoicing in the prospect of this happy day. First, the family planned to do a little yachting at a millionaire's estate on the Hudson; then they would proceed to Williamstown, Massachusetts, where Garfield was to speak at the commencement exercises of his alma mater, Williams College. It would be the twenty-fifth reunion of the President's class. Best of all, his old friend and personal hero, Mark Hopkins, who was still teaching at Williams, would go with them afterward into the White Mountains for some climbing. Garfield, who had taught school himself, liked to say that his idea of a college education was "Mark Hopkins on one end of a log and a student on the other." He wanted his two boys to meet Hopkins.

Now, after breakfast at the White House, the door was opened for them by Thomas Pendel, a curly-headed, stately Negro who often recalled that he had opened the door on an April night in 1865, when Abraham and Mary Lincoln had left for an evening at the theatre. On this July morning the presidential party, including several members of the Cabinet who were to see the Garfields off, travelled briskly to the railroad depot, at the site now occupied by the National Gallery of Art. At 9:20 A.M. a policeman opened the carriage door; when the President asked how much time they had, he answered, "About ten minutes, sir." So Garfield sat chatting sociably with Secretary of State James G. Blaine.

There was still no Secret Service, and, just as in Lincoln's time, the safety of the President was left to the local police. But Officer Patrick Kearney, on guard by the carriage, was sober, conscientious, and intelligent. He was no doubt sorry that Garfield had come so early, for there was something else he wanted to do. A few minutes before, he had overheard a stranger outside the depot ask a hack driver if he could "get away from the station in a hurry." The man had looked respectable, but Kearney had thought the remark vaguely suspect and would have liked to investigate. There was no chance for it now.

Garfield himself had never—with one recent and striking exception—shown any particular concern about his safety. He had been President only four months, but he had been in public life since 1863 as congressman from Ohio, and before that had displayed personal courage on the field of battle. The risk of assassination, he had written to a friend the previous November, "can no more be guarded against than death by lightning; and it is not best to worry about either." However, just two nights before this July 2, he had done an uncharacteristic thing. He had asked his Secretary of War, who was Robert Todd Lincoln, to sit down and describe in detail the assassination of his famous father. Garfield had never been personally very close to his Secretary of War. The President belonged to the liberal wing of the Republican party; Lincoln, a corporation lawyer, was a conservative and sat in the Cabinet chiefly because of his illustrious name. But of course he complied with the President's request, and for more than an hour, from his store of painful memories, answered questions. He may have told the story that Lincoln himself, shortly before his death, had dreamed of hearing weeping in the White House, seeing a coffin there, and asking a soldier who it was. "The President," the dream soldier had replied.

Now the ten minutes until train time was almost up. Garfield and Blaine descended and entered the ladies' waiting room at the B Street entrance of the station, walking arm in arm toward the main waiting room.

At the door between the two waiting rooms they disengaged, and the President walked ahead—but only for a step or so. Suddenly two quick shots rang out close behind him. He cried out, "My God, what is this?" and collapsed, bleeding heavily, as Blaine leaped

Leslie's Illustrated, JULY 23, 1881

Mrs. Garfield and fourteen-year-old Mollie, awaiting the President at Elberon on the New Jersey shore, rushed to his White House bedside. "From the moment he saw them," a reporter noted, "[he] seemed to gain in strength and spirits."

While soldiers guarded the house and doctors worked to save the patient's life, Lucretia Garfield ("Crete" to her husband) prepared special dishes, exuded confidence in the sickroom, and snatched a bit of rest whenever she could.

to his aid. The station had been sparsely occupied, and there was little commotion. A station janitor called police and doctors. Officer Kearney, meanwhile, had quickly arrested the assailant, who in fact made no great effort to escape.

It was the same man Kearney had noticed earlier querying a hack driver about getting away in a hurry—a slender, sallow man with thin, dark-brown whiskers. He had been loitering around the station since before nine o'clock. He was Charles Guiteau, age thirty-nine, accurately described by the *New York Times* as "a half-crazed, pettifogging lawyer, who has been an unsuccessful applicant for office under the Government, and who has led a precarious existence in several of the large cities of the country." In Washington, he had been known for not paying his bills at a succession of boarding houses, and in recent weeks he had begun to look almost like a tramp. Yet for this occasion he had managed a clean suit and a shoeshine. There was twenty cents in his pocket.

Now he declaimed, "I did it and will go to jail for it. I am a Stalwart and Arthur will be President." The Stalwarts were the anti-reform wing of the Republican party, including the political bosses and spoilsmen with whom Garfield had recently been at odds, and Vice President Chester A. Arthur was of their number. "The President's tragic death was a sad necessity, but it will **unite** the Republican Party and save the Re-

public," said a letter found in Guiteau's pocket. It was soon evident that he really did intend to go to jail. It was in anticipation of mob violence that he had arranged with a hack driver to take him away from the station, so that he could make his way later to the safety of jail. He had already been to the jail, in fact, to look it over in advance, and had decided that it would do. Some days earlier, when Garfield took his convalescent wife to New Jersey, Guiteau had planned to kill him at the station but had been touched, then, by Lucretia's frailty and by the obvious affection between husband and wife. He had also spied on the President in church—which seemed an ideal place for anyone to die—but had not drawn his gun for fear of hitting innocent persons. In recent weeks Guiteau had been sitting night after night on a bench in Lafayette Park, facing the White House, waiting for the President to appear, trying to make up his mind to shoot. He had no doubt been there on the evening of June 30 while Garfield had been speaking to Robert Todd Lincoln about his father's assassination.

A few minutes after Guiteau had been led away, the first physicians arrived, among them the District of Columbia Health Officer, Dr. Smith Townsend. He found the President still on the depot floor, still in shock. He administered half an ounce of brandy and aromatic spirits of ammonia, and ordered him carried upstairs and laid on a mattress in an office. Secretary

362

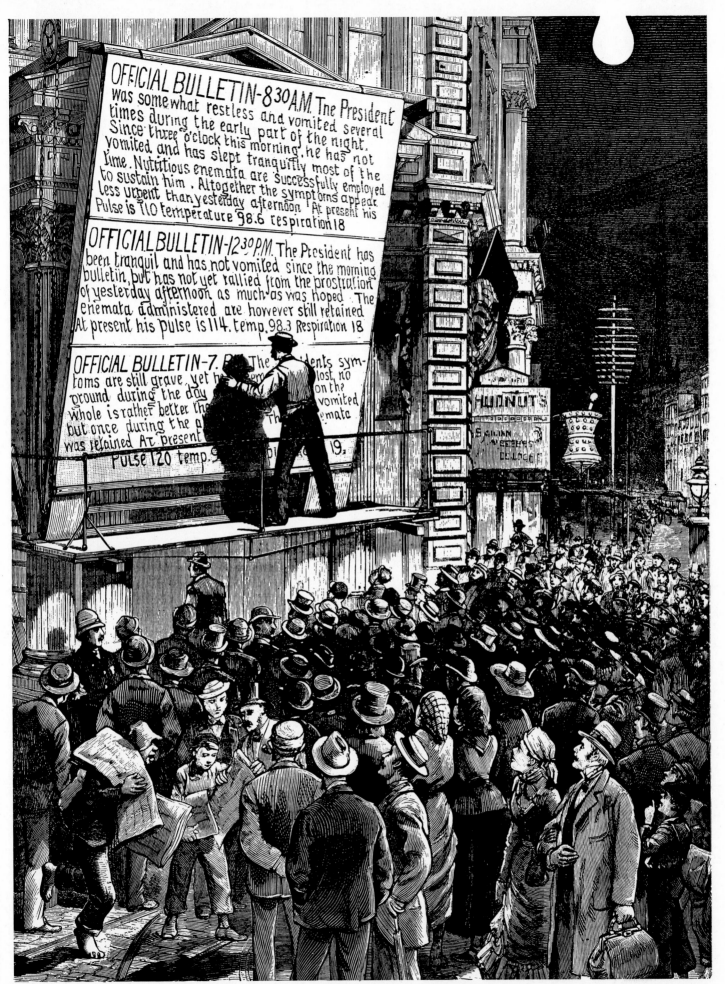

Frequent bulletins on the President's progress, like these outside the New York Herald's office, were relayed to eagerly waiting crowds.

Lincoln, meanwhile, had summoned Dr. D. W. Bliss, a physician who was a lifelong friend and old neighbor of Garfield's in Ohio. Bliss made the first examination of the President. One bullet had only grazed an arm, but the other had entered his back near the spine. He was extremely pale, apparently in "perfect collapse," and his pulse was feeble and fast. He had vomited and was sweating freely, but he was now fully conscious and complained of "a sense of weight and numbness," and of pain in his legs. Bliss gently probed the wound, but under the circumstances did not feel it safe to press down far. He ordered the President removed to the White House, and temporary dressings were applied.

Meanwhile the wounded man asked his private secretary, Colonel Rockwell, to send a telegram to Mrs. Garfield in New Jersey: "The President wishes me to say to you from him that he has been seriously hurt—how seriously he cannot yet say. He is himself and hopes you will come to him soon. He sends his love to you." Rockwell also arranged for a special train to bring Lucretia Garfield back to Washington, and then he telegraphed her, on his own, the comforting words spoken by young Congressman Garfield sixteen years before: "God reigns, and the Government at Washington still lives."

At 10:45 A.M., a police ambulance took Garfield home, followed by silent crowds who watched outside the White House as, to quote the *Times*, "the large fine form of the President was tenderly lifted from the vehicle, with the pallor of death stamped on his countenance." Looking up at the windows, Garfield recognized familiar faces, smiled, and raised his hand in military salute.

In downtown Washington, meanwhile, mobs—encouraged by premature obituaries in several papers—threatened to storm the jail where Guiteau was held; Secretary Lincoln sent troops to guard it. The District police were now clustered at the White House; Lincoln also arranged for troops to relieve them, so that they could prevent any rioting. Inside the White House, Garfield's bloodstained clothing was cut away and he was put to bed comfortably at last, more than two hours after the shooting. When an attendant, sent out for a pint of brandy, returned with two pints, the President joked that he was getting a double allowance. (He was personally quite ab-

Leslie's Illustrated, JULY 30, 1881

Well-meaning citizens sent many quack medicines and remedies to the White House.

stemious in his use of alcohol but had bitterly resented the attempts of Prohibitionists to enforce teetotalism on the White House.) Around three o'clock, when fifteen-year-old Jimmy broke into tears, his father said quietly, "Jimmy, my son, hope for the best . . . the upper story is all right; it is only the hull that is a little damaged." But when Dr. Bliss told him, "I do not think you can live many hours," Garfield said, "I'm ready to go if my time has come."

The house was full of visitors all day long. The Cabinet wives organized themselves into a nursing committee; their husbands could only wait. Secretary Lincoln, who had done such a good job all day, remembered his talk with Garfield two nights before and now exclaimed, "My God, how many hours of sorrow I have passed in this town!" Blaine was watching as the weeping Mrs. Garfield arrived about 7 P.M., and young Jimmy rushed out to greet her, pulling her close and whispering softly to her as they walked upstairs to the sickroom. Blaine, at this sight, broke down. But Lucretia Garfield, who stayed with her husband about fifteen minutes, said afterward that it was the President's calmness that restored her own composure. "Go now and rest," he told her. "I shall want you near me when the crisis comes." The doctors now expected that he might die in half an hour. "The bullet has pierced his liver," they stated—erroneously—"and it is a fatal wound."

By evening, shock waves had spread throughout the country. In most of the larger cities, shops and offices closed, and huge crowds gathered outside newspaper offices. In London, 500 Americans went to the Embassy to sign a message of sympathy for Mrs. Garfield, and Queen Victoria asked to be kept informed.

Yet the President did not die that night. With the aid of morphine, he slept. His eliminations became normal, and the liver theory was abandoned. Sunday morning, July 3, respiration and temperature were nearly normal, too, and he seemed rested and cheerful. Awed by his natural powers of recuperation, the doctors decided to leave well enough alone for the time being; they did not press the search for the bullet. On the morning of the Fourth of July, Americans saw with immense relief that the flags were still not at half-staff. Yet the doctors had been so pessimistic that Garfield was still assumed to be dying. It was decided to break the news to his old and failing mother in Ohio. She inquired of a reporter, "How could anybody be so cold-hearted as to want to kill my baby?"

He was her youngest child—the last President to be born in a log cabin, in Cuyahoga County, Ohio, in 1831. She once described his infancy in unaffected pioneer style. "The largest Babe I ever had, He looked like a red Irishman, a very large Head and Shoulders

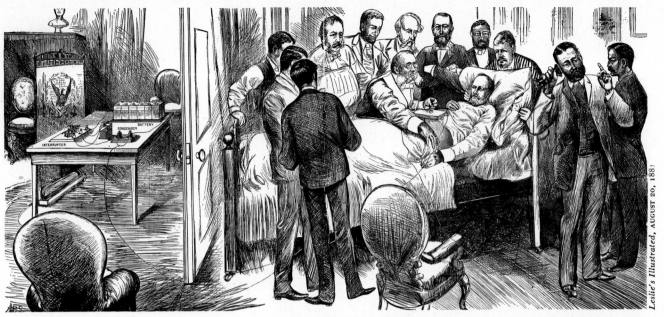

The X ray was not yet known to medicine. In an effort to locate the bullet, Alexander Graham Bell devised an "induction balance," which worked somewhat like a modern mine-detector. As the autopsy showed, its information was slightly in error.

Leslie's Illustrated, AUGUST 20, 1881

& Body equal to the Head and Shoulders. He was a very good-natured child, he walked when he was nine Months old, when ten months old he would climb the fence, go up the ladder a dozen times a day, he never was still a minute at a time in his whole life." Without changing very much, James had climbed the ladder to the top.

His mother was widowed when he was a small child, and before he was sixteen the boy was mowing hayfields, earning a man's wages of a dollar a day. Once, after reading a work entitled *The Pirate's Own Book,* and having glimpsed the great ships sailing on Lake Erie, he ran away to become a canal boy. In six weeks he licked a deck-hand bully twice his age, fell overboard and almost drowned, caught malaria, and came home —hoping to go back to the canal. But his mother, he wrote, "captured me." This she did by never once reproving him. She "simply went about her duties quietly and permitted things to work themselves out." This would be his own preferred method in politics, too. But he matured slowly.

"I was a very pulpy boy until I was at least twenty-two years old," he remarked once after examining his youthful writings of "slush and gush." At eighteen, he had joined the Disciples of Christ, an earnest sect that left its mark upon him. The Disciples largely avoided the hysteria and hell-fire preaching of the time, and laid great stress upon human rights, welfare, and education; they established several schools and colleges. Through one of these, the Western Reserve Eclectic Institute, young James began to work his way. He preached on Sundays, and drifted steadily toward the ministry—until he transferred to Williams. Here, too, he paid his way, with a little help from his remarkable

mother and a sixty-dollar loan from Mark Hopkins. He also learned to have fun, at college foolishness and at mountain climbing. ("I think you are in danger of being too sober and sensible and may get old too fast," he later cautioned a young Disciples friend he was helping through college.) Returning to Ohio, he taught at the institute, married Lucretia—a childhood playmate--and served briefly in the state senate until the Civil War swept him into a wider world. Elected commander of a volunteer regiment, he studied tactics and strategy—not, of course, neglecting Julius Caesar— while the boys drilled. He was a better-than-average field commander. He was elected to Congress from the Nineteenth Ohio District in the fall of 1862, while still in the Army; and he continued to serve, reaching the rank of major general before taking his seat in Washington in December, 1863. Even then he was somewhat reluctant; but Lincoln, who had good use for a Republican congressman with a knowledge of military affairs, urged him to resign from the Army. He complied.

It is easy to see why the Ohio voters kept sending Garfield to Congress. He was almost the embodiment of the Western Reserve itself, which had moved far beyond its log-cabin days. Though it favored the advance of science and education as the basis for a better material life for all, Cuyahoga County wanted no part of the scandalous Gilded Age that sprang up in Washington, New York, and Newport after the Civil War. Garfield, with his practical idealism, was their man. "The hand of God has been visible," he would tell the House, ". . . leading us by degrees out of our prejudices to see that the fortunes of the Republic and the safety of the party of liberty are inseparably bound up with the rights of the black man." He opposed monop-

365

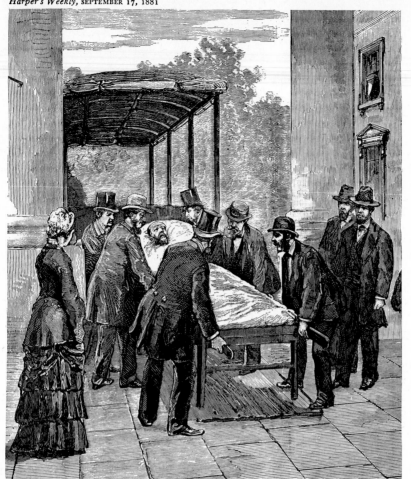

As August ended, the President still clung to life, but he was getting no better. Thinking the sea air would be a tonic, he asked to be moved to El-beron. On September 6 he was carried from his White House sickroom and placed in an Adams Express wagon (left) for the trip to the railroad station. There he was lifted aboard a specially equipped car (right) attached to a special train preceded by a pilot en-gine. While the doctors watched their patient closely, attendants wrote fre-quent medical bulletins on slips of paper and dropped them from the win-dows of the speeding cars; these were caught up eagerly and telegraphed across the nation. At Elberon (below), a special spur had been laid right up to the doorstep of the borrowed summer house where the President was to stay. The change of scene did him no good: in a few days he began sinking, and on September 19, at 10:35 P.M., he died.

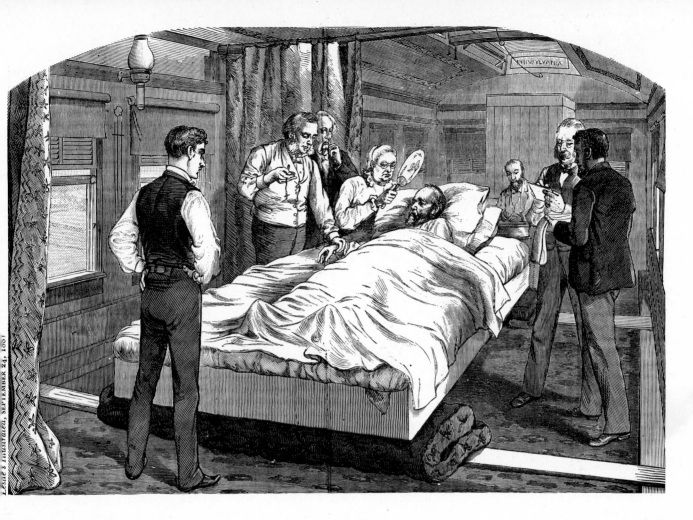

Leslie's Illustrated, SEPTEMBER 24, 1881

Leslie's Illustrated, SEPTEMBER 24, 1881

BOTH: *Harper's Weekly*, OCTOBER 1, 1881

Left: Vice President Arthur was at his home in New York when Garfield died on Monday night. Within three hours—at about 1:30 A.M. on Tuesday, September 20—he took the presidential oath in his own parlor before Justice John R. Brady of the New York Supreme Court. Later in the week, for the record, the ceremony was repeated in Washington before Chief Justice Morrison R. Waite, with former Presidents Grant and Hayes and a few other notables looking on.

Right: From Wednesday evening to Friday morning, the open casket lay in state in the Capitol rotunda, and thousands of citizens came to pay a final tribute. "Among them," a reporter wrote, "were hundreds of colored farmers from the country. . . . Their sorry-looking wagons and animals stood beside handsome carriages and richly caparisoned horses; and the ragged and toil-stained farm hands from Virginia and Maryland and the colored laborers of Washington moved side by side with the representatives of wealth . . . past the unpretentious casket . . . A few policemen were present outside, but their services were not required."

olies, hoped for an eventual world of free trade, backed the sound dollar against greenbacks. He introduced a bill establishing a federal office of education, and another to appropriate funds for the Naval Observatory to observe "the transit of Venus" (a subject upon which his conservative opponents were unbearably witty).

He was probably the best-read man in Congress. He could mentally escape from a dull sermon by translating an ode of Horace; but he also read new books constantly, in trains and omnibuses. "Give me something to read I don't know about," he used to tell the Librarian of Congress before starting a journey. He had an engaging way of expecting other people to share his enthusiasms. When the novelist William Dean Howells visited the Garfields in Ohio, and began to talk on their porch one evening about poets he had known, the Congressman could not contain himself. He jumped up and ran across the grass, waving his arms wildly toward all the neighboring porches. "Come on over!" he shouted. "He's telling about Holmes and Longfellow and Lowell and Whittier." Obediently, the shadowy figures of his neighbors followed him to the house. "Now go on," Garfield told his guest.

Like John F. Kennedy, Garfield won the presidential election by a tiny margin—9,464 votes out of over nine million cast—and to the country at large he was not very well known. His legislative box score could not be determined until Congress convened in December. Yet the proper test of a Presidency, John Kenneth Galbraith recently observed, is not legislation but the progress made in "dealing with those grievances and reversing those trends which otherwise could destroy us." And this test Garfield had already begun to pass.

There was then no civil service through which federal jobs were filled, and all appointments were controlled either by political bosses who used them to build the power of their own machines, or by the White House itself. This had been Garfield's particular bête noire. Of course, as a seasoned congressman he was quite used to dispensing government jobs, but on a retail rather than a wholesale level. Some weeks before the shooting, he wrote that the torrent of White House job seekers "swept away my day . . . I felt like crying out in the agony of my soul against the greed for office and the consumption of my time." He himself had never had to ask for a job in his life, and he soon came to hate the "Spartan band of disciplined office hunters who drew papers on me as highwaymen draw pistols." He had predicted, in fact, that civil service reform would come by necessity after "the wearisome years of wasted Presidents have paved the way for it."

But this was not the worst of the grievance, for the power of the political bosses and the spoils system always went hand in hand. Among the Democrats, Boss Tweed of Tammany Hall had but lately died in prison after looting New York City of uncounted millions. Among the Republicans the leading bosses were Senators Roscoe Conkling and Thomas C. Platt of New York, who during the two weak administrations of President Grant had virtually run the party and with it much of the country, exercising a veto power over all important federal appointments in

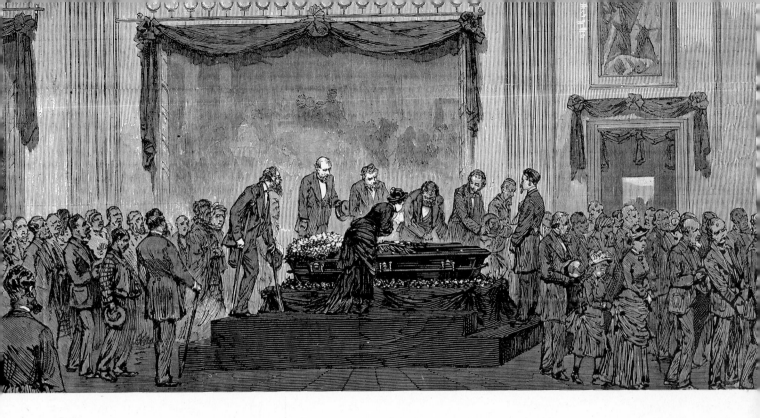

New York. They had been temporarily set back by the one-term, reform administration of Rutherford B. Hayes, which had split the party. In 1880, Garfield had been chosen as a compromise candidate who could patch things up between the Stalwarts and the other Republican factions, and win—which he had just barely done.

After his inauguration the country watched to see if he would knuckle under to the bosses. At first he seemed to, filling major appointments from a list approved by Senators Conkling and Platt. But when he came to the Collector of Customs, a choice plum in New York State, he decided to draw the line. Without consulting the two senators, he switched the incumbent Collector to a diplomatic post and sent his own nomination to the Senate.

"This," he said, "brings on the contest at once and will settle whether the President is registering clerk of the Senate or the Executive of the United States." If Conkling should attack, the President promised, "he will find it no rose-water war." The public was delighted to see its big, good-natured schoolmaster President stand up to a bully, as the canal boy long ago had done. Messages poured into Washington. ("My Dear Sir, Stick. The Constitution, the Lord God and the People are with you.") It was soon clear that the Senate would confirm the President's nominee, and the disgruntled Senators Conkling and Platt resigned.

It was thus a popular President who lay wounded in the White House in 1881, and a most unpopular assailant, the unsuccessful job seeker Guiteau, who settled comfortably in the District jail. The press was already raving, on this sad Fourth of July. "MURDERED BY THE SPOILS SYSTEM!" exclaimed the angry New York *Tribune*.

But the President, as a matter of fact, seemed to be improving. He received visitors daily, giving each a smile and a firm handshake. After July 9, when the doctors reported him actually on the road to recovery, even the job seekers returned. How many were admitted to the sickroom is not known. But nothing could keep the job seekers away, not even a grave series of crises which developed as summer advanced.

The doctors soon reported discharges of pus, which they called "of healthy nature," but the wound was not draining well. A channel descending toward the groin, which the doctors mistook for the track of the bullet, was really formed by pus that had not been able to drain out. On July 23 the patient had a "severe rigor," his temperature rising to 104 degrees. To improve drainage, the doctors removed a small piece of bone from a rib the bullet had fractured. It was apparently not thought safe to place the President under ether, but during this painful operation he did not murmur or complain. "Never had physician such a patient before," remarked Dr. Bliss. A small platoon of distinguished doctors was usually in attendance, but Dr. Bliss, whom Garfield had personally asked to take charge of his case, stayed close by the President night and day.

It was very hot in Washington in the summer of 1881; the public, reading the weather bulletins, suffered for their suffering President. They subscribed more than a quarter of a million dollars to a benefit

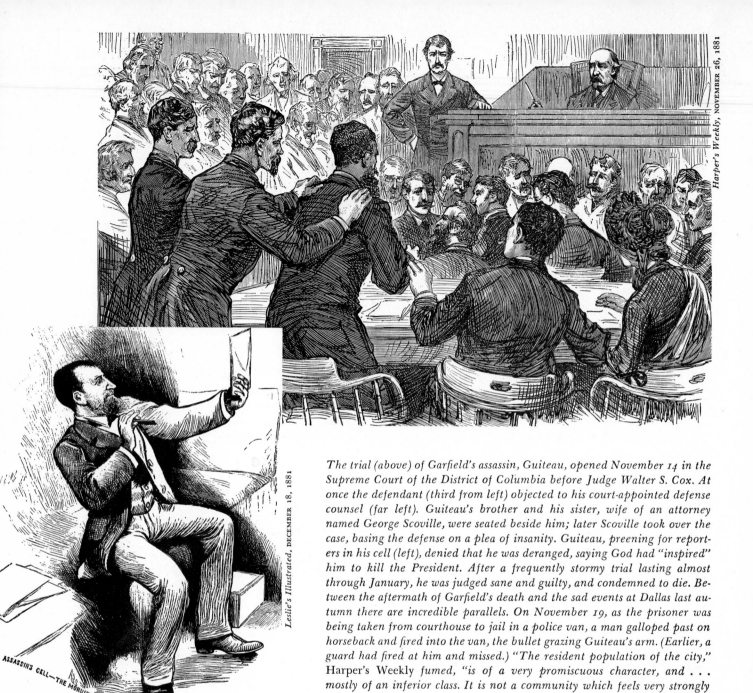

Harper's Weekly, NOVEMBER 26, 1881

Leslie's Illustrated, DECEMBER 18, 1881

ASSASSIN'S CELL—THE MORNING TOILET

The trial (above) of Garfield's assassin, Guiteau, opened November 14 in the Supreme Court of the District of Columbia before Judge Walter S. Cox. At once the defendant (third from left) objected to his court-appointed defense counsel (far left). Guiteau's brother and his sister, wife of an attorney named George Scoville, were seated beside him; later Scoville took over the case, basing the defense on a plea of insanity. Guiteau, preening for reporters in his cell (left), denied that he was deranged, saying God had "inspired" him to kill the President. After a frequently stormy trial lasting almost through January, he was judged sane and guilty, and condemned to die. Between the aftermath of Garfield's death and the sad events at Dallas last autumn there are incredible parallels. On November 19, as the prisoner was being taken from courthouse to jail in a police van, a man galloped past on horseback and fired into the van, the bullet grazing Guiteau's arm. (Earlier, a guard had fired at him and missed.) "The resident population of the city," Harper's Weekly fumed, "is of a very promiscuous character, and . . . mostly of an inferior class. It is not a community which feels very strongly the . . . responsibilities of citizenship, and it is . . . only laxly controlled."

Harper's Weekly, DECEMBER 3, 1881

fund for his family. They sent hundreds of letters and telegrams daily, with much medical advice. There was great fear lest the Potomac flats, traditionally called Foggy Bottom, should cause malaria, and Garfield was given quinine daily. The state of the White House itself caused anxiety. Rotten timbers in its basement and green, slimy brickwork were vividly described in Congress. A distinguished engineer came to look at the venerable plumbing.

Everyone tried to help. Alexander Graham Bell produced an electrical device, with primary and secondary coils, an interrupter, and a telephone hearing-piece, to locate the bullet in the President's body. The results were inconclusive, perhaps because of the metal bedsprings. It was not thought advisable to probe and remove the bullet. "We suspected and dreaded some internal injury which no mortal could have dared to explore," said Dr. Bliss. An air-conditioning unit put together by a specialist in ventilating mine shafts was more successful. Lengths of drenched cotton sheeting drawn tight on frames, an iron chest with 500 pounds of salted ice, and a fan turning at 1,400 revolutions per minute were the essentials of a system that forced cool air, purified by charcoal, into the upstairs bedroom. Its temperature was kept at 81 degrees or lower, a remarkable achievement.

Two more operations somewhat like the first were undertaken, and on August 6 the President again rallied—until August 14, when he had another high fever, which also subsided. The President begged for a change of scene. The Garfields had always been great believers in sea air, and the doctors agreed that he could go to Elberon, New Jersey. Streetcar tracks over which the horse-drawn ambulance had to pass to the station were packed with sawdust to prevent jolting. The President's bed was placed on heavy springs in a car cooled by iceboxes, and the train zipped along, sometimes at almost eighty miles an hour. Too fast? the President was asked. "Oh, no, let her go," he said.

And after the train rolled up over a special spur to a borrowed cottage, he did begin to rally once more. He even dismissed three of his doctors, and sent Harry and James off to enter Williams College, as he had planned. But he was very weak, and pitifully shrunken. Often he could take only liquid nourishment, and frequently he vomited. The doctors watched apprehensively. On September 17, the President had another "severe rigor," with chills and fever.

Now Garfield asked for a writing tablet. With his left hand, he wrote his autograph and added three words in Latin, which made it clear that he knew he was dying—and also, why: *Strangulatus pro Republica.* The following day he asked his secretary, "Old boy! Do you think my name will have a place in human history?" Colonel Rockwell answered, "Yes, a grand one, but a grander one in human hearts. Old fellow, you mustn't talk in that way. You have a great work yet to perform."

"No," said the President after a moment. "My work is done." The next morning, September 19, his temperature was almost 109 degrees. At 10:35 P.M. Dr. Bliss raised his head from his patient's chest and said, "It is over." And now autopsy found the hidden enemy at last. The bullet, although not quite where the doctors had supposed it to be, was harmless in itself. But a huge blood clot, almost the size of a fist, had formed within the congested bullet track and worked its way out by rupturing the splenal artery and finally breaking through the peritoneum into the abdominal cavity. It was at this point, the physicians believed, that death occurred; they listed a secondary hemorrhage as the immediate cause.

With X ray, antibiotics, anticoagulants, and other remedies not then available, Garfield's life could almost certainly have been saved. But with the equipment they had, the physicians were probably right not to attempt a deep probe, and instead to let their patient's strong constitution and serene temperament fight the battle. Unhappily, these were not enough.

As the bells of New York's old church, St. Paul's, and of All Souls in Washington began to toll simultaneously at 10:50 P.M., people wept at home, or sought each other's company. The Court of England, in an unprecedented gesture, declared a week's mourning. At the Capitol, where the President's body lay in state, mourners waited an average of three and one-half hours in line. It was the funeral train, however, that provided the closest link with the people. As she accompanied Garfield's body back to Washington, his widow—just as Mrs. Franklin D. Roosevelt would do on a similar journey in 1945—kept pushing back the window curtains to see the crowds of mourners at every crossing. From Washington to Cleveland, where the funeral was to be held, the train frequently passed over flower-strewn tracks, between kneeling Civil War veterans and workmen who stood at intervals holding pine torches through the night. The funeral procession in Cleveland was six miles long.

There was no electronic means to permit national participation in the funeral services at Cleveland, but the public flocked, at the same hour, to their own houses of worship, following frequently the same order of service. Many a stirring sermon was preached, and published. "Unmurmuring Submission" was the title of one.

But the people's mood was a long way from unmurmuring submission. They thought they knew what had killed Garfield, and their demand for civil service reform, which would end control of their federal government by political bosses, became irresistible. Within two years the former spoilsman, now President, Chester A. Arthur, recommended to Congress passage of the country's first civil service law; it was enacted in 1883.

Another direct consequence, of course, was the trial of Charles J. Guiteau for murder. It was one of the most spectacular, and revealing, trials ever held in this country. The three other accused assassins of Presidents have told us almost nothing. Death silenced both John Wilkes Booth and Lee Harvey Oswald before they could be brought to trial. Leon F. Czolgosz, the anarchist sympathizer who shot McKinley, was swiftly executed after a trial lasting little more than eight hours. But Charles J. Guiteau told all. In him stand revealed all the messianic traits and the delusions of persecution that so often have marked assassins throughout history.

"I come here in the capacity of an agent of the Deity in this matter," he declared to Judge Walter S. Cox, of the Supreme Court of the District of Columbia, at the opening of the trial on November 14. For two and a half months he ranted on. Sometimes the Judge reprimanded him severely, but for the most part Guiteau was allowed to have his say. (Cox, it was noted, had been counsel to two of John Wilkes Booth's associates in 1865 and was determined that this time there would be a full and fair trial, as had hardly been the case before.) Many of the facts of Guiteau's fantastic life were already known, and others came out, in garbled and distorted form, during his ravings.

It was just about a month before the shooting that Guiteau had at last been turned away, not only from the executive offices which he had been haunting but from the White House front door. He was one of the most persistent as well as preposterous job hunters who had ever come to Washington. Yet his interest in politics was really quite recent. He had turned to it after having failed at everything else.

Ten years younger than the President, Guiteau had grown up in Freeport, Illinois, the son of a respectable Republican, a bank cashier with only one marked eccentricity: the senior Guiteau was a devout follower of the Reverend John H. Noyes, founder of the Oneida Community, a collective farm where not only Christian communism but plural marriage and eugenic breeding were practiced, and where strange theories of divine inspiration were preached. Here young Guiteau, who had been a restless boy unable to settle down and concentrate, arrived in 1860. He was given unpleasant jobs in the kitchen and workshops, but apparently found some satisfaction in the religious teachings and

the companionship of the female members; he stayed throughout the Civil War. In April, 1865, he went to New York City with, as he put it, "the Bible for my textbook and the Holy Ghost for my schoolmaster." He lived over a bakery in Hoboken, New Jersey, on a subsistence diet, claiming to be in the employ of *"Jesus Christ & Co."* and drafting plans for a chain of religious dailies. Nothing came of that.

After another stay at Oneida and another unsuccessful sojourn in New York, Guiteau decided to try Chicago. There he managed to pass the bar—then a relatively simple matter—and practiced as debt collector, keeping for himself most of the money he collected. He met, and married, a good-looking sixteen-year-old girl who worked in a Y.M.C.A. library. Periodically he and his young wife were thrown out of their lodgings for nonpayment, or fled voluntarily just before rent day. He left a chain of bills at hotels, lodginghouses, and haberdasheries across the country. He never paid railroad fare, usually telling the conductor, "I am travelling for the Lord." If this didn't work, he would get off at the next station. After almost five years of this uncertain life, his wife divorced him for adultery; he did not deny that he had spent some of her money on prostitutes, and had caught syphilis.

About 1876 Guiteau began to attend prayer meetings of the Moody and Sankey revivals in Chicago, where he served as an usher and was sometimes permitted to preach. This started a new phase of his career. Now, wherever he could rent a hall or borrow a church, he began to lecture on the Second Coming, giving as his own the doctrines he had learned from the Reverend Mr. Noyes at Oneida. His audiences were sometimes a hundred or more, sometimes only two or three. He also sold copies of a book called *The Truth,* in which he plagiarized Noyes' ideas. But in the spring of 1880, having done poorly with a lecture called "Some Reasons Why Two-Thirds of the Human Race Are Going Down to Perdition," he began to be interested in the coming GOP national convention.

He expected General Grant to be nominated for a third term, and wrote a campaign speech intended for him. When Garfield was nominated instead, it was not difficult to revise the speech. Guiteau had copies printed and took them, uninvited, to an August meeting of Republican leaders at the old Fifth Avenue Hotel in New York. No one used the speech in the campaign—it was dreadful. But he did get from the politicians a few kind words, and somehow conceived the notion that the GOP owed him a job.

His days in Washington, where he arrived on borrowed money on March 5, 1881, were discouraging and lonely, but he persisted. Once, pushing his way through a crowd of office seekers, he managed to see

Garfield, who was of course courteous, and gave the President a copy of his speech. (He also sent him at least four other copies.) First, Guiteau asked for an ambassadorship; then for the consulship at Paris. In the White House he would help himself to stationery, write a note ("Can I have the Paris consulship?"), and leave it with a clerk. He also pestered Grant, Blaine, and Vice President Chester A. Arthur, and he asked many members of Congress to sign a petition on his behalf to obtain the consulship—with complete failure.

After he was barred from the White House door sometime in May, Guiteau wrote a vaguely threatening letter to Garfield—of the kind the Secret Service would automatically be notified of today. It went unanswered. And it was, naturally, about this time that he turned against Garfield and began to brood about the President's "removal," as he called it. On June 8, borrowing fifteen dollars from a cousin, he purchased

a .44-caliber British revolver with a white bone handle. (A cheaper model was available with a wooden handle but, he said later, he wanted one that would look well in a museum.)

"That will make a good noise," Guiteau told the gun-seller, who replied, "That will kill a horse." Guiteau, who had never fired a gun, went to some woods along the Potomac and practiced shooting at trees. Thereafter he began to haunt the President.

His trial was a spectacle. Crowded every day, the courtroom often resounded to boos and laughter. At first, Guiteau was allowed to receive visitors in his cell. He demanded that President Arthur, since he had achieved office by the "removal," should contribute funds for his defense. He attacked witnesses, the prosecutors, even his own attorneys, who were led by George Scoville, his brother-in-law. The defense plan was to plead insanity—but Guiteau demolished his own case

Leslie's Illustrated, JULY 8, 1882

An appeal to the United States Supreme Court having failed, Guiteau was hanged at 12:40 P.M. on June 30. In his cell he had composed his own epitaph: "Here lies the body of Charles Guiteau, Patriot and Christian. His soul is in glory."

373

by telling an alienist in jail, before the trial, "I knew from the time I conceived the act if I could establish the fact before a jury that I believed the killing was an inspired act, I could not be held to responsibility before the law."

Perhaps the most important parts of Guiteau's sayings and writings are those that reveal how verbal violence, following Garfield's defiance of Conkling and Platt, had given the assassin the backbone he otherwise lacked to commit murder. Garfield had not, of course, defeated the Stalwart bosses without causing fierce controversy. A marked editorial from the Brooklyn *Eagle,* found in Guiteau's pocket after he shot the President, had predicted the disintegration of the Republican party. Guiteau said, "After I saw the President and General Grant and Conkling and that kind of men were wrestling and at loggerheads, I saw that this nation was coming to grief." Enough Americans agreed with him so that he sometimes received in his prison cell as many as a hundred favorable letters and telegrams a day. Others so thoroughly detested him that while in custody he was twice shot at. Once one of his own guards fired at Guiteau; the bullet missed its mark. Again, an assailant on horseback fired into the police van which was taking the prisoner between jail and courtroom.

On January 25, 1882, after only about an hour's deliberation, the jury found Guiteau guilty. He was hanged on June 30, exactly one year after Garfield had talked with Robert Todd Lincoln about his father's assassination. Guiteau was allowed to recite on the scaffold a poem he had written that morning, purporting to be the words of a dying child; he told reporters that it would sound better if set to music. It went in part,

> I saved my party and my land;
> Glory Hallelujah!
> But they have murdered me for it
> And that is the reason
> I am going to the Lordy.
> Glory Hallelujah! Glory Hallelujah!
> I am going to the Lordy.

He was still saying "Glory," as the trap was sprung.

Harper's Weekly, JULY 23, 1881

A detail from At Liberty's Door, *the great Thomas Nast's moving tribute to the fallen Garfield in* Harper's Weekly.

The lamplight filtering through the haze and drizzle gave the streets of New Orleans an eerie pallor that October night in 1890. It was nearing midnight when Dave Hennessy, the city's thirty-two-year-old police chief, left his office and headed home, escorted by an old friend, Captain William O'Connor. There had been threats on Hennessy's life, but the popular and respected chief took them lightly. When the two men reached Girod Street, where Hennessy lived, the chief told O'Connor it was not necessary to accompany him any farther. The two men bade each other good night, and Hennessy headed up the damp and deserted street alone.

He had almost reached home when the silence of the night was shattered by the roar of gunfire. The shots came from a shanty on the other side of the street where a recently arrived immigrant Sicilian shoemaker was living. Hennessy was hit, but he managed to draw his service revolver and get off three or four shots as his attackers fled.

Captain O'Connor heard the gunfire, rushed to the scene, and found Hennessy on Basin Street, where he had collapsed after gamely pursuing his assailants. "Who gave it to you, Dave?" O'Connor asked. "The Dagoes did it," Hennessy murmured.

Within hours the police found five weapons abandoned in the gutters a block or two from the scene of the crime. One was an ordinary double-barreled shotgun. The others were curious pieces—shotguns with the barrels sawed off and the stocks hinged so that the guns could be collapsed to the size of a horse pistol and easily concealed.

These weapons had done their work well. Three large slugs had torn vicious wounds in the chief. His face, neck, arms, and legs were riddled with shot. Hennessy lingered through the night in Charity Hospital but died the following morning.

VENDETTA IN NEW ORLEANS

The city panicked with fear of the Mafia when the police chief was murdered

Three victims of mob justice lie sprawled in the prison gallery where they were shot down.

Hennessy's body was taken back to the house on Girod Street where the bachelor chief had lived with his elderly mother, and later to City Hall, where it lay in state. The thousands that came to mourn him rivalled the crowds that had appeared there some months before to view the body of ex-Confederate President Jefferson Davis. The chief's brutal murder was on everybody's lips. Feeling against New Orleans' Italian community ran at fever pitch. One grief-stricken mourner, a news-carrier friend of the chief, went directly from the funeral to the Parish Prison, where he asked to see one of the arrested suspects, Antonio Scaffidi, and shot and wounded him in the neck.

The shots that killed David Hennessy in October were the belated echo of a salvo of gunfire that had split the New Orleans night five months before.

By JOSEPH E. PERSICO

The right to unload fruit vessels landing in New Orleans had been fiercely contested by two gangs of Italian stevedores, the Provenzanos and the Matrangas, so called after their rival bosses. Initially, the Provenzanos had controlled the business. But Charles Matranga, the operator of a gambling den and dance hall serving New Orleans blacks, began to eye the fruit-handling concession covetously when police pressure on his other enterprises became too uncomfortable. Through persuasion and coercion Matranga managed to oust the Provenzanos and put his own men on the wharves.

Late one night in May, seven of Matranga's men, including his brother Tony, were driving out Esplanade Street in a wagon after unloading a ship at the Levee. As the wagon reached a tree-lined intersection at Esplanade and Claiborne a fusillade of shotgun fire erupted, and three of the men fell wounded, including Tony Matranga, who lost a leg in the ambush.

At first the victims clung to the ancient Sicilian custom of silence and refused to identify their assailants. Later they relented and accused several members of the Provenzano faction. Six members of the Provenzano group were convicted in June.

The verdict left Chief Hennessy dissatisfied, and not merely because he was a personal friend of the Provenzanos. The attorneys for the Provenzano men had filed for a new trial, and in making an investigation relating to this appeal Hennessy had obtained damaging evidence of perjury by the witnesses for the Matrangas. Further feeding his suspicions that justice had been subverted was the fact that a key witness for the defense had been murdered before he could testify. Hennessy suspected the Matrangas of the deed. The Provenzano trial was, in fact, so redolent of perjury that the court did grant a new trial, set for October 22.

Hennessy's probing had convinced

him that the Matrangas were guilty of more than perjury and an isolated murder. In the course of his inquiries he had been in contact with Italian police officials and now had reason to believe that the Matranga faction represented the New Orleans branch of the Mafia.

Opinion differed as to whether the Mafia actually existed in America. However, ever since Italy had been united in 1861, her government had conducted a vigorous, often ruthless, crusade to stamp out the ancient criminal fraternity. In Sicily, Mafiosi were gunned down like dogs. Surely, some authorities believed, among the thousands of Italians then streaming to America there might be Mafiosi fleeing the harsh hand of the Italian police. In New Orleans, according to a grand-jury report, the Italian consulate had the names of over a thousand fugitives from Italian justice living among the city's twenty-five-thousand-member Italian colony. The city's total population was then about a quarter of a million.

The Sicilian criminal element had captured Hennessy's interest long before, and the young chief had carved out a national reputation as an authority on the Mafia. Nine years earlier Hennessy, then a detective, had scored an impressive coup by arresting the internationally notorious Sicilian bandit Giuseppe Esposito in New Orleans. This brigand was wanted in Italy for premeditated murder, robbery, and extortion. British authorities were after Esposito for mutilating a curate in a £5,000 ransom scheme.

But arresting a suspected Mafioso proved far simpler than getting a conviction. American police, trying to solve crimes believed committed by the Mafia, ran into the ancient Sicilian code of *omerta*, meaning, literally, "connivance." *Omerta* held that justice was a personal matter, not something to be delegated or entrusted

to outsiders. A man's first duty was to avenge himself for any injury. To appeal to the public, the police, or the courts for redress was contemptible, the act of a traitor. The customary Mafia penalty for giving evidence to the authorities was death.

Thanks to this near immunity from the testimony of their neighbors, blackmailers and extortionists exploited their fellow countrymen virtually at will in the New Orleans Italian colony. Authorities pointed despairingly to ninety-four murders involving Italians in the twenty-five years preceding the Hennessy assassination; only five had resulted in convictions, and the other cases had been dropped for lack of evidence.

The deadly feud between the Matrangas and Provenzanos hardened Hennessy's determination to break the Mafia in his city. He had obtained from Italian authorities criminal histories of several immigrants now residing in New Orleans. His investigations convinced him that Charles Matranga, Joseph P. Macheca, a well-to-do merchant, and several other Italian-Americans were the leaders of a Mafia family operating in the city. He had planned to destroy this criminal cabal by sending its leaders to prison for perjury in the first Provenzano trial.

In ferreting out the motive behind Hennessy's murder, the chief's fellow officers theorized that the Matranga leaders had been tipped off that Hennessy intended to put them behind bars. Hennessy was, in fact, murdered on October 15, exactly one week before he was expected to unveil his case against the Matranga gang at the second Provenzano trial.

Of those suspected as Mafia kingpins only Macheca was a native-born American. He gave every outward appearance of being a substantial and enterprising member of the community. Twenty years before, Joe Macheca had pioneered the steamship fruit trade between New Orleans and Central America. He owned the first ship to make the run and had founded the firm of Macheca Brothers. He was prominent in Democratic politics and often served as a delegate to the party's state conventions. Ironically, seventeen years earlier he had saved the life of a New Orleans police chief by his conspicuous heroism during a civil riot. Now middle-aged, Macheca was a portly, pleasant-mannered, and popular gentleman, father of six, owner of a handsome house on Bourbon Street, and believed to be worth hundreds of thousands of dollars. He was now a suspected architect of assassination.

The New Orleans populace was so enraged at the brazenness of the Hennessy killing that the mayor, Joseph A. Shakspeare, felt compelled to take extraordinary measures. Shakspeare described the murdered chief as a "victim of Sicilian vengeance" and warned, "We must teach these people a lesson that they will not forget for all time." The mayor appointed a committee of the city's prominent and powerful to help bring Hennessy's assassins to justice and to root out any "oath-bound" or "hellborn" societies in New Orleans. The appointees, who came to be known as the Committee of Fifty, put up a substantial sum of their own money to engage the best detective skills and the sharpest legal talent in the case.

After scores of initial arrests nineteen men were finally indicted on December 13, 1890, for the murder of David C. Hennessy. Later, the state obtained an order of severance, and only nine of the nineteen were scheduled for immediate trial. The nine were the alleged ringleaders, Joseph Macheca and Charles Matranga; Pietro Monasterio, the shoemaker living in the shanty from which the attack had been staged; Bastian Incardona, an Italian criminal fugitive; Antonio Marchesi, a fruit vendor; his fourteen-year-old son, Gaspare; Antonio Scaffidi and Antonio Bagnetto, also fruit vendors; and Emmanuele Polizzi, an unstable Sicilian who had

once been fired by the Provenzanos for blackmailing them.

The public's vengeful feeling against the Matranga-Macheca faction now seemed to work to the advantage of the rival Provenzanos. When the Provenzano members were finally retried in January, after postponement of the October trial date, they were found not guilty of the ambush on the Matrangas.

The date set for the Hennessy murder trial was February 16, 1891, with Judge Joshua G. Baker, a gentleman described as "pleasant, dignified and punctual," presiding. The

Slain police chief David C. Hennessy
Harper's Weekly, NOVEMBER 8, 1890

defense retained a blue-chip battery of five lawyers led by Thomas J. Semmes, one of the South's most distinguished attorneys, a former Louisiana attorney general and Confederate senator. The defense also boasted a former district attorney and crack trial lawyer, Lionel Adams. The high quality of counsel tended to confirm accounts that the defense was lavishly financed. The *New York Times* reported that Italians all over the country had been asked to contribute two dollars apiece to help defend their countrymen. Sums large and small flowing into New Orleans were estimated to have swelled the

defense war chest to seventy-five thousand dollars or more.

The Hennessy trial seemed to offer a clear-cut confrontation: a contest between a society based on law and a society rooted in evil, and the case commanded nationwide attention. The *New York Times* billed it in advance as "one of the noted criminal cases of the age." The selection of a jury foretold the intensity of the coming struggle. More than 1,300 prospective jurors had to be summoned, and 780 were examined. It took eleven days to select twelve jurymen.

On February 27 spectators packed the courtroom as the trial began. An uneasy stillness fell over the crowd as the first witness, Dr. Paul Archinard, assistant coroner, recounted the terrible wounds in Hennessy's body. Then the prosecution produced four witnesses who testified that "Peter Johnson," the man who had rented the shanty from which the shots were fired, was actually Joseph P. Macheca. The rent had been paid in advance by Macheca, who installed Monasterio in the shanty as a shoemaker shortly before the ambush.

A Mr. Peeler, a painter who lived on the corner near the murder scene, testified that on hearing the first shots he had sprung to his balcony and seen Scaffidi, Incardona, and Bagnetto firing from in front of Monasterio's shanty. He had seen Scaffidi fire twice at Hennessy with a double-barreled shotgun, reload, and fire again.

A black youth, Amos Scott, told the tense courtroom how Hennessy had been set up for the kill. Amos said he had talked to Gaspare Marchesi, the son of Antonio Marchesi, in Poydras Market three days after the shooting. Young Marchesi told Amos that on the fatal night he had been stationed by the men to watch for the police chief. When Hennessy appeared, Gaspare ran ahead of him and whistled to signal his approach.

Altogether the prosecution produced sixty-seven witnesses, including several who identified some of the accused as the men they had seen actually firing weapons or fleeing the murder scene.

In building its case the state had enjoyed unusual extralegal support, since the Committee of Fifty disclosed later that a spy had been planted as an employee of the defense team. This man was actually on the city's payroll, and his duty was to file a daily report of everything seen and heard in the defense camp.

The antics of one defendant, Emmanuele Polizzi, provided lively copy for the journalists covering the trial. Polizzi, a short, swarthy man in his late twenties who was described by a *Times* reporter as "dull and ignorant," had already interrupted the trial earlier with his ranting and had been taken into the judge's private chamber, where, it was rumored, he had offered a confession implicating the other defendants for an assurance of immunity for himself. On March 6, the day the defense was to begin presenting its case, Polizzi rushed to a window and shoved his foot through the glass in an attempt to escape to the street outside. Deputy sheriffs finally subdued him, but only after having their hands bitten and their clothes torn in a fierce struggle. Court was adjourned to give the coroner time to determine Polizzi's mental condition.

On March 7 the defense finally called its first witnesses, and the weight of evidence began to seesaw. Where the state's witnesses had Antonio Bagnetto firing at Hennessy, defense witnesses had him watching over some fruit stands in the marketplace during the attack. Others swore that the Marchesis, father and son, were at their home, four blocks away. Still other witnesses placed Scaffidi at home, nursing a sick wife, at the hour Hennessy was attacked.

Almost from the outset of the trial an undercurrent of insinuation and suspicion had swirled about the integrity of the jury. Gossip around the courthouse had it that "big money might be made by going on the jury and doing right." The money reportedly pouring into New Orleans to finance the defense tended to substantiate widespread suspicion of jury tampering. Toward the end of the trial two agents of D. C. O'Malley, a private detective working for the defense, actually were arrested and charged with attempting to bribe prospective jurors.

On Friday, the thirteenth of March, an impatient throng milled outside the courthouse. The jury had been out since the previous evening, and its verdict was due soon. At 2:53 P.M. the jury re-entered the courtroom, and the foreman handed the verdict to Judge Baker. The judge stared at it a full minute before ordering the verdict read. In the case of Macheca, Matranga, Bagnetto, Incardona, and the Marchesis the jury found "not guilty." In the case of Monasterio, Polizzi, and Scaffidi the jurors had not been able to agree on a verdict and had declared a mistrial.

As the *New York Times* reporter saw it, "So strong a case had been made by the State, the evidence had been so clear, direct and unchallenged, that the acquittal of the accused today came like a thunder clap from a clear sky." Among the crowd outside the courtroom disbelief soon gave way to outrage. The air was acrid with shouts and ominous mutterings. The frightened jurors prudently melted into the crowd.

But if, after the trial, the jurors worried about the public's attitude toward them, they expressed no misgivings about their judgment. A reporter questioned them shortly afterward. Some refused to comment, citing a pledge they had all made not to discuss the case further. But others, including the jury foreman, were willing to talk and expressed a low opinion of the prosecution's case. Why hadn't the prosecution called such obvious witnesses as Captain O'Connor and another police officer who had happened onto the murder scene? How reliable were eyewitnesses late on a rainy night in a dimly lit street? And hadn't the prosecution let the defense alibis go uncontradicted? One juror, acknowledging that the verdict may have "astonished" people, concluded, "If anybody could do any better than we did with the evidence, let them try."

The nine defendants could not be freed immediately after the trial, since technically they still faced another charge, "lying in wait with intent to commit murder." But in a day or two the state could be expected to drop this charge and set them free. Back in their cells the nine who had just been tried and the ten men still awaiting trial rejoiced in the verdict.

Along the Levee, people from the Italian colony began to gather in a festive mood. Italian boat owners in Lugger Bay near the French Market hoisted two flags on their masts—the Italian flag above, the Stars and Stripes below, upside down.

But as Italians celebrated on the Levee angry men met in another part of town to denounce the verdict and ponder other paths to justice. Several members of the Committee of Fifty had reconvened to form a "Vigilance Committee." That the Hennessy jury had been tampered with, the jurors bought off, and justice perverted was outrageously obvious to these men. Hadn't the defense somehow secured the list of prospective jurors even before the judge released it? Hadn't they been approached at home or on their way to the courthouse by defense emissaries with insinuations or outright offers of payment? Hadn't two of these bribers actually been arrested just before the trial ended? And what about the huge sums the defense had available to work its will?

Members of the Vigilance Committee labored until midnight drafting an appeal for a mass protest. It was signed by more than sixty prominent citizens. Their work done, the committee sent copies of the statement to the local newspapers.

Saturday, March 14, the morning after the trial, dawned cool, clear, and sunlit after a week of steady rain. Sheriff Gabriel Villère read in his newspaper the statement the Vigilance Committee had issued:

Mass Meeting
All good citizens are invited to attend a mass meeting on Saturday, March 14 at 10 o'clock A.M., at Clay Statue, to take steps to remedy the failure of justice in the Hennessy case. Come prepared for action.

If the call for action worried Sheriff Villère, he must have brushed his fears aside when he got to the Parish Prison and found nothing out of line. At 8:30 A.M. the sheriff left the prison in charge of his deputy, Captain Lem Davis, and headed for his office in City Hall.

Out on the Levee the city's Italians renewed the festivities of the night before and prepared for a victory banquet. A mile away, at the statue of Henry Clay, the sun was drawing a crowd certain to please the Vigilance Committee. Just before 10 A.M. W. S. Parkerson, a leader of the committee's call for action, a respected attorney and prominent politician, arrived on the scene. After leading a brief march around the base of the statue Parkerson mounted the pedestal and began to address the throng.

"What protection, or assurance of protection, is there left us," he cried, "when the very head of our police department—our chief of police—is assassinated, in our very midst, by the Mafia Society, and his assassins again turned loose on the community?... Will every man here follow me and see the murder of D. C. Hennessy vindicated? Are there men enough here to set aside the verdict of that infamous jury, every one of whom is a perjurer and a scoundrel?"

"Hang the murderers," the crowd shouted back.

By now the crowd had grown so great that the trolley cars circling Clay Statue could not move. Spectators clambered on top of the blocked cars and cheered the speaker on.

Two more speakers followed Parkerson, but the crowd was growing impatient. "We have had enough of words," men shouted, "now for action." The last speaker, a newspaper editor, John Wickliffe, was unable to finish. "Very well, then, gentlemen," he said, "let's go and do our duty. Mr. Parkerson is your leader. Mr. James D. Houston is your first lieutenant. Your second lieutenant is myself."

The leaders then walked over to Royal and Bienville streets, where about fifty men armed with pistols and shotguns joined them. The crowd, now swollen to well over six thousand and whipped to a righteous fury, began to march down Rampart Street toward the Parish Prison.

At the prison a swelling mass of onlookers now lined both sides of the street in front of the main gate. The Italian prisoners had learned of the mass meeting and begged Captain Davis to let them out, or else give them arms to defend themselves.

Davis was becoming edgy. Why wasn't his superior on the scene? He phoned Sheriff Villère to tell him of the surging crowd. He kept the night watch on duty when the day watch came to relieve them. He sent a runner out to bring in deputies who lived nearby. The crowd hooted and jeered as the prison gate clanged shut behind these reinforcements.

The prison that Davis was trying to secure was a bleak fortress occupying an entire city block. The main gate on Orleans Street was guarded by iron bars an inch and a half thick. But on Treme Street only a small wooden door gave entry into the prison. Davis ordered his carpenters to barricade this doorway. Each report of the carpenters' hammer blows was echoed by more yells from the crowd.

Matranga   *Macheca*

Monasterio   *Bagnetto*

The Marchesis, father and son

Scaffidi   *Polizzi*

Davis' strategy to save the nineteen prisoners was first to lock all the other inmates into their cells. He then transferred most of the Italians to the women's side of the prison, where they were released and allowed to fend for themselves within the prison compound. Several of the men bolted for hiding places—in a trash bin, in the wash house, under a mattress. Two even managed to cram themselves into an oversize doghouse that had been made out of an old box for Captain Davis' bull terrier, Queen. But most of the Italians remained upstairs on the women's side of the jail.

By now all four streets surrounding the prison were thick with people. Davis checked the carpenters' work on the Treme Street barricade and decided it would hold. Suddenly a new sound riveted the captain's attention. He could make out in the distance the muffled roar of an approaching mob, the steady tramp of marching feet. As he listened two detectives pulled up to the main gate in a horse-drawn cab and shouted to him that the Vigilance Committee was headed for the prison "to lynch the Dagoes." Davis answered, "Let them come, they won't get in."

Pasquale Corte, the Italian consul in New Orleans, had also read the Vigilance Committee's call to action that morning in the papers. To Corte this threat was a direct summons to duty. At least three of the men accused of the crime were still Italian citizens and entitled to the Italian government's protection.

When Corte learned that a crowd was indeed gathering at Clay Statue, he raced his carriage to City Hall to find Mayor Shakspeare. There he met Sheriff Villère and the attorney general, Mr. Rogers, who told the consul that they too were looking for the mayor. But in Corte's judgment, "They appeared to me to be very calm and to be anticipating what was about to happen."

Corte, a tough and determined

agent of his government, then asked where he might find Governor Francis Nicholls. Told to try a certain lawyer's office, Corte hurried back to the carriage and tracked Nicholls down. The Italian diplomat pleaded with the Louisiana governor to send troops or a force of police to head off possible violence at the prison. Nicholls replied that he could do nothing until he received a request from the mayor; that he had already telephoned Mayor Shakspeare at the Pickwick Club and asked him to

Vigilante leader William S. Parkerson

come over at once. Nicholls suggested that Corte sit down and wait with him. Twenty-five agonizing minutes passed; then the telephone finally rang, and someone reported that the mob had reached the prison. Corte sprang to his carriage and headed at full speed to reach the scene of the trouble.

The mob arrived at the Parish Prison and demanded the keys from

Captain Davis. He refused. The iron-barred main gate looked formidable, but the barricaded wooden door on Treme Street offered the vigilantes a more vulnerable target. A pile of wood on the street provided handy battering-rams. Neighbors volunteered their axes for the task. A black man brought a heavy stone crashing down on the door. It burst open, and a roar went up from the crowd.

John Wickliffe stood guard at the shattered entrance and allowed sixty armed men to enter. The merely curious were excluded. Sentries were posted at every exit to shoot down any prisoner trying to escape.

Parkerson helped to lead a group of vigilantes, rifles slung over their shoulders, across the prison yard. The guards quickly backed out of harm's way. As the vigilantes entered the prison building they saw in one cell a face frozen in terror. It was Scaffidi, somebody said. Shots rang out and the man dropped, though they had missed him. He was not one of the nineteen Italians. The leaders asked for someone to come forward who could identify the right prisoners. Somebody shouted, "Go to the female department." The door to the women's section was thrown open, and an old black woman told the vigilantes they would find the men they wanted upstairs.

The avengers first discovered young Gaspare Marchesi but spared the boy because of his youth. His father, Antonio, had fled with Scaffidi and Macheca to the gallery for condemned prisoners on the third floor. A grated gate slammed and locked behind them. The gate at the other end of the corridor was locked too, trapping the three men like caged beasts. They tried to protect themselves by lining up behind a pillar in the gallery. The mob reached the third floor, but the locked gate kept them from getting directly at the prisoners. Scaffidi peered out briefly, and he was shot through the head. Marchesi stumbled over Scaffidi's fallen body and, while struggling to his feet, was riddled with buckshot. Someone unlocked the gate for the vigilantes. They moved in and made short work of Joseph Macheca. He slumped to the floor, and the avengers passed over him.

Six other prisoners had fled down a back stairway and hidden in a cell until discovered by half a dozen gunmen. They then burst into the courtyard, where they were finally trapped against a wall. The six huddled piteously on their knees, their hands over their heads, pleading for mercy. The executioners poured a deadly rain of fire into the crouching figures, who fell in a blood-soaked heap. Monasterio, still alive, raised a hand. "Give him another load," someone shouted. A revolver shot dispatched the shoemaker for good.

To satisfy the crowd, which had missed the action within the prison, Antonio Bagnetto was dragged outside and hanged from a tree, although the man was probably dead already from gunshot wounds.

The crazed Polizzi was found crouched under a staircase, babbling to himself. He too was dragged before the mob. A rope was thrown around his neck, and he was hoisted to a lamppost. Polizzi managed to grab the rope and pull himself up, hand over hand, until he reached the crossbar and hung there gasping. A young man climbed the post and beat him in the face until the prisoner lost his grip and fell to the ground. Finally, on the fourth attempt, with his hands tied behind him, Polizzi was hanged. The crowd gave out a deafening cheer.

One of those who arrived too late to witness the spectacle, or to help avert it, was Pasquale Corte. On reaching the jail the Italian consul realized the massacre was over and headed back to his office, where he would soon be occupied in the grim business of helping the families of the victims.

Twenty minutes after the Treme Street door had burst open, it was over. Eleven men lay dead. The other

Harper's Weekly, MARCH 28, 1891

Cornered in the courtyard by the angry avengers, six prisoners begged for mercy—in vain.

eight Italian prisoners were spared, either because they had not been found or someone had vouched for their innocence. For those who still had not seen enough, arrangements were made for small groups of ten to fifteen spectators each to pass through the prison to witness the vigilantes' handiwork.

Mr. Parkerson addressed the crowd once more: "I called you together for a duty. You have performed that duty. Now, go home and God bless you."

"God bless you, Mr. Parkerson," they shouted back, lifting him to their shoulders for a triumphal return to Clay Statue.

Among the original nine defendants who survived were Bastian Incardona and Charles Matranga. Incardona had hidden in a box of rubbish. Matranga, one of the suspected ringleaders, had taken refuge under a mattress, a crucifix pressed to his lips. His deliverance, he later told reporters, had confirmed his innocence. He expressed some doubts, however, about the innocence of the less fortunate prisoners.

As the *New Delta,* the city's leading Democratic daily, later described that March morning, "The work was rapid and comprehensive. The guilty were stricken, the innocent were spared." Perhaps so. But of the eleven dead men now stretched out in the prison, three had been acquitted, the jury could not agree on a verdict for three others, and five had never been tried at all.

When word of the lynching reached Lugger Landing, flags were quickly lowered, some to half-mast. By Sunday the only Italian flag still flying was one from the masthead of a steamship of the Macheca line. That Sunday afternoon the founder of the firm was carried from his Bourbon Street house in an expensive silver- and gold-trimmed casket. Twenty-five carriages bearing Joseph P. Macheca's relatives, friends, and associates followed the hearse to the funeral in St. Louis Cathedral and then to the cemetery.

The funerals of the other victims were less splendid. Most were simple family observances. Bagnetto's body was attended by no one. Three of the men were buried in potter's field.

The gunfire in the Parish Prison reverberated around the country and beyond. Italian-Americans meeting in Chicago fired off a telegram to Secretary of State James G. Blaine: "We, Italians by birth, Americans by choice, assembled in mass meeting, unanimously protest against the cowardly and lawless act of the New Orleans mob, aided by the tacit consent of the local authorities...." In New York six thousand members of the Italian community massed at Cooper Union in an orderly but angry demonstration. Outraged Italians gathered in Pittsburgh, Philadelphia, and Kansas City.

In Italy Premier Antonio Starabba di Rudini now faced a threat to his political survival. In office only one month, possessing only the slenderest parliamentary majority, Rudini was already in trouble on a tax-reduction pledge when the New Orleans incident broke. Since some of the victims were still Italian citizens, public opinion clamored for justice and the vindication of Italy's national honor.

Rudini took a time-honored stance, a show of strength abroad to mask his faltering grip at home. He demanded punishment of the murderers and indemnity for the families of the victims. In a lengthy exchange of diplomatic notes Secretary Blaine lectured the Italians on the fine points of American federalism, under which Washington could make no such assurances in a matter essentially involving the state of Louisiana. Naturally, this answer could not satisfy the embattled Rudini. He ordered Baron Fava, the Italian ambassador, home from Washington in order to register Italy's official displeasure.

Rumors now began to spread of Italian warships headed for the American coast. The threat, however fanciful, was just the tonic the American spirit thirsted for in 1891. The war scare, fanned by a jingoistic press, gave Americans a chance to demonstrate, after a quarter of a century, that the deep wounds of the Civil War were healing nicely and that the nation was, once again, whole. Confederate veterans from Tennessee and the Shelby Rifles of Texas volunteered to fight for Old Glory against Rome. Uniontown, Alabama, offered fifteen hundred men. An ex-Confederate wrote the Secretary of War, "... I will ... fight for the old flag as willingly as I fought against [it]." From Georgia the War Department received an offer of "a company of unterrified Georgia rebels to invade Rome, disperse the Mafia and plant the Stars and Stripes on the dome of St. Peter's." Not until the Spanish-American War would America have a better chance to satisfy the country's longing for a true test of renewed national unity.

On May 5 a New Orleans grand jury, convened to look into the Parish Prison murders, issued its report. As for the trial, the grand jury concluded that some of the jurors who had served on the Hennessy jury had been subject to "a money influence to control their decision." As a result six men were indicted for attempted bribery, including the private detective, D. C. O'Malley. Only one person was actually convicted, and he received a short sentence.

As for the lynch mob, the grand jury decided that it "embraced several thousand of the first, best and even the most law-abiding citizens of the city ... in fact, the act seemed to involve the entire people of the parish and the City of New Orleans...." And after thoroughly examining the subject the grand jury reported there was no reason to indict anybody for the lynching.

Not everyone who studied the case shared this judgment. During the diplomatic sparring between the United States and Italy, the Department of Justice had been ordered to look into the incident. After reviewing the eight-hundred-page transcript of the Hennessy trial, a U.S. attorney, William Grant, reported that the evidence against the defendants was "exceedingly unsatisfactory" and inconclusive. And later, all charges outstanding against those who had survived the prison massacre were dropped.

No matter. The mass of public sentiment across the nation leaned to the view that justice had triumphed—in the streets of New Orleans, if not in its courts. A scattering of civil libertarians might shake their heads sadly. The *Nation* magazine did say we had "cut a sorry figure before the civilized world." But New Orleans was content. "The hand of the assassin has been stayed," the *New Delta* reported. "The Mafia is a thing of the past."